£21.69

HARRY POLLITT
a biography

HARRY POLLITT
a biography

by

JOHN MAHON

"All his days he was on fire"

1976
LAWRENCE AND WISHART
LONDON

This biography of Harry Pollitt, by John Mahon, was first published by Lawrence & Wishart Ltd. in hardback edition in 1976. The Indexes were compiled by Pat Sloan.

[SLOAN]

Copyright © Mrs F. Mahon 1976

ISBN 0 85315 327 2

DEDICATED TO ALL WHO STRIVE
FOR THE CLASSLESS SOCIETY

Workers of all Lands, Unite!

Produced by computer-controlled phototypesetting,
using OCR input techniques, and printed offset by
UNWIN BROTHERS LIMITED
The Gresham Press, Old Woking, Surrey

PREFACE

On a wet Saturday afternoon in 1921 a workmate took me to a meeting where Harry Pollitt was to speak.

Socialism was already much in my mind; I had the good fortune to find on my father's shelves Marx's *Capital*, Engels' *Socialism, Utopian and Scientific*, Lissagaray's *Paris Commune*, Morris's *Dream of John Ball* and *News from Nowhere*. I had heard many Labour speakers—Snowden, eloquent but aloof, Ramsay MacDonald leaving me in a roseate trance, Jack Jones of the S.D.F., a wonderful voice, and H.M. Hyndman, kindly approving Marx but sternly disapproving Bolshevism. None of them gave me any definite idea of how we should actually get socialism, none explained what Lenin had done.

To hear Harry Pollitt was something entirely different. In making the case for representation at a congress of the Red International of Labour Unions, he opened a fascinating perspective of how the workers could, in striving for their daily needs, also gather strength to conquer political power so that instead of having to scramble for crumbs from the rich men's tables they could build socialism and master their own destiny.

Since then I have heard Harry Pollitt at hundreds of meetings. Whether his audience was a cheering crowd of thousands, or a handful of people in a smoky back room, he never failed to strengthen their socialist purpose, to inspire them to further effort in the cause of the liberation of mankind.

Such men are rare. My impulse to write this book arose from my feeling that Harry's life should be recorded before memories fade and documents disappear. For the rising generation of new fighters for socialism can draw strength from his example.

My aim has been to give an accurate account of Harry Pollitt's life, of the influences that shaped him, of the contribution he made to the labour, socialist and communist movement, and to present his views in his own words wherever possible.

I hope I have verified all data—if errors have crept in I should be glad to be told of them. The estimation in the final chapter is my responsibility, though I have listened carefully to others: the reader will find its basis in the previous chapters. I have made full use of such papers as were preserved by Harry Pollitt and of others given to me while writing the book. These papers and any which may yet be sent to me, will be later made available to those interested.

The necessary reading of many old socialist pamphlets and journals has more deeply impressed upon me how much the Labour movement of today owes to the pioneers who were not afraid to blaze an unknown trail.

They spoke up for socialism and carried on the class struggle in spite of abuse, victimisation and persecution.

It has been a deeply moving experience to talk to the few survivors who shared Harry Pollitt's early years, at Gorton Tank, in the Openshaw Socialist Society, in the British Socialist Party, and during the founding and formative years of the Communist Party, to feel the warmth of their recollections of his politics and his personality.

I should like to mention two of my problems. The first—whose names from among the hundreds who rightly considered Harry Pollitt a personal friend, should be mentioned? I have taken his own writings as a guide, though this may well omit many with whom he was in daily contact, since he had no need to write to or about them. The second—to give a full account of his activities as General Secretary of the Communist Party would be to go beyond the scope of this book, so I have selected those incidents and events in which I felt he was most personally concerned.

I acknowledge below, with much warmer feelings than a few words can convey, the generous help and assistance I have received in preparing this book.

Acknowledgements and Thanks

Of the many hundreds who knew Harry Pollitt, I have been able to contact only a small proportion. Most of the information and recollections given have been used in the book, and I hope that in due course all relevant information and documents, together with his writings and notes, will be accessible to those interested.

My grateful thanks are due:

To Harry's sister Ella, and to his wife Marjorie, for continuous help and information.

For access to journals and documents: John Gollan, General Secretary and Frank Jackson, Librarian, of the Communist Party of Great Britain; Daniel McGarvey, President, Amalgamated Society of Boilermakers, Shipwrights, Blacksmiths and Structural Workers; Michael McGahey, President and William McLean, Secretary of the National Union of Mineworkers, Scottish Area.

For discussion on problems: R. Page Arnot, Emile Burns, Rajani Palme Dutt, Maurice Cornforth, Peter Kerrigan, James Klugmann, E. Papaioannou, R.W. Robson, Andrew Rothstein, Ted Williams.

For assistance in research: Emily Ash, Robert Bailey, Kay Beauchamp, John Bloom, Frank Day, Jack Eighteen, Max Egelnick, Sid French, Edmund and Ruth Frow, Jack Gaster, Rosa Glading, Chris Gollaglee, Finlay Hart, William Laithwaite, James Jarvie, Ian McDougall, Harry Quinton, Betty Reid, Winnie Renshaw. On Harry Pollitt's evening schooling, John B. Elliott and John Senior of Manchester University, M.A.L. Nutt, City and Guilds Institute. On Gorton Tank: E.H. Fowkes,

Archivist, British Transport. On Manchester County Forum: J. Skelton on *Orion:* Miss F.M.M. Beall, P & OSNC

For personal recollections: On Droylsden, Gorton Tank and Openshaw: James Acton, Richard Allcroft, Ben Ainley, David Ainley, Mrs. Lavinia Brown (nee Smith), Miss W.J. Brown, Mrs. Calder, Sir Richard Coppock, Mrs. Beth Davies, Harold Fleet, Mrs. Jessie Kennerley (nee Rathbone), Charles Marks, Alderman Tom Regan, Muriel Roberts, Vic Summers.

On early years in London, R.I.L.U. British Bureau and the Minority Movement: Willie Allan, Frank Ayres, J.A. Bell, Harry Brown, Dave Campbell, T. Crawfurd, Mary Docherty, Rajani Palme Dutt, Kathleen Eaves (nee Strudwick), Aitken Ferguson, Percy Glading, Ted (Lord) Hill, S.C. Hutchings, Frank Jackson, John McArthur, Ena McCrae, Hugh McIntyre, Abe Moffatt, Ray Offley, Olive Parsons, Eva Reckitt, Robert Selkirk, Alec Squair, T.R. Strudwick, Ted Taylor, John Wood, William Zak.

On the period Harry Pollitt was General Secretary of the C.P.G.B.: W.G. Allen, Tony and Betty Ambatielos, George Baker, Minnie Bowles, Lawrence Bradshaw, Reginald Bridgeman, Norah Cockren, Idris Cox, Fred Douglas, Gladys and Sid Easton, Edmund Frow, Margot Heinemann, Frank Jackson, Julius Jacobs, Alice Jones, Mick Jenkins, J.W. (Bill) Jones, Solly Kaye, Peter Kerrigan, Joe and Bessie Leigh, B.M. Letsky, Betty Lewis, Alice and Jack Loveman, Beattie Marks, George Matthews, Bill Miller, A.F. Papworth, Will Paynter, Annie and Trevor Powell, D.N.Pritt, Rev. Jack Putterill, Mrs. Roberts, Bill and Louise Ross, William Sedley, John Speechley, Wally Spencer, Ken Sprague, Ebby Thomas, Ivy Tribe, W.H. Walker, Charlie Wellard, A. Wilson.

On the British Battalion in Spain: John Angus, Frank Ayres, Donovan Brown, Isobel Brown, Alec Digges, Nan Green, Alex Robson, R.W. Robson, Jim Ruskin, Sam Wild, Mrs. Dover Wilson.

On the 1960 Tour: *New Zealand*—G.E. Jackson. *Australia*—Joe Bailes, J.W. Bevan, R. Dixon, R. Gibson, Joe Goss, H.T. Johnson, Ralph Maddern, W. McDougall, Stan Moran, Jean Pollitt, Steve Quinn, Joyce Slater, Alf Watt.

And for invaluable and sustained secretarial assistance from Minnie Bowles, Rosa Rosen and last but by no means least, my dear wife Florence.

JOHN MAHON
Leatherhead, January 1975

CONTENTS

Chapter
1. DROYLSDEN, 1
2. GORTON LOCOMOTIVE WORKS, 12
3. THE OPENSHAW SOCIALIST SOCIETY, 23
4. OPENSHAW BRANCH OF THE BRITISH SOCIALIST PARTY, 34
5. AGAINST IMPERIALIST WAR: AUGUST 1914 TO NOVEMBER 1917, 46
6. THE IMPACT OF THE RUSSIAN SOCIALIST REVOLUTION, 54
7. LONDON, 1918–1919, 65
8. HANDS OFF RUSSIA, 76
9. THE COMMUNIST PARTY OF GREAT BRITAIN, 1920–1924, 84
10. BATTLE FOR TRADE UNION POLICY, 1920–1924, 98
11. RED FRIDAY AND THE GENERAL STRIKE, 115
12. POLLITT BECOMES GENERAL SECRETARY OF THE C.P.G.B., 136
13. GENERAL SECRETARY, 1929–1932, 162
14. FOR UNITY AGAINST THE 'NATIONAL' GOVERNMENT, 178
15. FOR UNITY AGAINST FASCISM, 191
16. THE FASCIST WAR ON SPAIN, 206
17. THE ROAD TO MUNICH, 232
18. WHAT KIND OF WAR?—1939, 244
19. THE WAR EXTENDS, 257
20. ANTI-FASCIST WAR, 271
21. WHAT KIND OF PEACE?, 294
22. THE LABOUR GOVERNMENT—1945–1947, 311
23. THE LABOUR GOVERNMENT—1948–1951, 327
24. THE BRITISH ROAD TO SOCIALISM, 349
25. TORY GOVERNMENT—1951–1955, 358

26. Visit to India, 372
27. Cyprus—1954, 389
28. The C.P.S.U. 20th Congress, 396
29. Party Chairman, 403
30. Australasia, 414
31. Harry Pollitt: a retrospect, 429

Notes on Chapters, 445

APPENDICES
1. Harry Pollitt's Early Reading, 489
2. The Openshaw Socialist Society, 497
3. Congress of C.P.G.B., with Data on Pollitt, 501
4. Congress of C.I. and Plenums of E.C.C.I., 502
5. Articles, books and Pamphlets by Harry Pollitt, 504
6. Diary of Main Events, 520
7. Pollitt's Last Writings on Trade Unionism, 532
8. Two Fabrications, 536
9. The Meerut Prisoners, 537

ABBREVIATIONS used in the Notes and Appendices

General Index 542
Names Index 548
Organisations Index 557
Places Index 562
Publications Index 566

Illustrations between pages 374 and 375

CHAPTER 1

DROYLSDEN

1. "The most active year". 2 No. 14 Wharf Street. 3. The Pollitt family. 4. Schooldays. 5. Introduction to socialism.

1. "THE MOST ACTIVE YEAR"

"Unquestionably the most active of all the years during the latter half of the nineteenth century from a social industrialist standpoint"—so Tom Mann,[1] himself a living embodiment of the workers' determination to shape a better life, described the year 1890.

The flame lit by the match girls and the dockers in London's East End the year before, spread far and wide. The downtrodden, the uneducated, the half-starved, ignored by Parliament, looked down on by the "respectable", excluded from the craft trade unions, decided that they had endured in silence long enough. Gas workers, printers, railwaymen, carmen, navvies, postmen, builders—they held meetings, they demonstrated, they struck work, they organised.

May Day in London saw the largest crowd in living memory gather in Hyde Park, not to dance round the maypole, but to cheer the trade union and socialist speakers demanding a legal limit of eight hours to the working day. From their West End balconies, the upper ten thousand had watched, amusement mingling with concern, two processions, each taking an hour to pass, workers of all trades behind the shield-shaped banners of the Eight Hours Day Committee and the "acres of splendidly painted silk" of the craft unions and the London Trades Council. The old unionism was typified by the "hundreds of gentlemen compositors, wearing kid gloves and top hats", the new unionism by "thousands of dockers marching in their rough working clothes", responding to the call of the International.[2]

In September the Trades Union Congress, meeting at Liverpool, found outside the hall "60,000 workers marching with the banners of 57 trades", and inside, for the first time, representatives of the new unionism. Controversy ran high, the two sides could easily be distinguished, for "the old unionists looked like respectable city gentlemen, wore very good coats, large watch chains and high hats ... were aldermanic in form and dignity", while "the new delegates looked like workmen, they were workmen ... not sticklers for formality or procedure, more guided by common sense".[3]

Tom Mann, his new union of dockers and labourers now 60,000 strong, stated his aims. "Poverty in our opinion can be abolished, and we consider it the work of the trade union movement to do this . . . our trade unions shall be centres of enlightenment . . . brotherhood must not only be talked about but practised . . . we are prepared to work unceasingly for the economic emancipation of the workers."[4]

The 1889-90 strike wave stimulated the organised labour movement to embrace all workers, not only craftsmen, while within it was voiced the aim to end capitalism, not only to reform it. In this year of storm and hope Harry Pollitt was born on November 22 at No. 14 Wharf Street, Droylsden, Lancashire.

2. No. 14 Wharf Street[5]

Droylsden was then a distinct village east of Manchester, three miles from Ashton-under-Lyne. From the city centre, Market Street crosses the now derelict Manchester–Ashton canal and, as Fairfield Road, runs almost straight to Openshaw.

A few minutes' walk from the centre, Wharf Street is a turning on the right. In 1890 it had a recently flagged pavement, but the narrow road was not made up; it had ruts and puddles and no proper drainage. A solitary gas jet lit its junction with Fairfield Road. At this corner a small shop sold a variety of household goods. Halfway along Wharf Street, an opening led to waste ground on the right. The street's northern end was closed by a two-storey brick building, on the other side of which was the canal with plodding, patient horses drawing narrow barges laden with cotton, coal, lime or manure. Passing the waste ground the canal went under a footbridge, through a double lock, and made a right-angled turn to the east, bathing with its green-fringed waters the footings of a great cotton mill, the dominant feature of the scene and of the life of Droylsden. Built in 1839, known by its original name of Benson's, this seven-storey steam-engine-driven mill, machines clamouring, tall octagonal chimney belching smoke, rows of windows glaring with gaslight, every morning eagerly, like a modern dragon, engulfed hundreds of humans, reluctantly releasing them each evening.

For sixteen years after Harry's birth, the Pollitts continued to live at No. 14, a terraced two-storey house of orange-tinged red brick. Without garden or area at the front, the street door opened direct into a sitting-room. Between this and the kitchen, a narrow stair led to a front and back bedroom. From the kitchen a back door opened onto a small cobbled yard enclosed by brick walls. This in turn gave on to an alley scarcely three feet wide into which opened the similar yards of similar houses in a similar parallel street.

In each yard were a little coal store and a brick built chamber containing an open privy midden, an inevitable encouragement to the domestic fly, regarded in 1894 by Dr Martin, a local Guardian, as a cause of the prevalent and often fatal infantile diarrhoea.[6]

Droylsden was colder and wetter even than Manchester and the prevailing west winds brought smoke, dirt and grime from the great factories in Openshaw. Droylsden had the highest infantile mortality rate in the country: an average of 190 of every 1,000 babies born alive died before reaching one year of age. The Lancashire average was 160—that of England and Wales 140. Conversion to water closets began only in 1909 and was not completed till 1931.

By working-class tradition the Pollitts' front room was the parlour, the "best" room, and the centre of daily life was the kitchen with a coal fire always burning—good coal was less than 10d. a cwt. It contained a stone sink with one cold water tap, a boiler heated by a small fire for washing clothes, a large cupboard under the stairs. An iron fireplace and kitchen range had to boil water, cook food, bake bread, toast muffins, and dry clothes. There was no bathroom, only a tub in the kitchen. For long, lighting was by candle or gas jets, and when about 1896 "father first lit an incandescent mantle, it seemed magic, the gloomy room where it was an effort to read became fairyland".

Food was simple and sometimes not enough. For breakfast oatmeal porridge, bread with beef dripping, bacon a rare treat on Sunday. Tea was hot, strong and very sweet; coffee was not drunk. Midday might be bread and cheese, or more often soup or stew, with cold apple pie or pudding. The evening meal might be of Lancashire hot-pot, a vegetable stew flavoured with a little meat, or baked potato pie. On Sunday, dinner would be a small roast and vegetables. The children often had a glass of milk, or a thick slice of bread spread with black treacle.

3. The Pollitt Family

Samuel Pollitt and Mary Louisa Charlesworth were married on March 31, 1888, "in the Red Hall Chapel Audenshaw according to the rites and ceremonies of the Methodist New Connexion". He was twenty-four, a smith's hammerman, she was nineteen, a cotton weaver, both from Droylsden families. His father, John, was a cotton weaver; hers, William, a cabinet maker.[7]

Mary Louisa bore six children. The first, a boy, lived only a few hours. Harry was born on November 22, 1890. Ella born on March 7, 1893, became Harry's childhood companion and close friend for life. Jack was born on June 1, 1900—the age gap and differing temperaments later made it difficult for him to fit in to the already formed family life. On June 16, 1901, came twins, but after two months the boy Stanley died of diarrhoea. The girl, Winnie, "with a face like an angel", became the darling of the family. Her sudden death from pneumonia when two years old was a terrible blow.

When Mary Louisa visited Samuel's parents in their Fairfield cottage before her marriage, she "always found a smell of baking and hams hanging from the beams, they kept one or two pigs". When Harry and Ella went there "it was a comforting home, with an air of opulence compared with Wharf Street". Later, Grandfather Pollitt lived with the family for a few years; he was short and slight with a little pointed beard and about seventy when he died. Granny Charlesworth frequently visited Wharf Street. In the family must be included Mary Louisa's younger sister, Emily, almost a second mother to the children.

The name Pollitt is not rare in that part of Lancashire, though a comparative newcomer to Droylsden, where the records go back to the thirteenth century; it is first recorded in 1698, spelt with one 't'. John Pollitt (1864-1915), boilermaker and A. Pollitt, secretary of the Openshaw Clarion Vocal Union were not related, nor were two namesakes: Harry Pollitt, chief locomotive engineer to the Great Central Railway and Harry Pollitt, contemporary student at the Manchester School of Technology. Harry's uncles included George Kidd, charge-hand at Gorton Tank, his brother William, with sixty years' membership of the Boilermakers' Society which he joined in 1844, and another (name not known), "a solicitor's clerk who sported chamois gloves".

Samuel Pollitt (1863-1933)

Harry's father was fair haired, a sturdy five feet four, with muscular shoulders, strong arms and straight back. His moustache, upbrushed quiff of hair and bold stance bore a hint of defiance. His expression was alert and cheerful, often laughing, singing or whistling, and he was known by his mates as "Happy Sam".

Going into the foundry at the age of eight, he became a blacksmith's striker. Woken by the knocker-up at 4.30 a.m., Samuel, whatever the weather, walked the long mile to his work at Gorton, never late, always arriving 15 minutes before the 6 a.m. start. "The striker grasps with both hands a long-shafted hammer, weighing about 2½, 7 or 14 lb. The last is sometimes known as a 'Monday hammer', its use producing a depressed feeling similar to that of contemplating a week's work ahead. Smith and Striker are a team, their integrated efforts produce the job."[8] Then after ten hours of arduous work, at 5.30 p.m. Samuel began the walk home. His wages were 18s. for a week of 55 hours. He was once off for sixteen weeks with a broken leg, and no sick pay. One day he was eating his mid-day sandwiches and a blacksmith remarked, "A bloody labourer with meat sandwiches". Samuel resented this superior attitude. The meat was only there because Mary Louisa got a skilled weaver's wages.

Quick-witted, intelligent, Samuel liked an argument. He took Blatchford's *Clarion* and *The Freethinker* every week; his reading included Gibbon's *Decline and Fall of the Roman Empire*, and the Bible, though he was not religious. He voted Liberal in opposition to the Tory establishment. Though a staunch member of the Smiths and Strikers Union, he had no confidence in his fellow workers and advised Harry, "Don't bother about them, they are not worth it, get tha feet under the table", meaning, get a comfortable job; but when Harry disregarded this advice, his father let him go his own way without pressure. From his closed circuit of arduous physical toil and the insoluble problems of poverty, he sought an escape or at least a respite, by drinking too much, spending money and time needed at home.

He was deeply attached to the children. When baby Winnie died he ceased to drink and to whistle for two years, and it was the canary who was heard in the house. During Harry's imprisonment in 1926, father's whistling again ceased. He believed in helping his children to help themselves. "Look in the dictionary and learn for yourself", was his reply when asked the meaning of a word. When Harry came home from school with marks of caning on his hands, and mother and sister were indignant, father commented, "You should behave yourself."

When he reached sixty-five Samuel was paid off without pension, and grieved to be a cost to his family. His last years were happy, though: he helped in his own home and that of his sister-in-law, did much reading and, relieved of pressure, ceased to drink. He died suddenly from haemorrhage of the spleen in October 1933 and was buried in Droylsden Cemetery.[9]

Mary Louisa Pollitt (1868-1939)

His mother's influence predominated in Harry's most impressionable years. She was the heart and soul of the family. Her loving care and devoted toil turned the unprepossessing little house into a happy home, and sixty years later her children's eyes would shine when they recalled her loving kindness.

She began work in a cotton mill at twelve years of age. During Harry's early years she rose at 4.30 a.m. to get ready for the 6 a.m. start at Benson's, leaving the children to be "minded out" by a neighbour. The 8 a.m. stop meant hastening home to give the children breakfast, taking her own while so doing, and rushing back to be in the mill by 8.30—for to be late meant losing pay. Dinner time, 12.30 to 1.25, brought another scramble—home, the children's dinner, tidy up, hurry back to work. In the afternoon the mill would be hotter and noisier, the air heavier. But her attention must not flag, for the weaver's work requires quickness of eye, dexterity of hand, unremitting attention to her four looms. How the afternoon must have dragged, how welcome the 5.30 bell, how good the air on the slower walk home, sometimes enlivened by the children meeting her!

The ten hours in the mill were the first round, at home began the second, the evening meal, then the endless cleaning, washing, mending, cooking, baking, looking after children, preparing for next day, calculating how best to spend the inadequate housekeeping money, to make clothes last longer, to keep the family well. The shining black hair, the rosy cheeks of youth, the velvety brown eyes, which so delighted Samuel that he likened them to pansies, faded too soon, but the smile and the caress for the children were always there.

A strongly built woman, five feet two, she had the reserves of physical and mental energy, a determination which defied fatigue, and the moral courage needed to cope with her life. Her features were regular and pleasing, the mouth generous and ready to smile with well-shaped firm lips, the glance kind but penetrating, the complexion good, the chin showing resolution.

Her home was plain but clean and bright, with spotless table, shining cutlery, always a few flowers. The steel fender and fire irons were polished bright, the brass candlesticks shone. The stone flags at the front door were regularly scrubbed and then rubbed with "donkey stone", leaving a white or cream surface. "She was the cleanest woman I ever knew," wrote one of Harry's school teachers.

Her neighbours and her fellow workers in the mill came to her with their troubles, and she never failed to respond. One neighbour wrote, "She was an inspiration to all around her. A working-class woman, she was a cultured lady in the best sense of that term. Good manners were part of her, and did not have to be, nor were, taught to her".

Mary Louisa Pollitt was one of the unrecorded thousands of working-class wives and mothers whose self-sacrifice sustained their men and their children in the never ending battle against poverty, ignorance and disease which was the lot of millions during the decades of the ruthless advance of industrialism and imperialism. And she was something more—she read, she went to classes in economics and industrial history, and to socialist meetings, she sought the roots and the remedy for poverty and injustice. Her grandfather a Chartist, her father a trade union pioneer, herself a trade union and co-operative member all her adult life, she carried on the Lancashire tradition of resistance to the rich. Joining the Independent Labour Party she found in socialism the hope of a new and better future for mankind.

4. SCHOOLDAYS

Children began school at four years, where the names and buildings were those of the religious denominations prior to the 1870 Education Act. "Independent" was nonconformist; "British", Church of England. Not till 1907 was there a Council-built school. Harry first went to the Infants School in King Street; at seven he transferred to the British school in Market Street, held in the gloomy basement of a church, reached from the street down a cinder slope and stone steps. There was no playground and no playtime.

The headmaster, Mr. J. Taylor, was strict, punishing naughtiness, lateness or truancy with the cane. There was a small room for the headmaster; the teaching was in a large hall with desks and benches for one class. Four classes went on simultaneously—one at the desks for writing, the others standing in the corners for oral instruction. Hats and coats hung on hooks around the walls. Girls had a clean pinafore each day, boys a clean collar. All wore clogs, boots were only Sunday wear. To rise from one class to another a written test had to be passed, so a backward child of ten might be in a class of eight or nine year olds. The children paid each Monday morning, one penny for the lowest class, rising to 7d. for the top.[10]

When Ella began school, after leaving mother at the mill gate, Harry would see her to the Infants School, then go on to his own. At dinner time they went home together; the pattern was repeated in the afternoon. The walk included crossing a main road, but Harry could trundle his iron hoop and Ella her wooden one without fear of sudden death. There was nothing more lethal on the road than the butcher's cart. the milk cart, the doctor's horse and trap. The only danger was delay by distraction by meeting the muffin man ringing his bell, the seller of fresh watercress, the man with yeast in a blue and white chequered cloth with a little pair of scales, the buttermilk seller—the Pollitts took a quart for 2d.—or the really great event, the man with the big bear who would dance for a penny.

Those were the years when Harry was "a sharp little boy with merry brown eyes and rosy cheeks in an innocent face, always something stirring when he was around". He and his companions, including nearby twin lads of his own age, got a reputation for mischief. They dared each other to teeter across the narrow top of the canal gates, jump off a high wall or cause unseemly diversions in Sunday school. During a lantern lecture at the Band of Hope, where strong drink was not approved "awful noises and loud miaows came from behind the organ"; Harry was found there and turned out. At the Christian Endeavour, invited to say a little prayer, he responded ingeniously but irreverently with "Hold the Fort for I am Coming, in a little Donkey Cart", and was duly excluded. He was doing well in the Confirmation Class until, when he was absent from the final test, the parson, "a great fat, well-fed man", found him cleaning the fire irons at home and warned him he was in danger of going to hell. Harry, "thinking of his mother slaving her inside out to get our living", told the parson to go to hell himself. His father was tolerant but sometimes the strap normally hanging idle in the kitchen was put to use, as when, unable to resist those dares, Harry with a broken arm still in a splint had been caught trying to walk the tightrope, and also after he had "thrust a piece of wood between the spokes of the milk cart, so that as it started the churn fell off and the milk ran down the gutter". At school too his tricks got him frequently caned; "The cane was long and thick and to hear it brought down with a swish made you feel quite sick".

It was at the Moravian Sunday School that Harry did best, being considered a very bright lad and given reading lessons. His teacher prophesied a great future for him as a preacher. From this school he enjoyed his first excursion to Mottram Old Hall, a six mile trip, paying 6d. for train fare, a bun and a mug of milk.

But other sides to his character came out. He was a great help to his mother in the house, each week doing an evening cleaning, as well as helping father who always did the washing up. On Friday Harry did the shopping at the Co-operative, spending his weekly halfpenny pocket money on sweets. On Saturday morning he brought from the Council offices the carbolic for the privy, emptied the night before by the Council men.

He was in much demand, even by the Sunday Schools which had expelled him, for his recitations from the Lancashire dialect poets.[11] Very popular was his rendering of the ballad "The Drunkard". In this the Drunkard is compelled to go teetotal when one day the publican refuses him any more credit; and as a result the former drunkard's home, previously abjectly wretched, is miraculously improved. Most appreciative of this fable was Harry's father, who on hearing it readily signed the pledge of abstinence, but never with such miraculous results.

Quick to sympathise with those in trouble, Harry was also quick to try and help—as when he went among his mates collecting Saturday pennies for a family with two sons suffering from tuberculosis.

He grew steadily closer to his mother. "When after Winnie's death Mary Louisa wept day and night, and would not eat, Harry put his arms around her and his face against hers and she seemed comforted for a time. Then the doctor, quoting a Chinese proverb that excessive grief for the dead is an injustice to the living, reminded her of her other children, and she pulled herself together."

There is a Moravian Settlement in Droylsden, its graceful church built in 1745. The beautifully proportioned and arranged houses, the spacious cobbled square, with its venerable lime and rowan trees and secluded alleys over-arched in verdure still produce an all-pervading atmosphere of serenity and harmony which made so deep an impression on Harry in his childhood that he recalled it fifty years later.

At Whitsun each Church had its procession, band and banners, children in white carrying flowers. The Moravians, with whom the Pollitt children usually went, were more sedate; they walked quietly into their Square and sang a few hymns during which Harry often disappeared. Then there were sports, games and races, prizes, buns and milk, perhaps even a trip in a canal barge, scrubbed and covered in turkey-red calico. Another annual event was the visit of Sanger's Circus, with its dinnertime procession of animals, clowns and other performers through the streets. And greatest thrill of all were the occasional trips to Manchester, to see the Carl Rosa Opera Company, or Henry Irving at the Theatre Royal.

The children got fun out of elections too. The rival candidates had wagons decorated with their party colours, swarming with their supporters' children, singing lustily, "Vote, vote, vote for our man so-and-so, He is sure to win the day, He is polling very fast and we'll have him in at last, And we'll throw old what's his name away".

One of his teachers, Miss Jessie Rathbone, summed him up as "a brilliant scholar and a leader among his playmates". Recalling that he once held the whole school enthralled with a talk on the evils of strong drink, she added, "when I read the wonderful little essays and original short stories that he wrote, I was myself enthralled". Her conclusion years later was: "If Harry could have been educated in accordance with his abilities and aptitudes, he could have become a Prime Minister instead of a leader of rebels". And for making him a rebel she held his mother responsible.[12]

Harry's first step into the world of work was a five hour Saturday morning job, wages 6d. in the Wharf Street rag store. "A loathsome job; being small I had to crawl into the dark little places and rats were there." Next, as his twelfth birthday approached, he walked the three miles to Ashton with other boys and girls to sit for the examination, passing which meant they could legally work half-time in the mills. They were worried lest the questions be too hard for them, but "You'd have to be deaf, blind and dumb not to pass, so keen were the employers to get child labour into the mills at 2s. 6d. a week, and they controlled the education bodies".[13]

So at twelve years of age Harry began work as half-timer helping his mother with her four looms. She regretted him starting so young, but she needed the help of a half-timer, and the 2s. 6d. meant more food for the family. So for a year he spent half the day at the mill and the other half at school, alternating morning and afternoon week by week. When starting at 6.30 a.m. in the winter he often fell asleep in school in the afternoon. When it was snowing or raining heavily he walked with his head under his mother's shawl for protection, or she would say "I'll manage till breakfast time, you stay in bed". Differences with his mother were rare, but once, when dissatisfied with his 4d. a week pocket money, Harry withheld paying over his wages, hoping to get more out of her. But "things went on as usual. No one said a word". He felt ashamed and put his wages on his mother's pillow.[14]

Like his pals, Harry occasionally added to his wages by selling programmes at the Co-operative lectures and concerts. The season was wound up by the annual dinner. Having heard gossip about the Committee members "doing themselves well" on these occasions, he thought why not the programme sellers too? So with that nice sense of timing which remained with him all his life he took his fellow sellers to the chairman just before the dinner began and said "Unless we get supper like the others, we won't sell the programmes". It was too late to argue, or perhaps the chairman had a sense of humour; the lads got their supper.

At thirteen he finished school, childhood ended and a full day's work had to be done. At Benson's he was transferred to the warehouse and acted as runner and helper to the cut-lookers,[15] a job which took him all over the mill, including the boiler-house and engine room, in which he was very interested. He was also sent to the homes of the manager and head mechanic to fetch their tea. The latter he had always heard referred to by the workers as "Mr. Pie Can". So he asked the woman who answered his knock for "Mr. Pie Can's tea". She did not like it, neither did Mr. Pie Can, who next day gave Harry a telling off.

Now his wages helped to pay for something never before possible, a holiday by the sea at Lytham, forty-five miles away. They left on a Saturday; Mother hurried home from the mill, Harry rushed for a cab. "For a shilling we were all driven in state to Droylsden Station, for a sixpence a porter got us a compartment to ourselves. After mother had put the finishing touches to us to her satisfaction, she leaned back and closed her eyes, too tired to even look out of the window."

But there was no future in this warehouse work, so there were anxious talks on what Harry should do. Most small boys then wanted to be engine drivers or cowboys; Harry's choice was boilermaker, but father said, "I've done enough slogging my guts out for one family". The Co-op had a vacancy for a butcher's boy and Harry was sent to be blooded at the slaughterhouse; but the piteous bleat of a lamb awaiting its fate touched his heart, he refused to become a butcher, and his mother backed him up. He persisted in wanting to be a boilermaker, and when his uncle George Kidd offered to "speak for him" at Gorton Tank, Harry got his way.

5. Introduction to Socialism

It was in his own home that Harry got his first acquaintance with socialist ideas. His father's radical trend, his mother's indifference to religion—the only time she ever entered even the Moravian Church was to hear Ella sing—the weekly reading of *The Freethinker* and *The Clarion*, all helped to produce an atmosphere of discontent, protest and would-be rebellion against the social injustice and class distinctions of which there was such ample evidence, including their own poverty and hardships. These feelings seem to have been given a definite turn to socialism when Harry was about twelve, and his Aunt Emily married a socialist workman, Alf Gerring, who took her to hear socialist speakers in nearby Openshaw where the I.L.P. had an active branch which Mary Louisa joined.[16] Aunt Emily and Mary Louisa, when she could find time, went to their meetings; in 1904 they launched a Socialist Sunday School in which Aunt Emily helped and Harry joined "like a shot". Among the "treats" arranged by this school were outings to the Vicarage Gardens of St. Margaret's Church in Altrincham, then a country village, where the Rev. Hewlett Johnson, later famous as the "Red Dean" of Canterbury, was deacon in 1905 and vicar in 1908.

The Openshaw I.L.P. gatherings were held in a small hall with adjacent kitchen facilities on the first floor of a timber structure at 135 Old Lane, off the Ashton Old Road. At a nearby corner it held open-air meetings, often very lively. No. 135 was the premises of a firm of plumbers, Messrs. Thomas Acton. Socialist branches then attached great importance to social gatherings with a club-like atmosphere, so the small hall was in almost constant use. Socialism was not then "respectable", but Mr. Acton was an independent-minded man and resisted suggestions that the lettings should be terminated. Having himself defeated the effort of the Town Board to charge the property owners in the Lane for resurfacing it by proving that it had once been part of the road from Manchester to Ashton, and was thus still a "Queen's Highway", perhaps he liked people who stood up to authority.[17] In this Hall Harry made his first and only appearance in opera, the Socialist Sunday School putting on the operetta "Lazyland" in which he played Mr. Merryman, his smiling face being eminently suitable.

Of the lectures he attended about that time two stayed in his memory. At the Droylsden Co-operative Hall, the socialist clergyman, Conrad Noel,[18] "made the audience gasp" by appearing on the platform in his priestly robe. In the Whitworth Hall, Openshaw, he heard Philip Snowden, then a militant and eloquent socialist speaker, later to be one of Ramsay MacDonald's Cabinet Ministers and to desert with him to the Tories in 1931. Harry's retentive mind seized upon one of Snowden's sentences—"only when capitalism has been abolished will it be possible to abolish poverty, unemployment and war". This thought became one of his basic tenets.

The year 1906 was a notable one in the political life of the Pollitts. The Openshaw I.L.P. held several open-air meetings in Droylsden,[19] at which the speeches of Mrs Emmeline Pankhurst and her daughter Adela (Emmeline),[20] who had just founded the Women's Social and Political Union, won the Pollitts for women's suffrage.

In the same year the Openshaw I.L.P., on his mother's proposal, accepted Harry as a member,[21] the chairman reading to him the statement of socialist policy and principles and giving him his membership card. Those present included a future national organiser of the Amalgamated Engineering Union, W. H. Hutchinson, and a future secretary of the National Federation of Building Trade Operatives, Dick, later to be Sir Richard, Coppock. In the autumn the Openshaw Socialist Society[22], was formed and became the hub of the Pollitts' political and social activities.

CHAPTER 2

GORTON LOCOMOTIVE WORKS

1. A new world.   2. Apprentice plater.   3. Life at 'the Tank'.   4. Evening school.   5. Trade unionism.   6. The labourers.   7. Craftsman and full member.

1. A NEW WORLD

On October 2, 1905, it was cold and dark when Harry, wakened at 4.30 a.m., set out to walk to the Gorton Works, where the locomotives of the Great Central Railway were made and repaired. It took its popular name, 'The Tank', from its most conspicuous feature, a large water tank surmounting a tower adjacent to the old round shed of the Manchester, Sheffield and Lincolnshire Railway, one of the earliest in Britain. Tower and tank had survived an extensive reconstruction of the works to meet the needs of the rapidly developing Great Central Railway.[1]

During his six years at the Tank, the working week was the then customary 53 hours, work from 6 a.m. to 8.30 a.m., half an hour for breakfast, work 9 a.m. to 1 p.m., an hour for dinner, work 2 p.m. to 5.30 p.m. On Monday the start was 9 a.m., on Saturday work ended at 12 noon. Beginning at 5s. a week, for some two years the apprentice did various minor jobs giving him the opportunity to get the general hang of things and acquire the vast variety of odd bits of knowledge essential in a workshop, while those in charge no doubt kept an eye on him and sized him up. He then chose the trade he wanted to follow, and began to learn the skilled work. Wages then rose each year to 15s. a week, of which, by Lancashire custom, 1d. in the 1s. was kept as pocket money, the rest going to mother for the family budget.

Harry's first job was heating rivets in a portable bellows-hearth with a coke fire; he had the rivets red hot to the command of the man doing the riveting. On this, his first job, Harry once unwisely mentioned his fear of rats and, when putting on his coat to go home, found a dead one in his pocket—and fainted. Next came a period in the foreman's office. A clerk did the paper work for the foreman, acted as timekeeper and issued workers' quarter-fare rail tickets. Harry's daily duty was to brew tea for these two worthies, at breakfast, dinner time and whenever else they fancied it. He ran various errands and, being found reliable, the clerk got him to collect the union dues for the Railway Clerks Association. This gave him opportunities to see all over the works.

He found a new world very different from Benson's Mill. The workshops covered fifteen acres, the running sheds another fifty. The 20 roads could hold 150 locomotives. The 65-foot diameter turntable had its own petrol motor. The breakdown train included a 20-ton steam-powered crane, replacing a hand-powered one of 15 tons. In the large and lofty machine shop the heavy tyre and wheel lathes, slotting and drilling machines were on the ground, while in a broad gallery were the lighter machines including the new 'automatics' for producing nuts and bolts. Other shops were equipped to produce templates, wheels, springs, copper and brass pieces. There was a brass foundry, one of the best equipped iron foundries in the country, a forge with two huge power-hammers, and a hydraulic flanging press "capable of 235 tons pressure and able to flange the throat plate of a firebox in one heat", Gorton being the first place where this was done.

So life was full of interest and occasionally came a glorious day, as when Harry and another lad, Harold Fleet, were sent to collect a stretcher from a hall about a mile away.[2] In the hall they found a billiard table and played till dinner time. They regained their strength from a couple of meat pies and, unable to resist temptation, went on playing till at 5 p.m. panic seized them and they rushed off at top speed with the stretcher, arriving just before finishing time. They expected an unholy row, but the foreman, Mr. Chaloner, had not forgotten that he once was a lad, and they got away with it.

2. APPRENTICE PLATER.

The works employed some 4,000 men, of whom a large proportion were skilled—boilermakers, coppersmiths, tinsmiths, patternmakers, tool-makers, fitters, turners, carpenters, joiners. Strongly organised, their conditions were above the average. The Tank was a complex of inter-related trades and skills, old manual processes and new machines. Its collective labour produced steam locomotives whose design underwent continual change as the railways were called upon to carry heavier loads at higher speeds.

Several types had been designed by Harry's namesake, the GCR locomotive superintendent from 1894 to 1902, whose last model was known to drivers and firemen as "Hell Fire Jacks". He introduced the tapered stove-pipe chimney, and gave some of his productions "almost feminine curves".

Early in 1907 Harry began "the real work on the marking-off slab and through the general run of plating", starting with light plating for tenders, side tanks and maintenance and going on to heavy plating including circular work. He was for the next five years in the heart of the Works, the boiler shop. It was large enough to handle up to 85 boilers at the same time, two bays were 300 feet long, three were 360 feet, the equipment was the most modern available, and 300 men were constantly at work.

A contemporary visitor[3] said that the incessant riveting hammers made "such a din that to a stranger it is impossible to catch a single word that may be spoken". He described the progress of the work. Huge plates of steel laid upon large flat blocks had the least shade of any buckle taken out. With their truth assured, an overhead crane transported them to machines for drilling rivet-holes—some did 22 holes simultaneously. Next the flat plate was changed to cylindrical form by passing through rolls bending it as though it were paper. Hydraulic machines able to exert pressure of 80 tons per square inch did the riveting. Seams were caulked with a tool using compressed air. The copper fire box was fixed in position, the dome seating added, tubes fitted in the cylinder, numerous minor additions made. Brass fittings were added and, after testing, the boiler went to the erecting shop to be fitted on to the locomotive frame. Here Harry saw locomotives weighing up to 80 tons suspended in mid-air from two travelling cranes. The visitor gave his final impression: "In the shops a locomotive is separated from its tender and is but an inanimate piece of machinery: in the shed it is almost a living being, with a history of its own, with its good points and its failings peculiar to itself, leaving its home for its day's work and returning when that work is accomplished."

This description shows that a boiler was no longer made as in the past, when one man did the whole job from marking the plates, to caulking, completing and testing. As boilers increased in size and complexity, "the employers found difficulty in getting enough men capable of all this, and split the job into platers, riveters and caulkers, so the commonly used term 'boilermaker' is now a misnomer. Today the plater does the marking off, punching and shearing, requiring a knowledge of mathematics and geometry. Platers work not only on boilers but also on bridges, gas holders, oil tanks, power plant, steel pipes, cement kilns, and bakers ovens. Platers made the dam-buster bombs."[4]

Harry was fortunate to find amid the machines men who helped him to become a good craftsman, a staunch trade unionist and a Marxist socialist. The champion marker-off in the boiler shop, Bill Unsworth, was "a marvellous craftsman though totally without book learning".[5] His two sons worked at the Tank. One of them, Jack, was an active member of the Openshaw Socialist Society, as was his wife, who taught at the Socialist Sunday School. Other socialist workmen who were friendly included Jack Gerring, whose son Alf married Harry's Aunt Emily. His cousins William and Arnold Kidd, also worked there. Among the apprentices were a school acquaintance, Harry Ware, who initiated him into rivet-heating; two years later, Harold Fleet, a Droylsden lad who visited 14, Wharf Street; and another two years on, Richard Allcroft, later to be an E.C. member of the Boilermakers' Union.

3. Life at 'the Tank'.

Harry was now in touch with all sorts of men and a great diversity of opinions. A feature of life at the Tank was the dinner-hour activity outside the main gate. On a fine day a variety of cheapjacks with catchpenny oddments and quack remedies competed for attention. When the racing tipster 'Old Man Morton' gave a winner he would be around for several days, expecting extra remuneration; if his horses lost he would not be seen for a while. An oriental doctor exalted the virtues of the galangal root, which chewed, grated or infused would "cleanse the blood". Another day might bring the Scot who offered boot and shoe laces, clip-on buttons for trousers and such small wares. The man who sold pills would first convince the listener that he was suffering from all the diseases in the book. The seller of embrocation had the advantage of being a fine physical type, well developed and muscular. Sometimes the hucksters went a bit too far in the lack of value they gave for the money they got, then the men would close round them and, when the hooter blew, rush them through the gate and into the works.

Harry enjoyed all this bustle, and often at home in the evening would stand on the horsehair sofa in the kitchen, reel off the patter he had heard and mimic the sellers, keeping the family in fits of laughter. If his grandmother Charlesworth were there she would wipe her eyes and say "That lad'll make a fine parson one day".

There was also serious fare. One man, H. H. Lawrie, a member of the Workers' Union, sometimes sold herbal remedies, and would make speeches too, always advising the labourers to join that union.

Prior to the 1906 general election, political speakers appeared at the main gate. Labour was contesting Gorton with John Hodge, a founder of the Steel Smelters Association, whose slogan was "Help for the helpless and work for the workless". The contest sharpened arguments between conservative-minded workers and those who inclined to the rising Labour movement, and even to socialism. The latter, including Harry who had put up Hodge's photo in the window at home, were greatly elated when he won. From then Labour speakers at the gate were more frequent, the Tories also sent their spokesmen. Harry began to be known for knowledge and ideas gained from his reading and at socialist meetings; the men encouraged him to have a go at the Tory speakers, though some felt he was too cheeky when he criticised Labour moderation.

Feeling for Labour continued to grow but there was a mixed attitude to the Socialists; some considered their propaganda to be extreme. Harry noted "derogatory expressions about workers known to be Socialists" including the jibe that "they were mere talkers who could not do their own job properly". From this he drew two conclusions: "to become as good a craftsman as possible" and "never to lay myself open to being sacked unless it could clearly be seen to be a case of victimisation", which meant acting in a way which the men could see was in their interest.

4. EVENING SCHOOL.

Any boyish elation in Harry's mind at leaving day-school soon gave way to realising that his education was insufficient for him to become a craftsman or to understand socialism. His mother, aided by a dictionary and a grammar, helped to improve his English, and at evening school[6] in Droylsden he took arithmetic, English and shorthand. In this he won second prize, a volume of Marmontel's *Moral Tales*—an odd selection. At Gorton Tank the apprentice had to study at the Manchester School of Technology and was warned that "unless the student has a fair command of English, of the elements of mathematics and of physics and chemistry he cannot with advantage enter upon the prescribed course . . . nor can he hope to achieve success in his studies unless they are pursued in a systematic manner and continued with intelligence and zeal". After two years preparatory courses in mathematics, applied mechanics and machine drawing at the Whitworth Hall he entered in September 1909 the imposing building of the School of Technology for the course in Metal Plate Work.[7]

The School was the product of nearly a century's effort to provide technical instruction for workers in industry. The first attempt, by the Manchester Mechanics Institute, founded by philanthropists in 1824, encountered an insuperable difficulty—the "utter inadequacy" or total absence of elementary education. Not until 1870 did Parliament empower local authorities to build schools and make attendance compulsory. The sponsor of the Bill revealed that in Manchester there were 16,000 children with no schooling at all. But elementary education was not enough, for "foreign competition was growing more effective" and could not be ignored. A Royal Commission after visiting competing countries found that the main cause of their success was the "efficiency of their educational means and methods both technical and general". An Act of 1889 then empowered local authorities to raise money for technical education.

Manchester Corporation made a rate, the government made a grant, so did the legatees of Sir Joseph Whitworth, who also gave land and transferred to the City the Whitworth Technical School and School of Art. The result was a six-storey building near the city centre in French renaissance style of Accrington brick, terra cotta and green roof slates, and splendidly equipped with lecture rooms, laboratories and workshops to give day and evening students technical instruction in all the major and many minor trades of Lancashire. Crossing the spacious entrance hall with its black and white marble floor and classical sculptures, or apprehensively awaiting questions in the first floor examination hall with its beautiful windows and dignified decoration, Harry had time to contrast these results of zeal to supply qualified workers to industry with the total lack of concern for the housing in which those workers lived.

The two-year course in Metal Plate work[8] was a stiff one. The lectures were followed by practical exercises in which the student had to construct models from drawings made by himself. Practical work included the use of the various hand and machine tools, the making of patterns, and production of an identical copy of a given model. Knowledge of plane and solid geometry was needed to mark off on the steel plate the places for holes to be drilled and the shape to which it had to be cut or bent, and to produce the correct result when the finished product had to be curved, angled or tapered in shape. Some knowledge of metallurgy was involved for hardening, tempering or softening metal, or making parts strong enough to sustain pressure or weight.

In the 1910 City and Guild examination Harry passed with an Ordinary certificate, second class. The following year he entered for the Honours Grade but got another Ordinary pass. In the autumn of 1911 he took classes in structural iron and steel, and in mathematics, presumably in line with his work on the job.[9] He continued evening studies for the next two winters, but details are not recorded. In 1914-15 he enrolled again for Metal Plate, but details are lacking and possibly the war interfered with his attendance.

5. Trade Unionism.

One Sunday in November 1910 Harry and his father walked the three miles from home to the Grand Theatre, Manchester, crowded to capacity to hear a debate on Syndicalism. Tom Mann, known throughout the English speaking world for his championing of the lowest paid, then at the height of his powers as orator, organiser and leader of men, had just returned from eight years in Australasia, where his experiences of Labour parliamentarianism led him to regard the industrial struggle as primary. To the question "Is Economic Organisation on the lines of Industrial Unionism the wisest and best method of realising Socialism?", he answered "Yes". His opponent was Frank Rose, a prominent Manchester member of the Amalgamated Society of Engineers, to which Tom also belonged. But the issue actually debated[10] was not syndicalism in principle but industrial unionism relying on direct action versus craft unionism tending to parliamentarianism.

The audience of trade unionists, unorganised labourers, and socialists of various trends followed the speakers closely. Tom Mann was applauded when he said: "The object of the employing class is that of controlling industry in such a fashion that they shall obtain ever increasing returns from the labour of the workers." And applause came again when he declared: "The workmen who organised, and by means of unions obtained reductions of working hours and an increase in the purchasing power of wages, also were largely, if not primarily, responsible for the agitations over long periods of years, that resulted in the Factory Acts, Mines Regulation Acts, etc. So that although the time came when Parliament was forced to apply those principles of regulation, the credit is due almost entirely to those men who had learned to appreciate the power of association."

These ideas were presented with all Tom Mann's enthusiasm, directness and vigour—"How he strode about that stage! How he hammered home his points! That's what I want to be like" Harry said to his father.[11] But it was when Tom spoke about trade unionism and the labourers that the applause was greatest. Here he challenged a conservative tendency in the movement. "Industry in future must be the unit, not the trade. It does not mean that there will be any action tolerating or approving the pulling down of the skilled man's pay. It does mean that with the unifying of the unions in each industry and the taking of common action embracing all labourers, the labourer shall receive the first and most important attention, because he is the lowest in the social scale." At the Tank Harry, "appalled at the way the platers treated their labourers, they might have been inferior beings from some remote planet", was already with others helping to organise them. Tom Mann's propaganda undoubtedly contributed to the advance of the labourers' movement, and to its support by the craftsmen.

6. THE LABOURERS

The demonstrations and strikes of the summer of 1911 which raised the pay and status of some 30,000 Manchester labourers were preceded by intense campaigning by active trade unionists, from craft and labourers' unions. It included Dick Coppock, bricklayer, Sam Hague, Labour Agent, Tom Higginson, boilermaker, H. Lawrie, Workers Union, Alfred Legge, Workers Union, and Harry Pollitt.[12]

The campaign focused on the demands: "£1 a week minimum for labourers; 2s. a week increase for semi-skilled; trade union organisation and recognition." The labourers' wage was then about 17s. a week of 53 or 55 hours, they had no representation and could be sacked at will by the foreman. The campaign was carried on at factory gates and in the unions. Harry Pollitt spoke in every trade union branch he could find in Openshaw and Gorton, sometimes invited, more often going along on chance, and in the back streets where lived so many of the factory workers. With plenty of topical illustrations and humour he made his key points: "The labourers will get nowhere without the skilled men, we need unity", "the unions must organise the semi-skilled", "there must be shop stewards and representation on the workshop floor, where piece rates are fixed," "the foreman's powers must be limited",—and always he urged joining the unions, "but where you are only a few keep quiet and gather strength". He explained why and how branches should be organised and records kept, for many men could scarcely read, and popularised elementary economics, explaining how the worker was deprived of the full fruits of his labour. He continued to help the labourers at Gorton Tank.[13]

Changing conditions in the workshop disposed the craftsmen to listen to these arguments. The need for mass production was bringing new machine tools which, once set up by the skilled man, could be operated by a new category, the 'semi-skilled', sometimes even by unskilled men. The old division into craftsmen and helpers was breaking down, the pay of the semi-skilled became a kind of 'floor' for skilled rates, and where piecework was done the co-operation of the unskilled was vital. Political factors were also at work; the judicial penalising of the trade unions through the Taff Vale and Osborne judgments had to be fought in Parliament, and to elect Labour M.P's the votes of labourers and semi-skilled were essential. The socialist propaganda stressed the class aspect of the workers' problems—the price of food was steadily rising and the initial proposal to limit the new Insurance Act to artisans, excluding those most in need, aroused discontent. Storm signals were flying. And the Gorton Trades and Labour Council, after intervening in a dispute in June at a Rubber works over trade union recognition, decided with commendable foresight to set up a Disputes Committee empowered to act. Its members were Councillors Fox, Hague, Higginson and Titt, all of the I.L.P.

In mid-July the management at Gorton Tank put labourers to work hitherto done by riveters, six hundred boilermakers went on strike, their district official Tom Higginson supported them, they won. Thus encouraged the semi-skilled, and the labourers at the Tank, followed by those at the associated Carriage and Wagon Works, ceased work. The Trades Council Disputes Committee negotiated for them and the management conceded the 20s. minimum for labourers and the 2s. increase for semi-skilled. The campaign had won the first round.[14]

The movement spread immediately. Some firms paid up at once; at others the men struck, the Disputes Committee to which, at the men's request, H. H. Lawrie and Alfred Legge were co-opted, did the negotiating. On the first Sunday of the strike the Alhambra Palace at Openshaw was packed with strikers, the speakers included Dick Coppock and Harry Pollitt. It was Harry's first strike meeting and in his excitement he strode up and down the platform—afterwards he took Coppock's advice not to do this but to make his emphasis by gestures.[15] The Strike Committee sent out organisers and speakers and opened a relief fund. At a press conference Tom Fox summed up the position of men taking home 17s., paying 4s. or 4s.6d. rent and having to keep dependents—"They don't live, they exist." Harry spoke again in Manchester's traditional popular meeting place, Stephenson Square, the crowd cheering the march in from Newton Heath of hundreds of railway labourers who had struck—"men for years underfed and underclothed, living in hovels, having no chance to obtain normal physical fitness. When they should be in the prime of life, they are worn out and squeezed dry, to be kept in hospitals and workhouses at the charge of the community." This meeting greeted with enthusiasm the announcement that the Strike Committee had negotiated a successful settlement at Crossley's.

By mid-August the strike spread to engineering and railway labourers in other parts of Manchester; many firms conceded but the number on strike reached 18,000. When some employers talked of bringing in outside labour, the Strike Committee warned "such a provocation would strain the patience of men on the brink of starvation". The craft unions instructed their members not to work with imported labour.

Hardship now became acute. The Strike Committee repeated its appeals, sent out street collectors "with four piano-organs", but could only pay to those in most desperate need 4s.7d a married man, 3s.4d a single, later reduced to 3s. and 2s.6d. A press man wrote[16] of his visit to a Gorton pawnbroker, "A young woman pale of face and frail of figure stepped in timidly and taking the wedding ring from her finger said 'I'm sorry it's got to go, how much?' The answer was 'It's nine carat, three shillings'. Asked if he got many wedding rings, the pawnbroker replied 'Plenty just now, they are usually the last, clothing went days ago, then smoothing irons, pictures, fenders, overalls, working clothes, goodness knows how they will redeem them. Now it will be quiet, they have pawned everything'."

Finally, with settlements at Beyer Peacock and Armstrong Whitworth, the solidarity of skilled, semi-skilled and unskilled gained the demands of the campaign.

But at a gathering organised by the Manchester and Salford Trades Council to mark the successes, Frank Titt said[17] "The concessions have left the men no better off than eleven years ago. At that time Booth and Rowntree said that 21s.8d a week was the minimum to assure bare physical efficiency. Today due to the rise in prices it would need to be 25s." It was this circle of hard won concessions with no prospect of ending the exploitation of the workers that was turning the thoughts of many, including Harry Pollitt, to the need for a social and political revolution.

7. CRAFTSMAN AND FULL MEMBER.

As an apprentice Harry was registered as such with the District Committee of the Boilermakers Society, as was then the custom; only in later years did an apprentice receive the 'half-card'. At the end of his apprenticeship, his friend Jack Unsworth proposed him for membership of the Society, at the December 1911 meeting of the Gorton Branch, paying the necessary entrance fee of 6s. At the meeting of 17 January 1912, no objections having been received, the Branch accepted him as a first class member, No. 78030.[18] The term 'first class' meant that he had completed five years apprenticeship and qualified to pay into all funds, including Superannuation.

The acceptance ceremony originated when trade unionism was illegal and new members had to take an oath of secrecy. It retained sufficient dignity and significance to induce in Harry a feeling of "very much awe".[19] The main feature was the solemn reading by the President of the Address to new members. One paragraph read: "Each individual member is expected to fully realise his position as a unit of our organisation and to try and grasp the idea that the success of all depends upon the efforts of individuals acting with loyalty to the principles they have pledged themselves to carry out." Another impressed that the new member "will be expected to conform to all our laws and usages to cultivate a kind of brotherly feeling amongst our members. Their cause must be your cause, their good your good, their troubles your troubles, and all past indifference must be transformed into a profound sympathy, and all prejudice into a sacred devotion for the elevation of the Order you are about to enter; and if these precepts are carried out in your everyday life you will at all times receive the approbation of your fellow members, and the shield of the Society will be raised to protect you in time of need."

Some Christian teaching was included, "not to do that to another which you would not have done to yourself", "it is better to give than to receive". A reference to being "expected to conform to the laws of the country" should be understood in the context of the trade union struggle for legality. The objects of the Society were given as "protection of its trade interests, the support of its members when thrown out of employment, the relief of the sick, the care of the aged . . . support to the widow and the fatherless, and other benevolent objects of a like kind."

Craft consciousness presented the concept of solidarity in strong and moving phrases, but limited to members of the Society. The concept of "class", as distinct from "trade" appears only in the negative "We are united not to set class against class but to teach one another that all are brothers".

Harry recorded "a great feeling of pride and craftsmanship in becoming a member, and hoped to bring as much credit to the organisation"[20] as his uncle, William Kidd, who entered in 1844 and had over sixty years unblemished record. On the job his first concern was to see that all the men were trade unionists and all cards kept clear. He usually became a shop steward, and as such the men's spokesman. In the political fight within the Society he never said or did anything to weaken its power and prestige. He saw clearly the limitations of the craft unions, he saw also that they embodied the effort and sacrifice of thousands of working men in a century's struggle for bread and rights. Recognition of the deep roots of the craft unions made him an adamant opponent of all tendencies to form break-away or new unions. He was confident that with experience and political education the members' outlook would broaden and develop to industrial unionism and class consciousness.

Since to remain at the Tank meant taking two years to reach the craftsman's wage, he chose the alternative of finding work elsewhere at full rate. In March 1912 he took home £2.1s., "the first slight easing from grinding poverty that my mother had ever experienced". At a makers of gas plant in Levenshulme he became shop steward of the Boilermakers and got the labourers organised. The manager was prone to "rush into the workshop and blow a referee's whistle", the nearest man then rushing to see what he wanted. The new shop steward called a meeting, and the next time the whistle was heard every machine stopped, every tool dropped, and every man rushed towards the manager who, astounded, went red in the face and temporarily silenced went back to his office. Next morning he tried again, with the same result. The whistle was heard for the last time.[21]

In July 1913 Harry got a job in Hyde, where the boilermakers observed tradition. The day following a holiday, they took their checks from the board and formed a ring in the yard. "The oldest boilermaker, resplendent in white moleskins and blue jacket, would pick up a brick, advance to the centre of the ring and announce 'If t'brick stays i' th' air, we start; if t'brick cooms down, we go whoam'." No instance is recorded when they did not "go whoam".[22]

Early in 1914 Harry began work at Beyer Peacock's foundry in Gorton, as a plater in the locomotive shop where his father was also working. After a few months the foreman asked him to take over the big furnace, a hot, heavy and highly skilled job, with the biggest money in the shop. In this firm it was practice that a worker who spoilt material paid for it out of earnings at so much a month. Harry, who was reading Marx's *Wages, Price and Profit* and explaining surplus value to anyone who would listen, decided that he could not accept this arrangement. His determination was put to the test in January 1915 when a copper plate being heated in the furnace shed "two pieces the size of a man's hand", some £90 worth of damage. The foreman argued with Harry to pay, pointing out that he could have a job for life. Harry argued that "the firm gets the profit out of me, it must stand the loss", and that afternoon, "to the astonishment of the whole shop", got his money and walked out.[23]

CHAPTER 3

THE OPENSHAW SOCIALIST SOCIETY

1. *The move to Openshaw.*   2. *Building the Socialist Hall.*
3. *A socialist centre.*   4. *A socialist speaker.*   5. *The county forum.*
6. *Coming of age.*   7. *The City elections.*   8. *21st birthday present.*
9. *Towards a Marxist Party.*

1. THE MOVE TO OPENSHAW

In the spring of 1907[1] the Pollitts moved to Openshaw, finding a better house at 4, Melba Street, near the junction of Fairfield Road and Ashton Old Road. The Gerrings were nearby at 32, Rock Street. Mary Louisa had decided to leave the mill and help her sisters; the elder was seriously ill and needed nursing, the younger, Emily, could only go to work if her baby was looked after.

Openshaw was noisy and crowded; along its axis, the Ashton Old Road, clanging trams were loaded with men in overalls from the big engineering works, women in shawls and clogs tramped to the mills. The Alhambra Theatre specialised in melodrama advertised in lurid posters. Samuel preferred his old haunts in Droylsden. But there were advantages; the daily walk to and from work was shorter, the occasional trip to Manchester centre was easier. For Harry too it was a shorter walk to work and to evening school. Mary Louisa and he were glad to be only a few minutes from the I.L.P. hall at Old Lane, and even less from the Margaret Street Hall, the centre of their social and political life. Visiting speakers, Tom Mann among them, sometimes came in for a meal.

Melba Street remained Harry's home until his marriage. When working outside Manchester, he always came home at Christmas. He would pay for hire of a piano, there would be a lively gathering of friends, Ella would sing, Harry would lead the choruses. Sometimes when he came for an odd week-end they made up a band with poker, tongs, a rattle and comb-and-paper.

2. BUILDING THE SOCIALIST HALL.

The Openshaw I.L.P. members in January 1905 were invited[2] to view the plans and a model for "a new Club House, a palatial edifice", and in December a grand bazaar to raise money was opened by John Hodge, Labour candidate for Gorton.[3] Land was secured in Margaret Street, a turning off the Ashton Old Road, almost opposite the Alhambra, well placed as a local centre. The hall as constructed did not occupy the whole vacant site; recollections vary as to whether to do so eventually was the original intention or not. Construction began in March 1907 and progress was chronicled by weekly reports in *The Clarion*.

Most of the builders were spare-time volunteers, skilled work which had to be done in normal working time was paid for. On a Saturday in March 1907 the site was boarded round and fifteen men lifted the first spadefuls of earth. Next Saturday twenty were busy with spades, picks and barrows. By mid-April nearly 300 tons of earth had been carted away, in one week 120 voluntary hours were put in. Three women took part "but they cannot wheel barrows along planks". By the end of May, bricklayers had begun their work. The writer of the weekly report remarked, "Navvying adds beauty to the figure, dignity to the bearing, strength to the limbs and variety to the language." Enthusiasm rose higher, volunteers gave part of their Whitsun holiday. On July 20 a procession "headed by the Crossley Brass Band and including 1,000 supporters, Socialists of all kinds, Clarion vocalists and cyclists, some with decorated bicycles, marched through Openshaw to the site." With John Hodge, M.P. presiding, three inscribed stones were laid at ground level, that of the Openshaw Socialist Society to the singing of 'England Arise', that of the Clarion Cyclists to the 'Red Flag', that of the Clarion Vocal Union to the 'Comrades' Song of Hope'. After three cheers for the Labour victory at Colne Valley where the socialist Victor Grayson had gained the seat, tea was served in two nearby halls, and the day ended with a grand concert in the Whitworth Hall. All went off without a hitch, socialists came from "within a 100 miles radius", a substantial sum of money was raised, "the whole affair was brilliant".

August saw the concreting of the cellars, vestibule, floors, steps and stairs—"ingredients measured to a cupful by the cognoscenti, then we shovel, mix, carry, smear and spread till we are tired." Spectators were advised against "coming in go-to-meeting clothes, work is so infectious and so dirty". Then came the smithying, pointing and drilling of the iron roof principles, "nearly like a shipyard", "work in the hands of men made of the same material as the Vikings". Winter closed down work till the spring. All through the summer work went on, until the grand opening took place on 26 September 1908.[4]

Again the Socialists of Manchester marched along the Ashton Old Road, the Hyde Brass Band leading, the cyclists in fancy dress, with the banners of the Independent Labour Party, the Social Democratic Federation, the Clarion Cycling Club and Vocal Union. This time the ceremonial opening was by the editor of *The Clarion* himself, Robert Blatchford, the most widely known Socialist in the country. Again tea and concert, "all a huge success".

The Hall was rectangular, the long side facing on Margaret Street, the elevation pleasant and dignified, presenting a series of arched windows and a handsome doorway on the right, topped by a stone inscribed "Socialist Hall 1907".[5] The visitor entered a vestibule from which rooms opening on each side, ended in a double stair leading to the big hall on the floor above. It could seat 400 and had an excellent parquet floor for dancing. Between the two entrances was a low platform; above, a gallery ran the whole width of the building; on the opposite wall was a large painting by Walter Crane; with scrolls bearing the words "When Adam delved and Eve span, Who was then the Gentleman?" The tall windows and high angled roof gave an exhilarating impression of light, space and elegance. The building had electric light. The ample basement contained more rooms, the boiler for central heating and a recess which could rapidly be sealed; a small flat-bed printing press was later installed.[6]

As though to emphasise the growth of the socialist movement, Robert Blatchford was again in Manchester a month later to open the Clarion Cafe, at No. 30, Market Street, on Saturday, October 31. Skilled men from eighteen trades had built, decorated and furnished it. The salon was imposing, with a Dutch tiled fireplace and a ceiling lantern. William Morris's poem "A King's Lesson" was pictured in a frieze by Bernard Sleigh. The windows had coloured glass figures representing Justice, Knowledge, Progress and Fraternity. On the floor above was the large and luxurious Clarion Clubroom, with murals by Walter Crane. The cafe part was electrically lit by ships' lanterns and had oak panels.[7]

The cafe soon became a meeting place for socialists and Labour people; Harry always went when in the town. Ella liked its "cosy and friendly atmosphere" and sometimes sang at the gatherings in the Club Room.

3. A SOCIALIST CENTRE.

The Hall was the centre of the varied activities of the Openshaw Socialist Society, the Clarion Cycling Club and the Clarion Vocal Union. There were members' meetings, public meetings and lectures, classes, choir practices, a drama group, an orchestra, socials, dances and concerts, and a Socialist Sunday School.[8] Refreshments were available and socialist books and pamphlets sold; also "Red Flag" cigarettes.[9] The traditional pattern of outdoor meetings in summer and indoor lectures in winter was followed. Occasionally the Whitworth Hall, seating 800, would be booked for a meeting.

Classes included one on economics, tutored by Joe McGhee, a tinsmith; Mary Louisa went to it; Dick Coppock took one on Socialism, using material by H. M. Hyndman and Harry Quelch with Harry Pollitt as a "most persistent questioner"; William Gee had a whole series on Socialism. Public lectures were given by socialists of varied trends from numerous northern towns; the first autumn series included 'Unemployment', 'Socialism and Religion', 'Socialism and its Critics', 'The Brotherhood of Man', 'Land Plunder', 'John Morley and Liberalism', 'Socialism and Life',

'The Crimes of Capital', 'Religion and Human Brotherhood'. From Manchester Miss Boltansky lectured on 'Eugenics'.

For the outdoor work, the local team were occasionally reinforced by men of national note, such as William Gee, the 'Socialist Dreadnought', and F. G. Jones, 'Silver Tongue'. Such practised orators were then a feature of the movement, they were self-educated men of considerable knowledge and reading, able exponents of socialism, each in his own style. Most of them were animated by love of the cause, gave their whole time to it, gaining a meagre living from collections at meetings or the hospitality of the local organisation. They conducted "Socialist Missions" for one or two weeks in a locality, speaking once, twice or three times a day, at traditional spots and breaking new ground. Bill Gee was Harry's idol, "my secret hope was to become one day as good a speaker as he". F. G. Jones had a commanding presence, a fine voice and perfect diction: "when he spoke the greyness of Openshaw faded and his audience saw instead the Openshaw that Socialism could—and will—create". Harry awarded him the ultimate in compliments—"the greatest orator I have ever heard".[10]

The work of the Openshaw Socialist Society, including the maintenance of the Hall, was voluntary. Mary Louisa helped in many ways, Ella sang at concerts and recitals, Alfred Gerring was Secretary and Emily helped in the Socialist Sunday School. Harry and his friend Charlie Openshaw, the literature secretary, polished the parquet floor of the big hall every Sunday morning and always gave a hand clearing up after a meeting. Other active spirits included the Crossley brothers, close friends of the Pollitts—Jim became "a sort of elder brother" to Harry and a life-long political comrade; Tom Halpin, who lept a drapers shop; Ted Somerset, a foundry worker, the treasurer; Dick Hollins, "an old Socialist stalwart", who liked taking Harry to meetings especially at the Secular Hall in Rusholme Road; Dick Coppock, Arnold Kidd, and Gilbert Roberts, who by virtue of his Marxist knowledge exercised considerable political influence.

4. A SOCIALIST SPEAKER.

The propaganda secretary, Jack Unsworth, long tried to persuade Harry to take the chair at the Sunday evening lectures. When at last he risked it he "spoke briefly and then shut up like a clam."

An indoor meeting where the audience is sympathetic is as the drill hall to the battlefield when the speaker ventures into the open air. The first problem is to get anyone to listen even to a single sentence, the second to keep them from immediately deciding they are not interested, the third to prevent a takeover by interrupters, hecklers and opponents. Harry's first chairing outdoors was on a Sunday night outside the Gransmoor Hotel and public house, standing well back from the Ashton Old Road. The speaker was the formidable Bill Gee, who gave Harry "enormous help with advice on what to read, how to study, how to get ideas across". Harry was well prepared, all went well, Bill's three imperatives—"start on time, boost the literature, finish before the pubs close, the workers like time for a drink"—were obeyed.[11] Indeed, Harry stuck to them all his life. When he was in the chair, the first speaker would find the meeting had started without him, if he was late. If the last speaker went over his time, his peroration, however brilliant, was mercilessly cut short.

The step from chairman to 'main speaker' is usually an ordeal, postponement of which is welcomed; but Harry was now itching for the chance and leapt at it one night at the Socialist Hall when the advertised speaker failed to arrive. When Harry was announced as substitute his mother's "eyes nearly came out of her head" and she "concentrated on noting his errors in grammar". From then on the traditional open-air meeting places—Old Lane, The Gransmoor, Taylor Street, the Half Way House—were Harry's happy hunting ground, though "few ever stopped to listen, and small blame to them either".[12] But it was invaluable training; and when later he stumped the back streets for the labourers' movement and the railway strikers, they did listen.[13] One lecture by him is recorded, on Engels "Socialism, Utopian and Scientific" to the Oldham branch of the British Socialist Party.

5. The county Forum.

A potent influence in shaping Harry's growing ability as an exponent of socialism was the Manchester County Forum, where members of all parties, and of none, debated politics, literature and art. Founded in 1812 by a radical, William McGuffin Greaves, it took pride in dispensing with written rules, minutes and membership. Its weekly meetings, open to everyone, were held in a succession of public houses and halls, for it frequently outstayed its welcome.[14]

Taken by Jim Crossley in 1910 to a session at the Ship Inn, Harry went frequently for four years "enjoyed every minute spent there and found it a first rate training ground". Among the regulars were Mr. Gray, Tory, and Mr. Whittle, Radical. The former was "equipped with bowler hat and umbrella", the latter with a voice "sounding like a bursting cloud, yet waxing louder still and still more loud" as he unfailingly responded to the call "speak up, Whittle".[15]

The socialists included Bonar Thompson, come from working in the glens of Antrim for 6d a day, to seek fortune in Manchester; Bob Whitehead, later the Openshaw Socialist Society candidate for the City Council, and the formidable Moses Baritz. A contemporary attender, Mr. Charles Marks, said: "Moses would overwhelm listeners with his capacity to present a broad case for socialism and his knowledge of Karl Marx. He spoke so forcibly that people were afraid to take him on, he could be withering in reply. Harry admired his wit, speaking ability and knowledge."[16] T. A. Jackson, also withering and witty, said of him, "If the

Lord had inflicted Moses Baritz on the Egyptians as the first plague, he would have needed no other," adding that Moses "was also a musical genius of the highest grade."[17] Moses ranged wide; one course of his lectures covered "The Materialist Interpretation of Literature, Ethics, Art, Drama, Music, History, Politics, the British Constitution, Transport, Morals, Science, Philosophy, and the lives of Marx, Engels, Lafargue and Lewis H. Morgan".[18]

In this somewhat daunting company, it took Harry two years to decide to enter a debate. "When he did, his ability even without experience made an impression. Moses Baritz commented that he spoke remarkably well, and with more study would become an accomplished exponent of Socialism."[19] Harry himself wrote that after the debate Moses spoke to him and "that started a friendship kept up to the day of his death, though I am bound to say that never again had Moses a good word to say for my politics. But next Sunday when I sailed into the debate with unbounded confidence, Moses got after me with criticism which knocked all the conceit out of me."[20] Mr. Marks, who was present at both debates, agreed that at the second, "Moses tore Harry to pieces, a compliment because it showed he regarded him as a serious speaker."[21]

Harry later wrote of the Forum debates that "they opened my eyes to the existence of all sorts of experiences outside the routine of home and work. They were one of the influences that created the desire for a fuller life in which culture and ideas should have their proper place. They helped put flesh and bone on the framework of Socialism."[22]

6. Coming of Age

The year of Harry's twenty-first birthday also saw his coming-of-age in industry and politics. He was active in the labourers' strike, emerged from apprentice plater to craftsman, and was Secretary of the Openshaw Socialist Society.[23]

Class feeling ran high that summer, and Manchester was one of the cockpits. Thousands of labourers were already on the streets when a national railway stoppage was called for August 17. The response in Manchester was "almost complete, mills, collieries and workshops closed for lack of coal". Memories of Peterloo were revived by the news that at Llanelly and Liverpool troops had fired, killing and wounding strikers, and that in Manchester companies of fusiliers had entered the city by night. Their deployment at rail depots caused considerable turbulence among the people, extra police had to be called in, but no shooting took place.[24]

We have already seen that Pollitt was immersed in the labourers' movement. With the additional excitement of the railway strike and the general strike at nearby Liverpool, meetings in the back streets and at factory gates multiplied and attendances grew. Harry's open-air practice

OPENSHAW SOCIALIST SOCIETY.
Municipal Election, Nov. 1st, 1911.

Socialism or Social Reform?

Probably one of the most prominent topics of the day is the question of Social Reform, and the assertion is frequently made that there is a connection between Socialism and Social Reform. It is necessary, therefore, to define these terms in order to see whether this is correct or not. The word Socialism implies a complete revolution in the internal workings of the system which we call Capitalism, or a transition from one form of Society to another, in order that, by a more scientific economic system, all the evils that arise from our Poverty problem may once and for all be eradicated. Social Reform, however, proposes nothing of the kind, because a reform only acts on external effects brought about by internal causes. Instead, therefore, of going right to the root of the problem, Social Reform only acts upon its effects, and not upon its causes. An example may make this clear. Suppose you have a chair and the wood it is made of is rotten, now no matter what colour, or how many kinds of paint you put on it, the chair still remains rotten. To make a good chair, you would have to construct a new one from new material. This analogy applies to the Capitalist system to-day, and ever since Capitalism originated you have constantly had social reforms, yet never in the history of the world was poverty greater, or the line of demarcation between the Employer and the Employé clearer than it is to-day. The fact that all these reforms have been given to us by the dominant class shows the futility of expecting social reforms to effect any permanent change in our economic status of to-day. Indeed, it is just because reforms will do nothing of the kind that Social Reform finds such favour in the Liberal, Tory and Labour platforms. One of the many contradictions of the present system is that, after a certain period of good trade, the markets get overstocked with various kinds of commodities, so that you have the absurd spectacle of seeing men thrown out of employment because they have produced too much. This is called a trade crisis, and with the intensification of the system, these crises are more frequently recurring. Now the result of this is that, after the workers have been out of work a time, owing to the lack of the necessaries of life they begin to physically deteriorate, so that when trade improves, and they are found work again, they are not in a state of physical efficiency to do justice to their work. In order to remedy this, various measures have from time to time been put upon the statute book, which enable municipal bodies to provide

P.T.O.

audience heard the Liberal receive a severe trouncing. His opponent stated that Harry Pollitt got his knowledge from penny pamphlets, such a splendid testimony that we sold a large quantity after the meeting."[14] But at Leeds it was a different story. Booked to speak for the B.S.P. in the afternoon and evening, Harry found on both occasions that on the next platform to him was Tommy Jackson speaking for the Secular Society. "He had the crowd, I had the chairman and myself. . . . The people were his; instead of proving what a wonderful orator I was, I found myself listening to a fascinating explanation of the works of George Meredith. The effect on me was that I stinted myself to buy Meredith's collected works."[15] In these years Harry looked so young that on first visits the comrades thought he was deputising for his father and were chary of introducing him as principal speaker. He also spoke at working men's clubs and trade union branches in Manchester, including the Stanley Street club in Openshaw and the Boilermakers Club at Newton Heath and for the Suffragettes at Old Lane[16]; and sometimes he attended the Higher Openshaw Literary and Debating Society at the Gransmoor.

2. "Don't shoot"

The industrial upsurge continued. In March 1912 a million miners struck for the principle of a minimum wage, the biggest strike yet seen in Britain. In Openshaw, for want of coal, factories and rail yards closed down or went on short time. The city made some coke available, but many people had no fire at home for a week. The Openshaw B.S.P. championed the miners' cause, giving out 6,000 leaflets and speaking in the streets. Again the government mobilised troops and this time Tom Mann roused the whole Labour movement to action. Speaking in Salford and Pendleton, he called attention to the preparation of temporary barracks in Manchester and protested at the prison sentences on those responsible for a leaflet headed "Don't Shoot!" distributed to soldiers. The text of this leaflet had first appeared in Jim Larkin's paper *The Irish Worker*, then in *The Syndicalist*[17] Tom Mann read the appeal in full, including . . . "When we go on strike to better our lot, which is also the lot of your fathers, mothers, brothers and sisters, you are called upon by your officers to murder us. . . . Boys, don't do it!"

Tom was arrested and charged at the Manchester Assizes[18] on May 9 with "Incitement to Mutiny". The public benches were packed, crowds outside could not get in. Dick Coppock and Harry Pollitt, who had taken food in for Tom in Strangeways prison, were in court and heard him state his full agreement with the spirit and object of the appeal.[19]

His grounds for pleading "Not Guilty" were that "in case of civil disobedience a command must be in accord with civil law, for a soldier assisting the civil authority is a citizen . . . murder cannot be lawful" . . . "the use of soldiers to shoot workers is murder and should not be various food dispensing stations for the benefit of these unemployed. This, however, is now failing to meet the problem adequately, so that the greatest piece of social reform that has yet been brought to light (the Insurance Bill) is going to be passed in order to do this work of keeping the workers in a better physical condition—not, mark you, to solve the unemployed problem, but only to act upon the evils resultant from unemployment and low wages; so that, with the position of the workers becoming more insecure, in order that they will not begin to be too aggressive and militant in their demands, social reforms are now put upon the Statute Book with the rapidity that the fungus grows in the night. Therefore, social reforms serve two very important purposes for the Capitalist Class: (1) They keep the worker in a better working condition; (2) they bolster and patch up all the evils that this capitalist system produces. It is no duty of the Socialist Party to propagate Social Reform, because as Socialists we recognise that, with the development of the system, the time is getting more and more ripe for the complete abolition of Capitalism altogether, because the productive process to-day has been brought to such a perfect pitch by the sub-division of labour and the introduction of labour-saving machinery that every commodity is a product of social human labour. Yet, despite this, individual appropriation still remains, so that you have the contribution of social production for individual appropriation, and Socialism proposes that for this we should substitute social production for social use. Therefore, we should turn all our attention to the study of the economics of Socialism, in order that we shall be in a fit condition to take over the mighty factors of wealth production, because the Capitalist Class will look after all the social reforms that they think are necessary in order to stave off the time of the Social Revolution. Therefore, on November 1, vote for the revolutionary Socialist Candidate, who realises that the only method by which we can solve the poverty of to-day is by the application of the principles of Social Democracy, which alone can redeem humanity from industrial chaos and anarchy. Therefore,

Register your Vote For the Principles of Socialism,

thus:

WHITEHEAD | X

Printed and published by Mark Buckley & Sons, Ferns Street, Openshaw.

now stood him in good stead and he "made a name for himself in support of the strikers."[25]

7. THE CITY ELECTIONS.

With the 1911 City Elections, political differences between the I.L.P. and the Openshaw Socialist Society came to a head.

Socialist elation at the Labour successes in the 1906 election was followed by considerable disquiet at what many felt to be the excessive moderation of the Labour M.Ps. In 1907 a militant socialist, Victor Grayson, standing against the wishes of the Labour leaders, won a by-election in Colne Valley. This success was regarded by militants elsewhere as a sign of mass discontent with the moderates. In June 1909 the O.S.S. voted by 107 to 100 to "secede" from the I.L.P.; in September it withdrew from the Gorton Trades and Labour Council; in 1910 it refused a hearing to the Labour candidate for the City Council; in 1911 it withdrew from the joint socialist election committee and decided to put up its own 'revolutionary socialist' candidate in opposition to the official Labour candidate, a member of the I.L.P.[26] The politics of this decision were expressed by Harry Pollitt in his first printed election leaflet.

In it he posed the question "Socialism or Social Reform?" He argued that socialism is revolutionary because it means the replacement of the capitalist system by a new and different system, based on "social production for social use". Socialism will end the private capitalist appropriation of the product of social labour, and thus abolish poverty and other evils arising from it. In contrast, Social Reform "acts only upon effects and not causes", and therefore can be made use of by the capitalists as a palliative to weaken working-class militancy and "a means of staving off social revolution".[27]

This leaflet showed that the Openshaw Socialist Society was in advance of the general Labour movement and of the I.L.P. in its understanding of the Marxist concept that socialism requires that capitalism be ended, not merely improved, and that to end it needs a political and social revolution. At that time the name of Lenin was certainly unknown in Openshaw, yet in this leaflet Pollitt expresses the same thought as Lenin did when fighting the revisionists who demanded that "Social-democracy must change from a party of revolution into a democratic party of social reform."[28] But the leaflet then dismissed reforms as of no concern to socialists, and in place of struggle for immediate demands advocated only "the study of the economics of socialism" in order that "we shall be able to take over the mighty factors of wealth production."

The Labour candidate was the same H.H. Lawrie who had been secretary of the Labourers Strike Committee. His agent pointed this out in a leaflet, adding that the strikes had put "a £1,000 a week in increased wages" into the electors' pockets. The Labour vote was 1,628, the O.S.S. got 148, and the Tory won by 126.

Together with the political issue there was a personal one. Lawrie had joined the O.S.S. in October 1910, been elected to committees, accepted the position of Election Agent for the revolutionary socialist candidate, and later agreed to be himself considered as O.S.S. candidate. In these twelve months he appeared to be fully in support of the O.S.S. policy. Suddenly he resigned from the O.S.S. and was announced as official Labour candidate.[29]

8. 21ST BIRTHDAY PRESENT.

For his twenty-first birthday Harry's mother gave him the first volume of Karl Marx's *Capital.* She could hardly have chosen a more appropriate present or one which would have been more appreciated. "I felt that I owned the world" was how he described his feelings on receiving it. This book extended the frontiers of his mental world and provided a scientific basis for his aspirations for a socialist revolution.

Capital embodied a lifetime of intense intellectual labour by one of the greatest thinkers mankind has produced. It is a critical study of the processes of capitalist production and of the accumulation of capital. It explains how capitalism arose, developed and is motivated. It shows that capitalist profit originates in the fact that the worker is legally robbed of a substantial part of the fruits of his labour, and that capitalist competition leads to the concentration of capital on the one hand and on the other to a massive working class whose basic interests are in the overthrow of capitalist rule and the establishment of socialism. It is an arsenal for the propagandist, an example of meticulous precision in scientific analysis and an eloquent expression of passionate feeling for mankind's well being, rights and dignity. Its pages animate the reader with the inspiration of a great mind devoting itself to a great purpose. Reading it gave further strength to Harry's growing determination to devote himself to the cause of the working people.

In this he received full co-operation from his mother. "She was my pal. I confided to her all my hopes and ambitions. She guided my every step", he wrote. She first explained economics and industrial history, then took him to socialist meetings. When he began public speaking, he would get up on a chair at home and practice his speeches on her, and after a meeting she wanted to know every question he had been asked and how he had answered. This interest she maintained all her life. And she offered sound advice: "Always explain a situation as plainly as possible, so that the workers will understand."[30]

9. TOWARDS A MARXIST PARTY

The O.S.S. expressed a revolutionary trend developing in the working class under the dual influence of sharp clashes in industry and the weakness of Labourism in Parliament. As the established national leaders of the I.L.P. were seen to be firm supporters of reformism and parliamentarianism, the militant trend came closer to the Marxists in the Social Democratic Party, as the old Social Democratic Federation now called itself. In August 1911, Victor Grayson, M.P. and others, including the O.S.S., launched a call for a united party with clearly defined socialist aims.[31] In response 218 delegates came to a conference in Salford in October 1911, 86 from the S.D.P., 41 from the I.L.P., 32 from Clarion organisations, 48 from Socialist Societies and 11 from already formed branches of the new party. They decided to call the new party the British Socialist Party, to come into being on January 1 1912.[32]

The O.S.S. delegates, Jim Crossley and Jack Munroe, voted for this decision. A special members meeting endorsed their action and agreed to become the Openshaw Branch of the B.S.P. Harry Pollitt as Secretary reported the decision to *Justice*, which on January 13 1912 announced that the B.S.P. Executive had accepted the Openshaw Branch.

In the five years of its existence the O.S.S. membership, their commitment varying from sympathy to dedication, reached about 300 at its peak. It began as a socialist social club and grew into a local political party led by Marxists. It was very active in outdoor and indoor socialist propaganda and education, but that it did not take root among the local workers was shown by the low votes for its candidates. Its leaders appeared locally mainly as speakers who played little or no other part in local life; its candidates for the City Council came from other parts of Manchester. Of the 20,000 workers in the Openshaw factories, many living locally, only a handful of the skilled men joined the O.S.S.

Such information as survives (see Appendix) shows that with a few exceptions the industrial members were not leaders in the trade unions nor in their factories; that there was a sprinkling of professional people and small shopkeepers; and a tendency to family membership.

Later Pollitt pointed to the weakness in the propaganda; "The speeches dealt with primitive communism, chattel slavery, feudalism, mercantilism, modern capitalism and socialism, hardly mentioning the everyday fight against capitalism, nor did we agitate for an immediate programme. That would have been reformism and anathema to us."[33]

But it is to the credit and honour of the Openshaw Socialist Society that, despite its separation from the mass labour movement, it courageously kept aloft the banner of revolutionary socialism and refused to surrender to the prevailing reformism.

CHAPTER 4

OPENSHAW BRANCH OF THE BRITISH SOCIALIST PARTY

1. Branch secretary.   2. 'Don't shoot'.   3. 'The Iron Heel'.
4. Clarion cyclists.   5. Class conflict in Dublin, 1913.   6. Problems of policy.   7. Gilbert Roberts (1881-1933), a Marxist influence.

1. BRANCH SECRETARY

From its inception till he left Manchester in February 1915, Harry was Secretary of the Openshaw Branch of the B.S.P. Its activities were partly reflected in his weekly reports to *Justice*. Of the 1912 B.S.P. annual conference he wrote that Openshaw looked to it "to place the party on a sound revolutionary basis", a remark indicating dissatisfaction, but not formulating what he wanted. He was a delegate to national conference only in 1913, but let his fellow delegate, Gilbert Roberts, do the talking. In 1914 he got six votes for a divisional seat on the Executive; the winning votes were 36, 35, 26.

At the Socialist Hall, meetings, lectures, classes, debates, social functions and, of course, the Socialist Sunday School were in full spate. The Clarion Cycling Club, the Vocal Union, the Clarion Choir and a Socialist Orchestra all met there. Once he appealed "sopranos and tenors are urgently needed" and invited "all lady socialists to choir practice", but did not report the results. Concerts and recitals were frequent, with Ella Pollitt among the singers.

He organised a lending library with "the cream of Socialist literature," and was often in the entrance hall near the display of books and pamphlets talking to members and suggesting what to read. The literature secretary, Charlie Openshaw, had Harry's full support; he considered it "a key position and selling literature our most important political duty". The penny pamphlet was then, next to the weekly journals, the main medium of education, and the appearance of a new one was an event. Books by Marx and Engels from the Chicago firm of Charles Kerr and Co. were always on sale.[1]

The internationalist spirit was strong. Harry proudly concluded the winter events programme with the words, "Socialism is international in its aspect, recognising no creed or colour. The British Socialist Party is affiliated to the Socialist International, a bond of brotherhood millions strong ... its aim is the world's wealth for the world's workers."[2] When the German Social Democratic Party won 4 million votes and 100 seats in the Reichstag, the Branch wired congratulations, adding that the German Social Democrats "had the full backing of the Openshaw Branch."[3]

Meetings and lectures[4] were enlivened by many visiting speakers, including the ever-popular stalwarts Bill Gee and F. G. Jones. Abel Bradshaw of the Manchester Microscopical Society illustrated his talks on science by lantern slides. J. Taylor spoke on "The Chinese Revolution", Ernest Marklew from Grimsby spoke several times; Harry "greatly admired his oratory". Miss Boltansky lectured on "Education and Heredity" and on the "Biological Aspect of the Woman Question". Some of the lecturers were from Owens College, which later grew into Manchester University, where Professor Weiss was developing extra-mural activities. The concerts and socials also had as appreciated visitors, Willie Paul, a powerful and expressive barritone who rendered songs of the Irish potato famine, and Bonar Thompson who recited "Cyrano".[5]

Harry's efforts to build "the sound and efficient organisation necessary for success" were unremitting—"There is every scope for good work, do your share", "our chalking squad to decorate the pavements is a fine chance for budding artists", "our summer campaign will be the finest ever if all comrades rally round the Red Flag", "Any comrade who can spare an evening can be filled in with that particular hobby of ours—work". He generously acknowledged what was done, and occasionally chided backsliders. Those who "signed forms but failed to become members" were told, "Sympathy without backing is no use; every hand is required to see that our ship reaches port in good time." Once he had to appeal for teachers for the Socialist Sunday School "or else it will close. Don't let this calamity happen." There was a response, for the School continued and counted 70 children and 30 parents attending an outing.[6]

The two most colourful visiting personalities were women. Madame Sorgue was sent by the French trade unions to tour Britain in support of a miners' strike in South Wales. A Brussels magistrate called her "the most dangerous woman in Europe". She was good looking, sturdily built, wore over her shoulder a "broad, bright red sash fastened at the waist. Straight back and prominent bust, she strode like a sergeant major on parade".[7] She nicely sized up Ramsay MacDonald: "He may raise himself to power; he will never raise the proletariat to a higher standard of life."[8] She had expected a big meeting, not a small club, and Harry had to go to her hotel to persuade her to come. She did come, and carried the meeting with her on the theme that "the workers by consolidating their forces can prevent a European war."[9]

Harry also mobilised Madame San Carolo, daughter of a countess from an ancient Venetian family who had married an English army officer. "She gave two magnificent recitals greatly appreciated by enthusiastic audiences. One filled the Whitworth Hall, the other the Socialist Hall. She began with a talk on Songs of the Revolution, including those against foreign aggression and against domestic tyrants. Her recitals included

'Scots Wha Hae wi' Wallace Bled', the 'Ça Ira' and the 'Marseillaise', a Hindoo song against the British, Chartist songs, and the war hymn of Garibaldi."[10]

In 1912, the engineering apprentices came out in September for 1s. a week rise. The strike began in Openshaw, was assisted by the Gorton Trades Council, and spread through Manchester. The press commented on the efficiency of organisation and picketing. The lads in Gorton Tank were well to the fore; one of them remarked "What a pity Harry Pollitt isn't still here, he would have been in his element."[11]

An incident in 1912 gave Harry an insight into one of the undercurrents of politics. A deputation of Branch members came to see him one dinner hour; representatives of the Tory prospective candidate for Gorton had proposed that a revolutionary Socialist candidate be put up, financed secretly by Tory money. Harry's indignation was by no means cooled when he was told that in 1910 when Bill Gee contested Ashton-under-Lyne Tory money was accepted by some of his supporters, though Bill knew nothing of it. Harry insisted and the comrades agreed that the Tory offer be turned down "with a bang".[12]

The climax of this year of extended collective effort was the 1912 city election campaign. Under the slogan "Openshaw expects every Socialist to do his duty", Harry mobilised every possible support. Bill Gee came for two weeks, F. G. Jones for one; speakers came from other B.S.P. branches, there were "meetings every night, better sales of literature, boundless enthusiasm". Madame Carolo sang, as did the Clarion Choir. But the Openshaw workers remained unmoved. Labour got 1,275, the revolutionary candidate "who never promised a single palliative" got 260. But Harry was not depressed: "The result," he wrote, "augurs ill for Labour misrepresentatives in future." Moss Side B.S.P., who had come to help, had doubts; such a vote in a purely industrial area with a branch of 300, good premises, and many years' standing, they thought, "needed explanation". There must have been doubts in Openshaw, too, for the members met to hear Sam Hague, the Labour agent, speak on "Socialist Unity and Policy". The Branch put up a candidate once more in 1913 when the vote fell to 183, Labour winning the seat by 1,617 against the Tory 1,433.

In these years Harry became well known as a speaker all over Lancashire and Yorkshire. In addition to the open-air meetings held on Sunday runs of the Clarion Cycling Club, he was invited by several B.S.P. Branches. In May 1912, Warrington reported "Harry Pollitt fairly captivated the crowd," and Liverpool said "Everyone should hear this young and experienced propagandist"[13]—a change from his visit when the chairman's introduction was still in full spate at 9 p.m. when Harry had to leave for home. On a glorious July evening Harry had his first public debate, also in Liverpool, the subject being "Liberalism versus Socialism", his opponent a schoolmaster. The Liverpool comrades reported "a large done and the working class are entitled to say so to soldiers who are members of that class." The judge sentenced Tom to six months in prison. A tremendous protest movement swept the country. At crowded meetings the full text of the appeal was read aloud, often with the audience repeating the words. The idea "Don't Shoot!" became alive in the minds of hundreds of thousands. Tom Mann was released after six weeks.

3. "THE IRON HEEL"

When in November 1912 the indefatigable Miss Boltansky again lectured at the Socialist Hall, she was Mrs. McKellen, and her husband sat at the back of the class. He got into conversation with Harry, to whom he gave a copy of Jack London's book *The Iron Heel*.[20]

Harry read for the first time this enthralling story, a vision of future revolutionary struggles against the big capitalist trusts, their mercenary troops and a corrupted labour aristocracy. He contrasted it to Blatchford's books "which gave an elementary understanding of socialism, but never imparted that bitterness against capitalism so essential in steeling one to do battle against the capitalist system as did *The Iron Heel* with its hatred and contempt for the rich and its merciless exposures of the capitalist system, its parasites and profiteers".

His favourite chapter was the one depicting the verbal battle between the socialist hero of the book, Ernest Everhard, and an assembly of hard-faced capitalists and their ideological apologists, to whose arguments Everhard replied with "scathing yet simple words, exposing their greed, their uselessness, their hatred of the poor". When the capitalist spokesman declared that they would use force to prevent the working class taking control and producing goods for the people's well-being, not for capitalist profit, "Everhard smites them hip and thigh with his supreme faith in the inevitable victory of the working class".

Harry at once set about getting others to read this sixpenny book. He "went round the streets of Openshaw, Ashton-under-Lyne, Salford, Manchester, Oldham, Leeds and Liverpool speaking about the book, then getting down from the mineral water box and selling it." Later, commending the book to young people, he wrote: "It will create in you a feeling of wanting to be up and doing with a heart for any fate . . . it will help to make you such a socialist that no one will ever be able to destroy your faith in the most glorious principles which have ever inspired humanity—the principles of socialism".[21]

4. CLARION CYCLISTS.

During the summers of 1912 and 1913 Harry and Ella shared in the delights of the runs organised by the Clarion Cycling Club. An enthusiast of the time describes what the advent of the bicycle meant to thousands of youngsters; "Here at last was the means of escape from city life after the round of daily toil was finished. The power to roam at large on the King's highway—a luxury hitherto almost the exclusive privilege of the rich. The rustic beauties of the country lanes and villages, the cloud-capped hills and scenic panoramas, the meres, lakes, tree-filled valleys, rocks and mountains, all—all could be seen and enjoyed by the mere possession of the magic wheel. Hence arose the Socialist cycling clubs".[22]

Meeting at Margaret Street—the greeting was "Boots", the answer, "Spurs"—they went into the villages of Cheshire and at a suitable spot would dismount and, led by Harry Fisher or Jim Crossley, would sing:

"In youth as I lay dreaming, I saw a country fair,
Where plenty shed its blessings round and all had equal share.
Where poverty's sad features were never, never seen,
And idlers in brotherhood would meet with scant esteem".

The unaccustomed sound of singing brought people to stand around, and Harry Pollitt would then make a ten-minute speech. "Very few ever remained to listen but we felt we had done our duty, and we would wind up with 'England Arise'. Returning in the evening we would repeat the performance in another village".[23]

A favourite run was the ten miles to the Club house at Handforth,[24] in a secluded position half a mile from the Cheadle-Wilmslow road. "A two-story brick and timber farm house was adapted as a country club. The old kitchen, with huge oak beams and fine oak panelling, had become a comfortable lounge. There were card and billiard rooms, a library, a dining room seating two hundred, and a well-equipped kitchen. The grounds included two orchards, a kitchen garden, an open air theatre, two tennis courts, football and cricket pitches. There were beds for 60 in summer and 50 in winter".[25] On a fine Sunday as many as 400 sat down to tea. Harry liked to spend a week-end there, but Ella was not allowed by her parents to be away from home for a night.

Handforth was an outcome of much effort and experience. The first venture at a weekend in the country had been a touring van and tents in a Cheshire field in the summer of 1895. The promoters had nervously awaited the results of their advertising the camp, wondering whether the food they had laid in would be eaten. Their wildest hopes were exceeded, in eighteen days 2,200 Clarion Clubbers "came on bicycle and tricycle, boneshaker and velocipede, on old prehistoric crocks, and some on 'Mohawks' built for speed". They ate "1,400 meals not counting snacks" and 464 of them slept in the camp.[26] The success was repeated the following summer. Then one of the supporters, who had read the description of the Guest House in *News from Nowhere*, William Morris's dream of a socialist society, suggested a permanent country house club instead of the camp. The idea took on, £500 was raised in 5s. shares, a detached villa near Altrincham was rented and in 1897 the resultant club, "a rendezvous of kindred souls bubbling over with the spirit of newly found Fellowship" was "indeed a taste of the joys to be had in 'the days a-coming'." But disapproving eyes were upon them. "The utter absence of Sabbatarianism, class distinction and moth-eaten convention . . . offended the local Mrs. Grundys and roused the ire of the Lord of the Manor."[27] There was no renewal of the five year lease and the search for another Garden of Eden began, Handforth being the result.

March 1913 saw Harry among the Clarion Cyclists off in force to the annual meet at York, where the programme included concerts, visits to the Minster, athletic events, river trips, and of course, meetings. The recorded attendance was 1,030. The Sunday night meeting had two overflows.[28] Harry was asked to speak at one from the Clarion van and did so, unprepared, "with a torrent of words". The next speaker, Fred Bramley, later Secretary of the T.U.C., remarked that he did not know the boy who had just spoken, but "thought that one day he might be a leading figure in the Labour movement."[29]

5. Class conflict in Dublin, 1913.

In the autumn of 1913 a bitter class conflict in Dublin held the attention of British socialists and aroused a wide solidarity movement. The Dublin employers were "determined to crush out trade unionism"[30] and the workers led by Jim Larkin and his Irish Transport and General Workers Union were as determined to secure its recognition. The names of Jim Larkin and his lieutenant James Connolly were familiar to Harry Pollitt; their paper *The Irish Worker* circulated in Manchester, they occasionally spoke at Socialist meetings and when in Manchester frequented the Clarion Cafe.

Jim Larkin, "a giant, six feet two inches high, breadth and depth in keeping, powerful body topped by a fine head with rugged features and alert eyes . . . the glamour and rich imagination of the Celt, the restlessness and vitality of youth, the vigour of a clean living, clear thinking man", personified the feelings, thoughts and aspirations of the Dublin workers. For five years prior to 1913 he organised them in one struggle after another, in his own words "lifted men and women out of the bog, put them on firm ground . . . gave them new hope . . . made them see the folly of fighting one another over religious and political differences".[31] Lenin, not a man given to extravagance, summed up—"he has performed miracles among the unskilled workers".[32]

In May 1913 Larkin, having secured union recognition from the Dublin port employers, began to organise the tramwaymen. The employers refused recognition, dismissed Larkinites and replaced them by non-union labour. The conflict spread, 400 employers locked out 25,000 workers, demanding as a condition of employment the signing of an undertaking not to belong to a trade union. Their demand was described by the British T.U.C. as a "direct attack on trade unionism" and by a government-sponsored enquiry as one that "no self-respecting workman could accept". The government thrice arrested Larkin, he was sentenced to seven months but a storm of protest secured his release after seventeen days. The police used batons without mercy, killing two workers in an attack on the union headquarters.[33]

The Openshaw B.S.P. popularised the cause of the Dublin workers, collecting food and money, as did the British Labour Movement as a whole. On September 26 the steamship "Hare" left Manchester docks at 5 p.m., flags and streamers flying, cheered by hundreds of workers on the banks of the Ship Canal.[34] She carried 250 tons of food in 60,000 packets ready to be distributed—tea, jam, butter, fish, biscuits, potatoes. The Co-operative Wholesale Society in 48 hours from signing the contract had supplied the food at cost, chartered the ship and made all arrangements, also ordering the baking of 30,000 loaves in Ireland. An eye-witness on the "Hare" recorded: "In ordinary circumstances we should have been fogbound all night at Eastham Locks but with heroic decision, skilful seamanship and sympathy for those who hungered, the skipper slowly cut his way through the terrible gloom of the night". The ship arrived at Dublin at 1.30 p.m. next day, welcomed by hooting sirens, ringing bells and cheers from thousands of men, women and children lining the banks of the "black, typhoid-infested Liffey". The sight of the starving on the quay side was "appalling and beyond description".

In November, when the employers brought in blacklegs, the Union withdrew its members from the Port. An eyewitness saw at the Union food distribution centre "hundreds of women and children lined up inside and outside, they are slowly dying of hunger, old and young, mothers and grandmothers, thin and spare, faces deathly white, eyes red, burning with hunger and suffering". Winter was coming "the women have coat and skirt but not a vestige of blouse or underlinen", the children had no boots or stockings, some were "clad only in sacking".[35]

Larkin was the soul of the resistance, "a stern rugged, uncompromising figure, minatory, denunciatory, eager, fierce, almost livid face thrust forward, arms swaying menacingly", "a great primeval force, his personality caught up, assimilated and threw back to the vast crowd that surrounded him every emotion that swayed them, every pain and joy they had ever felt, made articulate and sanctified."[36] But not enough food was coming and the employers could only be beaten if British labour would stop the transport of goods to and from Dublin. Larkin appealed for action and spoke at several great meetings, one in Liverpool.[37]

He had been billed for a B.S.P. solidarity meeting in Grimsby. When the Irish comrades learnt that the chairman, Ernest Marklew, had been involved in divorce proceedings, however, they felt that for Larkin to appear with him would enable hostile elements in Dublin to arouse

41

prejudice. The Grimsby B.S.P. then paid Harry the compliment of asking him to substitute for Larkin. This he did so successfully that the collection for the strikers was over £17, then a substantial sum.[38]

The decisive trade union leaders, who had always been lukewarm in their support, now went cold. They had earlier ordered Liverpool railwaymen back to work when they had refused to handle goods for Dublin, and likewise those at Crewe, Birmingham, Derby and Sheffield who supported them. In December, at a special Trade Union Conference in London, the leaders secured the defeat of a solidarity resolution. The T.U.C. delegation to Dublin and the Parliamentary Committee had declared that a "basic principle of trade unionism" was at stake in Dublin. But when confronted with the necessity of solidarity action to maintain this principle, they abandoned it and took a position which in fact lined them up alongside the Dublin employers, police and government against the workers. It was becoming evident that two opposing trends were at work in the trade unions.

6. Problems of Policy

The Openshaw Socialist Society had been a law unto itself; the B.S.P. had a Constitution and an Executive. Its dominant figure was H.M. Hyndman, one of those controversial personalities who arouse strong likes and equally strong, if not stronger, dislikes. Pollitt "disliked him for his arrogance and snobbishness from the first moment I set eyes on him on the platform."[39] This impression, for they were never in personal contact, may have arisen from Hyndman's habit of appearing with frock coat and top hat—symbols of his upper-class origin and public school education—or from his tendency to disapprove of trade unions, especially when on strike. The Openshaw Branch "was never very happy in the B.S.P., always in disfavour with Head Office". The political differences turned around basic questions—the Labour Party, trade unionism, and internationalism.

A major source of disagreement was the Openshaw opposition to official Labour candidates. Contesting against Labour conflicted with the policy of seeking to get B.S.P. members adopted as Labour candidates. The E.C. told the branch that "their splendid propaganda work had been depreciated by their election attitude". Hyndman went further. His comment on Pollitt's letter stating the Openshaw case was: "impossible anarchists"; and adding injury to insult, he spoke in Openshaw for the official Labour candidate, an action provoking protest at the B.S.P. 1914 Conference, and not forgotten[40] in 1920.

Openshaw also opposed B.S.P. affiliation to the Labour Party as being "in direct opposition to the principles of revolutionary socialism." The Executive favoured affiliation, acting on the International Socialist Bureau's proposal that the B.S.P., the I.L.P. and the Fabian Society amalgamate to form one party affiliated to the Labour Party. Hyndman, looking back thirteen years, "regretted they had left the Labour Party; they would have done better to stay in".[41] A B.S.P. ballot gave a majority for affiliation, and the application made in June 1914 was accepted by the 1916 Labour Party Conference. But Openshaw maintained their opposition till 1919. Harry did not support affiliation till 1920.

Openshaw's attitude to the Labour Party was connected with their view that a programme of immediate reforms "would obscure the class war issue". "Insofar as they entered into competition with the capitalist parties in offering to the people more reforms, they themselves would become a reformist party."[42]

The Hyndman attitude of dissociation from trade unionism was reflected in a May Day cartoon.[43] It depicted a tug-of-war between Capital, well fed, well clad, with police and military standing by, and Labour, thin, ragged, with hungry wife and children. The rope is inscribed "Means of Life". A beautiful female figure, watching with compassion, points to a picture of future plenty, "The Co-operative Commonwealth". The caption "The Real Tug-of-War" gives "The Message of the Socialist Party" as "Why not use your brains and strength to realise the Co-operative Commonwealth, where the full fruits of labour could be enjoyed with work and plenty for all?" This mixture of pity and superiority could only raise Pollitt's hackles.

But Hyndman went further. He wrote:[44] "Can anything be imagined more foolish, more harmful, more, in the widest sense of the word, unsocial, than a strike? ... Trade unions, by admitting wages as the permanent basis of the industrial system, virtually condemn their members to continuous toil for the benefit of the profit takers so long as that view prevails. The organisation of the trade unions is sometimes useful, their theory of society is hopeless. . . . Strikes, syndicalism, anarchy, are but varying forms of restless working-class ignorance or despairing revolts against unendurable oppression." This patronising disapproval of forms of struggle which Pollitt knew from experience to be essential in working-class life must have been all the more irritating because there was a germ of truth in its reference to the limitations of the trade union outlook.

Not all members of the B.S.P. agreed with Hyndman's views on trade unionism; many did responsible work in trade unions and in strikes. But the E.C. never challenged him and in the public eye he was the B.S.P. spokesman; he had earned this position by his years of indefatigable propaganda.

Later Pollitt wrote: "I heard Hyndman, Harry Quelch, Tom Kennedy, Dan Irving, Bill Gee when at the height of their fame—I cannot remember a single speech or article dealing with the necessity of activity in the unions or their role in a socialist state. Many a time Tom Mann told me the greatest mistake of the S.D.F. leaders was their contemptuous attitude to the trade unions. This was why he did not last long with them."[45]

A third issue was internationalism. The Openshaw Branch opposed Hyndman's support of British naval re-armament against Germany, and at the 1912 B.S.P. Conference voted with the majority who defeated him. The full implications of this difference became clear in the 1914 war.

7. GILBERT ROBERTS (1881-1933), A MARXIST INFLUENCE

The leading Marxist in Openshaw throughout these years was Gilbert Roberts, one of the founders of the Openshaw Socialist Society, though never in the I.L.P. Well read, an effective speaker and debater, he was repeatedly elected delegate to B.S.P. Conferences, and had much influence on Pollitt politically.[46]

Roberts' parents were strongly Conservative. As a youth he was a labourer in an engineering factory. Later he travelled widely for a Manchester hosiery firm. An attractive personality, handsome, immaculate in dress, appreciative of classical music, he wrote verse, sang, and played the flute. A great socialite and an excellent host, he gave parties with plenty of good food and drink, music and singing, at which he welcomed political friends and acquaintances.

His socialism was revolutionary and internationalist, he was consistently opposed to reformism, but assumed that any programme of immediate demands was necessarily identical with reformism.

From the start of the 1914 war he denounced it as imperialist and worked for the defeat of the pro-war group in the B.S.P. At the 1916 conference he criticised the Executive for "lukewarmness in recognising the service rendered by our imprisoned members". He refused on socialist grounds to do military service and was directed to "work of national importance" in Glasgow. In 1918 he said, "Bolshevik interests are those of the workers of the world" and denounced "those who had bathed Europe in blood for three and a half years and now pretend concern at bloodshed in Russia." In 1919 he supported the Communist International.

For some years he opposed B.S.P. affiliation to the Labour Party. By 1919 experience had convinced him to a change of view: among workers the call was being heard for a general strike for political ends, and "the B.S.P. should continue affiliation to constitute a revolutionary left wing in the Labour Party." In 1920 he wanted the Communist Party affiliated to the Labour Party because "on the verge of a revolutionary situation, the working class who would have to make the revolution, were not giving conscious thought to the problem", and the Party must be among them.

Roberts did not think that the socialist revolution could come through Parliament, nor could industrial unionism bring it about. He wanted revolutionary representatives in Parliament to be seen attacking capitalism and defending the working class. Marxists should be active in all trade unions; workshop organisation and socialist education were equally essential to develop class consciousness. He rejected the idea of "socialist unions as opposed to craft or industrial unions," and supported the 1918 B.S.P. conference resolution advocating industrial unionism based on recognition of the class struggle. In 1919-20 he worked whole-heartedly for the formation of a united Communist Party.[47] From what is known about him comes the impression of a sincere Marxist, prepared to learn from experience, and fearlessly taking a principled position on decisive issues.

CHAPTER 5

AGAINST IMPERIALIST WAR
August 1914 to November 1917

*1. Anti-war propaganda.   2. Shop steward at Armstrong Whitworth.
3. Strike at Southampton.   4. Gathering storm.*

1. ANTI-WAR PROPAGANDA

In August 1914 Harry Pollitt was not fully aware of the declared attitude of the Socialist International, for *Justice* had made only cursory reference to its 1912 resolution calling for international action to prevent war and, if war began, to struggle to stop it and end capitalist rule. But he felt not the slightest doubt that the 1914 war was "not one which the workers could support",[1] and he set out to tell them so.

He had a date to speak at the regular Sunday morning meeting of the Ashton B.S.P. soon after war was declared. On the walk there Jim Crossley thought "that being a barrack town, there might be a little bother". Their platform was a circus cart, and in the crowd were many red coats. Harry roundly denounced the war as imperialist and "called on the workers to use the opportunity to make war on capitalism". Mutterings grew into shouts, the crowd dragged the 'platform' round the Market Ground and only its high sides and the vigorous wielding of chairs by chairman and speakers saved the speakers from physical assault. "Lucky to escape without injury", they were escorted by police to the Openshaw tram and strongly advised not to come back. That however was what Harry did the next night, in his working clothes; his mother, aware of his intention, had taken his best suit round to her sister's. A bigger and more hostile crowd awaited him, but the same policemen were there, he was not allowed to speak, and again deposited on the Openshaw tram.

The Moss Side B.S.P. then decided to hold a meeting outside the Yeomanry Barracks, the speakers being a Liverpool comrade who was an authority on English Literature, and Harry Pollitt. The remarks on English literature were tolerated but as soon as Harry announced that he "would say a few words about the war and what the workers ought to do", the din drowned anything further, some soldiers demanded that he sing 'God Save the King' and on his refusal set about him with fists and feet. He was rescued by a woman who made her way by lashing out with a serviceable umbrella, seized him by the arm and got him away from the discomforted soldiers. Once out of the crowd she said, "I'm a suffragette, and used to rough handling, good night and good luck".[2]

Everywhere the jingo atmosphere made it impossible to hold public anti-war meetings and socialist premises were sometimes attacked. At a pro-war meeting staged near the Margaret Street Hall a speaker incited the audience to attack the Hall, where a dance was going on. Someone tipped off Percy Crossley, who got the band to continue playing, "then closed one half of the main door, and stood just inside the other half. He had a fist like a hammer, and by his side, sleeves rolled up, stood hefty Maggie Fleming who was afraid of nobody. When the raiders arrived, Maggie invited them to 'come on' but they did not accept and shortly went away".[3] For a time the whipped-up wave of pro-war hysteria continued to rise; "workers who you never thought could be swept off their feet by jingoism and flag waving, could by some incident or other be so transformed, though perhaps only temporarily, that they did not appear to be the same people."

The Openshaw Branch shared Harry's views and came into renewed conflict with the B.S.P. Executive, which together with the Labour Party had rapidly retreated from initial opposition to supporting the war as a war for democracy against Prussian militarism. When in September *Justice* called for support for recruiting, Openshaw was one of many branches which objected. It soon became apparent that the Executive was split and that opinions were hardening. Reading his *Justice* Harry found his conviction strengthened by declarations of the Italian Socialist Party, of Liebknecht, Luxembourg, Mehring and Zetkin in Germany and, clearest of all, the call of the Russian Social Democratic Labour Party, Lenin's party, for intensified class struggle against the war in all countries.

The B.S.P. leaders who supported the war gradually lost ground, until those who saw the war as the inevitable outcome of capitalism, with all the great powers equally responsible, got a majority of one on the E.C. during 1915 when no national conference was held. Openshaw consistently supported the internationalist position. In December 1914 it decided to cancel a concert if the singing of 'God Save the King' were insisted upon, and called for a special meeting of the International Socialist Bureau to formulate peace proposals acceptable to the whole international socialist movement.[4] In January 1915 it decided to reply to the pro-war manifesto circulated by "old and active members" of the S.D.F. and B.S.P.[5]

In February 1915 Harry Pollitt resigned his position as Secretary of the Openshaw B.S.P. and Jim Crossley took over. Meantime Harry was working as a plate leveller at the Openshaw factory of Armstrong Whitworth where 8,000 men were employed.

2. Shop Steward at Armstrong Whitworth.

Harry had soon become a shop steward at Armstrong Whitworths, with a "splendid bunch of workmates", including Ernest Tomkinson, and a new friend, Alfred Whitney, who later went with him to many jobs all over the country.[6]

This works was opened in 1880 by Sir Joseph Whitworth, who played a leading part in the introduction of accurate measurement, standardised screw threads and the systematised production of true plane metal surfaces, all essential to the making of precision machine tools.[7] A technical revolution in the engineering industry followed. Previously "with the exception of very important lathes and a few drills, the preparatory operations of construction were effected entirely by the hands of the workmen". Mating parts were fitted by hand, using calipers and ruler; inter-changeability was impossible; each product was unique. Whitworth's innovations made possible standardised accuracy to a ten-thousandth part of an inch and opened the way to modern mass production, and in so doing struck a mortal blow at the old division of labour between craftsman and helper.

Harry had found the factory almost entirely on war work. Soon the management began to put unskilled labour on to jobs done by skilled men without consulting the unions, and the workers gave notice of strike action unless this practice stopped. The management thereupon agreed to confer with delegates from all shops, a provisional agreement favourable to the men was arrived at and the strike notices were suspended. No more unskilled men would be put on skilled work, and those already so placed would get the trade union rate for the job. The unions were to be supplied with a complete list of unskilled men and allowed to inspect the credentials and the work of all new employees. The firm guaranteed that new workers classified as dilutees would be dispensed with at the end of the war. Such provisions if generally adopted would have defeated the employers' aim to use the incoming new labour, required to increase war production, including women, as a means of paying under the skilled rate, breaking trade union strength and preventing wage increases.[8]

But this provisional agreement was overtaken by events. In March, 1915, most of the national trade union leaders agreed with the Government for the duration of the war to give up the right to strike, submit to arbitration, relax established customs and practices, and accept dilution of labour, the suspension of the Factory Acts and the speed-up of production.

In June Harry decided to enlarge his experience by getting shipyard work. Changing jobs was frowned upon but not yet forbidden. The foreman asked him, "Have you no patriotism?". "I have that", Harry replied, "but your idea of patriotism and mine are two different things".[9] And with this parting shot he and several pals, including Alf Whitney, left to try their luck in the south.

3. STRIKE AT SOUTHAMPTON.

At Southampton Harry found new friends including the Boilermakers' delegate Harry Ratcliffe, with whose family he lodged. Since there was no local B.S.P. Branch he joined the I.L.P.,[10] who issued his membership card "with pleasure". He attended their lectures but did not accept their pacifist views. A job at Thorneycrofts on Admiralty work was his first experience of shipyard work; for a time "the terms in usage were double Dutch", but the Boilermakers were well organised and he transferred to their Woolston Branch.

In July Parliament rushed through the Munitions of War Act prohibiting strikes, and imposing compulsory arbitration. It abolished freedom to leave work in controlled establishments. Any workshop action or practice having the effect of restricting production, including refusal to do a new job whatever the rate, or refusing to work overtime even if not paid extra for it, was made an offence. Penalties included heavy fines or, if not paid, imprisonment. The effect was legal sanction to employers to break down conditions secured by generations of trade union effort, to hold down wages and maximise profits. Under this Act a Royal Proclamation was posted in South Wales declaring that to strike in the coal mines was a punishable offence. Two days later 200,000 miners went on strike for higher wages. This pretty problem was solved by the Minister of Munitions, Lloyd George, rushing to Cardiff in a special train and, as Sir George Askwith mournfully recorded,[11] "giving way on all the main claims and yielding to the strikers". Thoughtful shop stewards noted the results of this confrontation, but such mass solidarity of great numbers was not easy to achieve elsewhere.

Sometimes this Act had odd results. Sir George Askwith mentions a man released from his regiment as a 'riveter'. He turned out to be a street seller of oranges, and knew or cared nothing about riveting. His sergeant had wanted to be rid of him.

Thorneycrofts was now a 'controlled establishment' and at the end of August the Ministry of Munitions sent a high official, Dr. Macnamara, to ask the workers to give up their holidays while the war lasted. His scarifying account of what was happening to the men at the front had an effect on a delegate meeting, but Pollitt, one of the boilermakers' representatives, got up and said, "The responsibility is yours and your government's. The British and German workers had no quarrel, you are sending them to slaughter one another. Our stand for trade union rights is for the benefit of the lads at the front, if we give up what they have won they will never forgive us when they come home. There is no such thing as common sacrifice and you know it. Your class caused this war, mine wants to stop it." Macnamara was furious, but he did not get the agreement he wanted.[12]

When the question of non-union men being employed on boilermakers' work arose, the firm met the men and agreed to await a decision by the Munitions Tribunal. But the manager insisted on starting meantime six non-union men released from the Army. The boilermakers, who knew that squads of riveters were on commercial work, concluded that the firm was using the Act to introduce non-union labour, and stopped work. For two weeks every form of pressure was tried to get them back—abuse in the local press, and threats by the Admiralty, the Ministry of Munitions and the national union leaders, all failed.

Harry Pollitt was one of the elected Strike Committee, and was present at a mass meeting addressed by J. T. Brownlie, well known leader of the engineers. Brownlie began "supremely confident, the famous smile on his face. 'The ship of state is at sea, a storm comes on, all lives are in danger. The whole crew must pull together to get the ship safely back to port.' This nautical analogy was strangled at birth, for a boilermaker shouted 'That's fine, but you would not send piss pot jugglers into the engine room'. With that homely expression the meeting came to an end."[13]

Threats having failed, 50 strikers were summoned under the Munitions Act; but it was 300 who caused a sensation in Winchester by marching through its quiet streets to the Tribunal at the Guildhall. The case was adjourned, due to absence of assessors,[14] and resumed in Southampton on October 2. Before the Tribunal sat in the Bargate, an ancient structure spanning the road to the docks, a conference was held to induce the Strike Committee to call off the strike.

In the midst of the argument came the sound of bagpipes and the tramp of soldiers marching to the docks. Such departures were usually at midnight, this one had been thoughtfully timed. A solicitor led Harry to the window, pointed dramatically to the marching Highlanders and said, "Can you stand here and see those men on their way to the front and refuse us permission to go into Court and say you will start work on Monday?" "Sorry," was the reply. "If my policy were adopted those men would be marching away from the docks, not to them. They are being driven to France by the same gang that is trying to drive dilutees into the shipyards. We may not be able to stop the soldiers, but at least we can stop the dilutees." On a vote, every member of the Strike Committee was against a return to work.[15]

In Court—one of the Assessors was Ernest Bevin—the counsel for the Ministry of Munitions remarked, "We ourselves belong to one of the closest unions in the world and in the Courts no one not a member of our union is allowed to practice our profession." "Not even in war time?" asked the President. "No, not even in war time" was the reply, at which the boilermakers present applauded loudly.[16] Then the strikers were sternly admonished on duty to King and Country, and given the choice of a fine of £5 or three months in prison for impeding the production of munitions. A mass meeting that night unanimously endorsed the continuation of the strike. The union officials insisted on a further meeting next morning, where Pollitt was not allowed to speak. A ballot showed a majority for resuming work pending arbitration, the bulk of those present being under the false impression that on resumption of work the non-union men would be transferred to other work.[17]

The General Secretary of the Boilermakers' Society dismissed the strike with the words: "Trouble has come upon us . . . a handful of our members have been convicted of irregular cessations of work and in Southampton we have had a strike."[18] The Executive refused to pay the fines, because the men had acted contrary to their advice. The Strike Committee appealed, however, to boilermakers all over the country, who subscribed £790.

The case went to arbitration, where the decision was in essence based on "the principle that in time of war conflicting rights must be subordinated to the major issue of war . . . rights cannot be freely exercised if such exercise hinders the production of munitions of war."[19] However, there were positive results for the men. The six dilutees were gradually removed. Thorneycrofts never again raised the question of dilutees working with boilermakers, and certain provisions in the dilution scheme were not brought into operation till 1917. The men presented Harry with a suitably inscribed silver watch—and the firm put him on a job where he was isolated from other boilermakers.

Things being thus difficult for him at Thorneycrofts, Pollitt decided for a change. He left Southampton, the military authorities offering no objection, and in February began work in Nicolson's shipyard at Northam, on relatively light work on pinnaces and adapting luxury yachts for naval purposes.

4. GATHERING STORM.

During a flying visit home in January 1916 Harry found Openshaw and other B.S.P. branches taking an active interest in the shop stewards movement. War enthusiasm had been quenched by the fearful losses of British lives in Gallipoli and France. Trade unionists were increasingly discontented with the lag of wages behind prices and the stream of convictions under the Munitions Act.[20] An all-Manchester meeting of shop stewards "associated itself fully with the attitude of the Clyde workers . . . regarding their action as an historic episode in our class struggle".[21] This referred to the Clyde mass meeting's refusal to listen to Lloyd George and Henderson on dilution. In February a new paper appeared at Margaret Street. *The Call* spoke for the anti-war trend in the B.S.P. at whose Easter Conference the Openshaw delegates voted with the majority to defeat the pro-war group, who then left the party.

In 1917 Harry returned to live at home and, after a short spell at Armstrong Whitworth, worked for a Swinton firm making ventilation plant. Going round the country fitting it up limited his local activity and he did not accept nomination for the B.S.P. Conference. Part of the year he was on the Gorton Trades and Labour Council[22] and co-operated with other left-wingers in support of the March revolution in Russia. The B.S.P. celebrated the overthrow of Tsarism by a crowded meeting on March 17 at Pendleton. Harry was among those who responded to a call to be there in case of trouble. In the event, it was "a tremendous success and inspired those present to prepare for the next round in the class struggle."[23] This was not long in coming.

Among Harry's friends in the Openshaw B.S.P. was George Peet, a Branch Secretary of the A.S.E. and Secretary of the Manchester Shop Stewards Committee. In May this Committee, after a workshop vote, called the engineers out on strike. The issue was on dilution: a Rochdale firm had put women on commercial work for which the trade unions had not accepted dilution. The skilled men refused to instruct them; the firm insisted, the men struck, the strike spread. Manchester demanded that the Government should withdraw its Bill to legalise dilution on private work and should not withdraw the Trade Card exemption scheme, a part of the bargain for union acceptance of dilution. The Trade Card, issued by the unions to skilled workers, over-ruled a military call-up notice, and its withdrawal would leave the military tribunal the sole authority for exemption. Openshaw was a centre of the strike; when the King and Queen visited Armstrong Whitworth's they found production interrupted, but were consoled by being shown "a gun casting seventy feet long raised red-hot from a furnace and plunged into a deep well of oil".[24]

The strike spread to forty-two English munition centres; 200,000 men lost one and a half million working days.[25] The Government order and the Union Executive's appeal to return to work were ignored. On May 15 strikers' delegates met in London. The Minister of Munitions refused to receive its spokesmen, and seven leading stewards, including George Peet and P.H. Kealey of Gorton, were arrested.[26] Deprived of its key men, the conference failed to cope and handed over the dispute to the union executives on the understanding that the arrested men would be released, with no victimisation. After some confusion the strikers went back without gaining their demands. But subsequent events showed that this first nation-wide unofficial strike had influenced the Government. Extension of dilution to private work was dropped, and the leaving certificate, which meant six weeks unemployment for those who left without the employers' consent, was abolished.[27]

Industrial conflict was accompanied by a rising political movement. On June 3 a Convention of 1,150 delegates met in Leeds, sent a telegram of greeting to the Petrograd Soviet and enthusiastically endorsed the Soviet's peace policy.[28] Jim Crossley represented Openshaw B.S.P., Harry Pollitt was not present, but he kept all his life the Convention report in which he marked William Gallacher's prophetic utterance—"This Conference seems agreed that the Russian Revolution is definitely settled, but is it?

The Russian workers and soldiers have the biggest fight on, not against the capitalists of Russia, but against those of other countries, who have determined that the Socialists of Russia have to be beaten back"[29]—and his call to the delegates, "Give your own capitalist class in this country so much to do that it will not have time to attend to it."

The Convention's appeal for Councils of Workers and Soldiers Deputies in Britain proved unrealistic, but its campaign for immediate peace without annexations or indemnities and for full restoration of civil liberty in Britain was received with enthusiasm at numerous meetings. At one of these in Manchester's Stevenson Square, Harry Pollitt was among the speakers on "Socialism and Peace". The Watch Committee had refused permission for the meeting, but it took place none the less and endorsed Convention policy.[30] A further B.S.P. meeting on August 5 was broken up by rowdies. At the subsequent protest rally "an immense crowd" attended, but the police prevented the speakers from addressing them.[31]

CHAPTER 6

THE IMPACT OF THE RUSSIAN SOCIALIST REVOLUTION

*1.   November 1917.   2.   What happened to Lancashire?   3.   Violence.
4.   Working-class power.*

1. NOVEMBER 1917

Harry Pollitt was working in a small boilershop in Swinton in western Manchester when news came of a second revolution in Russia.[1] In Petrograd armed workers, soldiers and sailors of the Baltic Fleet had swept away Kerensky's provisional government and established a government of Soviets.

These events were the outcome of eight months of unprecedented mass political ferment following the March overthrow of Tsarism. Kerensky had emerged as the spokesman of a coalition of capitalist representatives and compromising socialists who supported the war against Germany and thought in terms of Russia becoming a capitalist parliamentary republic. Lenin, returned from exile, and leading the Bolshevik party supported by the workers in the industrial centres, stood for Soviet power, an immediate peace, and the transition to socialism. Events moved rapidly. In the summer Kerensky, under British and French pressure, launched an offensive against the Germans which resulted in tremendous Russian losses, defeat and military disintegration. Mass discontent was expressed in great demonstrations; Kerensky outlawed the Bolsheviks; but in September it was the Bolsheviks who organised the mass actions of the Petrograd workers to defeat a military attempt to set up a right-wing dictatorship. The Bolshevik idea that to secure peace required the overthrow of capitalist governments spread. The Kerensky government visibly failed to cope with reaction or with the rapidly growing crisis threatening economic collapse. All over the vast lands of the Russias millions of people swung to the left, the autumn municipal elections gave the Bolsheviks the majority in Petrograd, Moscow and other towns, the trade unions elected Bolsheviks to their Executives, the peasants went over to the Left Social Revolutionaries. Lenin called for insurrection, for "All Power to the Soviets". The erosion of support for Kerensky was so great, the mass upsurge in Petrograd so powerful, that on November 7 a single shot from the cruiser *Aurora* secured the surrender of the Ministers in the beleaguered Winter Palace.

On November 8 the Congress of Soviets formed a new government with

Lenin as Chairman. Its socialist and revolutionary policy was made clear by its first actions—an appeal to all the peoples for "immediate negotiations for a just, democratic peace . . . without annexations or indemnities", the expropriation of landed property without compensation and its handing over to the peasants; all nations in Russia to have the right to self-determination; complete democracy in the Army; workers' control over production; all power to the Soviets. "We must now set about building a proletarian socialist state in Russia."[2]

The impact of the Russian socialist revolution upon Pollitt was profound, it decided the future course of his life. Immediately, without hesitation, doubt or reservation, he took his stand in support of the Soviet Republic.

His decision was no temporary fit of enthusiasm, to evaporate as did that of so many others, as capitalist and reformist disapproval hardened into hatred and repressive intervention. It was not a vision of heaven on earth, an idealist dream to fade in the stern realities of the desperate struggle for survival. It was not a patronising intellectual approval made from moral heights to be withdrawn in due course on equally high moral grounds. It was conscious political support to be sustained, indeed to wax in conviction in the anxious years when the young Soviet Republic, attacked by fourteen capitalist powers, seemed doomed, and to endure for the remaining forty-three years of his life. It was a class conscious political understanding of the movement of history, of the significance to all working mankind of the breach of the imperialist front in Russia.

It was a passionate personal commitment impelling him to reject any prospect of his own aggrandisement through co-operation with the capitalist establishment and to devote his whole being to the service of the working class and the cause of socialism.

Pollitt's own explanation of the impact was: "The thing that mattered was that lads like me had whacked the bosses and the landlords; had taken their factories, their lands and their banks . . . that was enough for me. These were the lads and lasses I must support through thick and thin. I was not concerned as to whether or not the Russian Revolution had caused bloodshed, been violent and the rest of it. I had lived my life in Lancashire, had read and seen what kindhearted British bosses had done to the Lancashire working class. I knew about Peterloo."

"I had never heard of the dictatorship of the proletariat, or the expression 'Soviet Power' . . . . I did not understand the significance of the polemics between one section of social democracy and another. All I was concerned about was that power was in the hands of lads like me and whatever conception of politics had made that possible was the correct one for me."[3]

These simple and direct words came from depths of emotion and thought. They arose from experience, reading and discussion which we shall endeavour to outline.

2. What happened to Lancashire?

South-East Lancashire was the birthplace of large-scale capitalist production. From the late decades of the eighteenth century it was "converted from an obscure ill-cultivated swamp into a busy, lively region, multiplying its population tenfold in eighty years."[4] The main industry was cotton textiles. Hand spinning and weaving gave way to machines, water power to the steam engine, factories, still called "mills", multiplied, so did coal-mines, railways, canals and workshops making the required machines. Deprived of alternative livelihood, the workers were driven by hunger into the mills, where the owner reigned supreme and the only regulation was profit. The owner wanted to run his machines without pause, and by the cheapest labour. Hence the working day of 14 to 16 hours, the permanent 12 hour night shifts, cases of 30 or even 40 hours worked at a stretch with a couple of hours snatched for sleep, and the supreme abomination of child labour.

Blake wrote of the "dark, Satanic mills," Marx of the "factory hell", Frances Trollope told of what she found, "the ceaseless whirring of milling hissing wheels seizes on the tortured ear, and while threatening to destroy the delicate sense, seems bent on proving first, with a sort of mocking mercy, of how much suffering it can be the cause. The scents that reek around from oil, tainted water, and human filth, with the last, worse, nausea arising from the hot refuse of atmospheric air left by hundreds of labouring lungs, render the act of breathing a process of difficulty, disgust and pain." In these mills were working "hundreds of helpless children, divested of every trace of health, of joyousness, of youth". They were not only local children, the owners' agents scoured the country for orphans and foundlings. "Their lean distorted limbs, sallow and sunken cheeks dim, hollow eyes that speak unrest and most unnatural carefulness, give to each tiny, trembling, inelastic form a look of hideous, premature old age."[5]

Parliament could and should have put a stop to these horrors, but instead it prevented the workers from organising against them. The Combination Acts of 1799-1800 made trade unions, and efforts to organise them, illegal, thus giving the owners a free hand on wages, working conditions and child exploitation. The workers had no vote, undemocratic and corrupt elections ensured control of Parliament by the Tory landed interests. The movement for reform was met by Acts limiting organisation, assembly, speech and publication, enforced by centrally controlled police, troops and mounted yeomanry drawn from the middle classes. These were the forces in action against the Lancashire workers demonstrating for reform, the right to organise and to vote, in Manchester on August 16, 1819.

Peterloo

Early on that bright Sunday morning, Manchester and nearby towns were astir. The ranks of Reform were swelled by a severe trade depression, thousands were unemployed, weavers at work got at most 12s. for six days of sixteen hours each.[6] Processions with bands and banners marched to St. Peter's Fields: by noon 60,000 workers had gathered, their banners proclaimed "No Corn Laws", "No Borough Mongering", "Universal Suffrage", "Annual Parliaments", "Vote By Ballot". In a house overlooking the Fields were some Lancashire and Cheshire magistrates. In adjacent streets, in response to a call from the Lord Lieutenant of the county, Lord Derby, were the Manchester Yeomanry, "in a state of readiness, their sabres sharpened", hundreds of special constables, several companies of infantry, squadrons of Hussars, and a Royal Artillery troop with two 6-pounder guns.

The arrival of Orator Hunt and other speakers, escorted by a great procession, was cheered by the orderly and peaceful crowd. Before a word was spoken, the magistrates decided that "the whole bore the appearance of insurrection" and ordered the arrest of Hunt. The Yeomanry, primed with liquor and commanded by a mill-owner, charged for the platform, but lost their formation in the dense crowd. The magistrates ordered the Hussars to charge. They did so, slashing with their sabres till the Fields were clear. Eleven men were dead and hundreds wounded. Later, the Prince Regent expressed "great satisfaction" with the conduct of the magistrates, the Courts imposed heavy fines on arrested demonstrators and whitewashed the authorities.[7]

Lancashire never forgot Peterloo. In 1830 the government representative at the opening of the Liverpool-Manchester Railway was the Duke of Wellington. Approaching Manchester his train was showered with stones by a crowd of thousands. At the station more thousands prevented him from reaching the hall for the official luncheon. The train had to be reversed. He left amid jeers and boos. The people's banners told him "Remember Peterloo".[8]

The illegalisation of trade unions, the refusal of Parliament to regulate conditions in the mills, the violence of Peterloo were not aberrations. They expressed the deliberate policy of the propertied classes to extract the maximum profit from the workers.

In the pages of Marx and Engels,[9] Pollitt found the official documentation of the effects of prolonged overwork—chronic debility and disease, physical deformation, stunted growth, mental depression and vacuity, premature aging and death. One Commissioner wrote that "children have been worked a most unreasonable and cruel length of time daily ... adults have been expected to do a quantity of labour which scarcely any human being is able to endure. The consequence is that many have died prematurely, others are afflicted for life with defective constitutions and the fear of posterity enfeebled by the shattered constitution of the survivors is but too well founded."[10]

Fifty Years for Ten Hours

The early conditions were such that an eight-hour day or the abolition of child labour seemed utopian, the struggle for limitation centred on the Ten-Hour Day. For fifty years the millowners and their accomplices in high places used every possible means, within the law or in defiance of it, to refuse, delay or negate this limitation.[11] The step-by-step progress to its achievement resulted only from sustained agitation by the workers, aided by a handful of enlightened M.Ps. and later by the Factory Inspectors. Limitation of hours was not the only issue, but it was the most obdurate. In 1824 the workers forced the repeal of the Combination Acts. In 1832 the first Reform Act was passed, in 1839 the new Poor Law was modified to allow out-door relief in textile areas; in 1846 the Corn Laws were repealed. But the effective limitation of hours to 10½ per day did not come till 1853.

The Acts of 1802 and 1819 limited the hours of apprentices and of children under 12 to 72 (yes, seventy-two) per week. Both were inoperative, Parliament with tongue in cheek provided no means of enforcement. In 1832 the short-time movement described child labour regulation as "a mere farce"; a year later a Select Committee recorded the "thrashing of children to keep them awake in the afternoons",[12] its report made the factory question a national issue. Later it was officially admitted that prior to 1833 "young persons were worked all night, all day, or both, without limit".

Mass upheavals compelled the Tories to give ground on reform, but the property qualification imposed denied the vote to most workers, so the first reformed Parliament again rejected the Ten Hours. But it had to limit the working day to 5.30 a.m. to 8.30 p.m., with maxima of 8 hours for children and 12 for young persons. This Act in 1833 appointed Factory Inspectors with powers to prosecute for infringement.

The owners' riposte was to introduce a relay system dividing the working day into discontinuous periods nominally making up the permitted total hours, but in fact exceeding it. This complex arrangement made effective control impracticable. In 1844 Parliament made an ineffective attempt to stop this system. In 1847 the Tories, to avenge their defeat over the Corn Laws, voted the Ten Hours Act to come into force a year later. The owners, aided by magistrates who refused to convict on prosecutions, and by a High Court decision negating the 1844 Act, intensified the relay system so that for the fifteen hours of the working day the workers were now in, now out, for 30 minutes, for 60 minutes, in this room or that room, at this mill or that mill.

This was too much. The workers' movement became so menacing that the factory inspectors warned the government of the danger of social convulsions. At this, Parliament gave way and found the right words to establish a uniform 6 a.m. to 6 p.m. working day of 10½ hours work and 1½ hours meal times for women and young persons. It "forgot" to include children, who remained liable to the 5.30 a.m.—8.30 p.m. law, but in 1853 protest forced it to remedy the omission.

An M.P. pointed to the fearful price paid for these fifty years of delay—"During three generations of the English race the cotton trade has destroyed nine generations of factory operatives." Marx summed up: "Apart from the working-class movement that daily grew more threatening, the limiting of factory labour was dictated by the same necessity which spread guano over the English fields. The same eagerness for plunder that in one case exhausted the soil had on the other torn up by the roots the living force of the nation."[13]

Not "Things of the Past"

Pollitt's own experience and what he read in the current press showed the falsity of claims that overwork and starvation wages were "things of the past" or that reforms were modifying the blatant class contrasts. A lecturer at the Hyde Socialist Church spoke of women living, working and sleeping in small rooms sewing furs for 1s. a day; making dolls' hands for 1s. a day, or children's overalls for 2d. each, supplying their own cotton. Matchboxes were made for 2d. a gross; paper bags for 6d. a thousand; a man and wife jointly got 10s. a week for artificial flowers; a mother and daughter 5s. a week for 12 hours a day making sunshades.[14] One issue of *Clarion* reported a Camberwell girl keeping her mother and self on earnings of 8s. a week, paying 1s. 6d. rent; girls working 17 hours a day for 1s.4d. making artificial flowers; girls machining blouses for 8½d. a dozen.[15] In a Lambeth school, Lady Warwick found in Standard 1 "twenty boys told not to come home to dinner as there was no food; 16 had breakfasted on charity; 2 had no breakfast." In Standard 2 "Six had not breakfasted, 45 were habitually underfed, 34 had no dinner to go home to." In Standard 3, "Nine had no breakfast."[16]

In spite of gains whon by the organised workers, the contrast between poverty and riches was as great as ever. Openshaw was drab and dusty, but blue sky could often be seen. But in Manchester itself Pollitt could only see what its Dean described as the "black pall of smoke always over the city producing a physically C-3 people".[17] For a century this pall had been part of the city scene, lifting only during the 1842 general strike, its absence surprising the Chartist delegates on their return from London.[18] The kind of housing Pollitt saw[19] when selling *Merrie England* in the back streets was described by the Dean of Manchester: "9,000 people, five or six industrial works, two or three churches, three or four schools, crowded into a quarter of a square mile. The vicar and I have been in rooms where beds are so close that some occupants only get to their own by climbing over others." At holiday camps the Dean found "children who did not know how to use a knife and fork . . . they never had anything to cut; bread, butter and tea were their staple food." In contrast were the homes of the rich; "My own family was typical. One uncle, whose money was in coal, had a beautiful country house north of Wigan; another built a mansion in Warwickshire with superb panelling for the great library. My brothers had country houses, my father a beautiful grange in Cheshire". The Dean commented "the industrial wealth was perpetually creamed off... the City of Manchester perpetually robbed of the riches the industrial workers produced."[20]

A substantial portion of the cream went to "great territorial magnates with pervasive political influence". Such a one was the seventeenth Earl of Derby, known as the "King of Lancashire", his properties there being so extensive. A descendant of the Lord Lieutenant who mobilised troops for Peterloo, he owned 70,000 acres bringing him rents of £300,000 a year, due to the growth of factories and housing, and yielding a net income of £100,000 taxed at 1s. in the £. One of his largest houses, Knowley Hall—its dining room was 53 ft. × 37 ft.—with 28 servants and 29 gardeners, cost £50,000 a year upkeep. His outlook was reflected in his reply to a suggestion that his London home was an extravagance because so rarely used—"Well, Lady Derby must have somewhere to change when she comes up to the theatre."[21]

No wonder that Pollitt wrote "My experience in Lancashire generated in me a hatred of capitalism which I know will never leave me."[22]

3. VIOLENCE.

Pollitt not only "knew about Peterloo", but also that the state power frequently used violence against the working people.

1887: Trafalgar Square

On November 13, 1887, the Metropolitan Radical Federation asserted the right of free speech. Radicals, socialists and Irish marched against a government ban on a meeting. To enforce the ban were 4,000 police, a Guards detachment with bayonets fixed and 20 rounds apiece, and two squadrons of Life Guards. Approaching the Square the people were attacked by mounted police; for four hours the people strove to enter the Square, the Riot Act was read. Of the hundreds wounded three later died from injuries. The next Sunday came another demonstration; mounted police rode down and killed a bystander. Thousands marched to Bow Cemetery for his funeral, where William Morris spoke. The "Death Song" he wrote for this occasion

> "Not one, not one, nor thousands must they slay
> But one and all if they would dusk the day,"

was for some years sung at Socialist meetings. "Bloody Sunday", as it was called, was followed by the radical-socialist coalition winning the London County elections, and in 1892 the right to meet in the Square was officially recognised.[23]

1893: Featherstone

During a lock-out of miners the sale of accumulated coal "transmuted the misery of the miners into heaps of gold" for the owners. At Featherstone, Yorkshire, when hungry miners protested against the transport of coal from colliery stocks, the owners sent for the military. A magistrate gave the order to fire on the crowd; two men were killed and sixteen wounded. A jury "deeply regretted the extreme measures of the authorities".[24] In the Commons, John Burns said that those responsible "thought less of the interests of the community than of using soldiers and police for intimidating men whom they, as masters, were fighting."[25] The Liberal Prime Minister justified the firing.

1911: Llanelly

During the rail strike in 1911 the Home Secretary, Winston Churchill, charged the military "with protection of the railways and all railmen who continue at work," and suspended the regulation that a civil authority requisition for troops was needed. A blackleg-driven train was held up at Llanelly by railmen and miners. Troops fired, killing two and wounding several. Later the Commanding Officer claimed that he was empowered to open fire without an order by a magistrate.[26]

1911: Liverpool

With 200,000 workers on strike, no goods were moved without the authority of the Strike Committee. Strike leaders were speaking to a peaceful meeting of 6,000 men when a blackleg convoy escorted by "mounted and foot police, infantry with bayonets fixed, and a squadron of Hussars, forced their way through the mass". Troops fired, killing two workers. A union leader told the Home Secretary that those in charge could have diverted the convoy, but "deliberately drove in among the dense throng". On Sunday, August 13, 1911, police who were ordered to disperse a meeting in St. Georges Square "used their truncheons mercilessly, some taking deliberate aim at men's heads before giving them blows which despite the din could be heard yards away". There was a 12 ft. drop from the Square to a street below. "Men, women, boys and girls were pushed over the edge as rapidly and continuously as water down a steep rock. . . . It was a display of violence that horrified those who saw it."[27]

1912-14: Ireland—Tory Mutiny

When the parliamentary majority of Liberals, Labour and Irish Nationalists favoured Home Rule for Ireland, the Ulster Tories organised military style volunteers. Their declared intention of armed resistance was fully supported by the Tory Party leaders. In spring 1914, as the third reading of the Home Rule Bill approached, the Liberal Government ordered the Commander-in-Chief in Ireland to move troops to strategic positions in Ulster. He did not obey, but came to London to explain that his officers refused to move north. This was mutiny. The Ulster Volunteers seized 20,000 rifles and 3 m. round of ammunition illegally landed without the Navy noticing it. This was preparation for rebellion.[28] Field Marshal Lord Roberts said that for the army to be called upon to fight the Ulster Volunteers was "unthinkable"; and the Tory leader said "any officer who refuses is only doing his duty". Faced with an officers' mutiny, armed rebellion and Tory subversion, the Liberal Government crumpled, an amending act was passed at the same time as the Home Rule Bill, making its operation dependent on Irish agreement, and thus nullifying it. A Tory newspaper declared that "the army has killed the Home Rule Bill".[29] The Tory political and military chiefs successfully defied the parliamentary majority.

1916: Ireland—Irish Revolt

At Easter, 1916, Irish patriots took to arms, occupied the centre of Dublin and proclaimed an independent Irish Republic. This time the British Government did not hesitate: overwhelming military force crushed the rising. The President of the Provisional Republican government said, "We seem to have lost; we have not lost. We have kept faith with the past, we have handed on tradition to the future. . . . You cannot conquer Ireland, you cannot extinguish the Irish passion for freedom. If our deed has not been sufficient to win it, then our children will win it by a better deed."[30]

Pearse and thirteen others were summarily court-martialled and shot.[31] James Connolly, socialist trade union leader, wounded and unable to stand, was shot tied to a chair. The Government responsible for these "executions", regarded by the Irish, the socialists and many others as judicial murders, included Labour leaders.

1914-18: Imperialist War

The use of legalised and sanctified violence in the interests of the ruling class reached a new height in the imperialist war.

At Southampton in 1915, Pollitt saw the white hospital ships with their green bands and red crosses move slowly into the docks each morning, "an indelible picture of the agony and suffering they bore" was etched in his mind. He saw the *Mauritania* sail for the Dardanelles "every inch of space crammed with Lancashire lads". "Such spectacles turned to fever heat" his hatred of capitalism and war.[32] They were the prelude to the cumulative horrors of slaughter unprecedented—the *Mauritania* lads helplessly crowded in small boats trying to reach the shore; the men caught in the Turkish fire at Gallipoli where British losses reached 200,000; the 1916 battle on the Somme, on the first day 57,000 British dead and wounded, in four months 415,000[33]; the 1917 offensives in France, 350,000 casualties "with little to show for it but a sea of disputed mud"[34] and all the time the knowledge that the agony and death of Europe's youth was for capitalist profit and aggrandisement.

It was with this in mind that Pollitt "was not concerned as to whether or not the Russian Revolution had been violent".[35]

4. WORKING-CLASS POWER

Pollitt's study of capitalist development had led him to the conclusion that the essence of capitalism, the root of its evils, was the private ownership of the means of production, the legalised power to exploit labour. This exploitation of the industrial workers of Britain and of colonial peoples abroad was the main source of the riches of all sections of the ruling class—employers, landlords, shareholders, merchants, financiers, militarists.

The system was maintained by state power. Whether clad in traditional panoply, flying the national flag, or masked by pseudo-democratic procedures, the state power was in fact the executive committee of the capitalist class, particularly big business. It was authoritarian, ready to use the prison, the cudgel and the bullet to enforce capital's rights over labour.

Capitalism culminated in imperialism. The atrocities practised in Lancashire were re-enacted with greater ferocity in the colonies. Imperialism culminated in world war, the maiming and slaughter of millions for profit. The ruling class revealed itself dehumanised in its attitude to those from whose labour it extracted its wealth.

So to end capitalism it was necessary to end capitalist state power, to replace it by working-class power. The crucial question was, how could this be done?

The British Labour movement had developed a reformist parliamentary party; the war experience had shown that capitalist control of the state had not been challenged but reinforced by the entry of Labour leaders into the government. A revolutionary trend was growing in the British Socialist Party, but it lacked a basis in the trade unions and could not influence the course of events. The Second International was fragmented, the peoples seemed harnessed to the war machines.

To Pollitt and those who thought as he did, the November Revolution came as light in the darkness. "Power was in the hands of the workers", and "whatever conception of politics had made that possible" was what he was looking for. The conquest of power, the workers' state, the control of production, the Socialist Republic, were no longer dreams, they were realities. The Russian workers had found the way, had built a revolutionary party, had "whacked the bosses" and conquered power. And if Russian workers could do it there, British workers could do it here.

Pollitt felt that his road was clear, and went ahead.

CHAPTER 7

LONDON, 1918–1919

1. Speaking and teaching. 2. London ship repair. 3. The River Thames Shop Stewards Movement. 4. The Boilermakers' Society. 5. Militant trade unionism.

1. SPEAKING AND TEACHING

In January, 1918, Pollitt began work in London ship-repair, sharing a basement bedroom in Poplar[1] with Alf Whitney and two other boilermakers. His trade union activities centred on the Port, and will be described later. His political work was mainly speaking, particularly for "Hands Off Russia", and he took educational classes.

In the autumn of 1918 Pollitt was in touch with the I.L.P., probably in East Ham, for he wrote to the Openshaw B.S.P. asking for a testimonial[2] in support of his application for the post of I.L.P. Organiser there. In December the East Ham Labour Party asked him to speak in the general election for their candidate, Arthur Henderson. He did so at numerous street meetings, sometimes heavily heckled. The eve of poll meeting at the Town Hall was crowded out. Pollitt was asked to hold the people at an overflow till Henderson came out. When he did, Pollitt hurried to finish his speech, but before he could do so heard Henderson say, "Stop that man going on with that stuff", and later heard him "remonstrate with his agent, in language most people would not use to a dog, for allowing me to speak."[3] Pollitt told them both what he thought of them—unfortunately his remarks were not recorded.

He spoke also for the B.S.P. in Kentish Town and Victoria Park. He took a dislike to the Hyde Park audiences, suspecting them of being more interested in his Lancashire accent and George Robey eyebrows than in what he said. After speaking at Hammersmith he would drop in at a bookshop run by James Tochatti who had been in the Socialist League with William Morris. Tochatti held anarchist views, and engaged in discussions, particularly with young people, in a room behind his shop. All shades of anti-war and anti-capitalist opinion were voiced, from total pacifism to a scheme for producing home-made bombs. Here Harry found a kindred spirit in the militant carpenter, Frank Jackson, with whom he defended conscientious objectors on socialist grounds, disputing with Tochatti, who alternately favoured folded arms and shooting the officers. Sometimes they had first-hand news from Russia by someone returning from there.[4]

Pollitt at this time joined the Workers Socialist Federation and was more active for it than for the B.S.P., probably because it focused its activities on the dock areas. Its leading spirit was Sylvia Pankhurst, who declared[5] in 1918: "I am proud to call myself a Bolshevist." An outstanding champion of working women, not only for the vote, but on all economic and social issues, she had founded the Workers' Suffrage Federation, later renamed Workers' Socialist Federation, and edited its paper *The Woman's Dreadnought*, later *The Workers' Dreadnought*. Pale and calm of face, slight and frail of figure, she yet conveyed an impression of unshakeable resolution, especially when speaking from the platform. Pollitt wrote of her "remarkable gift of extracting the last ounce of energy, as well as the last penny, from everyone with whom she came in contact, to help on the activities she directed. She was loved in Poplar; and though I often heard she was difficult to get on with, I never found it so."[6] Her devotion and courage—she was fearless of police violence and unbreakable under the torture of forcible feeding—gathered around her a band of comrades whom Pollitt described as "some of the most self-sacrificing and hardworking it has been my fortune to come into contact with." One of these was Melvina Walker, once a lady's maid, then a docker's wife, alongside Sylvia all through the suffrage campaign, and like her, enthusiastic for the Soviet revolution and the prospects it opened for a new life for the workers. A popular speaker, she threw herself into the "Hands Off Russia" campaign with such devotion that Harry "felt for her the same sort of affection as existed between me and my mother".

Pollitt spoke frequently for the W.S.F. at the dozen or so weekly meetings it ran in the dock areas, and occasionally in Hammersmith, St. Pancras and Walthamstow.[7] He marched with them to Hyde Park on May Day. In the 1919 march their banners, inscribed "Hungarian Soviet Republic", "German Workers' and Soldiers' Council" and, strangely, "Soviet of Constantinople", drew from an irritated capitalist newspaper the comment "How long is this open propaganda of Bolshevism to be tolerated by the authorities?"[8]

That year Pollitt was in touch with a group calling itself, with little basis for so doing, "Workers', Soldiers', Sailors' and Airmen's Council". Apart from Eden and Cedar Paul, with whom he made friends, he did not take them seriously; but he spoke at their public meetings in defence of the Russian Revolution.[9]

A book[10] of 1919 press cuttings shows data used by Pollitt for his speeches. It includes a photo of the eviction of a farm labourer who fought at Mons; the huge profits of a coal company whose directors disapproved the enquiries of the Coal Commission; Atlantic freight rates per ton of bacon rising from 42s.6d. under state control to 93s.4d. under private control; secret official documents asking whether troops would assist in strike breaking, or parade for drafting to Russia; official instructions that troops ordered to fire on rioters must neither use blanks nor fire over heads; a bathroom and lift for the Lord Chancellor costing £3,800; a shipping firm calculating on an annual profit of £72,000 on a vessel costing £100,000; organised atrocities by the counter-revolution in Russia; an army instruction to burn copies of the *Daily Herald* addressed to troops; a Tory Colonel's suggestion that unemployment benefit to youths under 25 be stopped to promote army recruiting; British Government members' share-holdings in Russian corporations; figures of British war casualties; General Ironside's plan for an attack on Petrograd from Archangel.

He was tutor to Marxist classes run by the London Labour Educational Council.[11] In Stratford he took a Sunday afternoon six-lesson course[12] on Industrial History, outlining the exploitation of labour from slavery through serfdom to the modern wages system, mercantilism, the industrial revolution, capitalist expansion, and problems of the modern Labour Movement. As always, he recommended books for study. At this class, Harry, after explaining the influence of wool production in the British economy, added that he "preferred his lamb on a plate" and noticed the eyes of one student "twinkling with merriment". The student and the girl with him invited Harry to their home for tea. This was his first meeting with Percy and Elizabeth Glading[13] whose home he frequently revisited, particularly on Fridays when Elizabeth made fruit trifle with cream and sherry.

A class on political affairs held in Poplar for apprentices was less successful. Harry Brown, who took part, wrote: "We began on Sundays at 11 a.m., but when the pubs opened at 12, the students became restless. When the attendance fell to less than a dozen, Harry gave up, saying he would have done better with a course on sex knowledge."[14]

2. LONDON SHIP REPAIR

The Port of London Authority's area stretched from the tidal limit at Teddington Lock to Tilbury. The oldest dock was St. Katherine's, near the Tower, the newest, King George V at North Woolwich. The once flourishing Thames iron ship-building industry had faded out in 1860, but ship-repair continued to employ some 16,000 workers.

On January 23, 1918, Pollitt started work at the Blackwall yard of Green and Silley Weir, the largest firm in ship repair. His first job was to construct a chart house on a new continental ferry boat lying at Tilbury, where he found an air raid going on. He appears to have worked for this firm for about eighteen months.

During 1918 he had an accident at work and had an operation in Poplar hospital. Waking from the anaesthetic he found pinned to the bed-cover a text left by a lady visitor; it read "The Wages of Sin is Death". The ward was all accident cases, none could sit up, but when the parson came on Sunday "he played his little harmonium and invited us 'Stand Up, Stand Up for Jesus, Ye Soldiers of the Cross'."[15]

Returning to ship repair after working for the "Hands Off Russia" Committee, he was blacklisted in 1919 and had to get a job at Frasers boiler shop in Bromley-by-Bow. But on March 21 the spring sun shone so warmly that he and his mate decided on a day at Kew Gardens, had a glorious evening too, and did not go back to Frasers. But Harry's good angel was vigilant. A foreman boilermaker at the Graving Dock, a member of the Salvation Army, who objected to men being victimised, came to see him and promised him a job. Harry "jumped at the chance to get back to the shipyard."[16]

The intermittent nature of ship repair meant frequent spells of unemployment, when men waited each morning at the yard gates hoping for a job. Pollitt vividly described one such "call on" for the Graving Dock.[17]

"For many weeks things had been very quiet. The oldest hands had difficulty in remembering when trade was so bad. However, good news was to hand; a big oil tanker had been dry docked. Everybody was buoyed up with the hope of getting a start. True, it would be a day or two before the job would be opened up, but what's a day or two after weeks of enforced idleness? Besides, isn't it an oil tanker and isn't it extra money on such jobs? On Monday at 7.30 a.m. instead of the usual men there were 500 from all over London. Boilermakers, shipwrights, engineers, plumbers, carpenters, scalers, painters, labourers had turned up in force. 'Never seen such a lot of strangers' grumbled one of the regulars. 'We won't get a chance in this crush' said the older men. As 8 a.m. approached all eyes were fixed on the gate where the foreman would call on men who were wanted. Even if we are not called this morning, we must let the foreman see us, then perhaps our turn will come tomorrow. So everyone is getting as near the gate as possible, crushing and straining, swearing and hustling everywhere. Each man trying to hide his real feelings but hoping it will be him the foreman calls.

"Suddenly at 8.10 the gate opens. Three foremen emerge. A silence as of death falls on the crowd, not a sound, only the heavy breathing of those crushing us from the back. One foreman calls for two engineers, another for four labourers, the third says 'No more wanted, the job isn't being done till next trip.' In silence the crowd disperses, disappointment on every face, another hope smashed, another day gone. Now to sign on at the Labour Exchange, then home to break the news to the wife, to give pain and bitterness to those we love best. This scene is enacted daily in every ship repair centre, in fair weather and foul, morning after morning workers turn out, only to have this experience. Can you wonder there is great discontent and bitterness brewing, that one day they will be avenged, for having to suffer such inhuman and chaotic conditions?"

3. THE RIVER THAMES SHOP STEWARDS MOVEMENT

In the Port of London during the war dissatisfaction with trade union officialdom had grown, and the successes of the shop stewards in key industrial centres had been noted. The electricians and wood-workers launched the idea of an all-in shop stewards movement representing all yards and all sections, skilled and unskilled. Harry Pollitt spoke for this proposal at mid-day meetings and in trade union branches. Craft insularity was overcome and in October 1918 a demand for a 15s. wage increase for all went in and the River Thames Shop Stewards Movement came into being. It had a monthly printed paper *The Consolidator*[18] and its motto "Consolidate and Conquer" reflected the influence of the National Shop Stewards Movement. It called for 100 per cent trade unionism and the election of shop stewards committees in every yard. Individual cards were issued to supporters paying 3d. or 6d. a month. It had its own choir and orchestra, much in demand at meetings.

An electrician, Walter Day, was its "most efficient" secretary, the paper was edited by J. Gilchrist, a carpenter with "a remarkably fluent pen".[19] He and other B.S.P. members helped conscientious objectors who were on the run, and fitted up bunks for them in a disused laundry at Redbridge.[20] The orchestra was conducted by I. Borrodell Lambert.[21] Sam Bradley, the secretary of the official Joint Committee was "willing to help but fearful of the consequences". When secretary of the National Shop Stewards Committee during the war he was suspended by the A.S.E. Executive for two years, "however he came in with his full support. He was a very fluent speaker, given, like me, to flights of poetry".[22] Jack Tanner sometimes attended representing the national shop stewards' paper *Solidarity*, and James Tochatti reported mass meetings for the *Workers' Dreadnought*.

Harry Pollitt, known as "the Bolshie", was appointed paid organiser,[23] and "stumped every shipyard on the river" several times for the 15s. increase. On January 12, 1919, he spoke in the Poplar Hippodrome to a mass meeting which voted by 1,008 to 534 for strike action in 14 days if the 15s. was not granted. Two weeks later the same theatre was crowded by some 8,000 men. The Joint Committee reported unsuccessful negotiations, and proposed a ballot. For the River Thames Shop Stewards Movement Pollitt argued for a strike. He began: "You are like men in the boxing ring who have stripped for a fight, either you must let the trainer put the gloves on or get out and say you were kidding. The ballot proposal is too late, it should have been made a month ago." And he concluded, "Not a man in this hall but has tried to imagine a state of society in which his children would not be forced to toil and pinch as he has done. The history of the working class was one of sacrifice, workers had to tighten their belts, strive and suffer for every improvement. If they were not prepared to do so now, they would make no further progress, let them go home and hang their heads in shame." A forest of hands went up for the strike, 61 were counted against.[24]

On the dark, foggy and frosty morning of 27 January the strike began. Men took away their personal tools and stowed away those belonging to the firm, 15,000 were out including women,[25] for four weeks every yard was solid. Some union officials and district committees, including the carpenters, supported the strike; but the national executive opposed it and refused strike pay. The Thames Shop Stewards took collections only for the strikers' children, at that time no public relief was given to strikers' families. Pollitt and other members of the strike committee were active "from Chiswick to Tilbury, and when it was not strikers' meetings it was committee meetings". But hopes of an early victory, perhaps founded on the idea that the end of the war meant an immediate boom in work, faded. Delegates sent to other ports had found strikes going on for the 44 hour week but co-ordination proved impossible. The national officials wanted the men back and played on the differences between skilled and unskilled.[26]

Political differences also arose. The strike leaders freely expressed their sympathy with Soviet Russia. After one meeting, an old boilermaker said to Harry Pollitt, "I can see your game. This strike is to help Russia, not Poplar"—a remark which expressed the view of those who thought in terms of craft rather than class. "Not so," replied Harry, "it will help both."[27]

Recognising the change of mood, the Thames Shop Stewards called a meeting to decide whether or not the strike should go on. The Hippodrome was again packed, with an overflow at the nearby Queen's Music Hall. This time no cheers but fifteen minutes of hostility greeted Harry when he rose to speak. The vote was heavily for a return to work. Some did not approve the hostile demonstration, and one labourer wrote: "I don't think I felt so grieved in all my life. Fancy a man fighting for betterment of his fellows being shouted down"[28]. The R.T.S.S.M. was not daunted by the defeat, however. In September it supported the London Workers Committee, and its activities continued for some years. The display of solidarity had positive effects, trade union organisation improved and a year later new Port Rules brought improvements for the men.

4. THE BOILERMAKERS SOCIETY

Harry transferred to the Boilermakers London No. 11. Branch, where he remained a member for the rest of his life. His regular attendance, activity as shop steward and all round ability won the Branch's confidence and he was sent as delegate to the Society's London District Committee, who appointed him Secretary as from 1 January, 1919. It was an honorary post; the full-time official was the District Delegate, who, if not himself available, called on the secretary to act in negotiations with employers. Such talks required a thorough knowledge of the trade, of agreements, working rules and customs, and a combination of toughness and adroitness.

Most trade union members form their opinion of a candidate for union office on his ability to secure favourable results from negotiations. Harry's varied experience in railway shops, shipyards and general plating stood him in good stead, and those who later nominated him for the post of District Delegate wrote that "while District Secretary he was called upon to negotiate several knotty problems which brought credit to himself and benefit to us he represented".[29]

However, this was not the case when he visited the Southern Sewage Outfall at Crossness, where Society members had claimed additional pay for abnormal conditions.[30] He was taken down through the surface manhole to the main sewer, an indescribable spot. The members explained their claim by hammering on the sides of the sewer, the result being that the group were, in the words of a well-known parody, "covered all over from head to foot". Harry beat a fast retreat up the ladder, removed the offending muck from his person, and the following dialogue ensued:

"Have you withdrawn your labour?"
"No."
"Why not?"
"Because we have excellent relations with the management."
"How long have you worked under such filthy conditions?"
"Twenty years"
"And never done anything about it?"
"That's right"
"Well, if you've not solved this problem in twenty years, and now don't propose to do anything about it yourselves, brothers you can stick it until you do. Good day to you."

In 1919 and 1920 he wrote to the Society's *Monthly Report* on industrial and political problems. He welcomed the amalgamation with the kindred societies of Shipconstructors and Shipwrights, and with Blacksmiths and Ironworkers, as a step "to the time when our card shall represent all workers in the industry." Advocating social ownership of the means of production, he pointed to the succession of labour-saving inventions—the oxy-acetic burner, high-speed drills, electric welding, a machine to clean ships' hulls while afloat—which turned craftsmen into machine-minders. "Even the most conservative boilermaker," he argued, "should realise that allowing the means of production to be privately owned meant that instead of lightening toil, the machines intensified poverty and unemployment." The workers' only remedy was "organise to own the machines". He rebutted the view that trade unions should have nothing to do with politics. Asked why trade unions were necessary, he answered: "Because we live in a society where the struggle for existence compels us to combine to protect ourselves from our employers. They are able to be employers not by divine right but because the laws of the country, framed by employers through their concept of political power, make it legal for them to do what they like." He urged the younger members to "get out of that damnable rut of 'what was good enough for my father is good enough for me', because it is not."[31]

When London No. 11. Branch put him forward as a Labour candidate for Parliament, he claimed "a good knowledge of the historical development of society without which no one can represent the workers' true interests". He wanted the trade unions politically represented "In order that the status of our class can be permanently altered" and asked for the support of all "who are desirous of seeing the political life of our society placed in the hands of men who are determined opponents of capitalism and all that it stands for."

He advocated a militant policy on immediate demands, suggesting that a national conference of branch delegates should draw up a programme to "inspire enthusiasm and pride" among the members. His proposed demands included an increase of £1 per week, the 44-hour working week, raising the income tax exemption limit to £250 a year, merging all war awards and the 12½ per cent into the basic rate, nationalisation, ending conscription, and Hands Off Russia and Ireland. The conference would also discuss ways and means for pressing its demands and campaigning to arouse the branches. But the Executive Council refused to call any such conference and declined to publish Pollitt's protest. He thereupon accused them[32] of being an autocracy "working in a reactionary manner" and proposed to follow the miners' example of forming unofficial committees to campaign for a common programme and overcome lack of coordination on the Left—a forecast of later developments.

5. Militant trade unionism

The London Workers Committee

Pollitt was in touch with militants in the London Workers Committee, and its associated committees in East and West London. They included W. F. Watson, who in 1910 initiated an amalgamation movement aiming at one union for each industry. When it fused with the shop stewards in 1919 Watson, an effective speaker and writer, though given to extravagant language, became chairman of the London Workers Committee. He brought out a paper in February 1919, Pollitt being among those who sent messages of greeting.[33] Others prominent in the Workers Committee movement were, Victor Beauchamp, an official of the Painters, Ted Blackwell, Jack Tanner and Ted Lismer both engineers, and David Ramsey, who in September 1919 became organiser of the L.W.C.

The London Workers Committee originated in the discontent of militants with the Treasury Agreement of 1915, having been set up when Woolwich Arsenal Shop Stewards, who objected to the wages standstill, called first a local, then an all-London conference. This conference set up the Committee to carry on the struggle. Its Secretary was Tommy Knight, members included W. F. Watson, Tom Quelch and Frank Jackson. In February 1916 when meeting at Featherstone Buildings, Holborn, to discuss a possible strike at Woolwich, it was raided by the police and dispersed.[34]

In 1918 it was reconstituted as the London Committee of the National Shop Stewards and Workers Committee Movement and became very active. Pollitt spoke at its meeting for trade unionists at the Holborn Empire[35] on 1 December 1918. The dispersed and heterogeneous nature of London engineering proved an obstacle against its becoming based on factories in the manner of the Clyde or Sheffield Committees, however, and it became a propaganda centre for militant and revolutionary trade unionists. Its first big success was the 'Hands off Russia' national conference in January 1919 at which Pollitt launched a call for industrial action against intervention.

The L.W.C. held Trafalgar Square demonstrations at two of which Pollitt spoke, in August 1919 against the sentence on W.F. Watson for alleged sedition and in March 1920 in solidarity with the German revolution. It held several conferences: in June 1919 to demand the release of the 300 political prisoners in Britain; in September 1919, with Tom Mann speaking, to review the work and elect a new Committee; and in January 1920 when 63 delegates representing 7,700 workers voted for affiliation to the Communist International.[36]

Electricians—November 1918

An incident to which Pollitt often referred later was the action of the electricians in reply to a refusal to let the Albert Hall for a Labour meeting. The management were annoyed because at a previous meeting a speaker had expressed a longing "for the day when a sign 'To Let' will hang on Buckingham Palace", and the audience had not only sung 'The Red Flag' but draped the Royal Box with it. Telephoned by Bill Webb, London Secretary of the Electrical Trades Union, the manager refused to reconsider his decision. Bill then informed him that unless Labour had its meeting, no other meetings would be held and "as for your Victory Ball on the 27th you can cut that out". The offices of the Prime Minister and the Home Secretary when telephoned said it was not their business. What happened next was summed up by Bill Webb: "I reported to my Committee, who laid plans accordingly. The juice to be cut off on the night of the 27th and if any attempt to replace the links, everything to go down. We visited the key branch on Friday, they were impatient and decided to isolate the Hall on Saturday morning. I was therefore in attendance, saw the job done and accepted full responsibility. I left instructions that if . . . there were any attempts to replace the links, the power house to go down instantly, tubes and electric railways to follow. . . . In a couple of hours all London would have been at a standstill. Got the assurance that the chief engineer would make no attempt to replace, so went home as usual on Saturday. Was having a cup of tea at 5 p.m. when George Lansbury dug me out. He said the medicine had worked very well . . . we had a joy ride in a taxi, gathered the boys together and put the links back."[37] The Labour meeting was duly held.

Carpenters Amalgamation, February 1919

The two main unions for carpenters and joiners, the Associated Society and the General Union, were discussing amalgamation. A joint meeting of members was held at the Holborn Empire Music Hall, once the National Hall of the Chartists, and it was a recognition of Pollitt's knowledge of trade union problems that he, though not a carpenter, was invited to be the principal speaker.[38] The Thames Shop Stewards Movement's orchestra provided music. The feelings aroused are expressed in the following extract from a leaflet circulated at the meeting.

> "A lifelong struggle by those who have fought for Amalgamation
> Must not end in failure this time. It would be too bad,
> After all our sacrifices of time and money. *Never!*
> Let those who have opposed us come with us.
> Grasp our hand—the hand of Progress.
> All for each, each for all—must as workers be our motto.
> Move in the right direction: strengthen our position,
> And prepare for the fight that may come at anytime
> Turn this over in your mind, and you will see that
> Every vote given for AMALGAMATION is one for might."

Police Strike, August 1919

Among Pollitt's political acquaintances were some active members of the National Union of Police and Prison Officers, Jack Hayes the general secretary, Tommy Thiel a constable and a member of the B.S.P., and Harry Sell, a constable in Poplar.[39]

There had been socialists in the Metropolitan Police since before 1890, when two members of the S.D.F. founded a union which only lasted for a few months; it called a strike for better pay and conditions, which failed. Thirty-nine men were dismissed, none reinstated. Still earlier, in 1872, a strike for "the right to confer" also failed.[40]

The N.U.P.P.O. was popular in the labour movement because of its action in 1918, when an almost total police strike in London had secured pay increases and the reinstatement of a victimised man, but instead of recognition of the Union got only a promise of "representation". This strike had come as a surprise. The government in something like a panic had Grenadiers with rifles in Downing Street, Scots Guards in Scotland Yard and loaded machine guns in the Foreign Office courtyard. Having got the police to resume work the government set out to break the union. It appointed a new Commissioner, General Sir Nevil Macready, an astute disciplinarian who knew how to appear fairminded. A Bill was prepared offering the police a Federation, a kind of company union. This meant banning the N.U.P.P.O.[41] Against this Bill the Union called a strike for recognition, but the leadership had misjudged the mood of the men and only a minority responded.

One of the leaders, probably Jack Hayes, called on Pollitt to ask him to go "out on the street corners and explain the police case". He at once did so, as did others including Jack Tanner and Mrs. Walker. They did not have an easy time, for dockers had more than once felt police batons, and inclined to the view that "whatever the police got, they deserved it". But Pollitt saw solidarity as a matter of principle, and if the opposition was not convinced it was argued into silence. At Tower Hill "he showed he was fully conversant with the demands of the Union, and was loudly cheered when he mentioned Brother Spackman".[42] This referred to a constable, an active union member, who had been dismissed for a minor disciplinary offence. Later the Commissioner offered to take him on probation as a new recruit provided he left the union. To his credit he refused the offer.

The strike rapidly dwindled. Outside London it had only made an impact at Liverpool where tramwaymen were also out and troops fixed bayonets. Official Labour did not go beyond parliamentary speeches and resolutions of sympathy. The remaining strikers were dismissed and never reinstated. Macready's patience—"The patience of Job . . . did not bear comparison with that which I had to exercise until the time came"[43]—gained its objective, the union was broken and never revived.

CHAPTER 8

HANDS OFF RUSSIA

1. 1918—On whose side? 2. 1919—The call for Direct Action. 3. 1920—The 'Jolly George'. 4. Threat of general strike.

1. 1918—On whose side?

In 1918 as the capitalist military intervention increased, the slogan "Hands Off Russia" was heard in Britain. It was popularised throughout London's dockland by the Workers Socialist Federation. Harry Pollitt became known to thousands as an eloquent and well-informed champion of solidarity with the Soviet Republic. He made use of Russian revolutionary pamphlets reaching Britain[1], including the text of secret treaties found in the Tsarist Ministry of Foreign Affairs, and Lenin's *Lessons of the Revolution* of which thousands of copies were seized by the police in the B.S.P. office.[2] He organised wide distribution of illegally printed copies, supplied by Sylvia Pankhurst, of the *Appeal to the Toiling Masses* signed by Lenin, Chicherin and Trotsky. Pollitt knew it by heart and "thought that never before had there been such a flaming appeal to the class instincts, solidarity and international duty of the common people."[3]

In the summer of 1918 British troops landed at Murmansk, Archangel, Baku and Vladivostock, British warships bombarded the coasts of the Baltic and Black Seas. These operations, officially described as support for Russia against the German attack, aided the counter-revolutionary armies of the White Guard generals. After the mutiny of the German Navy, the overthrow of the Kaiser and the Armistice of November 1918, the British and French governments began to direct their main forces against Soviet Russia. A new appeal[4] "Are you a Trade Unionist?" signed by Lenin and Chicherin was widely distributed at British ports and to troops likely to be sent to Russia. Pollitt often read its concluding paragraphs at meetings:

"We, the workers of Russia . . . in October last swept the capitalists out of power, and declared that Russia belongs to the whole of the Russian people.

"We are not going to grow food for the rich to eat, or weave cloth for the rich to wear. The people will enjoy the product of their labour.

"Can you wonder that the capitalists of all countries should hate us? We have shattered their dreams of the vast fortunes to be made out of the great stores of natural wealth contained in our country.

"Besides, if they allow us to remain in existence, will not the workers in other countries follow suit, and do as we have done?

"They have decided therefore to crush us before we have time to consolidate the position. And you, English trade unionists, will be used for this purpose.

"The Russian capitalists do not stand an earthly chance against us by themselves. But your capitalists know that their interests are the same as those of the Russian capitalists, and they have come to their assistance.

"Why do you not recognise your class interest in the same way? You as trade unionists are fighting your capitalists: we have settled our account with ours.

"What are you going to do? Are you going to undo the work we have commenced? Are you going to do the dirty work of your enemies, the capitalist class? Or will you remain loyal to your own class—the working class—and support our effort to secure the world for labour? REMEMBER. . . .

"By fighting us you are not fighting for your country, but for the capitalists whom your fellow trade unionists at home are fighting. By fighting us you are fighting your fellow workers. Every blow you strike against us is a blow against yourselves. If you crush us, you will only succeed in strengthening the power of your capitalists to rob and exploit you.

"Fellow workers, on whose side are you—the workers' or the masters'?"

N. LENIN,
President, Council People's Commissaries
G. TCHITCHERIN,
People's Commissary for Foreign Affairs."

2. 1919—THE CALL FOR DIRECT ACTION.

On 18 January, 1919, a national conference met in London under the slogan "Hands Off Russia", its 350 delegates coming mainly from industry. It was called by the London Workers Committee, in association with the B.S.P., the S.L.P. and the I.W.W.[5] The resolution was moved by Pollitt, who represented the Openshaw B.S.P. and was known to industrial delegates for his work in the River Thames Shop Stewards Movement. The resolution pledged "to carry on active agitation to solidify the Labour Movement for the purpose of declaring . . . a general strike . . . unless the unconditional cessation of Allied intervention had been officially announced . . . and we are satisfied as to the truth of the announcement." Pollitt stressed the necessity of getting into touch with the organisations of miners, railwaymen and transport workers who could make such action effective. The resolution specified that "intervention" meant anything done against the Soviets "directly by the force of arms, indirectly by economic blockade, by supplying arms or money to internal opponents of the Bolsheviks or by any other sinister means." A Committee, including Pollitt, was elected to carry on work to implement the resolution.[6]

This conference, though much smaller in numbers than the Leeds Convention of 1917, raised the issue of specific action for a specific purpose—a general strike to compel the government to cease intervention. Conspicuous by their absence were the Parliamentary Labour leaders who at Leeds used such brave words about "Workers and Soldiers Councils".

As capitalist aid to reaction in the Russian civil war grew so also grew the understanding of the advanced workers of Britain that the future of socialism was at stake, and the realisation by the mass of the people, especially those in khaki, that they were about to be sent into another war. On April 3 1919 the T.U.C. and the Labour Party called on the government to withdraw all British troops from Russia, and to withdraw the Bill for conscription for further military service. In June the Labour Party Conference, against the will of the chief right-wing leaders, denounced the intervention as "war in the interests of financial capitalism, which aims at the destruction of the Russian Socialist Republic and as a denial of the right to self-determination". Reflecting the growing demand for action it called for consultation with the T.U.C. to enforce the demands "by the unreserved use of their political and industrial power". These demands were endorsed by the T.U.C. in September and presented to the government by a deputation which reporting to a Special T.U.C. in December expressed its "profound dissatisfaction" with the reply, reiterated the demands and decided to send a delegation to Russia which would report to another Special T.U.C.[7]

In May Harry Pollitt gave a lead which was to prove decisive—the direct appeal to dockers and shipyard workers "to refuse to touch any ship that is to carry munitions to Russia".[8] He was spurred on by the fact that in the London docks "British trade unionists are working every possible hour on barges being fitted out to carry bombs, munitions and aeroplane parts going to Russia to defeat and kill Russian trade unionists." His call to the rank and file was to bring the trade unions into action, to act through the union, not apart from it. "All of you who still have a heart that beats in sympathy with our comrades abroad, get busy in your branches and get the members to refuse to touch any ship that is to carry munitions to Russia. Only by such action can the British Labour Movement wipe out the stain that now tarnishes our ideals." This appeal was repeated at scores of meetings wherever dockers and shipyard workers could be reached.

In June 1919 the committee elected at the January Conference gave way to a more representative National 'Hands off Russia' Committee, set up by a conference in Manchester. Its President was A. A. Purcell, member of the Parliamentary Committee of the T.U.C., and it included C. T. Cramp, Industrial Secretary of the National Union of Railwaymen, Tom Mann,

General Secretary of the A.S.E. George Peet, secretary of the National Shop Stewards Committee and, by the end of the year, John Bromley, General Secretary of the Locomotivemen and Firemen, and John Hill, General Secretary of the Boilermakers, thus bringing in representative figures from the "big organisations" that could make a strike effective. Its Secretary was W. P. Coates and during 1919 its organiser was Harry Pollitt, with headquarters at the Margaret Street Hall, Openshaw, from which the great industrial centres of the North and the Midlands could more easily be reached.

Pollitt devoted his time to visiting trade union branches, helping to form local committees, and speaking at factory gates and public meetings.[9] Everywhere the idea of a national down-tools policy was popularised. In November a printed letter[10] circulated to the trade unions set out cogent arguments why delegates to the next T.U.C. should be instructed to vote for such a policy. It pointed out that the British intervention and blockade compelled the Soviets to give priority to military requirements, and thus promoted starvation in non-food producing areas, where 250,000 children were suffering starvation. It quoted from the evidence of Principal W. T. Goode, M.A., a Russian correspondent for the *Manchester Guardian*, Lt. Col. Malone M.P. who had just visited Russia and General Gough, ex-head of the British Military Mission to the Baltic States, who all gave factual eye-witness reports disproving the slanders that nationalisation of women, abolition of religion, neglect of children and absence of law and order prevailed where the Bolsheviks were in power. The letter concluded with a list showing that the orders the Soviet Government wished to place in Britain would be a substantial contribution to employment.

One result of this activity was that Pollitt, already well known in Lancashire, Yorkshire and East London, now became known all over the country. But as the intervention policy was intensified, he felt that not enough was being done to influence the decisive sections of trade unionists and that he "could do more for Russia in the docks and shipyards than in an office". He asked to be released to return to the shipyard.[11]

3. 1920—The 'Jolly George'

As 1920 opened the tension increased, it was beyond doubt that the government would not change course unless compelled to do so. The 'Hands off Russia' Committees redoubled their efforts. On February 28 the biggest meeting yet packed the Albert Hall in London, the speakers included Tom Mann, General Secretary of the A.S.E., John MacLean from the Clyde, Robert Williams of the Transport Workers, Israel Zangwill, Professor Goode and Commander Grenfell. Intellectuals attracted by the ideals and courage of the Russian revolutionaries were joining the movement.

In dockland, Harry Pollitt and the devoted band of W.S.F. members were active day and night with leaflets, meetings, talks and the *Workers' Dreadnought* which in every issue championed the Soviet cause. "Mrs. Walker of Poplar toiled like a Trojan. On a shopping morning you could rely on seeing her in Chrisp Street talking to groups of women about Russia and how we must help, asking them to tell their husbands to keep their eyes skinned to see that no munitions went to those trying to crush the Revolution."[12]

Seeking primarily to reach dockers and seamen, Pollitt's ardour seized the minds even of passers-by, one of whom wrote: "In the spring of 1920 I was a tailor's apprentice. One day I was taking some cloth to a shop in Burdett Road. Near the Seamen's Home a crowd was listening to a speaker. It was Harry Pollitt on 'Hands Off Russia'. What he said was a revelation to me. I listened entranced till the meeting ended. Then I found the shop closed, and had to take my cloth back again."[13]

In March the Red Army drove the southern counter-revolutionary troops into the Crimea. Feeling that it was now or never, the British and French Governments pressed Poland to invade Soviet Russia: in April Polish troops crossed the frontier. Immediately the news reached London, the 'Hands Off Russia' Committee wrote to every Labour and Socialist organisation declaring that "Russia is attacked solely because our class, the working class, is in power, and have demonstrated that 'Labour is fit to govern' ", emphasising that "more pious resolutions won't force the hands of the government, but resolutions backed by industrial action will", and asking for resolutions calling for a national conference and a national strike.[14]

Rumours of munition shipments flew all through London's dockland, the slogan "Hands off Russia" was heard and seen all over Poplar. Then came definite information—two large Belgian barges lying in the East Dock at the back of the Blackwall shipyard were being fitted to carry war material to Poland. Ordered to work on these barges Pollitt asked point blank, "Are they to help Poland against Russia?" and he was told "Yes". He then refused to work on them, got the sack, and was deeply disappointed to find that other men did the work, extra money being paid. From outside, the "Hands off Russia" appeal was repeated again and again. Ordered to work on a Sunday to finish the job, every man going in at 7 a.m. was handed a copy of Lenin's *Appeal to the Toilers*; many were spoken to personally. At 9 a.m. it began to snow, at 10.30 a.m. the men were sent home and paid double time for the whole day to offset the propaganda. Meeting that night at the W.S.F. Hall in Bow, Harry and his group all felt the position keenly. Afterwards an old workman said cryptically to Harry, "What are you worrying about? It'll come right in the end". A few weeks later news came that the towing rope attached to the barges had broken while crossing the North Sea, and the barges had sunk. "It almost looked as if his prophesy had something of inspiration about it!"[15]

Then rumour became fact: cases labelled "O.H.M.S. Munitions for Poland" were seen in the East India Docks at the same time as in Parliament the Government denied that war material was being sent. On May 1 the Danish steamer *Neptune* sailed with the munitions, attempts to stop her having failed. It was with heavy hearts that the W.S.F. group joined the march to Hyde Park, where Harry was one of the speakers. But all was not lost. Two revolutionary firemen were among the *Neptune's* crew; when she neared Gravesend, they came on deck, called the deck hands together, explained that the cargo was munitions for use against Russia, and asked what about it? The Captain then demanded to know what was going on and during the resultant argument a ship coming up the river struck the *Neptune* which had to be towed back into dock.[16]

The following week, Harry Pollitt led a deputation to the office of Fred Thompson, London organiser of the Dockers Union, whose District Committee had unanimously carried a resolution refusing to handle war material for use against Russia. This decision had been reached as a result of the widespread agitation throughout the country, particularly the dock-gate meetings held by Harry Pollitt and his colleagues. The deputation urged that munition shipments to Poland be stopped and asked for an interview with Ernest Bevin, the Acting General Secretary of the Union.[17] Bevin did not agree to receive the deputation but asked Thompson to note down their points and come to see him. This was done and the deputation awaited Thompson's return. He came back jubilant, Bevin had agreed after some thought to support any application for strike pay arising from a stoppage. Thompson then asked the deputation to help get early information of any munitions, not easy "with five unions and 90 miles of quays". They scoured every dock and wharf, and in the East India dock found munitions for Poland ready to load on the *Jolly George*. They determined to stop this ship at all costs.

On May 10 *The Times* wrote that the capture of Kiev by the Poles "is a great triumph for them and their Ukrainian allies, and a heavy blow for the Bolsheviks". That day the *Jolly George* was due to sail. The men began to load her so as to give her such a list that it would be unsafe to move her even in the dock. In reply to the men's enquiry Thompson sent two officials to tell them that a stoppage would be official. They returned and reported, "the men were eager to stop, and had stopped, leaving the ship with a very bad list". Two and a-half years unceasing activity had borne fruit, dockers and coal heavers had struck, the *Jolly George* could not sail. The news ran at lightning speed all through Poplar and all over Britain.

The immediate sequel was told by Fred Thompson.[18] "The War Office rang me and implied that troops might be sent to complete the loading. My reply that this would certainly mean a port stoppage brought matters to a head. After a period of argument, both sides using the best Billingsgate, they rang off." Then "the owners rang to know on what terms they could complete the loading and get their ship released. I told them: the cargo should be taken out with an undertaking given that they would not contract to carry further munitions. They pleaded that as common carriers it was not their business to enquire as to what use their cargoes were put. They found I could not be moved and rang off, but in ten minutes were back asking whether if they undertook not to carry further munitions without reference to the union, would the men unload the cargo and free the ship? To this I agreed. The cargo was unloaded, most of the munitions being landed in the open at Greenhithe where they were left to rot or until scrounged."

Events soon proved that the stopping of the *Jolly George* had lit the fuse to a nationwide explosion.

4. 1920—THREAT OF GENERAL STRIKE

The Government now admitted it had supplied munitions to the Poles since October 1919. It intensified its support for them and the "Hands Off Russia" movement intensified its campaign against intervention.[19] In June, weekly demonstrations outside the London Polish Embassy drew large crowds; in the same month the Labour delegation to Russia reported favourably on the Soviets. In July, the Red Army drove the Poles out of Russia. The British and French Governments sent an ultimatum that if Russian troops entered Poland, the Allies would aid the latter by every means in their power. The climax of the struggle in Britain was now at hand.

On July 21 the National "Hands Off Russia" Committee alerted the whole Labour Movement to the danger of a new war, and warned that "if attempts are made to send men, munitions or money to aid Poland, organised Labour can and will resort to direct action to prevent it."[20] The alarm spread, and when the Labour Party called for emergency demonstrations on Sunday August 8, the response was tremendous. On the 9th representatives of the T.U.C., the Labour Party E.C. and the Parliamentary Labour Party declared that the war being engineered against Russia would be "an intolerable crime" and "the whole industrial power of the organised workers will be used to defeat it". They then set up a Council of Action and called a national conference of trade union executives. This conference met, endorsed the formation of the Council of Action, instructed it to remain in being until it had secured "an absolute guarantee that the armed forces of Great Britain shall not be used in support of Poland . . . or any other military or naval effort against the Soviet Government", and authorised it to "call for any and every form of withdrawal of labour" to give effect to this policy.[21]

Everywhere the workers responded, 350 local Councils of Action were set up. It was clear to all that the call to down tools would mean a general strike. The Government, presented with Labour's demands, had to give way. As Winston Churchill later put it, "Under these pressures Mr. Lloyd

George was constrained to advise the Polish Government that . . . the British Government could not take any action against Russia".[22]

So after eighteen months of unremitting effort the aim of the conference of January 1919 had been achieved; by threat of general strike the capitalist government had been compelled to change policy. No one could dispute the statement in the Labour Party's annual report "There is no doubt whatever that the action of the Labour movement early in August prevented open war with Russia".[23]

The "Hands Off Russia" movement triumphed because it expressed the will of millions who wanted to avoid another war and of thousands of class-conscious workers who knew that the emancipation of their class was bound up with the preservation of the first Socialist Republic. Among many talented and devoted leaders of the movement Harry Pollitt stood out as having been the first to see clearly that success depended on Labour's will to use its industrial power; as the man who realised that the seamen, dockers and shipyard workers were best placed to strike the first blow; and who personally led the months of campaigning in the East London dock areas to convince them to act.

Years later, when the Labour leaders rejected the strike as a weapon of struggle against another war, Pollitt wrote: "To prevent, impede or sabotage a war demands constant and unremitting preparation, agitation, propaganda and organisation. But when the workers are won for direct action, then indeed the results of this action strike decisive blows against the war makers and can on occasion force them to change their whole political line."[24]

CHAPTER 9

THE COMMUNIST PARTY OF GREAT BRITAIN, 1920—1924

1. The first two years. 2. Shaping the Party of a New Type. 3. Communist affiliation to the Labour Party. 4. Parliamentary elections.   5. International solidarity.   6. The death of Lenin.   7. The First Labour Government.   8. Research and relaxation.

1. THE FIRST TWO YEARS

The formation of the Communist International in 1919 stimulated a growing desire for a unified revolutionary party in Britain. After much negotiation a Unity Convention on July 31-August 1, 1920, founded the Communist Party of Great Britain, section of the Communist International.[1] The B.S.P. was the largest element in the new party of which, by virtue of his membership of the Openshaw Branch, Pollitt was a foundation member. He was not a delegate to the Unity Convention, but attended as a visitor.

Division arose during the negotiations over the attitude to the Labour Party, to which the B.S.P. was affiliated. Pollitt had felt deeply enough on this issue to travel up to a special meeting of the Openshaw B.S.P. to vote against affiliation, and had carried the Branch with him. But when he heard from Gallacher and Tom Bell how Lenin had answered the anti-affiliation arguments, this made him "sit up and take notice; here was something more realistic and practical than we revolutionary dreamers had ever experienced". He saw that affiliation could be needed "for the sake of millions of workers attached to the Labour Party".[2]

Pollitt held no official position in the C.P.G.B. until 1922, though as a national speaker he went all over the country at week-ends and spoke at many evening meetings in London.[3] He was not attracted to some of the leading figures in the Party. "At that time the Revolution was in the way of being fashionable, many with 'big names' flirted with Communism to be in the swing of things." Some "did not hesitate to make workers like myself feel that we were very small fry indeed." But when police persecution began with the arrest of Albert Inkpin in 1921, many of them left the Party "and found comfortable careers in brighter limelight and with fatter salaries than ever the C.P. would be able to offer".[4]

One day when at work, Pollitt got news of munitions to be loaded for Poland and rushed, in his overalls, to King Street to get the news into the Party's paper. After some difficulty he penetrated the editorial sanctum and found Francis Meynell and Raymond Postgate poring over old books. "I told my story and saw at once that they were more interested in the books than in what I had left my work to report. So I went back to work calling them names their parents would have blushed to hear said about their offspring."[5]

The feeling of being regarded as an intruder at 16 King Street was not peculiar to Pollitt. For while Albert Inkpin was a devoted and efficient secretary, there was little collective work and no adequate arrangements to deal with those who came without an appointment. Perhaps there was also a political element of difference. *The Call* had never drawn conclusions from the strike on the *Jolly George* and the leaders from the B.S.P. still failed to fully appreciate the role of the trade unions.

Meantime Pollitt continued, with spells of unemployment, to work in ship repair. And it was his ability in the trade union field that was to pave the way to his advance in the Party leadership. This trade union activity of his will be dealt with in a separate chapter.

2. Shaping the party of a New Type

In 1921 the Communist International had declared that the immediate need in Britain was for working-class unity to defeat the mounting capitalist offensive. Pollitt had taken part in an international discussion on problems of unity and reported on it to the 4th Congress of the C.P.G.B. in March 1922, stressing that the Party strove for unity not for any partisan advantage but to advance the interests of the mass of the workers.[6] In his reply to the discussion he commented that the speakers had to some extent failed properly to grasp the problems of unity, but that the discussion did nevertheless reveal a deep concern at the continued domination of the right-wing Labour leaders and the consequent retreat of the working class.[7]

At this Congress many of the delegates were critical of the leadership given by the E.C. The principles of the Communist International, endorsed by the Party, were not being applied in its life, the E.C. leads were too general, and most branches were unable to cope with their tasks. Aware of weaknesses in organisation and propaganda, the E.C. proposed a Commission to examine them and make proposals. The Congress agreed—but insisted that the Commission be composed of personnel from outside the E.C. itself, and elected R. Palme Dutt, Harry Inkpin and Harry Pollitt as its members. Pollitt afterwards commented that he had found the association with Dutt "invaluable in collective work and thought".[8]

For five months the three met in evenings and at week-ends, each having his daily duties, Pollitt in the shipyard. They went through a mass of letters, reports and suggestions; there were meetings, interviews and discussions. Dutt was chairman and did most of the drafting; Pollitt contributed mainly on Labour movement problems, also speaking to membership meetings in Manchester and Liverpool. After two interim reports, the final one aroused a furore of discussion, and was accepted with enthusiasm at the 5th Congress in October.

This 40,000 word report[9] was animated by a central idea, the transformation of a loose association of socialist-minded people into a leading political party of the working class, capable of giving leadership in all aspects of the struggle against the capitalists and their state machine. This required a centralised executive supported by departments with qualified personnel, members educated and trained for political activity in the service of the working class, and an organisational base in the factories. Essential was a daily newspaper, for which the weekly journal would prepare the way, to give news and leadership, to agitate and organise.

Pollitt himself later referred to the report as bringing "a new conception of what a Communist Party is, the function of its press, the correct methods of work in the factories, trade unions and localities, and the decisive place that agitation and propaganda occupy in its work". But, he added, "it would have been better to concentrate on a few things rather than attempt so much at one time."[10]

One immediate result had far-reaching effects—the 5th Congress elected Dutt and Pollitt to the Executive. This was not to the liking of the old members, with the strange result that Pollitt, though put in charge of the Party's trade union work, was not appointed to the Political Bureau.[11] He met Palme Dutt every Saturday evening to prepare the next issue of *The Workers' Weekly*, which in 1923 replaced *The Communist*. Its aim was to focus attention on current issues, agitate for workers' demands, and give leadership in the struggle. It was the first paper "to give workers' correspondence its real importance". Pollitt later described it as "one of the most effective weekly journals ever published", and advised Party writers to look over its files to "gain inspiration and find a little more of the punch often missing in working-class journalism today."[12]

In the summer of 1923 the International set up a commission to examine the British problem, for while some changes for the better had followed the Commission's report, the general situation of the Party had not improved. Pollitt was among those who went from Britain, but had to return before the Commission met to attend the Labour Party Conference. During the proceedings, Dutt proposed that Pollitt should be the General Secretary of the Party.[13] The proposal reflected the growing opinion that the Party Centre, as the collective working at King Street, Covent Garden, was termed, was not meeting the requirements of the 5th Congress decisions. This proposal was not accepted, but significant changes were made soon after. Pollitt was included, with Dutt and Gallacher, in a new five-man Political Bureau; leading industrial comrades were brought on to the Central Committee; and new steps were taken to improve work in the factories and trade unions.

At the 6th Congress, in May 1924, Pollitt moved the resolution on the left-wing Minority Movement in the trade unions, emphasising the need to combine all the oppositional movements into one powerful force. He and Dutt again topped the poll for the E.C. After this Congress the First National Conference of Communist Women was held. Pollitt opened the discussion on agitation and propaganda among women, and became a member of the Committee of the Women's Department.[14]

3. Communist affiliation to the Labour Party

At the 1922 National Labour Party Conference the Labour Party Executive recommended rejection of the Communist Party's application for affiliation.[15] Pollitt, a delegate from the Boilermakers', moved reference back with instructions to open up conversations with the Communist Party. He argued that the Labour Party was by its constitution a combination of working-class parties and the trade unions. The Communist Party, an integral part of the organised working class, would make itself increasingly felt in the future and its influence ought to be expressed inside the Labour movement. Communist Party candidates were opposing official Labour Party candidates, but this could be the subject of negotiation. He suggested that the Labour Party put to the Communist Party the straight question "Will you, or will you not, abide by the Constitution of the Labour Party?" and let the Communist Party return a straight answer. The real objection was the fear that if they took in the Communist Party they would lose votes at elections, but the Labour Party in power would depend upon the men in mine, mill and shipyard where the bulk of the Communist Party happened to be. Affiliation should be considered in relation to the fact that the working class was not on a wave of revolution but down at the bottom and trying to find a way up.

The main opponents of affiliation were Frank Hodges, secretary of the Miners, and Ramsay MacDonald, who argued that the Communists were agents of Moscow bent on destroying the Labour Party. On a card vote the reference back was lost by 3,086,000 to 261,000. The conference also adopted a new Rule that no one should be eligible as delegate to the Labour Party who belonged to an organisation putting up candidates not approved by the Labour Party. In subsequent discussions in the Communist Party Pollitt argued for continuing the campaign for affiliation, fighting against the proposed bans on Communists and calling for immediate united front action against the capitalist offensive. At the 1923 Labour Party Conference affiliation was again rejected, this time by 2,880,000 to 366,000, but the Rule adopted the previous year was withdrawn and the right of Communists to be members and delegates was confirmed.

The 1924 Labour Party Conference was held "in an atmosphere of unreality and emotionalism" with "slavish adulation" for MacDonald. Any attempt to face fundamental issues would have brought strong criticisms of the Labour Government, and was suppressed. The expected general election was the dominant concern. The Executive, anxious to dissociate the Labour Party completely from the Communists and to clear the way for developments in policy which would appeal to the petty bourgeois and liberal voters, moved that Communist affiliation be refused and that no C.P. member be endorsed as a Labour candidate. Both resolutions were carried, with large majorities. A third resolution, that no C.P. member be eligible for individual membership of the Labour Party was carried by a narrow majority, 1,804,000 to 1,540,000.

Pollitt argued that the Labour Party Executive was taking "the first open step towards splitting the Labour movement" and wanted to expel the Communists "because they represented a growing alternative to the policy initiated by the gentlemen on the platform..." "The people who were trying to frighten them with the bogey of the dictatorship of the working class were themselves exercising dictatorship." He summed up the decisions as "the first steps to exclude completely the Communists from the Labour Party and the trade unions ... the leadership and the direction of the movement are at stake."[16] He strongly criticised the Left wing for remaining silent while MacDonald "paved the way to a bargain with the dominant classes", adding "we want a Labour Government not as guardians of capital but as fighters for the cause of Labour".[17]

4. PARLIAMENTARY ELECTIONS

Pollitt was not a candidate in the general elections of November 1922, December 1923 and October 1924.

Endorsed as Communist candidate for Gorton in 1922, he spoke with John Hodge, the Labour M.P., to announce his own withdrawal in the interests of unity. In 1923 the Paisley Boilermakers proposed him as Labour candidate, he met the local Labour Party, declared his pride in being a Communist Party member, his readiness to sign the Labour Party constitution, and "claimed the same rights as Maxton, Wheatley and others who differed from official Labour policy".[18] He was not adopted. In 1924 he was proposed as Labour candidate in Leith, but not adopted.[19]

He spoke in two by-elections contested by Communists, in August 1921 in Caerphilly, a South Wales mining constituency, for Bob Stewart, and in May 1924 in Kelvingrove, Glasgow, for his fellow boilermaker Aitken Ferguson.[20]

In the 1922 general election the Communist Party produced a daily paper with editions in London and Scotland.[21] The Executive, with a temerity never since equalled, placed Pollitt, an Englishman, in charge of the Scottish *Daily Communist*. There were four issues, 8,000 copies of each, price 1d., four large quarto pages. It gave news on unemployment, evictions, miners' conditions, argued for the united front and a Revolutionary Workers' Government, and featured the Communist campaign and its crowded, enthusiastic meetings. At one, Arthur MacManus asked the Labour candidate for three pledges—never to vote for war credits; never to make an alliance with a capitalist party; always to oppose any attack on working-class freedom. In Motherwell, Walton Newbold's most applauded remark was, "They dare not evict a man here, they know we'll put him back."

In Dundee, Churchill, National Liberal, referred to Willie Gallacher, Communist candidate, as a "dangerous and dismal revolutionary", adding for good measure "Trotsky is only Mr. Gallacher with power to murder those he cannot convince". Gallacher said this was putting it rather strongly, but he did not mind that so much as being called "dismal". Dangerous he might be, but "dismal" was more than he could stand. Gallacher said of Churchill, that he "was going to address a meeting sitting down as he was unable to lie standing", and quoted with zest from a just published book: "From his youth Churchill has loved with all his heart, all his soul, all his mind, all his strength, three things—war, politics and himself."

A year later Pollitt recalled a midnight incident in this election. A meeting was still in progress in Albert Square when Gallacher turned up from a series of meetings so worn out he had to be lifted on to the lorry platform to make his final appeal. He said, "Whether top or bottom of the poll, the fight goes on."[22] Dundee, a two-member seat, was won by the Prohibitionist and official Labour candidates. Fred Douglas, a leading figure in the C.P. and among the unemployed wrote "The credit went not only to the Labour man, Morel, a quiet but effective public figure, but to the Communist campaign and to Harry Pollitt who led, spoke, and set the pace. Harry also spoke for Newbold in Motherwell. At one meeting Newbold had to leave after his speech, the crowd began to leave too, but in a few minutes Pollitt had their attention and held them for the rest of the evening. His ability to present a case and his passionate eloquence were the essence of his platform powers."[23]

In 1924 Pollitt was again in Dundee to help the Communist candidate, Bob Stewart. Two local branches of the Boilermakers asked the Liberal candidate to debate with Pollitt at a meeting of the shipyard trades. The Liberal refused, saying that Pollitt was not a Dundee voter. When it was pointed out that neither was he, he still refused, this time "because Pollitt was out to subvert the trade unions".[24]

During this election a curious incident occurred in Fife, where there were two miners' unions, the left-wing Reform Union and the "Old Union" dominated by Adamson, an extreme right-winger, Secretary of State for Scotland in the Labour Government, Labour M.P. since 1910. In 1923 Philip Hodge, Secretary of the Reform Union, opposed Adamson and got 6,459 votes. Hodge wanted to stand again in 1924, but largely due to Communist influence, the Reform Union E.C. did not allow him to do so. He then wrote in his paper that Adamson was the greatest and most vindictive enemy of the Reform Union. Their duty was "to defeat or discredit him at the ballot box and thus deprive him of his power to misrepresent us". This meant in fact advising the miners to vote Tory. When the matter was brought to Pollitt's attention he urged Hodge to withdraw the article and call on the miners to vote Labour.[25]

5. INTERNATIONAL SOLIDARITY

The Russian Famine

Tom Mann on his return from the famine areas of Soviet Russia gave a graphic report[26] of the conditions there, and he and Pollitt arranged to publicise the Relief Fund. The Openshaw C.P. was among those who organised aid: in one march Pollitt carried a banner, in another a collecting box. In a butcher's shop a woman who had refused to give "for Russians" was asked by him "Will you give for hungry children?" and did so immediately.[27] The Gorton Trades and Labour Council actively supported the Relief Fund, raising over £1,000. Tom Regan was in charge and invited Pollitt to speak at a public meeting. He agreed, but the right wing objected and got the meeting called off. Pollitt sent Regan a friendly letter and then spoke at the Alhambra at a Communist meeting.[28] Pollitt also assisted the formation of a British Joint Labour Aid Committee for the Workers' International Relief, which later issued Workers Loan Bonds—Pollitt held Nos. 250200-1—and appealed for "every kind of tool used by builders, engineers, woodworkers, instrument makers, clothing workers".[29]

Germany

Pollitt was in Germany in July 1921, July 1922, May 1923 and December 1924, and saw the rise of the Communist Party of Germany in bitter class struggles.

Returning to Britain to attend the 1921 T.U.C. Pollitt and Ellen Wilkinson broke their journey at Berlin to get first-hand information on the German situation from the correspondent M. Philips Price.[30] He described the "brutal, uncivilised terror carried out with design and efficiency" by the military against the left-wing revolutionaries, and gave a first hand account of the general strike of the Berlin workers which defeated the putsch led by General Kapp, and of the military reign of terror imposed in the Ruhr. He was also able to give an eye-witness account of the 1920 conference of the Independent Social Democrats who formed the Communist Party of Germany. In the debate at this conference the representative of the Communist International, Zinoviev, said that Soviet Russia had no desire to dominate the C.I. and would not object to a transfer of its headquarters away from Moscow.

In 1922 Pollitt saw the printing plant of the German Communist Party, "a handsome building, clean and airy rooms, modern machines and equipment. Each day it prints two editions of *Die Rote Fahne (Red Front)*, the Berlin paper of the C.P.G., each in 40,000 copies, bundled in twenty-fives. It also prints *International Press Correspondence* twice weekly in four languages. The C.P.G. has 35 dailies, a 24 page fortnightly for trades unionists, papers for women, co-operators, children, for Party members on internal affairs, and a daily news bulletin. The R.I.L.U. Bureau has a weekly and a monthly bulletin." Contrasting this mass of publications with the meagre resources of the C.P.G.B., Pollitt commented "I could have wept."[31]

In June 1923 a fusion conference of the Second International with the so-called Two-and-a-half International (a kind of temporary left-wing stop gap for internationalists who wished to keep away from the Communist International) was held in Hamburg. Pollitt was one of a delegation sent by the International Committee of Action against the French Occupation of the Ruhr.

At Hamburg, he saw the leading figures of international social-democracy, stout, elderly gentlemen who knew how to dine and wine, "they gave me the impression that they felt they had more to gain under capitalism than under socialism." At the Trade Union House where the fusion conference met there was no red flag; it was the flags of capitalist countries that were flying, including Mussolini's Italy and Tsarist Russia. In two great marches that passed the hall, the Communists carried red flags, the Social Democrats the black-and-gold of the Weimar Republic. The International Committee delegates were denied any opportunity to present their proposals and were escorted out of Hamburg by the police.[32] Philips Price recorded that nevertheless the British I.L.P. delegates at the fusion conference did receive them.[33]

Pollitt's undelivered speech was later published.[34] He said that the International Committee of Action was neither asking for a theoretical discussion nor to start a revolution, it was asking for "united action in joint committees, mass demonstrations and a one-day general strike against the Ruhr occupation, the war danger and fascism". While the French in the Ruhr increased the exploitation of German workers, fascism was spreading from Italy to the Balkans, Austria, Germany, Poland and Spain. The British had abrogated their trade agreement with Russia, their Chief of Staff was in Poland, their Royalty in Italy. Their purpose was to promote new attacks on Soviet Russia and supply arms, munitions, ships and money. Told that fundamental differences between social democracy and Communism offered little prospect of an understanding, that the Communists denied the democratic princple and wanted a small clique to dictate to the proletariat, the delegation replied that "the R.I.L.U. and the Communist International saw their main task as winning the majority of the proletariat, but in spite of differences of opinion, united action was possible in partial struggles".

In 1924 Pollitt spoke for the Communist Party of Germany in the December election campaign. He travelled by train, in conditions far worse than British third class, to Berlin, Cologne, Leipzig, Halle, Stettin, Bremen, and Altenburg. Everywhere factories and shipyards were being reconstructed with up-to-date equipment. Workers streamed into the meetings, faces gaunt and pinched, clothes shabby and much brushed, few had good boots. The skilled shipyard worker got 28 to 30 marks weekly, the British equivalent was 47 marks; the unskilled German 18 to 22 marks—British 37. "When asked why they stood such wages, they spoke of repeated betrayals by leaders, lack of a common policy, bloody suppression, thousands in prison." Pollitt commented, "The mood of what's the use of anything is the price for social democracy."[35]

Ireland

In March 1923 the British police arrested 110 Irish Republican supporters, and handed them over to the Free State Government, then shooting Republican prisoners in revenge for the assassination of Michael Collins. The Communist Party called for "Hands Off Ireland"; protest meetings were held, and among those where Pollitt spoke was one organised by the West Ham Trades and Labour Council.[36]

Maud Gonne MacBride on behalf of the Political Prisoners Committee in Dublin wrote to Pollitt asking for public campaigning for the release of over 100 Irish political prisoners held in British gaols. She recalled that in the eighties . . . "the Irish parliamentarians refused to demand the release of Irish freedom fighters held in English prisons", and that when she visited Portland in 1896 she found Irish prisoners who had not received a visit for ten years; five of them had become insane. Accusing the Free State Government of a similar conspiracy of silence she named prisoners held in Leeds, Maidstone and the Isle of Wight, with the sentences: 4 of seven years; 6 of eight; 3 of ten; 1 of twelve; 2 of fifteen and 1 of twenty-one years.[37]

6. THE DEATH OF LENIN

On his way to Moscow early in 1924 Pollitt was refused Polish, Latvian and Lithuanian visas and had to travel as a stowaway on a ship from Stettin to Reval. Going ashore after nightfall he found groups of workers, many wearing black armbands, talking softly. It was Wednesday, January 22 1924, and they were discussing the news of Lenin's death.[38] In Moscow, Pollitt found that he had been chosen as one of the Guard of Honour who stood in turn around Lenin's bier, set in a blaze of light on a crimson catafalque under tall palms in the columned Hall of the Trade Unions, in

Tsarist times the Club of the Nobles. "Outside the Hall queues a mile long stretched for four days and nights as workers and peasants waited their turn to pass and salute their beloved leader for the last time. Train after train was coming into Moscow bringing representatives from towns and villages all over the Soviet Union ... Countless meetings were expressing their sorrow and pledging their determination to defend the Revolution and carry on the struggle for Socialism." More than a million filed past the bier.

On Sunday at 7 a.m. the Hall of Columns was packed with people. The last Guard of Honour, the leaders of the Soviet Union and the Communist International, and Lenin's wife Krupskaya, took their places, the Funeral March was played and "as the last notes died away, massed bands struck up the *Internationale* which rang out like a death knell to pessimism and defeatism, the answer of the Russian workers and peasants to those who, like ghouls, saw in Lenin's death the removal of a barrier to their hopes of being able to destroy the Revolution. All is silent. The coffin is closed and carried slowly down the stairway, out into the windswept streets. Outside, a sea of faces, red banners fluttering against a background of snow."[39]

On the short march to the Red Square, Pollitt was one of four bearers of the banner of the Communist International, which with that of the Russian Communist Party followed the coffin. It was bitterly cold, 30 degrees below zero, the coldest, they said, since 1912[40]. A dim red sun tried in vain to pierce the mist over the frozen town. There was an absolute prohibition to bring children into the streets. Lenin's coffin was placed where it could be seen from every part of the huge Square, over the temporary wooden mausoleum which workmen had toiled day and night to complete in time.[41]

"There are no speeches, for who can speak at such a moment? A comrade reads the names of the provinces and towns represented. The Guard of Honour is mounted, to be changed every ten minutes. The Kremlin chimes break the silence, it is ten o'clock. A comrade cries 'Workers of the World, Unite', the 'Internationale' is sung, the great march past begins." It went on, the whole town moving towards the Red Square, and with a brief halt at 4 p.m., continued through the night. At four o'clock, cannon crashed out the final salute. All over the Soviet Union people stood in silence and transport stopped for five minutes, Lenin's body was carried down to the vault within the Mausoleum. "The bearers were his oldest comrades, those who under his leadership, in exile, in prison, or working illegally had built up the Party which carried through the Revolution and won power for the workers. For seven long years they withstood the assaults of counter-revolution, blockade, famine, civil war and the open hostility of world capitalism. They have won through, as we in Britain will win through."[42]

Back in Britain, Pollitt spoke at many meetings in honour of Lenin. Outstanding was one at the Manchester Free Trade Hall, of which a young man who had a year before joined the Communist Party gave the following account:

"Every seat was taken, every inch of the great platform occupied, the doors were closed with hundreds trying to get in . . . In an atmosphere of expectancy Harry got up to speak. In a voice that seemed no louder than a whisper, but every word clear and distinct, heard by everyone in that vast audience, he told of the scenes in the Hall of Columns, of the never ending stream of workers, peasants, intellectuals and foreign visitors, come from near and far to pay their last respects to Lenin. How simple peasants had expressed their gratitude for the freedom he had brought them from Tsarist oppression and taxation, how hardened Bolsheviks who had suffered prison and exile, had fought in the civil war, broke down and wept. He told of a people oppressed and exploited, but militant and fighting; of a working class whose conscious element had embraced Marxism with its revolutionary teachings of social progress, of how they had formed the militant party of the working class, the Communist Party, of its leadership, its revolutionary skill, its self-sacrifice, of the civil war and intervention. And how the audience rose when Harry lifted the curtain of the future and gave us a gleam of what these revolutionary workers were fighting for, of what their sacrifices would bring. He talked of the great leaders of our people—of John Ball, Robert Owen, William Morris and the pioneers and how their dreams were being made realities today. And he asked 'if the Russian workers and peasants can maintain power against world imperialism and reaction, if they with their terrible legacy of backwardness and privation can so confidently tackle the future—what could we do with our tremendous economic and industrial resources and our skilled working class?' He sat down ringing wet and utterly exhausted, he had spoken for over an hour and put everything into that speech. That night Pollitt became my hero."[43]

7. THE FIRST LABOUR GOVERNMENT

A new development in British political history took place in January 1924. By decision of the capitalist parties, for the Labour M.P's were a minority in the House, a Labour Government took office. "Tremendous hopes and not a few illusions were aroused among the workers that at last a real battle would be joined between the capitalist class and the working class. How little these workers knew the character of the men who had come to power on the basis of the workers' sacrifices and activities!"[44] In industrial matters the Government followed the example of its Liberal and Tory predecessors.[45]

The Communist International had meantime fixed August 1 as a day of international action agaist imperialist war. Pollitt drafted an appeal to the men in the armed forces to be published in the *Workers Weekly*. He read his draft to the editor, J. R. Campbell, and got "a rather old-fashioned look"—but Campbell agreed to publish it as an "Open Letter to the Fighting Forces". After doing so Campbell was arrested.[46]

The Open Letter followed the tradition of Tom Mann's "Don't Shoot" appeal. It reminded the men that most of them had joined the forces because of prolonged unemployment, spoke of the repressive and irksome military regulations and said that in war "the enemy consists of working men like yourselves". It recalled the earlier use of troops in industrial disputes, the firing on workers in Llanelly in 1911, the warships used against dockers in 1912, the miners lock-out in 1921 when Hyde Park became an armed camp, and how the current Labour Government used Emergency Powers and sent naval men against strikers. It then urged: "Let it be known that, neither in the class war nor in a military war, will you turn your guns on your fellow workers, but instead will line up with your fellow workers in an attack upon the exploiters and capitalists, and use your arms on the side of your own class."

At Campbell's arrest "a great outcry arose from the whole Labour Movement. So great did the campaign become that when the case came on Sir Patrick Hastings was forced to state that the Government did not intend to proceed with the prosecution."[47] This in turn produced a censure motion in the House and the government fell. At the resultant general election the Tories were returned with an overall majority. To make sure of it, following the furore of "The Campbell Case", the notorious forged "Zinoviev Letter" had been sprung on the public.

Pollitt said[48] that the Labour Government fell not because the capitalists were dissatisfied with MacDonald but because the working class was showing a rising opposition to his policies. The lesson was that a government claiming to represent the working class could not rely upon Parliamentary majorities but must rely solely on the support of the organised working class. Later he wrote that the Labour Government's defeat was due to its refusal "to organise the masses for active fight to improve their conditions, against imperialist war and to develop the mass movement to the stage when the decisive struggle for power could be placed on the order of the day".[49]

8. Research—and relaxation

In the early twenties Pollitt's passion for hard facts led him to the Labour Research Department. The association continued all his life; in his speeches he frequently quoted L.R.D. publications, and when in London attended its Annual General Meetings. In 1923 he was nominated for its executive, was elected the following year, and re-elected each year until 1935 when pressure of other work made him unable to serve.[50] Beginning in 1912 as the Fabian Research Department, the L.R.D. became independent in 1917, based on the support of affiliated organisations, mainly trade unions. When Pollitt first visited it, the Secretary was R. Page Arnot, the Assistant Secretary Rose Cohen, the International Secretary R. Palme Dutt. G.D.H. Cole and Margaret Cole were associated with it.

Harry's mind was not entirely occupied by research and politics. He enjoyed social life and was a frequent visitor to a flat shared by a trio of young women active in the Department, Rose Cohen, Olive Parsons and Eva Reckitt. The latter had a cottage at Houghton, in West Sussex, a base for delightful walks and week-end expeditions. "Harry was an all-round person, a great lover of the countryside. He spent a great deal of time between the cottage at Houghton and that of another friend at Middleton. He liked nothing better than to sit, look at the downs or at the sea, and be quiet."[51] One favourite walk was to Houghton Bridge over the Arun, with its boats, tea places, the Bridge Hotel for a drink, and then on to Amberley. Another walk was to Clymping, once a possession of Earl Godwin, father of Harold the last Saxon King. After the conquest it passed to Roger de Montgomery, part of his reward for command of the Norman centre at the Battle of Hastings. Passing the pre-Norman church, they reached the pebble shore, with its wooden breakwaters and a low stone wall, a favourite spot to sit watching the waves or a passing ship.

The cottage was secluded but not isolated. And at the inn not far away the publican took a great liking to Harry, and in later years would stand looking out over the curving downs, and say "Mr. Pollitt, a travelled man, been all over, says there's nowhere as beautiful as this."

Harry was at this time "a rather gay young man, always cheerful even in adverse moments, very attractive though not particularly good looking". He was greatly attracted to Rose Cohen, who had black hair, red cheeks, flashing eyes, a provocative smile and a quick wit. But she refused to take Harry seriously, married a representative of the Comintern and went to work in Berlin and Moscow.[52]

Olive Parsons, whose husband was later secretary of the L.R.D., and Eva Reckitt became Harry's life-long friends. Eva was an acute observer and wrote of him: "He was not a simple character, but if he gave his word he always kept it. That made him able to borrow money for the work, a thing most people on the left don't find easy. When he gave a date to repay, he kept that date. You felt Harry as someone who would make a decision: people asked him what should be done. He always seemed active among ordinary workers and attached importance to them; he was not among those who were always squabbling. He combined personal friendship, remembering your interests and your birthday, with the fact that he was a Communist and wanted everybody to be. Many of us thought only the best of the working class was good enough. Harry was yea-saying not nay-saying—he wanted everybody in. He had that feeling that it was not enough just to write what was needed—you had to write so that ordinary people could understand and appreciate, so that it was not merely a lot of words, but got inside them. Another thing was that he always gave you a straight answer, sometimes straighter than you wanted."[53]

CHAPTER 10

BATTLE FOR TRADE UNION POLICY, 1920–1924

1. R.I.L.U.—the British Bureau. 2. R.I.L.U.—First World Congress. 3. To stop the retreat. 4. The unemployed. 5. Strikes and lockouts. 6. The trades councils. 7. T.U.C., 1922-24. 8. The National Minority Movement.

1. R.I.L.U.—THE BRITISH BUREAU

In June 1920 Soviet trade union representatives discussed with British and Italian trade union leaders the promotion of a revolutionary trade union International (the Red International of Labour Unions—R.I.L.U.) in opposition to the newly revived International Federation of Trade Unions, led by advocates of class collaboration. The two British leaders, Robert Williams of the Transport Workers and A. A. Purcell of the Furnishing Trades, agreed as individuals to the calling of an international congress for this purpose. In July a more widely representative meeting drafted provisional rules, called on revolutionaries not to leave the existing unions but to work within them against collaboration, and set up a provisional committee to prepare a world congress. Williams and Purcell were not present, having returned to Britain.[1]

Among the first affiliations to the Provisional Committee was the British shop stewards movement; their representative J. T. Murphy served on it, and in November, with the Russian Tomsky and the Frenchman Rosmer, signed its appeal *To the Organised Workers of Great Britain*.[2] After hearing Murphy's report, the National Committee of the shop stewards initiated the formation of a British Bureau composed of leading trade unionists, with an office in Manchester. Pollitt, who had closely followed these developments, was asked to form a London Committee, and did so. An energetic campaign began for delegates to the World Congress.[3]

Events disposed trade unionists to listen to the propaganda. There were two million unemployed. The Government precipitately decontrolled the coal mines, the owners demanded big wage cuts and locked out the miners. A State of Emergency was declared, troops were sent to the coalfields. The miners called on their partners in the Triple Alliance, the railwaymen and the transport workers, for solidarity action. The alliance decided to strike and the Co-operatives and the National Council of Labour to give support. For a moment it looked as though the great days of August 1920, with its Councils of Action, were to come again. But on April 15, known later as

Black Friday,[4] the rail and transport strike notices were withdrawn. Isolated, the miners were defeated, employers in other industries imposed cuts.

On Black Friday Robert Williams defected from the policy of united struggle. He was not the only one. Pollitt recorded that many leaders previously associated with the British Bureau "one by one severed their connections with us."[5] And it was the workers who had to pay for their collaboration policy.[6] For four months the ship joiners were on strike against a wage cut, the employers sent the work to continental ports, the Union Executive did nothing about it. "This blacklegging," Pollitt wrote, "proves the need for the Red International"; but the Executive forbade branches even to read correspondence from the Bureau.[7]

The London Committee was very active: in two months its speakers addressed 85 trade union branches. Pollitt was "very happy" to be doing this night after night, particularly when, as soon as he arrived, he was invited into the branch room and heard the Chairman say "Rules do not provide for the presence of strangers, but we know Brother Pollitt, he can listen to our business till the time for his address." In his talks he emphasised that "the main work must be done by the advanced section of the rank and file in the trade union branches ... show the inseparable connection of national and international affairs ... not simply abusing yellow leaders but making action an issue in every branch room and workshop."[8]

Others active for the London Committee were Jack Tanner, militant engineer and editor of *Solidarity*, Alec Squair, a leader of the unemployed, Tommy Knight of the London Workers Committee, and later Fred Thompson of the dockers, and Wal Hannington, a young engineer. The minutes[9] of the Committee, kept by Pollitt, show detailed attention to many union problems. The work bore fruit: in May 354 delegates from 217 trade union branches,[10] after hearing Pollitt, elected Tom Mann their delegate to the coming World Congress. All this attracted the attention not only of trade unionists but of the Duke of Northumberland, who described Pollitt as "a very interesting gentleman".[11]

Pollitt also spoke for the Bureau at provincial conferences and mass meetings. In 1921 the police were very active against Communists, of whom 150 were before the courts that year[12]—and after two meetings at Plymouth in May Pollitt was charged under the Emergency Regulations with "an act likely to cause disaffection among the civilian population". The police case was that he had urged "have a revolution now", and was a prominent member of the Communist Party whose object was to overthrow Parliament. Pollitt, who defended himself, said that his speech dealt with trade union problems and that statements attributed to him by the police were in fact quotations from Tory speeches in 1914 against Home Rule. The police witnesses admitted that their notes were made from memory after the meeting. The police testimony, hardly describable as evidence, was in fact ludicrous, for no Communist of Pollitt's understanding would invite people to "have a revolution now", as though it were a plate of fish and chips. But Pollitt was fined £10 or 28 days, a woman in court paying the fine.[13]

2. R.I.L.U.—First World Congress

The Bureau elected Pollitt as one of its delegates, and he and Tom Mann boarded the *Baltanic* at East India Dock for his first visit to Soviet Russia. He had worked in this dock and men who knew him gave him a send-off; one shouted "Are you sure its safe to go, Harry?" and was assured that it was. They disembarked at Reval and entered Soviet territory at Narva. After tea, bread and eggs they took a train to Petrograd, where Tom Mann's name ensured a warm welcome, with tea and bread but no eggs. On to Moscow and a few days sightseeing before the Congress opened. They were invited to join an excursion to Tula, by a train with a new kind of engine fitted with a propellor, but they missed the bus to the railway station. It was as well, for the train met with an accident in which several delegates were killed, among them the Welsh miner Will Hewlett.[14]

Invited to the concluding sessions of the Third Congress of the Communist International, they were waiting in a corridor leading to the Great Hall of the Kremlin when Lenin appeared, striding briskly, papers in hand, due to report on the tactics of the Russian Communist Party. "Tom Mann stepped forward, Lenin's face lit up as he told Tom how he had followed his revolutionary activities all over the world." For Harry there was a handshake, "My name meant nothing to him, but that handshake meant everything to me and I seemed to walk on air to my place in the Congress."[15]

On 3rd July the red trade union Congress opened with 380 delegates from 41 countries, the majority non-Communist. For two weeks it thrashed out the basic principles of the new International, named Red International of Labour Unions. There was a serious division of opinion. Many syndicalists distrusted on principle or from experience all party politics, they wanted the trade unions to be independent and opposed subordination to any political organisation. So strong was this feeling that the Communist International, which had envisaged direct trade union affiliation,[16] agreed to organisational independence for the R.I.L.U. On this basis the Congress succeeded in uniting syndicalists, communists and other revolutionary trade unionists. A subsequent attempt of some anarcho-syndicalists to form an International of their own petered out.

At this Congress Pollitt first met Alexander Losovsky, later known to millions as secretary-general of the R.I.L.U. till 1939, and during the second world war as spokesman for the Soviet Information Bureau. An attractive personality, with a splendid head, pointed beard, alert blue eyes, and a keen sense of humour, he spoke and wrote fluently in half a dozen languages. Sentenced in Tsarist Russia to exile in Siberia he had escaped to France. The experience gained there enabled him to discuss with first-hand knowledge trade union problems in the capitalist countries and to avoid misconceptions easily arising in the minds of those who knew them only from documents. Pollitt acknowledged that the skilful leadership of Losovsky greatly contributed to the success of the Congress.[17] In his own summary Losovsky spoke of "long and heated debates, struggle and mutual concessions. The resolutions are the crystallised experience of the labour movement of all countries"[18] and stressed without ambiguity that the R.I.L.U. was for "winning the reformist unions, not smashing them". As Pollitt put it: "The platform of the R.I.L.U. is to win the trade unions away from the policy of class collaboration to that of class struggle; for affiliation to the R.I.L.U. instead of the Amsterdam International; to unite every trade union struggle; to work out a common policy and tactics suited to the differing conditions prevailing in each country."[19]

The R.I.L.U. Constitution declared its aim "To organise the working masses throughout the world for the overthrow of capitalism, the emancipation of the toilers from oppression and exploitation and the establishment of the Socialist Commonwealth".[20] It provided for affiliation of revolutionary minorities in unions remaining within the I.F.T.U. Its organisational principle was that of industrial unions with the workplace as branch unit. Losovsky made clear that these aims required the breaking of the ideological grip of reformism on the workers' minds, and to do this, with the revolutionary tide on the ebb, would require long-sustained and skilful struggle by the R.I.L.U. adherents.[21]

3. To "stop the retreat"

Inspired by the Congress, Pollitt returned to Britain to grapple with the grim situation following Black Friday. Unemployment was rising, defeatism was rampant in the Executives, thousands were leaving the unions. Previous slogans of the Bureau were outdated, the lead now given was "Stop the Retreat", and "Back to the Unions".

In the next six months the Bureau developed an integrated strategy, with Pollitt as its leading spokesman. The main ideas popularised were: mass direct action to resist attacks on wage and hours and for a programme of united working-class advance; the T.U.C. General Council to become a general staff for the movement; industrial unions based on the workplace to replace sectionalism; international solidarity through the R.I.L.U. and world trade union unity; united advance to working-class power and control of industry.

At the 1921 T.U.C., the first which Pollitt attended representing the Boilermakers, he championed the policy of the R.I.L.U.[22] J. H. Thomas, PC, MP, extreme right-wing leader of the Railwaymen and crony of George V, was moving a resolution on disarmament, and Pollitt began a duel which lasted as long as Thomas was in politics. "It was idle to talk about disarmament," Pollitt declared, "when armaments were as necessary to perpetuate the capitalist system as was unemployment." The leading personalities of the I.F.T.U. deserted internationalism in 1914 and the real way to disarmament was through world-wide revolution. He moved a resolution on the 44-hour week, but it was held over, and also spoke for a grant of £1,000 to the Russian Famine Fund, reminding his hearers that Russia was surrounded by hostile states supported by English munitions, money and spies.

The veteran Ben Tillett congratulated Pollitt on his "fiery eloquence", adding "you recall my young days, we were all like you then, but you, like all of us, will mellow with age. Good luck and stick to your guns." Pollitt stuck not only to his guns, but also to his revolutionary ideas. Tillett introduced him to Edo Fimmen, fraternal delegate from the I.F.T.U., a left-winger, and to Ernest Bevin. Fimmen was warm and friendly, Bevin cold and aloof. He recalled their first meeting at Southampton, but "no words of encouragement, only a recognition that we should always be fighting one another". This Congress replaced the Parliamentary Committee by a General Council, with very little power.

At a London Conference in October 650 delegates from 300 trade union branches heard Pollitt report on the R.I.L.U. Congress and Tom Mann on the Russian famine.

In a letter from the London R.I.L.U. Committee in January, 1922, Pollitt presented the Bureau's policy in terms which aroused wide support. The opening struck a realist note: "R.I.L.U. adherents should participate in every action and question concerning the trade unions. It is not enough to call for the revolution, we must relate our principles and experiences to the everyday struggles of the trade unionist." The current situation was starkly described: "Unparalleled unemployment, unions unable to maintain conditions won during the war, wage reductions the order of the day, working hours in danger of being extended. Union funds depleted, members leaving in thousands, the morale of the movement gone, faulty leadership, poor vision." A constructive policy followed. One union for all in one industry, irrespective of craft and occupation, must be the reply to the displacement of craftsmen; "if exploitation is common to all workmen, then all workmen must organise in a common union to abolish exploitation". Unemployed trade unionists should join the local Unemployed Committee which organises all irrespective of grades. The slogan should be "Work or maintenance at full trade union rates". If this is impossible under capitalism then "urge the abolition of such an inhuman system". The General Council should issue an ultimatum to the employers that no further wage reductions would be tolerated and a special T.U.C. should plan the resistance and challenge the employers' right to run industry. Workshop organisation, with all grades and departments represented, Pollitt stressed, had as its purpose united action, not waiting for a full-time official to arrange things; its business was not only workshop conditions but included consultation on changes in the production process, or staff appointments and the education of the workers "in the idea that the factory will one day be theirs to administer in the interests of the community". The letter concluded with suggestions for the election of the best men to trade union positions.[23]

During 1922 the Bureau's activities[24] greatly increased; in the autumn seven district conferences attracted 905 delegates representing trade union branches with 166,000 members and Trades Councils, District Committees and Unemployed Committees with a total affiliated membership of 851,000. Pollitt reported at London, Newcastle and Barrow—and one by-product of the Barrow conference was the largest revolutionary poster[25] ever put on a hoarding in this country. These conferences reinforced the core of militants of the Workers Committees, on whom the Bureau originally relied, by the efforts of thousands of active trade unionists to win their organisations for the Bureau's policy.[26] In 1922 the Bureau office was transferred to London. *Solidarity* had closed down in the previous May, and in January the Bureau issued its own monthly, *All Power*, edited by Pollitt with the help of Tom Quelch, Nat Watkins and Frank Jackson. In the first issue[26] Pollitt set out the paper's aim: "to show that the reformist belief that improvement in conditions of labour would lead to socialism was in contradiction to the increasing violence of the class struggle; and that the trade unions needed to be revolutionary because without a violent overthrow of capitalism the working class cannot abolish wage slavery", and concluded with Jack London's words, "We, the working class, want in our hands the reins of power and the destinies of mankind."[27] As from June 10, the Scottish organ of the Bureau was the Glasgow weekly, *The Worker*, Pollitt later contributing a "London Letter".

Apart from unsigned articles and notes Pollitt rarely wrote for *All Power* but he ensured that it dealt with the key problems of struggle. Frequent contributors included Tom Mann, Nat Watkins, J. T. Murphy, Ellen Wilkinson, Tom Quelch, George Hicks, Frank Smith and later W. MacLaine, Ness Edwards and Walton Newbold.

Later in 1922 emerged the first nationally organised 'Minority Movements', those of the miners and the engineers.

The Miners Minority Movement began in South Wales, the signatories to its first statement including S. O. Davies, later a well-known Labour M.P. and A. J. Cook, later Secretary of the M.F.G.B.[28] It spread to all major coalfields and, largely due to the untiring efforts of its capable organiser Nat Watkins and his fortnightly paper *The Mineworker*, was able to hold regular national meetings and express its policy in every miners' conference. A similar movement of engineers was stimulated by Wal Hannington and Frank Smith. These developments led Pollitt to the conclusion that "there could only be a real drive inside the trade union movement if this were carried out on a centralised and organised basis".[29]

Pollitt's contribution to the Bureau's activities up to August 1924 may be further considered under the headings—Unemployment, Strikes and Lockouts, Trades Councils, the T.U.C. and the National Minority Movement.

4. THE UNEMPLOYED

Pollitt's association with the unemployed began in autumn 1920 when, speaking for the East London Workers Committee, he advised them to organise. Soon a London District Council of Unemployed was leading demonstrations with the slogan "We Refuse to Starve in Silence", and in 1921 Wal Hannington emerged as leader of the National Unemployed Workers Committee Movement. Pollitt spoke publicly for the unemployed and campaigned in the trade unions for action by the whole Labour movement to secure work or full maintenance.

The Labour leaders were reluctant to go beyond Parliamentary action and calls to vote Labour. In January 1921 a joint T.U.C. Labour Party committee called a national conference where the idea of a one-day general strike was mooted; but the conference adjourned for a month to enable the trade unions to take the opinion of their members.

Pollitt was at the conference when it re-assembled. It was, he said, "as carefully stage-managed as any modern revue". Only one union had balloted on the one-day strike, and the platform brushed aside all proposals other than parliamentary. This desertion of the unemployed by the Labour leaders in February foreshadowed their desertion of the miners in April.

The Labour leaders "out of the workshop for 10, 15 or 20 years have forgotten what a nightmare unemployment is to the worker . . . have not the slightest intention of doing anything to solve or alleviate this terrible problem . . . refused to allow a spokesman from the unemployed and after two hours closed the conference before the arrival of the unemployed march".[30]

Throughout 1921 the unemployed marched, demonstrated, occupied workhouses and public buildings. These activities stiffened the whole working-class struggle. Alec Squair, their representative on the London R.I.L.U. Committee, wrote "Harry Pollitt was always ready and willing to address our meetings, street corners or elsewhere. An effective propagandist, he made a convincing case, seasoned with humour, the crowd liked a laugh. On one occasion we were refused Trafalgar Square and met in Hyde Park. Pollitt spoke, then the call was made 'Who's going to the Square?', the answering shout was 'All of us'. Pollitt was among those at the head of the march. At the entrance to the Square was a cordon of police. The banners were furled, the marching ranks broke, the crowd rushed through the police ranks into the Square. Pollitt was also with us when, on Armistice Day 1921, thousands of unemployed from all over London assembled, many with pawn-tickets for war medals pinned to their coats. A wreath was inscribed 'In Memory of those who died for Rent, Interest and Profit. From the survivors of the Peace whose sufferings are worse than Death'. In Whitehall we were held up till the official ceremonies had ended. The police wanted us to go to Hyde Park, we insisted on going to the Cenotaph".[31]

Another national Labour conference on unemployment was held in December 1921, where Pollitt was again a Boilermakers' delegate. In a report[32] which the editor of the Society's journal did not publish, he described the conference as sparsely attended, the atmosphere cold, no enthusiasm: "One felt that nothing tangible could come out of such an assembly and the proceedings bore out this premonition." The platform's resolution "would not have caused any consternation at a Liberal conference . . . no amendment was permitted, only safe men were allowed to take part in the discussion". This conference dispersed early, just as an expected march of the unemployed began to arrive. A handful of delegates, Pollitt among them, joined the march to nearby Clerkenwell Green, where Pollitt gave them an account of the conference.

In 1922 the numbers of unemployed rose, so did their activity. It reached record heights when 2,000 Hunger Marchers from all over Britain arrived in London at the end of November and for three months made their case a daily issue before the public.[33] Pressure on the General Council of the T.U.C. brought their agreement to a Joint Committee with the N.U.W.C.M. and the calling of joint demonstrations of employed and unemployed all over the country on Sunday January 7, 1923. The London demonstration was "enormous, filling Trafalgar Square and extending far down the Strand, Northumberland Avenue, Whitehall and Charing Cross Road, the sight of a lifetime". But the General Council, ignoring proposals for a one-day strike, did nothing farther.

When its Third Annual Conference met in April, the N.U.W.C.M. was firmly established. It decided to affiliate to the R.I.L.U. For the next fifteen years, becoming better known as the National Unemployed Workers' Movement, the N.U.W.M., it championed the unemployed, earned the proud description of "blackleg proof" and prevented fascism from making use of the unemployed.

5. STRIKES AND LOCK-OUTS

Meantime the call to "stop the retreat" had aroused a wide response. A series of industrial disputes confirmed Pollitt's view that the rank and file were willing to fight for their standard of living and that it was in leadership and policy that changes were needed.

1922: March to June—ENGINEERS

With 80,000 engineers out of work, the employers demanded the right to decide without consulting the union on the amount of overtime, what grade of worker should man the machines, and workshop practice in general, thus opening the way to increased intensity of labour and lower earnings. A.E.U. leaders advised acceptance; the members voted against by a big majority. On March 1st the employers locked out 250,000 A.E.U. members, two months' later they extended their demands to the other unions in the industry and locked out another 600,000 workers. After negotiations by T.U.C. and Labour Party leaders, the other unions deserted: the A.E.U. continued the struggle till forced to return to work in June. The R.I.L.U. Bureau issued a special number of *All Power*,[34] convened a solidarity conference and sent speakers to many meetings. It argued that to defeat the employers required united action of all under attack, led by the General Council, not mere intervention in negotiations. Pollitt also showed that engineers and shipbuilding workers had a common cause, for while the former were resisting autocracy on the job, the latter were fighting a wage cut of 22s.6d. weekly. If the employers won either of their demands, their next step would be to impose the other.

1922: March to September—BOILERMAKERS

Since Black Friday the shipbuilding employers secured without resistance a wage cut of 6s. weekly, then another of 12½ per cent. In March they demanded a further cut of 22s.6d. The men by ballot rejected it, and were locked out. After three weeks the men rejected a proposal for a cut of 16s.6d. in three slices, without prejudice to a further demand for 10s., but the officials ordered them back on the rejected terms. This was the last straw: revolt began, the Thameside men remained out. In September when the third slice of the cut of 16s.6d. had taken effect, the employers promptly demanded another 10s. Pollitt urged a vote for rejection plus the demand for the General Council to organise united resistance. "If the 10s. is accepted in the shipyards it will be imposed on engineers and railmen. United action is not for sentimental solidarity, but is a vital necessity if other unions are not to be dragged down also."[35]

In October, after nearly two years' absence, Pollitt was back in the shipyard. There he found that a heavy price was being paid for official sectionalism and defeatism. "More work done for less money than ever before. Charge hands more bullying, and workers more subservient. When we take our mid-day meal . . . general hesitation about opening our grub packets. I have never seen men eat so little, or be prepared to eat the stuff they are doing now and call it dinner. Pay on Friday night, everybody broke by Monday morning. It is a revelation how far spirits have been crushed."[36]

Following the lock-out, engineering conditions were "Wages down with a run, factory discipline tyrannical, unemployment more pernicious, employment made casual and difficult to retain." A miner's leader wrote of "prolonged starvation, rampant unemployment and broken organisation" in the coalfields.[37]

1923—DOCKERS

But resistance grew and in July 1923 dockers in all major ports struck unofficially against a wage cut of 1s. a day imposed under a cost-of-living clause in an agreement signed by the T.&G.W.U. It was a "spontaneous revolt, not against the union, but against wages that mean starvation".[38] Outside London the men were in the T.&G.W.U.; in London, dockers and lightermen were in that union, the stevedores had their own union. A three-cornered struggle for leadership developed.[39] T.&G.W.U. officials, led by Bevin, ordered a return to work on the grounds that an agreement must be honoured and that there was an organised effort to use the strike to break up the T.&G.W.U. Some leaders of the Stevedores and the Lightermen at first covertly and then openly worked for a new union in opposition to the T.&G.W.U., but the R.I.L.U. supporters urged that all efforts be concentrated on winning the strike and that talk of new unions should be condemned, for reactionary officials could only be shifted by systematic work within the existing unions and not by leaving them. Pollitt led those who supported the R.I.L.U. policy, but their influence was seriously weakened by the action of Fred Thompson, a T.&G.W.U. docks official who had a well earned reputation for militancy, but on this occasion actively supported Bevin, possibly because he had inside information of the intention to form a new union.

The first phase of the strike from July 2 to July 10 saw the strikers solidly rejecting all calls to return. A national unofficial conference turned down both Bevin and Thompson. Smithfield Meat and Covent Garden fruit porters, Hull railmen, many road transport men, and German and Norwegian seamen blacked goods from the striking docks.

The second phase from July 11 to July 30 saw the strike solid in London, but weakening elsewhere, mainly due to Bevin's energetic propaganda. He got the London Strike Committee to recommend return; the strikers repudiated the committee and elected a new one. Pollitt met this committee and found it composed of 13 stevedores, 13 lightermen and 13 dockers, an ominous sign. It had no left-wingers on it, and refused any help from Communists. It also refused any contact with provincial ports, an action which accelerated the trend there to return to work. London continued solid, however; a huge indoor meeting refused to listen to Bevin and Gosling, there were street marches with bands and banners every night, and the 'Dead March' was played outside the houses of blacklegs or officials who refused support. Two thousand turned out for an all night march to picket Tilbury.

The third phase began with the Strike Committee's claim on July 23 that the employers must meet them as the only accredited representatives of the men. On July 30 the Watermen and Lightermen broke away from the T.&G.W.U. and together with the Stevedores formed the Amalgamated Society of River and Waterside Workers, which included dockers. Bevin at once claimed this as proof he had been correct. T.&G.W.U. dockers began to go back, and on August 18 the Strike Committee called off the strike.

Throughout the dispute Pollitt was personally active. In the first phase he rallied most of the R.I.L.U. militants but failed in his efforts to get Thompson to change his mind. When the Strike Committee decided on a bulletin, Pollitt helped one of the members, Bill Sturrock, to get out two issues on July 10 and 14. It gave news from various ports and vigorously argued the strikers' case—"those who frame cost-of-living figures never had to try and keep a family on 10s. a day . . . union leaders who urge us to accept it would not attempt to keep their own families on it . . . casual labour over a month brings it down to 5s. a day." Its nine demands—no wage reductions, revision of the agreement, no work till these are conceded, no separate agreements, all in or none, no leaving the unions, union recognition and strike pay, strikers to go to the Guardians for relief, co-operation with the unemployed—were a programme for success.

In the second phase Pollitt was one of a very effective team of speakers—including Tom Mann, Ernie Cant, Melvina Walker—who at dockers meetings argued for concentrating on winning the strike. When the new Strike Committee refused to continue the strike bulletin, he organised strike editions of the *Workers Weekly* appearing on July 23, 24, 25 and 28.[40]

In the third phase an Open Letter from the Communist Party was given out, warning of the dangers of isolation or breakaways and making constructive proposals for effective unity. Another letter was issued to the mass meeting on August 11.[41]

Though this strike failed to stop the wage cut, the militancy of the dockers had its effect and in February 1924 the T.&G.W.U. called an official national strike for a 2s. a day increase. In Speakers Notes for solidarity meetings, Pollitt gave the facts on the wage demand, quoted the port employers' chairman's remark that an increase for dockers would be "a signal for raising wages throughout the country", and proposed to the T.U.C. to organise solidarity and launch a campaign for all-round increases.[42] During this strike anonymous posters went up in Liverpool with such phrases as "All Power to the Coming Revolution", "All Power to the Communist International", "To Hell with the Labour Government, the Union and their Dupes". Pollitt declared that "the poster was not put up by our people. We had nothing to do with it. It is a dodge of the fascisti movement."[43]

1924: February—April: SOUTHAMPTON SHIPYARDS[44]

Southampton shipyard wages were from 10s. to 17s. a week lower than in other ports. In February, 8,000 men came out for a local 10s. increase. The Strike Committee showed that in "Britain's premier passenger port, with the largest liners afloat, the Last Word in Luxury" a skilled man in the shipyard got £2. 7s. 6d. for 47 hours, less than a tram conductor or a docker, and only 3d more than a refuse collector. An unskilled man got £1. 18s. 0d., while a builder's labourer got £2. 6s. 9d. for 44 hours.

Several Labour M.Ps. spoke for the strikers. So did Pollitt and Gallacher, who also helped with publicity. Pollitt was applauded when he said, "When London tried to get an increase the employers replied that they could get the ships repaired more cheaply elsewhere. It is time to put an end to one port helping to keep down wages in another." The Strike Committee recorded appreciation of the assistance given by Gallacher and Pollitt on behalf of the R.I.L.U.

The national employers came to the aid of their Southampton colleagues. They refused to discuss the union's claim for a national increase of 10s., and threatened a lock-out unless Southampton went back. Pollitt commented, "This solidarity and generalship was an example to the workers." The Southampton men stood firm, a national lock-out began on April 11. The union leaders took action, succeeded in dividing Southampton, expelled woodworkers and shipwrights who refused to return. On April 25, Southampton went back on the understanding that uniformity in pay at London and Southampton would be discussed by the unions with the employers. It was—and the issue remitted for arbitration. Pollitt summed up:[45] "For nine weeks Southampton kept the fight going, a signal to the rest of the country. Had the union leaders any courage it could have been turned into a national revolt. The Southampton men were betrayed."

The experiences in these and other disputes were closely examined in the columns of *All Power* and in the British Bureau of the R.I.L.U. It was now clear, they concluded, that the dominant trade union leaders were not so much weak or confused as deliberately pursuing a policy of damping down struggle. Pollitt connected this policy with the fact that while the workers had sacrificed to build up their trade unions, "the dominant class with their skill in governing have succeeded in utilising these organisations for the purpose of defending their class interests."[46] In face of this collaboration of employers and trade union leaders, spontaneous militancy and sectional unofficial action were not sufficient to win the workers' demands, since the employing class was able to concentrate all its forces against each section in turn.

6. THE TRADES COUNCILS

A major achievement of the Bureau was its campaign for the revival of the

Trades Councils. "The credit for seeing the potentialities of the Trades Councils and doing the main propaganda work on their behalf, must be given to our comrade Tom Quelch who conducted a ceaseless campaign . . . so that they could become all-embracing centres of every sphere of working-class agitation and organisation."[47]

Local trades councils originated in industrial areas by the joint action of various unions, usually to aid strikers. They helped to form the Trades Union Congress in 1868, and could affiliate to it up to 1895. After the 1914-18 war they were numerous and active, became local centres for militant activity, often uniting trade union and political branches. In 1922, the Birmingham Trades and Labour Council, whose Vice-President, William Brain, was an R.I.L.U. adherent, convened in July a local conference on the unification of the trade union movement and then a national conference of trades councils in October.[48]

In total 127 trades councils responded, 67 sent 126 delegates; 60 sent letters of support; $1^{1}/_{4}$ million workers were represented. With Alex Gossip, militant secretary of the Furnishing Trades Workers, in the Chair, the conference called for "one national organisation for all workers, with departments for industries or crafts". It also called for trades council representation at the T.U.C., the transformation of existing trades councils into "the dominating local Councils which objective conditions imperatively demand", declared itself the first Annual Conference of the Federation of Trades Councils, and set up an Executive Committee.[49]

Of the activity of the E.C. little is recorded, except that it sent out an appeal in support of the building workers in January 1923.

Prior to the 1923 Conference, Pollitt said that coming after the Plymouth T.U.C. it would be "watched by millions of workers who are waiting for a lead." He went on: "What is wanted is a rallying centre to face up to the mistakes that have been made and give a new lead to the movement. . . . The General Council is a head without a body, only the Trades Councils can supply the body and the life blood." It was their role to voice the workers' demands, carry through the common campaigns, and "they are also compelled to take the initiative in endeavouring to force a lead on the central organs."[50]

The 1923 Conference was attended by 120 delegates from 72 trades councils. Pollitt in his Presidential Address stressed the need for united action—"two million of our class out of work; real wages lower than for a generation"—and outlined the concept of a unified working class acting "with its entire strength on wages, hours, unemployment, housing, rents, co-ordinated by the Trades Councils and directed by the General Council on lines decided by Congress". But they were "not in antagonism to the T.U.C.", he emphasized, "they wanted it to express the feelings of the mass movement." He concluded that it was in the struggle for immediate demands that "strength would be gathered for the struggle for working-class power and control of production."[51]

The Conference resolved that "Trades Councils become the true guardians of all working-class interests" and that "all bona fide working-class organisations—industrial, political, co-operative, social"—should be affiliated. A report on the R.I.L.U. Congress was approved[52], and a constitution adopted including the aim of industrial unionism. The decision to advocate industrial unionism was a defeat for the concept of 'one big union' as adopted the year before.

Increased trades council activities followed, mostly along the lines indicated by the R.I.L.U. Bureau. The General Council of the T.U.C., however, felt the need to exercise control, and at a conference to which it omitted to invite the Federation set up a Joint Committee of representatives of trade councils and of the General Council. From 1925 the annual conference of trades councils was held under T.U.C. auspices. In 1927 the General Council showed the right-wing motivation of its control by refusing recognition to any trades council affiliated to the National Minority Movement, the successor of the British Bureau of the R.I.L.U.

7. Trades Union Congress, 1922-1924

In 1922 Pollitt began a practice he continued annually: before each T.U.C. he wrote on the problems it faced and suggested policy; after it, he summarised its results. These articles became a guide to action for militants.

For the 1922 Southport T.U.C. his main proposal was that the General Council become an efficient general staff, with power to take any action necessary to win strikes or lock-outs, up to and including a general strike. The capitalists, he argued, had long realised the need for centralised direction: in 1916 they had set up the War Cabinet and the Federation of British Industries; in 1919 the Cabinet had helped the railway companies by organising road transport and a skeleton rail service, but the railwaymen got no help from other unions, only more negotiators. The recent disputes had shown, he continued, that inter-union consultation and even financial aid were not enough; it was united action that was needed, yet no large union had put down a resolution for common policy and action. While arguing against sectional opposition to more power to the General Council, he warned of the danger of a General Council "whose members are obsessed with the idea of an industrial truce".[53]

The proposal for more power to the General Council was defeated at Southport but the resolution for the 44 hour working week, moved by Pollitt, was carried, though more as an aspiration than with intention to act. It would, Pollitt declared in his speech, "stiffen the backs of the men we represent, make clear that in these days of depression we have not lost all hope. Even though the employers see in the coming winter a time to extend working hours it will act as an effective counterfoil to their demands".[54]

As Boilermakers' delegate to T.U.C. and National Labour Party Conference Pollitt was also their delegate to the General Federation of Trade Unions Conference. In 1922 they met at Dumfries and he criticised the presidential remarks about peace in industry as "far from reality." He added, "the platform setting was the most appropriate possible"—there were stained glass windows and portraits of three Scots preachers.[55]

The 1923 T.U.C., at Plymouth, again defeated the "more power" proposals. Pollitt stressed again the urgency of united action by the T.U.C.—with all working-class organisations at home for work or full maintenance for the unemployed; with the French and German trade unions against the French occupation of the Ruhr and the dangers of war and fascism. But instead of positive measures there was recrimination and confusion. Pollitt summed it up as "a complete failure of leadership; no attempt at a serious programme or policy". Others were critical, too. Tillett said it revealed "the ugly side of the movement", Sexton "it was not a Congress but a laundry", J. R. Clynes, "of the bad T.U.C's, this was the worst".[56]

Pollitt then made two proposals. The first was a five-point programme for common action—a national minimum wage, a six-hour day, full maintenance for the unemployed, a common fight against unemployment, the General Council to act as Labour's general staff. He invited discussion. Among well-known leaders responding were Emmanuel Shinwell, A. J. Cook, Will Lawther, A. A. Purcell, John Jagger and Victor Beauchamp. Opinion favouring common action was growing. The second proposal was co-ordinated effort to get militant resolutions on the T.U.C. agenda and to elect militant delegates so that lack of an organised opposition would no longer leave the Congress in the hands of the General Council.[57]

Pollitt's proposal that the General Council should have power to act as Labour's general staff was an essential element in his policy that the T.U.C. itself should adopt a militant class policy, make it binding on the General Council and elect leaders who wholeheartedly supported it. Such unity of purpose was essential to end the danger that a left resolution carried by the T.U.C. could be negated by the simultaneous election of a right-wing General Council.

The 1924 Hull T.U.C. saw such a contradiction develop. In the discussions an accord of opinion between the small number of revolutionary delegates and a larger, more nebulous left, resulted in two substantial advances. Congress carried the motion giving some more power to the General Council and decided to raise within the I.F.T.U. the question of international trade union unity.

8. The National Minority Movement

The activity of the British Bureau of the R.I.L.U. greatly stimulated workers' resistance to the capitalist attacks on wages and conditions. In the strikes and lock-outs, among the unemployed, and on the trades councils, thousands of trade unionists rallied to the slogans launched by the Bureau. Among miners and engineers organised militant minorities had taken shape. The widespread frustration caused by official defeatism was being replaced by a growing and well informed understanding that changes were needed in trade union policy and leadership. The total failure of the Plymouth T.U.C. to give leadership stimulated the scattered revolutionary workers to come together.

At a national conference in August 1924 some 270 delegates representing 200,000 workers formed a movement for organised activity within their respective trade unions and co-operatives. A nine-point programme of economic and political demands was adopted:

(1) increase of £1 a week in wages, a minimum wage of £4;
(2) a 44-hour week, abolition of overtime;
(3) Workshop Committees, members guaranteed against victimisation;
(4) affiliation of Trades Councils and Unemployed Committees to the T.U.C. and their representation on the General Council;
(5) power to the General Council to direct the movement, with the obligation to the T.U.C. to use that power;
(6) workers' control of industry;
(7) control of the Labour Government, reversal of present policy, repeal of anti-Labour laws;
(8) campaign against the war danger;
(9) international trade union unity.[58]

The name National Minority Movement "was felt to express what we were for the time being", and was chosen "because we were referred to as the 'rebellious minority'." Tom Mann was Chairman, Harry Pollitt Honorary General Secretary of the National Executive, and there were industrial sections for mining, metal, transport and building.

The first action of the N.M.M. was to circulate a Manifesto[59] to the 1924 T.U.C. delegates. It restated the now familiar case for common action and in addition raised the political issue of the Labour Government and its policy. This it declared was "not outside trade unionism but the central question for the trade union movement... trade union questions are inseparably bound up with politics. Economic and political questions far beyond the control of any individual union govern the living conditions of the workers and compel them if they are to go forward at all, to handle these forces." That was why "the combined power of trade unionism has been organised into the Labour Party to win the power of the Government". But, the Manifesto asked, what was the Labour Government doing? And replied, "It threatened to operate the Emergency Powers Act during the tramway strike, ordered naval men to unload mail during the dockers' strike, threatened to use naval men in the power stations during the rail shopmen's strike. On no single occasion has it used its power to help the workers to fight the capitalists. . . . It is supporting the capitalists against the working class. At home and abroad it has declared itself the servant of the capitalist state and of all the commercial and financial interests. It has failed to take one single step towards the only object of working-class organisation—the conquest of power, in order to break the power of capitalism and establish working-class control of economic and social conditions." The Manifesto concluded by calling upon the T.U.C. to make the programme of action the official programme of the trade union movement.

The N.M.M. thus set out to promote unity of purpose among trade union militants on the basis of a deeper understanding of the class relations between workers and capitalists. It worked for unity of trade union action to achieve immediate practicable demands while simultaneously spreading comprehension that the full satisfaction of trade union interests required working-class power and socialism.

CHAPTER 11

RED FRIDAY AND THE GENERAL STRIKE

1. *Trade union unity.* 2. *Kidnapped by fascists.* 3. *Red Friday and after.* 4. *Scarborough T.U.C. and Liverpool Labour Party Conference.* 5. *Marriage.* 6. *Arrest and Trial.* 7. *Defence and Sentence.* 8. *Wandsworth.* 9. *Prison thoughts.* 10. *Release.* 11. *The 1926 Margate Labour Party Conference.* 12. *Helping the miners.* 13. *Jellied eels at Woolwich.*

1. TRADE UNION UNITY

There were sensational developments on this issue in 1924. In July, the R.I.L.U. Congress proposed a single united International, open to all unions—I.F.T.U., R.I.L.U., and unattached. The I.F.T.U. view was, however, that unity meant accepting the I.F.T.U. constitution and affiliating on I.F.T.U. terms which the Soviet T.U.C. could not accept. In September, the British T.U.C., with Soviet delegates present, favoured negotiations with the Soviet T.U.C. In December British delegates attended the Soviet T.U.C., and "after doubts and hesitancy" agreed in principle to an Anglo-Russian Trade Union Committee.[1] Pollitt, at this Congress as a member of the R.I.L.U. Unity Commission, gave a full report on his return to a gathering of 617 delegates representing 750,000 trades unionists.

In January 1925 the General Council endorsed the proposal for an Anglo-Russian Unity Committee, and it was set up in April. In a new monthly magazine, *Trade Union Unity,* Purcell, Hicks, Fimmen and other leaders supported unity. The British unity initiative[2], particularly the idea of convening an all-in world conference, aroused violent hostility in the capitalist press and among I.F.T.U. leaders. But Pollitt, in stressing the great opportunities now opening up, also gave warning that "Unity is not a question of trade unionism pure and simple, but is a class question intended to rally the workers internationally on the basis of the class struggle against capitalism". The workers would be able to maintain trade union conditions only "to the degree that in that struggle we are loyal to our fellow workers, locally, nationally and internationally".[3] Unity was not an end in itself, he deduced, but a "means to more effective struggle against capitalism and to the gradual development of working-class power up to the point that it is able to overthrow capitalism".[4]

Continued struggle with the right-wing leaders was therefore necessary.

"They now in Britain control the Labour Party", and were placing their men in key positions in the I.F.T.U.—Hodges as Secretary of the Miners International; Shaw of the Textile International. The next British T.U.C. would see, Pollitt predicted, "a struggle to marshal forces for reactionary trade union leadership in this country".[5]

2. KIDNAPPED BY FASCISTS.

On Sunday, March 15, 1925, Pollitt was due to speak at Liverpool. After leaving work on an oil tanker at Tilbury on the Saturday, he telephoned his office and was told of an enquiry as to the train he would travel on so that he could be met. This was usual, and he thought nothing of it. He went on an evening train from Euston, and just as it started another man entered his compartment. When the train drew in at Edgehill, the carriage door was thrown open and a group of men on the platform shouted "Come on, comrade, we have a car for you." "This was so unusual that I smelt a rat, and stated I had no intention of leaving the train. The men then dragged me from the carriage, the other passenger was in the gang. My bag was torn from me in the struggle, the handle left in my hand. Out on the platform, the train disappearing, I was dragged to the barrier, struggling violently. The barrier is a narrow one, but on this occasion the gates were wide open and no ticket was asked for[6]—the collector had been told that a dangerous lunatic from London might give trouble. I was hustled into a car and driven away; the men crowded round me so that I could not attract attention. Eventually we got to a small hotel in North Wales. I had been ill with bronchitis and during the night had several bouts of coughing which rather frightened one of the fascists, for when left to guard the window he apologised for being mixed up in the outrage. I was told that as long as I did not try to escape no physical violence would be offered, the only intention was to prevent me speaking at the Sunday night meeting. On the Sunday afternoon I was taken to Shrewsbury, and got a train to London."[7]

Another meeting at Liverpool was promptly fixed for the next Sunday, and Pollitt got a great welcome from 2,000 workers.[8]

The kidnapping received considerable attention in the capitalist press; most papers tried to pass it off as a joke. Several men were arrested and committed at a magisterial hearing. The name "Rowlandson" was mentioned and a London enquirer received from him a letter dated April 5, 1925, and headed "British Fascisti, Liverpool Divisional Headquarters, Justice Chambers, Hatton Garden, Liverpool", signed in typescript "Jack H. Rowlandson". The writer admitted being "the organiser of this little affair", "the Rowlandson referred to in the papers", the address given being "merely to keep away the press and avoid unnecessary publicity."[9] After giving names of his associates, the writer said Pollitt was "a man whose ideas are in opposition to the ideas of people like you and myself and the class we represent and who is out to abolish the principles and means through which you and I obtain our living. In the strictest confidence, I can inform you that the Police and Government and all concerned are on our side and it is we who wish to force the pace." Pollitt was to hear from Rowlandson again.[10]

Late in April the case was heard at the Assizes before Mr. Justice Fraser.[11] Pollitt wrote: "The fascists had briefed Sir Henry Curtis Bennett, K.C., but one look at the jury convinced me they need not have gone to so much expense to make sure that bunch of middle class Liverpudlians did not convict them. For though in his summing up the judge gave a clear and straightforward direction to the jury to find a verdict of 'Guilty', they returned a verdict of 'Not Guilty'. The judge could not hide his disgust and abruptly left the bench after ordering the release of the fascists."[12]

Among many expressions of support, Pollitt received one from the group publishing the *Nine Elms Spark,* the first railway depot paper of the Communist Party. In a letter of thanks he wished the *Spark* good luck in "assisting many workers who do not yet realise their position in the fight against the master class. Such incidents as Liverpool are but a part of the struggle and show that our movement is making headway."[13]

The jury decision had a sequel at the 1925 Labour Party Conference whose resolution described it as "an instance of class prejudice on the part of juries". Herbert Morrison for the Executive said it was "because Mr. Pollitt's views were what they were that a British court of justice disgraced itself by giving a verdict contrary to the evidence".[14]

3. Red Friday and after

In popularising trade union unity, Pollitt emphasised that the struggle was political as well as economic. "In these days of declining capitalism, questions of wages and hours are issues of revolutionary politics. This is nowhere better exemplified than in the mining industry where there is now chaos and stagnation. The only way out is for the people to take over the mines. That raises an even bigger problem—not only taking over a single industry, but taking over the power of the State as a whole." Drawing attention to current talks between the miners, engineers, rail and transport workers, he said "unless a decision is taken for a united struggle, we can look forward to more disaster than we have experienced since Black Friday."[15]

In July events moved rapidly:[16]

> June 30: The mine-owners give notice of terminating the wages agreement at midnight July 31.
> July 1: Owners demand big wage cuts, longer hours, guaranteed profits, abolition of guaranteed minimum wage, district negotiations.
> July 3: Miners delegate conference rejects owners' terms.

July 10: Miners state their case to the General Council, who record "complete support".

July 13: Government appoints a Court of Enquiry.

July 15: Miners refuse to attend the Court, but are ready to negotiate with owners when present demands are withdrawn.

July 17: Unions in heavy industry discuss an Industrial Alliance.

July 20: T.&G.W.U. Conference empowers E.C. to call a strike in conjunction with T.U.C. if necessary to aid the miners.

July 23: Miners place their case in hands of General Council.

July 24: Special T.U.C. on unemployment hears miners' appeal not to be left to fight alone.

July 25: General Council, rail and transport unions agree to embargo on all coal movement if there is a lock-out of miners.

July 27: Prime Minister hears T.U.C. urge notices be postponed and owners demands withdrawn.

July 28: Owners refuse. Cabinet discusses crisis.

July 30: *Morning*—Special conference of Trade Union Executives; 1,000 delegates hear miners report being told by the Prime Minister that "all workers in this country have to face a reduction in wages". Conference agrees to embargo, empowers General Council to give financial support and to issue strike orders.

Evening—Four major unions and General Council issue official instructions to halt coal movements from midnight on railways, docks, waterways and roads.

Night—Special Cabinet meeting.

July 31: 3.45 p.m. Prime Minister tells General Council and miners that owners have agreed to suspend notice; there will be an enquiry and the government will give financial assistance until May 1, 1926.

The first round ended in a victory for the workers, but both sides realised that there was only a truce and that the major battle lay ahead.[17]

Aug. 2: The Home Secretary at Northampton says that "the thing is not over, sooner or later this question has got to be fought out", and puts the issue as government by Parliament or by trade union leaders.[18]

Aug. 6: In the House government spokesmen make clear that the struggle has yet to be won and that the issue will be—who rules the country.[19]

Aug. 7: The Communist Party says that "an unstable truce cannot lead to industrial peace but only to renewed class conflict".[20]

Aug. 19: The Chairman of the Miners Delegate Conference says: "No need to glorify about a victory. It is only an armistice."

Pollitt, when he heard the news on the 31st remembered he had previously cancelled his holiday with the Workers Travel Association at St.

Malo. He found there was a spare place in the party leaving the next night, and booked it. On the shore at St. Malo whom should he see but Ernest Bevin. "We eyed each other. Ernest got his blow in first. 'Oh, so while you were agitating for a general strike to start this week-end, you were going on your holidays, eh?' Smiling, I told him the facts of life and he said he had done the same as me. I often wish I had kept the snapshot of Bevin and Pollitt paddling in the sea side-by-side."[21]

The holiday was brief, for the Second Annual Conference of the National Minority Movement was only four weeks ahead and much had to be done. The attendance of 683 delegates representing 750,000 workers showed the growing desire among the mass of trade unionists for adequate preparation for the next round.

4. SCARBOROUGH T.U.C. AND LIVERPOOL LABOUR PARTY CONFERENCE

1925 T.U.C.

Following Red Friday, an atmosphere different from previous years prevailed at Scarborough. The President, A. B. Swales of the Engineers, struck a militant note. "This movement has learned many lessons during these years of reaction, one is that a militant and progressive policy constantly and steadily pursued is the only policy that will unite, consolidate and inspire our rank and file." He added that many who once taught that there was no remedy other than the abolition of capitalism "now appeal for a united effort to patch it up with the aid of the possessing class".[22]

Pollitt was particularly concerned with the resolution[23] which condemned imperialist domination of non-British peoples as capitalist exploitation, declared for the right of these peoples to self-determination and independence, and pledged support for the organisation of trade unions and workers' parties in all parts of the Empire. J. H. Thomas was "more than usually lavish in praise of the Empire, and called on Congress not to make itself 'ridiculous' by passing the resolution". Pollitt, speaking after Thomas, gave facts to show that the Empire was "tyranny and exploitation"— appalling conditions in Indian textile mills, women working 36 hours at a stretch in mines; slavery in Kenya, troops firing on strikers; peoples with no right to organise and no legal redress. "It is not a Wembley Exhibition Empire of coloured fairy lights, it is an Empire with every yard of territory drenched with the blood of British soldiers and of native soldiers who tried to keep the British out." Congress carried the resolution by 3,082,000 votes to 79,000. It was Thomas who looked ridiculous.[24]

Summing up the Congress,[25] Pollitt singled out as its positive features: the inclusion in trade union aims of the overthrow of capitalism; repudiation of class collaboration; approval for factory committees; the go-ahead for an all-in International; the condemnation of the Dawes Plan[26] and of imperialism.

As negative he saw the failures to give a lead on unemployment, or on the seamen's strike, and the reluctance of the left on the General Council to fight for its point of view. Also "considering that the Government is making every preparation for a fight next May, when the Coal Commission findings will be a screen for an all-round attack on wages and conditions, it was a serious weakness not to agree to affiliation of the N.U.W.C.M. and of the Trades Councils, nor to give the General Council powers to mobilise the whole movement in a common struggle."

The Scarborough decisions aroused enthusiasm on the left, but the composition of the new General Council was a danger signal. It included Arthur Pugh, J. H. Thomas and other right-wing leaders for whom class collaboration had long been a way of life.

1925 Labour Party Conference

With the government preparing for a new clash over miners' wages, and the T.U.C. moving to the left, the Labour Executive used the National Conference to dissociate the Party from class struggle and from the Communists. The chairman endorsing the actions of the Labour Government, said "In our practice we transcend the conflict of classes, we ask for the co-operation of all classes", declaring that it was "impossible to reconcile the constructive activities of Labour Ministers with the traditional doctrine of the class struggle." He gave no call to support the miners but talked about the danger of "Revolution by force", a figment of his imagination.

Pollitt challenged MacDonald's analysis of the political situation as "totally wrong, as though imperialism were a thing of the past". There was no recognition that the class struggle was sharpening, and that "the Organisation for Maintenance of Supplies is an organised expression of fascism". On the Dawes Plan, Pollitt said that by a procedural device the E.C. was denying the Conference a direct vote for or against. The E.C. members who supported the plan had failed to make clear what it meant, though capitalist authorities had made it clear enough. He quoted Professor Cassel: "A systematic plan for sucking the juice of a nation", and Sir Josiah Stamp: "For Germany a lower standard of living, longer hours of work, greater efficiency per working hour." British workers were already feeling the adverse effects of reparation payments.

The E.C. proposed that Communists be ineligible for individual membership of the Labour Party. Pollitt moved the reference back, arguing that this was a first step to a deliberate splitting of the movement. It was intended as a gesture to the nation that "they had once and for all cleared out the Communists, bag and baggage". A year previously MacDonald had told Parliament that the Labour Party Conference was still in the hands of the constitutionalists, and that the decision to expel the Communists showed they were on the right lines. But "did that make the capitalist class any more lenient in their treatment of Labour? Not a bit of it." If the Labour Party was wide enough to include those on the right who fraternised with the upper class, it ought to be wide enough to include the others. The T.U.C. had realised the need for unity and to work with Russian Communists. It should be possible for British Communists and the Labour Party to work together for a capital levy and for nationalisation.

MacDonald in reply presented the issue as the Labour Party being for a parliamentary victory and the Communist Party for civil war. The reference back was lost by 321,000 to 2,870,000. A second E.C. proposal that trade unions be advised not to elect Communists as delegates to Labour Party Conference was carried by 2,692,000 to 480,000.[27] The immediate political effect of the Conference was to make clear to the Government that there would be no official Labour support for the Communist Party if the latter were attacked.

Years later Pollitt said of this conference that it was "MacDonaldism of the most snivelling kind, hoisting the white flag. It contained the germ of the sell-out in 1931. The new programme adopted was remarkable for the fact that almost every real socialist demand included in 1918 was removed."[28]

5. Marriage

In October, 1925, with his thirty-fifth birthday in sight and "feeling autumn in the air", Harry proposed to Marjorie Brewer and was accepted. They were married on the 10th at the Caxton Hall registry office. Percy Glading was best man; he and Tom Mann were witnesses.

The bride was 23 years of age, good looking, vivacious, well informed. Born in Marylebone and brought up by an elderly woman, she won a scholarship to the oldest girls' school in England, Christ's Hospital. She strongly opposed the 1914-18 war, not on political grounds, but because of jingo hooliganism against a neighbouring baker whose shop bore a German name. His windows were broken, his small boy beaten up at school, and he himself interned. She thought, "If this is what war does to innocent people, its a horrible thing and I'm against it." When she left school she joined the Independent Labour Party.[29] From 1922 she taught in an elementary school in Hoxton. Of a class of fifty 12-year-old girls she wrote that they knew nothing of London other than their own back streets, "the majority had never seen the Thames or Highbury Fields a mile away, or any green except scrubby bits in Pitfield Street". For a composition she gave the theme "If my father was a millionaire". The resultant essays gave glimpses of the children's lives and ambitions. One wrote that she would have "fish and chips for tea every night", a second would "have my shoes mended when they let in water", a third would "have proper gym shoes, not slippers made from an old felt hat". A fourth dream of wealth was "a day trip to Southend". Only one had the idea of what such riches could really mean. She built public libraries, endowed hospital beds, paid for a new Town Hall, and concluded: "We would not go on living in a basement in Crondall Street but move to a splendid mansion in Barking Road."[30]

Harry and Marjorie first met on holiday at St. Malo in 1924, where Harry was with Percy Glading and Marjorie with two girls from the West Ham Socialist Sunday School, one of whom knew Percy. To help make an impression, Harry borrowed a particularly fine wrist watch from Percy. In later years when he had come off second best in a tiff with Marjorie, who always had a mind of her own, he would say to Percy, "Its all you fault for lending me that bloody watch." The holiday acquaintance was kept up when they returned to London. Harry got her to help on the *Workers Weekly* and at the Minority Movement office. She joined the Communist Party, and went through a new members' class tutored by Tom Wintringham, learning "political truths which over the years I have found invaluable".[31]

The newly-weds spent the week-end at the Red Lion in Dorking. Noticing a benevolent-looking gentleman alone in the lounge, Harry promptly invited him to have one; he as promptly accepted, and returned the compliment. Next morning, having bought the newspapers, Harry lent them to the same pleasant gentleman, and was profusely thanked. They were soon to meet again.[32]

Harry wrote to a friend, "Marriage, as you say, is a big thing and with the right girl, provided she has an interest in Party life, can be made a big success. I think the girl who has decided to change her name to Pollitt will develop into a very good comrade for the Party and so far as speaking in public is concerned, I shall soon have to take second place to her."[33]

If we may anticipate events, Harry's forecast proved to be fully realised. In a letter on behalf of the Party Executive congratulating Marjorie on her 50th birthday, he spoke of her sterling services in many capacities, "a speaker with unrivalled capacity to put a case, you have also trained scores of others in the art . . . as Parliamentary and local government candidate your campaigns have been a model" . . . and of her "knowledge of the Labour movement, understanding of the feelings and aspirations of the working people, political grasp and Marxist understanding." The letter ended on a personal note: "No General Secretary of a Communist Party could have wished for a better wife and comrade. To be wife of a General Secretary must be one of the most unenviable occupations known to woman. All the trials and tribulations involved you have borne with patience, forebearance and fortitude, and have never ceased to be a help and inspiration in every problem the years have brought."[34]

6. Arrest and Trial

The capitalist press applauded the Labour Party Conference's anti-Communist decisions; one paper[35] had an article by J.H. Thomas headed "Smash the Reds or They will Smash Us!" The Government lost no time in having twelve Communist leaders,[36] including Pollitt, arrested. On the surety of George Lansbury, Pollitt was granted bail. He went to Scotland Yard to recover belongings taken from him on arrest, and found there the benevolent gentleman whose acquaintance he had made in the Red Lion at Dorking. "My sense of humour got the better of me and I had a good laugh at having been so thoroughly taken in."[37]

The hearing at Bow Street was before Sir Chartres Biron, described by Gallacher as "an ideal subject for Dickens, majestic, pompous, fully convinced of his high responsibility as custodian of the law and safety of the realm."[38]

Sir Travers Humphreys for the prosecution described the twelve as "leaders and principal executive officers of two illegal organisations" and betrayed somewhat slender knowledge by announcing that "Communism hails from Russia". The prosecution put in a cartoon published in the *Workers' Weekly* showing the Prince of Wales reading with a pained expression a paper bearing words familiar to so many unemployed, "Not Genuinely Seeking Work". Pollitt pointed out that this cartoon had appeared later in another paper without any legal action being taken.

On the charge of seducing the armed forces, Pollitt asked the police witness, "Do you believe that the whole Labour Movement hold the opinion that under no circumstances should troops be used against strikers?"

The Magistrate: "Even if it is necessary in the interests of public order? You have got to go that far because it is the only circumstance in which troops could be legally used."

Witness: "I don't think the whole of the Labour Movement would go as far as that."

The Magistrate: "I should hope not."[39]

The accused were committed, George Hicks giving surety for Pollitt. The trial began at the Old Bailey on November 16 before Mr. Justice Swift: the charges were conspiracy on three counts—seditious libel: incitement to mutiny; seduction of members of the armed forces. Prosecuting, the Attorney General, Sir Douglas Hogg, contended in a four hour speech that the Communist Party was illegal because it "stood for the forcible overthrow of the existing state of society". He quoted Pollitt at the 7th Congress of the C.P.G.B., "Communism is no longer a spectre haunting Europe, it is a definite menace to every capitalist institution."

Hogg then commented that if this meant it was a menace to a state institution "that is a good reason for its activities being brought to an end".

Pollitt questioned one of the policemen.

Pollitt: "Why at the office of the Young Communist League did you represent yourself to be a Communist?"
Witness: "They regarded me with some suspicion."
Pollitt: "If I went to Scotland Yard and represented myself as one of you, what would happen to me?"
The Judge: "I don't think that is a question which the witness can answer."[40]

On the removal of papers from the Communist Party office to the address of one of the accused, Pollitt, to establish that there was nothing secret about it, asked a witness:

Pollitt: "Would you be surprised to learn that a London evening paper came out with scare headlines about 'secret removal'?"
The Judge: "I would not think he would be surprised at anything appearing in a newspaper."
Pollitt: "The point is that the press is creating prejudice."[41]

Of the wholesale appropriation of documents by the police, in some cases without a search warrant, Pollitt suggested it was "a serious encroachment on the liberty of the subject to take everything and sundry from the Minority Movement office without a warrant".[42]

In the course of his defence Pollitt wanted to quote from seditious speeches by Tory leaders—Lord Birkenhead, Lord Carson and Sir William Joynson-Hicks.

Mr. Justice Swift: "I cannot give you permission to do that. I do not see how seditious speeches by them can be of assistance to the jury or have anything to do with this case. You could have preferred a Bill of Indictment against them if you had wished to do so. We cannot have their seditions mixed up with yours."

Pollitt: "When we are members of the government we will satisfy you that action shall be taken."[43]

7. Defence and Sentence

Campbell, Gallacher and Pollitt, defending themselves, followed the socialist tradition of using the dock to expound their political views. Legal formalities aside, it was the Communist Party that was on trial, and their three speeches made an exposition of Communist politics, theory and practice which thousands of workers read with appreciation.[44]

Pollitt's 15,000 word speech took three hours.[45] He began by explaining the political motivation behind the prosecution—on the eve of the maturing of the coal crisis, the government sought to remove from the political arena the most effective exponents of united action by the working class to aid the miners. And he warned the jury against the newspaper build-up of prejudice against the Communists. He then showed that the Attorney General in referring to documents of the Communist International had, by selected quotations and omissions, sought to picture the Communists as trying to "make people do by force what they are not prepared to do as a result of lawful conviction." He rebutted the allegations that the Communist Party was a foreign-inspired conspiratorial body, intent on using force and violence, by describing how it carried forward long-standing British traditions of struggle for a new order of society, how its propaganda was publicly organised and directed to persuasion of the Labour movement and the mass of the workers. The prosecution had put in, among other documents, "The Draft Programme of the Communist International". Pollitt went through this, with occasional homely illustrations, to show how capitalist control of the means of production extended also to control of the State, of education, and of the opinion-forming press, so that the country was ruled in the interests of the capitalist minority; how the class war arose, not from communist propaganda but from inherent conflicts of interest within capitalist society. Capitalism gave rise to big business, the world market, and colonial exploitation. It brought imperialist war and out of that came "the destruction of Monarchies, of Tsardom, not as the result of Communist propaganda, but as the result of conditions created by capitalism."

Asking the jury not to be misled on the subject of peaceful persuasion, he said that "when history has instituted social changes in this country of a violent character they have taken place not because one or two men wanted them, but because the economic conditions of the time compelled that change to take place in that particular manner".

He directed the jury's attention to the paragraph in the Draft Programme calling on the Communist Parties to win over to their views the majority of the working people. A juror asked what was the meaning of the word "hegemony" in the sentence "bring under its influence . . . the petty bourgeois elements in general and thus to achieve the political hegemony of the proletariat". Pollitt replied: "That is, to secure preponderating control."

After correcting the distortions of Communist policy indulged in by the prosecution, Pollitt re-stated with no ambiguity some essential tenets of the Party. "The Communist Party will never look upon the Forces as some neutral body completely cut off from the rest of the working class. In industrial disputes it might very well happen that a particular regiment is sent to a particular mining village, and may be ordered to shoot strikers (which has been done before) and amongst the strikers may be the fathers or brothers of the soldiers who are called upon to do the job. In those circumstances our Party declares 'Don't Shoot Workers'."

"The Communist Party believes that force is inevitable not because we want to believe this, but because our past and present experiences have convinced us.... The Chartist agitation in England, the Revolutions in '48, the French Revolution in 1789, the South African war, the Russo-Japanese war and the Imperialist War 1914-18 ... did they not all occur under circumstances which necessitated the use of force by the ruling classes? ... The lesson of history is that whatever ruling class is in power, it will retain that power peaceably and constitutionally if it can, and if it cannot it will resort to other methods."

He concluded: "We are looked upon as the vanguard of the working-class movement. Progress can be hindered and can be retarded, but it can never be stopped. Communism today is a general political issue which cannot be wiped out by persecution or repression. I confidently ask you, members of the jury, to return a verdict of 'Not Guilty'."

But after a hearing of eight days, the twelve defendants were found guilty on all charges. Five, including Pollitt, who had previous convictions, were sentenced to twelve months in the second division. The Judge offered to bind over the other seven if they would have nothing more to do with the Party or its doctrines. They refused, and were each sentenced to six months.[46]

The spectacle of "an ex-Tory M.P. sitting in judgment upon the Communists and offering them liberty at the price of apostasy" aroused considerable criticism. Walter Citrine, Secretary of the T.U.C. said, "In my view a most unsuitable judge was selected", Col. Wedgwood Benn, M.P. "the sentences are perfectly iniquitous. The Judge's summing up was extremely biased." In the House, Ramsay MacDonald, referring to a speech of the Home Secretary allegedly forecasting conviction of the defendants, asked "How did he know? Was he in touch with the Judge?" With unconscious humour Mr. Justice Swift's biographer disposes of all these criticisms by remarking: "The plain fact is that when a barrister who has been a party politician ascends to the Bench he sheds his politics completely."[47] In the House an Opposition motion that the prosecution was "a violation of the traditional British rights of freedom of speech and publication of opinion" got 127 votes against the Government's 251.

The Government later published a 136 page blue book of "Communist Papers"[48] selected from the mass of documents seized. Of the 52 documents, only 5 referred to Pollitt—a letter from Losovsky referring to the textile industry and the N.M.M.; an unsigned copy of a letter from the British Bureau to Losovsky on financial and personnel problems; a letter from Inkpin mentioning that Pollitt was on a finance sub-committee; a memorandum allocating £300 for Pollitt's election campaign in Leith, which was cancelled; data on the N.M.M's colonial activities. Presumably the selected papers were those considered most relevant, but a strong political prejudice of mind would be necessary to regard any of these as evidence of conspiracy either to forcibly overthrow the existing State or to incite to mutiny.

8. Wandsworth

The first night at Wandsworth was also the first clash with prison authority in the shape of the parson who, according to custom, came to "console" the newly arrived prisoners. Knowing that three photographs were allowed in the cell, Pollitt had put on the wall those of his sister's two children, one aged three years, the other three months. The parson looked at them and no doubt recalling the recent newspaper headlines about the "Red Bridegroom" remarked severely, "Born out of wedlock, I suppose?". Unfortunately Pollitt's rejoinder is not recorded.[49]

The prison routine included work, classes and chapel. Reading in the cell and a study notebook were permitted. Being deprived of smoking made the first days extremely trying. To get through the time as easily and quickly as possible, Pollitt had made up his mind to keep fit by exercise and study, and whenever possible to see the funny side of things. Of the twelve convicted Communists, six worked in the tailoring shop and six, including Pollitt, on producing mail bags. This work was done in a large hall with a cutting table, where Pollitt, Inkpin and Hannington were seated a couple of feet apart. They could chat quietly without being bothered. On either side of the hall a warder on a raised platform kept watch, two others were in charge of the work. Gallacher, Bell and Rust sat at a table nearer the door. On their first day in the workshop a prisoner managed to ask them, "Are you the Reds? How long have you got?" When they said, "Yes, twelve months", he said, "Serve you bloody well right, you've no respect for private property." He was a burglar by profession.

Among the regulations was one banning the Marxist classics, of which they had hoped to make a thorough study. Books sent in to prisoners had to go to the prison library, and Marxist works might corrupt other prisoners. Then there was the practice of washing greasy plates in cold water, and "the stupidity of many prison officers, whose ignorance and brutality made those who were exceptions stand out as men of really fine character." Pollitt attended chapel regularly; it broke the monotony and there was a bit of a concert at the end. One week-end a man appealing against a death sentence was brought to Wandsworth and the prison atmosphere became tense. That Sunday the helpful chaplain preached from the text "The wages of sin is death," but the man won his appeal.

A "Release The Twelve" campaign was getting going; workers marched from Hyde Park, Trafalgar Square and elsewhere to Clapham Common, where regular Sunday meetings were held, and then with bands and banners to the prison. The shouting of the crowd, directed by megaphone, caused great excitement and encouraged the twelve to hope it would have an effect on the Government. They had rebelled against insanitary shaving facilities and, their request to have their own razors being refused, had grown magnificent beards. On Christmas Eve their cell doors were opened and they were marched to the Governor's office, thinking "This is it—we're out". But it was not release, it was to receive the razors sent in by their wives, and on Christmas Day the beards were no more.

Pollitt attended classes in French, English and General Knowledge, taken by teachers organised by a Mr. Bell to cover London prisons. The General Knowledge teacher was a tolerant man, who used Shakespeare's *The Tempest* as a textbook and would ask a student to read part of it, or himself recite from it. When he tried to draw a religious moral, Gallacher, who had joined the class with an eye on the fact that tobacco could be obtained from one of the prisoners there, got into conflict with him and was reminded by Pollitt, "Its a very pleasant class and we don't want it broken up." On the last night of this class, Pollitt suggested to Gallacher that he pay tribute to the teacher for his erudition, patience and tolerance. Gallacher did so, the teacher was pleased, and referred to "appreciative scholars". Then Mr. Bell came in and Pollitt congratulated him on the success and beneficial effect of the classes he had so thoughtfully organised, for which all who attended felt a debt of gratitude.

The release campaign filled the Albert Hall on March 7 and on the 14th the demonstration outside the prison totalled 15,000, repeating *en masse* the words "We call on all soldiers, sailors and airmen to refuse under any circumstances to shoot down the workers of Britain and we call on all working-class men to refuse to join the capitalist army".[50]

In April, the congenial company in the mail-bag hall was reduced by one; Bill Rust was among the seven released on completion of sentence, and was greeted by an enthusiastic rally in Hyde Park.

As May approached, it became more and more difficult to keep the mind on study and to see the funny side of things. The coal subsidy would expire, the mineowners would attack wages, the government having used its nine months for preparation would be ready. That the miners would stand firm the five did not doubt, but what would the T.U.C. do? It was bitter to be dependent on the weekly news synopsis given by the parson and on the daily prison rumours; galling to be powerless to raise a finger or say a word when the greatest class confrontation in Britain's history took place and nine million workers downed tools. Gallacher circulated, on toilet paper, a thesis on the Party's tactics; Pollitt got some relief by telling the Governor and the parson what he thought about the latter's "excessively outrageous remarks about the miners". Most bitter of all was the knowledge that the general strike had been betrayed and miners were fighting on alone.

In June, Pollitt raised the question of being allowed to attend the T.U.C., due to begin on September 6, his release being timed for the 10th. The General Secretary of the Boilermakers asked the T.U.C. to make representations to the Home Secretary, who wrote[51] "Even if it were shown to me that the attendance of Mr. Pollitt was important for the purposes of the Congress, I could not regard this as a sufficient ground for recommending the remission of a sentence of imprisonment", and concluded with an elephantine touch of humour, "No doubt a very large number of prisoners would like to have their sentences shortened in order that they might attend to business important to themselves or others."

Mary Louisa's birthday was on August 11, and Pollitt, explaining that he had never missed writing to his mother for that day, asked the Governor for a special letter. "He listened quite unmoved, but when I had finished, said to the Warder in as gruff a voice as possible, 'See that A44 has a special letter'."[52]

9. PRISON THOUGHTS

After associated activities there were many hours of isolation in the cell. Harry's Prison Notebook[53] shows that he continued his normal mental discipline and planned use of time. When it was not possible to read there were "Things to Ponder On", listed in one of the early entries as: (1) The Economic Situation, its Political Reflections, its Problems; (2) The Coal Commission's Report; (3) The Budget; (4) The Left Wing Movement, Trade Unions and Labour Party; (5) The Future here of the Party; (6) Future Policy of the Minority Movement; (7) Series of Short Stories a la "The Traveller's Guide"; (8) The Trade Union Movement; (9) Workers' Control; (10) Simple Methods of teaching the Workers.

The Notebook for "General Study", with a stern warning "for this purpose only and no other," was issued to Pollitt on April 10 1926, and was examined by a prison official on May 24 and on July 26. It contained 46 numbered leaves size 8½" by 9¼" ruled on each side with 27 lines, in a brown cover, the insides also ruled, the back one numbered 47. Leaves 2 and 3 have been removed, the remaining 88 sides are filled with writing. French lessons occupy 41 sides, notes on books 22, his own thoughts 25. On the inside of the back cover he made a calendar from November 1925 to October 1926, each day crossed through from November 25 to September 4. Visiting days are circled, letter days in a square.

The books dealt with are: *The History of our Time* by G. P. Gooch; *Richard Cobden* by Paul Leroy Beaulieu; *The Town Labourer* by J. L. and Barbara Hammond, *The French Revolution* by H. Packwood Adams, *A History of the Chartist Movement*, by J. West. Extracts include paragraphs giving the essence of the argument, sometimes accompanied by Pollitt's own notes.

From the Hammonds he quotes examples of the conditions of child labour. The Bradford employers described their labour system to a West Indian slave owner, who said "I have often thought myself disgraced by being the owner of slaves, but we ... never thought it possible for any human being to be so cruel as to require a child of nine years old to work twelve and a half hours a day". The session of the House of Commons committee on child labour: "Before this Committee there files a long procession of workers, men and women, girls and boys, stunted, diseased, deformed, degraded, each with the tale of his wronged life; they pass across the stage, a living picture of man's cruelty to man, a pitiless indictment of the rulers who in those days of unabated power had abandoned the weak to the rapacity of the strong". Pollitt then makes three comments on the book: "Note the fear of the ruling class . . . of the effects of the French Revolution. A similar fear today . . . about the effects of the Russian Revolution." "The Church absolutely on the side of wealth and oppression. Both the Church and nonconformity the cloak for shielding the most pitiless exploitation, for breaking any spirit of revolt and for inculcating a spurious doctrine of patience and the promise of an eternal heavenly reward." "The instinctive class-consciousness of the Volunteers and the Militia. The same factor operates today and should never be overlooked. The simple bread and butter appeal of one worker to another, whatever station they occupy, can always be made the via media of a class appeal."

From *The French Revolution* he made a calendar of dates, while the extracts mainly showed the influence of economic issues upon events and the class interests behind the political conflicts. The first extract is: "Ideas are certainly strong, but never so strong as when they get into the heads of those whose interests lie in having them turned into facts", and the last one: "Until the unprecedented control which man has gained over natural resources can be placed in the hands of chosen and trusted persons and used, for the purpose of freeing from the degrading motive of individual hunger the servants of humanity, there can be no realisation of the ideal of political liberty."

Nine pages of extracts from the book on Chartism show Pollitt closely concerned with the lessons it offered to the working class today. They deal with: a daily paper for the workers: leadership will get response: agitation to arouse the will to act on a given issue, propaganda to explain its causes: the division between reformist and revolutionary. Others point to problems besetting the Chartists and relevant today: the influence of economic conditions on the rise and fall of political activity; relations between the wage earners and sections of the middle class; moral and physical force; the capitalist use of the people's movement for their own ends.

One extract is a poem from the *Poor Man's Guardian*, 7th January 1832:

"Wages should form the price of goods yes, wages should be all,
Then we who work to make the goods should jointly have them all.
But if their price be made of rent, tithes, taxes, profits, all
Then we who work to make the goods shall have—just none at all.
One of the Know-Nothings"

Pollitt's own writings, apart from short notes, are: a moving description of the early morning call for ship repair work; his view on the current position of British capitalism; and a 6,000 word examination of the problems of international trade union unity, masked by the heading "Sidney Webb's 'History of Trade Unionism' ".

On British capitalism he notes as major post-war factors—the rise of nationalist movements in the colonies, American colonisation of Europe, re-emergence of German competitive power, the importance of Socialist Russia and the Orient. On the prospects he writes: "Stabilisation on the pre-war basis is impossible, but there is no possibility of a rapid collapse. Due to the weakness of the Labour Movement, British capitalism has turned the worst corner, but the loss of world supremacy means a change in the character of the political parties. The Conservatives will attract the right-wing Liberals, the left-wing Liberals may join the Labour Party."

On the Labour Movement: "it must as a whole go left if capitalism cannot very quickly recover and give the workers better conditions. As the movement goes left two important developments are likely—overtures by the right wing to certain Liberals to come into the Labour Party with promise of Cabinet seats in the next Labour Government, and the strengthening of the organised left wing and the Communist Party. The Party's most important task is preparation for this; at present more dangers arise from the unorganised character of the left wing than from the right wing ... we should consider concentrating on the left wing in the localities and extending the Minority Movement as an all-in oppositional movement."

As this is the first entry in the Notebook, it was almost certainly written within a day or two of April 10, that is, prior to the events of the General Strike.

10. RELEASE

At last came September 10 and release. Off went the five to the Party Centre, crowded with comrades come to welcome them. Pollitt was immediately asked for a message to the readers of the *Labour Monthly* and wrote a thousand words on the "central theme of the L.M. since its inception ... the rapid disintegration of capitalism, in particular the rapid and permanent decline of Britain and the new political problems arising therefrom."[54]

On the Saturday they were all invited to a grand dance organised by the London Trades Council where Wal Hannington, an active member of the Council, was guest of honour.[55] The souvenir programme was decorated with broad arrows. On the Sunday a huge crowd assembled around five platforms in Hyde Park gave them a roaring welcome. There was a galaxy of Left speakers—George Lansbury, Mrs. Despard of the Irish Workers Party, Saklatvala the Communist M.P., Joe Vaughan for the London

Trades Council, A. H. Hawkins for the *Sunday Worker* and R. W. Postgate for Lansbury's *Labour Weekly*. Two general strike prisoners, one a Councillor, shared in the honours. A Communist Party meeting at Shoreditch Town Hall on the Monday was a more intimate gathering. The celebrations concluded on the Tuesday, when the three mail-bag cutters were together again, this time with their wives, to see "The Co-optimists — a Pierrotic Entertainment", appropriately at His Majesty's Theatre.[56] After a brief holiday with Marjorie in Cornwall, Pollitt prepared for the battle expected at the Labour Party Conference at Margate.

11. The 1926 Margate Labour Party Conference

The Conference met while the deserted miners entered their sixth month of semi-starvation. The first clash came when Pollitt broke tradition to criticise the Chairman's address. Robert Williams had likened the miners "to the sightless Samson feeling for a grip on the pillars of the temple, the crashing of which will engulf this thing we call British civilisation," and had described the call for an embargo as "magnificent, but not war". Pollitt protested at the implication that defeat for the miners was inevitable, and proposed that "in view of the insolent attack from the chair on the policy of the miners, the conference take the mining crisis as its first business". The Chairman refused. Later an Executive resolution congratulated the miners on their "magnificent resistance", protested against government support for the owners and called for the nationalisation of the mines. This meant refusal of any practical aid. David Kirkwood, M.P. moved and Pollitt seconded the reference back, calling for an embargo on coal transport, a financial levy for the miners, and a general election. The resolution was carried by 2,159,000 to 1,368,000.

The question of Labour–Communist relations came up once more. The Executive had disaffiliated 13 Divisional Labour Parties or Trades and Labour Councils for refusing to expel their Communist members. The E.C. action, Pollitt said, would create "wholesale disunity" in the movement. He moved reference back, but a huge majority endorsed the E.C. action, including a recommendation to trade unions not to elect Communists as delegates to the Labour Party.

Later Pollitt did not mince words in exposing the full significance of the Margate decisions. The Labour leaders had neither helped the miners nor challenged the Tory Government. Verbal sympathy for the miners was mere camouflage, the real policy was refusal of embargo and levy. Instead of rousing the working class against the government, the conference had consolidated the alliance of the middle-class liberals and the old school trade union leaders, who decided policy without discussion with their members and forced it through with their block vote. Their policy was to use the workers' own organisations to stifle the rising tide of workers' demands, to open the way to all-round collaboration and to rivet the grip of MacDonaldism on the movement. Pollitt concluded that a new leadership was needed and to achieve it would take years of steady, organised activity. A militant Labour Party left wing working with the Communists was a first step; the basic necessity was work to win the trade unions for a change of policy and to develop new leaders. This could only be done in the course of struggle for the workers' demands, to resist all attacks on the unions, to bring down the Tory Government and put in its place a militant Labour Government.[57]

Events over many years were to show the realism of this analysis.

12. Helping the miners

In October Pollitt was one of several Communist leaders who went into the coalfields to help the miners. Going first to the Midlands, he met on the railway platform at Leicester Herbert Smith, M.F.G.B. President, who after a friendly talk gave him a note of introduction which stood him in good stead with the miners. At Coalville Pollitt heard Herbert Smith appeal to men who had gone back to work to come out again. "It was bitterly cold and the men looked cold, an astonishingly large number of women were present, all very interested. Of the 5,000 men in the district 4,500 had resumed work on an 8-hour shift and drawn a full weeks pay. One said said 'We'll be back on bread and margarine on Monday even if working', and a woman 'We're starving when working, might as well be out fighting with the rest'. A coal-owner had said that the miners could stand a cut, for they spent 5s. a week on going to the pictures. Smith asked him where he was the previous night, he was in a 5 guinea box at a theatre."[58]

Pollitt then joined Nat Watkins in a series of miners' meetings in Notts and Derby and adjacent coalfields. "At Hucknall 3,500 miners and their wives came to the meeting, their grim determination made itself felt throughout the huge building. My speech was a plea for national solidarity, for district settlements would mean longer hours. A miner's wife looking tired and half starved jumped up and exclaimed, 'Harry, go and tell them that before the men shall go back to longer hours, we'll eat grass!' ". A miner who had gone back to work after being out 23 weeks came to Pollitt to explain why. "I live with my mother who is 80. We had pawned all we had. All men in our yard went back and when they had their first week's pay it broke her heart that she had no money. She cried every day, I could not stand it and went back."[59]

Pollitt and Watkins found that the cause of the return to work was poor district leadership, and bad organisation. The Mansfield Area Committee of lodge delegates was inactive and without funds; they persuaded it to resume campaigning and splendid meetings resulted. Lack of Labour strength on the local Guardians meant no relief and great hardship for the miners. In South Yorkshire there was police terrorism, meetings prohibited under the Emergency Powers Act.[60]

The miners' M.P's Spencer and Varley were largely in control and had broken their pledge to work loyally with the M.F.G.B. In August the owners had demanded district agreements and an extra hour on the working day, but the M.F.G.B. insisted on national negotiations. Spencer's speech in the House on that occasion earned the compliments of a Tory coal-owner M.P. who said that had Spencer been in control of the M.F.G.B. negotiations there would have been no stoppage or, if there had been, it would months ago have been over.

Spencer's attitude was reflected in the fact that on September 29, when the national total of men returning to work was 81,000, just over one-tenth of the voting membership of the M.F.G.B., in Notts and Derby and the Midlands it was 60,000, just over one-half. At the M.F.G.B. conference on October 7 Spencer admitted negotiating in Notts for a return, adding "I don't regret it and I don't plead extenuating circumstances". The chairman commented, "I would rather be shot than do what you have done" and ordered Spencer out of the conference. On October 15 the M.F.G.B. decided to campaign to bring out those who had gone back. The Notts. miners balloted, stood by the M.F.G.B. by 14,331 to 2,875, and suspended Spencer.[61]

Meetings in October and November reduced the numbers at work, and Pollitt expressed the view that those who had gone back "could be got out again if M.F.G.B. speakers and Labour M.P's would tour the coalfields". But the T.U.C. was increasing its pressure on the M.F.G.B. to accept district settlements, the transport unions refused an embargo on coal, Spencer prepared a break-away. On November 21 Pollitt was due to speak in Derby, and was prohibited by a police order under the Emergency Powers Act. Another comrade delivered the speech from the extensive notes it was Pollitt's habit to prepare, while Pollitt sat beside him on the platform.[62]

On November 23 Spencer announced the formation of his breakaway union, "The Nottingham & District Miners Industrial (non-political) Union." On November 29 the majority of the miners resumed work. After seven months heroic endurance of semi-starvation, every kind of intimidation, betrayed by the T.U.C. leaders and abandoned by the other unions, the miners were forced by hunger back to work on terms dictated by the coal-owners. The Spencer break-away union, which the owners supported, set out to form branches in other coalfields, and the struggle against it went on for ten years.[63]

13. JELLIED EELS AT WOOLWICH

Towards the end of November Pollitt, back in London ship-repair, received a letter from the Labour Manager at Woolwich Arsenal saying that they wanted a plater, and referring to his application for such a job seven years previously. An interview proved satisfactory, so Harry was told to hand in his insurance cards, get vaccinated and then start work. Arriving home that night with a red band on his arm, Marjorie asked if he was not red enough without advertising it. On his punctual arrival at the Arsenal he was not allowed to start work but sent to another interview, this time with a higher official who, after first saying that a regrettable mistake had been made, finally admitted that instructions had been received not to employ Harry Pollitt. Pointing out that he had given up a good job and been put to a lot of trouble, Pollitt successfully claimed two weeks wages in lieu of notice, and also received an invitation to lunch. Having £7.10s. in his pocket, he countered by offering to act as host at a jellied eel establishment nearby. His offer was politely declined.[64]

CHAPTER 12

POLLITT BECOMES GENERAL SECRETARY OF THE C.P.G.B.

1. Class collaboration at a new level. 2. Solidarity with oppressed peoples. 3. Libel action, 1927. 4. 38 Great Ormond Street. 5. Thomas Robert Strudwick. 6. Pollitt excluded from T.U.C. and Labour Party Conference. 7. A. J. Cook broken. 8. Mondism in action at Dawdon. 9. General election, May 1929. 10. Pollitt becomes general secretary.

1. CLASS COLLABORATION AT A NEW LEVEL

After hunger had forced the miners back to work the Conference of Trade Union Executives was recalled to endorse the General Council's actions. Pollitt's view was that the call-off of the general strike by the General Council was a betrayal—not an isolated or unpremeditated act, but the culmination of right-wing policy. The left leaders shared responsibility by their collapse at the crucial moment. In 1924 they had endorsed common action, and had they fought to realise it the official direction of the movement would have been different. The unanimity of response to the strike call had shown that the workers realised that the miners were fighting for the whole working class, and it showed the potentialities of the class spirit given militant leadership.[2]

Unless the movement could put an end to the General Council's policy it would lead to "more surrenders, wage reductions, the end of the power of trade unionism." The only alternative policy was a "united class fight of the whole trade union movement" for the interests of all workers. For this a centralised leadership was essential, but it must be "a General Council preparing for battles, not grovelling for peace". Pressure on the existing leaders was not enough, it was necessary to struggle for "a complete change in structure, policy and leadership" and only in such a struggle would new leaders develop.[3]

The Minority Movement did not want splits. It wanted its policy to become by majority the official policy of the unions, "to become the Majority Movement by the conversion of the unions from supporters of an industrial system controlled by capitalists for profit, to one controlled by workers for use."[4]

But the General Council had no intention either of leading a united class fight or of allowing the Minority to become the Majority by democratic persuasion. At the 1926 T.U.C. one of its members, speaking against allowing trades councils to affiliate to the N.M.M., said that if the General Council allowed such affiliations, "it is obvious that if we go on these lines, within a short period the Minority Movement may become the majority".[5] In April 1927 the General Council decided against recognition of any trades council affiliated to the N.M.M.

This action was also a signal to Union Executives to do likewise. The General and Municipal Workers ordered their branches to sever all relations with the M.M., disbanded those who did not obey, and obliged candidates for office to sign a denial of C.P. or M.M. membership. Other unions imposed similar bans.[6]

In 1927 the T.U.C. General Council opened up talks with the employers for a joint policy and broke off its relations with the Soviet trade unions, an act Pollitt described as "a crime against the working class of the world, equalled only by the betrayal of the general strike".[7]

The next two years saw the parallel development of surrender to the big employers and sustained attacks on revolutionary workers. The Mond–Turner conferences[8] led to unions' acceptance of the effects of rationalisation—speed-up, longer hours, less wages. Disputes were to be settled by conciliation, the strike weapon was not to be used. Pollitt wrote that the General Council was trying to persuade the workers that rationalisation would lead to a new period of prosperity. It was pre-supposing a peaceful transition to socialism via economic democracy within the capitalist system. It was renouncing class struggle.[9]

"Rationalisation requires peace in industry to facilitate new attacks on the workers. Peace in industry requires a leadership that will surrender the whole trade union fight and will attack the revolutionary workers."[10]

The bans on the C.P. and M.M. had a dual purpose—to preserve right-wing domination and to deprive the trade unions of militant leaders. The attack was led by the new General Secretary of the T.U.C., Walter Citrine. His ability to ignore inconvenient facts, lack of working-class principle, and complete subservience to capitalist thinking. combined with administrative efficiency and command of procedure, made him eminently suitable for harnessing the trade unions to Mondism. He worked hard for the knighthood and peerage with which his capitalist patrons subsequently rewarded him. In defence of collaboration Citrine wrote a pamphlet on what he called "Communist disruption". Pollitt answered every point in his *Reply to Citrine* which sold 50,000 copies in three weeks.[11]

The most flagrant right-wing violation of trade union democracy took place in the Scottish Miners Union. In Fife, three successive ballots with 90 per cent voting gave decisive majorities to left-wing candidates. They were elected as county agents, as members of the Scottish Executive, and nominated for Scottish Executive positions. Together with left successes in Lanark, this meant a left majority at the Scottish Annual Conference. The sitting right-wing officials thereupon refused to call the annual conference and manoeuvred to secure the disaffiliation of the Fife Union. The right-wing M.F.G.B. leaders supported this defiance of a democratic majority decision.[12]

The 1928 T.U.C. met at Swansea. Banned as delegate, Pollitt this time was outside, speaking on the sands to thousands of workers who had marched from all over South Wales to demand a militant policy. In the Congress the General Council got block-vote endorsement for Mondism, the attack on the M.M., and a break with the organised unemployed. This T.U.C. made clear that any fight against rationalisation would have to come from the workers themselves and would meet the strongest opposition from trade union officialdom.

2. SOLIDARITY WITH OPPRESSED PEOPLES.

Among the political documents cherished by Pollitt was the Communist International's *Thesis on the National and Colonial Questions*.[13] It developed the concept that the working people of the imperialist countries and those of the colonies both stood to gain from the ending of imperialism and should act in conjunction for its overthrow. Pollitt never tired of explaining that until the British workers ceased to support in any way the subjection and exploitation of other peoples, they would not be able to free themselves from capitalist exploitation. Active solidarity with the colonial workers and national independence movements against the common enemy was indispensable for the advance of British labour. It was a question of practical assistance as well as propaganda.

In 1924 Jim Crossley went to the Near East and Percy Glading to India to gather information. In 1925, George Allison, a leading Fife miner, went to India to help in building trade unions, and in 1927 was sentenced to 18 months in gaol. Another experienced trade unionist, Ben Bradley, an engineer whom Pollitt had met in the "Hands Off Russia" movement, went to India in the autumn of 1927. The Indian trade unions grew rapidly, and in 1929 some 30 leaders, including Bradley, were arrested and committed for trial at Meerut.[14]

In 1927 Pollitt arranged for Tom Mann to go on an R.I.L.U. delegation to China[15], and to attend the Pan-Pacific Trade Union Conference in Hankow in June. On February 25, Tom Mann spoke at a mass meeting in Canton to protest against the landing of foreign troops in China; 40,000 people marched. On March 23 he wrote to Pollitt: "In seventeen days since we left Canton we travelled 120 miles by rail, then reached Souchon by river and road. Our party was 150 strong, including armed guards, in four boats each worked by 16 coolies. Six pulled from the shore, or in the river, others shouldered poles. We went upstream at 3 to 4 miles per hour for three days. No seats except on your own luggage. Then 40 miles tramp through the mountain passes, rice fields and peasant farms, over the summit and down to another river running north, again boats worked by hand. On the whole journey not a horse, cart, wagon or lorry. Oh, the awful labour of the Chinese people! But the revolutionary spirit was everywhere, meetings enthusiastic and crowded, delighted at messages of solidarity from other lands." In May, Pollitt received a cable from Tom Mann "Mobilisation of warships at Hankow includes ten British vessels ready for bombardment. This shameful assault can only be stopped by direct action on the part of the workers in Britain... Chinese trade unionists ask help".

Pollitt said of Tom Mann on his return that he was "the first Englishman to enter China, not for imperialist aims or propaganda, not for Christianising the Chinese, but to convey a message of solidarity from comrades in the trade unions of this country."[16] The report of the visit was widely circulated.[17]

Pollitt actively supported the League Against Imperialism in which organisations in imperialist countries and in the colonies could co-operate for the freedom of oppressed peoples. Of the foundation conference in February 1927, where 200 delegates represented 134 organisations in 37 countries, he wrote: "I never sat in a Congress where I was made to feel so bitter as I felt at Brussels, as I listened to the burning speeches of representatives from countries exploited by imperialism, glad to have the chance of stating their suffering and oppression, a story of the lust for profits and cheap labour, of robbery, violence, forced labour, the loss of all rights, confiscation of their land, destruction of all freedom. A Zulu comrade said 'They told us the Union Jack meant freedom, we who have been deprived of our land, our cattle killed to force us to leave our homes, go down their mines and live in their filthy compounds. With the colour bar against us, the political parties won't look at us, only the Communists treat us as equals'. When an Egyptian Nationalist said he did not believe in force, only in evolution, a worker from the French Congo told a story of outrage, rapine and ill-treatment that made one's blood boil and asked 'What would you do in our place?' And so it went on, from Japan, China, Africa, South America, speaker after speaker exposed the hypocrisy about the 'civilising mission'. We saw imperialism as it really is—a system of extracting colossal wealth as a result of unheard of exploitation, suffering and misery."[18]

His pledge of support to the League included the exposure of the realities of imperialism to "our comrades in the army and navy in order that they will do their class duty", and to trade unionists to promote strike action against the movement of troops by rail or ship. He signed the invitation to a conference in July 1928 to establish a British Section of the League. He was again a delegate at the League's Second Congress in July 1929, when it had sections in seventeen countries. The Labour Government had made no change in Britain's imperialist policy in Egypt and Palestine. James Maxton, M.P., Chairman of the I.L.P., made the opening speech at the Congress, but failed to even mention, much less condemn, the Labour Government's actions. Under criticism, he declared before the end of the Congress that facts imposed upon him the duty of strongly opposing this pro-imperialist attitude and of striving for the adoption of an anti-imperialist policy.[19] But on his return to Britain, Maxton failed to publicise or implement his declaration. Pollitt publicly attacked him for this, and the League proceeded to expel Maxton for actions incompatible with its principles.

For the 1929 Annual Conference of the N.M.M. Pollitt arranged with the Labour Research Department the preparation of a documented survey of workers' conditions in the colonies.[20] It gave facts on East and South Africa, Malaya, India, and on forced labour, and its exposures were in sharp contrast to official whitewash, including that by the Labour Government. In a preface Pollitt quoted J. H. Thomas at a luncheon on July 26; "The Labour Government was as anxious and as jealous, and would maintain the integrity, improvement and development, and were as proud of the development of the British Commonwealth of Nations as any government that either preceded it or that would follow it." Pollitt commented: "It is to place the real facts of imperialism before the workers and to expose the Thomas school of imperialists, that the Minority Movement is giving such prominence to the whole problem of imperialism."

To meet the costs of publishing this survey, Pollitt wrote to some who might help, including Bernard Shaw, who replied, "I cannot give money to the N.M.M. because that would commit me to the delusions of the middle-class idealists of 1848, to the class war, the revolutionary proletariat and the other figments of British Museum Socialism. But your kindness in sending me a copy of the report reminds me that I forgot to send you a present on your last birthday, and I hasten to repair that deplorable omission."[21] A cheque for £5 was enclosed. But when Pollitt tried to get H. G. Wells also "to repair a deplorable omission," the reply was brief. It read "Dear Pollitt, If I were you, I wouldn't keep a birthday. Yours, H. G. Wells."

3. Libel action

One summer morning in 1927, on his way to the Party office after waiting in vain for a call at the docks, Pollitt saw in the Strand some boilers being transported to a hotel. He asked if there was a job, and was taken on to erect the superstructure.

A few days later he was notified of an action for criminal libel taken against him by David Scott[22], a member of the National Union of Seamen, whose President was Havelock Wilson.

Militant in his early days, Wilson later became an ally of the shipowners. To be signed on a seaman had to have a valid form, Port Consultant No. 5, issued by the N.U.S. only to union members financially in order.[23] This system gave the N.U.S. official power to deny work to a man. In the 1926 general strike, Wilson ordered the seamen to remain at work, applied for an injunction to prevent union branches paying strike pay, and gave the High Court the opportunity to declare the strike "contrary to law". Wilson's policy and his dictatorial attitude within the union were publicly criticised by Pollitt. In turn, Wilson lost no opportunity to denounce "the Reds". The antagonism came to a head when in 1927 Wilson took the N.U.S. out of the Labour Party, and offered an interest-free loan to the Spencer breakaway union for miners, an action denounced by Pollitt at the T.U.C. If it be added that Wilson said of Edward VII when Prince of Wales, "I found him a real English gentleman, and I can say without qualification that there is nothing finer in the world",[24] it will easily be understood that politically Wilson and Pollitt were poles apart. The R.I.L.U. also criticised Wilson, holding that his policy adversely affected seamen of other countries.[25]

In February 1927 Wilson printed Scott's allegations[26] of wrongful arrest, detention and deportation from the Soviet port of Novorossisk, and as part of his campaign against the Labour Party challenged Lansbury to take up the case.

The Seafarer, a Minority Movement paper, printed an article from the R.I.L.U. replying to Scott, and containing comments libellous in English law. When Pollitt saw the proof he gave instructions not to publish, but the paper had come off the press.[27] Wilson obtained copies, action followed against Pollitt, T. R. Strudwick and R. Beech, the two latter office holders of the Transport M.M. The case was heard in October by the Recorder of London, Sir Ernest Wild, K.C., at the Old Bailey. Mr. Oliver, K.C. and Sir Travers Humphreys were for the prosecution; Pollitt defended himself. Sergeant Sullivan, K.C., who defended Sir Roger Casement in a famous treason trial in 1916, appeared for Strudwick and Beech.

The trial turned on two issues—was the action bona-fide or an abuse of law to further a political campaign? was Scott's life in Novorossisk "sober, industrious and respectable", or, as the defence claimed, that of a "pimp, contrabandist and thief"? Prosecution witnesses were mainly Wilson's officials, not all as crude as the American who described Wilson as "the greatest labour leader in the world."[28] Defence witnesses were mainly officials from Novorossisk.

The prosecution stressed the revolutionary aims of the Minority Movement and appealed to anti-Soviet prejudice. Counsel claimed that the M.M. "advocated the employment of Soviet money for propaganda", then added, "I have not read these passages for the purpose of prejudicing the defendants". Sergeant Sullivan remarked, "You are to bear something in mind for the sole purpose of putting it out of your mind . . . why was it put in at all?"[29] Sir Travers Humphreys spoke of "Moscow, where the heads of this so-called government live," and, referring to a disorderly house, "Perhaps it is not an offence in Russia."[30] Mr. Oliver said on the application for release of the Soviet witnesses, "the country will be glad to get rid of them". Only after the Recorder had expressed regret and disapproval did Oliver apologise. His anti-Soviet zeal exceeded his political knowledge, for his reply to a question from the Recorder was that "international bourgeoisie meant everybody who was not a Communist."[31] When a Soviet witness described himself as "secretary of a national minority organisation" Oliver informed the Court that the "Minority Movement in this country is the same as that in Russia!"[32]

Witnesses from Novorossisk brought copies of their official records. The prosecution intimated they would challenge such documents as forgeries; but on grounds that under English law Soviet administrative tribunals could not be classified as Courts, the documents were not admitted.

Addressing the jury, Pollitt claimed that the proceedings bore out his contention that "the case would not be discussed apart from politics", the prosecution was primarily part of a political campaign against those who sympathised with the Russian Revolution. "A stranger in this Court . . . might well have imagined that the Russian Revolution and its methods were on trial."[33] Pollitt countered several of the prosecution's attempts to create bias. On the remark that Soviet political police did not all wear uniforms, he said he knew "half a dozen people sitting here as members of the Political Branch of Scotland Yard, it is a political trial of interest to them". Oliver asked of the Russian bourgeoisie "were they killed?". Pollitt pointed out that "wives and mothers in Amritsar uttered that cry in regard to their husbands and sons".[34] Oliver stressed that the ruling Communist Party was a minority of the Russian population and did not publish a list of its members. Pollitt asked "Is not the Conservative Party in this country a minority? Does it publish a list of its members, or where it gets its finances?"[35]

Pollitt drew attention to the fact that when asked in the House whether it would seek compensation for Scott, the Government had twice replied that "it was not a case in which compensation could be claimed".[36] He added that a Sunday newspaper had given what it considered to be the reasons for the government's attitude. "They discovered that the aggrieved person had got off very lightly . . . he had set up a traffic in souls on a wholesale scale . . . and a little smuggling in dope as well."[37] Cross-examined by Pollitt, Scott said he would have taken action against anybody who made allegations against his moral character. Asked why he had not taken action against the Sunday newspaper, he said he had not seen the article referred to. Pollitt pointed out that *The Seafarer* had reprinted the article in its May issue, a copy of which Wilson had shown to Scott without directing his attention to the reprint. Pollitt asked "Why not, if the prosecution is for personal honour?" and suggested it was because "the politics of the Sunday paper are not those of the Minority Movement, but those of the N.U.S."[38]

One evening after the Court had risen a man told Pollitt that the

Registrar of Shipping had "the full record of Scott at sea, not just the discharges" in the book on which Oliver examined Scott. After the resultant search, further cross-examination of Scott shed light on his unsavoury record, including drunkenness and venereal disease. On subpoena the Home Office produced their record of the woman with whom Scott had consorted in Novorossisk, and whom he had presented as "honest and hardworking". Her record showed that in Britain in 1918-19 she had been fined for indecent behaviour as a prostitute, convicted for keeping a brothel, sentenced to 21 days for assault and battery and deported as undesirable.[39]

Sir Ernest Wild's summing up, a hundred foolscap pages long, gave the impression to the lay mind of the present writer, of aiming at a scrupulously balanced presentation. But the jury had to bring down the balance and its very fineness meant that the prevailing anti-Communist prejudice would bring it down against the defence. The verdict was "Guilty".

The Recorder reminded the defendants of their right of appeal, "in such a way as gave the impression that if we agreed not to appeal against conviction, the sentence would be lighter".[40] Pollitt stated there would be no appeal. He was bound over to keep the peace for a year and ordered to pay £100 towards the cost of the prosecution. Strudwick and Beech were similarly bound over and ordered to pay £50 each.

For reasons which do not appear to be on record, a decision was taken in Pollitt's absence abroad, to appeal. On February 24 1928 it was dismissed by the Lord Chief Justice sitting with two other judges.[41]

4. 38 GREAT ORMOND STREET [42]

From 1925 to 1929 the Minority Movement office at 38 Great Ormond Street was a hive of activity, rarely quiet before midnight. From two inconvenient rooms on the fourth floor the M.M. moved to a first floor annexe in what had been a garden. The door bore the words "Room No. 14"; in fact there were four rooms, or rather two, one for the Hon. General Secretary and his super-efficient private secretary, one for the general office, and two cubby holes. The owner of the building was a formidable dark-browed lady who viewed the M.M.'s activities from a purely business standpoint. Police intrusions, libel actions, press photographs were all ammunition in her ceaseless campaign to raise the rent. She took a fancy to Pollitt and would lie in wait to entice him in—her two rooms were off the same corridor—for a cup of tea and an argument which she dearly loved, especially when she could state a case for more rent. He thought of the most ingenious objections and often found a loophole in her case.

In the basement another lady, darker browed but not quite so formidable, kept a café; and as many of the M.M.'s visitors, and those of the C.P. London District Committee and the national Y.C.L. who were on the top floor came straight from work, she did quite an evening trade. Scotland Yard found the café convenient, their representatives would sit there, usually deep in a paper, and no doubt picked up a lot of information. Less responsible jokers would exchange ideas as to who was police, and having picked out their man would engage in an audibly whispered conversation about some outrageous proposal in the hope that he would mislead his paymasters. One selected victim of this trick turned out to be an old friend of Harry's, who warned him that dangerous secrets were being talked about. Harry was furious and put the café out of bounds for a week, to be himself waylaid by the proprietress demanding to know why everyone was avoiding her.

Harry was unquestionably in charge because of his outstanding abilities, but he did not believe in a one-man band and went out of his way to give responsibilities—and credit—to others, whether full-time or volunteer workers. Mining matters were always dealt with by Nat Watkins, who seemed to know every coalfield and every militant personally. He was a foundation member of the C.P., having represented the Doncaster Workers Committee at the 1920 conference. He would occasionally put on his collar back to front and hold forth in a parson's voice on the iniquities of the Reds. He was no lightweight, neither was Wally Hannington who shared one of the cubby holes with him, though not often there due to his work for the N.U.W.M. When Wally and Nat were both in, there was room for just one visitor; if George Hardy came in too, the door could not be shut. The plain-clothes police often stood at the front entrance scrutinising the visitors; and one day when George Hardy came in with some documents from Hamburg and was discussing them with Nat and Wally a comrade rushed in, shut and bolted the No. 14 door which usually stood open, and announced that the police were on their way up. There was a back way out, a somewhat perilous drop into a yard and then over a wall. If a photo had been taken of George, Nat and Wally negotiating this exit, it would not have been believed. It eventually turned out that the police had gone up to see the Y.C.L.

The rules of the Boilermakers required that members accepting nomination for the T.U.C. had to be working at the trade or signing the vacant book, unless they were officials. For most of the year Harry was therefore in the shipyard. This meant an early morning start from home, walk to the station, train to Fenchurch Street, another to the docks, perhaps even to Tilbury. The morning post would bring a batch of stuff prepared by him the night before for typing; in the dinner hour he would telephone for a precis of his correspondence and dictate replies, notes or an article; about 5.30 p.m. he would arrive looking fresh as a daisy, deal with his letters, dictate more, prepare notes for his evening meeting and see people. He rarely had a free evening for amusement. At week-ends he spoke outside London, often travelling back during the Sunday night.

Meticulous in preparing his speeches, packing them with relevant facts and arguments, Harry never wasted a word or a minute. He insisted on time for questions and carefully noted every one and the effect of his answer. He said that though he could not guarantee that every questioner could learn from him, he could guarantee that he would learn from every questioner. He enjoyed the speaking, and made it an art and a science. For novices in the office, including the present writer, he took a speakers' class, and corrected our faults without embarrassing us. One of his hints was "Without the sympathy of your audience you won't get anywhere, to win it you must begin by saying things they understand and agree with. When you want them to accept something new or controversial, don't unload it suddenly; explain the problem and gently lead up to the answer."

Harry liked to claim, not to say boast, that the Boilermakers were the salt of the earth. The Engineers could not accept this and one of them asked him why, if the Boilermakers were so good, so few were in the M.M. Harry took this to heart and after a talk with his bosom pals, collected two pounds off them and got out the first issue of a monthly duplicated paper—then a favourite method of M.M. group work—for sale at 1d. *The Boilermaker* first number sold 500 copies and the orders rose to 1,500, about the limit of what could be produced. It became in many features a model of how to arouse the interest and widen the outlook of members of a union traditionally concerned primarily with their own craft affairs. It ran for nearly two years.[43] Harry liked to edit it himself, but once or twice when an issue was due and he had to leave London he would ask the lads to send their letters to the present writer whom he sternly warned, "Don't start improving what they write, just make sure the commas and full stops are right."

Harry had a great admiration for David Low the cartoonist. One of his cartoons, in a series "If Bolshevism came to England" showed a revolutionary tribunal in session, the Justices being Pollitt, Gallacher and Campbell. Before them stood Winston Churchill, in full oratorical spate, hand on heart, arm uplifted. The caption said: "Winston is called upon to justify himself before the Revolutionary Tribunal and does so with such moving eloquence that he is appointed leader of the Revolution."[44] On this effort Harry's comment was brief—"What a bloody hope!"

In 1925 the Committee of the General Workers M.M. was composed of comrades Moody, Wild and Savage. The following year it was Moody, Wild, Young and Wooley. "We drew Harry's attention to this, he said it was well named and then threw his arms around us."[45]

During March 1927 Pollitt's attention was drawn to an interview between the Labour Correspondent of the *Morning Post* and Mr. G. A. Spencer M.P. The latter was alleged to have repeated a statement made to him by John Bromley, M.P., to the effect that in 1926 two prominent M.M. members asked him to get them tickets for the gallery of the House. He did so and in conversation asked them not to make political capital out of the miners, who were seeking only to protect their wages and conditions, for some ulterior purpose. "These men then said, 'Is your mentality no higher than to think that we care a damn what becomes of the miners? We are going to use them for a purpose, we are out for a revolution.' " Bromley then tore up the tickets. Pollitt wrote to Bromley on March 22 quoting the report, saying that he thought a press statement necessary and asking Bromley for the names of the "two prominent members" so that he could get their views. No reply was received. On March 29 Pollitt repeated the request, registering the letter. Again no reply. So he published both letters,[46] but Bromley's silence remained unbroken.

5. THOMAS ROBERT STRUDWICK[47]

Potential capacity for leadership among trade union militants was quickly recognised by Pollitt, and he often helped their development by entrusting them with responsibility. Such a one was T. R.—"Tommy"—Strudwick, who on the formation of the National Minority Movement was a consistent voluntary helper.

Born in 1886 of poor parents living in Southwark, he enlisted when 14 years of age. Drafted to Reserve in 1906, he married and got work on the London Electric Railway. In the 1914-18 war he served again; on discharge he returned to railway work. There were ten children; his eldest daughter wrote of their life in the early twenties, "Then Southwark was really a slum, our house about the worst, two tiny bedrooms, kitchen and scullery. We went there to find a pile of refuse reaching halfway up the downstairs windows. Adjoining was a yard where wood was chopped and a traction engine stood. The children slept 'top and bottom' in two double beds, one in a bedroom, the other in the kitchen. The Saturday night bath was in a tub before the fire, the water warmed up after each child from a kettle on the hob. Each week part of the wages got our Sunday clothes out of pawn, to be 'popped' again on Monday. Money lasted a couple of days, then I often had to borrow a few shillings for food. On Tuesdays I and other children went over London Bridge to Leadenhall Market to stand opposite a shop, and be called across to receive a bag of pieces. My mother was ill most of the time; she took a punishing, she slowly disintegrated under the pressure. These half-forgotten memories still make me boil at a reference to the 'good old days' ".

Tommy's war experiences, the contrast between his life and the promised "land fit for heroes" and the innumerable discussions he had, led him in 1919 to join the B.S.P. Walworth Branch. He became well-known as a Communist at the Browning Socialist Hall and the Newington Working Men's Club, where he often took his wife and elder children.

A fluent, popular speaker, he expressed his ideas in homely terms with colour and animation. Generous in the extreme, his last coppers often went on fish and chips and tea shared with someone unemployed, and he walked several miles home. Entirely self-educated, he read socialist literature avidly. Respected on the job for his sincerity, he made many new members for the union and helped initiate the joint Trams, Omnibus and Tubes movement for unity. Pollitt recognised his qualities, helped him to study, gave him responsibilities, and spoke of him as "one of the salt of the earth".

He became Secretary of the Transport Minority Movement and found new problems, particularly among dockers and seamen. Unconcerned with personal gain, he fearlessly advocated what be thought to be right. Arrested in the 1926 General Strike, a duplicated news sheet was found on him. Though neither its publisher nor writer, he got two months' hard labour. When he came out and reported for work, the L.E.R. demanded an undertaking that he would cease political activities. He refused; they sacked him. For a year alternately unemployed or in casual work, in his spare time he worked voluntarily for the M.M. In 1927 he was involved in the Scott libel action.

Later he worked full time for the M.M. and for the International of Seamen and Harbour Workers, formed in 1930. He was several times on missions for the R.I.L.U., he liked to recall the beauty of Japan's cherry orchards in bloom. Back in England he worked till the second world war, when he lived in Cornwall. His wife died in 1946. Over 60 years of age he took what work he could get, in hotels, kitchens, house portering, selling from a barrow. Life became difficult, his health gave way, in and out of hospital, two operations. But he never lost his enthusiasm for the socialist cause: the world around him was his life, he did not count his own misfortunes.

His last years were easier, spent in New Zealand near his youngest daughter, Rosa, named after Rosa Luxemburg. His last public effort was in protest against legal limitation of trade union rights for seamen. He died suddenly but peacefully on July 31, 1970, aged 84.

6. POLLITT EXCLUDED FROM T.U.C. AND LABOUR PARTY CONFERENCE.

In the planned campaign of the right-wing leaders to deprive their opponents of democratic rights, it was essential to prevent Pollitt's voice from being heard at T.U.C. and Labour Party Conferences. Here the Executive of the Boilermakers played a decisive part.[48] Their Secretary, John Hill, was a member of the General Council, dependent for his seat on the votes of the big unions and vulnerable to pressure.

Following the 1926 Labour Party Conference moves against Pollitt began. He did not accept Hill's draft for the delegates' report, but Hill vetoed Pollitt's and nothing appeared in the *Monthly Report*. Pollitt's version of Margate was refused publication, indeed from then onwards none of the articles he sent for the *Monthly Report*, not even one which Hill had approved, was published, the decision being that of the E.C.

When asking for nominations for the 1927 T.U.C. and Labour Party Conference, the Boilermakers E.C. publicised the Labour Party's appeal to trade unions not to elect Communists as their delegates, on which a national newspaper commented that it would be interesting to see whether "this has the effect of excluding the familiar voice of Mr. Pollitt",[49]. It did not, since Pollitt was again elected by the usual majorities to both conferences.

The next stage in the attack on Pollitt was the rejection of his report on the 1927 T.U.C. Hill's report, which Pollitt refused to sign, was then published. In it Hill said that policy questions had been "forced" on Congress to the detriment of discussion on wages and hours; blamed Russian interference in British affairs for the breakdown of the Anglo-Russian Unity Committee; and alleged that Pollitt "spoke as a representative of the Minority Movement and in favour of the Russian point of view against our own".[50] Pollitt's reply to this attack was refused publication[51] and he had to circulate it by post. He pointed out that his Communist views were always known to those who voted for him and that "for six years the Boilermakers have preferred an honest fighter, even though they may not agree with all his opinions, to a deaf and dumb delegate who goes to national conferences for a holiday at a good rate of pay". He was attacked because of his criticism of those "who betrayed the general strike, capitulated on the Trade Unions Act, broke with the Russian trade unions, and have now agreed with the industrial peace propaganda of Havelock Wilson". He quoted capitalist praise for some of the decisions of the T.U.C. and Labour Party and asked, "Do Boilermakers want me to support the policies that call for such praise by enemies of the working class? If so, I am not your man." His view of the duty of a delegate to a national conference was to "think out the implications of the resolutions submitted, and make a contribution to the debates, not from the viewpoint of a section, but from the standpoint of the working-class movement as a whole".[52]

The E.C's next move was to announce their intention to ban Communists from standing for election to T.U.C. or Labour Party Conference, thus going beyond the Labour Conference appeal, which had no reference to the T.U.C., on the grounds that the C.P. "opposes our industrial methods and constitutional parliamentary efforts, and takes its policy and orders from a committee of dictators in Russia".[53] An appeal against this decision was lodged by Aitken Ferguson of Glasgow No. 1. Branch, on the grounds that it was "unjustifiable, anti-working class and contrary to the customs, rules and usages of our Society, as well as the rules of the Labour Party and the T.U.C." The E.C. decided on a ballot on the question at branch meetings in May, and issued a 1,200-word statement, the main points in which were: the objects of the C.P. were opposed to those of our Society; the Minority Movement was a branch of the C.P. formed to undermine the trade union movement; members of trade unions, including Boilermakers, "were invited to Moscow, appointed full-time paid agents of the Russian Communist Party, with secret orders to discredit trade union officers, make our constitutional procedure impossible and bring along an armed revolution".[54]

The London No. 11 Branch circulated a letter asking members to vote against the E.C.'s decision, saying that the issue was not the merits or demerits of Communist policy but was "whether members of the Society who are in full benefit and fulfil every trade union qualification in accord with the rules are to be discriminated against and penalised because of their political opinions".[55]

The wording on the ballot papers—its full significance appeared later—was:

"For Ferguson's Appeal and Communist Representation:
"Against Ferguson's Appeal and Communist Representation:"

At that time voting in the Society was by attendance at the branch meeting and filling in the ballot paper. Voting anywhere else or by post was against the rules. Of 68,307 members entitled to vote 6,531 did so. Of 383 branches, 274 sent in returns. The result was announced as—For 1,520: Against 5,011.

The final phase of the attack immediately followed. In June Pollitt was nominated for the E.C. and duly applied, giving a nine-point policy.[56] The E.C. refused to accept the nomination on the grounds that the ballot on the Ferguson appeal "involved the whole policy and constitution of the Society" and that the majority vote had decided "against Communist representation of the members".[57]

The E.C. operation had a double success—the Labour Party Executive and the T.U.C. General Council were relieved of their most formidable opponent at conferences, and the sectionalist leadership of the Society relieved of the organised challenge to their domination. The capitalist press applauded this limitation of the democratic rights of trade union members at the same time as it applauded the parliamentary limitation of the democratic rights of the trade unions.

Allegations of irregularities in the conduct of the ballot were made, but the E.C. refused an enquiry. London No. 11 branch challenged the Limerick vote, officially recorded as 42 against the appeal, none in favour, whereas the total recorded membership of the branch in December was only 33. Hill replied that there was a mistake in the records, the membership was 45. As three apprentices had no vote, this meant that every member of the branch must have attended the May meeting. The Belfast No. 2. total branch membership, 363, cast a vote of 6 for the appeal, 317 against. The entire Irish vote looked odd, 31 for the appeal,

1,426 against—a total of 1,457 votes cast, while the Irish totals of the four previous ballots were respectively 212, 121, 175 and 114. Pollitt himself was present at one branch where five of its members attended and the official return showed 5 votes for the appeal, 25 against. In this case Hill admitted in a letter to London No. 11 branch that there were irregularities. Pollitt offered to give the names of other branches, one where 8 members were present and the return showed 88 against the appeal, a second where 13 were present and the return showed 213 against the appeal.[58]

7. A. J. Cook broken

In May 1928 the M.F.G.B. Executive received the Scottish officials who had been defeated in the Scottish ballot, the majority having voted for Communists or Minority Movement members. The democratically elected officials were given no hearing, a proposal for M.F.G.B. officials to visit Scotland and investigate was turned down, and the Executive proceeded to adopt a resolution condemning "the Communists and Minority Movement and their tactics, particularly in Scotland". In July the M.F.G.B. annual conference endorsed this resolution without discussion and without enquiry. This was equivalent to a refusal to accept a ballot result in which Communists or Minority Movement members were elected to official positions.

Eighteen leading miners, including A. J. Cook, signed a protest against this resolution. At the Executive meeting on October 12 Cook was told that if he did not repudiate his signature he would be suspended from his position as Secretary; S. O. Davies of South Wales and Harry Hicken of Derbyshire were similarly threatened. The Executive then agreed to enquire into the Scottish position and to declare that the Annual Conference decision did not mean "the dismembering of individual members on account of their political beliefs or associations", after which Cook and the others withdrew their signatures. The capitalist press was jubilant over "the climb down" of A. J. Cook and the Minority Movement spoke of "A. J. Cook's grave mistake", adding that if Cook considered that the decision to enquire into events in Scotland meant negating the Annual Conference resolution he was mistaken; the enquiry would be made by those who had openly declared themselves in support of the officials whom the members had rejected.[59]

Pollitt had first met Cook in 1921 at the King Street bookshop[60] and subsequently kept up a close association with him, actively supporting his campaign for the M.F.G.B. secretaryship. Cook was one of the founders of the Miners Minority Movement[61] and continued to co-operate with it after his election.

On October 25, 1928, Pollitt wrote a letter marked "Personal" beginning, "Dear Arthur, Glad to hear of your recovery but amazed at the sharp turn of events so far as your policy is concerned. I believe that your present line is the most dangerous to yourself that you have ever taken. Unless you are more than careful, you will find that more dirty actions will be taken by the M.F.G.B. in your name and over your signature, against the militant miners, than have ever been taken before." He went on, "Your Notes in last week's *Sunday Worker* were appalling"—opponents of the M.M. had in fact quoted them with approval. "I wouldn't presume to write you, only for our close friendship, and no one knows better than I do all you have gone through. But you know you have had our backing and help as well. For the last two weeks I have been speaking all over Lancashire on the Swansea T.U.C., stating the fight you put up there, getting support for you, making your position clear, and then you throw it all away in a misguided conception you are doing the right thing. You are not. You could sweep all the coalfields on the one union issue, but unless you break with them now, you'll find it too late." The letter concludes with passion, "I beg of you, for the sake of the miners' best interests and your own, to repudiate your present policy. Resume your open fight. It will rally to you all that is best in the movement. When you have been fighting the hardest, you have had the greatest mass support. On your present lines you'll not only lose it, you'll knock the heart out of thousands of the M.F.G.B. best lads. Is it worth it? Of course it isn't. They believe they have got you down. They'll wipe their feet on you. They won't forget all they have to pay you back. Fight them now, let them see they only gained a Pyrrhic victory over you when you were weak and distraught. But you will have to do it now, or it will be too late."[62]

Cook's reply was written in pencil, undated and showing signs of haste and anxiety. The full text was:

"Dear Harry, Regret delay in answering your letter but was delayed at home. Am much better but not yet A.1. Now don't worry shall not go over to the reactionaries they wait for my body. Tactics may be wrong but I am up against difficult proposition when to force issue cannot explain by letter but should like to see you as they are out for a smash. Future must be thought out do not blame rank and file but b—— machinery which keeps rank and file at bay. Their Power in machine when and how to test it. You surely have had bitter experiences of machine. I am firm on One National Union and want to swap coal fields but when and how. See me soon.
I have nought to fear in a fight. My reply in W.L.
                                    Yours ever for the workers
                                    A.J.C."[63]

Pollitt's warning that weaknesses would lead Cook into the clutches of the right-wing leaders was justified. In 1929 Cook ceased to advocate industrial militancy by the M.F.G.B. and operated Mondism without protest.[64] He no longer criticised MacDonald, but assured the miners that a

Labour Government headed by him would "in the first session repeal the Eight Hours Act" and would "nationalise the mines, minerals and by-products"[65] Instead of championing Labour and Communist unity in action, Cook repeated the anti-communist slanders circulated by the right wing.[66]

In the general election of 1929 the Labour Party sent Cook to Seaham Harbour to speak against Pollitt and for MacDonald. Pollitt describes an incident: "I knew it was a task he would detest and if he had been at all firm he could have got out of it on some pretext. So I decided to stand on the street corner by the Miners' Hall at Dawdon, where he would be bound to see me, thinking that at least his conscience would prick him a little. Up he rolled in a big car which stopped just where I was standing. He waved a friendly greeting to me which I studiously ignored. I knew he would be upset and he was ... We never spoke to one another again after this incident."[67] Those who may feel that Pollitt was unduly harsh should remember that he realised that it was the workers who would have to pay for Cook's political retreat and its consequences.

8. Mondism in action at Dawdon

The principal coalowner in the coastal constituency of Seaham Harbour, south of Sunderland, was the Marquess of Londonderry, owner of thousands of acres in Durham, Northern Ireland and South Wales. He was a worthy descendant of a family of exploiters the most famous of whom was that Viscount Castlereagh, cheered by the people only on the news of his suicide, of whom Byron wrote: "So Castlereagh has cut his throat! The worst of this is—that his own was not the first."[68]

In February 1929 Lord Londonderry, having secured one wage cut at his Dawdon colliery, demanded from about half the men another averaging 3s. per shift. Men and boys numbering 3,800 rejected the advice of their union leaders and ceased work. Pollitt was in the constituency preparing for his general election contest and did all he could to help the Dawdon men.

His reports in *The Worker* gave a picture of the men's determination, the hostility of the M.F.G.B. officials, national, county and lodge, and the activity of rank and file militants. "There is no strike pay. Single men get no relief. The Strike Committee calls no meetings." The Miners Minority Movement held frequent meetings and issued a bulletin advising: "Election of a new Strike Committee excluding those who favoured surrender, extension of the strike to Londonderry's Seaham colliery where men are working below the minimum, call on the whole county to fight for a new agreement when the existing one ends in two weeks time, organise communal feeding, demand relief for single men and school feeding for children"[69]

The miners elected a Vigilance Committee to prevent the fight being lost by the hostility of the Lodge Committee, which in seven weeks had taken three ballots hoping to get the men back, though each gave an increased majority against accepting any reduction or arbitration.[70] The national office of the Workers International Relief sent £30 to open a Fund and the county secretary then wrote to the Lodge Committee asking their co-operation in opening a feeding centre. After three weeks came their refusal to start their own kitchens or allow the use of their hall and its cooking equipment. The Vigilance Committee and the W.I.R. made a public appeal for funds, the *Daily Herald* refused to publish it, the M.F.G.B. paper alleged that the Communist Party used such monies for its political purposes. But the money came in. When the Vicar was prepared to allow the Parish Hall for use as a communal kitchen, the Lodge Committee persuaded him not to. The Workers International Relief began by giving out 300 food parcels, of tea, sugar and milk, supplied by the local Co-operative. Then use of the Co-operative Hall was obtained and Pollitt was able to report that the Fund had reached £180 and "Last Saturday we fed 301 meals and gave 301 parcels—let's make it 1,000!"[71]

After ten weeks struggle, the Vigilance Committee appealed for its extension: "Dawdon is the strongest and best organised lodge in the county, if we go down every pit will suffer reductions similar to ours." Conditions since the ending of the 1926 lock-out were summed up: "We have all gone through hell. Every sacrifice by the men the jumping off ground for another demand from the owners. Thousands not getting the minimum. Thousands on piece work in bad places on starvation pay. Increasing accidents, victimisation, insults from bullying managers and hangers-on." Then the issues were put for common action "not in defence of us, but for immediate wage advances for all classes of Durham miners."[72]

The dispute went on through the general election during which Pollitt at every meeting championed the cause of the Dawdon men. But MacDonald did not speak in Dawdon and when asked why he did not give a fighting lead to the men replied that he "knew his job better than to interfere in what was trade union business. The Labour Party, unlike the Communists, was not out to exploit the industrial difficulties of the Unions."[73]

After three months semi-starvation, the unremitting hostility of the union officials brought about a return to work on the reduced wage, with a formula including arbitration. The Fund had reached £324, and 14,880 meals and 1,200 parcels had been issued.[74]

The vote for the arbitration representatives demonstrated the men's feelings—100 for A. J. Cook, 90 for Lumley, a local Communist, and 82 for Harry Pollitt, and for three officials of the Durham Miners Association—72, 45 and 1 respectively. Cook was unable to attend, Lumley and Pollitt accepted, but the proceedings broke down due to failure to agree on an impartial Umpire.[75]

Pollitt regarded this conflict as one of "the first signs of a great strike movement that will develop in this country over the heads of the reformists. Having got the Mondist–T.U.C. collaboration the workers are now experiencing the results and fighting against them."[76] Dawdon certainly was an example of collaboration—"Lord Londonderry issued a press statement saying he had no quarrel with the miners officials, national, county or local. This statement was never repudiated even by the local officials who were actually facing the men".[77]

9. GENERAL ELECTION MAY 1929

In this general election Communists for the first time opposed official Labour candidates; previously they stood either as endorsed Labour candidates or where Labour had no candidate. The change followed the Labour Party's exclusion of Communists, designed by MacDonald to prevent any effective campaign within the Party against his pro-capitalist policy. Pollitt used the election to rouse the workers against rationalisation which he described as "a means whereby the capitalist can lower wages, intensify exploitation, abolish long standing customs and practices in the workshops, adopt a merciless rate cutting policy to those on piece work, force speeding up to disregard of human life and safety." Giving examples of the workers' resistance in transport, motors, shipyards, wool and mining, he warned that "the means of breaking this resistance is not the old-style methods; the breakers of the workers resistance are the trade union and Labour Party leaders, the open agents of the capitalists now in control of the machinery of the movement."[78]

These Labour leaders who were asking to be elected as a government, "carry through rationalisation on a tremendous scale, hastening the coming of war, which the imperialists are making inevitable and which will come the sooner, the quicker rationalisation takes place." "The problems confronting the workers can only be solved by smashing the capitalists and their allies and by the formation of a Revolutionary Workers Government. This is the basic fact to place before the workers." "Advantage must be taken of an awakened interest in politics to bring out the whole implications of the present period and the present leadership. The new line of the Communist Party and the Minority Movement will be accepted by all the best elements in the working class because it is the only policy the workers can adopt."

At Seaham Harbour, one of the safest Labour seats in the country, Pollitt as Communist candidate against MacDonald set out "to raise the banner of independent working-class struggle against the three capitalist parties and to carry forward under the battle cry of class against class the revolutionary fight both inside and outside Parliament".

The campaign began by Pollitt and his agent, Dave Ramsay, a stalwart of the earlier Workers Committee Movement, doing the chalking and bell ringing for the adoption meeting. At the first attempt not a single person turned up. They tried again, sixty-three people came, listened attentively, asked questions, gave a good collection. From then on they gathered a small but splendid band of workers, meetings growing in size and interest were held all over the constituency, the prodigious task of addressing and filling 58,300 envelopes was completed. The only committee room to be got was the front room in the house of a disabled miner. They had no car until the eve of poll, when they got "a baby Austin which aroused either tears or mirth" from onlookers.[79]

Pollitt's election address[80] was a call to action for the demands of the working class—the seven-hour day for miners, united resistance to wage cuts, work or full maintenance for the unemployed, free meals for school children, repeal of anti-working class legislation, abolition of workers' contributions to national insurance, repudiation of the Dawes plan, recognition of and trade with the Soviet Union. The Tories were the dominant party of Empire slavery and robbery, the Liberals had essentially the same platform. Labour professed socialist aims but its practical programme was capitalist reorganisation. A Labour Government of the then Labour leaders, "all proved traitors to the workers", would only be an instrument of capitalism.

Pollitt put squarely the only alternative, "the complete transformation of society—the abolition of all class divisions, privilege, monopoly and exploitation which today condemn the mass of the population to slave labour and misery for the profit of the few." To achieve a free and equal Socialist Republic a Revolutionary Workers Government would break the power of the ruling capitalist machine, give independence to all peoples of the Empire, take over the land, banks, mines and all large scale industry, run them with workers' control on a plan in the interests of the working class. These revolutionary ideas aroused enthusiasm among a few and hostility among others. Marjorie Pollitt who came to speak at week-ends was once pulled off the box by angry miners.

That Pollitt had reason for his dislike of MacDonald—"I hated that conceited, self-satisfied creature"[81]—may be seen from the comments of observers who in no way shared Pollitt's politics. Beatrice Webb described MacDonald's thinking as "conservative collectivism tempered by muddle-headed utopian socialism".[82] Francis Williams wrote: "his personality, superficially distinguished, was in its real texture amorphous—a peg built to hang myths on"; "he did not so much succumb to the aristocratic embrace as fling himself into its arms"; "he was sustained in his position by mass loyalty based on an almost total misunderstanding of what he really stood for". No serious socialist hearing MacDonald at a big meeting could dispute Winston Churchill's remark that he "used the largest number of words to convey the smallest amount of thought."[83]

MacDonald was politically summed up by the veteran Socialist Mrs. Despard, in a letter of support for Pollitt: "When I claimed his support for Irish prisoners and deportees (he was leader of the Opposition) he did nothing, he made no protest. Instead of fighting our great foes, imperialism and capitalism, he has played the double game of diplomacy, refused to support the really forward movement of the workers, preached expediency, agreed to compromise and checked enthusiasm. During his brief period of power, did he put forward any one measure antagonistic either to capitalism or to British Imperialism? What has he done for the miners? Where was he on the day when all London was moved with enthusiasm and sympathy for the Hunger Marchers?"[84]

Pollitt and MacDonald met twice on polling day. Touring the polling stations in his baby Austin, its red ribbons ruined by being pelted with mud and rotten vegetables, Pollitt's arrival in Murton coincided with that of MacDonald in his shining Rolls Royce. As they passed, the wheel of the Austin came off to the delight of MacDonald's cheering supporters. At the count, MacDonald entered half way through and circled the room "graciously shaking hands with all and sundry. When he came to Marjorie and me, he said in a tone of voice for which I could have killed him, 'How do you do? How do you do?' I could not resist saying 'I beg your pardon. I have not been introduced to you'." The result was MacDonald 35,615, the Tory 6,821, the Liberal, Haslam 5,266, Pollitt 1,451. He summed it up: "a fight which had been abundantly worth while, one of the most valuable political experiences I ever had, although one of the hardest campaigns."[85]

10. Pollitt becomes General Secretary

The Communist Party discussion culminating in the election of Harry Pollitt as General Secretary went through three phases. First: Differing estimates of Labour Movement problems, expressed at the 8th and 9th Congresses led to the appearance of a majority and minority in the Executive; both presented their views to the 19th Plenum of the C.I. in February 1927. This Plenum adopted a new policy, known briefly as "independent leadership". Second: Intense criticism arose of the presentation of the new policy by the E.C. and it was widely felt that its leadership of the 10th Congress had failed to rise to the occasion. Third: The struggle to secure an Executive able to apply the new policy led to decisive changes in leadership in August 1929. Pollitt played a leading part in these discussions and in the public presentation of the issues involved.

At the 8th Congress the E.C., in its thesis on the general strike, repeated the previous call for pressure on the Labour leadership for a militant policy, with the addendum that the existing Labour leaders should be replaced by new ones with a left policy. In contrast, Pollitt emphasised that a new element had appeared, an agreement of the old school of trade union leaders and the middle-class liberals in the Labour Party "to use the machinery of the movement to stifle the rising tide of working-class demands because it leads to class conflict". Pollitt not only called for a new

Labour leadership, but also maintained that to achieve it "it is necessary to work in the trade unions for a change of policy and the development of new leaders. It will take years of steady, persistent organisation."[86]

The 9th Congress spoke of the aim to replace the Tory Government by a Labour Government "under control of the Labour Party E.C.", later altered to "pursuing a working-class policy under control of the Labour Movement". Subsequently two distinct opinions in the E.C. were submitted to the E.C.C.I. 9th Plenum, in a majority thesis and an alternative prepared by R. Palme Dutt and Harry Pollitt. The main differences between the 'theses', and the differences between them both and the view in the Plenum, were as follows.[87]

C.C. majority: The situation in Britain is not so revolutionary in 1927 as in 1920.

Dutt–Pollitt: The present stage of revolutionary development is higher than in the temporary boom period of 1920.

Plenum: The resistance of the working class to bourgeois policy will cause the class struggle in Britain to become more acute.

C.C. majority: "The Party in 1928, no less than in 1920, must help to push a Henderson–Snowden Government into office to help the workers convince themselves by experience that reformism is worthless."

Dutt–Pollitt: Lenin did not declare that the disillusionment of the majority of the working class is necessary before the C.P. can undertake its direct fight against Social Democracy. It is the fact of the exposure and of continuing exposure that makes it possible for us to fight for and win the majority of the working class.

Plenum: In 1928 the campaign is not under the slogan of a Labour Government. The objective is to mobilise workers under our banner for future class battles with the slogan of a Revolutionary Workers' Government.

C.C. majority: Party support for a second reformist Labour Government renders more than ever necessary the struggle for the election of Communist M.Ps.

Dutt–Pollitt: The majority say that Communist candidates should oppose official Labour candidates only in exceptional cases. But to set the two alternative policies before the working class on a national scale it is necessary to place Communist candidates against Labour Party leaders.

Plenum: The Party should contest the elections to the maximum extent of its power and resources to mobilise the maximum of working-class support and focus the fight nationally against selected Labour Party leaders.

C.C. majority: The Party cannot exclude the possibility of having to change its tactics in the event of a sharp change in the situation.

Dutt–Pollitt: This possibility is recognised without making it dependent on whether the majority of the working class is disillusioned or not. With this the whole case of the thesis falls to the ground. "Sharp changes" are admitted for the future; those that have happened are not recognised.

Plenum: The experiences from 1924 to 1925 make it necessary for the Communist Party to come out clearly as an independent party and to replace the slogan of a Labour Government by that of a Revolutionary Workers Government. This general change determines the electoral tactic.

The Dutt–Pollitt document also set out four reasons why the Communist Party should develop its independent fight against the Labour Party leadership: (1) because the political division was increasing between the workers' leftward advance and the rightward consolidation of the reformist leaders; because the official Labour Party had become the coalition partner of the capitalists, with Baldwin and MacDonald agreeing on many issues; because Labour Party discipline now made impossible any adequate expression of the revolutionary fight at the next election; because there had been a serious decline in C.P. membership.

Dutt and Pollitt were not at the Plenum. Their views were supported at it mainly by R. Page Arnot, and the final resolution, which was unanimously accepted by the British delegation, came very close to them. An E.C.C.I. member later wrote that the Pollitt–Dutt document contained "a precise criticism" of the fundamental mistakes of the majority, he approved its tactical line, though not all its conclusions.[88]

The subsequent Party discussion on the Plenum resolution showed, however, that unanimity of acceptance did not extend to interpretation. The Political Bureau considered that where demanding basic changes in the Party's attitude to the Labour Party and Labour Government, the Plenum resolution still carried forward much of the previous policy. But Pollitt, opening discussion in London, said it was "a complete change in Party policy."[89]

In 1928 the 4th Congress of the R.I.L.U. and 6th Congress of the C.I. further developed the concept of independent leadership. Pollitt singled out a point made by Losovsky on strike strategy: "It is the business of the revolutionary wing not only to tell the workers when to strike, but also to be able to lead them against both the employers and the trade union machine."[90]

The C.I. Congress warned that "unless Communists strengthen their positions in the trade unions they may become isolated from the organised workers". Losovsky spoke of the need for "the united front from below" in leading economic struggles "against the reformist trade union apparatus if it sabotages the fighting will of the masses". On Britain, an E.C.C.I. member said: "It is necessary to have a new orientation of the whole Party."[91] And the resolution on Britain declared that the 9th Plenum "implied a definite change in the whole work of the Party" and called for a wide discussion.

All this stress on industrial struggles and complete change in policy gave warning to the British E.C. of tough problems ahead. The collaboration policy of the reformist leaders was resulting in suppression of strikes, the outlawing of the Minority Movement and bans on the Communists. How, then, was the workers' struggle for immediate demands and for socialist aims to be carried on, when the official machines of the workers' organisations were collaborating with the capitalists? This question now became acute in the everyday life of the Party and was at the core of the inner-Party discussion. The 9th Congress did not answer it clearly, and the members looked with increasing concern to the 10th Congress for a decisive lead.

In the pre-Congress discussion,[92] Pollitt stressed that the Party's job was to win influence over large numbers of workers in action for immediate demands, and transform the unions into militant organisations. He proposed to present the new policy as a line of fight against two enemies, the capitalist class and the collaborating Labour leadership. To do so it must be explained why the Party's policy had to be changed; and it was necessary to intensify the Party's factory and trade union work, and to secure a united front with local Labour Parties and trade union branches. However, the only task allotted to him by the E.C. was to move a resolution at Congress in favour of paying the political levy in the trade unions. He did so, arguing that this was a means of raising political issues and of ensuring that the unions conduct political campaigns instead of allowing the Tories to remove them from political life. J. T. Murphy opposed, arguing that the levy was merely money for the Labour Party. The resolution was carried by 100 votes to 22.[93]

The E.C. did not present any general line for discussion at the 10th Congress, but put forward only resolutions on separate issues. It claimed that its policy was correct and made no self-criticism. And while its documents used phrases from International decisions, the line and spirit of advance to independent leadership were absent. This left a widespread feeling that the Congress had not met the needs of the Party, and Tom Bell, Harry Pollitt and William Rust went to the C.I. for further talks.

The outcome was a "closed letter"[94] from the E.C.C.I. Such letters ("closed" for discussion within the Party, or "open" for publication) were not unusual but rarely did any contain such far-reaching criticism. This one began by stating laconically that the 10th Congress "marked a step forward" and then for the rest of its eight foolscap pages dealt with deficiencies and what should be done to correct them.

The main criticisms were that the E.C. had not fully understood the temporary nature of "capitalist stabilisation" and the approach of revolutionary class conflicts; had failed to explain the policy of independent leadership, presenting it as a continuation of the previous policy, of which it was a repudiation; had seen its application mainly in electoral terms, not appreciating its significance for industrial struggles and trade union work; and had failed to launch the campaign for a daily paper, indispensable to the fight for the new policy. The letter then expressed "great consternation" at the failure to strengthen the E.C. by new men from the factories, and spoke of the danger "of a small group of leaders insufficiently linked with active Party life and with the workers' struggles". Finally it made proposals to apply the new policy in all fields.

In discussion of this letter throughout the Party, the feeling hardened that the leading group in the E.C. was unwilling or unable to develop independent leadership, and that changes in personnel would have to be made. The E.C's formal reply to the letter did nothing to weaken this feeling. A District Secretary remarked that "for the E.C. the closed letter was a dead letter".[95] The discussion was interrupted by the general election in May, and was resumed with increasing sharpness on the formation of the second Labour Government in June.

In July the 10th Plenum of the E.C.C.I. met. In his speech[96] on Britain with its "army of unemployed over 45, for whom there is no hope at all", Pollitt said that while in 1924 votes for Communist candidates were votes for "a Labour Government, but make it fight", in 1929 they were for something very different, "a Revolutionary Workers Government", that is, votes against the Labour Party and the Labour Government. The biggest danger was the belief that disillusionment arising from the Labour Government would mean an automatic turn to the Communist Party.

The 9th Plenum resolution of the E.C.C.I. meant that the Party had to fight independently on every field of the class struggle, he declared, but in the Party discussion it had been interpreted as limited to an election tactic. "We have no roots in the factories and no daily paper. Our mistakes and vacillations have meant that the workers do not see us as an alternative to the existing Labour Party." Pollitt differentiated his own position from that of Rust when he asked, "What has been the policy of the C.P.G.B. during the last eight years?" And answered, "Rust referred to it as if it had not been the policy of the C.I. If we have been only a revolutionary left wing in the Labour movement, that is as much the responsibility of the C.I. as of the C.P.G.B. Our line and policy has always been that of the C.I."

Before the 10th Plenum report was available, the demand for a Special Congress was rising in the C.P.G.B. on the grounds that the E.C. had done little to implement the closed letter. The Tyneside District Committee, the National Committee of the Y.C.L. and the London members, by 206 votes to 13, with 15 abstentions, supported the demand.[97] The Report of the 10th Plenum declared that the British Party was "not fulfilling its obligations", there was political unclarity and the leadership was not carrying out the correct political line.[98]

Under this further pressure from the C.I. and faced with the rising revolt in the Party, the E.C. meeting in August recognised that changes had to be made. Three leading members were removed from the Political Bureau, including the Party Secretary, Albert Inkpin. In his place, Harry Pollitt became General Secretary.[99]

The great majority of the Party membership welcomed the changes, but some of the older members associated with the B.S.P. were not convinced that it was necessary to remove the man who had been Secretary of the Party since its foundation. Albert Inkpin, though not a commanding platform figure, was widely respected for his devoted service, and for his unshakable staunchness and loyalty during the prosecutions when as Secretary he was always a target.

Pollitt was widely accepted as the most able of those who had initiated, developed and publicly championed the policy of independent leadership. His selection to oppose MacDonald at Seaham Harbour was a recognition of his standing as a Communist leader. His popularity with scores of thousands of workers was due to his ability as a Communist spokesman and his contact with and understanding of the Labour Movement. He was esteemed as a leader who practised what he preached, personally took part in all aspects of Party work, and was always ready to answer questions and give a helping hand. Supported as he was by R. Palme Dutt and William Gallacher, there was in fact no comparable rival.

Pollitt himself had no doubts. For him the appointment was "the fulfilment of an ambition cherished ever since I came into the revolutionary movement". All previous experiences were only "steps in my training, serving my apprenticeship until my comrades considered I was fit to become their Secretary".[100]

CHAPTER 13

GENERAL SECRETARY, 1929-1932

1. Responsibility.   2. Whitechapel, Dec. 1930—Oct. 1931.   3. Strike problems.   4. Trade union problems.   5. Visit to Belgium, May 1931.   6. Communist Party advance.

1. RESPONSIBILITY

To approve and carry out the changes proposed, the Party needed another Congress. Discussion on what the new policy meant was stimulated by open admission of previous failures.[1] Pollitt simultaneously pressed forward the necessary preparations to publish the long-talked-of *Daily Worker.*

The 11th Congress[2] met in November 1929. The delegates, deeply disturbed by the C.I. Plenum's declaration that the Party was failing to meet its international obligations, listened closely to Pollitt's 2½ hour report. It was too serious, even grim, for applause. It ruthlessly exposed weaknesses and spelt out the changes needed to remedy them. It stressed the urgency of the whole Party coming into action to achieve these changes.

The policy of "class against class", of independent leadership, was overwhelmingly endorsed. Changes were made in the C.C. personnel, with Pollitt, Dutt and Gallacher emerging as the leading core. It was a beginning: the next three years revealed the full extent of the task which had been undertaken.

The class struggle was intensifying. The "greatest economic crisis capitalism had witnessed"[3] gave rise to mass unemployment, big wage cuts, and ominous political developments—the advance of German fascism toward dictatorship, and the Japanese invasion of China. Meetings of the Communist International and the R.I.L.U. in 1931 stressed the urgency of united working-class action on all these issues. In September 1932 the 12th Plenum of the E.C.C.I. declared that "a new round of revolutions and wars" was approaching, that "the right-wing Labour and Socialist leaders were everywhere supporting capitalist policy" and that it was of "decisive importance" that the Communist Parties won the majority of the working class for struggle.[4]

In Britain the 1929 election resulted in a minority Labour Government taking office by permission of the capitalist majority. It pushed on capitalist rationalisation, depriving the coal miners of the seven-hour day and cutting cotton wages by arbitration, imposed means tests and cuts in unemployment benefits, and subjected India and other colonial countries to a wave of repression, including jail sentences, shooting and Air Force bombing. In the credit crisis of August 1931 the Labour Government split and fell. Ramsay MacDonald and Phillip Snowden, its Premier and Chancellor, deserted to the Tories, forming with them a "National" Government. The widespread cuts in wages and benefits then imposed provoked street demonstrations of a size and temper not seen since the general strike, and a mutiny in the Atlantic Fleet. But in October a general election gave the Tories and their "national" allies a majority. The new National Government intensified attacks on workers' standards, and war preparations.

The situation showed the necessity of independent leadership, but Pollitt had to face the fact that the Party was less than 3,000 strong, largely isolated from the organised workers. To give a new orientation to its activities was essential, but not enough: it was also necessary to transform it so that, as Pollitt said, "it should be a Party *of* the workers, not *for* the workers". This required continuous mass political work, an organised base in industry and a much larger membership.[5] There was only one way to begin this transformation—to plunge into the struggle and learn from experience.

An impression of the efforts made and problems encountered in industrial and unemployed struggles may be gained from the remainder of this chapter. The Charter campaign and the first strike experiences showed that workers acted on issues arising in their particular circumstances rather than on general demands, and that without previously established influence and organisation it was very difficult to lead strikes. The general election showed that Communist leadership on economic issues did not of itself bring Communist votes.

The *Daily Worker*, first published on January 1, 1930 and boycotted by wholesalers, brought numbers of Party members and supporters into action to distribute, sell and finance it.

Following this election, Pollitt initiated a commission of active members to examine the practical activity of the Party branches and to propose what should be done and how to do it. The resultant resolution[6] of the January 1932 Central Committee dealt in practical terms with the development of workers' movements and Party building, it declared political work in the factories and trade unions to be decisive, called for mass sales of the *Daily Worker* to combat the influence of the capitalist press. The prerequisite for winning the majority of the workers, it said, was the daily struggle against reformism.

Pollitt then led the whole Political Bureau in directing work to implement the resolution in the major districts.[7] About 150 of the most capable members of the Party were allotted for personal activity at specified work-places and trade union branches, and to discuss the problems arising. In most cases after a few weeks, positive results appeared, workers' activity increased, new members were made, Party influence rose. It was proved possible to battle the way out of isolation, a new pattern of organisational work was set, the examples spread.

2. Whitechapel, Dec. 1930—Oct.1931

In December 1930 the death of Harry Gosling, Labour M.P., caused a by-election in Whitechapel and St. Georges. This was a constituency with a multiplicity of trades and a large Jewish electorate, many descended from immigrants from Tsarist Russia and highly conscious politically. The announcement that Pollitt would be Communist candidate brought offers of help pouring in; he was endorsed by a representative conference of workers' delegates. Money came in, too. But even Harry was at a loss for a reply when a well-known local character handed him a 10s. note and added confidentially, "I can make as many of them as you like."[8]

Living and working conditions were appalling: in one year, out of 31,870 houses inspected by the local authority, 23,425 were condemned as unfit in some respect for human habitation; the infantile death rate was 88 per thousand, the all-London rate being 70; food inspectors condemned 282 tons of food to be destroyed. Unemployment was widespread. "The accumulated evils of generations of sweated and casual labour, a damning indictment of capitalism", Pollitt described it.[9]

His election address called for the complete transformation of society—the abolition of all class divisions, privilege, monopoly and exploitation, the creation of a free and equal Workers' Republic—and then presented the immediate demands. To the plea that the Labour Government was in office but not in power, he replied, "You have seen that this Government that has not power to give you better conditions, has the power to worsen them", and gave examples of wage cuts in textiles, conditions in the coalmines, and misery of the unemployed.[10]

There were marches of Pollitt supporters, local and from all over East London. The largest, 3,000 strong, was organised by the London Charter Committee, and at a mass meeting en route 5,000 listened to Pollitt and to Jim Larkin Junior, come over from Ireland. Two thousand people heard an open-air debate between Pollitt and the Liberal candidate,[11] in which Pollitt made play with an article in the *News Chronicle* which declared that "nowhere in Europe would people be found better clothed, better nourished or better behaved than in Moscow". His speech was applauded and dockers carried him shoulder high to his next meeting in a nearby school. Communist canvassers, who sold 4,000 copies of the Charter pamphlet, found Pollitt well known, and usually referred to by his Christian name. One who opened with "I hope you are voting for Harry" was surprised to get the reply "Well, I've done it for twenty years, and I'm not likely to change now." This elector had failed to note that the previous

M.P. had passed on. Pollitt was invited in to one of the billiard clubs in the area. The boys took no part in politics, but he spoke their language and they listened. One lad who made a living by putting on bets for illiterates, asked what would happen to horse racing under communism, and there was laughter when Pollitt replied, "As you are so keen on it, we'll put you in charge of it."[12]

Asked "What can one man do in Parliament?" he replied that the struggle must be seen as a whole, in and outside Parliament. Then work in Parliament could be made a means of tearing down the mask of hypocrisy and deceit, and intensifying the struggle. Small representation in Parliament could be backed by powerful organisation outside. On Palestine, he stressed that colonial problems must be understood free from religious or nationalist bias, and that Jewish and Arab workers should stand together against imperialist and native exploiters.[13]

Pollitt got 2,106 votes, showing what could be done by a Communist Party local organisation with good local standing and a popular candidate. Labour held the seat with 8,544, the Liberal polled 7,445 and the Tory 3,735.

When the Labour Government fell in October 1931, Pollitt stood again, his main slogans, "Class Against Class—Not a Penny from the Workers" and "Forward to Socialism Through the Workers' Dictatorship."[14] In a four-page election special he contrasted the local poverty and anxiety with the wealth and luxury of the West End, and declared that the workers' dictatorship would confiscate without compensation the wealth of the rich, the banks, large-scale industries, land and means of communication, end for ever exploitation by landlords, bankers and employers and organise the country's resources to satisfy the workers' needs. This time there were even more meetings, all ending at 10.15 p.m., to be followed by a march to a spot in Vallance Road. The Eve of Poll Rally was 5,000 strong.

A representative of the Communist International, who was in the country clandestinely, came to hear Pollitt speak. His verdict was brief—"All rhetoric". He asked for Pollitt to discuss with him, but the plain-clothes police were trailing Harry as usual. The comrade who kept in touch with the C.I. man was walking along with Harry talking of possible meeting places, when they passed a huge poster advertising a Liberal meeting. "That's the place and time", said Harry; and they had their chat unmolested.[15]

Before a meeting at Brick Lane Palace, Harry said to a comrade who was very keen but inclined to neglect his personal appearance, "I want you to get your hair cut, put on your best clothes, and be outside the hall at 8 p.m. sharp. A rich woman is coming to hear me, take her to a good seat, see that she's all right, and afterwards I'll ask her for a donation." She arrived in her big car; the comrade, all polished and smart, did his stuff. She listened very attentively, and when the meeting ended, waited for Pollitt to come and speak to her. Then she said, "Mr. Pollitt, having heard you I now realise how dangerous a man you are." And that was all he got. At another meeting the audience included some businessmen. Noting that Harry had only the use of his feet to get away when it was over, they decided to arrange a car for him. They fixed a really posh one and a well-dressed driver. One day when Harry was getting out of it, two dockers passed by and one commented loudly to the other, "They're all the bloody same." Said Harry to his driver, "The workers' instincts are sound." Four navvies working in Whitechapel Road got a copy of the 'Special', and one came to the Committee Room to ask Harry if he would go and talk with them. Someone told him that the candidate could not spare the time to talk to only four people. When Harry came in and heard of this, he said, "You should never say that. I'll talk to one person if he is interested"; and off he went to devote his time to the four.

One of the most active of Harry's workers recollected, "I was living at my sister's and she asked me why I was so busy every night, so I took her to hear Harry speak at Premierland. Going home afterwards we passed a fried fish shop, and there was Harry in the queue. She was quite upset. 'What', she said, 'Such a fine man and none of you take him home for supper!' So she took his arm and brought him home with us, and for the rest of the election he slept at our house, in my bed as we had no spare room. After supper when my sister went to wash up, Harry said 'Oh no', sat her down at the table and served her, and got the boys to wash up. He was first up in the morning, usually waking at 6 a.m. and singing 'Arise ye starvelings from your slumbers'. He cleaned out the grate, lit the fire, left everything neat, and then went out. The friendship thus begun lasted till she was killed in the first air raid in 1940. Harry was terribly shocked and angry. He was due to speak in Manchester that night and was so distraught that the comrades at the Centre were doubtful whether he should go. He insisted and after the meeting the comrades said he had never spoken so movingly."

The 1931 election result in Whitechapel was: Liberal 11,013, Labour 9,864, Communist 2,658 and Fascist 154. The increased Communist vote and the wide support in the Labour Movement became the basis for a considerable advance of the Communist Party in Stepney and for some years Pollitt continued to work with the local organisation.

Immediately after the poll Harry left for a meeting in Moscow, before the declaration, which required his signature, was ready. Great pains were taken to fabricate it. When the agent took in the papers to the Town Hall, the Clerk said to him, "The figures are all clear, but next time take more care with the signature."

3. STRIKE PROBLEMS.

After the RILU 4th Congress Pollitt began systematic discussion of all strike experiences. Passive resistance, folded arms and "leave it to the leaders" were proved inadequate strike tactics. The rank and file strikes of Rego Clothiers, Dawdon miners, Austin Motors, London busmen and many others, all against the will of the trade union leaders, showed that new strike tactics were needed.

South Wales miners—January 1930:

The mass miners' strike in South Wales, a traditional militant area with the left holding many trade union positions, revealed that its preparation and carrying through had been handicapped by differences among the militants, which Pollitt summed up as follows:

> *The old view*: We work in the unions to win the leading positions.
> *The new view*: We work in the unions, on the job, also among unemployed and unorganised to win the working masses for action.
> *Old*: We need trade union unity at all costs, the opposition must keep within the limits of official policy and rule.
> *New*: We need trade union unity to advance the workers struggles.
> *Old*: So long as the right wing is in control of the union machine, they must be forced to fight; leadership cannot be taken from them until the left, by arguing more effectively for their policies, are elected to the leadership.
> *New*: The right cannot lead a mass movement in the workers' interests; if they do lead, it is to defeat. To win, the workers must from the start establish their own independent leadership.

To transform independent leadership from an aspiration to a reality, Pollitt proposed that the militants should stimulate widespread discussion on the necessity of leadership independent of the right-wing officials and explain what it meant: the democratic election by the workers of their own Strike Committee, or at an early stage, their Committee of Action; this committee to organise groups to carry out picketing, publicity, relief, and other activities; a decision to begin or end a strike to be taken only by the workers.[16]

Yorkshire Woollen Workers—Spring 1930:

In 1929 employers, Labour Government and trade union officials combined to enforce wage cuts on the Yorkshire woollen workers; the workers resisted by numerous local stoppages and by a big majority in a ballot. In February 1930 a Labour Government Court of Enquiry recommended a 10 per cent cut and a ballot rejected it by four to one. The union officials then proposed a 5.8 per cent cut. Consistent propaganda by a few Minority Movement wool workers and two respected Communist local figures, Isabel and Ernest Brown, had led to the setting up of a Committee of Action. And when the employers imposed the cut the mills stopped, the strike became general, for eight weeks a Central Strike Committee held mass meetings, organised publicity and relief. But it was not able to build independent leadership on a mill basis, nor to challenge the officials in the top union committees. When the officials got the key section, the wool combers, to go back, the rest followed.

From this first large-scale attempt to lead a strike Pollitt concluded that to develop independent leadership during a strike was "a hard, almost impossible task" in the absence of systematic preparatory work in the unions and on the job. "You can explain and strikers will agree, but your work is ten times harder than it ought to be because the strikers have not had the experience while at work of an organised group defending their interests. Where such a group exists, strikers will turn to those of whose leadership they have had daily experience."[17]

London Boilermakers—July–August 1931:

In spring 1931 the London ship repair employers demanded a 20 per cent cut, the men refused and after three months' negotiations were locked out. The Minority Movement members were few, but held influential positions. A Lock-Out Committee was set up representing all Branches, including No. 11, Pollitt's branch. He became an unofficial publicity officer, reporting to the press and helping to get out special issues of *The Boilermaker*.[18] The 20 per cent cut was "only the first move", he warned. For the employers' aim was to divide the men by payment by results, cutting prices to get piecework production for day-work rates, also to reduce the London differential and allowances, abolish demarcation and restrictions on labour-saving machines. So the lock-out was "a life and death struggle for our very existence, unity and solidarity can win".

The employers argued that acceptance of their demands would bring trade to the port. Pollitt replied that since 1918 wages had been cut by £700,000 a year, one port had been played off against another, and trade was worse than ever. Official figures of average weekly earnings were:

	Miners	*Engineers*	*Labourers*	*Bricklayers*
1920:	£4. 9. 9	£4. 9. 7	£3.10. 9	£5. 0. 0
1930:	£2. 3.10	£2.19. 0	£2. 2. 0	£3.10. 6

Pollitt asked where had these cuts led to trade revival?

For seven weeks he helped sustain the will to struggle by touring the port and speaking and writing about what he saw. Men sacked twelve days before the dispute were disallowed benefit. At the Court of Referees the employers agreed that this was so, but argued that work was now obtainable. The Court allowed the men's claim, the Insurance Officer appealed; during the delay no benefit was paid. Many men had to apply for relief, it was only granted to wives and children. Pollitt urged demonstrations to demand relief, public assistance, feeding of school children, and that food centres be set up: "This is a time for fighting, not for starving. Respectability does not fill empty bellies." To show how the intermittent nature of ship-repair work intensified the effects of wage cuts, Pollitt published figures of how many weeks' work members of the Lock Out Committee had had in the previous twelve months. One had 30 weeks, one 18, one 10, one 8. One had 9 weeks in two years, one 3 weeks in 18 months, one only one day in 18 months.

The Lock-Out Committee held mass meetings, though not twice a week as Pollitt suggested. One meeting voted 500 to 1 against bringing the Union's Executive into the dispute because that "would be the best way to defeat".

This situation was very different from that of the wool workers, but it strengthened Pollitt's argument on the necessity of winning the trade union branches to oppose the right-wing policy of surrender.

Lancashire Cotton—1932:[19]

Following the successful strike of 1931, mass strikes of weavers in August and of spinners in November showed the textile workers' growing resistance to collaboration, and likewise that the officials in the absence of independent leadership in the mills and union branches could break up even solid strikes. The Cotton Minority Movement did much to raise the workers' resistance to strike level; beginning in Earby and Burnley, the weavers' strike against working more looms spread till 150,000 were out. Union branch committees, mostly with no M.M. members, played an important part; some mills elected strike committees, the Cotton M.M. gave way to a broader Solidarity Movement. But when the union officials agreed to a wage cut of 1s.8d. in the £, and to working more looms, the Solidarity Movement was unable to continue the strike. It remained in being, however, and published a monthly paper opposing collaboration. Pollitt again drew attention to the failure of the militants to get elected to the union committees, where they could have proposed meetings of strikers to elect strike committees.

The employers then attacked the spinners; their officials agreed to a wage cut, but 140,000 workers struck. After two weeks, the officials announced a ballot on acceptance of a 7 per cent cut. Again the absence of militant activity within the unions made itself felt. On a brief visit, Pollitt had to comment on "lack of elementary information which would have made a great difference to our campaign". He had to go to the union office to find out how and where the ballot would be taken, and he had to correct the omission of how the ballot paper should be marked in the Solidarity Movement's leaflet calling for votes against acceptance. He warned that the officials would call off the strike and the mills would be open, even if the ballot went against acceptance. The Solidarity Movement had not the necessary organisation to provide the mass pickets necessary to prevent a return to work.

London Lightermen—January 1932:

This dispute began with no Communists among the Lightermen. A member of the Communist Party's Stepney Branch Committee recorded: "One night we were meeting in a room in Cable Street when Harry came in, asked to see the agenda, and when he saw it burst into flames, saying that a strike was coming which would tie up the river, and it was about the only thing not on the agenda. The Lightermen had voted to strike, we must get in touch with them. He went out himself, found a lighterman born in Manchester,— they were like old pals united."[20] Pollitt drew up an account of the lightermen's conditions, got it into the *Daily Worker*, and sent copies to leading lightermen. It was read out by a branch chairman to a meeting of 500 strikers. This began the building of Party influence; twenty strikers joined the Party.[21]

London Busmen, 1932–33

This was undoubtedly the most successful rank-and-file movement of the period; one settlement it secured was described by the T.&G.W.U. as "one of the biggest victories the union has achieved". Pollitt singled it out as an example worthy of study and emulation because it linked the fight for the workers' immediate demands with that for a change of union policy and leadership, always acting as part of the union. It was initiated by the successful efforts of a handful of militants to convince their own union branches to come into action for what the members wanted and to form a leading committee consisting of branch delegates. The discussions of this committee arose from branch proposals, its decisions were reported to the branches for confirmation and action. The branches received its speakers at mass meetings, gave out its leaflets, sold its pamphlets and its monthly printed paper, *The Busman's Punch*.[22] Its support spread to the majority of the bus fleet, its leading figures were elected to union positions.

The power of this movement was such that in January 1933 a

six-day strike over half the bus fleet compelled the Traffic Combine and the top union officials to accept the men's demands. Pollitt summed up, "The Rank and File Committee draws its authority from the garages and branches which were looked to for leadership in the fight against the employers, a fight independent of the union officials, but with the full force of the trade union branches and garages behind it."[23]

The busmen's outstanding spokesman was the secretary of their Chelverton Road branch, A. F. Papworth, later elected to the Transport & General Workers Union Executive and to the T.U.C. General Council. The editorial committee of *The Busman's Punch* accepted the assistance of Emile Burns, a member of the T.&G.W.U., though not a busman, a member of the C.C. of the Communist Party and a close colleague of Pollitt.

In the disputes above mentioned, and others occurring in these years, experience confirmed Pollitt's view that if the employers' attacks were to be successfully resisted, the workers themselves had to take action and provide leadership, independent of the Mondism-dominated officials. The sustained activity of militants was indispensable to the success of independent struggle, and the first aim had to be to convince the active trade union members to transform the shop steward and union branch organisation.

4. TRADE UNION PROBLEMS.

As the right-wing leaders extended their bans and expulsions, the main channels of Minority Movement influence in the unions were severed by denial of the right to associate with it or to elect its members as officials, and by the intimidation of sympathisers. The fall in trade union representation at the 1929 Conference showed that M.M. activity was being limited to that of individual members, not all of whom were prepared to face the hazards of militancy on the job when deprived of union support. The loss of Pollitt as its general secretary was keenly felt by the M.M., and intensified by the fact that his influential successor, Arthur Horner, did not in fact function in that post due to differences on policy.

The urgent need for mass resistance to collaboration led the Minority Movement in summer 1930 to launch a campaign for a Workers' Charter. In an explanatory pamphlet[24] which sold 100,000 copies in two months, Pollitt recalled the days of Chartism when, to co-ordinate diffused discontent into a powerful movement, the Six Point Charter was formulated with the result that "agitation was conducted and organisation built that made the ruling class tremble". It "left a lasting imprint on the fight for freedom and was of tremendous international significance". He declared that T.U.C. and

Labour Government collaboration with capitalism made it high time for a new Charter to express the interests of "employed and unemployed, organised and unorganised, of whatever political opinion or religious belief."

What had collaboration brought? "Into over two million homes the gaunt spectre of unemployment has entered, bringing misery and want, sickness and anxiety", while to those at work the speed-up brought physical exhaustion, illness, "a time-rate wage for piece-work speed, fear of the sack, worker against worker in a grim struggle to keep jobs". The Labour Government at home used arbitration to cut wages, lengthened miners' hours and planned to reduce unemployment benefit. Abroad it imprisoned trade union organisers and fired on workers and peasants in India, and sent warships and troops to Egypt and China. "The whole capitalist world is in crisis . . . millions starve, millions need boots, clothes, houses, decent conditions because too many things they need they cannot afford to buy."

Pollitt saw the Charter demands as a means of arousing new forces and unifying them into a mass movement strong enough to defeat the capitalist offensive.[25] The existing members of the M.M. were to be responsible for winning these new forces to revolutionary principles.[26] The Charter Convention was to begin a still wider campaign, breaking new ground, forming numerous Charter Committees able to carry on propaganda and to initiate struggles, thus building up the workers' counter-offensive. He visualised a new general strike, this time led from below by the workers' own leaderships.[27] This rather complicated and grandiose conception was not widely understood, however; and one trend of M.M. opinion regarded the campaign as a diversion from the struggle in the unions.

On the bright but cold morning of April 12, 1931, the Sunday calm of Southwark was broken by the cheering of marching delegates, headed by Harry Pollitt and George Allison. At the Bermondsey Town Hall, Tom Mann, greeted with enthusiasm, opened the Convention. A nine-point draft emerged from numerous suggestions, and became the Workers' Charter. There were 788 delegates, half of whom had never previously attended an M.M. conference; but trade union and workshop representation was less than at the 1929 conference of the M.M. New ground had been broken, but the industrial workers bearing the brunt of the struggles against rationalisation never saw the Charter as a unifying force.

Moving the main resolution, Pollitt said that the growing resistance of the British workers and the rising revolutionary wave in India made up a common struggle against a common enemy. Re-stating the need for an independent workers' leadership able to organise the counter-offensive, he showed that where the workers followed the official collaboration policy they lost; where they fought it they gained.

Calling for an intensified campaign he stressed that for the Charter to be a unifying factor it had to be related to the issues, however small, arising in factory or union.[28]

The campaign continued, and made its contribution to the struggle to break through collaboration. But in the outcome it did not achieve the hoped for advance.

The R.I.L.U. 5th World Congress meantime faced problems similar to those facing the M.M. In Germany, Communists were expelled in thousands from the trade unions, in which democracy had reached vanishing point, wage settlements being agreed without reference to the members. The international conclusion was that a "Revolutionary Trade Union Opposition" to defeat the collaboration of capitalism and social democracy was essential. The Congress envisaged this opposition as combining work in the factories with activity in the reformist unions.

In Britain, the term "revolutionary trade union opposition", without capital letters, was first used by Pollitt early in 1931. It meant that in the factories and trade unions, with workers' leadership independent of the right-wing leaders, a mass militant opposition to collaboration had to be organised and would eventually take the place of the Minority Movement.

At the R.I.L.U. Central Council in November 1931, Pollitt, always ready to speak his mind on problems of the British movement, clashed sharply with Losovsky on the form of this development. Losovsky saw the advance through the extension of the existing M.M. organisation during the struggle for independent leadership. Pollitt pointed to the rank and file movements emerging among engineers, railwaymen, busmen and builders. He condemned as wrong the viewpoint held in the R.I.L.U. that these were barriers to the M.M. "These militant workers not yet associated with us are seeking to express their hostility to the trade union bureaucrats. Our task, far from stifling these movements, is to encourage and stimulate them so that at a later stage, with their development, and our leading work, it will be possible to get political and organisational consolidation." He argued that the new policy needed new methods and new organisational forms. First must come mass movement on the workers' own demands; only when that was a fact should there be a national centre for a revolutionary trade union opposition. The M.M. should campaign to develop action and independent leadership on the workers' own demands, not on a pre-designed programme. He also criticised the R.I.L.U. for allowing the impression to continue that work in the reformist unions was not essential. "A drive to carry out this work has not been made by the Executive Bureau and certainly not by the International Propaganda Committees."[29]

The differences were not resolved at this session, but later the R.I.L.U. accepted Pollitt's view.

It was never R.I.L.U. policy to advocate the general formation of "red" unions in Britain, though some comrades, generalising from experience elsewhere, did raise the question. In the case of the National Union of Seamen which, under Havelock Wilson, was in 1927 difficult to distinguish from a company union, the R.I.L.U. spoke of the need for "a class union for British seamen". This was interpreted by the M.M. as meaning a Marine Section of the T.&G.W.U. When the T.U.C. expelled the N.U.S. in 1928, Bevin did launch such a section, but abandoned it when, after Wilson's sudden death, the N.U.S. returned to the T.U.C.[30] The M.M. then had to change its position. Some leaders of the Seamen's M.M. wanted a new union and built up the individual membership of the Seamen's Minority Movement with this perspective. The Transport International Propaganda Committee of the R.I.L.U. and later the associated International of Seamen and Harbour Workers proposed that this new union be inaugurated on January 1, 1933.

Pollitt at the R.I.L.U. Central Council argued that no basis for such a union existed. Of the 2,000 members of the Seamen's M.M., 64 per cent were unemployed, the N.U.S. paid affiliation fees to the T.U.C. on 59,000 members out of 156,000 employed seamen. The view of the British delegation was "not a suggestion of the liquidation of the perspective but a categoric statement that it will be a crime against the whole of our work if with no mass contact, no perspective but unemployed seamen, a new union is formed on January 1."[31] This declaration was worded to secure unity in the delegation between those who were totally against a new union, including Pollitt, and those who agreed that circumstances were not ripe but did not reject the perspective. In the outcome, Pollitt's speech meant the end of the proposal.

In fact, Pollitt had always been against the idea of "red unions" in Britain. He accepted and worked loyally for the United Mineworkers of Scotland, formed as a reply to the rejection of ballot results by the officials of the Fife and Scottish Miners Unions. But when circumstances changed he was foremost in advocating re-entry into the old unions[32] The United Clothing Workers Union was formed without consultation with him, and he never considered the decision correct.[33]

5. Visit to Belgium, May 1931

Appointed fraternal delegate to the Congress of the C.P. of Belgium, Pollitt took a ticket from London to Brussels via Calais. At the Franco–Belgian frontier two imposing frontier guards examined his passport, questioned him, took his attaché case and asked him to follow them to their chief's office. Protest was useless. He was not allowed into Belgium. When they found he had neither a return ticket nor money to buy one, they gave him a travel document and put him on a train for Calais.

Arriving back in London he got some money from his office and rushed to Liverpool Street Station to book for Amsterdam via Harwich. At Amsterdam he asked a friend whether he could get him over the Belgian frontier. The reply was, "Yes, but it will not be a comfortable journey". Late that night they arrived at the frontier, slept on hay in an old barn, got up at dawn and took a long walk through a wood. Pollitt was shown a footpath, told to keep to it, and he would arrive at a Belgian village from whence he could get a bus with connections for Seraing where the Congress was being held. He arrived just before it ended, and made his fraternal speech. He travelled home via Brussels and Calais. "When my smiling face turned up at the frontier, the gendarmes could not believe their eyes, but they did when I showed them a Belgian newspaper with my photo and my Congress speech."[34]

6. COMMUNIST PARTY ADVANCE.

The 12th Congress met in an expectant mood, and Pollitt's report[35] rose to the occasion. A new kind of report, it gave a general line of advance, setting the main problems in relation to the basic reason for the Party's existence, the conquest by the working class of political power. It presented the views of the Communist International in terms of the responsibilities of the British working class.

The report was permeated by a sense of urgency arising from facts showing that "a new round of wars and revolutions" was opening. Pollitt saw the von Papen government as the first phase of fascist dictatorship in Germany, the Japanese attack on China as the first phase of a new war for the re-division of the world, the triumph of the Soviet Union's first five-year plan as the establishment of an unbreakable basis for socialism. The 'National' Government of Baldwin and MacDonald was driving down the standards of the people, while it supported Japanese aggression, ruled India by repression, and prepared for war on the Soviet Union. In the growing resistance of the British workers Pollitt saw the emerging force which with Communist leadership would bar the way to imperialist war and fascism.

He focused on the problem of winning the workers away from Social Democracy, now an active instrument of capitalist policy. The Party had proved that independent leadership could gain successes, *Daily Worker* sales had doubled in eighteen months, but much more had to be done. The Party membership of 2,756 in June 1931 was now

5,400. With supreme confidence that the workers would respond to a political lead Pollitt put before this small number no less a task than changing the course of the Labour movement. He did it without rhetoric, using the lessons of three years effort to show how united action could be initiated on issues raised by the workers themselves, how in the course of this reformism could be exposed in effective propaganda and strong positions be gained in the factories and trade unions. The "great difficulties of work in the factories" were faced up to. "Two members inside are worth a hundred outside. Keep them in, add to them, understand their problems, help them. Guard by correct methods against victimisation, don't make it an excuse for not doing political work."

The necessity of activity in the trade unions was put in the clearest possible words: "They play a decisive part, without winning decisive sections of trade unionists there is no future for this Party. I say that fully conscious of the responsibility of this statement." He stressed the need, whatever the difficulties, to continue the struggle to win elective positions in the unions. Then came a correction to those who saw independent leadership as something apart from the unions. Work in the unions with the aim of winning trade union members, branches and district committees for the line of independent leadership and struggle "is a vital part of our work in the factories".

There was a clear lead on the future of the Minority Movement. "The workers have formed unofficial movements with greater influence and power than the sections of the M.M." Examples were the Engineers' Rights Movement, the London Busmen's Rank and File Movement, the Port Workers' Unity Movement. "We must initiate and develop such movements in every industry. But they do not represent 100 per cent the platform of the R.I.L.U., the principles of the Minority Movement. They are the first beginnings". He proposed that the Communists in the rank and file movements should develop their political understanding as well as widen their influence with the prospect of unifying them on a district and national scale "under such a name as Trade Union Militant League" for revolutionary opposition to collaboration.

He also spoke of measures to equip the Party members with the theoretical and political understanding needed to explain convincingly what the Party stood for, and to bring new people on to the Party committees at all levels.

The effect of the report, received with enthusiasm, was to extend Party activity among the workers, and to correct the tendency to neglect or even disparage work in the trade unions. Pollitt's presentation of problems, his use of experiences to build up political understanding, confidence, and a deep sense of personal and collective responsibility, was a major factor in producing the intense activity and devotion of thousands of Communists in the next decade, acknowledged with envy by leaders of other parties.

CHAPTER 14

FOR UNITY AGAINST THE 'NATIONAL' GOVERNMENT

1. Japan begins the Second World War.   2. Rhondda East and Clay Cross.   3. C.P. and I.L.P., 1932.   4. Belfast.   5. Hunger March and National Congress.   6. Trial at Swansea.   7. Meerut.   8. London Boilermakers' Strike.   9. Boilermakers' Centenary.

.1. JAPAN BEGINS THE SECOND WORLD WAR.

In 1931 Pollitt estimated the Japanese seizure of Manchuria as "the commencement of the new world war for the re-division of the world and for armed intervention against the U.S.S.R." for which all imperialist countries were preparing on "a scale never witnessed before."[1] The British Foreign Secretary said in the House, "We should view with sympathy and conciliation" the Japanese position, and an official delegation of the Federation of British Industries was sent to the Far East. Pollitt denounced "the ceaseless sending of munitions" to Japan from Britain and, recalling the strike on the *Jolly George,* called for direct action. The *Daily Worker* printed the names of ships bound for Japan; Pollitt spoke at anti-war meetings and marches in the dock areas. A leading Scottish Communist wrote: "When speaking in Edinburgh, a Leith seaman told me he was working on a Ben boat due to take on an arms cargo in London before sailing for Japan or Korea. I got into touch with the Party Centre and was asked to be in London the morning the boat was due. Dock gate meetings had been arranged and there were leaflets on the Ben line's imperialist connections and profits. We found that the crew were mainly Lascars, the ship was to be loaded further down the river from lighters. This frustrated the attempt to get action by seamen and dockers. Arrangements had been made to meet my Leith friend in an East End pub. In a preliminary talk one comrade suggested that if we could do nothing better our seaman friend might make a public gesture against the support of the war by jumping his ship: we could get him any legal help necessary. Pollitt smouldered while this idea was put, came down heavily against it, and was as serious as I have ever seen him. He was against any cheap substitute for mass action. If conditions did not favour the re-enactment of the *Jolly George* demonstration, he was not going to let it degenerate into a more or less farcical affair of one seaman jumping his ship. We worked out what could be done; leaflets for the Lascar crew, telegrams to the lightermen's officials, and contact at Hong Kong, the first port of call. Then Pollitt and I went to keep the date with the seaman and talked it over and he agreed to keep in touch."[2]

2. RHONDDA EAST AND CLAY CROSS.

In two by-elections in 1933, Communist candidates challenged the 'National' Government policy.

In Rhondda East the Communist candidate was Arthur Horner. His agent, Idris Cox, described Pollitt as the "driving force in the campaign from first to last".[3] The constituency included Mardy, once the pride of the Rhondda for its trade union strength, and after 1926 the target of the coal-owners' vengeance. First they had kept the pits closed, then opened them but excluded every leading militant; in 1927 they had demanded heavy wage cuts. The Mardy Lodge led by Arthur Horner refused, and was expelled by the S.W.M.F. officials, who opened a new 'loyal' Lodge. The owners refused to employ any man belonging to the old Lodge.[4] And the men, driven by starvation, had slowly gone back to work.

Horner, when he stood as Communist candidate in the 1931 general election, got 10,359 votes. Later he helped to defend the home of a miner threatened with eviction. The bailiff was sent by the Rhondda Urban District Council, the police by the County Council—both had Labour majorities. There were 39 arrests and heavy sentences. Horner got 15 months hard labour. When he came out in December 1932, the Mardy miners elected him as a checkweighman. At this, the owners closed the pit "till further notice."

Horner's election address in the 1933 by-election called the constituency "a capitalist graveyard for the workers". Pollitt, on his speaking tours, saw scores of closed shops; those open had hardly any customers. Of the 48,000 electors, 10,000 were unemployed, their wives bought meat only on Friday or Saturday nights when perishable goods were sold off. Only second-hand clothes were bought. Police harrassed miners scrabbling on coal tips to keep their fires burning.

The method of selecting the Labour candidate added to the bitterness of the contest. Normal practice was for Lodges to nominate and the miners to decide by ballot. On this occasion the S.W.M.F. President said Horner's nomination was out of order, he belonged to the expelled Lodge; there would be no ballot. The official candidate was W. H. Mainwaring, one-time militant, now agent responsible for the "loyal" Lodge.

Pollitt initiated an Election Conference: 46 delegates came from 28 organisations and four mass meetings. Horner and his platform against unemployment, collaboration, war and fascism were endorsed and a Central Election Committee and four area committees were set up. In addition to Horner, Pollitt, Tom Mann, Pat Devine, all superb speakers, the Communist team included organisers and canvassers. After a two-day whirlwind tour Pollitt wrote "Our comrades, badly fed and badly clothed, work with an enthusiasm that puts other districts to shame." A few days before the poll a sensation was caused by news that the owners, following a deputation led by Mainwaring, were re-opening the No. 3 pit. This gesture, which meant jobs for 200 men, reflected the owners' concern at the impact of the Communist campaign. The local press gave the credit to Mainwaring and was silent when a few days later the owners closed a pit some miles away.[5]

Horner's vote was 11,228, an increase of 869. Labour won with 14,127, a drop of 7,959 in their total vote and of 2,986 in their majority. The Liberal got 7,851.

In September a by-election in Clay Cross, a Derbyshire constituency with miners, rail, steel and agricultural workers, gave Pollitt himself the opportunity to oppose Arthur Henderson, a key right-wing leader. There was a wide response to Pollitt's appeal for funds; £340 financed the election address, a four-page Special and a small team of volunteer helpers. The campaign began without the Communist Party having a single member in the constituency.

Many miners worked only two days a week, taking home 8s. or 9s. after stoppages: 7,000 were unemployed. The Means Test operated without mercy: a lad of 17 had his allowance cut to 7s. because he lived with his mother. Miners' dwellings were such that a correspondent walking along the backs was "in momentary uncertainty whether they were houses or stables". Two water taps in a yard served ten houses. There were open middens, water closets were rare. In one house, the father had lost one eye in the war, the other eye was bad, he had no pension. The mother had reared twelve children, five still lived at home, two working, three at school. A lad of 17 worked in a colliery; pay slips for 22 weeks showed that after stoppages and 5s.7d. for a colliery house, he brought home 5d. a week. The other son was a joiner. They all had to be fed on his £2 a week. The food on the table was bread and dripping; that day the mother had eaten only one slice. Miners' wives baked their own bread. "Imagine rows of little brick kennels, a woman in each, spending hours at a stove doing work for which automatic machinery had long reached perfection, but miners were too poor to buy its products."

Living in such conditions, the miners flocked to Pollitt's meetings. They appreciated his directness. He struck home with the class contrasts. "The luxury of the rich mocks the starving workers; stocks of coal at the pit heads mock the workers without coal in their homes. While the Labour leaders draw fat salaries, the working men and women of Clay Cross are worried to death trying to make ends meet." "What are we to do? Starve quietly and wait for the next general election? The Communists say, No! Let them apply their means tests to the bankers, landlords and royalty, and to Mr. Henderson who took £5,000 a year as Minister in the Labour Government while getting his £1,000 a year as Labour Party Secretary." Charged with wanting violence, Pollitt replied, "I don't want you to get rifles, I want you to get trade union cards", and in answer to a sneer from Henderson about orders from Moscow, "Let Henderson take his orders and money from the capitalists; I am proud to be associated with those who carried through the Russian Revolution."[6]

In his election address, Pollitt showed local events in the light of the international capitalist drive against workers' standards. In Germany the collaboration of the Labour leaders had led to fascism. Class unity could be developed in the fight to realise the workers' demands. "If we workers who hew the coal, weave the cloth, build the ships, make great engines and machinery, unite our forces against those who rob us, no power on earth can prevent us taking these things for the use of the working people, and setting them to work for the needs of the starving masses, instead of making profits so that an idle class can live in luxury." "The workers' dictatorship, which is simply the organised power of the working class over the capitalist class, will take over the means of production, give complete independence to the colonial peoples, assist them to open up their countries for socialist industry and agriculture, and raise the living standards of millions in those countries and in Socialist Britain."

The result was Henderson 21,931, National Liberal 6,293 Pollitt 3,434. After the declaration, Henderson in his speech began, to the disgust of his supporters, to praise the Returning Officer, known locally as a reactionary Tory. Pollitt was standing nearby with his little daughter, Jean, in his arms, as there was nowhere to leave her. As Henderson approached his climax, "the child stated in her clear, penetrating voice, 'Daddy, I want the lavatory'. This brief remark expressed the feelings of almost everybody in the room, and was greeted with a spontaneous roar of laughter which brought the speech to an untimely end."[7]

Later, Pollitt's summary of the 1931-1935 record of "Baldwin and his Tory friends masquerading as a National Government" showed the correctness of his forecasts. At home— cuts in wages and benefits; reduced expenditure on housing, education and all social services; higher food prices; the Sedition Act passed, and the vestiges of democratic administration of unemployment relief swept away. Only mass resistance had forced the government to suspend starvation scales for the unemployed. Abroad—a tariff war on Ireland; a more oppressive constitution for India; no parliamentary government for Egypt; connival at Japan's seizure of Manchuria and Hitler's increase of armaments; toleration of Mussolini's preparations for war on Abyssinia and no effective action when it began; refusal of friendship with the Soviet Union.

3. C.P. AND I.L.P., 1932.

One effect of the poor showing of the second Labour Government was that Fenner Brockway, Chairman of the I.L.P. 1932 Annual Conference, declared that the political situation required their policy to move "from reform to revolution".[8]

At a subsequent debate with Brockway[9] before 2,000 workers Pollitt recalled that in 1920 the I.L.P. left the Second International, flirted with the Third and formed a new one—at once dubbed the "Two-and-a-Half"—only to return to the Second in 1923. He described the I.L.P. as "not a socialist party with different tactics from those of the C.P., but a party of capitalism." He then gave his view of a revolutionary party. "Immediate demands not an end in themselves but a means to strengthen the fight against capitalism and to go forward to the conquest of power. The Communist Party sought to strengthen the daily fight of the working class until it was possible by revolutionary action to destroy the apparatus of the capitalist state and the domination and exploitation it represents. In the crisis of capitalism the issue was revolution or starvation. Only by the maximum unity of action could the workers defend their conditions, learn discipline, develop political consciousness. The Communist Party strove for solidarity between the British workers and the workers and peasants of Ireland, India, China and Africa, for their immediate demands and for the complete independence of all colonial peoples."

Within the I.L.P. a Revolutionary Policy Committee appeared, based mainly on the London Division, where it had majority support. It sought to clarify what was meant by the move "from reform to revolution", and to give the I.L.P. a constitution and organisation appropriate to a revolutionary party. It was critical of the Communist Party, but advocated a united front of all workers as "possible and desirable".[10] At the I.L.P. Special Conference in July 1932, the R.P.C. leader, Jack Gaster, emerged as the most capable and consistent advocate of a revolutionary policy. This conference debated a proposal to disaffiliate from the Labour Party. Pollitt and Gallacher at a meeting to which the conference delegates were invited, declared the readiness of the Communist Party to work with those I.L.P. members who wanted united action, but warned against a repetition of the 1920-23 manoeuvre.[11] The I.L.P. decision to disaffiliate carried by 241 to 142 caused a political sensation. Pollitt's first reaction was critical. "The separation staged at Bradford is only temporary; the events of 1923 will soon be repeated." He accused the I.L.P. leaders of using phrases about "Socialism the only hope" to hold workers back from struggle, and of manoeuvring to distract them from finding their way to Communism.[12]

Later he gave a broader estimate. The decision, made under pressure of widespread dissatisfaction with Labour in government and in opposition, "represents a tremendous change in the traditional attitude that the party which formed the Labour Party should now leave it". He continued to be critical of the I.L.P. leaders but in discussing the united front urged: "We must make a determined effort to win the rank and file of the I.L.P., at the same time avoid creating the impression that there are no fundamental differences between our party and the I.L.P."[13]

At the 12th Congress of the C.P.G.B., Pollitt posed the question—should the C.P. only seek to win individual members of the I.L.P., or set out to win decisive sections of it to join the C.P? Advocating the latter he proposed a two-point campaign—to draw every I.L.P. militant into some kind of united activity and simultaneously to promote discussion within the I.L.P. on working-class power and socialist revolution. His criticism of the I.L.P. leaders was sharper, they were "past masters in using left phrases", in speaking about a Marxist policy for the I.L.P. they aimed at "building a barrier between leftward moving workers and the C.P.". It was by "tearing away spurious revolutionary phrases and putting them up against straight answers to straight questions", that they would be compelled to show their true colours. Of the Revolutionary Policy Committee he said that "the language of their amendments could deceive workers into thinking they believed in Communism". He did not spare his criticism of the "sectarian and supercilious attitude" of those Communists who saw in the appearance of I.L.P. and C.P. speakers on a united platform an "opportunity of knocking hell out of the I.L.P.". It was by "convincing and correct arguments" that I.L.P. members would be won and the policy of I.L.P. leaders exposed. In his reply Pollitt had to record that his challenging presentation of the I.L.P. problem "seemed to have passed over the head of the Congress"; it had not been taken up in the discussion and he re-stated it emphatically in his reply.[14]

4. BELFAST.

On Sunday morning, 15th October 1933, Harry Pollitt stepped off the Heysham boat at Belfast. That evening he was on the boat back again, escorted by two detectives who had served him with a deportation order under the Civil Authorities (Special Powers) Act of 1922. It prohibited Pollitt from entering the Six Counties on the grounds that he was "suspected of being about to act in a manner prejudicial to the preservation of peace and the maintenance of order". Tom Mann had been similarly deported in October 1932. He had arrived on Friday 14th to attend the funerals of two workers shot dead on the previous Tuesday. One funeral in the morning Tom Mann could not attend owing to other duties. He did attend the afternoon one, of Samuel Baxter. On leaving it he was taken to the office of the police chief who asked if he intended to address any public meetings. On replying "Yes" he was served with a deportation order and taken to the boat.[15]

Pollitt had been invited by the Belfast Communists to speak at a public indoor meeting, but he was not allowed to reach the hall. The other speaker, the Secretary of the Communist Party of Ireland, Sean Murray, from Dublin, evaded the police and entered the hall. As he stepped on to the platform, two detectives served him with a deportation order. He protested that he had come on a peaceful mission and was determined to speak. The organisers of the meeting supported him and asked the police to leave. Gripping Murray by the arms, the detectives forced him towards the door, the shouting crowd closed in upon them, the detectives drew their revolvers, menaced the people with them, and hustled Murray into the street, where a strong force of police were waiting. The meeting protested against the deportations, and against the banning of an unemployed demonstration four days earlier, and declared that it was these provocative measures that menaced public order, not the peaceful expression of workers' demands.[16]

5. Hunger March and National Congress.

In the autumn of 1933 the Government, boasting that in two years it had "economised" £54½ million on unemployment relief—£27¾ million by a tighter Means Test and £26¾ million by reduced benefits—brought in a Bill to extend the Means Test, conscript the unemployed into camps and training centres and remove thousands from unemployment benefit to local relief. The responsible Minister, with a salary of £80 a week, advised local authorities that an adult could live on 5s.1½d. a week, 8½d, less than the B.M.A. subsistence minimum.[17]

Pollitt initiated talks leading to nineteen well-known leaders from the N.U.W.M., the trade unions, the Labour Party Left, the I.L.P. and the C.P. issuing an appeal for a united fight by employed and unemployed against the government policies, and proposing a National Hunger March and a United Congress. The response was immediate and determined. In mid-winter the Hunger March began: 2,000 men and a women's contingent planned publicity and agitation in 146 towns; a London Reception Committee planned a huge turn-out to welcome the marchers in Hyde Park; the National Congress was fixed for February 24 and 25. In popularising these actions at meetings in Glamorgan, Pollitt and Mann were arrested and charged with sedition.

When the Congress opened nearly a million workers were represented by 1,494 delegates from 949 organisations and branches.[18] Pollitt and Mann being in court, two empty chairs bearing their photographs were on the platform. Pollitt's speech was read by William Gallacher. It showed the effects of the government's attack on the working class. From 1928 to 1934 wages fell by £150 million a year. Rationalisation had increased unemployment and also the output of those at work. Loco repairs at Crewe previously took six weeks, now six days. Austin Motors in 1922 employed 55 workers per week per car produced; now 10. Miners' wages in 1920 averaged £4. 5s. 9d. per week with an output of 14.54 cwts. per shift; now they averaged £2. 1s. 11d. with an output of 21.92 cwts. per shift. It was time to declare that "the trade unions have finished with Mondism, finished with unity with the capitalist enemy and all of us are going forward for the fighting unity of employed and unemployed".

To "hurl in the teeth of the parasites the accusation that the workers do not want work", Pollitt proposed specific measures to provide for two years, at trade union rates, work for 1¼ million workless, at a cost of £350 million a year, less than the annual payments for past and future wars. This was the first time such a specific programme for constructive work of social value had been put forward. It included: half a million new houses, "decent, commodious, conducive to health and comfort, at rents workers could pay"; new schools, "in many existing schools bad lighting and ventilation leads to defective eyesight and sickness"; new hospitals, "thousands now suffering pain do not get proper treatment due to overcrowding"; universal provision of proper lighting and sanitation, with piped water where now lacking; adequate safety measures in mines and factories; four million more acres of land to be cultivated. The cost of this programme to be got "by taxing the rich who could well afford it". The programme of actions to follow the Congress included activities around these demands.

When Pollitt and Mann arrived—on bail—at the Sunday morning session, the Congress greeted them with acclamation.

The National Committee elected by the Congress continued the movement during 1934. The full results of the agitation were seen when in February 1935 mass upheavals[19] compelled the Government to suspend Part II of the Unemployment Act and repay cuts in benefits made under it.

6. Trial at Swansea.

The evening before the National Congress, Pollitt was arrested as he left the Party office at 5 p.m. Tom Mann was arrested at his home. Next morning they were charged at the Stipendary Court at Pontypridd with edition, alleged to have been committed at meetings at Ferndale and Trealaw on Sunday February 18.[20] This Court was notorious for its hostile attitude to active Communists. Pollitt remarked that "It is well-known in South Wales that when Communists come into court, justice flies out of the window."[21] The magistrates remanded the case for a week, the police opposed bail; it was granted on a rather high sum and with a broad hint that further bail after the adjourned hearing would depend on the conduct of the accused in the meantime.[22] "By this manoeuvre they were to some extent muzzled" for some weeks and prevented from speaking at the Congress on the 24th and in Hyde Park on the 25th. Both were committed for trial at the Swansea Assizes in July. The committal aroused widespread indignation. The International Labour Defence got 75,000 signatures to a protest petition presented to the House by James Maxton M.P. Conferences of workers' delegates in Carmarthen, Glamorgan and Monmouth elected a workers' Legal Commission to scrutinise the trial. A

Defence Committee organised marches to Swansea, and protest meetings.[23]

The night before the trial Sir Oswald Mosley held a Blackshirt meeting in a Swansea cinema. Outside, thousands of hostile workers gathered, there were collisions with the police, and many arrests. Inside, a questioner was struck by blackshirt stewards; the gallery rose like one man, the blackshirts had to leave by the back door. The workers marched to a meeting and demanded the release of those arrested, and of Mann and Pollitt.[24] As the trial opened on July 3, contingents from all over South Wales marched into Swansea. Kept away from the court by massive ranks of police, they held a continuous meeting on the beach.

It had been agreed that Mann, whose case came first, be defended by D. N. Pritt, K.C.[25] If he were acquitted the Crown would probably drop the case against Pollitt. If Mann were not acquitted, Pollitt would defend himself and "make a first class political battle with no holds barred." The police excluded from the public gallery those they considered to be Communists, their test being "whether he was poorly dressed". The complaint of the excluded was passed by Pritt to the Clerk, and by him to Mr Justice Talbot, whom Pritt described as "of quite icy impartiality, capable of trying a question of alleged sedition by a Communist with as little emotion as a question of the quality of tin plate." The Judge entered twenty minutes late and, stated that he had been considering the situation in chambers, where he had ruled that every citizen, whatever his views, had the right to sit in the public gallery so long as he behaved himself. He had insisted on those excluded being given seats.

Policemen claimed in evidence against Mann to have taken down his speech in shorthand. An expert who examined their notebooks said that what they had written "was not shorthand at all". When something was read to them at moderate speed, they were unable to get it down. One policeman said he only wrote down what was seditious.

Pritt: You listened to a sentence, decided whether it was seditious or not, and if it was you wrote it down?
Witness: Yes.
Pritt: What happened while you were writing, did you ask Mr. Mann to wait?
Witness: No.
Pritt: How did you decide what was seditious? Did you hold as seditious anything you disapproved of?
Witness (firmly); Yes, Sir.

The next day the prosecution decided not to proceed further on the Ferndale speech. After the Judge had remarked that there was only one passage in the Trealaw speech which might be capable of being construed as seditious, the jury found Mann "Not Guilty" on both counts; the prosecution offered no evidence against Pollitt, who was also found "Not Guilty."

At a huge meeting on the beach, Mann and Pollitt called for the fighting spirit shown in their defence to be carried into the struggle against the whole policy of the National Government.

.7. MEERUT[26]

In January 1933 the trial of thirty-two leaders of the Indian working class, including three Englishmen, came to an end. Immediately after their arrest in 1929, Pollitt had helped to form a Meerut Defence Committee in London, and during the four-and-a-half years' duration of the trial he campaigned ceaselessly in their support. On Pollitt's suggestion, J. R. Campbell agreed to go to Meerut to report on the trial, but government permission was refused.

Meerut, known to every British schoolboy as the starting point of the great revolt of 1857, was selected for the trial because of its remoteness from the industrial centres and because the jury system did not operate there.

The prisoners were charged with "conspiracy to deprive the King-Emperor of his sovereignty over British India". Pollitt showed that the arrests were an attempt to disrupt the rising trade union movement in India. They followed the great strikes of 1928 when over half a million workers came out against attacks on wages and conditions, including 150,000 Bombay textile workers and 200,000 Calcutta jute workers. In both towns the workers left the old associations subservient to the employers and formed militant trade unions. These events and the formation of the Workers and Peasants Party marked the emergence of the Indian working class as an independent political force. The Government replied by new repressive regulations, firing on strikers by troops and police, and widespread arrests including the Meerut defendants, all of whom had been elected to leading positions in the militant unions, All-India T.U.C., or Workers and Peasants Party.

Pollitt's opinion was shared by Jawaharlal Nehru, President Elect of the All-India T.U.C., who described the trial as a "blow at the whole working class". Later a government report said, "There can be no doubt that the arrests ... placed the authorities in a commanding position and created a vacuum in the leadership of the movement."[27]

When the arrests took place there was a Tory Government in Britain, but Labour was in office when the Meerut Trial began. That Pollitt's allegation of Labour complicity in the repression in India was well founded, was shown in official documents published later. The Labour Secretary of State cabled the Viceroy on 17 January 1930, "If ... you find it necessary to make use of extraordinary powers ... I have every confidence in your judgment and will support you fully." Ramsay

MacDonald added his prime ministerial message, "Keep up moral authority of government. . . . Maintain policy of reform while handling with firm determination revolutionary leaders. . . . Go ahead with calm assurance. I add my sympathies to my pledge of confidence."[28]

When the full text of Ben Bradley's defence became available, Pollitt quoted with pride the following passage: "Unless the workers come out of the struggle with added knowledge, much of their suffering is in vain. . . . I have justified the right of the Indian workers to receive assistance, financial and moral, from their fellows in Russia, Britain, and elsewhere. . . . We are not ashamed of these activities. We are proud that the workers approved of them and that the employers found them so inconvenient that they had to pull wires and get us arrested. Today, as before our arrest, the workers need to have their well organised and centralised militant industrial trade unions. It is essential to organise the widest masses of the working class, to defend their day-to-day interests and to maintain the general revolutionary struggle of the masses of India."[29]

The judge took 4½ months to prepare his judgment. He found 27 of the prisoners guilty, ignoring the opinion of his three assessors who found only 17 guilty. Sixteen prisoners were sentenced to transportation, one for life, five for 12 years, three for 10 years, three for 7 years, four for 5 years. Eleven got rigorous imprisonment, four were acquitted, one had died. A great wave of protest arose in India and in Britain. On appeal the High Court in August 1933 reduced all sentences.

8. LONDON BOILERMAKERS STRIKE

In June 1934, the London ship repair employers, disregarding procedure, imposed wage cuts of 1s.6d. to 10s.6d. for time workers, 10 per cent to 50 per cent in piece rates, and adverse changes in working conditions. The boilermakers struck with full backing of their branches and District Committee. Ted Hill, an outstanding militant and an old pal of Pollitt, was now the responsible full-time official. On the first morning of the stoppage Pollitt made suggestions, including a press statement, a daily bulletin, a democratically elected and fully representative strike committee, and solidarity actions; and he offered his personal help.[30]

Touring the port to get news for the *Daily Worker*, he found the yards silent from London Bridge to Tilbury, the pickets confident, the strike headquarters a hive of activity. He gave an example of what was so strongly resented by the men, the continuous attacks on customs and practices. An acetylene welding device which gave off fumes, dangerous in enclosed spaces, caused an accident. Eleven men were gassed, one died. Since then the boilermakers had insisted that two men be on the machine and get danger money at time-and-a-half. Now the employers demanded only one man, and a cut in the danger money, as well as the wage cut.[31]

The traditional solidarity of the boilermakers was reinforced by effective publicity. The Dispute Committee put their case to a big conference in Bermondsey Town Hall, and Pollitt, with strikers on the platform, spoke to 1,500 workers at a solidarity meeting called by the West Ham Communist Party. In the fifth week, after the strikers refused to return as a condition of discussion, the employers agreed to withdraw their proposals and go through procedure. A mass meeting agreed to ballot; it also called for the release of Thaelmann and other imprisoned German Communists. The ballot was 335 to return, 205 to stay out. The minority were expressing the demand for a wage increase. The return was accompanied by inspection to ensure 100 per cent union membership and more shop stewards. In one yard, four blacklegs were found and the men did not return till they were removed.[32] Throughout this dispute the rank and file, the union branches, district committee and district officials acted together.

9. BOILERMAKERS CENTENARY

On August 20, 1834 fourteen working boilermakers met in Manchester, undeterred by the savage sentences of transportation imposed on the Six Men of Dorset,[33] to found the "Friendly Boilermakers Society" and adopt Rules.[34] Pollitt was of the opinion that the best centenary celebration would be to increase membership, organisation on the job, and attendance at Branch meetings; to argue for amalgamation with other unions in the same industry, end the bans on Communists and "give the Society a class purpose, solidarity with our fellow workers, undying hostility to our enemies and those who stand for Mondism."[35] But the E.C. decided on a grand march, high tea, and meeting in Manchester.

Manchester weather put on its best blue skies and brilliant sunshine as the procession was formed to march from Ardwick Green to Belle Vue.[36] Pollitt was among those greeting old friends and workmates as they found their places in the ranks. The silken surfaces of the banners gleamed in gold, crimson, silver, blue and green displaying the emblems, mottoes and allegorical figures delighted in by trade union blazonry, and picturing the locomotives, ships and bridges embodying the skills of the boilermakers. The marchers were in high spirits, in their best clothes; most wore the centenary badge. At the head were the national officers and the banner of the oldest branch with a continuous record, Bolton. The superannuated members got special attention, some rode on the Salford State Coach, loaned by the Labour Council. The grand old man, Edwin Rickard of Swansea, 90 years of age, had to his credit 70 years of membership, and had never drawn benefit. He said the day was the happiest of his life and recalled the sacrifices of those who founded the Society, as an example to the young members who had to mould its destiny in its second century.

At Belle Vue a 5 p.m. tea, in full Lancashire style, was followed by a meeting in the Kings Hall. Among those in the hall were many known to

Pollitt. From his old branch, Gorton, were a fellow apprentice at the Tank, Richard Allcroft, now Secretary, the President, T. Worrall, and his namesake, J. B. Pollitt. Three came from Woolston No. 1, and from London No. 11 the Secretary, Sid Chaplin, the Treasurer Harry Flint, and of course, Alf Whitney. On the platform were two other old friends, Ted Hill, London District delegate and Harry Ratcliffe, district delegate in Southampton, in whose house Pollitt had stayed in 1915. Among the national officers was John Hill, General Secretary, a prime mover in getting Pollitt banned from the T.U.C.

The speeches were tuned in to the prevailing brotherly harmony, though some grim features of the current scene could not be ignored. Giving the civic welcome, Alderman Titt asked those under 40 not to judge trade unionism by the experience of the years of negotiating falls in wages, but to compare with 60 years ago to realise the tremendous difference the movement had made. The E.C. Chairman spoke impressively of the new techniques where by pressing buttons great forces were set in motion, and claimed that only by combination could workers reap the benefits of scientific advance. John Hill spoke of thirteen years depression having crushed half of the men out of the main industries, and put half the rest out of work. These years had meant an expenditure of £2½ million in benefits plus £½ million in administration, while contributions had been £2 million. The Society got by only by using up the previous balance of £834,000, and £200,000 from investments. But though men walked the streets idle for months and years, they never lost faith in their union.

Pollitt later commented that the speakers had lost a great opportunity. The only lead given was to work for a Labour Government. It was left to the younger members to bring about a common strategy and policy in strike struggles.[37]

The great event terminated with cheers and "Auld Lang Syne", and the Boilermakers, ranks closed and banners high, marched into their second century, certain of the truth of their first motto "Unity Is Strength", perhaps a little underestimating the meaning of the second one, "God Helps Those Who Help Themselves."

CHAPTER 15

FOR UNITY AGAINST FASCISM

1. Hitler in power. 2. Communist call for unity. 3. United action in Hyde Park. 4. Dynamite in the Dock, May 1935. 5. Seventh World Congress of the Communist International. 6. Abyssinia, September 1935. 7. General election, November 1935. 8. Communist affiliation to the Labour Party. 9. Hitler in the Rhineland. 10. Fascism means war. 11. C.P. and I.L.P., 1933–36. 12. A ceremony for children.

1. HITLER IN POWER.

In January 1933 the German ruling class placed the state power in the hands of Adolf Hitler, leader of the National Socialist German Workers Party, the German fascists. After a month of preparation, the Nazis launched terror all over Germany, suppressed all opposition, and began massive rearmament.

For some years German capitalism had been in crisis, one government after another ruled by Presidential decree, the equivalent of Britain's Emergency Powers Act. The President, Field Marshal von Hindenburg, had been elected with Social Democratic votes as "the lesser evil" to Hitler. In November 1932 a general election gave the Nazis 196 M.Ps., the largest single party but not a majority, in the Reichstag.[1] Hindenburg called Hitler to the post of Chancellor; Hitler formed a government with three Nazi Ministers and eight Nationalists. But Hitler did not want a coalition with Nazis in a minority; he wanted a Nazi Government with an absolute majority. New elections were fixed for March 5 1933. The Nazis were in difficulties; in November their vote had fallen and the Communist vote risen. The Nazi M.Ps. were fewer than the combined working-class parties. Unless something extraordinary happened there was no reason why a new election should give them the majority they wanted. They saw to it that something extraordinary did happen.

On February 24 the press announced that the new Nazi police chief claimed to have found in the Communist Party offices documents showing that acts of terror were being prepared. At 9 p.m. on the 27th fire broke out in the Reichstag building.[2] A supposed Communist, conveniently found in the building, was arrested. Official reports blamed the Communists, connected the fire with the documents allegedly found by the Nazi police chief, and said that the fire was the signal for widespread Communist outbreaks. Outbreaks there were, but of Hitler terror. That night 1,500 arrests, next day fascist storm troops invaded the working-class districts, attacking the premises of organisations, raiding homes, beating up, arresting. Official decrees suspended freedom of speech, of the press, of meeting. An anti-communist campaign of propaganda and physical assault raged up to polling day. Under these conditions, though the mass of Socialist and Communist voters stood firm, the March elections gave the Nazis 288 M.Ps. and the Nazi-Nationalist coalition a clear majority. With the outlawing of the 81 elected Communists the Nazis alone had a majority.

From then on Nazi terror became continuous, it was extended from Communists to Socialists, to Liberals, to all who opposed Hitler, accompanied by imprisonment and torture on a mass scale. The flower of the German working class, of the intellectuals and humanists were done to death in Hitler's concentration camps and prisons.

2. Communists call for unity

In March 1933, in face of the fascist coup in Germany, the Communist International appealed for a working-class united front against Hitler, urging all Communist Parties to approach the Socialist parties for joint action. Pollitt sent this appeal, with the C.P.G.B's proposals for Britain,[3] to the Labour Party, T.U.C., Co-operative Party and I.L.P. Only the I.L.P. responded.

At many meetings, organised by the C.P. and by anti-fascist committees which sprang up, Pollitt exposed the complicity of the National Government in Hitler's advance. British imperialism wanted a counter-revolutionary war on the U.S.S.R., Japan was on the Soviets' eastern border, Hitler spoke openly of conquering the Ukraine; hence British loans, arms, political support to Hitler and Japan. In February 1934 Hitler claimed "equality of rights" in armaments, and the British Foreign Secretary said the claim "cannot and ought not to be resisted". In breach of the Versailles Treaty, British heavy tanks and aero engines for warplanes poured into Germany.

In July 1934 Pollitt welcomed as "a tremendous thing" the French Socialist–Communist agreement on united action, "a 10 to 1 majority of the Socialist rank and file . . . if done in France, we can do it here." Urging "Let us get together before it is too late", he proposed joint Labour and Communist demonstrations in August for unity against war and fascism. In September the Blackshirt offensive in Britain was opposed on the streets by thousands of workers. In October the fascists in Spain opened fire on workers. On each occasion the renewed Communist appeal for united action was rejected or ignored by the Labour leaders.

3. United action in Hyde Park

Sunday, September 9 1934 was warm, fine, with clear skies. Hyde Park was still green. Anti-fascist contingents streamed in and mingled with a huge crowd already waiting. The Blackshirt column, "hemmed in by long lines of police on either side and resembling so many prisoners", passed through long avenues of jeering spectators.[4] With police clearing the way, Mosley mounted his platform, the Blackshirts massed around it, the police lines encircled them. Then an empty space of some yards, then another police cordon, then an immense human sea, a vast and impenetrable mass of people from whom, as Mosley stepped to his microphone, there arose a roar of anger, hatred and contempt. Mosley gesticulated, the roar went on, beyond his circle of Blackshirts not a word could be heard.

Near the trees some distance from the great mass was another crowd, small in comparison, but numbering several thousands. Pollitt was speaking from the anti-fascist platform. His audience listened intently to his case for the united front of all workers and democrats against the fascist menace. The audience grew until even his far-carrying voice could not reach its edge. So it went on for an hour and a-half till Mosley gave up and, heavily guarded by Blackshirts heavily guarded by police, left the Park amid boos, jeers and curses from the still swelling crowds.[5]

The capitalist papers at first suppressed the news that a counter-demonstration was being organised. The anti-fascist publicity campaign directed brilliantly by Ted Bramley of the London Communist Party, found means to break the silence barrier. For a week there was spectacular showering of leaflets from the tops of buses, the windows of government offices, the roofs of Oxford Street and other big stores. Then on September 3 the *Daily Express* reported that three anti-fascists had called over a microphone at the Queens Hall for a march against fascism on September 9. From two of London's biggest cinemas came similar broadcasts. From then on, nothing could stop the propaganda. The plinth of Nelson's column was painted in letters a yard high calling on workers to do their duty, walls were painted and streets chalked all over London. A train steamed into Kings Cross station, its engine bearing in great white letters the words "Right Away to Smash Fascism". The *Manchester Guardian* reported that "a daring and brave man" had climbed the facade of the Law Courts and, in full view of the crowded street, unfurled a banner "March Against Fascism on September 9". Newspaper cameramen tipped off to be outside the heavily guarded B.B.C. headquarters at mid-day on the 7th saw a giant banner similarly worded unroll from the highest window in the building. Next day the Labour headquarters at Transport House unwittingly displayed a streamer with the words "The United Front from Below is on Top". The 'unauthorised' broadcasts continued, one from a Strand restaurant on the first evening of the new B.B.C. Droitwich transmitter. All this, plus innumerable loud speaker street announcements and door to door 'knocking up' in working-class areas, resulted in all London's attention being fixed on September 9.[6]

Pollitt described the anti-fascist turnout that day as "the biggest break through ever made against the ban on the united front imposed by the

Labour leaders."[7] The workers had in action answered not only Mosley, but also the Labour leaders who had advised "Stay away". On September 10 the *Manchester Guardian* put its finger on the spot when it said, "If this counter-demonstration, which outnumbered Mosley by 20 to 1, could be gathered from such a small party as the Communists, with large numbers of Londoners acting on their own initiative, on what scale would the opposition have been had it had the whole force of organised Labour behind it?" The *Daily Herald* achieved a distortion of facts rarely if ever equalled when it ascribed Mosley's eclipse "to splendid police organisation and the good sense of London's workers who observed the direction of the T.U.C. and took no part in the counter-demonstration".

4. Dynamite in the Dock, May 1935

On May 4, 1935, Pollitt sent to the Royal Commission on the Private Manufacture and Trade in Arms a Memorandum and proposals prepared by the Communist Party, and on May 23 he gave verbal evidence.[8] The Memorandum presented a mass of facts to substantiate that Britain was the main pillar of the world traffic in arms, that the government with the complicity of the capitalist class bore direct responsibility for the traffic and that it was blocking adequate enquiry into it. It argued that the proposal for a state monopoly of the arms industry was inadequate to end the evil, and that in addition to prohibition of the private manufacture and sale of arms and munitions, there should be a total ban on their export.

Pollitt in evidence brought out many significant facts. "While the League of Nations was trying to check the Japanese aggression on China, British arms manufacturers were supplying the means for it to be carried out." British amphibian tanks were being used against the Chinese Communists; British warplanes were sold in South America. Most serious of all, British firms were arming Hitler. Speeches by the Chairmen of Vickers and of I.C.I. had shown that the distinction between the private arms trusts and the State was only a formal one. The appropriation of the profits was by private shareholders, but the operations of the trusts were in complete collaboration with the government, and he gave names to show the interlocking of the arms firms with government offices and committees. The system of export by license made it possible for the arms trusts to supply both sides in a war; for example, that between Bolivia and Paraguay. The trusts could operate through subsidiaries in other countries, thus concealing from the British public the real destination of the arms. As for the profits, among arms shareholders were politicians, Ministers of the Crown, royalty, the church and the nobility—he gave the names—and many banks.

When Pollitt suggested that the Commission should protest against the restriction of the scope of its enquiry, the Chairman, who had several times shown impatience as Pollitt piled up his facts, became indignant.

Chairman: Are you really suggesting this is a matter we ought seriously to consider? Do you think it rests on a Royal Commission to complain of the terms after they have accepted the appointment?

Pollitt: I consider, Sir, that in this eve-of-war situation, anything you can do, despite all the attempts of the Government to limit the scope of the Commission, should be done by you in the interests of humanity as a whole, and we put it forward most seriously and earnestly.

Chairman: Very well.

Pollitt then gave data substantiating that the Government had exerted diplomatic pressure to prevent documents involving British interests being brought before the Arms Enquiry in the U.S.A.

Chairman: You say that "the evils of the armaments traffic can only be overcome by the overthrow of capitalism and the establishment of a world socialist society in which armaments will no longer be necessary and production will be organised for use, not profit". That is your view of the only possible real cure, is it?

Pollitt: Absolutely.

Chairman: Well, I suppose you would agree with me that it is not a cure that is likely to be immediately effective?

Pollitt: More's the pity!

5. Seventh World Congress of the Communist International

The 7th C.I. Congress was held in Moscow in July-August 1935[9] It "laid down lines for developing the united front on a broader basis than ever before contemplated". It opened far-reaching perspectives—immediate united action against fascism and war, giving rise to the united front of the Socialist and Communist Parties and going on to unify the Labour movement. Pollitt himself had made a substantial contribution to this new development by his criticism at the E.C.C.I. of the practice of making united action dependent on conditions unacceptable to Labour and Social-democratic workers[10] and his call for greater efforts to follow up the withdrawal by the Labour and Socialist International of the ban on its sections co-operating with Communist Parties.

The Congress proposals arose from experience. In France, united action had stemmed the fascist advance, impelled the government to a peace pact with the U.S.S.R., unified the trade union movement and led to an alliance of the workers and large sections of the middle class. Such an alliance in Germany would have prevented Hitler establishing a social basis prior to coming to power.

The rise of fascism heightened the danger of war: the Communists were vitally interested in preserving peace and in the past had shown that well organised actions could prevent war. But the situation was complex, a mere negative attitude was not enough. In a war for national liberation—such as resistance to a fascist attack on Poland or Czechoslovakia—the Communists "will support their ruling class in defending the attacked nation because to surrender such countries to German fascism would prepare a rod for the backs of the Russian workers and for all workers".[11]

Defining what was meant by unifying the Labour movement, Pollitt was precise—in each country, a single trade union centre and one united revolutionary party of the working class, and internationally, one trade union international, one working-class political international.

Pollitt's speech at the Congress[12] reinforced the call for unity by concrete proposals: the basis for united action to be the workers' own demands, however "small"; a distinction to be made between lower officials in reformist organisations who wanted to move left and those higher up who used left phrases merely to deceive. He argued that the only guarantee that the opposition of the top Social-democratic leaders could be overcome was the establishment of the united front in the factories, trade unions and localities. This required from the Communists ability to adapt to rapidly changing situations; to formulate slogans which every worker would feel he must fight for; to prove themselves in deeds the best defenders of the workers' daily interests; to relate the immediate issues to the struggle "for Soviet power" and the fundamental principles of Communism.

In Britain, said Pollitt, tendencies to fascism were likely to increase as the difficulties of British imperialism increased. The National Government was strengthening the coercive apparatus of the State and limiting working-class rights. Mosley with his openly fascist party, semi-military formations and lavish funds, advocated full-blooded Nazi-style German fascism. "The ruling class holds Mosley in reserve while the National Government carries through its preparatory work, taking advantage of the mass hatred of fascism as expounded by Mosley to present its own policy as upholding the traditions of British democracy. The fight against fascism is seen largely as a fight against Mosley. The tendencies towards fascism in the policy of the National Government are not seen as a vital danger making its defeat imperative."

6. ABYSSINIA

In the summer of 1935 Italian fascism made clear its intent to attack Abyssinia. Pollitt called for working-class action to stop the supply of war materials to Italy, and to boycott Italian ships. He rejected the official Labour reliance on the National Government. Labour should itself organise mass pressure for closing the Suez Canal to Italian ships, banning arms and loans to Italy and for full League of Nations sanctions. Success in saving peace and Abyssinian independence would check Hitler's advance in Europe, strengthen the anti-fascist fight, and encourage the millions demanding national independence in India, China and Africa.[13]

On September 25, with Italian forces poised for the attack, the Communist International wired the Labour and Socialist International proposing joint action, and appointed a delegation to discuss this. On the 26th, Pollitt proposed that the British Labour Party convene an international meeting of Socialist and Communist Parties and the trade unions, to express "the workers' determination to preserve peace".[14] On the 27th the C.I. delegation of Cachin, Thorez, Pollitt and Sverma met in Paris and informed the L.S.I. they were ready to talk. On October 3 at the Labour Party Conference in Brighton the L.S.I. Secretary, Adler, told Pollitt that their Executive had not yet discussed the C.I. telegram. Back in London that evening, Pollitt learned that the Italian attack on Abyssinia had begun, and at once wired the conference Chairman.

Next morning, on entering the hall, the Labour Party Conference delegates were handed a copy of the *Daily Worker*, with the text of Pollitt's telegram. It began, "London evening papers declare Adowa bombed, hundreds dead. We beg you in the name of humanity to agree to the proposal of Dimitrov for common action between the Socialist and Communist Internationals", and concluded, "We appeal to you in all sincerity to take the initiative in this fateful hour to ensure workers' international unity that can still save the world—Harry Pollitt."[15] The Labour Executive declined.

On October 12 in Brussels the L.S.I. Executive discussed the C.I. proposal. The majority favoured acceptance, but five parties, headed by the British Labour Party insisted on rejection.[16]

7. GENERAL ELECTION, NOVEMBER 1935

The question of electoral unity to return a Labour Government at the coming General Election was raised by Pollitt at the end of 1934. He had no illusions about the policy of such a government; "There is nothing in common between the aims of the workers under the influence of the Labour leaders and the policies these leaders are carrying out." Nevertheless he saw a class movement in the swing to Labour in the by-elections. "We need to see not so much the Labour leaders as the workers behind them", and an election victory would encourage these workers "to press forward a class line."[17] The Party's aim was "to sweep away the National Government, return Communist M.Ps. and a Labour majority".[18] This would create new conditions for pressing forward the whole working-class fight. The Party accordingly contested only two constituencies with Communist candidates, elsewhere pressing Labour candidates to declare for united action. The slogan of a Revolutionary Workers' Government was replaced by "Vote for a Labour Government to fight capitalism".

Arthur Horner, having been elected to a trade union position, was unable to stand in Rhondda East, and Pollitt became Communist candidate there. Urging the miners to vote for Pollitt, Horner commended his trade union standing and experience as second to none, adding, "The return of Pollitt will give every miner and his family the guarantee that our case will be presented with facts, arguments, lucidity, power and feeling that will find a response not only in Parliament but throughout the country." Ted Hill, on behalf of the Boilermakers' London District Committee, also sent support.[19]

Speaking at Porth on November 1, Pollitt detailed the needs of young people, pledging himself to fight for the six-hour day, proper training, raising the school leaving age to 16, places for young miners at 21 at the full minimum, and concluded, "It is time a holy crusade was carried on to save the youth of our country from capitalism's slaughtering of their hopes, prospects and ambitions".[20] A local paper found the election as a whole "dull", but "Mr. Pollitt is having inspiring meetings. Not ashamed of his gospel, he is a Communist and proud of it."[21]

Pollitt estimated[22] that the change in election tactics had brought an "unofficial and very elementary form of united front", in addition to the return of a Communist, Willie Gallacher as M.P. for West Fife. But the National Government got back with a larger majority.

Why, after four years of the National Government's anti-working class policy, were not the workers able to defeat it at the polls? Pollitt replied that the main reason was the Labour leaders' failure before and during the election to give a class lead, and their rejection of unity. The fighting spirit shown against the Blackshirts, in the miners' campaign for a wage increase, in the unemployed marches and the actions which defeated Part II of the Unemployment Act, showed what could be done when the class spirit was roused; but the Labour leaders made no effort to campaign among the workers, preferring to fall in behind the government on the Royal Jubilee campaign, the gas drills and other war preparations, and refusal of the essential oil sanctions to halt the Italian aggression in Abyssinia.

8. Communist affiliation to the Labour Party

The National Government had now another five years of power to further strengthen Hitler, unless a mass movement brought it down. To overcome the Labour leaders' resistance to such a movement, it was essential within the Labour movement to deepen the understanding of what was at stake. Discussion was stimulated by the Communist Party's new application for affiliation to the Labour Party.[23] Pollitt wrote that the Communist Party, while retaining its revolutionary point of view, would work sincerely for strengthening the working-class movement and winning a Labour majority on local bodies and in Parliament. He gave the lie to the assertion that Communists wanted to destroy the Labour Party: on the contrary, they would contribute to a policy around which the whole Labour left could unite and which could become Labour Party policy.[24]

The Labour Executive took two months to refuse.[25] They argued that nothing had happened to justify a change from the 1922 decision to reject affiliation and that differences on policy were irreconcilable. Pollitt in reply pointed out that Socialist–Communist unity against fascism now existed in France, Belgium, Austria, Italy, Switzerland and Spain, and that unity in Britain would now mean unity between the Socialist and Communist Internationals. Discussion spread; by June 1936 1,300 local Labour and trade union organisations, and the miners' Executive, had recorded support for affiliation. Herbert Morrison then stated the official case against; Pollitt replied, point by point.[26]

Morrison: The Labour Party is a constitutional political party recognising Parliamentary and municipal institutions. The Communist Party is a revolutionary organisation, highly disciplined, believing in the forcible overthrow of democratic institutions and their substitution by a political dictatorship. There is a fundamental difference between the political objectives of the Communist Party and of the Labour Party.

Pollitt: Communist Party discipline is based on the policy of class struggle and socialism. Expulsions are directed against those who injure the workers' cause. Such measures applied in the Labour Party might have prevented the harm done by MacDonald, Snowden, Thomas and Spencer. We have never disguised our view that socialism will only be finally won by the revolutionary conquest of power and the establishment of the dictatorship of the proletariat over our class enemy, and experience since 1917 has proved us right. Millions of socialists in Germany and Austria now regret the price they are paying for believing otherwise. The French Socialist Party is also on record for the same belief.[27]

Morrison: The Communist purpose is to remove the existing Labour leadership and substitute their own, convert Labour policy into Communist policy and, as Dimitrov said, "amalgamate the forces of the working class into a single revolutionary party".

Pollitt: The immediate issue is to defeat the National Government and return a Labour Government. Our affiliation to the Labour Party, by closing the workers' ranks, would help bring about a mass movement for this purpose. In the Labour Party we would certainly fight to get the leadership and policy necessary to achieve this. Dimitrov's aim of one revolutionary party would fulfil Marx and Engels' slogan "Workers of the World, Unite" and would mean unity, victory, power and socialism for the world's workers.

Morrison: We can no more form an alliance with the Communists than we can with the fascists.

Pollitt: Come off it, Herbert. Tell your next public meeting, "I can no more work with Harry Pollitt, Tom Mann and Willie Gallacher than I can with Sir Oswald Mosley", and see what happens.

Morrison: Prior to the disciplinary decisions made by the Labour Party we were weakened by Communist activity inside our ranks. We are stronger since we have protected ourselves from it.

Pollitt: That this is not true is proved by your lack of numbers and effective opposition in Parliament, by the discontent on your back benches, and by the fact that a National, not a Labour Government is in power.

Morrison: Association with the Communists would lose us hundreds of thousands of votes. C.P. affiliation is not the path to power, but the road to ruin.

Pollitt: This phrasemongering is not worthy of a leader in the present grave situation. It is not the opinion of the 1,300 local organisations who want Communist affiliation and a united front.

9. Hitler in the Rhineland

In June 1935, Britain agreed that Hitler should have a navy, including battleships and submarines, four times the size allowed by the Versailles Treaty; and to help him finance his rearmament the National Government allowed the Bank of England to loan him millions of pounds. The Bank's Chairman gave the reason, "The Nazis are a bulwark against Communism." That Hitler should use his arms, not against the West but against the Soviet Union—this was the wishful thinking of dominant British political circles. A journal close to the aeroplane industry[28] wrote in reference to the massing of aerodromes in North-West Germany that the obvious explanation was "as far west as possible to get them out of the range of Russian bombers. Germany has no fear of war against us." It went on, "If and when we join Germany in throwing the Russians from civilised Europe, these aerodromes will be quite nice as first landing places for our aerial reinforcements."

A few days later Hitler marched into the Rhineland and denounced the Locarno Treaty. "He would never have dared", said Pollitt, "had he not received British loans, arms, naval pact and support for his vast rearmament."[29]

At the same time Hitler offered a 25 year peace pact with some countries, not including Austria, Czechoslovakia and the Soviet Union. He then included the first two, making all the more glaring the omission of the Soviet Union. Many leaders of British public opinion treated this offer as serious. Pollitt wrote: "They would do well to ask 'Can Hitler be trusted?' Hasn't he broken Locarno which he had promised to respect? If the Soviet Union were attacked could such a war be localised? It is worthwhile remembering that while Hitler shakes his fist at the Soviet Union, he marches West. Hitler is the chief war aggressor, he cannot be tamed by pledges and paper documents; he can only be tamed by the overwhelming opposition of the peoples who desire peace."

10. Fascism means war

During the Rhineland crisis the leaders of the L.S.I. and of the I.F.T.U. met in London, but there were no public meetings. Pollitt commented,[30] "Everything behind closed doors. Everything to fit in with the requirements of the National Government and the League of Nations. Can anyone imagine that if the Communist International were allowed Executive meetings in London that Dimitrov, Thorez, Ercoli, Pieck, Pollitt and others would not have addressed great masses of people, roused them to the struggle for peace, to a white hot hatred of fascism?"

At meeting after meeting Pollitt replied to questions and arguments.[31]

Q: "War should be welcomed because it would bring revolution."
A: "Communists reject this false theory. War would bring death to hundreds of thousands of workers and weaken the revolutionary movement."
Q: "To fight war we must fight capitalism in general, for all wars and government policies are alike."
A: "This is the idea that it is 1914 all over again. It is not. In 1914 no-one could say which imperialism was the aggressor, all were equally to blame. In 1936 the actions of the fascist powers define them as aggressors fomenting a new world war. And today there exists the Socialist Soviet Union, a powerful bulwark for peace."
Q: "Should Hitler's offer of 25 years peace pacts be accepted?"
A: "No. Their aim is not to maintain peace, but to facilitate his attacks on other countries. They exclude the USSR, so we can only assume that if Britain and France get 25 years security it will be at the expense of the U.S.S.R. Besides, Hitler breaks pacts when it suits him to do so."
Q: "Surely sanctions mean war?"
A: "It is lack of sanctions that leads to war. Japan and Italy, because sanctions were not seriously applied, continued their aggression on China and Abyssinia. This in turn encouraged Hitler. Sanctions should be accompanied by treaties of mutual assistance against agression and by international working-class unity. If the peace front enforces boycott of the aggressor, refuses credits and loans, stops ships and commerce, there is less likelihood of the fascist madmen risking war."
Q: "Can't we keep out of it?"
A: "In face of fascist aggression there is nothing neutral about the attitude of neutrality. It helps the aggressor by holding back opposition to him."

A dangerous proposal to placate Hitler was that of a world economic conference to give Germany a greater share in access to raw materials and to investment in underdeveloped countries. Pollitt condemned this as "giving Hitler a share in the imperialist exploitation of the colonies" and, by strengthening his economic and military position, making him a still greater danger to peace. "Colonial peoples are not cattle to be bartered by imperialist interests. The duty of the working class is to help the colonial peoples to attain complete national freedom and independence."

While fully recognising the need for an international peace front against fascism, Pollitt saw the peace movement in Britain as the decisive factor: "If Hitler is a menace in Europe it is because of Baldwin." To end National Government support to Hitler was the task, and to achieve it required a mass movement, powerful enough to force its will on the government, or bring it down. That in turn required "the ending of all policies of class collaboration by the Labour Movement and a united front of all sections in common struggle for immediate economic, political and social demands."[32]

11. COMMUNIST PARTY AND I.L.P., 1933-36

The I.L.P. Annual Conference decisions on relations with the Communists may be summarised[33] as follows:

1933: Disaffiliation from L.S.I. endorsed. A united front with the C.P.G.B. and co-operation with the Communist International accepted. But the elected N.A.C.[34] remained opposed to affiliation with C.I.

1934: For an "all in" International including L.S.I. and C.I.; rejection of "sympathetic" affiliation to C.I.[35]; joint activities with C.P.G.B. endorsed; N.A.C's attacks on C.I., C.P.S.U. and Soviet Government's peace policy accepted.

1935: Joint activities with C.P.G.B. endorsed unification of C.P.G.B. and I.L.P. rejected; N.A.C's increasingly critical attitude to Communism accepted.

1936: The C.I. condemned as "opportunist" and the C.P.G.B. as "reformist".

Pollitt regarded the I.L.P. leaders as themselves opportunist and reformist, not Marxist, and throughout these changes his aim was consistent—to clarify the role of reformism, to secure any possible unity of action, to win I.L.P. members for Communist policy. He saw three trends at the 1933 Conference: the right were for immediate return to the Labour Party; Maxton and Brockway were for a centrist I.L.P. not affiliated to the Labour Party; the left wanted a revolutionary policy and organisation.[36]

The leaders' opposition to the C.I. was reflected in the way they carried out the 1933 decision. Pollitt described their letter as "formal, bureaucratic, with no proposals"[37]; they sent no delegation. But an agreement with the C.P.G.B. was drawn up in May and listed specific issues on which both parties were to bring their members into activity. Pollitt commented that "only daily activities in co-operation in the factories, trade unions and streets will give it life". The resultant joint activity and its extension in 1934[38] were warmly welcomed by workers alarmed at Hitler's successes. Audiences at joint meetings were larger, many local and some national trade union and Labour Party leaders associated with joint appeals or spoke on joint platforms. There was mutual support at by-elections. Notable meetings were in Manchester on October 21, with I.L.P., C.P. and two Labour Party E.C. members speaking against fascism. A week later in Trafalgar Square, speakers against the Sedition Bill were again from I.L.P., C.P. and Labour Party E.C. members.

More impressive was the response to joint calls for action—particularly for the Hunger March and National Congress in February 1934. At the Congress a difference arose between the two parties over a reference to the T.U.C. leaders, and when it was settled by agreement the prolonged applause showed the delegates' concern to maintain unity. Later in 1934 came big rallies against Mosley and in February 1935 the mass upheaval against Part II of the Unemployment Act. Pollitt summed up these results as "undoubted achievements having a profound effect in the Labour Movement, though millions are not yet drawn in."[39]

Parallel to the joint actions the I.L.P. leaders campaigned against the C.I. and for their idea of a new "All in" International. Brockway said that both the L.S.I. and C.I. were bankrupt.[40] The National Administrative Council (N.A.C.) of the I.L.P. published a new journal[41] with long articles by Trotsky and others whom the C.I. regarded as renegades. To the C.I. proposals for sharper struggle against reformism, I.L.P. affiliation to the C.I. as a sympathising party, and the formation with the C.P.G.B. of a united revolutionary party, the N.A.C. took a negative attitude. The anti-C.I. campaign secured the rejection in 1934 of the proposal to affiliate and ended I.L.P. negotiations with the C.I.

By December 1934 difficulties had arisen in I.L.P.-C.P.G.B. co-operation. Pollitt, approached by I.L.P. members who wanted to join the C.P., had advised them to remain in the I.L.P. and work for its affiliation to the C.I. The I.L.P. leaders objected to this as "Communist faction work" in their party. Pollitt complained that lack of activity by the I.L.P. was reducing the joint agreement to a piece of paper. These differences were not resolved but it was agreed to jointly issue a New Year Appeal for ending the "class collaboration and retreat" imposed by the reactionary leaders. This appeal, a joint leaflet supporting the Austrian workers and the exchange of fraternal delegates at the 1935 Party Conferences, created a public impression that C.P.-I.L.P. relations were improving; in fact, as I.L.P. hostility to the C.I. hardened, they inevitably deteriorated.

As fraternal delegate to the I.L.P. 1935 Annual Conference, Pollitt, said that similar joint activities in France had compelled the Socialist leaders to accept the united front. He proposed joint work in the trade unions, help to the growing opposition in the Labour Party, and regular meetings of members and leaders to discuss immediate issues and fundamental questions. Welcoming tendencies towards communism in the I.L.P., he declared that there was no middle course between the Second and Third Internationals. "Attempts to find one may result not in going forward to revolution but back to reformism." The creation of a united revolutionary party in Britain would "attract thousands of revolutionary workers at present unattached." Later he commented, "Conference opened with 30 minutes from Maxton, 25 explaining why he was not going to make a speech. I was called immediately after; my speech went flat as dishwater. Every anti-Party, anti-Soviet, anti-C.I. reference cheered by big sections, especially the strong Glasgow delegation. Good speeches from Cullen, Hilda Vernon, Gaster, but they had not campaigned."

The Conference, in the grip of a centrist-right alliance, moved to the right; N.A.C. spokesmen extended their attack from the C.I. to the C.P.G.B., calling its leaders "commercial travellers paid by Moscow gold". Closer co-operation with the C.P. and the proposal for one party, were rejected; the concept of an "All in" International was endorsed. In this context the decision to continue joint activity with the C.P. rang somewhat hollow. After the Conference, the N.A.C. took steps to disrupt the London Divisional stronghold of the Revolutionary Policy Committee. After the 7th World Congress of the C.I. had opened new perspectives for unity, the I.L.P's. Revolutionary Policy Committee called on its supporters to leave the I.L.P. and join the Communist Party.[42] To the N.A.C., however, the 7th Congress was a "new opportunist line" and the C.P's application for affiliation to the Labour Party a "reformist turn". The N.A.C. without formally renouncing the agreement with the C.P. abandoned it in practice. Relations were at this low level when the fascist attack on the Spanish Republic in July 1936 aroused a new surge for unity in the Labour movement.

12. Ceremony for Children

On Sunday, April 26, 1936, Harry, Marjorie and Mary Louisa took Jean, then aged aged 4½, and baby Brian, to the Fulham Socialist Sunday School to be ceremonially "named", the socialist equivalent of christening. Alex Gossip, whom Harry had first met in the "Hands Off Russia" campaign and who remained a staunch militant through all his years as General Secretary of the Furnishing Trades, conducted the ceremony. In addition to the children who were members, their parents and relatives and delegates from sympathising organisations had been invited. First the parents promised to so order their lives and the home that the children "may grow up in comradely socialist surroundings and be given such simple socialist training as a child may understand—ideals of social justice, common humanity, peace, freedom and brotherhood." Then Alex Gossip "under the Red Flag of Socialism, on behalf of our national and international socialist fellowship, whether free or oppressed" named the children Jean Marjorie and Brian Harry, and wished them "a full and useful life in the interest of the common people of all lands, irrespective of race, creed or colour". The children of the school then presented flowers to Marjorie, the initiation certificates to Harry, and presents to Jean and Brian. Alex Gossip then reminded the audience that children in other lands were suffering hunger and lacked hope, conditions which socialism would put an end to. The ceremony ended, as it had begun, with a socialist song. The certificates, inscribed with words of welcome "as a scholar and as a worker for the cause of socialism" hung above the children's beds for many years.[43]

CHAPTER 16

THE FASCIST WAR ON SPAIN

1. The Spanish generals revolt. 2. Chamberlain aids Franco—Labour leaders aid Chamberlain. 3. British Battalion. 4. First visit—Jarama, February–March 1937. 5. Second visit—Madrid, June 1937. 6. Brunete and Aragon, July to November 1937. 7. Third visit—Teruel, December 1937. 8. Fourth visit—Catalonia, April 1938. 9. Fifth visit—Ebro, August 1938. 10. Fall of the Republic.

1. THE SPANISH GENERALS' REVOLT.

The fascist war on Spain began on the night of July 17-18, 1936, when generals who had twice sworn allegiance to the Republic led an armed rising of troops and fascist bands. In the big towns the people immediately fought back.

Sylvia Townsend Warner described the first hours in Barcelona: "The workers were in the factories when the soldiers came from the Montjuich barracks into the town centre. People thought it was just another parade. Then the soldiers opened fire; women out marketing, breakfasters in the cafes, street vendors showing their wares, gardeners planting flower beds, looked up and saw people falling dead around them. Troops occupied the Hotel Colon, their machine guns commanding the central square, the Plaza de Catalunia, and the boulevard of the Ramblas. Others went down the boulevard, entering churches en route. The police ranged themselves with the people, fighting side by side with professors, journalists and intellectuals. The police carried arms, the people ran to gun shops taking sporting guns and ammunition, automatics, and when nothing better was left, knives. A tram hastily blinded with sheet metal went at full speed down the Ramblas through a machine gun barrage from a church. Where soldiers had gone in, tramloads of men followed, took the kingdom of heaven by storm, and put the machine guns out of action."[1]

When, after three days of hesitation, the Republican Government armed the workers, the fascists were crushed in Madrid, Barcelona, the Asturias and most of the mainland, but they held Navarre, Western Andalusia, the islands and Morocco. It was clear that only help from abroad would save the rebel generals. German officers, technicians and munitions came through Portugal, Italian planes flew in by the score. Thousands of Moors and Foreign Legion mercenaries were brought from Africa in German ships and Italian planes.

As soon as the generals' revolt was known in London, Pollitt appealed[2] with passion—"as never before in my life"—to the British working class to do all in its power to ensure complete victory for the Spanish people "who are defending democracy not only for themselves, but for all peoples". He showed the complicity of Hitler, Mussolini and Chamberlain, the two former supplying the rebels with men and arms, the latter with political support, and all working for a fascist victory.

In a thrice reprinted pamphlet[3] Pollitt showed the falsity of the claim that Franco was a patriot defending Spain against a "Red" seizure of power. The programme of the Spainish People's Front which had won a majority in the February 1936 elections was not socialist. Its government was entirely Republican without one Socialist or Communist, its policy England would call Liberal. Its social economic and democratic reforms were to meet urgent needs of the people. The fascist generals were mutineers against a legitimate, democratically-elected parliamentary government. Franco's shock troops were not Spaniards, but mainly mercenaries and Moors, officered by aristocrats, financed, armed and equipped from foreign sources. The revolt was a concerted move of the fascist powers to strengthen their strategic position for war on the democratic countries, particularly France. The stories of "red atrocities" in Spain were a cover for the fascist policy of systematic slaughter of their political opponents, such as the massacre following the capture of Badajos.[4]

For the next three years Pollitt lived every hour on the heights of endeavour in the anti-fascist struggle. He showed what the war meant for the British people, how Chamberlain's mis-called "non-intervention" strengthened Hitler in aggression and brought world war nearer. Stressing that working-class direct action was indispensable to a democratic victory, he simultaneously strove for wider unity of action in all forms of aid to Republican Spain—political, military, medical, material.

In response to the call in July for medical aid, Pollitt asked Isabel Brown, an eloquent and moving speaker with wide experience in relief work, to take the initiative. Her ability to win support was such that in less than three weeks the first British Medical Unit left for Spain, including four doctors, six trained nurses, eight dressers, medicines costing £500 and equipment for a 30-bed field hospital. Thus began the Spanish Medical Aid Committee. In 1937 the crew of the British ship *Linaria* loaded in Boston with nitrate, refused to sail her to Franco.[5]

London engineers and builders stopped work in protest at Chamberlain's policy. But the greatest response of working-class and democratic opinion was to Pollitt's call for a British Battalion of Volunteers to fight in the army of the Spanish Republic. This direct involvement raised solidarity to a new height and gave a tremendous stimulus to the anti-fascist movement.

2. Chamberlain aids Franco—Labour leaders aid Chamberlain

Pollitt publicised[6] every step of Chamberlain's support for Franco—official visits by naval officers to Franco's headquarters, detention of Republican trawlers by British destroyers, refusal of oil and coal at Gibraltar, and denial of Tangier to Republican ships. That these were not isolated actions but a consistent policy was shown by the British Government being the first to deny the Spanish Government its legal right to buy arms and by British pressure on France to do the same and to initiate the so-called "non-intervention" policy. Under the threat that the British guarantee of the French frontiers would not remain valid if France supplied arms to Republican Spain, the French Government proposed the "non-intervention" policy and on September 9 an International Committee was formed to operate it. In practice this policy meant that France and the U.S.S.R. were prevented from sending volunteers, arms and planes to the Republic, while Hitler and Mussolini poured in troops, planes and armaments to Franco.

To politically sustain "non-intervention", the Labour leaders' support was vital to Chamberlain. It was given by the National Council of Labour on August 28. Pollitt described the decision as "treason to democracy and peace."[7] At the Labour Party Conference, the Executive supported "non-intervention", imposing silence on its members who were opposed to this, including Morrison and Hicks. Delegates from the Spanish Socialist Party were not allowed to speak before "non-intervention" had been endorsed. And in the debate an Executive spokesman asked, if the non-intervention Pact was not being observed, "why cannot the T.U.C. General Council get evidence of it?", whereupon a delegate interjected, "Because they are not looking for it." When the Spaniards did speak they gave such evidence of German and Italian intervention that the Conference declared its firm conviction that the Pact had been broken, and sent delegates to ask the government to investigate, and, should the intervention be proved, to restore to the Republic the right to buy arms.[8]

In the face of all evidence, the Labour leaders persisted in support of "non-intervention". A great discussion followed throughout the movement, with Citrine and Bevin the chief spokesmen for "non-intervention", Pollitt for aid to Spain. The main arguments briefly stated were as follows:[9]

Citrine: Any course other than neutrality would lead to war with the fascist countries.

Pollitt: To refuse decisive action when the fascist powers aid Franco is not to avoid the risk of war, it is to encourage Hitler and Mussolini to further aggression. "A fascist victory in Spain will plunge the world into war, with democratic France surrounded by fascist states and disrupted from within by a Hitler-controlled fascist movement."

Bevin: The assumption that we will never defend ourselves is not true. Fascism is not going to saddle itself on the whole earth either by intrigue or the methods employed in Spain.
Pollitt: This means allowing fascist aggression today, but threatening we will hit back tomorrow. This line of argument has led to the present situation, and if maintained it will lead to fascism dominating Europe and to an inevitable war, with fascism in a much stronger position than now.
Citrine: The only way to restrain Germany and Italy from supplying arms to the rebels is to place a naval blockade round the coast of Spain.
Pollitt: This is true, and had the League of Nations been asked to declare that to arm the rebels was a break of international law and a threat to peace, a blockade of the rebels' ports could and should have been imposed. But the point at issue is not that we should restrain Italy, Germany and Portugal from violating international law, but whether fear of an attack by them should restrain us from giving the Spanish Government its rights under international law.
Citrine: The fact that the French Communist Party, while agitating against neutrality, will not vote against the Blum Government shows the hollowness of the situation.
Pollitt: The French Communist Party and others are trying to get the Blum Government to change its policy, not to throw it out and get a right-wing government in its place.
Bevin: The British Communists said scarcely a word about intervention till the National Council of Labour made its decision, then they thought it was a ground of attack.
Pollitt: Not true. On July 25 and August 1 and frequently since we demanded that the British Government supply the Spanish Government with what it needed.

Urging rejection of 'neutrality', which "would place millions of lives in jeopardy", Pollitt wrote, "If the British workers could see regiment after regiment of Spanish Socialists, Communists and trade unionists marching into battle with sticks and bare fists as their only weapons, they would blaze with anger at the policy of the British Government and their own leaders." At a Communist National Conference in October, he pointed to the growth of opposition to "neutrality", declared that "the fate of the working class is in our hands" and called for fresh efforts to help Spain, including Volunteers and a mass campaign against "neutrality".[10] In that same week the Spanish Communist Dolores Passionaria said: "If the men of Madrid will stand weapons in hand, the city is invincible. If there are not enough rifles, we will use sticks and stones. If there are no stones, we will use our fists. And if there are no men left, the women will carry on the battle."[11]

Assured of official Labour support, Chamberlain took every opportunity to help Franco. He allowed Franco to use London as a propaganda centre, while refusing facilities to the Spanish Government. He placed obstacles in the way of sending food to the Basque country and of removing Basque children to safety from fascist bombing. He refused to invoke the League Covenant against the fascist aggressors. In the autumn of 1936 he made it illegal for anti-fascist volunteers to go to Spain.

During 1937 the fascist bombardment of Madrid and other cities, including the total destruction of Guernica, the massacres of civilians and prisoners such as at Badajoz, roused wide circles of British public opinion against 'non-intervention', but left the Chamberlain Government unmoved.

"When in April Sir John Simon declared that Britain would not be unmoved by brutality and bloodshed, he was not referring to the current bombing of women and children in Madrid, but to the fact that British birds had illegally participated in a cock-fight in Calais."[12]

Pollitt summed up the Chamberlain policy on Spain as bearing "the main responsibility for the increase of the war danger and the menace of fascism to all mankind."[13]

3. BRITISH BATTALION

The first British volunteers were Communists who when the fascist revolt began were in Barcelona and promptly joined the People's Militia. The young artist Felicia Browne was killed on the Aragon front on August 29. Two London tailors, Nat Cohen and Sam Masters, were in the unsuccessful attempt to seize Majorca.

In September the C.P.G.B., in response to the call of the Communist International, began organising volunteers. Pollitt arranged for one of the most capable Party organisers, R. W. Robson, to personally interview all volunteers and to warn them of the dangers and difficulties. The only political test was sincerity in anti-fascism; there was a medical examination. Precautions were taken to keep out spies and fascist agents. The enrolment was at first open, but became clandestine when the British government made it an offence and the French closed the Pyrenean frontier. About 2,500 men were accepted, the great majority proved of high reliability. The few who were unable to sustain the strain of battle were either given other work or returned home.

The Republic recognised the International Brigades in September and gave them Albacete as their base. Groups of British attached to the Thaelmann Battalion and a French battalion fought in Madrid "holding on with their old rifles and jamming machine guns" in November, and on the Cordoba front in December. As the numbers mounted, Pollitt proposed the formation of a British Battalion. This was done in January 1937, when four companies were in training. The British, with French, Belgians, Slavs and Americans formed the XV Brigade.[14]

During 1937 and 1938, Pollitt visited Spain five times. He went about in the streets, the training camps, at the front, in the hospitals, "watching, listening and noting experiences, to sense the opinions and feelings not only of the leaders, but also of the people."[15] He was punctilious in the necessary calls on the authorities but he wanted to spend the maximum of time with the men of the British Battalion.

Unheralded except by rumour, his short, stocky figure would turn up, his large black briefcase bulging with scores of letters in its indexed compartments, the specially made giant pockets of his brown leather fur-lined coat bursting with cigarettes and chocolate. He greeted almost every man by name, often was able to give him news of his family. He would take letters or note messages to be delivered on his return. When the Battalion was in the line he "went right into the trenches".[16] "He made no bellicose speeches or calls for heroism. He went from one individual to another talking quietly, showing concern for the suffering, noting messages for relations, showing confidence in each man. It was a great contribution to morale."[17] He visited those resting or in reserve, chatting informally with as many as possible and answering their questions. If conditions permitted he spoke on the home or international aspect of the struggle. Every man felt stronger for what he said and how he said it. He never failed to get a list of the wounded, find out what hospital they were in, and visit them. Sam Wild, Battalion Commander, wrote, "other leading Communists were respected and admired by the Britons in Spain, Pollitt was loved. I knew men give up their leave because they wanted to meet him. A sacrifice made only for him. His approach to the welfare of our Battalion and our nurses was unique; he thought of things most people would not dream of. His appeal in the *Daily Worker* for compasses and map reading material got a terrific response. Another appeal made possible on my 30th birthday, August 19, 1938, an issue of cigarettes to all the British and half the Yanks."[18]

On his return from each visit he would recount in detail to meetings what he had seen and heard at the front, in the hospitals, in the bombed towns and villages, with such vivid imagery and homely terms that the hatred of fascism rose higher and higher, and a continuous stream of volunteers came forward.

He received numerous requests, "six all-wave wireless sets", "gramophone records, flexible ones that don't crack", "portable gramophones", "cigarettes by the million"; "Dr. Taylor wants a water-analyser". The Battalion command asked for "a standard in the colours of the Republic, without Party symbols". He saw for himself that binoculars were needed. All these requests he met. The Battalion banner was magnificent in red, purple and gold, its symbols the clenched fist of the Popular Front and its slogan "Freedom, Democracy, Peace".

He replied in detail to many letters.[19] Some were critical of lack of accurate information about casualties. He explained that when official information was received about men missing, wounded or killed, he let relations know, but sometimes information was sent by post and the Censor blacked out names, or it turned out to be a rumour. He added "If the whole organisation of the work was in our hands, it would be different, but it is not, we have to make the best of other people's arrangements".

Then there were personal problems. "This man left his sole remaining relative, his father, in care of friends in Dublin. Unemployment compelled them to move to Liverpool. He is anxious about his father who the medical people say needs an early operation. He asks for a dependent's allowance for his father until he is able to return home". Some requests were straightforward, "I have been wounded and feel I can't go on. I am not a coward but would like to go home." Another, "I have been at the front and injured, I am 45, the doctor says I am not fit for service, I think I could be more use at home". Others, "I am now a widower and have five dependent children and am being asked to return and look after them." "I have been wounded and am unfit for service, and am informed my wife is pregnant and dangerously ill." For nearly a year Pollitt did what he could on all such letters, later the Dependent's Aid Committee took on most of the work. Some requests were a pleasure, such as that of the South African Friends of the Spanish Republic who asked him to secure and despatch, at their expense, an ambulance. He did so, it bore an inscription "Springbok Ambulance—South Africa" and "Springbok Ambulans—Suid Afrika". Occasionally a lighter note was struck. A woman volunteer wrote from Albacete, "This is to confess that I am disobeying your order not to get married to a foreigner. Well, you can blame it on to our countrymen, who have had the same chance but failed to take it."

Pollitt encouraged volunteering by his political explanation of the significance of the war. Party officials and leading members who volunteered did so on their own initiative. If individuals asked for advice he said they should make their own decision after taking all circumstances into account. Oxford comrades who responded to Pollitt's appeal for binoculars, when they heard of the death of the writer Ralph Fox, felt that they ought to do more—to volunteer themselves. They went to see Pollitt about it. One of them wrote, "We discussed very thoroughly. Pollitt advised us to think it over very seriously, to remember that we needed revolutionary intellectuals here and could not afford to send everyone to Spain. He said we must make our own decision, he would not like to be the one responsible for sending us."[20]

"The British Battalion" said Pollitt, "has retrieved the honour of the British Labour Movement." "General Kleber declared that when the British are in a tight corner calling for coolness and courage, what they are defending will be held to the last." "These comrades are flesh of our flesh, blood of our blood, bound to us by a thousand ties. We have the right to be proud of them and to shout their bravery to the skies, so that it shall be a power in the movement towards the People's Front. . . . We must see that the fund for maintenance to their families is higher, help those who come back wounded, and when fully recovered we must help them to get jobs, never let them be forgotten."[21,22]

4. First visit—Jarama, February–March 1937.

In mid-February Pollitt heard that the British were in action and suffering heavy losses. He at once made arrangements to visit them. Refused official permission to enter Spain, he went to see friends in Paris. A day later a Senor Pedro Acebal, complete with Spanish documents, was drinking coffee in an airport restaurant wondering how, with a knowledge of the Spanish tongue limited to his name, birthplace and similar details, he would get through the controls. After delays due to bad weather, his plane, an ancient, battered and camouflaged Douglas, appeared on the departure ground. At this sight every official disappeared and Senor Acebal together with six other coffee drinkers departed, officially unseen, unheard and unrecorded. The plane lurched abominably, there were no seats, there was an unexpected landing at Toulouse. Then over the Pyrenees, down the coast to Valencia, a night in a hotel, a car to Albacete, where he met Peter Kerrigan who had been with the Battalion at Jarama.

Here we interpose a brief account of the fighting at Jarama.[23]

Franco's direct attack on Madrid having failed, he planned an encircling movement. A northern thrust would cut the road to Catalonia, a southern thrust that to Valencia. A steel ring would close at Alcala de Henares, Madrid would be isolated.

Some twenty kilometres from Madrid the Valencia highway crosses the Jarama, runs through Arganda, then crosses the Tajuna. By reaching Arganda or commanding either of the two bridges, the fascists would cut the vital supply route and imperil Madrid. On February 6 the attack of 25,000 fascist troops, including German planes tanks and guns, broke the thin Republican lines and approached the west bank of the Jarama at San Martin on the road to Morata. Republican H.Q. sent an urgent call to Albacete and four battalions of the International Brigade left at once to form the left flank of the defence.

The British Battalion reached the San Martin–Morata road early on February 12, they had hardly left the lorries when the order came to take battle positions. They advanced towards the river, in line parallel to the road. They reached the crest of a ridge, and saw the grey cloaks of the Moors ascending the slope, and opened fire just in time to prevent the fascists occupying the ridge.

Toward the centre of the ridge—nicknamed "Suicide Hill"—was a small white house. On its right rose a conical hill. Both were occupied by the British. Still further to the right was a knoll adjacent to the San Martin road. Beyond the road were Republican guns and other International battalions. To the rear of 'Suicide Hill' the ground fell for several hundred yards, then came a second but lower ridge, behind this a sunken road. The

British machine guns and H.Q. were on this second ridge. Nearby were olive groves. Behind and to the left of the British there were no Republican troops, and no reserves at Arganda or Chincon. So the order was "Hold on at all costs". The fascist artillery, machine guns, automatic rifles and tanks developed such heavy fire that the Republican forces on the British right had to retire. This enabled the Moors to occupy the knoll and enfilade the British positions.

A ceaseless steel rain came down hour after hour, but the rifle companies held their front all day. The British machine guns were silent, ammunition had not arrived. So great were the casualties that in the evening the order was given to retire from 'Suicide Hill' and concentrate on the second ridge and the sunken road. The Moors now confident of victory were advancing to overwhelm this last defence when the long awaited ammunition arrived. When the Moors were 150 yards away the nine heavy machine guns slaughtered them with a stream of bullets.

At the end of the first day of battle, the British had less than half their men on their feet, the first ridge was lost. But the second was held, the machine guns were intact, the remaining riflemen rallied on their flanks. Spanish troops under General Lister were coming up on the left, the dangerous gap on the right remained. The night was bitterly cold.

The fascist attack was resumed at dawn. Again it was broken by the death-dealing machine guns. But on the British right the fascists gained more ground, their artillery concentrated on the British machine guns for several hours. Then came a lull and a crowd of fascists advanced singing *The Internationale* and giving the popular front salute of the raised fist. Not doubting it was a desertion the British held their fire. But it was a trick, the machine gunners and their guns were captured, with their commander Lt. A. J. Fry.

The second ridge lost, the sunken road now became the front line. The Battalion Commander, Captain Tom Wintringham, was wounded in the thigh and had to be carried off. Jock Cunningham took command. It was the end of the second day.

The dawn of the third day found the British remnant cold, hungry and exhausted but tenaciously holding the sunken road. From Brigade H.Q. Major Nathan brought news. The Lister Brigade was now covering the left flank, the French-Belgians had come up on the right. A Republican tank attack was timed for 1 p.m. But it was the fascist tanks that appeared. They were soon in the sunken road, followed by Moors. The Republican line gave way.

Captain Frank Ryan, leader of a group of the Irish Republican Army who had joined the International Brigade described what happened next: "Now there was nothing between the fascists and the Madrid road but disorganised men dispirited by heavy casualties, by defeat, and by lack of food. Worn out by three gruelling days, they seemed to have reached the end of their resistance. Walking along to see how many men we had I found myself deciding to go back on the line of the San Martin road and take the Moors on their left flank. I hitched a rifle to my shoulder. Men stumbled to their feet, fell in behind. Up the road Jock Cunningham was assembling more men. We joined forces, we two at the head, men behind us marching silently. Remembering a trick of the days of banned demonstrations, I jerked my head back and shouted 'Sing up boys'. At first quavering, then more lustily, then resounding, arose the chant of the *Internationale*. What had been a routed rabble now marched again into battle. They were joined by stragglers, by a group of Belgians, then by a Spanish battalion. At the olive groves we deployed to the left, were back on the ridge, again in the thick of the battle—this time advancing. As night fell we dug in on reconquered ground."[24] It was the end of the third day.

That night the British were within 300 yards of their first positions; this advance proved to be a turning point in the battle, though attack and counter-attack, bombardment by fascist guns and planes went on without intermission for the next seven days and nights. Then the fascists weakened and by February 21 had lost the initiative.[25]

The stubborn resistance in which the British had played a decisive part had given time for the arrival of substantial Republican reinforcements. The battle of Jarama officially ended on February 27, though less intense fighting continued. The fascist drive to cut the Madrid–Valencia road was defeated. Jarama was a Republican victory.

Pollitt arrived towards the end of February and with Peter Kerrigan found the British, now less than 200, just arrived at Morata for a brief rest behind the lines. Unkempt, unshaven, inexpressibly wearied in body but with a feeling of pride that they had held the sector, they crowded into the little church to hear Pollitt. He looked at the upturned faces of men who had faced death every hour of seventeen days and nights. "At first words would not come, then the look in their eyes brought speech. I don't know what I said, I only know they hung on every word. At the end they surged round and, summoning strength from goodness knows where, surged into the street, hoisted me on their shoulders and marched in tattered ranks through the village singing the *Internationale*." Two days later they were back in the line.

Kerrigan and Pollitt returned to Valencia to attend a conference of the Spanish Communist Party. Then Pollitt visited a hospital. "Ward after ward—in one I recognised a sleeper, a Labour Party comrade from West London, who had thrown up a good job to go to Spain. I asked 'What is the matter with you?' He replied, 'Nothing', but I could see that one arm was missing. In another ward was a Dundee lad I knew, Willie McGuire. He was dying. He wrote on a piece of paper, 'Please send my watch to my mother. Long live the Y.C.L.' In another bed was Douglas Springhall, the London Secretary of the Communist Party. A bullet had gone through his cheek. I shook him and he woke. His first question was to ask for the result of the L.C.C. elections."

Back in Britain Pollitt asked "If there can be unity on the battlefields, why cannot we have it here?" Of Jarama he said, "Not a man who went out there was promised a penny. Every one was a genuine volunteer, and understood that he was going out to face death." This did not stop a capitalist paper[26] writing that Franco's British prisoners had been promised by Communists work at £6 per week "then found they were given arms in the Red's front line."

After Jarama Pollitt wrote, "The dream of Marx and Engels has been realised, the dream which dominated them when they formed the First International, that one day there would arise a single world party that could mobilise the best of the people in every country to come to the assistance of comrades in other lands fighting a deadly enemy."[27]

5. SECOND VISIT, MADRID—JUNE 1937.

For six days and nights Pollitt travelled by car over Republican Spain and noted a new optimism and confidence resulting from the efforts of the Negrin Government to secure a unified military command, an efficient war industry and an end to sabotage and disruption.

He found the British Battalion resting. He got a great welcome, gave them the latest news of the political situation, distributed many letters and took as many to be posted on his return. Some comrades were on duty on the Madrid front where he went to see them. George Brown, previously Manchester organiser of the C.P. and now a political commissar, and the writer Ralph Bates took him over the city. Shelling and bombing went on day and night. "Great buildings smashed like a pack of cards, whole working-class streets were blown to atoms, huge steel girders once supporting vast edifices now twisted into fantastic shapes like streamers thrown across a dance floor. Lying in bed one hears the shriek of heavy shells—what has that one hit? Will this building be the next?" At the front at the Casa del Campo the scream of shells and boom of artillery was deafening. In one of the worst shelled areas a single barricade remained. "It seemed to epitomise the challenge of the dauntless Spanish people to Fascism: across it was the slogan 'Release Luis Prestes'[28] A people who in their own agony and sacrifice can think of Luis Prestes in far away Brazil is a people whom it is an honour to support." George Brown gave a cheery good-bye, neither of them could know that a few days later, on July 8, he would meet his death on this same Madrid front. Among others Pollitt met were Frank Ryan and Malcolm Dunbar.

Frank Ryan, big, always cheerful, a magnetic personality, had an outstanding record in the Irish Republican Movement. He and his friend Paddy O'Daire had represented the Irish Republican Army at the founding congress of the League against Imperialism in 1927. In 1934 they helped form the Republican Congress Party, whose slogan was "Workers and Working Farmers, Unite! On to the Workers Republic!"

But in two years it had faded out and in November 1936 both were among the first Irish Volunteers for Spain. On meeting him Pollitt exclaimed, "My word, Frank, you've lost some weight since I last saw you." He replied, "When you last saw me in London, I asked you if it took a long time to walk to Spain. Well, it does, and how long my waist line will tell. Believe me, there's no straight road and no road goes down hill all the way, but it's good to be here with the boys."

Malcolm Dunbar and his pals were "full of beans though drenched to the skin for there had been the worst thunder storm ever and the boys in the trenches were up to their waists in water. But rain could not wash their smiles away when letters and Woodbines were handed out. One comrade got a packet of Players, the way the others crowded round him you would think I had taken him the Crown Jewels straight from the Coronation."

The Spanish Communist Party had proposed to the Socialists the formation of one united working-class party. Pollitt saw the enthusiastic response at three mighty demonstrations in Madrid where Socialists and Communists spoke in favour. He then set out to visit all the British wounded, they were in eight hospitals. He chatted with George Turnhill of Worksop, Patterson of Glasgow, Learmouth of Motherwell, William Watson and Danny Boyle and Pat McIlroy of Dublin.

In one dimly-lit ward a nurse asked if he would speak to Arthur Raven,[29] one of the first Americans to volunteer. "How are you, I am very glad to see you", said Pollitt as he took his hand. The reply was, "Comrade Pollitt, I have seen your photo in the American *Daily Worker*, I am very glad to take your hand, but now I shall never see you". Pollitt bent down and saw that he was blind. "A hand grenade blew my eyes out", he said, "I can't fight in Spain any more, but back in New York I can tell the people what fascism has done in Spain." Pollitt wrote, "I am not ashamed to say that tears streamed down my cheeks, I could not find words to reply. What could one say? Never again to see flowers, one's children, the blue sky, a bird rising to pour out its melody. This is what lies in front of Arthur Raven, yet with sublime and indomitable courage he wants to get back to America to continue the struggle against fascism." "Moving down this ward I saw Ron Hurd, a Canadian well known on the Liverpool waterfront. 'Fancy seeing you,' he said, 'and fancy me lying here, after going through all the February battle and then getting knocked down by a lorry!' "

Elsewhere Pollitt saw another Canadian, Jack Brent, shot in the base of the spine, the legs paralysed. Skilful treatment was bringing back the use of his limbs. "I went to his bedside but he was in such terrible pain it was impossible for either of us to speak. The comrade with us said, 'I know what he wants to ask—how has the Annemasse meeting between the two Internationals gone?' "[30] Pollitt was "asked this question everywhere, for all the Battalion instinctively knew that if the united strength of the

Communist and Socialist Internationals were used, victory would be achieved."

Back in Valencia Pollitt was told of another comrade, McLerie of Glasgow, who for 4½ months had been in a Spanish hospital but untraced by the Battalion. Pollitt went back specially to Madrid to see him and found him recovering but unable to fight again. In the same room was a German, both eyes covered with a shade. He also asked about Annemasse and why the British Labour Party was so opposed to the united front with the Communists? Pollitt explained but wrote, "I would rather have left it to J. S. Middleton and Dr. Dalton to answer for themselves."

Hundreds of wounded Spanish Republicans were in this hospital. Pollitt waited in the entrance to the wards to get an idea of the spirit of the visitors. "They streamed in and eagerly rushed to the bedside of their loved ones. With what pride they greeted them! Every visitor, from the oldest mother to the youngest child, raised the clenched fist with the exultant cry 'Salud!' "

Returning to Valencia Pollitt passed the evacuation lorries taking women and children out of the danger zone. "In one village a lorry had broken down. Sitting on what passes for a pavement women and children weeping bitterly looked back in the direction of Madrid and the homes and relatives they had lost. The villagers offered food from their scanty store to those driven from their homes." "A lovely little lad was sitting there. I speak no Spanish, but I could not resist stroking his head, trying to convey sympathy and a pledge to do more to help the Spanish people."

"Everywhere I was struck with the regard and love for the Soviet Union. On barricades, hoardings and walls are the words 'Viva U.S.S.R.' Sir Walter Citrine, H. N. Brailsford and Fenner Brockway may not like the Soviet Union but the Spanish people have no illusions as to which country has shown solidarity in their hour of need. Had the Spanish Government been strong enough to take decisive measures against saboteurs, spies and traitors as the Soviet Government has, the civil war would have been ended long ago—or more correctly it would never have started. But this is one of the truths that are unpalatable to our sentimental Liberals and pseudo-revolutionaries who prate about 'the pacifist technique of revolution'."

"The whole military might of fascism, the most devilish instruments of death sent to Franco by Hitler and Mussolini have failed to destroy the morale of the Madrid population but instead have inspired them with a fiercer determination than ever to be avenged for every crime that has been suffered. Sorrow and tears there are in Madrid but also a holy anger and a relentless will, moulded and steeled in this fiery furnace of Fascist war and terrorism."

"Bombing and shelling has affected the health of all the population, especially of expectant and nursing mothers. Babies eagerly clutch at breasts that are either dry or yield milk like water with no nourishment. A comrade I met in February told me with what joy he and his wife looked forward to the birth of their first baby. In June I met him again and asked after them. He said 'Better if it had never been born. My wife has no milk, we cannot get milk substitute.' The babies die in hundreds, those who survive bear the marks of appalling malnutrition. To think that a people fighting for the democratic peoples of the whole world cannot get even from democratic Britain milk foods to stop babies dying."

6. Brunete and Aragon, July to November 1937.

At midnight on July 6 the Battalion went into action in a Republican offensive in the mountains north west of Madrid. The British stormed Villanueva de la Canada street by street, Spanish brigades took the town of Brunete. But the attempt to capture the fortified key ridge failed due to fascist artillery and air superiority. Then the fascist counter-offensive slowly drove back the Republican line, retaking Brunete.

The British were involved with one brief interval in three weeks of continuous marching and fighting, mainly on steep hillsides, lacking shade, water and regular food in the broiling heat of the July Spanish sun. Bombing, air strafing and shelling went on day and night, often the ground was too rocky for trench digging. Attacks had to be made up slopes under sustained fire from fortified heights. The 300 British who stormed into Villanueva de la Canada numbered 37 when they came out of the line, and of these 27 were at once ordered to hospital.

Following Brunete the British Battalion went into rest billets in Mondejar, a village sixty kilometres east of Madrid. The XV Brigade was re-organised to consist of English-speaking volunteers, from Britain, Ireland, Canada, the U.S.A., Australia, and Cyprus plus a Spanish battalion.

At the end of August a Republican offensive was launched on the Aragon front in the direction of Saragossa. It was necessary to break through fortified fascist positions in the hills and villages stretching from the Ebro to Belchite. The key to the town of Quinto was Purburell Hill on which the British began the attack. They were held up by heavy fire from the fascist fortifications, later found to be of steel and concrete including tank traps and deep dugouts, the gun positions protected by barbed wire, all constructed by German military engineers. The Battalion Commander, the Irishman Peter Daly and the Commissar, the Welshman Jack Roberts, were both wounded on the first day, the former fatally. Next day the British resumed the attack and with the help of the anti-tank battery and heavier Republican artillery stormed the hill while other battalions occupied Quinto. During the main Republican attack on Belchite the British were for three days and nights continually in action in the hills near Medina to the north of Belchite. When that town fell the British had a spell in reserve.

In October the Republicans sought to break through the fascist entrenched lines before Fuentes del Ebro, fifteen miles from Saragossa, by a combined attack of planes, tanks and infantry. It was not successful, the British again lost their Commander, Harold Fry who had returned after being released from a Franco prison, and their Commissar, young Eric Whalley. The offensive petered out due to lack of reserves. The British returned to Mondejar and intensive training went on till in December they were moved to the north of Teruel.

7. Third visit, Teruel—December 1937

On his third visit, from December 15 to 27, Pollitt noted that the Peoples' Army was better equipped, its discipline and training improved, morale high and under unified command. Production in the war industries was rising. "A resolute purpose seems to have gripped the population. There is no longer romanticism or belief in easy victory, but a grim realisation that every available resource is needed to conquer." Great strides in education and culture, the light of learning and understanding spreading among millions previously kept in ignorance by reaction and clericalism. Fascist bombing and shelling of civilians continued, food and fuel were short, there were streams of refugees, but the slogan seen everywhere was "No compromise—crush Franco."

Pollitt was at International H.Q. in Albacete when news came that the Republicans had taken Teruel. The night was very cold and thick with fog when to the sound of bugles a spontaneous march began, soldiers and the people singing and cheering, the Republican colours ghostly in the fog. Next morning was bright, and every battalion and organisation in the district was in a triumphant march through the town. The whole Republic celebrated the victory, gained entirely by Spanish troops, a combined operation, unexpected by the enemy, and forestalling the much publicised Christmas offensive.

On their way to Teruel Pollitt and Bill Rust saw something of the difficulties facing the Republican troops in the environs of Teruel, great mountains, roads edged by precipices, hairpin bends, destroyed bridges, all deep in snow, freezing cold. When in sight of the city, the anti-aircraft guns began to bark, the car stopped, all ran to throw themselves flat away from the road, "bombs fell thick and fast. When the planes were driven off we went on. The city with its great high coloured buildings, the churches—every church in Spain seems to have been built with an eye on its military importance—and the bull ring standing out above all else, were bright under the now brilliant sun." Clouds of smoke were rising, the fascists were seeking to avenge their defeat by bombing Teruel out of existence. "Hundreds of women, young and old, carrying babies, dragging little children, were running for their lives. As they reached the Republican lorries ready to carry them to safety the look of terror on their faces immediately changed to relief and hope." On the outskirts of the city they could hear street fighting, the fascists were making a last stand. They were not allowed to go further.

From Teruel they drove to Madrid. "When you see the bombs the fascists have dropped—they come up to my shoulder and are fourteen inches across—your breath leaves you, they are terrifying, ghastly. That man can devise machines to fly like swallows in the sunlight and then suddenly fling down missiles which smash buildings and scatter blood and limbs in all directions brings a new meaning even to 'non-intervention'." Across the road a bookshop displayed 'Peter and Wendy'. "The tears came to my eyes. I saw all the children who will go and see Peter Pan this festive season. May they grow up and never witness what the children of Madrid have witnessed! But if we are to save them we must turn out the Chamberlains." Walking through the working-class quarters, destruction was everywhere. Shells boomed overhead and turning a corner "we saw, as though in Poplar or Cowcaddens, washing hung across the street —pants, knickers, a blouse, a shirt, socks, nappies—oh God, what a mad world it is. We turn to go, on a half destroyed wall is written 'They who talk of compromise are enemies of the people' and further on a banner, put up for November 7, 'The youth of Madrid greets the Soviet youth on the 20th anniversary of the Russian Revolution'."

An old friend of Pollitt's bumped into him: "It was captain Giovanni Galligaris of the Garibaldi Battalion of the International Brigade. When his six years in prison for belonging to the Italian Communist Party had expired the war in Spain broke out, and he felt it his duty to go at once to fight fascism. He was wounded four times, in the ear, the neck, the hip and the feet. He will never walk properly again. We embraced, recalled earlier meetings, pulled out photos of wife and children. 'Tell your people' he said 'that the people of Italy are not all for Mussolini.' I looked at his wounds and thought, By Christ, they aren't."

Leaving Madrid, they saw many soldiers getting into trucks, off to the front. "One was embracing his wife, his baby, his mother. She had the last kiss, she clung to him. I could read her thoughts. This was the child she had borne, reared, watched play in the busy streets, and loved. Now he was going, perhaps to live, perhaps to die. He shook himself free, climbed into the truck, while wife and mother raised their clenched fists and cried 'No Pasaran'."

At the British Battalion, resting behind the Aragon front, Pollitt's first meeting was with the anti-tank battery, consisting of three 45 mm guns with a seven mile range, and manned by forty picked youngsters. Its first commander was Malcolm Dunbar with Hugh Slater as political commissar. The former was promoted to the Staff of the XV Brigade, and then to the Division, Slater became commander. When Pollitt arrived Slater was in hospital with fever but "found his share of Players as good a dose as the best doctor's medicine." A concert followed the meeting, "Everybody vied with everybody else to do a turn." A series of meetings followed, all battalions of the Brigade, British, Canadian, American and Spanish, were eager to see and hear Pollitt.

The British were now commanded by Fred Copeman, Bill Alexander was adjutant, Wally Tapsell political commissar. Its leading Company named after Major Clement Atlee M.P., leader of the Labour Party, who with Ellen Wilkinson M.P. and Philip Noel Baker M.P. had visited Spain in the autumn, was commanded by Sam Wild, back from a spell in Manchester to recover from wounds. There was an exhilarating battalion parade, with the banners of the Republic, the battalion banner sent from Britain and a banner given by General Miaja, commander of Madrid. The Brigade General, an old and tried Yugo-Slav revolutionary, Lt. Colonel Copic, and Pollitt took the salute at the march past. Then speeches, from Copic on the past achievements and future tasks of the Battalion; from Pollitt on the position in Britain and the Aid Spain campaign now joined by the Labour Party. The day concluded with a dinner, at which veal cutlets appeared from an undisclosed source. Then songs—Copic sang Italian and Mexican folk songs in a clear impressive voice, American, Canadian, Yugo-Slav, Cuban, Spanish and Irish comrades followed. Toward midnight they adjourned to the village cinema where British and Spanish were holding a festival. More songs, flamencos and Spanish peasant dances, the British with 'Goodnight My Love'. Then with raised fists "everyone joined in that grand song 'The Internationale', sung in a medley of languages. We could not understand each other but we knew that the sacred words bound us in the common cause. And so ended a great night."

The Teruel victory had raised spirits in the hospitals too. At the American hospital Pollitt was greeted by everyone who could walk or be pushed in chairs into the yard. The vote of thanks for his speech was proposed by a French comrade, seconded by a Spaniard, and supported by an Englishman and an American. Next to the hospital at Huete, taken over and supplied with equipment and staff by the British Medical Aid, Dr. Tudor Hart in charge. If at all possible British wounded were sent to this hospital to be well cared for and helped to recovery. A Christmas atmosphere pervaded Huete, decorations, paintings and presents for children.

The British also had under their wing a convalescent home in what had been a convent at Valedeganga. Here Pollitt found Len and Lilian Kenton of Whitechapel, Lilian specialising in orthopaedic treatment. Under her instructions the patients had fitted up a kind of gymnasium with appliances for various exercises to recover the use and strength of limbs. The political commissar was Frank Ayres who was surprised to hear Harry recall the occasion when they first met fifteen years before. "There were also some lads whose morale was down, a frame of mind which could lead to desertions, our job was to get them back to a soldierly outlook. Harry did not have a formal meeting or set speech, but a little gathering and a friendly talk. After this came quite a turn in their attitude. He always had this very interested, kindly, personal touch, never shouting or giving orders."[31] "One incident showed that even Pollitt's memory was not infallible. We had a badly wounded Canadian comrade, an expert mechanic. On the way to recovery he fixed up all kind of gadgets such as a stove and chimney made of tin cans. It not only worked but according to Pollitt it was the warmest stove he met in all his visit. The Canadian had completed the reconstruction of an old motor car, improvising for the lack of proper tools and spare parts. The day Pollitt arrived the engine was running for the first time. Harry was very interested in the Canadian and his gadgets, asked how he came to be in Spain and so on, putting it all down in his vest pocket notebook. But when the pamphlet on this visit reached us, the Canadian was furious to find his achievements credited to someone else. Either Harry had misremembered or the printer had misread. The pamphlet said 'Williamson', it should have been 'Tazzaman'."[32]

On Christmas Eve it was dark at 7 a.m. at Tarrazona, where new English speaking recruits and selected Spaniards went through training for the Battalion. The platoons were on parade in the village square, to the sound of bugles the red, gold and purple flag of the Republic was hoisted and saluted. The parade marched past the Commander, the American Major Johnson and Pollitt, and into a public hall where Pollitt spoke.[33]

From Tarrazona to Benicassim on the coast where more convalescents were planning Christmas festivities. Here was George Watkins with a badly wounded leg. Pollitt asked him "Weren't you told in London you were not old enough to fight in Spain?" "Yes", he replied, "but I was determined and I got here." He got to Spain by saying he was 22, his real age was 16.

Late on Christmas Eve Pollitt left Benicassim to drive through the night, he was due to spend Christmas Day with the Battalion. They lost their way and in a little village got out to make enquiries. "I saw a hammer and sickle sign on a wall and beside it a wall newspaper with a photo of Stalin. A light shone underneath a door, we knocked. We presented our credentials and were made welcome. It was the local branch of the Spanish Communist Party and the comrades were hearing a report of the Central Committee. A comrade took us to another house and was making us some supper when his wife came in, a young child in her arms, half asleep but saying 'Bombas, bombas, refugio, refugio.' We knew what was going through his little mind, the village was continually bombed, he thought the planes had come again and we were going down into the dugout for refuge. How long will this be allowed to go on? How long before the democratic people of Britain fulfil their responsibilities to Republican Spain?"

On Christmas day they missed the morning parade but arrived in time to see the giving of presents to the village children, amid great excitement. In other villages the Americans and Canadians were doing the same. Then the great event of the day, the Christmas dinner, the guests being the

General of the Division, the Brigade Staff, Professor J. B. S. Haldane, Harry Pollitt and Bill Rust. "After one look at Hookey Walker, the quartermaster, we knew by his serene smile that it was going to be some dinner. It certainly was. Where it all came from only God and Hookey know, and the secret is secure with them both." After the meal, the toasts, the revolutionary songs of all nationalities. "Then the individual efforts, Lieutenant George Fletcher, his chair on the table, 'One Finger, One Thumb keep moving', and did we get into a mess trying to follow? I'll say we did. Quiet Dr. Bradsworth of Birmingham singing 'How can a guineapig show he's pleased if he hasn't got a tail to wag?' An Australian nurse with 'The Shade of the Old Apple Tree', comrade Gibbons from Canada with 'The Rose of Tralee'. Then the old time choruses 'I saw the Old Homestead', 'The Old Mill by the Stream' and 'Nellie Dean'. Oh Gertie Gitana, you have had some music hall audiences singing that song! I have heard it after closing time in streets all over Britain but never was it sung as we sang it this Christmas night. We sang on, Sam Wild with 'Frankie and Johnnie', Bill Rust 'Come Landlord fill the Flowing Bowl', Wally Tapsell showing that the Carl Rosa Opera had missed a treasure. Then we adjourned to the local Ball. The comrades had organised a band Jack Hylton would have been jealous of if he had heard it. You couldn't move, let alone dance. So the songs began again, I had to make another little speech, the ball ended with cheers for victory for Republican Spain, loud enough for Franco to hear in Salamanca. We went round the billets and back to headquarters to say farewell."

On this visit Pollitt had more time to acquaint himself with the organisation of the Albacete base. The town was convenient but not impressive. Fairly good roads radiated from it, east to Valencia and Alicante, south to Murcia and Jaen, west to Madrid. It was on the Madrid-Valencia railway line. Mountain peaks were visible almost all round it. Easily accessible villages on its radial roads were utilised as battalion training centres or rest billets, the Brigade Staffs were in the town itself.

He found British representatives in most of these. Lt. Cummings, still convalescent from wounds, at the General Staff building, discretely tucked away in a side street; Harry Evans in Transmissions; Bill Rowe in the recently organised cadres section; John Mahon in the Political Commisariat; the surgeon Dr. Crome in the Brigade hospital; a wizard mechanic at the Autopark, but curiously enough none at Supplies. A British plumber had been and gone leaving behind him a shower yard which would take up to two dozen men at once. Tarrazona, the British training base was to the north. The favourite resting base was Madrigueras, where excellent relations were established with the local people.

8. Fourth visit—Catalonia, April 1938.

In January 1938 the fascist counter-attack on Teruel was spearheaded by planes and heavy artillery poured in by Hitler and Mussolini. The British were in action in defence of the city and later 100 miles to the north near Segura de los Banos in an effort to threaten the fascist left flank, and were commended for their conduct by the General in command. After a period in reserve they went for rest at the end of February but were hastily plunged back into the line when on March 8 Franco launched a new offensive. The fascist powers were now openly sending whole military formations to Franco: 800 planes, 1,000 pieces of artillery, hundreds of tanks and armoured cars, 50,000 Italians, 30,000 Moors and 10,000 Germans were hurled against the Republic's Eastern front. It broke, the fascist flood swept through Belchite, Alcaniz, Caspe and on toward the sea. From March 10 the British were continuously in action for six days and nights, retaining their cohesion under most difficult conditions, retreat alternated with entrenched resistance to infantry attacks supported by heavy bombing and shelling. On the 17th they went to rest and refit at Batea. Republican reinforcements were arriving in large numbers, Generals Lister and Modesto were now in command.

On March 17 a leaflet signed by Harry Pollitt was issued in Britain in half a million copies.[34] It quoted Chamberlain's remark in the House the previous day, "We can't burn our fingers", and continued: "That same night in Barcelona thousands of men, women and children were torn, mangled and burned by bombs from Hitler's and Mussolini's planes." Pollitt asked "Who is responsible for those planes being allowed to pour into Spain?" and answered, "Chamberlain, who has covered up the fascist invasion of Spain and refuses to respond to the demand which Labour, Liberals and all who stand by British traditions are making: Let the Spanish Government have the arms it needs! Call a halt to the ghastly infamies of the Italian and German butchers." Chamberlain had refused to stand by France in its desire to help Spain and Pollitt warned "The fascist war against European peace and democracy is in full swing. If it is to be stopped it is now or never. If we allow Spain to be sacrificed by Chamberlain to Hitler and Mussolini, this means the fascist encirclement of France and menaces the very existence of an independent Britain."

On their way to the front on March 26 the British were ambushed by enemy tanks at Calaceite, 150 were killed or wounded, 140 captured, the rest broken up. Some 60 joined a mixed force which rallied to prevent the fascists debouching from the Sierra de Pandols on to the roads to Mora de Elbro and Tortosa. In an inferno of fire from artillery, tanks, planes and machine guns they held out all day while vital war material was withdrawn, the Ebro bridge blown up and the Republican line reformed. During the night they got away, crossed the Ebro and rejoined their division. Wounded men returned from hospitals, the base at Albacete had been cleared, new recruits came from Britain. The Battalion was again 300 strong when its Diary[35] recorded on April 14 a surprise visit from Harry Pollitt. He "had hurried over from Britain immediately on hearing of the

Battalion's losses—a characteristic action, the boys appreciated it. As usual he brought a pile of letters and took replies for home. The boys know they can trust Harry to do a job for them. Not once has he let them down." The record continues, "Before he left Harry addressed the Battalion. He reminded us how often during the first seven years of the Soviet Republic its death had been prophesied, and pointed to its strength today as the answer to those who thought the days of the Spanish Republic were numbered. His speech helped to strengthen the spirit of confidence"

Driving to Tortosa Pollitt saw "a stream of refugees, a ghastly procession, carts filled with goods and chattels, men, women and children walking alongside. The looks on their faces penetrate one's very soul. Anguish, pain, grief, leaving land and homes into which generations have put their blood and sweat. But they prefer leaving to risking the future offered by Franco." Next day in Tortosa news came that the fascists had reached the coast at Vinaroz some 30 miles to the south. The Republic was cut in two. Pollitt wrote: "Calmness and order reign. The Republican soldiers are energetically carrying out their jobs. The advance of the interventionists has been due to machines not men."[36]

At Tortosa, "Not a single house, shop or building remains intact. Beams, girders, rafters, ruins, in the most fantastic shapes. Once a lovely town, now a huge graveyard. Such walls as were left gave the impression that any moment they would crash to the ground. On one a pot of still blooming flowers leaned crazily, it seemed trying to give sweetness to a town where only bitterness could be found. In a small mechanic's shop the lathes, forge and anvil were twisted but on a beam a clock was intact, a calendar advertised the goods of John Bedford & Sons, Sheffield. A worker's house was dust and debris, a smashed rabbit cage. I picked up an exercise book, that of a child learning one, two, three, four. I was hit as hard as if it had been a book of my Jean. In this mass of death and destruction I saw the face of Chamberlain, heard his phrase 'We can't burn our fingers'. But his fingers and his policy have helped to burn and destroy Tortosa.

"Over the ruins of what was once the main public building of the town, in honour of the Republic's anniversary, the flag of the Republic was flying, a challenge to the world. Round a corner at an entrance to what had been an air raid shelter, a few old women were sitting. They would not leave the town where they were born, fallen in love, had their children. On a heap of rubble a woman clutched a six-months babe on her knees while she ravenously devoured a piece of bread. One look and I knew this poor soul had gone mad. I wish every person in England could see Tortosa, for then surely they would sweep Chamberlain from power."

On his way back to Barcelona Pollitt spent a few minutes at the H.Q. of the Commander of Army of the Ebro, Colonel Jose Modesto. "In candlelight and within sound of the heavy fascist guns, Modesto tired but confident was tracing the military position on the map. He said to me 'Tell the British people that so long as one piece of Republican Spain is left, the war is not over'."[37]

In Barcelona Pollitt wrote an article under the significant heading "If we fail the Spanish people now, Who will help us?" From his window he saw out in the Mediterranean "right opposite the villa of Mr. Leeper the British representative, the great battle cruiser *Hood*, at anchor, small craft moving around her. In Tarragona and Reuss the people flee from death from the fascist planes. Death comes from the Balearic Isles. Death comes in the form of 'non-Intervention'. The Union Jack protects it and in doing so dooms people like you and me to the same misery, pain and death."[38]

In the autumn the food shortage became acute. Supporting the international appeal for food Pollitt said: "Republican Spain fights on, but it is hungry. The winter is coming. Women and children not only look at the sky in dread, they look on tables that lack food. Workers faint at their machines, exhausted for lack of food. Republican Spain is getting one-fifth of the food it needs. Queues form for meals, many are turned away, the food supply is exhausted. Women search dustbins for scraps. Malnutrition takes its toll. Babies pine and die for lack of milk."[39]

9. Fifth visit—Ebro, August 1938.

From April to June the British were undergoing intensive training. Visitors included the Spanish Foreign Secretary, Alvarez del Vayo and the Indian leaders Jawarharlal Nehru and Krishna Menon. During this period Pollitt received a copy of the "Book of the XV Brigade", with an inscription signed by the Brigade Commander V. Copic and the Political Commissar John Gates. It read "To Harry Pollitt, Spain's best friend in Britain. We present to you this short and incomplete history of the XV Brigade, a history in which you have played a great part. Your relentless fight against fascism has given inspiration to many heroes featured in this book who have fought for Spain's independence against foreign intervention. June 10 1938."

At 1 a.m. on July 25 the British were in the vanguard of the Republican surprise attack over the 80 yards wide 20 feet deep Ebro, most of them rowing across near Mora in small boats with padded rowlocks. The last platoons came over a hastily assembled pontoon bridge, already under fire from fascist planes. The British went on for fifteen miles to the outskirts of Gandesa. The key to the town was the heavily fortified Hill 481. For six days they fought to take it, but failed. They had only machine guns and mortars, for the heavy guns and tanks could not cross the Ebro. They had a week in reserve. The fascist counter attack began and they were rushed to defend Hill 666. They held it, with heavy casualties, for eleven days and nights, under continuous bombardment and attack. On August 26 they were withdrawn, on the 28th Pollitt arrived.

After crossing the frontier he was "stuck at the Spanish customs office, wondering how to get to the Ebro with my two great suitcases filled with cigarettes, letters and parcels for the British Battalion. After sitting on the roadside for some hours hoping for a lift, a car drove up, I thought I recognised comrade Jose Diaz, the General Secretary of the C.P. of Spain. Knowing he had been seriously ill, I was not quite sure it was him, but before I could reach him, he called out my name. He told me he had been urged to accept an invitation to go for treatment in the Soviet Union. I explained my difficulties and my troubles were ended. He put his car at my disposal, telling the driver what to do in Barcelona. Then we embraced, he passed over the frontier on his way to Moscow."[40]

In Barcelona Pollitt recorded that the Negrin Government had removed from their positions an insignificant minority who wanted to capitulate and that the mood of the people in the factories, houses, cafes, the rank and file army men, the Generals, the trade union, Socialist and Communist leaders, the members of the Government, everywhere was "We fight on, we will never give in" and always the question "How long are we to fight alone?"

Long before reaching the Ebro, they heard the thud, thud, thud of continuous bombing. "At Mora la Nueva and Mora de Ebro, not a house is standing. Civilians not killed have long been evacuated. But the bombing goes on. Other fascist planes drop leaflets 'Surrender'! Soldiers tear them up in scorn, shaking fists at the planes. Fists are no match for bombs, but behind the fist is that unconquerable spirit which cannot be crushed. In another village, bombed to bits, the terrible smell of rotting bodies, I vomit. Then the bombers are overhead, we throw ourselves on the ground. Close by a peasant, his wife and two children do the same. No time to stop that mule going round and round turning the irrigation buckets of a well. I watch it, fascinated. Round and round to give life to the vines, while death strikes from above." "Nearing Corbera we see clouds of dust and debris as the fascist heavy guns bombard the town. Tears stream down the face of our driver. He explains that he was born in these parts, and when the fascists took the village where his mother and sister were hiding in a cellar, they shot them. Nobody spoke. What could be said? The country was entrancing, on all sides vineyards thickset with green or black grapes, fig trees, nectarines, nuts, apples. A year's toil come to harvest but no hands to gather it. The peasantry gone, from dawn to dusk the fascist bombers, the only harvester, Death."

At the staff of the XV Brigade Pollitt asked what made possible the recent successful crossing of the Ebro and got the reply, "Organisation and audacity on the part of the troops who with great enthusiasm charged the Franco artillery, car park and aviation, taking them by surprise. In one day we reached the command posts of a fascist division." After lunch Pollitt went to the Battalion, talked individually with as many men as possible and in the late afternoon under some trees, with enemy aviation overhead, gave a picture of the international scene.[41]

The Battalion had just come from the front where for eleven days under continual fire by day and night they had repeatedly repulsed fascist attacks. "Their clothes were torn to shreds, they had a fortnight's beards. It was difficult to make out who was who. I thought—if only they could stand as they are now on the platform at the T.U.C. No speeches would be needed, the delegates would rise in their wrath and take action to force Chamberlain to alter his policy or be thrown out of office."

On the Ebro front Pollitt met once more, Sam Wild, George Fletcher, Paddy O'Daire, Bob Cooney, Hookey Walker, Hughie Barber. Then there was Lt. William Gregory of Nottingham Y.C.L. wounded for the third time. Asked what brought him to Spain he replied, "I hate fascism and was keen to fight it here". Councillor Tom Murray of Edinburgh and his brother, their sister Anne nursing somewhere in Spain; Ted Edwards, "the best handwriter I ever saw"; young Hanlon, son of a London taxi driver, wounded while driving an ammunition truck. "He had strict orders not to leave it. Nearing the front enemy bombers were overhead. Comrades shouted 'jump for it', he did in the nick of time, the truck went up in a direct hit. Jim Loban of the Vale of Leven had a beard that would make George Halkett gasp. I hope his mother got the letter I wrote as soon as I got back. I also met the comrade who in London hoisted over the German Embassy a banner with the words 'Release Thaelmann', stretched an anti-fascist slogan across Fleet Street as the King and Queen passed, and raised an anti-fascist banner on the roof of the Law Courts." Returning to Divisional H.Q. "We met the Staff, what youngsters they are! I am old enough to be their father. They are the new Spain. They are rejoicing in the honour conferred by Negrin on Modesto for the Ebro offensive, an honour for all who took part in it."

In the drive back to Barcelona Pollitt had the company of Peter Kerrigan, then *Daily Worker* correspondent in Spain. Pollitt recalling that Kerrigan had been a leading political commissar in the early days of the XV Brigade said that his despatches to the paper were got "not by watching from afar, but in it up to the neck, bringing in wounded, jumping out of a wagon a minute before it was bombed, swimming the Ebro to get his reports rushed to Barcelona and phoned to London. Tireless and fearless."

10. Fall of the Republic

In September the British alternated between intense fighting as shock troops rushed to hold the line where the fascist attack was fiercest, and brief periods of respite. Their last action was on September 23, for Negrin had decided on the withdrawal of the Internationals. On October 18 the Brigades, the British Battalion among them, marched through Barcelona, the people lining the streets to cheer them on their way out of Spain. The British reached London on December 7. Most of the other nationalities languished for weary months in the barbed wire pens in which they were kept by the French Government.

Meanwhile the fascist powers were pouring in whole brigades, divisions, batteries, tank regiments, air squadrons, to aid Franco. On November 15 the Republicans had to recross the Ebro. In January 1939 a new offensive broke the Republican front, on the 14th the fascists were in Tarragona, on the 26th in Barcelona, on February 9 at the frontier.

At this moment of anguish Pollitt wrote,[42] "It is Chamberlain whose policy of refusing international rights to the Spanish Government has made it possible for Barcelona to fall into Franco's hands. In the defence of Catalonia against foreign invaders, as fresh Republican troops went into the front line trenches they had to take rifles from the men they relieved and collect others from the dead and wounded. Franco had nine pieces of heavy artillery to every one the Republicans had; twenty anti-tank guns to every one Republican; five light machine guns to one, fifty anti-aircraft guns to one, fifteen planes to each one Republican. Against this tornado of metal and high explosive, flesh and blood cannot stand. But Spain is not conquered yet, the Republican flag still flies over one third of her territory. Given arms to equip the thousands offering their lives to keep Spain free, the Spanish government can yet drive the fascist invaders out of Barcelona, out of Catalonia, out of Spain," and he called for the use of every possible form of industrial and political action to force the Chamberlain government to allow arms to reach Spain. He gave a grim warning, soon to be realised: "Chamberlain's policy is taking us every day nearer to war, in circumstances when Britain may very well be isolated in her hour of need."

After the end of Catalonia, the Negrin government endeavoured to continue the war from Madrid and Valencia. On March 5 a plot by army and navy officers came to a head, a group headed by Colonel Casado and General Miaja seized power in Madrid and opened the front to Franco.

On March 7 Pollitt spoke to a crowded and deeply disturbed meeting in Lambeth.[43] He declared that Chamberlain bore the main responsibility for the fall of the Spanish Republic, and went on: "After the fall of Barcelona, the British and French Governments exercised maximum pressure on Negrin for unconditional surrender. With British naval help Franco was allowed to occupy Minorca. Then Franco was recognised. The prearranged resignation and flight of the President of the Republic, Azana, took place. A fascist rising in Cartagena gave the officers of the Republican Fleet an excuse to sail to Africa and surrender it. The Casado-Miaja coup in Madrid then opened the offensive not against Franco but against Negrin and the Communist Party. The defection of Miaja came as a surprise to those in Britain who knew him as the successful defender of Madrid. But observers had noted that during the Republican offensive on the Ebro, no supporting offensive was developed in central Spain by Miaja."

Pollitt continued, "There are those who cannot understand the apparently sudden collapse of the resistance, but workers will know how to approach the problem correctly"; and he drew an analogy with the experiences of prolonged strikes when those who say "It has gone on long enough" become "a prey to every lying rumour that the employers circulate". But he emphasised that even after the losses the Republic had sustained, the Casado–Miaja coup could not have been carried through without the open intervention of Chamberlain and Daladier against the Republic. To those who asked whether all the sacrifice of life and effort had been in vain, Pollitt answered, "If one thing has been proved since 1933 it is that had fascism not been resisted, it would be today riding rough-shod over the world. The Austrians were right to resist in 1934, the Abyssinians were right to resist in 1935, the Spanish a thousand times right." Their prolonged resistance had "awakened millions to political consciousness, to recognition of the danger of fascism, and had evoked the greatest demonstration of international solidarity the world has ever seen", the sending of food and medicine, raising money and above all the International Brigades of volunteers.

Pollitt declared that Negrin was right in wanting to continue the struggle and that resources to do so existed, "a powerful army, war materials, strong defensive positions, changes in the international situation". That was why Chamberlain's nominee, Casado, was required to hand over to Franco the political and military leaders of the Negrin government and of the Communist Party of Spain, why thousands of Communists were arrested and the working-class quarters menaced by tanks and artillery. "Every sincere anti-fascist understands that the leaders who left Spain in order to avoid being shot acted in the present and future interests of the Spanish people." He stressed the urgency of intensifying the struggle against Chamberlain, "responsible for the continued advance of fascism" and against those "Labour leaders who see bastion after bastion of democracy go down, and yet refuse the unity which can save the working class and the people of Britain."

It was a dark hour, but Pollitt, confident that the fascist triumph was temporary, declared, "Fascism is not all conquering. It is not all powerful. It can be driven back and defeated. But the conditions for this are working-class unity and the People's Front."

CHAPTER 17

THE ROAD TO MUNICH

1. *Unity campaign, 1937.* 2. *C.P. and I.L.P., 1937.* 3. *The Left Book Club.* 4. *Aid for the prisoners of fascism.* 5. *China, 1937.* 6. *Working-class unity and the People's Front.* 7. *Austria, March 1938.* 8. *Munich.* 9. *Caribbean cruise.*

1. UNITY CAMPAIGN 1937.

In autumn 1936, under pressure of the events in Spain, Pollitt and William Mellor, Editor of *Tribune*, discussed informally the possibilities of united action by the Socialist League, the I.L.P. and the Communist Party.[1] Sir Stafford Cripps, who had set up the Socialist League to counteract the dominant right wing of the Labour Party, secured agreement in principle and chaired negotiations on a declaration of joint aims. "Cripps proved admirable in getting us working together after a long period of hammering each other." To influence the Socialist League against the Communist Party, the Labour E.C. issued an appeal "for Party loyalty", but the Socialist League conference decided for unity rather than "loyalty" to Labour's right wing, and on January 18 1937, the joint Declaration was signed.[2] It set out the objectives of joint activity by the three organisations to secure unity of all sections of the working class against fascism, reaction, war and the National Government, for the workers' immediate demands, and for the return of a Labour Government as the next stage in the advance to working-class power. Unity was to be built within the framework of a democratised Labour Party and trade union movement. And unity, it was declared, would defeat fascism and save the peace. This unity would bring support to the colonial peoples fighting imperialism and, at home, improve the position of unemployed, employed and pensioners, bring in nationalisation of the mines and control over the banks and Stock Exchange, and make the rich pay for social amelioration. The declaration concluded: "We stand for action, for attack, for the ending of retreat, for building the strength, unity and power of the working-class movement."

The campaign began with a great demonstration in Manchester, when the Free Trade Hall, the Princes Theatre and the Theatre Royal were all packed on the same night. The speakers were Cripps, Mellor and Horrabin of the Socialist League, Maxton and Brockway of the I.L.P. and Pollitt, for the Communist Party.

Cripps wanted them all to dine with him in the Midland Hotel, so Pollitt declined the usual big Sunday dinner at his mother's. At the Midland, Mellor and Pollitt sat opposite each other, and their "faces were a study in still life as Cripps ordered his usual frugal salad, Maxton a poached egg on toast, Horrabin thin bread, butter and banana. Mellor winked at me, I winked back and ordered steak and chips and a pint; Mellor said 'the same'. Alas, the head waiter gravely explained 'the bar and grill room do not open until seven o'clock, Sir'. So gone were my fond dreams and we had to be satisfied with poached egg on toast. At that moment of agony, my mother and Henry Parsons were passing the hotel on their way to the meeting, she saying scornfully, 'There they are, dining and wining on the backs of the workers'."[3]

The meetings responded with enthusiasm to the call for united action. Among Pollitt's points were: "The campaign is not directed against the Labour Party. On the contrary. It is to bring all sections into what should be a united, all-embracing and all-powerful Labour Party." . . . "In blood and tears, in prison and concentration camp, in torture and the headsman's axe, workers in other lands have paid the price of disunity. Let us learn before it is too late." . . . "If Spanish, French, Italian, German, Polish and Belgian workers now find common agreement, why can't British workers?"[4]

The Labour Party Executive, stung by the successes of the campaign, disaffiliated the Socialist League and later declared membership of it incompatible with Labour Party membership. The Socialist League then dissolved so that its members could work within the Labour Party. Pollitt, while not responsible for this decision, thought it preferable to expulsion from the Labour Party.

Throughout 1937 the campaign held crowded meetings all over the country. Pollitt estimated that its influence was reflected in the election of Cripps, Laski, Pritt and Ellen Wilkinson to the Labour Party Executive in October 1937, a result which gave greater scope for progressive activity by local Labour Parties.

The Labour Party Executive warned that members associating with the campaign faced expulsion, and in March 1938 gave notice of intent to expel Cripps, Aneurin Bevan, George Strauss, Commander Young and Trevelyan. Bevan and Strauss withdrew, Cripps maintained his position but fought at the Conference on constitutional, not political, grounds. Pollitt watching from the gallery "felt he had lost the chance of a lifetime, and it was a mistake that Bevan did not defend him."[5] Those who did not recant were expelled.

Pollitt thought "every minute of the unity campaign was worth while, it gave new hope to tens of thousands, helped to strengthen solidarity and to revive faith in Socialist principles". Cripps was "a good comrade to work with. In his Chambers one afternoon the telephone rang, he kept saying with increasing emphasis, 'No!' When he finished he told me that he had decided to devote himself to political activities and not to take any more legal work. The phone call was from one of the largest banks asking him to take a case for them at fees amounting to £35,000."

As speakers, Pollitt found Cripps and Maxton very different. "Cripps paid as much attention to preparing his political speeches as he did to his legal briefs. He was clear, logical, making full use of facts and arguments, but I thought a little cold in tone, which was the last thing he wanted to be. Maxton I never saw either make notes or speak from them. When travelling together to a meeting, Cripps, Mellor and I would polish up our notes; Maxton would make jokes and tell us not to be too serious. He seemed to wait till he saw the audience, felt its pulse, and then relied on his experience. Usually it came off, especially when he knew the correct moment to thrust his hand across his brow and sweep back his locks of black hair."[6]

2. C.P. AND I.L.P., 1937.

Relations between the Communist Party and the Independent Labour Party improved in the first months of the Unity Campaign, then deteriorated when the I.L.P. added hostility to the Popular Fronts in France and Spain to its continued criticism of the Communist International.

The I.L.P. did not support the British Battalion in Spain, but sent a small group of its own volunteers to Catalonia where they worked with the P.O.U.M.[7], generally considered to be Trotskyite. To this party the Spanish struggle was "not between democracy and fascism but ... between fascism and socialism"; it opposed the Popular Front and called for a "government of workers and left petty bourgeois parties". In May 1937, the P.O.U.M. took part in an unsuccessful armed putsch in Barcelona to overthrow the Catalan government.

In November, the Communist Party stated "it is impossible for the Communist Party and supporters of working-class unity to co-operate with the I.L.P."[8]

3. THE LEFT BOOK CLUB.[9]

The Left Book Club made a considerable contribution to the struggle against war and fascism. In 1935 Pollitt discussed with the manager of the Workers' Bookshop in London the latter's proposal to form such a club, but they could not find the necessary capital. It was Victor Gollancz, the publisher, who in spring 1936 launched the Left Book Club, to publish a book a month, with himself, John Strachey and Harold Laski to choose the books. By the end of the year there were 31,850 members. Discussion groups and other activities were stimulated by the Club's monthly *Left News*, and in 1937 there were 600 groups. Pollitt was among the speakers at each of the Club's three greatest public meetings, at the Albert Hall in February 1937, and again in 1938, and at the Empress Hall in April 1939, all packed to capacity.

At the first of these Pollitt made clear[10] that while the Club was not a communist organisation, "its publications and discussions revealed for the first time in Britain a hunger for Marxism." It brought forward new writers who "expressed in their creative writing an understanding of what Marxism means and are influencing sections to whom a short time ago the name of Marx was a bogey". He suggested that the Club should sometimes make a Marxist Classic the Book of the Month, but the idea was not taken up.

At that time the success of the People's Front in France was on all lips. Pollitt in his speech stressed that the political conditions in Britain were totally different. "Here the decisive majority of the population are industrial workers, the most class conscious are already organised industrially and politically. Our first job is to bring about unity within our Labour Movement." This unity would be an irresistible magnet for all the progressive forces in Britain. There was a great field for the Club among professional people and the middle class. "Tens of thousands hitherto holding comfortable positions, and able to see their sons and daughters educated and similarly placed" now realised the problems of the distressed areas, of unemployment, and of war and fascism, and he suggested how Club members could influence such people.

A year later, in the same hall, Pollitt spoke of the Club groups "feeding and enlivening the existing Labour, Liberal, cultural, peace and professional movements," and called for books to arouse the social and moral conscience of the people, as Robert Blatchford had done with a million copies of *Merrie England*. At the same time there should be lighter literature. "All our books need not be leading articles in bound form. We have the romances, we have the thrills—Dimitrov's fight at the Leipzig trial, the workers' exploits in the Russian Revolution, the Long March of the Red Army in China, the heroism of our lads in Spain, the drama of our fight for socialism here. The stories of our own heroes, dramatised, told as a tale for our children, can provide our writers with enough material to make every newsagent's shop and bookseller a feeding place for the imagination of those who in time will see the political implications of what they read."[11]

The April 1939 platform was the broadest and most influential yet assembled by the Left.[12] It included David Lloyd George, who insisted that he should not be personally compromised by having to shake hands with Pollitt. "It was agreed that to avoid a meeting between us he should not come into the speakers' room till the very last moment, so he sat in his car outside. At the very last moment he came in. Then Sir Stafford Cripps, who knew all about the fuss that had been made, immediately went up to him and with fiendish delight said 'Allow me to introduce you to Mr.

Harry Pollitt'. It was a very, very cold hand that was extended to me. But when in 1941 I had an interview with him he said, 'You got a reception at the Empress Hall that any man would be proud of, and I apologise for my fears in meeting you on that occasion."

Pollitt was "very popular with V. G., the initials by which we were allowed to refer to Victor Gollancz, and got a lot of quiet laughs when travelling round the country with what was privately called 'the circus'. It was a delight to walk down the platform and see V. G. puffing at his cigar in a first-class carriage, while Muggins went piously to his third. Not that V. G. boggled at my going first, nothing would have given him greater pleasure, but I never did." "He was a terrific worker and when speaking would travel all night to be in his office by 8.30 a.m. In his car were hot water bottles and rugs galore. I would sit with the driver and he would stretch out at the back. If he had forgotten his cigars he would say when passing an R.A.C. hotel, 'Stop, Garrett, and get me a cigar'. I knew from experience that Garrett would come back with two, one for Victor, one for me, and Victor would say, 'That's right, I forgot Harry!' The more amusing the things that Victor said or did, the more unconscious of the fact he was. In Moscow he asked if I could arrange for him to meet Dimitrov. I did so, and Victor went off with a light in his eye to meet the hero of the Leipzig trial. The light shone brighter on his return. Asked how he had got on, he said with pride, 'Do you know, Harry, Dimitrov thinks about the Left Book Club the way I do'. I am sure we both slept soundly that night."

When war with Nazi Germany broke out in 1939 acute differences developed over the character of the war. Gollancz at first wished to maintain the Club as an open forum for all points of view, but abandoned the attempt. Anti-Soviet books began to be selected, Gollancz became suspicious of Communist influence in the Groups, and closed them down. The Club continued, with the heart gone out of it, till 1948.

In recollection, Pollitt said of the Club during 1936-39, "It rallied against fascism masses of people whom it would not have been possible to organise otherwise. The majority of the 115 books it published stimulated progressive political thought. It strengthened the bonds of international solidarity on behalf of the Spanish, Austrian, Chinese, Indian and Czechoslovak peoples. It helped to create a broad popular front and to strengthen the campaign for Labour Movement unity. It brought into political activity thousands who had not previously been to a political meeting or belonged to a political party." And he added, "Gollancz out of his great religious charity will forgive me if I now write that it was the work of the Communist Party which gave the Club its mass basis and enabled it to carry through its manifold activities."

4. AID FOR THE PRISONERS OF FASCISM.

Pollitt was tireless in action on behalf of the political prisoners in fascist gaols and camps.

Thaelmann

In March 1936 he appealed[13] on behalf of Ernst Thaelmann, the leader of the German Communist Party, arrested after the Reichstag fire and held in the Moabit dungeons. Pollitt wrote, "Just sit back and imagine those three years, every minute an hour, every hour a day, every day a year. The cries of the tortured, the defiant shouts of revolutionaries going to their death. Told your trial will begin tomorrow, then it is postponed, then a new indictment is ready, then that is withdrawn. What has forced these vacilations on the fascist ghouls? The worldwide demand that Thaelmann be freed. Why don't they bring Thaelmann to trial or publish the indictment? Because they fear another Leipzig Trial, another Dimitrov in the person of Thaelmann accusing them before the world!

"Comrades all, torture and death are not ever present visitors in our homes—they are in Hitler's prisons. Think of the agony of Richard Claus and John Scheer, secretaries of the German Communist Party, tortured before execution. Let an eye-witness speak. 'The fire in the stove was glowing red; they placed Scheer before it; they demanded a confession. Scheer made no reply. With rifle butts they pressed him against the red hot stove. Scheer cried out, he could be heard everywhere. When the cleaners entered later, they were struck by the stinking fumes of burnt flesh.'"

Pollitt repeated the words of Henri Barbusse. "We must win Thaelmann like a battle." "Organise for Thaelmann the same victory in the world fight against fascism that we secured for Georgi Dimitrov."

Gramsci and others

In the summer of 1937 Pollitt called for solidarity with the Italian anti-fascists. News had come of the death of Antonio Gramsci, the leader of the Italian Communist Party, in hospital, his health undermined by long years in Mussolini's dungeons. An amnesty announced in February did not apply to political prisoners. When they had served their sentences they were not released but deported to islands ravaged by tuberculosis. Pollitt drew attention to the Communist Terracini, 11 years in prison, the Socialist Pertini, 7 years, the Liberal Republican Roberto, 7 years, the woman Camilla Ravera, all deported and seriously ill. Pertini was taken off an island prison and imprisoned in Naples, accused of propaganda against Italian policy in Spain. Pollitt pointed out that he was typical of thousands of brave Italian men and women fighting fascism—soldiers refusing to go to Spain, sailors refusing to man ships carrying troops or munitions, sabotage in munitions factories, propaganda in the armed forces, money for the anti-fascist fight, volunteers for the Garibaldi Battalion of the International Brigade in Spain.[14]

5. China, 1937.

"You who read this, did you not shudder with horror at the accounts of Japanese bombers raining death and destruction upon innocent women and children in Nanking?" Thus began Pollitt's protest[15] at the murderous Japanese air onslaught on defenceless Chinese cities. Shanghai preceded Nanking, Nanking preceded Canton. "Thousands killed, thousands more wounded and mutilated, fires all over the city, red blood runs on the pavements, the maimed cry out in dreadful agony, little children raise their hands to the skies before life leaves them." Calling on the British people to act, he said, "We know the attitude of the Chamberlain Government, it will let this death and destruction go on, for it is anxious for Japan to strengthen its position in China, to become, as the *Daily Telegraph* said during the 1931 attacks on Manchuria, 'a bulwark against Bolshevism in the Far East'." He called for demonstrations to the Japanese Embassy and Consulates, for pressure on the Government to demand that the League of Nations act against Japan, for the trade unions to act to stop the loading or unloading of Japanese ships in British ports.

In December 1937 Southampton dockers refused to handle 200 tons of Japanese goods on the *Duchess of Richmond*. Local officials supported the men. When the ship returned to Canada, these goods were marked in large blue letters "Cargo refused by Southampton dockers". Pollitt approved a leaflet on this incident.[16] At Glasgow, dockers refused to unload Japanese goods from the *Letitia* and *Hector*. Union officials overruled them, but when unloaded the goods were largely useless, the hooks had been used rather carelessly. In January 1938 Middlesborough dockers refused to load iron for Japan on the *Haruna Maru* or the P. & O. *Bhutan*. On Jan. 31 the *Haruna Maru* docked in London, where the iron had been sent by rail. Pollitt, also Tom Mann at 81 years of age, joined in a dockland-wide appeal to black the ship, which sailed on Feb. 4 leaving the iron bars in their railway trucks.[17]

6. Working-class unity and the People's Front.

After the dissolution of the Socialist League and the breach with the I.L.P., the Communist Party launched a new "crusade" advocating unity against the threatening advance of fascism.[18] At Aberdeen in January 1938, Pollitt proposed that the Labour Party, the T.U.C., the Communist Party, and all the peace and progressive forces, including the Liberals, should unitedly demand from the National Government: immediate improvements in conditions for employed and unemployed; support for Spain and China; a foreign policy to build a Peace Front of Britain, France, the U.S.S.R. and the U.S.A. The Communist Party was eager for such co-operation and would place at the united campaign's disposal its hall-bookings, speakers, press, and thousands of active workers. It was good that left leaders were elected to the Labour E.C., but as long as the most active section of the movement, the Communist Party, was not affiliated, "so long are the Citrines, the Bevins and the National Government able to rejoice". In meetings Pollitt described the class contrasts in the town where he was speaking, giving facts on the differences in incomes and housing to support his argument that the National Government's failures to check fascist aggression abroad or to end unemployment at home sprang from the same root—its concern with the interests of the rich, not those of the people. The emphasis on economic issues expressed the concept of not peace alone but "Peace and Plenty", and reflected Pollitt's recognition of the weight of economic factors in the workers' minds.

Hitler's seizure of Austria stimulated the political pressure for unity and a People's Front, in which Liberals began to show an interest. The Labour Executive again rejected both. Their arguments and Pollitt's rejoinder are summarised below.[19]

Labour E.C.: The proposals would have less electoral appeal than the present policy of Labour.

Pollitt: The E.C. fails to recognise the tremendous electoral appeal of a common alliance of the peace forces. This political bankruptcy enables Chamberlain to proceed with his pro-fascist policy and to boast of "national unity".

Labour E.C: The situation requires a government coherent and decisive in leadership and able to count on resolution and unity from its supporters.

Pollitt: A People's Front Government would rest on a mass basis of the will of the people, their votes, their organisation, their firm determination that its programme should be achieved. Its foreign policy would have the support of France, the Soviet Union and all democratic states.

Labour E.C: Experiences of the first and second Labour Governments show that the Liberals are unreliable.

Pollitt: The analogy is misleading. Labour and Liberals were then elected on programmes that had nothing in common. A People's Front Government would be elected on a common programme.

Labour E.C: Communist Party policy is devoid of any certainty. They are committed to manoeuvre rather than principle.

Pollitt: C.P. policy is determined in relation to the situation and guided by Marxism. Today facts show that the people are confronted by the need to defend peace and democracy. The last few years have shown the C.P. as the most consistent defender of the interests of the people.

Labour E.C: A weak and indecisive Left government in Britain in time of crisis would make a rapid reaction towards conservatism not unlikely. A grave danger of fascism might arise.

Pollitt: This can only mean that with the National Government in power there is less danger of fascism than there would be with a Left Government. The Labour Executive refuses to understand that in aiding fascism in Spain, Austria and elsewhere, the National Government is paving the way for fascism in Britain.

Labour E.C: Entry into the People's front necessitates the abandonment of socialist principles. The road to peace lies through socialism.

Pollitt: The People's Front does not involve any sacrifice of socialist principle or weakening of the Labour Party. On the contrary, by defeating the forces of reaction and war, it strengthens the Labour movement and prepares conditions for the advance to socialism.

The discussion spread throughout the Labour and democratic movements, and in June Pollitt commented:[20] "The People's Front is not exclusively an alliance with the Liberals, it is a mass movement to defeat Chamberlain and get a new type of Government. It is not a retreat from socialism, it is the force which under present conditions protects the daily interests of the people and accelerates the fight for socialism. It does not endanger the Labour movement by placing it under other leadership. No People's Front can ever be a reality in Britain unless the Labour movement forms its basis and driving force. The opposition of the dominant clique in Transport House can be summed up in a sentence—it is not because they desire socialism or are afraid of losing their independence, it is because their political line is one of unity with Chamberlain and his government."

7. Austria, March 1938.[21]

On March 11, 1938 Hitler occupied Austria. Its minerals, timber and electric power were useful to his war economy; above all it would enable him to attack Czechoslovakia from three sides. His immediate purpose was to prevent the plebiscite to be taken two days later in which the expected big majority for an independent Austria would have shattered the Nazi claim that the Austrians wanted unity with the Reich.

The invasion was the culmination of four years of Nazi pressure from without and disruption from within. In 1934 the Nazis murdered the Austrian Chancellor, Dollfuss, but their putsch misfired. In 1936 Hitler agreed to mutual non-interference in home politics, but maintained in Germany an Austrian Nazi Legion which printed and smuggled illegal literature. In February 1938 Hitler compelled the Austrian Chancellor to include Nazis in his Cabinet. One of them controlled the Ministry of the Interior, including the police. The Chancellor, Schuschnigg, declared this to be a limit beyond which Austria would not concede more, and would fight to the death. He launched a campaign for independence, huge demonstrations were held, his supporters began to co-operate with the illegal trade unions, socialists and communists, the plebiscite was fixed.

Chamberlain had made clear that Austria could not expect protection from the League of Nations. "Why should we mislead them by giving them an assurance of security, when such security can only be a delusion?" Pollitt commented. "This is not weakness on his part. It does not mean that he believes in not interfering in Europe. No, the point is that Chamberlain and those who now rule Britain want Hitler to win. They want fascism to triumph."

Pollitt called for "Britain's united forces of peace and democracy to demand Hitler's withdrawal from Austria, the expulsion of the German Ambassador from London, a boycott of German goods and shipping, an end to the Chamberlain Government", and concluded "Fascism's next step will be to attack Czechoslovakia. Abyssinia, China, Spain, now Austria—the circle is closing round us. Let us unite with the peoples of France, the Soviet Union and the Spanish Republic to oppose fascist oppression."

8. MUNICH.[22]

In the summer of 1938 the campaign for the Peace Front focused on Hitler's aggression against Czechoslovakia; from May to September 195,000 copies were sold of Pollitt's three pamphlets exposing Hitler's aims and their meaning for the British people. Hitler wanted to eliminate the only surviving democracy in Central Europe, to control raw materials and agricultural resources, to seize the great Skoda arms works employing 35,000 workers, and to get a jumping off ground to seize Romanian oil and Yugoslav wheat. He had three weapons—the German army on Czechoslovakia's borders, the Sudeten Nazis' demand for autonomy, and the pro-fascists in the British and French Governments, upon whom he relied to secure the isolation of Czechoslovakia and the nullification of its pacts with France and the U.S.S.R.

Pollitt argued that the fate of Czechoslovakia was very much Britain's business; to sacrifice it to Hitler would lead to "either the surrender of British freedom and democracy to German fascism or a long, desperate war in which Britain, isolated because it refused to stand firm while there was still time, must go down to defeat". The alternative was for the British people to compel the government to join with France and the U.S.S.R. in defence of Czechoslovakia.

Hitler, knowing his Chamberlain, went ahead. In May he concentrated troops on the border while the Sudeten Nazis began disorders. The Czech Government sent troops who restored order and took up positions to repel a German attack. France and the Soviet Union declared readiness to fulfil their obligations. Chamberlain sent Lord Runciman to Prague to demand concessions to Hitler. Under British pressure, the Czechs agreed to a "fourth plan", asking that if it was rejected Britain should join France and the U.S.S.R. in guaranteeing their independence. While the British declared that the fourth plan was modifiable, Hitler demanded complete and speedy self-determination for the Sudeten Germans, otherwise he would move to their aid. It looked like war. Britain and France took preliminary mobilisation measures.

On September 30 Chamberlain flew to Munich and with Daladier, Mussolini and Hitler, without consulting the Czechs, signed an agreement to hand over to Hitler Czech territories with a German-speaking majority, evacuation of Czech troops to begin immediately.

The same day the Communist Party circulated a million copies of an appeal[23] written by Pollitt for popular action to repudiate the Munich Agreement, "the most complete and shameful surrender of peace, freedom and democracy. The peace of the world has not been saved. It has been betrayed to the custody of Hitler, to be broken when he considers the time favourable for his next act of conquest." Chamberlain went to Munich "not to save peace and help the Czechoslovak people, but to save Hitler, break the democratic peace front and open Europe and Britain to fascism and new wars". In a pamphlet, Pollitt wrote of Munich as "one of the most shameful agreements of all time. Britain and France agreed to sacrifice their ally to satisfy the fascist dictators. The appetite of the fascist tigers grows with every fresh kill. Can we be so blind as not to see that our turn will come unless we make a stand now?"

9. Caribbean cruise.

Pollitt's gross overwork during this period resulted in such exhaustion, plus bronchitis, that the doctors ordered him complete rest for three months.[24] He agreed; but the three months became two, for he insisted on speaking "by special permission" at the Empress Stadium celebration of the twenty-first anniversary of the Russian Revolution, and also on attending the *Daily Worker* festival ball at the Queens Hall on December 30. The two months were mainly spent on a Dutch boat cruise to the Caribbean. In addition to holiday amenities it had a Communist group among the crew, who made a great fuss of him. The album[25] of photographs they gave him shows that the boat called at the Azores, Madeira, Barbados, Trinidad, several Venezuelan ports and islands, the Panama Canal entrance and, on the return voyage, Jamaica; and that he had a good time in the swimming pool, on the sun decks, sea bathing and on shore fraternising with the children, white, black or mixed.

At one of the British colonial islands he was served with a notice banning him from landing. On board was an official delegation; they were invited to dine with the Governor. Two of them were left-wing trade unionists. The Party lads among the crew rigged out Harry in suitable clothes and got him down the crew gangway without the police noticing. The delegation then took him along with them, explaining to the Governor that they were sure had he known Harry was on board he would also have been invited, so they had brought him along. The Governor, who had authorised the ban, took it well and a good dinner was enjoyed by all.[26]

CHAPTER 18

WHAT KIND OF WAR?—1939

1. 'The hot flames are on our cheeks'. 2. Chartist centenary. 3. Soviet-German non-aggression pact. 4. War. 5. A change of line. 6. Removal from general secretaryship. 7. Looking back. 8. Death of Mary Louisa Pollitt.

1. 'THE HOT FLAMES ARE ON OUR CHEEKS'.

Following the fall of the Spanish Republic, and Munich, the fascist powers accelerated their aggression. On March 15, 1939 Hitler marched into Prague and occupied all Czechoslovakia. On the 21st he occupied Memel. On April 7, Mussolini invaded Albania; on the 26th Hitler denounced the Anglo-German Naval Treaty and the German-Polish non-aggression pact. Pollitt said[1] "It is said that no one wants war, yet we can feel the hot flames already on our cheeks." But he vigorously rejected the idea that war was inevitable, and tirelessly advocated the policy to prevent it. All that spring and summer there was a furore of popular discussion throughout the country; Pollitt, in continuous demand as a speaker, answered many questions at meetings, in articles and pamphlets.[2]

War or Peace?

The issue would be decided by what the people did. The nations who wanted peace could defend it "without the need to drop a bomb or fire a bullet" provided they pooled their resources and made the fascists understand they would be used to stop aggression.

Chamberlain's Policy?

Chamberlain represents those big capitalists who want fascism. He is "not a weak old man deceived by Hitler, but a cool, scheming leader consistently seeking to weaken the working class and to strengthen capitalism. He and his reactionary die-hards, who envy Hitler's and Mussolini's destruction of the Labour movement, have joined the fascist conspiracy to crush democracy by a terrorist dictatorship. They want to solve the crisis at the workers' expense, a forcible re-division of the world and war upon the Soviet Union. Chamberlain refused the democratic peace bloc because he wanted the imperialist anti-Soviet bloc."

Appeasement?

This policy expresses Chamberlain's aim to direct the main fascist offensive against the U.S.S.R. To him, the dangers appeasement brings to Britain are secondary to the danger to the whole structure of capitalism should the collapse of German fascism open the way to socialism in Central Europe.

Defence?

The main question is not technical or financial—it is political—who and what is to be defended? Chamberlain's defence is for the power and privilege of the rich, for their right to exploit the people. For this he wants fascism. Workers' and democrats' defence is for the people's lives and liberties, for their right to decide their own destiny. For this they must fight fascism.

Conscription?

The issue is not more man-power for war, but a policy to preserve peace. It is hypocrisy for the man who handed Spain, Austria, Czechoslovakia, with £160m. worth of armaments, and all the resources of the Balkans to Hitler, to pretend that conscripting 300,000 young men means protecting Britain.

Democracy?

Pollitt rejected the argument that democracy based on a capitalist economy is not worth defending. Certainly it is a democracy with contending classes, but it is the best form of government under capitalism because it offers the best conditions for workers' struggle. Victorious fascism destroys all workers' organisations and economic and political rights. It is easier to struggle for socialism under capitalist democracy than under fascism. "Does anyone think that the British battalion fought in Spain for an abstract democracy, or to make it safe for millionaires? They gave their lives for a democracy that meant economic and political rights for the workers—the things fascism destroys."

2. Chartist centenary.

Of all the crowded political indoor meetings organised that summer by the Communist Party, the most enthusiastic and successful was that which filled 10,000 seats in London's Empress Hall on July 22. An illustrated paper[3] reported: "The three big features were a pageant to celebrate the centenary of Chartism, the march in of the British Battalion of the International Brigade, and a speech by Harry Pollitt." In half-an-hour

£2,163. 3s. 0d. was raised for the Wounded and Dependents Aid Fund of the Battalion; 916 new members for the Party were enrolled. "Harry Pollitt, tanned, stocky, powerful, spoke at high speed for 45 minutes. He made few gestures, talked through bursts of applause without stopping." Points which aroused most applause—his attack on pacifism, his praise for the International Brigade, explanation of the Peace Pact negotiations, better hospitals and medical services, his greeting to the German and Italian peoples. A week previously, Mosley got his biggest cheer for an attack on the Jews; Pollitt got his for his message "to all peoples of whatever race, colour, creed or religion, the Communist Party sends its greetings."

In his speech Pollitt spoke of the shadow of imminent war, of the urgency of defeating Chamberlain, of the measures needed to defend the people from poverty, war and fascism.

Prior to the meeting, Pollitt had answered questions from this same paper,[4] including:

Q: "How does the C.P.G.B. contemplate getting into power?"

Pollitt: "The existing social order is based on the domination of the ruling capitalist class. This power has to be broken before it is possible for the working class to take over the means of production. This can only be accomplished by the power of the organised working class once it has reached consciousness of its class aim. To realise this conquest of power and the building of socialism, it is the task of the Communist Party to build the unity and organisation of the working class; to win a majority of the working class to Communist policy and leadership; to draw into association with the working class those other sections of the population whose interests lie in unity with it."

The Pageant[5] in which a thousand men and women took part, showed the struggle of emergent democracy against an entrenched, authoritarian Establishment, from the Chartism of 1839 to the mass movement of 1920. Scenes, costumes, dialogue were based on historical research. The words of Chartist workers and leaders, of the Prime Minister, a General and a Judge were spoken, Chartist songs were heard, there were glimpses of the Working Men's Association, the Chartist Convention, the Central Committee of the Communist League. Continuity of presentation was secured by the switching of spot lights from one to another of six platforms in the darkened arena. The concluding scenes revived the atmosphere of 1917-18 to 1920, the Russian Socialist Revolution, the strike on the *Jolly George*, the Councils of Action.

Pollitt spoke the final words: "The Communist Party is proud to inherit the Chartist tradition. Behind the Charter was a vision realised in the Soviet Union today, and that will be realised in Britain tomorrow. When the workers who till the soil and man the machines unite, nothing on earth can break us. With power in our hands we will conquer poverty, abolish class inequalities, free the colonial peoples, help them to construct socialism. We proclaim our faith in Communism, the noblest principle the world has known. Communism, that inspires all who accept it, will triumph. We have been too long kneeling, it is time to rise."

3. SOVIET-GERMAN NON-AGGRESSION PACT.

This pact, which took all sections of opinion in Britain by surprise, including the Communists, was preceded by the following diplomatic events:

March 18: Britain asks U.S.S.R.'s attitude on the Hitler threat to Romania. U.S.S.R. proposes a conference of Britain, France, U.S.S.R., Romania, Poland, Turkey to resist further aggression.

March 19: Chamberlain rejects conference as "premature".

April 12: Chamberlain guarantees Poland and Romania against aggression and three days later asks if U.S.S.R. would do the same.

April 16: U.S.S.R. proposes British–French–U.S.S.R. pact to resist aggression everywhere.

May 7: Chamberlain again asks U.S.S.R. for one-sided guarantee.

May 17: U.S.S.R. again proposes mutual pact.

May 27: Chamberlain agrees to discuss a pact limited to Poland, Romania and Greece. U.S.S.R. proposes that the pact apply to all countries, forbids a separate peace, provides staff talks, and includes resistance to 'indirect aggression', i.e. a traitor government inviting Hitler in. Chamberlain objects and sends a junior official to negotiate.

July: Molotov points out urgency of staff talks. Chamberlain sends by slowest route junior officers without power to agree. He also stops political negotiations, declaring that failure to agree is due to Soviet proposals which might encroach on the independence of the Baltic States. The U.S.S.R. denies this, saying its sole concern is to prevent the fate of Czechoslovakia befalling them.

August: U.S.S.R. declares readiness to send troops to aid Polish armies should Poland be attacked. Under British pressure the Polish government refuses to agree to Soviet troops entering Poland, thus nullifying negotiations for mutual aid.

August 23: Soviet-German Non-Aggression Pact signed.

That summer there were frequent Communist open-air meetings in central London. On the Sunday following news of the Non-Aggression Pact, which the capitalist press distorted into a Soviet-German alliance, an enormous crowd gathered to hear Pollitt. With German divisions on the Polish frontier, British reserves called up, evacuation of children announced, the atmosphere was electric. Pollitt gave a complete review of the situation and dealt with three questions that were burning in all minds:[6]

Q: Why had the U.S.S.R. signed the Non-Aggression Pact?

Pollitt: Chamberlain for years had helped Hitler and refused a peace pact of Britain, France and the U.S.S.R. When forced by public opinion to discuss with the U.S.S.R., he procrastinated to avoid agreement. The Soviet Union took 16 days to prepare its replies; Chamberlain took 59. Meanwhile he handed the Czech gold to Hitler, exported to him stocks of nickel, copper and shellac, supplied Japan with war material. His consistent aim was to embroil the U.S.S.R. with Germany and Japan, with Britain pretending to be neutral; in fact, aiding the fascists as in Spain. He rejected every peace proposal of the U.S.S.R. Now the rejection recoils on the heads of the rejectors, a defeat for those who wanted a fascist war on an isolated Soviet Union.

Q: Does the Soviet-German Non-Aggression Pact rule out a Pact of Mutual Assitance between Britain, France and the U.S.S.R.?

Pollitt: Such a pact can be brought into being any moment providing it is a real pact to secure peace for all countries, not merely to help British and French imperialism.

Q: What if war should come?

Pollitt: If Britain takes its place in any common front against a fascist attack, the Communist Party will do everything in its power to bring about the defeat of fascism. But we openly declare this cannot be done with any guarantee of success as long as Chamberlain is in power. His record and his deeds prove he is not the enemy of fascism, but its friend. You cannot fight fascism if the head of the country proposes to impose fascist methods on the British people. You cannot fight if you are placed in chains. Fascism can only be fought on the basis of democratic rights which strengthen the power of the people to defeat it.

That is why our democratic demands include: full liberty of working-class meetings, press and organisation; full rights for those in the Forces to take part in meetings and organisation and to read their chosen publications; promotion of officers from the ranks; removal of all officers with pro-fascist opinions; A.R.P. and civilian defence under democratic control; nationalisation of the arms industry; clearing out of all Nazi agents and suppression of all pro-fascist bodies; emergency powers to tax the rich, take over their establishments and resources for the service of the people. There must also be defence against poverty, for only a strong and healthy people can conquer fascism.

Pollitt emphasised that it was still not too late to save peace, provided that all who wanted it united to clear out Chamberlain. He recited the long list of acts of collusion by the Labour leaders who shared Chamberlain's responsibility for bringing "the terrifying shadow of death and destruction over our country and Europe". "The rank and file of the Labour movement also have their share for not repudiating and energetically fighting against the policy of their leaders." Now "every member of the working class must understand that no one can save them except themselves."

4. WAR.

Friday, September 1: The early morning radio spoke of German bombs on Warsaw; German armoured divisions speeding over the Polish frontier. A British ultimatum gave Hitler till Sunday midday to withdraw his troops. In Whitehall the messengers rushed with the orders to open the War Books.

Saturday, September 2: A manifesto of the Communist Party declared its support of all measures necessary to secure the victory of democracy over fascism, the first and most vital step to victory being a new government.

That evening saw an unprecedented spectacle, a Saturday night session of the Commons. Pollitt sitting in the Visitors' Gallery recorded[7] "the roar of disapproval that greeted Chamberlain's proposal to give Hitler more time, and the fact that Greenwood saved the government from defeat by refusing to divide the House."

Sunday, September 3: At midday the radio announced that Britain was at war with Germany; a few minutes later the air raid sirens sounded.

In a 32-page pamphlet, *How to Win the War*,[8] Pollitt restated his analysis of events leading to war, particularly Chamberlain's aid to fascist aggression and refusal of the Soviet proposals for a peace pact. He then explained why the Communists supported the war.

His central theme was that for the British people it was a just war, the issue was democracy or fascism. That the British and French rulers had declared war for their own imperialist interests did not alter the fact that their action, taken under pressure from their peoples, was for the first time a challenge to the Nazi aggressors. The British workers were in the war to defeat Hitler, because a German victory would mean the imposition of fascism on other countries.

He was confident that the anti-fascist will of the British people would defeat Chamberlain and determine the character of the war, despite the simultaneous existence of imperialist interests. He proposed measures to give effect to this anti-fascist will, the most vital being the replacement of Chamberlain and the Men of Munich by men without imperialist motives or any sympathy with fascism. Without mentioning names, he said they could be found in the Labour and Democratic movement. Such a new government would send representatives to the U.S.S.R. and to the U.S.A. to secure an anti-Hitler alliance, aiming to restore independence to Austria, Czechoslovakia and Poland; peace without annexations or indemnities; help to the peoples of the fascist countries to establish democratic governments.

He then spelt out the economic and social measures needed to secure the exertion of the full power of the British people. Believing that the peoples of the empire were as vitally interested in the defeat of fascism as were the British people, he called for immediate full democratic rights and representative governments for India and all colonial peoples so that they could fully enter the anti-fascist struggle.

He summed up: "The prosecution of this war necessitates a struggle on two fronts. First to secure the military victory over fascism, and second, to achieve this, the political victory over the enemies of democracy in Britain."

The line of this pamphlet and the manifesto of September 2 were endorsed throughout the Party.

5. A CHANGE OF LINE.

On September 14 a Moscow broadcast included the sentence—"There is no doubt in the minds of the Soviet people that this war is an imperialist and predatory war for a new redivision of the world, a robber war kindled from all sides by the two imperialist groups of powers." Two days later, a London paper[9] reported that in a Moscow interview the Secretary of the Communist Party of the U.S.A. had spoken of "an imperialist war".

Pollitt and others, aware of the broadcasts of course, realised that the Moscow view was in contradiction to the position of the C.P.G.B. But when preparing his report for the Central Committee, Pollitt maintained his position.[10] He agreed that mistakes had been made in not expecting the Soviet-German Non-Aggression Pact, the British declaration of war, and the Polish collapse. He recognised the significance of the lack of movement on the Western front. But to the question whether the line of the Manifesto of September 2 should be changed he answered "No". The line was correct, but it was necessary to sharpen the fight against the Chamberlain Government. "Britain is in danger every hour it remains." He re-stated the reasons for working for victory over fascism. "We have fought for peace and failed; we are now in the war—we cannot run away now. The war will go on to a finish, the Fifth Column has the door wide open for a peace meaning victory for fascism, but things have now gone too far."

The Communist International had an attitude to an imperialist war, to a war for national liberation, to a counter-revolutionary war on the Soviet Union, Pollitt continued, but it had not provided for the contingency that had actually taken place. As Marxists we have to analyse the situation as it exists and formulate our policy, he argued. He did not accept the argument that it was an imperialist war as in 1914. For some years we had been saying that we were in the era of the second imperialist war, but our line had always been to support any country or people resisting fascist aggression. Whether it was the second or third imperialist war, if in it there was a chance of smashing fascism or fascist aggression, that was justification for the line of September 2. The central question was not how to get peace, but how to win the war. There was no divergence of aim between the British people fighting to crush fascism, and what the Soviet Union was doing in Poland.

He reiterated the urgency of Labour taking the initiative for a new government, but added "We have to face facts. Labour cannot form a government that can win this war on its own. My personal opinion is that you can't win this war unless you have in the new government not only representatives of Labour, but men like Lloyd George, Eden, Churchill and Duff Cooper—all imperialists. But we have to win this war and to win it with people who are going to be ruthless."

The Central Committee met on September 24, and Pollitt reported on these lines. Some members expressed doubts; the majority of the speakers that day agreed with him. That evening D. F. Springhall, a C.C. member who had been working in Moscow, returned with the information that the Communist International characterised the war as an "out and out imperialist war to which the working class in no country could give any support".[11] Germany aimed at European and world domination, Britain at preserving her imperialist interests and European domination against her chief rival, Germany. That Chamberlain was not concerned with Polish independence was shown by his refusal of Red Army help. The war had opened up a new situation, the differentiation between fascist and so-called democratic countries had lost its former significance, and a new perspective opened of shattering the capitalist system everywhere.

The C.I. analysis made no mention of the factor to which Pollitt attached so much importance, the anti-fascist will of the people; nor of the differentiation in the British ruling class; nor of the warning by Molotov, which Pollitt quoted, not to read into the Soviet-German Pact more than it contained.

The Central Committee was thus faced with two mutually exclusive theses: its own Manifesto of September 2 reinforced by Pollitt's opening report, and that of the Communist International, carrying the full weight of international authority. It decided to take time for consideration, and adjourned till October 2.

When it met again the report of the Political Bureau was presented by R. Palme Dutt, who had been deputed to do so during the Bureau's intervening discussion. It proposed the withdrawal of the Manifesto of September 2 and of the concept of "the fight on two fronts", and the adoption of the line of the C.I. that the war was between imperialist powers for profits, markets and world domination; the British and French ruling classes were seeking to use the anti-fascist sentiments of the people for their own ends. Chamberlain and Churchill were bracketed as enemies of democracy and oppressors of colonial peoples.[12]

Pollitt adhered to his views, and together with J. R. Campbell voted against the resolution and for maintaining the line of September 2.

6. Removal from General Secretaryship.

On October 11 it was announced that in view of the differences of opinion, the Central Committee had decided that Harry Pollitt should not continue as General Secretary but should undertake other duties. Pollitt stated that the decision was correct, and taken after discussion in which he had had full opportunity to express his views. "The differences have nothing to do with the policy of the Soviet Union, with whose policy I am in entire agreement." He concluded, "I shall give the decision my fullest support and work for the Party in any way the Central Committee may decide." He rejected as "nonsense and wishful thinking the attempts in the press to create the impression of a crisis in the Party".[13]

The capitalist press made the most of its opportunity. Papers which normally showed not the slightest interest in Pollitt's speeches or his welfare began to find flattering phrases, "the most typical representative of the British working class among the Party leaders", "the ablest politician produced by the British Communist Party". One paper offered him £20 for a thousand words of "free expression of your views on war". He wrote vigorously rejecting this offer—"I am afraid you will never understand that a Communist can have differences with his Party and yet remain absolutely loyal to it and its declared policy."[14]

Just before his first public meeting after his removal, Pollitt wrote: "Am just off to the Rhondda for some meetings to popularise the Party policy. I will be in a difficult position, but will manage it alright. Feel more like emulating Garbo and her 'alone' feeling just now."[15]

At Trealaw he said to 800 miners; "As a man who believes in the Communist Party before anything else in the world, it is my duty to expound its policy." And "it was a splendid thing for working men to know that the Communist Party was strong enough to depose leaders who disagreed with its policy—if the Labour Party had adopted a similar practice we should not be in the position we are today."[16] At Tonypandy, referring to the Soviet pacts with the Baltic States and the liberation of Western Ukraine, he said "Russia has done more to weaken Hitler in two weeks than the rest of the world in six years".

Pollitt received many letters,[17] most expressed sympathy and regret. To C.P. members who continued to think that the line of September 2 was correct, he invariably replied asking them to do their Party duty and to give full support to the decision of the Central Committee. Harold Laski wrote, "I had hoped in early August for such an Anglo-Soviet policy as meant the unity of all anti-fascist forces against Hitler. Now I cannot understand the Stalin line. The only line I can take is: (i) in the interests of the workers all over the world we must destroy fascism; (ii) we must fight towards a Workers Government here as the essential medium of victory. My warm regards." Sir Stafford Cripps expressed his "deep and sincere personal friendship" and opined that the removal from General Secretaryship meant "the end of an effective C.P. in this country in the circumstances of the present time".

Of all the letters, Harry valued most the one from his mother. It read: "One thing I do know. I would not lose my dignity by having an office boy's job and being dictated to by someone half as competent, because the tools are still in the vaseline. I think you yourself ought to make a statement in defence of your policy so that people can judge your position for themselves. Of course, I know your answer to that! To you, to me, it is a blow. But it is the greatest blow to the Party. If this war is fought to a finish, great things will happen to you, because you have a clean record. Be of good cheer! Twelve months ago you were amongst the Distinguished Invalids in the Evening News: tonight you are in the 'Stop Press'."

Pollitt would not have been human if he had not felt the removal as a severe blow, personally and to his political line.

His action in publicly explaining with all his ability the policy decided by the Party, and resisting all suggestions to publicise his own views, was in accord with Communist theory and practice. There is a difference between agreement with a decision and acceptance of the obligation to carry it out. Political agreement is a matter of individual conviction, an intellectual attitude arising only from discussion, consideration and voluntary consent. The obligation to carry out a decision is a political necessity if the Party is to act as a unified force. A decision is made after discussion by majority vote, the only democratic method. A member who thinks it is incorrect has the right to reserve his opinion and in proper course to argue for changing it, but he is nonetheless bound to carry out what the majority have decided.

In mid-November Pollitt wrote[18] to the Central Committee declaring his "unreserved acceptance of the policy of the Party and of the C.I." and pledging full support in "explaining, popularising and helping to carry it forward", a pledge which he honoured to the full.

7. LOOKING BACK.

Many readers may raise the question, in the light of subsequent events, who was right in 1939, the Communist International leaders, or Pollitt? The C.I. dissolved in 1943 without having answered this question. The C.P.G.B. has not expressed an opinion. Stalin, who was silent on this matter in 1939 but may be assumed to have agreed with the C.I., said in 1946 "the second world war from the very outset assumed the nature of an anti-fascist war".[19] Pollitt never re-opened the issue but in 1956 said: "In 1939 I thought it an anti-fascist war. I thought it then and I think it now . . . but I was outvoted in my party and as I am a democrat I accepted the decision."[20] As he did not refer to his arguments in 1939 we may assume that he still considered them valid in essence.

The difference in opinion, for the purpose of comparison with the course of events, may be summed up as follows:[21]

What was the nature of the War?
C.I.: Out and out imperialist, two groups of imperialist powers fighting for world supremacy.
H.P.: Alongside the imperialist interests pursued by the governments was the anti-fascist will of the peoples, this element given leadership could be decisive. It was a People's war.
What should be the attitude of the C.P.G.B.?
C.I.: The working class cannot support such a war, the experience of the Bolshevik Party in 1914–18 shows how to achieve peace.
H.P.: Support for the military defeat of fascism, for which the political victory over the friends of fascism in Britain is essential. It is a fight on two fronts, against Hitler and against Chamberlain.
What of the difference between the fascist and the capitalist democratic states?
C.I.: It has lost its former significance.
H.P.: Capitalist democracy is preferable to fascism, but to preserve democracy a mass struggle for a new, People's Government is essential.
What is the perspective?
C.I.: The shattering of the capitalist system everywhere.
H.P.: A truly anti-fascist government in Britain which would mobilise every resource for the defeat of Nazi Germany and reach out to the U.S.A. and the U.S.S.R. for mutual assistance to that end.

When Pollitt spoke of "something in the war that did not fit into the pattern of 1914" he referred to five new factors. There now existed a powerful socialist state, the U.S.S.R. One reason for British and French government support for Hitler was his declared hostility to the U.S.S.R. There was a Soviet-German Non-aggression Pact, but Hitler broke pacts when it suited him, and each of his conquests was used to strengthen the German war machine. To the old imperialist aim of world domination, the Nazis had added—the total destruction of democratic rights and organisations by terror and brute force; the enslavement of conquered peoples, physical extermination of their opponents and active subversion within the democracies. In the democratic countries the mass anti-fascist movements were increasingly uniting the working class, sections of the middle classes and even some capitalists. The rulers were divided, some saw their main danger as from the working class and socialism, others saw Hitler Germany as the main enemy. These new factors had not been fully provided for by the C.I. division of wars into imperialist and counter-revolutionary, both unjust, or for national liberation and the defence of socialism, both just. But the C.I. had always supported states attacked by fascism and had sent or offered aid to Spain, Czechoslovakia and Poland.

What Pollitt meant by the fight against Chamberlain and the friends of fascism was shown in his proposals for a new government. It would be composed of men determined to end fascism and replace it by democracy and for this purpose seek the co-operation of the U.S.A. and the U.S.S.R. to win the war by defeat of Nazi Germany. It would restore the independence of countries conquered by fascism, and help the German people to fight Hitler. It would give democratic rights to India. It would remove all pro-fascists from responsible posts and mobilise the entire resources of Britain for victory.

Subsequent events, particularly the replacement of Chamberlain by Churchill, Hitler's attack on the Soviet Union and the growth of the Resistance throughout Europe are well known. With hindsight Pollitt may well have seen no reason to change his 1939 view, for even if it did not cover every aspect of what happened, he could claim that these events showed broadly speaking that he was correct.

8. Death of Mary Louisa Pollitt.

As though the political reverse was not enough, fate struck Pollitt the hardest personal blow—his mother died suddenly and unexpectedly on November 1. The first he knew of her illness was that she had been taken to hospital with thrombosis. He rushed to Manchester: it was too late.

The day before the funeral he walked once more through Droylsden village, re-visiting the places he and she knew so well—the house where she had borne and reared him, the mill where he had so often waited for her, the Co-op. where she had shopped, the canal bank where they sometimes walked, the schools he went to, the calm of the Moravian Square. Each spot evoked its memories of her, each seemed to whisper "never, never again shall we see her".

On November 4, 1939 Mary Louisa was buried alongside her husband in Droylsden Cemetery.

At the graveside were many old friends of the Margaret Street days. One wrote afterwards; "I wanted to speak words of comfort, instead my tongue clung to the roof of my mouth. When one has lost one's dearest and is full of grief, words do not offer consolation. During these few minutes the years slipped away, and once again we were waiting to go home with Cissie from the Sunday School classes. We knew we would get some sweets because she lived at a toffee shop."

A stream of letters[22] of condolence came. Frank Allaun, for the Manchester Left Book Club, recalled the regular attendance at their discussions of Harry's mother and his sister. Phil Piratin wrote on behalf of the Stepney C.P., Frank Bright for the Manchester Communists who "loved and respected her", Salme Dutt (the wife of R. Palme Dutt) "I feel as if I had lost my own mother", Eva Reckitt "a mother in a thousand", Albert Inkpin "I know the close bonds of love and comradeship between you", Tom Mann "What a shock, my sincere condolences", H. H. Lawrie "the real sympathy of fellowship in your loss", Jim Crossley "she was not in the limelight, but her unselfish and unstinted efforts behind the scenes made it possible for others to carry on in the vanguard", Ted Lismer of the early R.I.L.U. days, "The movement has lost a great comrade and you a greater".

D. N. Pritt "proud to have met her at Tom Mann's birthday dinner". Alex Gossip recalled, "her visit to our Fulham Socialist Sunday School, her pleasant, homely look". Krishna Menon, "I want you to know that some of us feel with you and share your sorrow." Nellie Lansbury, Arthur Horner, Nat Watkins, Stafford Cripps, Victor Gollancz, and many more. George Lansbury, whose kindness rose above political controversy, wrote "the joyful memory of a mother, comrade and friend will cheer and inspire you to carry on the work of human endeavour to which she devoted her life".

When subsequently in Manchester, Pollitt always went to Droylsden Cemetery and placed fresh flowers on her grave. In 1949, the London No. 15 Branch of the Furnishing Trades levied their members for a token of appreciation to Pollitt on his completion of twenty years service as General Secretary of the Communist Party. With the money he bought a stone urn,[23] and placed it on the grave. It was inscribed "In Memory of Mary Louisa Pollitt from her loving Son, Harry."

CHAPTER 19

THE WAR EXTENDS

1. Pollitt honours his pledge. 2. Silvertown. 3. 'Serving My Time'. 4. 'France has fallen—arm the workers'. 5. The people and the war. 6. The People's Convention. 7. 'Daily Worker' banned. 8. Death of Tom Mann. 9. The shipyard once more. 10. Hitler's deputy. 11. Hitler attacks the Soviet Union.

1. POLLITT HONOURS HIS PLEDGE.

The day after his mother's funeral Pollitt was in Glasgow—he had refused cancellation of the meetings—the one at St. Andrews Hall was full 45 minutes before starting time, and with an overflow totalled 3,500 people.[1] For the next twelve months he spoke all over Britain explaining the policy of the Party to audiences as large and attentive as in any of his campaigns.[2]

In the winter of 1939-40 he worked mainly from the office of the Party's Lancashire District, keeping his habit of early morning arrival. David Ainley, then working on the circulation of the *Daily Worker*, came in just after 9 a.m. and found Pollitt already at work. "You're late", said Harry. "I'm not" was the reply, "I start here at 9." "Then you're the only one who does", said Harry. The office could hardly be described as luxurious, in cold weather it felt freezing. Harry came in one day and found his old friend Mrs. Knight talking to the organiser. She asked, "What are you doing here?" "Its my Siberia" he replied. Said she, "It'll be mine too if somebody doesn't mend that fire."[3]

In December 1939 the Party, being opposed to the electoral truce, contested in the Stretford by-election. To break the press silence barrier there were loud-speaker street tours and factory-gate meetings. Pollitt helped organise the campaign, canvassed, drafted leaflets and raised money. Speaking at factory gates and in the streets he strongly defended the Soviet action in Finland. "The Western Front is quiet because efforts are being made to transform the war into a joint Allied-German attack on Russia; Finland to be the jumping off ground." At the same meeting Prof. J. B. S. Haldane said that the Soviet Union had acted to prevent the bombing and blockading of Leningrad, only twenty miles from the Mannerheim line. "The Soviet Union was right to defend itself, and I am glad it has."[4]

From January to May, Pollitt combined explanation of the Party's position on the war with championing the people's needs for adequate air-raid shelters, better education for the children—many schools had been taken over by the fire services—and better food distribution. He spoke at a series of local meetings in Lancashire, and another series in South Wales; at three delegate conferences to discuss Labour's attitude to the war, at meetings of Communist Party members on Merseyside and in Manchester; two or three times a day in the whirlwind ten days contest in the Silvertown by election; at public meetings in Nottingham, Lancaster, Birmingham, Cardiff, West Ham, Chiswick: all this sandwiched in between major meetings, in the largest halls available, in London, Liverpool, Manchester, Sheffield, Newcastle and Edinburgh.[5]

Travelling to and from meetings in blacked-out and crowded trains was time-consuming and exhausting. After going from Manchester to Birmingham to discuss with Communist engineering workers, he wrote: "I went to Birmingham and spent exactly ten hours in the train there and back. It was very good of the lads to put up the fare, you can tell them it was dead right to the ten-thousandth part of a penny."[6]

May Day found him once more speaking in Hyde Park. Marches were banned, but the First of May Demonstration Committee held a meeting in Chenies Street at 2 p.m. to protest against the ban. The Hyde Park meeting was held at 4 p.m., and at 8 p.m. the Holborn Hall was crowded. Pollitt also spoke to factory workers in West Hendon.

2. SILVERTOWN: FEBRUARY 1940.

At Silvertown, in London's East End, a national leader of the Communist Party contested a war-time election for the first time; financial support and requests for Pollitt's election address were widespread. The electorate was almost entirely working-class. From the start he struck the class note. "The Communist Party is the only party wanting to strengthen the working-class fight against capitalism, war and the Chamberlain Government. It alone stands to end the war by victory of the British, French and German workers over Chamberlain, Daladier and Hitler." Pollitt contrasted the millions of pounds going to shareholders in docks, shipping, sugar, flour and chemicals with the low wages, casual labour and bad housing of the workers whose labour produced these profits—class contrasts increased by war-time speed-up, rise in unemployment, inadequate air raid shelters and breakdown in children's education.[7]

It was a critical moment. Finland, ruled by Marshal Mannerheim, who had slaughtered socialist workers by the thousand in 1918 and later with German collusion built the fortified "Mannerheim Line" twenty miles from Leningrad, was in armed conflict with the Soviet Union. For the Soviet Union, with Hitler on its borders and faced, too, with the hostility of the allies, could no longer tolerate the danger Finland represented. It offered a mutual aid pact and, when Mannerheim refused, took military action to end the menace. Now Chamberlain, with the support of the suggestion of stopping the paper by the staff." It was "the only paper which exposed the grievances of the people and the Communist Party was the only party that stood against fascism whether from Hitler or Churchill and Morrison."[23] The ban was not lifted till August 1942.

3. Death of Tom Mann.

Tom Mann's apparently inexhaustible energy gave signs of flagging towards the end of 1939, and he went to live quietly in Grassington in Yorkshire, where Pollitt several times visited him. In March 1941 he took a turn for the worse. Pollitt rushed to Yorkshire and arrived just in time to shake his hand for the last time. He died aged 85 on March 13. Four days later, his coffin, draped in the banner of the Communist Party, was followed by many of his life-long comrades, delegates from workers' organisations and hundreds of men and women to Lawnswood Crematorium in Leeds.

Pollitt described the ceremony: "In silence, pregnant with love and reverence that few can command; the revolutionary Funeral March was played in a way that moved many to tears. Ben Tillett, one of Tom's oldest comrades, paid his last tribute in words of grief and eloquence. Arthur Horner followed with appreciation of all that Tom had done for trade unionism in general and for the miners in particular. Krishna Menon, on behalf of the India League, paid impassioned tribute to Tom's internationalism. William Gallacher, M.P., for the Communist Party, surveyed Tom's life of activities and his twenty years leading role in the Party. The orations ended, all present rose, the strains of 'The Internationale' resounded, Tom Mann passed slowly from sight."[24]

In an eloquent tribute, Pollitt described Tom Mann, as "one of the greatest men the international labour movement has ever produced—a giant, towering incomparably over all his contemporaries . . . the first British working-class leader to be known and trusted by workers throughout the world; the first to fight from start to finish for international solidarity and for the freedom of the colonial peoples . . . Summoned by the workers themselves, regarded with fear and hatred by their rulers, he agitated, organised, worked, fought and studied in Western Europe, Canada, the United States, South Africa, New Zealand and was first to plant the Red Flag in Australia. . . . At the centre of his thoughts were those who were worst paid and suffered most from unemployment. This made him a rebel against the craft prejudices and sectionalism that characterised the trade union movement of the 1880's, though no worker was prouder than he of his craft and his unbroken trade union membership from 1881 when he joined the A.S.E., then the A.E.U., till he died."

Pollitt characterised Tom Mann as a revolutionary. "From the agitation he began in 1886 for the eight hour day, his aim was always to break down rights; adequate air raid protection; friendship with the Soviet Union. In October, 500 men and women influential in the Labour and democratic movements, Pollitt among them, signed an appeal for a People's Convention.[19]

On January 12 1941, the Convention met, 1¼m people were represented by 2,234 delegates, the majority from industry, many from professional and cultural organisations. The policy adopted covered the issues already mentioned, with two additions—the use of Emergency Powers to take over for the people certain industries and services; independence for India, self-determination for all colonial peoples, ending forced partition in Ireland.[20]

Pollitt was among the delegates and wrote[21] of their determination, "eager to formulate a common policy, with a common leadership and strategy". There should be no false optimism about the stern character of the struggle ahead. The Convention brought together only the fringe of the decisive masses, but it "represented forces that, *if they will*, can win these masses". The Convention was not out to destroy the Labour movement but to revitalise it. The struggle for the Convention programme was the answer to the gathering offensive of the government and the employers. They wanted to refuse wage increases while prices rose, impose heavier taxes, maintain a shortage of food and fuel; introduce industrial conscription; and to use the Labour and trade union members in the government to prevent resistance.

7. 'DAILY WORKER' BANNED.

The Government evidently saw the Convention as a danger signal, for on January 24, 1941 the *Daily Worker* was banned by the Home Secretary, Herbert Morrison. There were also proposals to ban other left-wing publications, including *World News and Views, Labour Monthly, Challenge*, and *New Propeller*. The Security Executive favoured banning the Communist Party entirely and interning a number of its leading members. Morrison brought these proposals before a War Cabinet Committee. He realised that such measures might lead to unrest in industry such as occurred in 1914-1918. Ernest Bevin, Minister of Labour, was also dubious; he argued against such action until some of the shop floor grievances were overcome. The proposals were dropped.[22]

Pollitt called for mass pressure to get the ban lifted. He said it was significant that the suppression coincided with the move to impose industrial conscription. Allegations that the paper encouraged sabotage and lower production he described as "lies—and those who utter them know they are lies". Morrison said that the paper's machine room staff had twice struck against the paper's policy. Said Pollitt, "That is a lie; Morrison prefers to take the word of a copper rather than a resolution of the machine room workers' chapel. There has never been the slightest

'Don't let on to the old man.'" Pollitt then recounts another lad's experiences in air raids. "The shelter he goes to is packed like sardines with children and their parents, damp, no proper ventilation, so dimly lit you cannot read. They talk in whispers so that the kids can sleep. They have an Anderson in their garden, the old man concreted it in last summer, you need a life-buoy before you go in, there's a foot of water in it. His old man said, 'They tell me butchers eat their own sausages, but I'll bet neither Anderson nor Morrison sit in their own shelters'. Mother has put on years since the blitz began. The old man is like a bear with a sore head. He says that if there's an All Clear and he goes to the local for half a pint, Hitler seems to know he's there, and off go the sirens again."

About the youngsters, Pollitt writes: "We brought them into the world, we have a social responsibility as well as our duty as parents. What we have to put up with it is natural that youth should rebel against, and we should encourage them to rebel. We can help them a lot more than we do; see that they become good craftsmen and women when they are learning a trade, and where they are not, advise them how to do their jobs so that there are possibilities of advancement. As trade unionists we can see that they get proper wages and conditions, and don't work excessive overtime. This may mean speaking sharply because of the attraction of a little extra money to splash at weekends or buy a suit or costume that they think makes them look like a film star." He suggests means of rousing their interest in political and trade union matters, and encouraging them to read and study. This will take time, but "Bill, if you and I and a lot more like us would see that time spent on helping youth was the best investment we ever made, we would soon find the time."

Another pamphlet made the case for workers' action to secure wage increases to meet rising prices. Of the talk about "common sacrifice" he wrote: "It only comes up in a crisis, a strike, trade depression or war. It is hypocritical, the sacrifice is always one-sided." Of Churchill's Minister for Labour, "The capitalists do not mind Mr. Bevin's lavish use of the phrase 'I have decided'. They smile, for big as Ernest is, he is not big enough to see that the capitalists decided he shall be the medium to put over industrial conscription." He recalled that Bevin once impressed a Tribunal by displaying a paper of fish and chips and became known as the Dockers' K.C., "but now the ship-owners still have halibut and smoked salmon, while there is not two-pennorth of fish-and-chips for the dockers".

6. The People's Convention.

During 1940 there was a steady growth of popular anxiety and discontent. In August, a London People's Vigilance Committee was set up by a representative conference. In September it held a 15,000 strong meeting in Hyde Park. A variety of committees sprang up in the industrial centres, the common issues including defence of living standards and democratic

"If a Winston Churchill has the right to call on the German, French, Italian and Abyssinian peoples to take independent action, a Harry Pollitt has the same right to call on the British people to take their independent action to defend themselves from their enemies within and without."

"In this solemn hour when the world is far from being a Midsummer Night's Dream, when the flower of humanity faces death and destruction, we call upon you to take your places, stand to your posts and hold the unshakeable and unbreakable working-class front in the fight for a people's government, a people's peace and a People's Britain."

5. THE PEOPLE AND THE WAR.

In 1940 Pollitt wrote five pamphlets; three were informal "Letters to Bill", written with plenty of humour.[17]

The first dealt with work-shop problems, noting differences compared with 1914–18: "It was easier then to explain the causes of war because the complication of fascism did not enter." Today there were far worse working conditions, "greatly increased speed and strain of production, a seven day week and overtime every night." He answers Bill's question as to what he would do if he were now in the workshop. He would see that his workmanship was of the best quality, and his timekeeping strict. "I would not lay myself open to getting paid off because some toady whispered to the foreman 'He's a Red'." His second care would be to challenge excessive overtime, "which by increasing sickness, accidents and exhaustion in fact results in falling production". Attempts to suspend parts of the Factory Acts because "there's a war on" should be resisted. "Glasgow shop stewards have insisted that Saturday afternoons and alternate Sundays be free, and that after three nights' overtime, any proposal for additional nights be considered separately." Finally, he stresses the need to maintain trade union organisation and propaganda, to elect shop stewards for all departments, and to back them up.

The second letter took up political questions. Bill has remarked that the workshop was now discussing Soviet policy in a sympathetic way, and that he had been wrong over Russia during the Finnish events. Pollitt detects in Bill's mind the idea that only Russia can get Britain out of the mess she is in, and says, "Isn't it more pertinent to ask what we British workers are going to do about it?" And to answer "We are going to get rid of the present government and get a new one. Then things will change, for we will get into touch with the Soviet Government and the workers' organisations of all lands to bring peace and security for all working people."

The third letter[18] offers Bill some advice about his difficulties with a daughter of eighteen and a son of sixteen. "You asked me to tell him about the facts of life because you would feel ashamed if you did it. Well, I tried my hand and found he knew a few that were new on me. 'Only', he said, factories to save the people", a long deep-throated roar of approval rose from the dense crowd.[15]

He described[16] the situation as "the greatest crisis in the history of this island". Disaster could happen here too, for in high places were men with the same policy as those who opened the door for Hitler in France. The Labour Movement had to decide one of three courses—continue support of the imperialist war, surrender to Hitler, or bring to power a People's Government to defend Britain from fascism within and without.

The attraction of fascism for the ruling class was that, once in power, it destroyed all workers' and democratic organisations in order to get more work done for less wages, more profit for big capitalists, a stronger drive for world domination. That was the political basis for the pro-fascists who surrendered France, represented here by men like Chamberlain, Simon, Hoare, Kingsley Wood and General Ironside. The Churchill Government, with official Labour support, kept like-minded men in high office, and identified defence with the maintenance of empire and ruling-class control. But real defence of the people required a complete break with the policy of the ruling class, for they had led Britain into its present position."

"In this hour of mortal crisis the Labour leaders, instead of leading the fight against capitalism, rush forward to save it. They applauded Blum when he justified the suppression of the French Communist Party, and demanded the suppression of British Communism. No one has a greater responsibility for what has befallen France than Blum. Let it be a warning to Bevin and Morrison."

The responsibility fell on the organised workers to break the alliance with big business and give the lead for the formation of a People's Government to organise the true defence of Britain on a programme of urgent, essential measures: (1) remove supporters of fascism from all commanding positions; (2) conscript wealth and nationalise banks, mines, transport, armaments production; (3) elect Workers' Control Committees in the factories; (4) arm the workers in the factories; (5) increase Forces pay and allowances, break down the class system in appointing officers; (6) adequate air-raid precautions and evacuation; (7) withdraw all limitation of free speech, press, meetings and organisation for the workers; (8) full freedom to India and all peoples of the Empire, end the partition of Ireland; (9) fraternal relations with the U.S.S.R. and the workers of all countries for freedom and peace.

"This is no time for pessimism and doubt. It is a time for activity. The power to act is in the hands of the workers, the shop stewards, trade union branches, trades councils. Do not be afraid of this power; use it for the working class and the common people of this land."

He concluded: "They say we are anti-British. It is a foul lie. We love these islands so well, we love our people so much that we want to rid them of the parasites who betray them and aim to lead us to still further calamities."

one of the not-too-numerous band who turned up the same as ever. If you look up the files you will see I was not only writing but working steadily for months thereafter." No copy of Pollitt's reply is available, but a few days later Postgate wrote, "I am very glad to know you did not mean me". Mention of his name was deleted from later editions.[14]

The book was an instantaneous success among Communists, trade union militants and left-wingers. It was reprinted, twice in 1941, again in 1950, again in 1960, and was translated into German and Russian.

4. 'FRANCE HAS FALLEN—ARM THE WORKERS.'

On May 9, 1940, German Panzer Divisions crossed the frontiers of France. Some swerved to the coast, cut off the Belgian army and drove the British into the sea at Dunkirk. Others outflanked the Maginot Line and drove on towards Paris. Appalled Londoners saw a succession of newspaper placards—"Germans in Lille"—"In Arras"—"In Amiens"—"In Compiègne"—reviving memories of 1914. But this time there was no miracle of the Marne. On June 14 the placards screamed "Germans in Paris" and on the 17th., "French Surrender", an incredible pendant to "Dutch Surrender" and "Belgian Surrender".

Gradually the pieces of the jigsaw came together—French generals, taken by surprise, leaving vital bridges intact; streams of refugees blocking the roads and preventing the movement of reinforcements; burning oil tanks deluging Paris in black smoke; nine-tenths of the Parisians fleeing to the South and West on roads machined-gunned by planes; chaos in the administration; the Government in flight to Bordeaux, then to Vichy; the entire Maginot Line taken from the rear; heroic three days' defence of Tours; general military collapse; a new government headed by the defeatist Marshal Petain with the fascist Laval as moving spirit; armistice; France divided into Occupied Zone controlled by German fascists and Unoccupied Zone, controlled by French fascists. The completed picture read "France betrayed by the fascist fifth column".

The fall of France opened many eyes in Britain to the full meaning of what public opinion had dubbed the "phoney war". The heroism and determination of the crews of every small craft that could be mobilised rescued the army from Dunkirk, but its guns and stores were totally lost. For the first time since Napoleon, Britain faced invasion.

London workers expected Pollitt to speak at moments of crisis; Sunday, June 23 saw Chenies Street thronged by thousands who listened intently as he revealed the cause of the French catastrophe, the true nature of the peril to Britain, and the responsibility of the working class in defence of all past gains and all future hopes. His usual humour and cracks were absent, it was a grim speech for a grim situation, arousing not applause but a growing sense of urgency and determination. When his outline of what had to be done reached the crucial demand "Arm the workers in the one strength, hope and inspiration. There is no sacrifice too great to be allowed to serve the working class. . . . I have supreme confidence in the working class from which I have sprung and from which nothing will ever separate me. I know that one day they will conquer power in Britain and overthrow the decadent and corrupt clique who rule this country today. I know, too, that the Communist Party will lead this struggle to its successful issue."

Reviewing the book R. Palme Dutt wrote:[11] "At a time when slander of the Communists is the cheap diversion of every hack, renegade and political coward, this book is a breath of fresh air from a revolutionary working-class fighter." He contrasted its story, "full of life and racy humour, enthralling to read as a novel", with the tedious reminiscences of "self-important bigwigs of the ruling class" going through the routine of their ready-made lives.

Sean O'Casey wrote:[12] "Only a hundredth part of what Harry Pollitt has done can be recorded in this book, yet an amazing amount of work is pictured in it. Harry has well and truly laboured for his fellow workers, so different from those who left the workers' movement for a handful of silver or a ribbon to stick on a coat."

Such capitalist papers as noticed the book ignored its political content and selected humorous or emotional items—Bernard Shaw's gift of £5, Pollitt's handshake with Lenin, his mother's letter on his dismissal from the Secretaryship.

Many workers sent their comments. Among them Jim Godfrey, a leading militant locoman, wrote: "I particularly like the story of your young days, the tribute to your mother, the Southampton strike, your crossing the frontier of the U.S.S.R., Moscow at Lenin's death, your splendid justification when the Party was on trial. May you live to see realised the dream you portray, the mirage that all rebels see in their dreams that will some day materialise." Fred Bower, associated with Tom Mann in the "Don't Shoot" appeal of 1912, wrote "How your book revived me. I am now living on old age pension, have angina pectoris, sometimes have a struggle to breathe, so can only hark back to the battle from afar in my little cottage by the Dee. I did go to Russia three years ago to view the promised land, and found it good."[13]

A different response came from Raymond Postgate. Pollitt had mentioned him as present at the founding conference of the C.P.G.B., and went on to refer, without giving names, to those who had left the Party when police persecution began. Postgate first said that he thought the C.P. attitude to the war "was objectively nothing more nor less than aiding and supporting the Nazis", and went on: "I have always found you honest and accurate in your criticisms. I don't think you would intentionally write a false statement about me or anyone else in the Labour Movement." He then stated: "I was not at the Conference you mention. When Inspector Parker came to arrest Albert Inkpin, so far from leaving the office I was

Labour leaders, was sending huge supplies of munitions to Finland and preparing to follow up with a heavily armed force of 100,000 men.[8] Chamberlain and Daladier evidently saw the Finnish-Soviet conflict as their opportunity to "switch the war" and attack the U.S.S.R. Pollitt spoke in every backstreet of the constituency warning against the danger and recalling the example of the *Jolly George* and the Councils of Action of 1920.

Among Pollitt's helpers were Lawrence Bradshaw, painter and sculptor, and Ken Stitt, a commercial artist. Together they prepared posters and cartoons on high prices and other local issues, relating them to Pollitt's election policy. Displayed outside Committee Rooms, and changed every few hours to keep them topical, these drawings aroused great interest, especially when Bradshaw enlivened them with sketches of people in the crowd. Sometimes they invited people in to discuss the drawings; women and children were mostly interested; the children took leaflets to give out. Bradshaw was criticised because he put "too much of a come-hither expression" into some of the girls' eyes.[9]

Another active supporter was the militant socialist priest, Jack Putterill, whose church was not far away. He went canvassing, and one day was asked what he would do if the Red Army came to Silvertown. He replied that he would welcome them as soldiers of Christ, for they, too, advocated holding all things in common. When Pollitt later spoke in that street, he was surprised to find a desire for detailed information about the Red Army and was startled when told, "You've no bloody right to invite them to come here." Jack Putterill had an eye with a twinkle in it, he noted everyday things, such as Committee Room volunteers having a cold lunch. Next day and after he came with his cassock pockets full of baked potatoes, piping hot.[10]

The vote was: Labour 14,343; Pollitt 966; Fascist 151, on a poll of 55 per cent. Under the political truce, no Tory or Liberal stood.

3. 'Serving My Time' March 1940.

This book first appeared in March 1940, Pollitt dedicated it to his mother. It included accounts of significant episodes of his life and the full text of some of his documents and speeches. The conclusion gives his declaration of faith.

"We Communists are not activated by malice, jealousy and uncharitableness, but we do hate capitalism and all who uphold it. We hate to see the workers poor and anxious in a land where poverty and anxiety could be abolished tomorrow if all who pretend they are socialists fought for socialism and did not defend capitalism. We do want unity of the workers' forces for the genuinely sincere reason that we want the working class to be as strong as possible against all its enemies, against all its false friends.... There is no other class but the working class for me. They give the barriers between skilled and unskilled, and to make trade unionism a revolutionary weapon by the inspiration of Socialism." Tom Mann was the only leader of his generation who always saw ahead, never satisfied with things as they were. "He never went after positions of security, wealth and power. It was direct action he wanted, that was why he welcomed the Russian Revolution." A foundation member of the Communist Party, "he carried on the habit of his life, always to march with the vanguard."

The tribute concluded with a vivid sketch of Tom Mann as he would be remembered "by millions who knew and loved him, who quickened with life as he strode briskly on to the platform to explain things in simple socialist language; millions whom he roused to wrath by his exposure of capitalism and inflamed with determination to get together for unity, militancy, solidarity and direct action. At the end Tom would command them to stand and put up their hands if they agreed with what he had said, and swiftly taking out his handkerchief, he would call for 'Three Cheers for Unity!' This was no ritual on his part, it was a serious thing, a pledge taken, a decision made, an audience won for action. To send workers home feeling warm with comradeship and revolutionary fire—this was always his aim. Age was never allowed to dim his burning, passionate faith. Always the light of Socialism and Internationalism shone bright for Tom Mann."[25]

On April 15 1956 at a Poplar meeting to mark the centenary of Tom Mann's birth Pollitt renewed the pledge "to keep alive his fighting, socialist spirit and all it stands for."

9. THE SHIPYARD ONCE MORE.

Early in 1941 an Order was made for men who had left the shipyards to register for war work there. Pollitt went to see the Boilermakers' London official, Ted Hill, who later described what happened. "I phoned the leading employers and asked for a job for Mr. Harry Pollitt. Each replied that no work was available, and when I asked to speak with the leading man, he was not available. The next Monday happened to be the meeting of the Port Conciliation Committee composed of representatives of the Admiralty, the employers and the unions. The chair was taken by the Admiral of the Port, Sir Martin Dunbar-Nasmith, who got the V.C. for penetrating the minefields in the Dardanelles and sinking enemy craft in the Sea of Marmora. I asked for an additional item on the agenda, and when it came up explained that I had a first-class plater who wanted a job, but was not wanted because he was a Communist. The Admiral said, 'We need platers, and I'm not concerned whether he is a Communist.' The employers all wanted to please the Admiral and said they would take the man on. I asked whether the London Graving Dock wanted him, and the representative said 'I'll have him'."[26]

Pollit began work in the Graving Dock, Poplar, on April 21 "and received a warm welcome from the salt of the earth, the boilermakers, on returning to the fold." On the first day members who thought he was down and out offered monies totalling £250 to help him.[27]

On May 11 1941, Pollitt wrote: "This morning I walked from Old Street Tube Station to a Poplar shipyard after the great blitz. Everywhere fires, destroyed buildings, homeless people, for miles I walked on broken glass. I could not help thinking how the Amerys declare that the people of India are not yet fit to be trusted with the government of their own country—when this is the state of affairs in London and Berlin after centuries of so-called government by the cultured Christian capitalist ruling classes."[28]

One of his jobs was on a damaged destroyer, "a torpedo had passed right through the crew's quarters. We went below to see what repairs were necessary. We found a terrible mass of twisted steel and shattered human bodies, bodies of young men, too young to have known much of life. I am sure some of them had faced death in the belief that by doing so they were giving their fathers and mothers, their sweethearts, their children, a chance of a better life than they had ever had before."[29]

When Pollitt was again General Secretary of the Communist Party, he asked to leave shiprepair, because in that case he could "do more effective work in mobilising all possible support to achieve victory over fascism," than in the shipyard. The application was at first rejected. Pollitt appealed, won his appeal, and left the yard.[30] But the Admiral's eye was wide open. Ted Hill got a phone call from him: "This man Pollitt has left. He can't do that without permission. I can't have anyone privileged." Ted Hill explained that the Minister of Labour wanted him. The Admiral said, "He can't be released till he reports back at work. If he does it, thousands more will want to. There must be a proper release." On being told, Harry saw the point, went back to the job,[31] and finally got his release dated August 8.

10. HITLER'S DEPUTY.

In May 1941, Hitler's deputy, Rudolph Hess, landed in Britain to seek contact with the Duke of Hamilton. The Government allowed a veil of mystery to envelop this event. Pollitt was one of many who regarded it as an attempt to negotiate a deal between Hitler and British Tories. This view received wider credence when a few weeks later Hitler launched his blitzkreig against the Soviet Union.

Pollitt was one of those against whom the Duke of Hamilton took proceedings for libel, alleging that in certain publications he had been presented as a friend of Hess, plotting with the enemies of this country. The case was heard in the High Court on February 18, 1942. Counsel for the Duke said that he was on duty in an R.A.F. Operations Room when a German plane landed near Farne Island off the Northumbrian coast. Later, the Duke was informed that the pilot claimed to be on a special mission to him, and had intended to land near his home. The Duke and an interrogation officer then saw the German who asked to see the Duke alone, and announced: "I am Rudolph Hess." The Duke immediately got into touch with the authorities.

Pollitt stated that he had no responsibility for the publications complained of, and the Duke accepted his statement. The other defendants admitted responsibility and undertook to apologise and to pay costs.[32]

11. Hitler attacks the Soviet Union.

On Sunday June 22, 1941, the early morning radio announced that without warning Hitler had hurled hundreds of divisions and thousands of planes and tanks across the Soviet frontiers. Hitler proclaimed his reason: the Russian military presence on his Eastern borders tied up such German forces that the German High Command "could not vouch for a radical conclusion of the war in the West." Later that day, Churchill came to the microphone to declare that, without changing his views on socialism and communism, he recognised that Britain and the Soviet Union had "one aim, one single purpose—to destroy Hitler and every vestige of the Nazi regime," and that Britain would give what help she could to the Soviet Union. Stalin at once greeted this as "an historic utterance", and added that "aid would be on a reciprocal basis". On June 24, Britain and the U.S.S.R. agreed to co-operate and to exchange Missions. On July 12 they signed a Pact of Mutual Aid, pledging no separate peace.

The Central Committee of the C.P.G.B. met, recognised the vital change in the war and restored Pollitt as General Secretary. Greeted with prolonged cheers at a great meeting in Montague Place on June 26 Pollitt declared the supreme task to be "to develop the resources, leadership and strategy necessary to wipe fascism from the face of the earth".[33] It was the first of a series of statements to end any ambiguity in the workers' attitude to the war.

"The Churchill Government and the Soviet Union are fighting side by side, a fact which if some Communists did not expect it, neither did Hitler, nor other powerful forces in the world." The Party was for "a united national front of all who are for Hitler's defeat. Our fight is not against the Churchill Government, but against those who are secret friends of Hitler."[34] "The war for the defeat of Hitler is now the supreme issue before the whole of democratic mankind. . . . It must govern the action of a united people and rule their attitude to every question posed to them."[35] "For the first time we now have a real fight against fascism. Now it is a people's war in which the people of Britain and the Soviet Union are working and fighting side by side."[36] "This is a People's War. One that only the common people can and will win. To think otherwise is to have no faith in the working class and its mass organisations."[37]

To the taunt about "another change of line", Pollitt replied that the situation, including Churchill's attitude to the U.S.S.R., had changed. Communist policy took this into account. To those who spoke of dictatorship from Moscow, he said, "The Communist Party is dictated to only by the common interests of the British and Soviet peoples."[38] Speculation on how long British-Soviet co-operation would last he condemned as "defeatism, lack of faith in the sound instinct of the people". As for the past, "In the light of today, what does it matter what Gallacher said about Attlee, the *Daily Worker* about *The Times,* or that twelve Communists were in prison when Churchill was editing the *British Gazette?*"

CHAPTER 20

ANTI-FASCIST WAR

1. Programme for victory. 2. For the Second Front—1941. 3. For the Second Front—1942. 4. For the Second Front—1943. 5. Herbert Henry Bailey. 6. D-Day. 7. India. 8. Daily life in wartime.

1. PROGRAMME FOR VICTORY.

An essential element in support of the anti-fascist war was the programme[1] of measures necessary for victory, formulated by Pollitt in the summer of 1941.

The main features were:
 For British-Soviet aid to be reciprocal there needs to be a unified strategy and a Second Front in Western Europe.
 The Men of Munich and all friends of fascism must be removed from all positions of influence.
 The solution of the problems of production requires a combination of governmental measures and the democratic initiative of the workers.
 To maximise the war effort requires a leading part in all its aspects be played by the workers' organisations.
 India needs be treated as a full ally against fascism and have its own democratic and independent government.
 The ban on the *Daily Worker* and all similar restrictions hampering the war effort must be removed.
 Government propaganda, especially the B.B.C., must be improved and democratised.
 More must be done in the spirit of equality in sacrifice to meet the people's needs for improved air-raid precautions, higher war allowances, better food distribution, and other wants.

This programme did not include any socialist measures, it concentrated upon what was necessary for winning victory over fascism in the shortest possible time. It was democratic and national in content. It recognised that the people and in particular the organised working class were a decisive force in carrying the war to victory, and that political support for the Churchill Government did not mean subservience to it or unquestioning acceptance of everything Churchill chose to say or do.

Here Pollitt's policy stood in sharp contrast to that of the Labour leaders, who shared Churchill's views on the need to preserve British imperialist interests, and were content to allow him to determine at each stage what should be British policy.

The Communist Party's activities from 1941 to 1945 were on a scale greater than from 1936 to 1939. Pollitt consistently popularised all the main features of the policy for victory. We will limit examination to two issues—the Second Front and self-government for India—on which political differences and their class basis were most clearly revealed.

2. For the Second Front—1941.

From the start, Pollitt presented the Second Front as essential to British interests. "The British and Soviet peoples face unparalleled danger. We have to throw into the fight everything we can in order that from North and South, East and West, we can batter hell out of fascism."[2] "Only combined British-Soviet blows will bring down Hitler. In her own interests Britain must strike in the West by land, sea and air."[3] "The decisive question for speedy victory is the creation of the second front in the West."[4] "Hitler says that he could not finish off Britain because of Russia, so he will finish off Russia first and then turn everything against Britain without fear of what may happen in his rear."[5] "What the Russians have done in the last ten weeks has saved London."[6] "Because there is no second front, Hitler is allowed to fight his enemies one by one. He is allowed to push against Russia all he has, even divisions withdrawn from the West, so that he can attack Britain later in circumstances exceedingly dangerous for our people."[7] The Second Front meant strenuous effort and sacrifice: "We have no right to demand a second military front unless we create a fighting front in the mines, shipyards, aircraft and munitions industries."[8] "The Second Front means great sacrifices, but if we are not prepared to make such sacrifices, we have no right to expect others to make them for us."[9] "The second front will require a production front to achieve the maximum from the productive resources of Britain."[10]

Lloyd George

In July and August the German mechanised offensive swept on, their armoured divisions approached Moscow and Leningrad. Alarm grew in Britain at the absence of any move to open a Western front. Lloyd George said[11] "During the last war, Russia sacrificed her army at Tannenburg to save us and stop the march on Paris. She lost her army, but achieved her object. Now Russia is fighting for her life and if the German general headquarters are to be believed, she needs assistance. What now are we doing to help her? Absolutely nothing!" Pollitt, while recognising the "intense R.A.F. air activity carried out in the West",[12] considered the alarm fully justified, and in stressing the urgency of the Second Front made concrete proposals for increased production of everything this would require.[13] At the Ministry of Information "Brendan Bracken pleaded he was too busy to see me and pushed me on to the late Mr. Thurtle, who had not the slightest idea of what I was talking about. *The Times* asked me to see its Labour Correspondent. But Lloyd George asked me to come and see him at Churt. I did. He made me very welcome; told Miss Stevenson and Mr. Sylvester he wanted to be alone with me. The first thing he did was to apologise for what he called his 'ungracious conduct' at the Empress Hall in 1939. We then talked for two hours."[14]

Pollitt outlined[15] what he saw as negative features—cynicism in the factories over production, the exaggerated ideas about American help. Russian scorched-earth policy was approved but with no recognition of its real meaning to them or to us. Complacency that "we can leave it to the Russians" was mixed with suspicion that "we intend to let the Russians do the dying" and speculation about "a switch against them". Cheers for the Second Front didn't mean understanding what it meant for production. The Government had lost its grip on the people, the press and B.B.C. did not arouse enthusiam.

Pollitt recalled Lloyd George's speeches at Limehouse and elsewhere, in support of his pre-1914 budgets and the immense wave of popular support aroused. He then said, "Today someone with authority, prestige and popular sympathies needs to do a similar job. You are that man. You have a quite special position in home and foreign politics. The people are waiting for a lead—to be told the grim facts, what is expected of them, to be lifted out of the present dream world. They will respond if only the lead will come." He suggested that Lloyd George should call for a special meeting of Parliament, give a broadcast message to the nation, and one to the Soviet people, and initiate a public campaign of newspaper articles, meetings and demonstrations. Unfortunately Lloyd George's reply is not recorded.

The fact that Pollitt made such proposals suggests that he regarded Lloyd George as closer to the people than the Tories were, and that he realised that Churchill's adherence to the Anglo-Soviet Pact was intended only to advance the interests of British imperialism.

Moore-Brabazon;

While public support grew for compelling Hitler to fight on two fronts, a sensational incident threw light on thinking in high places. At a meeting[16] where reporters were not allowed, the Minister for Aircraft Production, Colonel Moore-Brabazon, said that he hoped "the Russian and German armies will exterminate each other", and leave Britain the dominating power in Europe. This speech was reported to the Trades Union Congress and aroused wide indignation. Churchill neither repudiated nor removed his Minister, but excused him for "unpremeditated indiscretion".

On September 9, Churchill gave Parliament an outline of government policy, from which Pollitt concluded that the Second Front "is not contemplated at this stage" and that the failure to repudiate Moore-Brabazon meant that "while his statement and government policy may have been differently phrased, from the point of view of practical effect, they were not very far removed".[17] Quoting the eminent military writer, Captain Liddell Hart, "Few people expected that Soviet Russia would for long withstand a German blitzkreig, and the higher the quarter the lower the expectations tended to be".[18] Pollitt commented that "having such higher ups so grossly misinformed, so secretly hoping the worst will happen" threw a flood of light on the reasons for British defeats and the refusal to open the Second Front.[19]

At a shadow factory building site the Works Committee, with management permission, invited Pollitt to speak. Stewards were waiting to meet him when, a few minutes before the meeting was due to begin, there was a flutter of officials, brasshats and lesser lights—the Home Secretary had banned Pollitt from entering the site. But if Morrison was quick, the men were quicker. An improvised platform went up just outside the job, the word went round. One listener wrote, "Despite police interference, Pollitt had a better meeting than he would have had inside. He was at his best, spoke of the need for war in the West and of overcoming absenteeism. He asked what would we think of an airman instructed to bomb Germany who went instead for a West-End jaunt, and showed how narrow were our objections to payment by results compared to the issue of Fascism or Freedom. He advocated recognition of the Works Committee, the use of all resources, an end to inefficiency and graft, and wound up with a scathing denunciation of Moore-Brabazon and all he represented. The meeting pledged solidarity with the Soviet building workers, demanded suspension of Moore-Brabazon, protested at Morrison's ban, and gave Pollitt three rousing cheers."[20]

German defeat near Moscow.

Events soon gave the lie to the prophets of Russian collapse. On November 7, Stalin said in the Red Square; "The German invaders want a war of extermination against the peoples of the U.S.S.R. Well, if the Germans want a war of extermination, they shall have it." Shortly afterwards the Red Army inflicted such a defeat on the Germans near Moscow that Hitler's offensive was brought to a stop.

Pollitt commented, "The Red Army has smashed the legend of fascist invincibility, one of the greatest military victories of all time has been won. The German people are realising this fact, for truth cannot be placed in a permanent concentration camp." His speech[21], three days after Christmas 1941, was relayed from the crowded Stoll Theatre, London, to nine other full halls. Communist technicians in their spare time had overcome problems arising from the varieties of amplifying equipment involved, the Post Office provided transmission over telephone circuits. It was a novel experiment attempted by no other Party. One listener wrote, "Pollitt spoke with an eloquence as effective when relayed as in the Stoll itself." The 12,000 strong audiences gave £1,174 to the Party, and 683 people joined.[22] The central theme of his speech and of the nation-wide campaign which followed, was that the successes of the Red Army marked a turning point in the war and that, provided the Second Front was opened and the full resources of the allies brought into action, the decisive victory over Hitler could be won in 1942. But he stressed "the deadly seriousness of the fight still to be waged, the sacrifices still to be made, the titanic efforts still to be exerted".

Production.

Pollitt had no illusions as to the problems in the field of production. The system of government payments on the basis of "cost of production plus 10 per cent" was itself a "root cause of waste and corruption".[23] There was no effective planning and control, instead "thousands of non-producers floating around impeding production by their multiplicity of directions".[24] Deeper difficulties arose from the structure of industry. "The great monopolies are their own controllers; their policy is profit, extension of their monopoly, safeguarding their post-war position. The needs of war production are fitted in to these interests."[25]

A combination of government measures and workers' initiative was required. "We need works committees to check mismanagement, waste and corruption and to ensure maximum production".[26] It was essential for the government "to end cost-plus; to plan production centrally; to control mining, transport, aircraft, engineering, iron and steel; to eliminate private monopoly interests and exhorbitant profit; and to give plenary powers to Production Committees".[27] But to implement such measures "it is urgently necessary that the factory workers should feel their own power and be confident in exercising it. Once the men and women on the job are really angry at what they see going on, and fight to put it right, then things will begin to move, and not before".[28]

Pollitt's intimate knowledge of industrial matters gave him considerable influence with leading militants in the trade unions. His ideas on production were reflected in a conference called by the National Council of Shop Stewards in the Engineering and Allied Trades, where 1,237 delegates from 330 factories decided on practical steps to "immediately increase production and mould industry into a tremendous force against Hitler". Their subsequent activities were decisive in the success of the Joint Production Committees.[29]

3. FOR THE SECOND FRONT—1942.

On January 29, Churchill countered a motion in the House urging changes in the government by asking for a vote of confidence. Pollitt acknowledged Churchill's determination to carry through to the end the war against Hitler and his recognition of the decisive role of the Soviet Union. But his refusal to reorganise the government meant that "he takes under his protection notorious incompetents and Munichites; his silence on India was ominous, and above all his refusal to open the Second Front imperilled the whole future".[30]

On February 15, Churchill broadcast a plea for complete confidence in his government. To Pollitt this was unacceptable. "The people have lost confidence in so many members of the Government." The loss of Singapore, the passage of Nazi warships through the Channel, the Nazi advance in Libya, above all the contrast between the Red Army offensive and the absence of a Second Front, made it essential that Churchill act against the incompetents. "To protect such people is not leadership, but inability to fight against reactionary Munichites totally incapable of leading the struggle".[31] Ten days later Churchill did make changes. Moore-Brabazon was among those dismissed. He was given a peerage—whether for his ban on production meetings in aircraft factories, or his "unpremeditated indiscretion" was not stated.

To Pollitt the changes were only a beginning. The new government must have a new policy. He recalled Churchill's admission of complete underestimation of Russian strength and Noel Baker's remark that little assistance had been sent because the government had been advised that Hitler's attack would bring a Soviet collapse. He added, "The same lack of confidence exists now. The full meaning of the Soviet victories is not understood. The contrast between Soviet confidence and British pessimism stands out a mile".[32]

May 1: Stalin speaks of a new phase in the war, "the liberation of Soviet lands from Hitler". At London's May Day, 20,000 hear Pollitt declare "Victory in this war depends on the Second Front in Europe".[33]

May 10: Churchill approves demonstrations "demanding most vehement and audacious attacks".

May 23-24: At a National Conference C.P.G.B. Pollitt says: "There is no substitute for the Second Front, the main enemy is Hitler, the only place he can be smashed is Europe. The danger of waiting is to prolong the war".[34]

May 24: Pollitt speaks to 50,000 in Traflagar Square. A resolution calling for the Second Front, freedom for India, and lifting the ban on the *Daily Worker* is carried with acclamation.

June 11: The signature of an Anglo-Soviet Treaty of Alliance and Friendship is announced, British, Soviet and U.S. representatives, having reached "full understanding with regard to the urgent task of creating a Second Front in 1942".[35]

End of June: Hitler's second great offensive threatens Voronezh and Stalingrad. Pollitt: "Hitler advances because there is no Second Front in Europe and he hopes his friends will prevent it being organised."[36]

July 1-2: The Commons by 475 to 25 defeat a motion of "no confidence in the central direction of the war". Churchill stands firm on the Anglo-Soviet Alliance, is silent on the Second Front and says "I have never shared the view that this would be a short war; it is far more likely to be a long one". Pollitt describes those voting against the alliance with the Soviet Union as "pro-fascists who from Hitler's seizure of power to Munich, yielded every strategic position to the Nazis, bringing Britain to the brink of destruction. Their aim is still alliance with Hitler against Russia. They want to instal leaders who will come to an understanding with the Nazis".[37]

July 4: Hitler takes Sebastopol after eight months' siege.

July 7: U.S. Chief of Supply says "U.S. ready and able to send men and materials on large scale to Europe".[38]

July 7: C.P.G.B. proposes to Labour Party common action to press for immediate opening of the Second Front.

July 10: "Britain's confidence in U.S.S.R. must be translated into positive assistance" (*Times*)

July 13: "We are pledged to establish the Second Front. When are we going to keep our promise?" (*Daily Herald*).

July 14: "The British people are restive with desire to strike a heavy blow in Europe" (*News Chronicle*).

July 16: "Must we stand as spectators at Armageddon, like racegoers who have placed their bets and can do no more than shout to affect the outcome?" (*Evening Standard*).

July 26: Bevin says the Second Front "may be a great contributory issue, but it is not the only one and not the only way to win the war".[39]

July 26: A British Government representative in U.S.A.: "The real Second Front is the bombing of Europe."

July 26: 60,000 people overflow Trafalgar Square to hear a platform of wide opinion call for the Second Front without delay. Pollitt: "Britain and Russian stand or fall together. Among the people there is anger that we play the role of spectators when all peoples at this fateful hour are at the crossroads of history".[40]

July 28: Air Marshal Harris broadcasts that air bombing is Britain's way to defeat Hitler.

July 29: 1,500 delegates lobby for the lifting of the ban on the *Daily Worker* and for the Second Front.[41]

August 1: Lady Astor says she "is tired of hearing about Russia."[42]

August 6: "Lack of Second Front in the grave military situation makes Allied strategy uncertain" (*Times*).

August 6: Shop Stewards from Manchester representing 150,000 workers and from London representing 100,000, lobby for the Second Front.[43]

August 7: Parliament adjourns for four weeks.

August 16: Ilya Ehrenburg in *Reynolds News:* "Britain and America are in danger. Neither the Channel nor the Atlantic will replace the Red Army."

August 17: Announcement that Churchill has been in Moscow; talks agreed on "common aim of complete victory over fascism." No mention of immediate Second Front.[44]

August 22: In South Wales 24 simultaneous demonstrations call for Second Front.

August 29: Pollitt: "The situation on the Soviet front is critical in the extreme for one reason—absence of the Second Front. No appreciable effort is being made to take off strain from the Red Army which faces the main war strength of Nazi Germany, Italy, Romania, Finland, Hungary, with all Europe a gigantic munition factory for Hitler".[45]

August 30: In London, 80 meetings with 33,000 people (Pollitt at Hammersmith with 2,5000) call for the Second Front.[46]

On September 8, Parliament returned from holiday to hear Churchill report. German Panzer divisions had forced the suburbs of Stalingrad. The Red Army was fighting street by street under a deluge of bombs and shells. *Pravda* had written. "Hitler has hurled all his reserves into the battle. He has risked denuding the Atlantic coast to attain success on the German-Soviet front".[47]

Roused by the danger, the demand for the Second Front reached new heights; all Britain expected Parliament to give the lead. Instead, Churchill's speech contained nothing new, the much-publicised debate was a fiasco. Pollitt described[48] what had happened as a "blow in the face for the nation. The country expected deeds from Mr. Churchill, it got words. The agreement to open the Second Front was deliberately side-stepped. It was the duty of M.Ps. not to rush out for lunch, but to challenge the weakness revealed by constructive proposals," But instead there was "a political demoralisation at the centre of the Government and in Parliament, with no counterpart in the ranks of the common people".

At the October meeting of the C.P.G.B. Central Committee, Pollitt directly associated Churchill with the decision to delay the Second Front. He spoke of "unease and disquiet, a growing sense of no clear strategy and leadership, a lack of confidence in the Government, the beginning of insistent questioning of the position of Churchill". The resolution he moved said "the Government has failed to carry out its pledged word to establish the Second Front in 1942. It has failed to overcome the defeatist activity of the pro-fascists. For this the Prime Minister bears a heavy personal responsibility."[49]

He reminded his audience that following the Soviet counter-attacks in the winter of 1941–42, "the Nazi army reached the point of collapse. Goering said conditions were such that normal people would have thrown their hands in.[50] Had we struck then from the West victory would have been certain. That chance was thrown away."[51]

"Widespread popular opinion for the Second Front has not arisen because of armchair strategies or irresponsible agitators. It has been formed because the facts of the situation can be understood by everyone. The one thing no one can understand is—what is Britain waiting for? The only explanation is that those who influence the Government's policy either do not want an early Allied victory (because like Moore-Brabazon they hope the Russians and Germans will exterminate each other) or are too timid and feeble to seize the opportunity the Russian resistance has given to the Allies."[52]

How close Pollitt was to the truth was shown when in 1946 the diary of General Eisenhower's Aide, Captain Butcher was published.[53] The entries included:

July 10 1942: "The Chiefs of Staff have been considering a quick thrust across the Channel during the summer of 1942 ... the British appear to favour an attack in North Africa ... Ike would prefer to cross the Channel."

July 19 1942: "Ike finished the basic proposals ... for the second front in France by October this year ... these are momentous days."

July 23 1942: "The proposal for the Second Front this year has been definitely turned down by the British. Ike and Clark deeply disappointed. Ike thought that July 22 could well go down as the 'blackest day in history', particularly if Russia is defeated."[54]

During October the fighting at Stalingrad reached a peak of intensity. Every day a fresh German Division was thrown in; the Russians fought street by street, house by house, floor by floor, room by room. By concentrating an enormous weight of metal on a small front the Germans stormed the workers' settlement, but the battle continued. Pollitt stressed the contrast—"The Red Army fights red eyed through lack of sleep in a burning inferno; workers' battalions, men and women alike, fight in Stalingrad streets, while all is quiet on the Western front, and in Britain we calmly discuss whether it is right to call on women to do firewatching."[55]

Pollitt proposed an emergency national conference of Labour organisations to agree on a win-the-war policy—remove Amery, Grigg, Halifax, Simon and Hoare from the Government; establish collective leadership in the War Cabinet; organise the Second Front; unify Allied strategy; make changes in the General Staff to operate this policy. Then call a conference of all anti-fascist parties to campaign to strengthen the government.

On October 25, Trafalgar Square again overflowed with supporters for the Second Front, the speakers included Labour M.P.s Dr. Haden Guest and Aneurin Bevan, the Editor of the *Sunday Express* and Ted Bramley of the Communist Party. On November 6 it was made known that the Red Army was fighting 179 of Germany's 256 Divisions, plus 61 divisions of her allies. Asked how it was possible for Germany to muster these forces, Stalin replied "Because of the absence of a Second Front in Europe."[56]

Two days later, following the British victory at Alamein, substantial British and American forces landed in Algeria and began a major offensive to drive the German-Italian forces out of North Africa.

Pollitt, recognising that this development, while not in itself the Second Front, opened new possibilities, wrote: "Attention has to be concentrated, not on the past, but on utilising present possibilities to secure a unified strategy and the speediest advance to a Second Front in Europe." "Everything possible must be done—in production, in policy, in strengthening the government to ensure the success of the offensive and its extension into Europe. Anything but its success would be not only a military disaster but would give new opportunities to reaction, pro-fascist or imperialist, to gain positions for attempts at appeasement." "While the Churchill Government has failed to open the Second Front in 1942, it does rule out any compromise peace with fascism. However wrong its strategy, its basic aim is the destruction of Hitler Germany, and in that it is at one with the Soviet Union and the U.S.A."[57]

On November 19 a Soviet offensive began; on the 22nd the Red Army at Stalingrad struck the first blows which culminated in the greatest defeat ever suffered by Germany, the surrender of Von

Paulus with the entire command and all the troops left of the German Sixth Army. This complete defeat of Hitler's second great offensive proved how well founded was the confidence that a Second Front could have finished him in 1942.

4. For the Second Front—1943.

On July 5 1943 Hitler launched his third great offensive. On a front of 170 miles at Kursk-Orel, 211 German Divisions attacked with 70-ton heavy tanks, mobile heavy artillery and thousands of planes. The attack gained ground at tremendous cost until July 14, when it was halted. Next day the Soviet counter-offensive began. On July 24 Stalin announced that all lost ground had been regained, the German offensive had failed. By August 5, German losses totalled 112,000 officers and men, 5,126 tanks, 2,492 aircraft. There were no German reserves capable of halting the Red Army's steady advance.

Pollitt described this victory as surpassing Stalingrad, adding "the most important lesson from the epic achievements of the British, American and Soviet armies is quite simple. If at the same time as the Red Army was fighting in the east, British and American armies were in direct combat with Hitler in the west, the war could be won in a very short space of time. If the Second Front were now in existence, the end of the war could be in sight. Every political, military, technical argument calls out for utilisation of the Allies' gigantic resources in a Second Front in the West now".[58]

To defeat Hitler's first and second offensives had taken long months of sacrifice and bitterly fought battles. His third offensive was literally crushed out of existence by the Red Army in one month. The decisive initiative had passed to the Soviet forces. For the third time came the opportunity for action in the West and an early end to the war. But still Churchill did not open the Second Front.

September 8: Italy surrenders unconditionally.

September 10: Germans occupy Milan and other towns in northern Italy, rescue Mussolini and occupy Rome.

September 19: Pollitt in Trafalgar Square[59] "The policy of allowing Italy to stew in its own juice has helped Hitler. There was reluctance by Britain and America to accept the anti-fascist forces in Italy as our real allies. Instead there was reliance on the King and the Italian generals. Hitler has used our weakness to his advantage."

"Mr. Churchill in his Quebec broadcast apologising for the absence of the Second Front, said that 'our soldiers' lives are expended in accord with sound military plans and not squandered for political considerations of any kind.'" Pollitt asked, "What considerations still hold back the creation of the Second Front?" He gave five reasons: (1)

Pressure by reactionary monopolists that Russia and Germany be allowed to exhaust themselves and thus make Europe safe for domination by Britain and the U.S.A. (2) Pressure by pro-fascists for a negotiated peace leaving the basic structure of fascism unchanged. (3) Belief that Hitler is no longer a deadly menace to Britain and the U.S.A., and that they can turn their principal attention to Japan. (4) Big sections of capitalists think that a Second Front would mean a speedy victory and a people's peace, the workers winning the post-war world. They don't want such consequences. They refuse support to the anti-fascist movements and seek through Allied military government to impose domination by big business. (5) The theories that bombing can defeat Hitler, or that there is some easier way to victory than heavy land battles in Europe. These boil down to wanting Russia to find the manpower while our contribution is metal and machines.

Pollitt criticised Citrine for stating at the T.U.C., when opposing the demand for opening the Second Front, "air power might easily be the decisive weapon in this war with an economy of loss of manpower on land". Pollitt said, "Citrine has proved himself wrong on every vital issue before the T.U.C. since he became General Secretary, on Mondism in 1928, on Spain in 1936. We are confident he will be proved wrong on his bombing theory. We know that Harry Hopkins, Roosevelt's confidant, declared that all our bombing had only dislocated Germany's production effort by 10 per cent. We know that Hitler's blitzes failed to put our war industry out of action or demoralise our people. If these theories fail to achieve their object, the danger is the long war Churchill warned against."

The Second Front, because it would compel Hitler to divide his forces, would give the United Nations superiority in East and West, Pollitt argued. It would bring into action the anti-fascist forces in every occupied country. It would enable the Red Army to make giant strides in its offensive. The Second Front alone would shorten and win the war. We should brand as traitors to Britain those who wanted to prolong the war in order to make great profits, consolidate their business interests, secure appeasement or fascism, and maneouvre a general election to return another Tory majority.

In his report[60] to the Communist Party Executive in October, Pollitt spoke of the political effects of the Red Army's advance, and of the need for British Labour to strengthen the fight against reaction and the pro-fascists.

Without minimising the achievements of Britain and the U.S.A., it was the Red Army which was dealing the main blows at Hitler. "Its days of retreat are over for ever. Each day takes it nearer the final destruction of Hitler." These victories were encouraging the resistance movements and creating dissentions in Germany, but different feelings were rising among the ruling class in Britain. Those who wanted the Red Army to weaken Hitler, but the knock-out blow to be given by Britain and the U.S.A., so as to claim the main prestige for Hitler's defeat, now began to fear speedy joint victory with the U.S.S.R. and the Resistance menacing their dream of making all Europe safe for capitalism. They wanted to throw the main burden of sacrifice on the Soviet Union.

"The Government takes little heed of the growing lack of confidence in its policies. This is dangerous because the fight for victory demands not less but more national unity than exists today. By national unity we do not mean capitulation to the vested interests: we mean a unity in which a policy for the people continually advances against the fifth column and monopoly interests. There must be more insistent mass pressure to reorganise the Government. We are not out to defeat the Government but to strengthen it by removing weak and incompetent elements and bringing in proved anti-fascists who will insist on a People's Win the War policy. Such people can be found in the Labour Party, the trade unions, the Co-operatives and the Communist Party." "The moment the Nazis were annihilated at Stalingrad and swept out of Africa, the die-hard Tories, thinking only of their class interests, bank books and future profits, began to show their traditional hatred of the popular and progressive forces. They demand immediate post-war restoration of private rights of exploitation, oppose post-war planning, attack the Labour movement and the Soviet Union. The only firm and lasting basis for progressive policies is in the Labour movement. The moment has arrived when Labour must speak and act for Britain. Unless the working class can be roused in time, it can be robbed of the possibilities of post-war social advance. Those Labour leaders who foster inactivity among the vanguard of organised labour must be put on the spot in the same merciless way we treat the die-hard Tories, for objectively they play into each others hands." "Our Party has to develop the class spirit of the working class to show what is at stake."

November 1943: The Chief of the German General Staff, General Jodl, reports to a meeting of Nazi Gauleiters that "the armed forces of Germany and her allies are strained to the utmost... In the West, Germany has 1,373,000 men. In the East, the Russians have 5,500,000, we have 4,183,000... It is totally incomprehensible that the Anglo-Americans should have avoided forming the Second Front in the West, which their Russian allies have demanded for two years. A successful penetration of the Western defences would soon break through to Belgium, North French and West German industry and so prove fatal."[61]

5. HERBERT HENRY BAILEY (1905–1943)

Among politicially-minded young people who found inspiration in Pollitt's leadership, and whose progress he followed with attention, was Herbert Henry Bailey, known to friends as "Bert".

Bert was born in Tottenham on February 13, 1905, the third son of working-class parents, the father a tailor, an active radical and a public speaker, often carrying his own platform to the local 'Speakers Corner'. The mother bore nine children, of whom six survived. In 1916 the father left home, and the burden of bringing up the children fell upon the mother who took in washing and did house cleaning to supplement the father's inadequate and irregular payments. In a small house in Hornsey, their poverty was acute. "Mother frequently visited the pawnshop. Food was the plainest. The Sunday dinner was cheapest scrag mutton; the left-overs did for Monday. Then three days of soup from bones, split peas or lentils, fish and chips on Friday. The kids queued at the bakers in early morning with pillow cases to be filled with 'make-weight' bread. No scrap of anything was wasted. The three boys slept in one bed with cheap, grey wartime army shirts as night wear. Mother began work at 4 a.m. lighting the old-fashioned copper to heat water, with a metal bath on a chair in the stone-floored scullery. For many hours she rubbed clothes on a scrubbing board, then hung them to dry on a line in a yard; in winter draped them on the kitchen range. At intervals in this day of slavery, she got meals for the children."[62]

From Marxist books, loaned by his brother Robert, with whom he had a lifelong bond of affection and friendship, Bert learned that hardship and poverty were not peculiar to his family, but were the effects of capitalist exploitation on millions.

Robert joined the Communist Party on its foundation, Bert joined the Young Communist League when he was 18, and became a leading member. He lost his first job, in a City shipping firm, for being found in possession of a copy of the Communist Party's weekly paper. Later his trade union, the National Union of Shop Assistants, Warehousemen and Clerks, employed him in full-time work.

He joined the National Minority Movement and at its 1925 conference stated the case for union organisation of young workers and full backing for their needs.[63] For two years he served as youth representative on the N.M.M. Executive.

Experience deepened his political convictions, he joined the Communist Party. Particularly interested in the struggle against militarism and imperialist war and believing that working-class solidarity included the men in the armed forces, he helped to secure effective distribution to soldiers of leaflets advocating democratic rights for the forces, exposing imperialism, and in 1926 explaining the reasons for the General Strike.

In 1928, the Shop Assistants Executive demanded that the union's officials sign a repudiation of the Communist Party and the Minority Movement. Bert refused to sell his principles for a job, was dismissed and expelled, as was his senior official, E. R. Pountney. Widespread protest failed to secure reinstatement. Bert found himself black-listed. After long unemployment he got work for a company selling Russian oil. He became an active member of the T.&G.W.U.

Called up in 1940, he volunteered for the Tank Corps, saw action in North Africa in 1942 with the 50th Royal Tank Regiment, was wounded in Sicily and later fought in Italy. His letters[64] give glimpses of a man ready to give all in the struggle for the people's bright future. On Sept. 29, 1942, he wrote "I am quite confident as to the ultimate outcome, but under no illusions as to the price to be paid." On October 25, "Action has raised morale to a high pitch ... you should understand what it means to us after spending our lives in the struggle when we confront a situation which means either winning or losing all we have fought for." He then writes affectionately of his mother, and adds "Take her along to some of Harry's do's, if he would have a five minute chat with her, she would be mighty pleased, she thinks such a hell of a lot of him." On April 26 1943 "If I get back to England, and the chances appear more remote each day, then Harry will have got back a lad much more steeled and resolute, more bitter in hatred of the causes of war, more class conscious than ever." On June 13, "I note Harry was enquiring after me. Tell him I'm fit as a fiddle. I often think of his tireless efforts." On September 14 "I don't get browned off, any tendency that way and I just think of our boys all over the world. Remember that the British army has never come up against more than 1 per cent of the Germany army. We have great armies: why are they not being used! Is it because of the spectre haunting Europe; are they being kept to see that it never takes flesh?"

On September 10 Pollitt wrote: "Dear Bert, I hope you have got over your recent illness. I must say your photo does you more justice than any photographer has ever made out of my dial ... Things go well now on all fronts; we are only waiting for the biggest front of all to give Hitler the knock-out ... The family is going on well, with problems and difficulties, but growing all the time", and in a covering note—"Give Bert my greetings. He is one of the best that ever lived and has a warm spot in my heart." On November 5 Bert acknowledged Harry's message, and on the 27th. wrote: "I have passed it on to all our lads as a personal greeting to them. I'm sure Harry would have wished it that way."

On December 10 Bert was commanding a Bren carrier returning from action when a long range enemy shell burst in front of it. He was killed instantly. His troop leader wrote of him as "very popular, had distinguished himself in action in Sicily"; his squadron leader—"he died as he had lived, as a soldier. I mourn his loss." He rests in the Sangro River Military Cemetery under an inscription concluding "A Fighter Against Fascism—Defender of the Common People—Brave Heart."[65]

6. D-Day 1944.

June 6, 1944: Between 6.30 a.m. and 7.30 a.m. British and American forces landed on the coast of Normandy, and established a formidable bridgehead.

Pollitt: "The final Nazi legend has been smashed, in a manner few believed possible . . . the present battles are the prelude to the advance into the heart of Nazi Germany. Never before have we seen advancing armies received with such warmth and enthusiasm by those they are freeing from a black and shameful terror. This is the measure of the difference between this and all other wars . . . it is a war of the peoples, for the people and by the people, so that the outcome shall be a new people's world. At this moment ensuring the speediest continuity of supplies for the Western Front is our main task. We at home must help to make up any leeway by the rapidity with which we help to repair ships, tanks and planes, get coal, turn round ships in the docks, load them again to cross the Channel, clear the railway sidings, abstain from needless travel, repair the locomotives, keep the permanent way in fine fettle, help in the hospitals, help the farmers. The Communist Party can be proud of the work it has put in to bring about the present favourable political and military situation . . . . It must be kept up and surpassed. Personal example day after day will bring victory nearer, however trivial the tasks may seem, they are all urgent and necessary, all fit in with the mainstream of effort now sweeping the country. Hard fights lie ahead, pain and bereavement, setbacks and disappointments, but nothing can now stem the onward march. The German war machine will be smashed, never again to menace the peace of the world, and then we shall know how to utilise for constructive purposes the initiative, planning and organisation that has made possible the new offensives."[66]

Early on D-Day, Pollitt wrote a duplicated letter[67] to every Communist Party member on his list of those in the Forces. "There were thousands of them, I nearly lost the use of my right hand signing them."[68] He began with "Warm fraternal greetings at this moment when the decisive battles for destruction of the power of fascism are beginning", and went on to express pride and confidence in their ability to set an example in discipline, initiative and courage. He pledged "fullest support for everything your fight and sacrifice will demand from the Home Front, including public vigilance for the welfare of your families". The letter ended by referring to "our historic goal of Socialism, when for ever shall be abolished poverty and want, unemployment conquered, war outlawed for all time and mankind stand forth in all its majesty and glory constructing the new classless society in which all endeavours are dedicated to serve the wellbeing of the people."

His sense of Communist responsibility found expression in the pledge that "the Communist Party will do everything in its power to ensure that the most difficult and arduous military, naval and air undertakings are carried through to success. In industry Communists will set an example by speed of output, quality of work, readiness to teach others, timekeeping, production and transport of all essential war supplies under any conditions, however strenuous, dangerous or protracted."[69]

7. INDIA—1942.

In his policy for victory Pollitt gave high priority to self-government for India. A few hours after Britain's ultimatum to Hitler expired, the Viceroy declared that India, too, was at war. The House of Commons gave him dictatorial powers. All this was done without discussion with Indian opinion. On September 14 the Indian National Congress reiterated India's adherence to democracy and liberty, asked the British Government to declare whether the war was being fought for these principles or for defending the Empire, and if the war was for democracy and liberty, how would they be given effect in India and the colonial empire? These questions were not answered. On October 10 Congress demanded that "India be declared an independent nation". On October 18 the Viceroy proposed a consultative committee to aid the war effort, ignored war aims and independence. Congress declared non-cooperation; eight of the eleven provincial governments resigned.

The Japanese thrust into South-East Asia, and their attack on Pearl Harbour in December, 1941, had already made clear that India was menaced, and that her co-operation against the Japanese was essential to her own defence and that of Burma, Malaya and Singapore, Pollitt, welcoming the release from prison of Nehru and other Congress leaders, pressed for the release of all the political prisoners and for a declaration that the Atlantic Charter would be applied to India, Malaya, Burma, the Dutch East Indies and the Philippines. This would help win these countries for active struggle against the Axis powers.[70] A few days later, at a celebration of Indian Independence Day, he said "India is more and more a centre of international problems, and Britain's success in the war will depend more and more on her treatment of India."[71]

The Government remained passive until the Japanese occupied Malaya and Singapore, and taking Rangoon on March 8, 1942, were poised to attack India. Then Churchill, sent a Mission under Sir Stafford Cripps to negotiate with the Indian leaders. His proposal was that the existing government of India continue till after the war then Dominion status would be given to an Indian Union. Pollitt pointed to the lack of any proposal for an Indian Provisional National Government, or for a democratic National Assembly to draw up a Constitution. "The outlook which denies responsibility to the Indian people is the outlook which lost Malaya, Singapore and the Dutch East Indies, and seems to be losing Burma."[72]

The Cripps Mission failed, Nehru explained that Congress rejected Dominion status because it would fragment India. It wanted full independence. It would put aside the question of the future if a responsible Indian National Government were put in charge of national defence, the armed forces remaining under the Commander-in-Chief. Cripps' proposal that the Viceroy be Prime Minister with power of intervention and veto was unacceptable.[73] The Government then withdrew its proposals and placed responsibility for further steps on the Indian leaders.

Pollitt expressed regret that Cripps had lent his name to terms which continued the old "divide and rule" policy, and rejected his decalaration that "nothing more can be done". There was no agreement between Britain and India to meet the Japanese threat. "The only way to win India's co-operation is to negotiate with Congress on recognition of Indian independence and an Indian National Government. India as a fighting ally can stem the Japanese advance, spearhead a mighty anti-fascist movement throughout the Orient, release thousands of British troops for the Second Front in Europe.[74]

In a telegram to the Communist Party of India, legalised in July 1941 after eight years underground, Pollitt spoke of the "new opportunity to rally the people of India in defence of their country",[75] and commented that legalisation showed that one "if so far only one of the lessons of Burma and Malaya had been learned".[76]

Prior to the August Congress Committee meeting, Gandhi made known that he favoured civil disobedience unless Britain agreed to an Indian National Government. Pollitt in a personal letter to Nehru[77] affirmed his complete solidarity with the cause of Indian independence. "I can write to you all the more frankly because you know that I have no special axe to grind, I am not one of those suddenly concerned about India because of the danger to their own vested interests." "I hate British imperialism as deeply as you do; my whole upbringing and experience has taught me to regard the ruling class with a hatred that no circumstances will ever damp down or allow me to forget." "I am deeply conscious of all the provocation to which India has been subjected, how wrongly advised Cripps was to go to India with such indefensible proposals. . . . I admire the forebearance Congress has displayed, despite the insults put upon it and the senseless persecution of its leaders, in not doing anything to embarrass Britain's struggle against fascism."

He went on to argue against deciding on civil disobedience, because "now the future of world progress is being decided upon the battlefields of the Soviet Union . . . there is one single consideration guiding every anti-fascist, every socialist—to assist in the defeat of fascism. Everything else is subordinate to this; everything that makes life worth while depends upon our formulating policies with this aim . . . Non-cooperation now would weaken the active struggle against fascism, bring serious danger to the entire people of India, and make serious difficulties for those in Britain who fight for Indian freedom." But he pledged that even if Congress did adopt non-cooperation, "We shall fight for re-opening negotiations with Congress and for India having complete independence".

He concluded that Congress would immensely increase its world influence by taking its place alongside the Chinese, Russian, American and British peoples against fascist aggression. "Co-operate and fight alongside us, the common people, now, and you make the independence of your country a surety even if the Government is misguided enough not to grant it now. The revolutionary change taking place in the outlook of millions, awakening to political consciousness for the first time, is the guarantee that the victory over fascism will be a people's victory."

On August 8, Congress stated that when India was declared independent a Provisional Government would be formed with the primary function of defending India and resisting aggression with all the armed, as well as non-violent forces at its command. It recorded the anxiety of Congress not to embarrass the defence of China or Russia or jeopardise the defensive capacity of the United Nations and again appealed to Britain to recognise India's claims. It decided to sanction the starting of a mass national struggle on non-violent lines "against the imperialist and authoritarian government".[78] The government immediately arrested Congress leaders and banned its newspapers.

Pollitt on August 9 urged British public opinion to press the government to reverse these "stupid and provocative measures and to negotiate for a National Government for India". The Congress stand for armed resistance to fascism and for alliance with the United Nations was "a serious offer of a settlement full advantage of which should be taken" but the Government was concealing it. Deploring the threat of civil disobedience under the leadership of Gandhi, "whose proclaimed views are equivalent to appeasement", Pollitt said that both were consequences of the reactionary British official policy, and that a settlement with the Indian leaders was in the interests of Britain and the United Nations.[79]

On August 21 Pollitt urged the Prime Minister to re-open negotiations on the basis of recognition of Indian independence.[80] He wrote that the exclusion of any possibility of a National Government was "a blow in the face for Indian aspirations". The threat of civil disobedience was "a last desperate expedient when every other attempt to win consideration for their claim to participate as a free ally in the war, had failed". Congress had made clear its wish to negotiate before launching civil disobedience. "The arrests of August 9 were not justified and served only to precipitate disorders neither directed nor sanctioned by Congress." As well as at many Communist meetings, Pollitt spoke to 1,500 people at an India League meeting to protest at the repressive measures, including arrests, collective fines, a whipping order, baton charges and firing on unarmed crowds. S. O. Davies, M.P., the Dean of Canterbury and Krishna Menon also spoke.[81]

When a new Viceroy, Mountbatten, took office in August 1943, Pollitt drew his attention to the urgency of securing the full co-operation of the Indian people in their own defence; all sections of responsible Indian opinion wanted such co-operation. The new Viceroy could end the deadlock by a new policy—release the imprisoned Congress and other democratic anti-fascist leaders; allow representative Indian leaders to prepare immediate proposals, and negotiate with them to reach a settlement; and take immediate steps to meet the food crisis, including requisitioning stocks and forming representative People's Food Committees. Such measures would correspond to majority democratic opinion in Britain and rapidly transform the situation in India.[82]

8. Daily life in wartime.

Various letters and notes by Pollitt give glimpses of wartime daily life.[83]

26-6-44: "The flying bombs made people reluctant to go out. In some streets in early evening when the alert was on, you found everybody in the shelters. So our Hendon Anglo-Soviet Week was a flop; I feel very sorry for Marjorie who worked like a Trojan for it."

28-6-44: "I firewatched in the street last night, and tonight will be on at the office. The Barnet School, where Jean goes, got all windows blasted today and the children were sent home for a few days. It was examination week. They ought to make allowances for this situation when kids are sitting trying to solve problems in geometry and French that their parents could never solve."

28-6-44: "One of our higher-ups coming back from the Soviet front was asked whether the Red Army had anything to teach us. He replied, 'No, its a pretty low grade front over there.' Class and breeding will tell, you see."

6-7-44: "I have asked Walter Holmes to write in his 'Notebook' a tribute to the London doctors and nurses for what they are doing just now. Brian is quite mad because he has 'never heard one drop'. The other night they were thudding thick and fast in the distance. I carried him down to the shelter, and half asleep he said, 'Don't forget the comics tomorrow, daddy.' How wonderful to be a kid. I can't sleep at night."

"Four of our staff at the office are bombed out; three others with children have left to go away. Percy Glading has roof and windows out, I met him for a chat. Early this year his factory was bombed out, a man from the Air Ministry congratulated him on the way he got the workers to tackle the damage and then to continue work on an urgent job in the open air."

6-7-44: "I keep my sister Ella on the go in Manchester visiting wounded comrades. She takes some of the murder stories I leave at her house. She found a Lieutenant in hospital reading Keats and Yeats, but he kept the murder stories. His wife will stay at my sister's when she visits him."

"A week-end at home, managed to get a lot of sleep."

10-7-44: "Saw the Russian Newsreel 'Justice is Coming' at the Tatler. Inside I found half our staff. Coming out they declared in unison it was their dinner hour. If I had the power I would force every cinema in the country to show it and chain the patrons to their seats to see it through. Some of the stills can never leave one's mind after seeing them."

10-7-44: "Reports from all over the country tell of the growth of hatred for the Nazis, and more common use of the word 'German' instead of 'Nazi'. After the flying bombs and the shooting of R.A.F. officers there is a greater tendency to believe stories of German atrocities in Russia."

18-7-44: "You will never convince me about what I call the 'La-di-da' schools. I am for utilising for the whole of the children the best every phase of education can provide, but I was miserable when Jean and Brian were at the 'La-di-da' type during the blitz, and breathed freely when they were back at Council schools among people they will work and live among. Marjorie never mentioned to me about sending our kids to a Child Guidance Clinic, and a good job too. The other night I caught the gang shooting little stones through windows with a catapult. Of course I stopped them, but I didn't send for a child guidance expert. I remembered the tricks I did when I was a kid."

27-7-44: "Up to the eyes, with the booklet and speaking. Hendon and Wembley now evacuation areas so we get the billeting allowance for two children."

31-7-44: "On Saturday morning, Manchester had the usual downpour but in the afternoon Brian and I had the time of our lives at Belle Vue, the paradise of the Lancashire proletariat when they can't get to Blackpool. In the evening at one of my old haunts, an old man whom I know to have only one song, came up and asked what he should sing. Never batting an eyelid, I said 'Sing your best'. Out it came, 'Broken Hearted Clown.' I led the chorus. It went fine. I noticed one and then another go out and come back with little parcels. Back at my sister's I had four new-laid eggs, a large piece of ham, two meat pies and a packet of cakes. My sister, her husband, their three kids said in one voice, 'We know where you've been—"Broken Hearted Clown".' On the Sunday at Rochdale[84] for the Co-op. Centenary. The Board and the Education Committee came to the meeting. Afterwards their spokesman said, 'Eh lad, tha can spout; its ben a treat to hear thee. We never thowt owt special about centenary. When we see you folk had got up a meeting we thowt we might as well come, nobody would come to ours'."

"Travelled all night to London to be best man at Jean Campbell's wedding. I remember her being born. Makes you feel old to see them off like this."

9-8-44: "Two days at home, bed and lying about the garden. Enjoyed it very much. On Bank Holiday night felt the desire for a pint of beer, but in an hour and a half could not find a pub open, brought home the fact there's a war on. Tonight finished the booklet."

15-8-44: "In South Wales. London children in all the valleys. They seem very confortable and happy. The miners and their wives seem to be repaying help given them in past grim struggles."

23-8-44: "Mrs. Mann is to have her leg amputated below the knee—gangrene. She has been ill for months, the way she sticks it is marvellous.

"This Friday I have meetings in Scotland, Newcastle, Sunderland, then back to London, settle things at the office, then Cornwall for a few days' rest. I admit I'm tired, working night and day without rest took more out of me than I bargained for."

8-9-44: "In Newquay with Marjorie; weather was lousy, but we walked and walked over the cliffs and got the wind and rain. Years have rolled off me."

24-9-44: "Coventry to launch campaign for a Tom Mann Memorial

Hall. Back to London by car, punctures and burst tyre made journey last from 4 p.m. to 12.15 a.m."

25-9-44: "So many comrades ill its a full time job keeping up correspondence. George Hardy had an accident in Manchester, broke a leg in two places."

9-10-44: "Rhondda same as ever only more so. Amazing difference in people's food, clothes and appearance. What a comment on civilisation that it takes a war to do this."

9-10-44: "Gallacher had a hard knock from a car, is worried because his wife takes it badly."

14-11-44: "Yesterday decided to break my London-Birmingham journey to visit Joan at Oxford. Fought my way on to already crowded train at Birmingham; stood all the way to Oxford. Found my way to the hospital, asked very sweetly to see her, and was equally sweetly informed that she had left for St. Albans. Then two hours' wait on Oxford Station, trains late due to fog, another fight to get on, stood all the way to Paddington; arrived home full of the milk of human kindness."

12-12-44: "Looking forward to three days at home doing what I like, eating without feeling I am taking it out of other people's mouths, getting as much sleep as I can. The busiest year of my life, it seems impossible to have so much travelling—105 big meetings by 21 December when I finish at Dover."[85]

26-1-45: "The Red Army is going places these days. One fellow said he wondered how soon it would be airborne to the Western Front!"

CHAPTER 21

WHAT KIND OF PEACE?

1. Policy for democratic advance. 2. Thaelmann. 3. Greece. 4. Coal. 5. Paris. 6. For electoral unity. 7. General election, 1945. 8. Rhondda East—a near miss.

1. POLICY FOR DEMOCRATIC ADVANCE.

As the final defeat of Hitler came into sight, millions began to ask what peace would bring. Pollitt stated the Communist view in a 40,000 word booklet[1] combining factual data, proposals and remarks on Marxist theory (*How to Win The Peace*). It answered three questions—What would be the main features of the post-war situation? What democratic advance was possible in Britain? What about Socialism?[2]

Post-War Situation

The peoples allied against fascism differed in social development. The Soviet Union was a socialist state; Britain, France and the U.S.A. were capitalist democracies; China and India were struggling for national independence. The defeat of Hitler fascism, "a decisive victory for democracy in the capitalist countries and for socialism in the Soviet Union," made possible a true people's peace very different from 1918. There were three essentials to realise it: continued Five Power Co-operation; national independence of the colonial peoples; democratic advance in the major capitalist countries.

The alternative was that the capitalist states would rupture the wartime alliance by returning to imperialist policies. This would lead to a repetition of crises, war and fascism. The attempt to impose Anglo-American capitalist domination through Allied Military Government showed that this danger was real.

Comparing 1944 with 1918, there were great changes. The Soviets, then weak and encircled, were now a first rank world power. The Resistance in Europe had brought Socialist-Communist unity in many countries. Liberation would mean democratically elected governments including Communists. The strength of the national movements in the colonies would compel British imperialism to a policy of co-operation. In this framework the British people, a People's Europe, and the U.S.S.R. could jointly shape a new world.

The people knew what state control of national resources had done for war; they wanted it applied to peace. The capitalists differed among themselves. The die-hards opposed state control, nationalisation and social security, and were in active alliance with European reaction. The more far-sighted, however, realised the growing strength of the people, feared a world economic crisis and supported peace-time co-operation of Britain, the U.S.A. and the U.S.S.R.

Pollitt defined the people's wants as first of all an enduring peace, not merely a breathing space but ending war for ever. Then, work for all with good wages, homes and decent living conditions, social security, a healthy nation, democratic education, a fuller life with recreation, travel, study and culture. All public and social institutions to be democratised, class privilege and snobbery to be ended. These things required a government acting for the people, not for the propertied classes, and a massive increase in production.

The Tories wanted to return the economy to private control. Pollitt proposed to extend the war-time co-operation of government and people in production. The state would own and expand basic industries—coal, gas and electricity, iron and steel, air, rail and long-distance road transport—and take over big landed estates, banking and insurance. State and privately-owned industries would work within a state plan. Unified national policies for fuel and power, and for transport would secure maximum efficiency. A national food policy would provide adequate nutrition for all . Agriculture would be of prime importance and be assisted to supply all dairy and vegetable produce needed and a higher proportion of cereals, meat and fruit. The state would control prices and profits.

Increased production would be accompanied by legislation for shorter hours, holidays with pay, trade union rights, social security, a full national health service, free education from nursery school to university.

Jobs for all would be secured by: a high-wage policy, rising purchasing power and living standards; the re-equipment of industry and transport; extensive house and social building; big trading developments following the independence of the colonial peoples, and trade with all nations to mutual advantage.

To the question what government would carry out such a policy, Pollitt replied: "A Labour and progressive government, based on a majority at the coming election and backed by a united Labour movement including the Communist Party." It would not be simply a parliamentary fight, the power of such a government would rest as much on the activity of the Labour movement as on the traditional forces of the state. The organised workers would be the main driving force. The state machinery would be modernised, made more democratic, give greater scope to the people's voluntary organisations.

Socialism

He showed the relation of democratic advance to the struggle for socialism. "It is not how 'left' the immediate programme may be in itself that determines whether it carries us forward towards socialism. It is the degree to which the workers and the people can be united to fight for it, their enemies isolated and exposed; the degree to whic h the progressive forces can increase their power. Workers will not unite and fight for things they believe to be impossible; they will fight for what they consider just, fair and reasonable."

"As capitalism becomes monopolised and the individual factory part of a nationally organised network, so the big decisions about wages and hours cease to be of concern to workers and employers alone, and inevitably become matters of national concern. The working class should have no illusions about a 'pure' industrial struggle in which only 'trade union' issues arise. A change of power in the state is necessary to give full effect to the growing strength of the workers in the factories and trade unions...."

Such a democratic advance would require a more intense struggle against reaction than ever before, because "instead of hitting at only one employer or group of employers, extracting this or that concession, we are fighting for control and power at key points in the system of monopoly capital. We must fight for a government which would assert the sovereign power of the people instead of the sovereign power of a few big businessmen."

2. THAELMANN.

On August 18, 1944, the Nazis murdered the leader of the German Communist Party, Ernst Thaelmann. Pollitt wrote:[3]

"This murder shows the ghastly face of the Nazi beast at bay, slavering with sadistic intention to pull down with itself as much of humanity's treasures as it can. With Thaelmann, Communist, died Breitscheid, Social Democrat. In the concentration camp there was unity. In death there was unity. The Nazis did not discriminate. How many more lessons like this before we obtain unity in life? Thaelmann was a great German. So, too, was Breitscheid. They represented German workers, scientists, poets, writers and people who believed in freedom of thought and worship. They wanted a great and noble Germany, they were millions strong, but in the face of the fascist enemy they were weak because they were not united.

"We tried to win freedom for Thaelmann, but some in this country shrugged superior shoulders. He was, after all, a Communist. Why worry?

The same political prejudice that divided the German people was spread in Britain. Forces strong enough to have compelled a change in government policy were kept weak by disunity. The disastrous years of appeasement followed. The men who engineered the Munich Pact retained their hold because those who could have moved them out were weakened by division.

"Unity could have saved Thaelmann, Breitscheid and all those other fine German people who have gone. Unity could have saved us this war. Today, unity, even incomplete, is making it possible to destroy the monster that disunity permitted to grow strong."

At the crowded memorial meeting, the first central London Communist rally after the big flying bomb attacks, Pollitt outlined Thaelmann's life. His father, a militant Social Democrat, had been in prison for organising socialist meetings in defiance of Bismarck. Born in Hamburg in 1886, Ernst Thaelmann at 16 years of age joined the Social Democratic Party. Then, working in the docks, he was an active militant in the transport workers' trade union. In 1914 he opposed the war, and was sent to the front. When demobilised he joined the Independent Social Democrats in Hamburg, and led them into the newly formed Communist Party in 1920. At the 3rd Congress of the Communist International, he spoke with Lenin. In 1924, when Pollitt first met him, he was a member of the Reichstag. In 1925 he polled 2 million votes as Communist Presidential candidate, and in 1932 at the head of the anti-fascist struggle, his vote was 5 million. That October he created an international politicial sensation by appearing illegally before 20,000 Paris workers at a Communist meeting together with Maurice Thorez, and calling in prophetic words for the unity of French and German workers against fascism and imperialist war. "We Communists in Germany, as in France, fight for the daily interests of the masses and at the same time for their socialist future. One cannot be separated from the other. We German Communists are in the front ranks of the international struggle against fascism. Our struggle is at the same time your struggle."

Pollitt concluded, "In paying tribute to Thaelmann, we pledge to assist in rebuilding the German Labour movement. Had Thaelmann lived he would have led the fight for a new Germany: that is why they murdered him. But what he stood for cannot be destroyed. The Germany of Thomas Mann, Thaelmann and Breitscheid will rise again.

"Think of it; the agony of 11 years in prison, the uncertainty, to live with death for 4,015 days and nights, and to remain firm and loyal to the cause. A comrade has written of Ernst Thaelmann[4]—

'Long years he waited behind walls of steel,
   His ears tuned in to every sound and shock,
The grinding of a key moved in the lock,
   The steps that meant a whipping or a meal.

>   Tortured and maimed, he yet refused to kneel,
>   But rugged and unflinching as a rock
>   He waited for the turning tide to knock
>   Against his feet. He made no last appeal.
>
>   But how the accusing silence of the years
>   Has stripped the gilding from the counterfeit;
>   The killer not the killed reveals his fears
>   And with his last lie damns his own deceit.
>   Thaelmann, our Thaelmann does not need our tears
>   But lives to speed the killer's last retreat'."

As Pollitt read this poem, the entire audience spontaneously rose to their feet and stood in silence until he ended, when they joined in singing the *Internationale*.

3. Greece.

Early in December, alarming news came from Athens. A B.B.C. correspondent eye-witnessed the Athens police, collaborators in the German occupation, fire on a peaceful demonstration, killing 12 and wounding 148 people. Two days later royalists, fascists and the Athens police jointly attacked the Greek Liberation forces and on December 6, British troops joined in the attack.

Pollitt immediately[5] denounced Churchill as planning to aid the return to power of the royalist clique, and using British troops to protect the reactionaries and fascists. "It will be a crime against our own soldiers to call on them to use their arms against those who for four years fought side by side with them."[6] Churchill committed that crime. Churchill's telegram—not published till three years later[7]—ordered the British general in Athens to "stop being neutral between the Greek parties; shoot at the communists without hesitation". Without proof and in contradiction to British pressmen's reports Churchill asserted that the national liberation movement, E.A.M., was out to set up a communist government.[8]

The preceding events may be summarised as follows.[9] In 1941 Hitler seized Greece, the Royal Government fled, the reactionaries and the fascists collaborated with the Germans, the people began to resist. In 1942 the progressives—Liberals, Agrarians, trade unionists, Socialists and Communists—formed a National Liberation movement (E.A.M.) and a guerrilla army (E.L.A.S.) joined by many Greek army officers. In 1943 Churchill supported the royalists in arming bands (E.D.E.S.) who fought against E.L.A.S. Early in 1944, E.L.A.S. had liberated more than half of Greece, Greek forces in the Near East mutinied against the Royal Government in exile. Churchill brought Papandreou from Athens to Cairo and made him premier in a re-shuffled Royal Government there.

E.A.M. accepted this as a provisional government of national unity until liberation and a general election. The Red Army advance compelled the Germans to withdraw from Greece; E.L.A.S. rapidly liberated the rest of the country, Papandreou went to Athens, took three E.A.M. members into his government; Churchill ordered British troops to Greece. In November Papandreou proposed that E.L.A.S. disarm: they agreed, provided E.D.E.S. also did so. Churchill sent to Athens Greek Royalist troops who had spent the war in Egypt. The E.A.M. demand that they be disarmed was refused. The E.A.M. Ministers resigned. The police and fascist attack began.

Greek seamen in Britain were deeply perturbed by these events. Their impulse was to strike, but recognising that the war against Hitler had still to be won, they sent a deputation to Pollitt to discuss political action.[10] Its spokesman was Tony Ambatielos, a militant of the Greek Seamen's Union and a member of the Communist Party of Greece. After Hitler seized Greece, he was among delegates of ocean-going Greek crews who met in New York to discuss their future. He was sent to Cardiff to help organise the Federation of Greek Maritime Unions, and became its Secretary. The Federation did much to increase the numbers of Greek seamen serving the Allied war effort, negotiated improvements in their pay and conditions, and became their accepted representative. Its Cardiff premises included offices, a hostel, a well-equipped club and an excellent restaurant. The Cardiff Communists helped its publicity work, and their propaganda secretary, Betty Bartlett, became Mrs. Ambatielos. In summer 1942 Pollitt was in Cardiff when the Greek seamen's club was opened, and was invited to the celebration. Greek hospitality ensured a good supper. On the tables were oranges, impossible to find in Britain at that time. Pollitt was told that a seaman had brought them from New York. "Just think of it", he said, "millions of our children have never seen an orange."

The Greek seamen's deputation was received by the Political Committee of the C.P.G.B., their decision not to strike and their proposals for political action were welcomed.[11] A wave of public indignation spread, and at short notice a crowd estimated at 20,000, a third of them in uniform, thronged Trafalgar Square on December 17. Pollitt and Tony Ambatielos were among the speakers.[12] The Communist Executive had called for an end to British armed intervention, a cease fire, and negotiations for the formation of a Greek national government[13] representative of all sections of the Resistance.

The Labour Party Conference met that December. Procedural maneouvres and the personal appearance of Bevin to defend Churchill prevented the condemnation of Churchill's policy in Greece. Among Bevin's sharpest critics was Aneurin Bevan, M.P. who said, "Only three bodies of public opinion in the world are on record in his support—fascist Spain, fascist Portugal, and the Tory majority in the Commons."[14]

Assured of official Labour support, Churchill intensified the intervention. After his personal visit to Athens during Christmas 1946, an all-out attack by three British Divisions with tanks, guns and planes compelled E.L.A.S. to leave Athens, though the struggle continued in other parts of Greece.

4. COAL.

Early in 1945, when unusually cold weather made people acutely aware of the coal problem, Pollitt critically analysed a plan drawn up by Mr. Robert Foot.[15] With no previous experience in coal, he was appointed "independent Chairman" of the Mining Association in April 1944 at a salary of £12,500 a year. Pollitt remarked, "I should be the last to say that it is impossible for an intelligent and fair-minded outsider to understand the problems of mining . . . Indeed I claim to know something about them myself, though no one paid me £12,500 a year for learning. My quarrel with Mr. Foot is not that he knew nothing about the industry, but that after seven months' tour of the coalfields, he does not seem to realise how serious the position is."

Pollitt outlined the situation. Output was falling: 237 million tons in 1938, it was 195 million tons in 1943. Each year there were 25,000 fewer miners. By old age and injury, more were leaving than could be got freely to enter. Boys had to be conscripted, most preferred the forces. Output per man shift, far behind other countries due to lack of machines, was falling still further. Owners were saying they could not afford improvements. The price of British coal was high, double that of U.S.A. These known facts were the reason for the wide demand for nationalisation.

Foot had no suggestions as to how production could be immediately increased. Pollitt proposed: government supply of the latest types of mining machines, priority production of essential spare parts; concentration of production in the best pits and seams; production committees in each pit, the management to adopt their proposals; full application of safety regulations; more rations and clothing coupons for miners; pithead baths at all pits; a government pledge of emergency measures to remedy housing conditions.

Foot's overall proposals and Pollitt's comments on them were as follows:

Control: Foot wanted a Central Board of owners and managers with power to reorganise the industry and fix prices. Pollitt—This means no government control and no trade union representation. It is the old policy of 'self government' in industry leading to big business domination, high prices, restriction of output.

Inefficiency: Foot wanted the Central Board to survey every pit for necessary re-equipment. If the owners cannot find the cost, the Board to raise money or loans. Pollitt—This leaves the owners to determine the standard of efficiency, and their yardstick is private profit. As to cost, modernisation does not offer good profits to financiers. With ascertained profits on mining proper at some £12 million a year, no capitalist will advance the £150 million to £300 million required unless profits are boosted up. The industry cannot be made efficient pit by pit; to win coal economically needs long term planning and lay-out in each coalfield. Finally, coal must be planned as part of fuel and power as a whole.

Manpower: Foot favoured "a wage, stability of employment, and general conditions to give the miners a good standard of living throughout their working life", Production Committees in the pits, and better safety regulations. Pollitt—"Such changes are inevitable if any miners are to be recruited at all . . . There is no criticism of the owners, all shortcomings are put down to economic circumstances. The miners are asked to forget their long experience of the owners' bitter opposition to every concession and to believe in a new regime of goodwill, while full authority is restored to the colliery managers."

Pollitt summarised the Foot plan as making service to the nation secondary to profit on capital, keeping the industry under private ownership and control. It would not result in efficient coal production by modern methods, with good wages and moderate prices. He finally re-stated the case for nationalisation as the only means to attain these aims.

5. Paris.

In April 1945, Pollitt spent a few days in Paris, where he found rationing of essentials, food shortages, black market, no heating, restrictions on light and power. Every day another 7,000 deportees and war-prisoners returned. The Resistance had high standing. The French Communist Party was re-establishing its organisation and preparing for the municipal elections. Pollitt attended two meetings—one of 2,000 teachers, another of 4,000 students to hear the Party leaders. Thorez's call for the avoidance of provocation and isolation was generally "regarded as common sense". There was anger at the return of Pétain, the Munich and Vichy elements "were seeking to get close to Gaullist circles". Nationalisation of some industries was a democratic necessity. Relations between the Communist and Socialist memberships were cordial, but the Socialist leaders were following Transport House. The Communist Party was proposing united Resistance lists for the elections, there were many such local agreements, but reactionaries were making big efforts to split the Resistance.

Pollitt drew the conclusion: "Do not under-estimate the efforts reaction is making to prevent the people reaping the rewards of their military victory over fascism. To achieve the political and moral destruction of fascism will require as arduous and sustained effort as did the military struggle."[16]

6. For electoral unity.

At the Communist Congress in October 1944, Pollitt emphasised that government policy during the first years of peace would determine Britain's future for many years. Therefore the over-riding necessity was to break the hold of the dyed-in-the-wool Tories and to form a new government based on a solid majority of Labour and progressive M.Ps. with Labour holding the key positions. To this end the Communists proposed that the Labour, Communist and Liberal Parties, together with other progressive groupings, should consult to avoid division of the anti-Tory vote. If Labour leaders at national level refused, there could be democratic conferences in each constituency to agree on one anti-Tory candidate. If the Labour Party prevented such an agreement, the Communist candidates would not withdraw. But agreement between the Labour and Communist Parties was possible and would be received with enthusiasm by the Labour movement.[17]

Trade union support for the Communist proposal included the Miners, Engineers, Electricians, Fire Brigades, Painters, Vehicle Builders and Locomen. In a speech at Huddersfield prior to the Labour Party Conference, Herbert Morrison said that if there was powerful Communist influence in some trade unions "it had not been done by straightforward conversion of a majority, but by the type of back-stage maneouvre in which these people were expert."[18] Pollitt commented that Morrison had said nothing about public disquiet on Churchill's hostility to the Resistance in Belgium, Italy and Greece, or the die-hard Tory activity in Parliament against social security, but had exclusively attacked the Communists. "No man has done more than Morrison to flout the declared will of the Labour movement on issues such as Mosley, Ramsey, and amounts payable for industrial injury, yet he dares to accuse others of being undemocratic." "Morrison also said that the real answer to Communist activities is to show 'more vigorous fighting enthusiasm, to get clear about the meaning of our policies, and then go all out for them.' I have said on countless occasions that the Labour Party needs the Communists for precisely these reasons."[19]

Morrison accused the European Communist Parties of working with all sorts of reactionaries. Pollitt replied, "He gave no examples, he could not do so", and went on to show that these parties were laying a basis to ensure that the governments in the liberated countries were purged of pro-fascists. He quoted a report[20] that in France the people remembered that the Communists chosen to be shot as hostages after the killing of a German officer went to their deaths singing the *Marsellaise*; they remembered how disciplined and efficient was Communist clandestine action. Also it should be remembered that out of 154 French Socialist M.Ps., 90 were ejected for collaborating with the Nazis; of 73 Communist M.Ps. one was expelled for collaborating.

The Labour Conference in December rejected unity by a narrow majority. The Executive spokesman said, without substantiating these charges, that Communist policy was fundamentally different from Labour's and the aim of the Communist Party was to destroy the Labour Party. Pollitt commented that against the Executive's wishes the Conference had reflected a rising swing to the left by its decisions on Greece, nationalisation, rent control and an Indian National Government. The unity campaign should be continued, especially in the trade unions.[21]

Pollitt saw in the decisions of the meeting of Stalin, Roosevelt and Churchill in February 1945 at Yalta, in the Crimea, confirmation of the view that in post-war Britain there would be far-reaching democratic advance. Pollitt estimated[22] the pledge to continue three-power co-operation "to remove the political, economic and social causes of war" to be "a turning point in world history". He anticipated "the removal of Nazi and militarist influence from the life of the German people, the freedom of the peoples of Europe to choose whatever form of government they desire, and the creation of the essential conditions for secure and lasting peace." He based this positive estimate on the "radical change" in the line up of world forces compared with 1919 and 1939. "Instead of an alliance with fascism against the Soviet Union and Communism, there is a firm alliance with the Soviet Union and Communism against fascism." But he warned against illusions that the Crimea policy would go through without opposition. "Reaction never gives up. Defeated in one field it will immediately try to find new battlefields." In Britain a Tory Government giving way to vested interests would not "be capable of carrying through the Crimea decisions and the vast social changes necessary at home. Hence the urgent need for electoral unity to win a Labour and progressive majority and a new Government."

To answer questions about the effects of changes in the relation of world forces he wrote a new booklet,[23] in which he raised for the first time the question of whether a peaceful transition to socialism was possible in Britain.

In March 1945 came Churchill's proposal to follow the end of the war in Europe by a general election and a continuance of national unity. Pollitt favoured national unity to complete the victory and win the peace, but, since the Tory majority was unrepresentative of existing public opinion, considered that it should be replaced by a Labour and progressive majority. This majority should be the basis of a new, democratic, national government, with representatives of all parties supporting the Crimea decisions, international economic co-operation and a minimum social programme including full employment, good wages and shorter hours. Once more urging Labour to conclude a progressive electoral alliance, Pollitt said that the number of Communist candidates was being reduced "to limit the contests where a split progressive vote could lead to the return of a Tory".[24]

April 26: Red Army takes Berlin.
April 30: British and Red Armies link up; Germany surrenders unconditionally.
May 8: Victory in Europe Day.

In May, Churchill demanded that the Labour Party choose between continued coalition till the end of the war with Japan or an immediate general election. The Labour Party Conference overwhelmingly rejected continuation and decided for an election in which it would fight on its own programme. As Churchill's ultimatum had made clear that for him a national government meant Tory domination, Pollitt welcomed the Labour decision.

At the Labour conference the right-wing leaders took advantage of the atmosphere of crisis to evade the issue of electoral unity. The Standing Orders Committee refused time to debate resolutions in its favour. Procedure allowed only a motion for reference back of this report, and the merits of the resolution could not be discussed. The reference back was lost by the narrow majority of 95,000. Among the 1,219,000 votes in its favour were those of the Engineers, Distributive Trades, Miners, Railwaymen and Electricians.[25] Pollitt considered that had discussion been permitted, a majority would have favoured negotiations for electoral unity. He added, "It is a thousand pities that we do not go into this battle as a united Labour movement in agreement with other progressive forces. This cannot but be an advantage to the Tories who in many cases will be opposed by two or three candidates."[26] He suggested local conferences to secure unity behind one anti-Tory candidate.

7. GENERAL ELECTION, 1945.

At the May meeting of the Communist leaders to launch their election campaign, Pollitt showed that after the death of Roosevelt—"one of the world's greatest anti-fascists"—the international situation was deteriorating, President Truman and Churchill were moving to the right.[27] He gave a 16-point guide to the Communist propaganda.

The Tories: Their programme contains not one thing that they could not have carried out when in power between the wars; they are responsible for the rise of fascism; their foreign policy caused the war and can lose the peace.
Russia: The U.S.S.R. played the chief role in winning the war, its policy is the chief guarantee to winning the peace. As for the gossip about war with the U.S.S.R., the working class will not go and fight the Red Army.
Europe: Spread understanding of the political awakening, the role and power of the Resistance.
Japan: Speedy victory over Japan requires speedy victory over the Tories.

The war, he continued, was not won by one man, but by the nation, in which the working-class was in the majority. The term "nation" must not be allowed to be monopolised by Tory propaganda. Britain's resources could either be used for the needs of the people or for the benefit of the monopolies—Churchill had chosen the monopolies.

Labour leaders attacked the Communists, but it was their own policy that prevented a united working class from moving forward to victory and socialism. Every Communist should set an example in the anti-Tory fight, whether for the Communist candidate or by unconditional help to Labour.

Pollitt broadcast[28] on June 28, when the Communist Party, with 21 candidates, got eight minutes after the six o'clock News a week before the poll. He said that the people had the opportunity to return a government which would see that everyone in the country had a home and a job, plenty to eat, a chance for the children, and security in old age. Private enterprise had failed to meet the nation's needs before and during the war. Public enterprise had succeeded through state control during the war. When planes, ships and tanks were needed, the national resources were concentrated to supply them. The men who manned them were kept fit by the best doctors and scientists. To supply munitions the country as a whole was better fed than before the war. What had to be done to win the war was now necessary to give the people a good life in peace.

The Conservatives could not deliver the goods, their vested interests stood in the way. Coal, steel, transport, the land, the Bank of England, must be publicly owned. Coal was a case in point. It was the only industry which had not increased production during the war because of the inefficiency of private ownership. Silicosis, a disease which petrified the lungs and burst a man's heart as he died coughing for breath, was increasing. In Rhondda, 69 cases were reported in 1937 for medical inspection; in 1944 nearly 4,000 were reported.[29] The increased coal output essential to the country could only be got by new technical and mechanical methods, and by planned production and distribution. That required nationalisation.

A firm and lasting peace needed friendship with all the United Nations, especially Russia. Between the wars the Labour movement stood for collective security abroad and planned prosperity at home. Now voting for Communist candidates, and elsewhere for Labour, would return a Labour and Communist majority. "All who have followed the activities of Willie Gallacher, M.P. will agree that 21 Communist M.Ps. will greatly strengthen Labour's fight for the people."

8. RHONDDA EAST—A NEAR MISS

The five weeks prior to the poll on July 5 Pollitt spent in the Rhondda save for an occasional speech elsewhere.

The constituency consisted of the area of Rhondda Fach plus three polling districts, Penygraig, Dinas and Trealaw of Rhondda Fawr.

Mountain springs in northern Glamorgan give rise to the two rivers Rhondda. About two miles apart, they flow from north-west to south-east, nearly parallel for ten miles, separated by a high ridge, till they swerve towards one another to converge at Porth. After four miles as one stream they join the Taff River at Pontypridd. Descending with the eastern and lesser stream, Rhondda Fach, we pass through villages or townships, mainly grouped in relation to collieries, of Maerdy, Ferndale, Tylorstown, Pontygwaith and Ynyshir. The western and larger stream, Rhondda Fawr, flows through Treherbert, Pentre, Gelli, Llynypia, Tonypandy, Trealaw and Dinas.

For centuries a scattered population lived mainly by forestry, sheep and cattle rearing. Both valleys and ridges were luxuriously wooded, including much fine oak grown for naval timber. Trout and salmon were plentiful in both streams. This rural peace ended with the industrial era and its insatiable demand for coal. The first colliery opened at Dinas in 1809, working steam-coal of high quality began at Treherbert in 1855 and Ferndale in 1862. Seven years later annual output totalled 1 million tons; by 1890 it had leapt to 7 million tons, transported by rail to Cardiff, Barry and Swansea, nearly half the annual coal exports from South Wales. The peak came in 1914 when 66 pits produced 9 million tons.[30]

Many seams comparatively near the surface and offering the coal companies high and speedy profits were exploited with a total disregard for the welfare of the miners or for the future of the industry. The owners failed to provide adequate safety equipment, to mechanise production, or to provide capital to work the deeper reserves of coal.[31] In their low-wage policy and vindictive anti-trade unionism, Tory and Liberal Governments gave them police and military assistance. The class struggle assumed exceptional bitterness, the South Wales miners became throughout the country the symbol of solidarity and militancy.[32]

With the Rhondda were associated such famous trade union personalities as "Mabon", Will Hewlett, A. J. Cook and Arthur Horner. Marxist education was on a mass scale. In 1921 a Federation conference voted for affiliation to the Red International of Labour Unions, prompting Lenin to ask whether it was in South Wales that a mass Communist Party and a workers' daily newspaper could first be established.[33]

The decline of coal production in Rhondda began after the First World War and accelerated after the miners' defeat in 1926. In July 1927 there were 39,177 employed in Rhondda collieries, by July 1936 there were 19,873.[34]

During the war Pollitt was in the constituency for one week-end every month. On these visits he stayed with Annie and Trevor Powell in Llwynypia.[35] Annie was a teacher in a local school; she was well known as a forthright champion of people's rights with an outstanding ability to express communist politics in popular terms. On one occasion a group of miners' wives, referring to a Communist speaker the day before, said to Harry, "We don't know what he was talking about; send us the girl with the pots and pans speech." Her home was familiar to scores of local people and when it got round that Harry was there, they would knock and ask to see him.

Usually he was asked for advice, but sometimes he got it. The local Secretary of the Communist Party, waiting in the next room while Harry shaved, said he agreed with the content of Harry's last speech but did not like the manner and preferred that of Idris Cox, who was then the Party's South Wales Organiser. Overhearing this and touched on a sensitive spot, Harry came in and asked "What's wrong with my speaking?" He was told, "Too much and too quick. Idris is calm and deliberate." Harry went out and finished his shave.

Though he was neither Welsh nor a miner, the people in their homes and clubs, as well as at meetings, accepted him as one of themselves, the school children talked about him. He was popular, "very likeable and with the ability to distinguish between behaving as a leader when on the platform, and as a rank and filer on the floor."[36] He respected the Rhondda customs and traditions, "adapted his conduct to the company" and "always remembered a name and a face."[37] He was careful of people's dignity: when a speaker was critical of slum housing, Pollitt reminded him, "Remember a slum is also someone's home." He always drank the cup of tea offered to him, and it was always "the best cup I've had today".

At Trealaw was the Judge's Hall, so-called because donated by a local judge, to be run for popular use by an elected committee. Holding over 800, it was usually full when Pollitt spoke. When in 1939 he came to explain why he was no longer the Party's General Secretary it was crowded. A police inspector told him that he would be held responsible for any disorder. Pollitt replied, "I shall be talking to workers and have every confidence that whatever happens, they will see fair play." At another meeting there he was asked by a well-known opponent of Communism, "Why have you no religion?" He said "Don't put words into my mouth, let me put it my way. When we get to the next world, God will take care of us; while we are in this one, let us take care of one another."[38]

In the war time evacuation the peak total of London children and mothers officially billeted in Rhondda reached 33,000. In August 1944 Pollitt wrote that "everywhere in the valleys the children seem very comfortable and happy, the miners and their wives are repaying help given in past struggles."[39] That summer, meetings and weather were both good. "In Rhondda they say I always bring rain, but this time, the first since 1919, I never had to wear my raincoat." One evening he felt energetic enough to climb the mountain overlooking Llynypia and spent an hour at the top, with its wonderful view. "It was splendid, I felt as though I had been on holiday for a month. The local comrades won't believe I have done the climb, but fortunately I was recognised at the top, so the news is all over the place." Evidently London was sceptical too, for a week later he wrote "the comrades here are so convinced they are prepared to send unbelievers an illuminated certificate."[40] During the war, when beer was short, Pollitt and a local comrade taking a walk came to one of the miners' clubs. They were willing to serve Pollitt but not his companion. Harry would not go in, but said, "Thank you, if you can't admit George, you can keep the beer."[41]

In 1945 the Rhondda Labour leaders refused proposals for unity behind one working-class candidate. Pollitt's campaign began early in June. Nine Communist Committee Rooms became centres for canvassers, who reached half the electors, sold 3,000 pamphlets and 18,000 copies of the *Daily Worker,* gave out 80,000 leaflets and 40,000 election addresses. Audiences at 207 meetings, at 99 of which Pollitt spoke, totalled 22,000.[42] The contest was complicated by a Welsh Nationalist candidate. A local paper commented on the "intense interest, record attendances at many meetings".[43] The poll was 87 per cent, a record, the previous highest being 80 per cent in 1929.

Pollitt's message to electors[44] in the forces struck his keynote. "The fight in this election is to save Britain from Tory rule, from depressed areas, lower wages, social insecurity and economies at the workers' expense." His aim was "a Labour and Communist majority, and a new government to organise the new Britain which you have sacrificed so much to win". He specified measures to secure peace, house the people, greatly expand industry and agriculture, control prices, with extensive nationalisation. He warned, "Without an unbreakable alliance with the Soviet Union there is no worthwhile future for our country." He pledged priority to the needs of servicemen and women—speedy demobilisation, jobs with good pay and prospects, training where necessary, compensatory pensions for those disabled.

He planned his speeches, indoor and outdoor, so as to give every elector the chance to hear the constructive Communist case on all issues. At many pithead meetings he dealt in depth with the coal problem, arguing for "nationalisation of the mines so that the basic industry of Rhondda East be brought to efficiency and prosperity, with effective safety and health measures in the pits. To prosper in the future coal must be mined for the nation and not for capitalist profit." He argued for preparation of suitable sites to attract new industries, such sites "will abound once an end is made of the scrap and junk along the railway lines, which now give a totally unjustified impression of decay".

At Pontygwaith: "Churchill pretends he cannot sleep at night for fear of a dictatorship by the Labour Executive. That Committee is democratically elected, but how is the Tory Executive elected? Only the Tory bosses know, and they won't tell."

At Trealaw: "Behind the Tory decision to rush this election was their knowledge of the swing to the left all over Europe. They want to cash in on

Churchill's personality before left tendencies express themselves here. They rush a general election here, and prevent one in Greece."

At Trealaw on Polling Day a five-year old boy waited some hours to see Mr. Pollitt. When he arrived, the mother said, "Here is Mr. Pollitt." The child in an awed voice asked "Do you mean we can see him for nothing; haven't we got to pay?"[45] At Tylorstown, Pollitt spoke from the tailboard of a van at the top of a cliff overlooking a steep path up which the miners walked from the pit below. For the 11 p.m. shift the van was lit up. "They say, let Churchill finish the job. We ask, what job? Cleaning up fascism everywhere, organising prosperity for the people—or refashioning reaction to make Britain safe for profiteers and millionaires?"

At Porth, Pollitt attacked Lord Beaverbrook, whose papers were denigrating the Labour campaign. Reminding his audience of how the coal combines had closed down pits and sacked men, he quoted Beaverbrook's reference to forming his first combine—"I was not concerned with the consumer. My first interest was to make money, my second to sell the public a sound security and enhance my rising reputation as a merchant banker."

At Treforest: "Nine great combines grip the food of the British people. They control 336 companies, seize the best sites, fix wholesale prices, advertise lavishly, cut out competition by 'rings', buy up commodities in short supply, drive small traders bankrupt. No wonder Rhondda has 318 empty shops."

At Ynyshir: "The Communist Party is proud of its consistent support for Socialist Russia. From the first days of November 1917 we have defended the Soviets when Labour and Tory leaders alike misrepresented and attacked them. Now their foreign policy is to make certain of a permanent peace."

Arthur Horner continued to have great influence in the Rhondda. He and Wal Hannington signed a leaflet in support of Pollitt. It was traditional for the South Wales Miners Executive to call on them to vote Labour against the capitalist candidates, and in 1945 Arthur Horner, as President, signed this appeal. The Executive agreed to his proposal to issue it only where the seats were not safe—meaning it would not be used in Rhondda East. But two days before the poll, the Rhondda Labour election machine flooded the constituency with it. The contradiction between these two leaflets told against Pollitt, for there was not time for an effective explanation.

The result, with the Armed Forces vote, was Labour 16,733, Communist 15,761, Welsh Nationalist 2,123. Pollit had polled the largest vote yet given to a Communist, but lost by 972. Idris Cox thought he would have won had there been earlier mobilisation of local support, a more positive attitude to Welsh national issues, and greater active support from influential Communist miners.[46]

The loss to the Labour movement by Pollitt's defeat was apparent in the next five years. Had he been in Parliament, his capacity in debate, influence among trade unionists and ability to attract mass audiences all over the country, might well have had a decisive influence in uniting the Labour left and centre against the right-wing policy of subservience to the City and the Americans.

CHAPTER 22

THE LABOUR GOVERNMENT—1945–1947

1. Labour victory and danger signals. 2. Norway. 3. Bevin, Foreign Secretary. 4. Morrison, Laski and affiliation. 5. Home policy. 6. The squatters. 7. Year of crisis. 8. Looking ahead. 9. A letter to the Prime Minister. 10. For a Left Labour Government.

1. LABOUR VICTORY AND DANGER SIGNALS

The overall majority of 180 meant that for the first time a Labour Government could legislate independently of Liberal support. Pollitt estimated this as a "gigantic victory for the working class" but "only a beginning". The election programme had struck the workers' imagination as a "minimum guarantee of peace and prosperity", but to carry it through would require the active support of the millions who voted for it.[1] The Communist Party had to influence the workers "to help the government to carry out Labour's declared policy, and not to make new demands upon it". While recognising "the traditional desire of some Labour leaders to serve the interests of the ruling class" he combated the idea that a right-wing betrayal was inevitable.[2] Whether or not the programme would be carried out would be decided by the struggle of the mass Labour movement against capitalist reaction. "Our main fight is not against the Labour Government—it is against capitalism and the capitalist ideas influencing members of the movement and of the government." This struggle was as essential on foreign policy as on home affairs, since a wrong foreign policy would jeopardise social advance at home. Solution of the problems of reconstruction and ensuring a lasting peace would at the next election bring "an even more decisive victory and a stronger Labour Government. Failure would bring disillusionment, a smaller majority, sectional and not class politics, the growth of fascism in new forms."[3]

The Communist attitude was summed up by Pollitt as "full support to the Labour Government when fighting to carry through its election policy."[4] But in two years the Government's retreat from the election programme had gone so far that Pollitt had to describe it as "active partner in the imperialist camp"[5] and to call for "a new, left, Labour Government." We shall outline the developments leading to this change.

Amid the jubilation of victory came unmistakeable danger signals. The first was right-wing dominance in the government. Attlee, Prime Minister, Bevin, Foreign Secretary, Morrison, Home Secretary, all shared with

Churchill responsibility for the anti-Soviet policy of delay in opening the Second Front. Bevin and Morrison were noted for long-standing antipathy to the Labour left as well as to the U.S.S.R. With Sir Walter Citrine in charge at the T.U.C. and Morgan Phillips at Labour headquarters, the commanding heights of the movement, as well as of the government, were firmly occupied by men dedicated to collaboration with capitalism.

The second came in broadcasts to the U.S.A. by Attlee, Cripps and Laski. When he read them Pollitt commented, "A cold shudder went down my spine. It was clear what was afoot. No broadcasts to the socialist countries, assurances to America that Britain had not 'gone Red'."[6]

The third was the visit of Professor Laski and Morgan Phillips, representing the Labour Party, to several European capitals for the purpose of preventing the continuation of Socialist-Communist unity achieved during the Resistance.

2. NORWAY.

In August 1945 Pollitt was in Oslo to attend the Congress of the Communist Party of Norway.[7] He found the city undamaged, but with many shops empty, shoe repairs taking six months, plenty of wood but no coal. The people welcomed liberation but resented Allied commandeering of thirty of the best hotels. Two Communists were in the government; one was the first woman to be a Minister. The Communist Party had 30,000 members, of whom 75 per cent had joined during the Resistance in which the Nazis shot all of the Communist Party's Central Committee. Its paper *Freheiten* had a sale of 95,000, the second largest in Norway.

Success in Labour-Communist co-operation during the war led to pressure after the liberation for one united working-class party. Unity negotiations initiated by the Norwegian T.U.C. brought rapid agreement on a general election programme, but differences on questions of organisation. A joint Unity Congress was proposed for September 2. The Norwegian Labour Party wanted representation in proportion to established membership, and immediate fusion. The Labour Party being composed of affiliated trade unions, this proposal meant for them a decisive majority. The Communists wanted a period of parity in representation in local committees to prepare for fusion. The two T.U.C. representatives in the Unity Committee—there were three each from C.P. and L.P.—voted with the L.P. When the Communists did not pledge to accept all decisions of the Unity Committee, the T.U.C. called off further discussion, and on September 2 the two Party Congresses met separately.

They were preceded by two demonstrations, Labour on August 30, Communist on September 1. Laski spoke for the Labour Party: he had been at the conferences of the Danish Labour Party and the French Socialist Party, both of which had rejected unity. In Oslo, Laski had been well publicised, but Pollitt felt that his ten-minute speech disappointed the

10,000 workers present. It contained polite compliments, but no policy. Next day, Pollitt was in the Communist march of 15,000, and spoke at the meeting.

The Communist Congress was opened by the oldest delegate, aged 77; he reminded Pollitt of Tom Mann. It sent a delegation to the Labour Congress, proposing a united election campaign for a working-class majority in Parliament and the renewal of the unity negotiations. The Labour Congress heard the Communist case, but rejected both proposals. This attitude Pollitt attributed to the activities of the veteran right-wing leader, Tranmael, and the influence of the British Labour leaders.

Later he summed up this affair: "Laski and Phillips in Norway prepared the way for Bevin's anti-Russian policy, as Bevin subsequently prepared the way for Churchill at Fulton."

3. Bevin—Foreign Secretary.

Bevin's first speech as Foreign Secretary showed continuity of policy with Churchill. He kept British troops in Greece and Indonesia,[8] lined up with U.S. imperialism against the Soviet Union and described the New Democracies in Europe as "replacing one kind of dictatorship by another". Pollitt pointed out that this did not correspond with the Labour election programme of consolidation of relations with both U.S.A. and U.S.S.R. He called the speech "a tragic example of the wrong kind of theory". Bevin denounced alike the fascist use of force against the people and the people's use of force against fascism, while himself using force against the Greek anti-fascists. "This conception of democracy can only help those who want the Labour Government to fail."[9]

When the U.S. struck Britain a severe blow by ending lease-lend and compelling payment in cash for U.S. goods, Bevin made no protest. In September at the Conference of Foreign Ministers, Bevin called Molotov's attitude "Hitlerian". Molotov rose to walk out, and Bevin had to withdraw.[10] In November, Britain and the U.S.A. agreed to share atomic know-how, but to give no information to the U.S.S.R. Defending this in the House, Bevin said that "war between Britain and the U.S.A. was unthinkable" with no similar reference to the U.S.S.R. At the 1945 Labour Party Conference Bevin had described British-Soviet-American friendship as "our insurance premium against war."

Perhaps sensing that Bevin's anti-Sovietism was reaching a point of no return, perhaps for the satisfaction of a confrontation, Pollitt asked for a personal talk. They met[11] at the Foreign Office on 14 November. Bevin opened brusquely, "Sit down and tell me what you want."

Pollitt said that he had come, not for personal reasons, but because he believed that foreign policy would determine Britain's future. The workers were moving to the left, Labour's foreign policy was moving to the right. If the spirit of Bevin's 1920 speech defending the Russian

Revolution was now applied, it would transform the international situation. "I ask you—cannot a new approach be made in Britain's policy to Greece, Indonesia, the Balkans, and especially to the U.S.S.R? I appeal to you to think it over." Later Pollitt described Bevin's reaction. "Then Ernie started. He was not afraid of Tories or Americans; he knew how to stand up to the Russians. No one was going to tell him what to do. 'What an impudence you have, with your record of disruptive activity, to lecture me.' All this accompanied by banging on the table and the use of language which left no doubt of his working-class origin. We both enjoyed the slanging match which followed, and as the cockney song has it, we parted on fighting terms. Afterwards, whenever we saw one another, it was a nod and pass on."[12]

In February, Pollitt called for pressure from the Labour Movement to change foreign policy. "It is time the nation saw the danger in which it is being placed. Labour foreign policy stands at the cross-roads."[13] He asked why Bevin's fury was always directed against the Soviet Union, never against reaction and fascism. Why trade agreements with fascist Spain, and deadlock on Anglo-Soviet trade? Why keep British troops in Greece and Indonesia? Why pay £500,000 every week to Anders' Polish army in Italy? Why the reluctance to purge Nazis from the administration in the British Occupied Zone? He described as "shameful" the statement of Bevin's principal assistant, Hector McNeil, M.P., that Bevin and the Labour Government could be relied upon to stand up to Russia, "the Russia that gave 15 million of the flower of its youth, that we might live." Michael Foot, M.P. had remarked[14] in connection with the differences between Russia and Britain, "the argument is also between Social Democracy and Communism." Pollitt commented, "It is nothing of the kind. The argument at rock bottom is whether Labour's foreign policy shall be a working-class policy or a continuation of Tory policy . . . since Labour came to power Tory leaders have not made one single criticism of the foreign policy, but on the contrary, applauded it."

As though to make crystal clear what Bevin was doing, Mr. Churchill at Fulton, Missouri, with President Truman approving, called for a "special relationship" between Britain and the U.S.A. because "nobody knew what Russia and its Communist international organisation intended to do in the immediate future".[15] His proposal was described by 105 Labour M.Ps. as "a military alliance between Britain and the U.S.A. for the purpose of combating the spread of Communism."[16] Attlee refused time in the House to discuss this motion; neither he nor Bevin, then or later, ever dissociated themselves from Churchill's Fulton policy.

Pollitt condemned[17] the Fulton speech as an appeal for "an anti-Soviet bloc and a bloc against the working class and all it stands for in social progress". The timing, too, was significant. It coincided with the opening of an offensive against Labour's programme by the Tories and big employers. Churchill, for whom Bevin had prepared the ground, was "seeking to use Labour for reactionary ends meant to lead to war on the U.S.S.R., to slow down Labour's domestic policy, to strengthen reaction all over Europe".

After Fulton criticism of Bevin's policy grew among Labour M.Ps., and in the movement generally; but the opposition was not strong enough to deflect Bevin from his course. His speech at the Labour Party Conference showed, said Pollitt, his determination to strengthen the Anglo-American bloc against the Soviet Union.[18] In November Bevin breached the Potsdam agreement by conniving with the U.S. to unify the British and American occupied zones of Germany.

In 1947 the Labour Government accepted the Truman Doctrine and the Marshall Plan. The former provided for the use of American money and armed force against what the U.S. might choose to call "communism". The latter spelt out the economic, financial and political conditions qualifying a government to receive this "aid". Bevin assured the House "there is no political motive behind the plan other than the over-riding motive to help Europe help herself".[19] Pollitt commented, "The over-riding motive is to help American financiers and industrialists to help themselves to Europe's markets, raw materials and overseas colonies and to build a Western bloc war base, against the Soviet Union and the new democracies." "The Western bloc is Hitler's Pan-Europe in a new dress, an attempt to partition Europe to bolster up the capitalist order in the West." Noting the approval of Bevin's speech by Churchill and the U.S. State Department, Pollitt said, "All pretence that Britain is pursuing an independent course has been abandoned. Britain is openly ranged in the imperialist camp as the willing accomplice of the U.S. Labour Ministers have thrown off the mask and come out in full support of Churchill's Fulton policy".[20]

The capitalist press lauded Bevin as the Great Man of the Government. In January 1947, reviewing a biography of Bevin by Trevor Evans, Pollitt wrote: "The book brings out very strongly the price working-class leaders must pay if they neglect the study of Marxism. . . . Behind the facade of the Great Man theory you get the attempt to cover up political weaknesses and blindness by bluff and bluster. Bevin is one of those Labour leaders who believe it to be important to prove that they can make capitalism work more efficiently than the capitalists, and who become tools of the most aggressive sections of monopoly capitalism—as Bevin proves by his willing servitude to American big business."[21]

Here we may interpolate something written twenty years later by Lord Butler in a foreword to a biography[22] of Sir Pierson Dixon "One of Dixon's greatest services was as private secretary to Ernest Bevin . . . It was largely Dixon's work to bring out the greatness in the man. At the same time, Dixon was able to conduct a bi-partisan foreign policy through his friendship with Eden . . . It was a tribute to Dixon that one Labour M.P. was heard to remark when Bevin sat down after speaking on foreign affairs, 'How fat Anthony has grown'." The biographer himself wrote "throughout this period Bevin worked closely with Eden on the implementation of a bi-partisan foreign policy. Dixon was the liaison between the two men."

4. MORRISON, LASKI AND AFFILIATION.

Bevin's policy was soon recognised by the Labour left as a departure from election pledges but for some three years home policy was seen as a fulfilment of them, even if slow and piecemeal. The right wing was aware that if criticism on foreign policy was swollen by discontent on home affairs, it could endanger their position. This made Communist affiliation to the Labour Party a crucial issue. With electoral unity so narrowly defeated in 1945, by 1,219,000 votes to 1,134,000, additional trade union support might carry affiliation in 1946. Entry of the Communist Party would strengthen the pressure to implement the whole election programme to a stage where a conference majority might not merely criticise but repudiate right-wing policy. Against this danger the right wing went into action.

Pollitt described[23] their first move. Attlee, Morrison and Morgan Phillips invited selected trade union leaders to dinner at the Savoy on March 15, the ostensible purpose being to discuss the future of the political levy after the repeal of the Trade Union Act. At the dinner, Morrison attacked the Communist Party, arguing that affiliation would mean Communist M.P.s, and make it difficult to resist a Communist claim to enter the government; and no honest man could sit in a government with a Communist, for the Communist Party did not have just one or two Soviet spies in it, the entire Party was such an organisation. The trade unions were wrong to allow Communists the right to be elected, the officials would pay a price for this, for the Party would get them out of their jobs. Morrison proposed that they should try to get decisions in support of affiliation changed before the Annual Conference. If this failed, they should vote against and explain why to their next union conference. Pollitt described the allegation that the Communist Party was an organisation of spies as "deliberately dishonest" and challenged Morrison to defend his speech in public.

While Morrison incited trade union officials to vote against their union's decisions, Professor Laski, who in 1936 supported affiliation but was now chairman of the Labour Party, provided some melodrama for the public. He alleged[24] that the Communists had applied for affiliation because Lenin's advice to enter Social Democratic parties to destroy them had recently been repeated by Dimitrov. Challenged by Pollitt to justify this allegation, Laski failed to do so, but repeated it.

Laski in the *Daily Herald*, April 23: "As is well known Lenin urged Communists to enter Social Democratic Parties to destroy them.[25] I suggest that what is taking place in relations between Social Democratic parties and Communist Parties in no way differs in principle today from the relations Lenin recommended. Then as now, it is the policy of the stab in the back."

Pollitt to the *Daily Herald*, April 24: Readers "will not have failed to notice that Harold Laski could not produce a single sentence from Dimitrov's recent speech which in any way implied that the policy of the Communist Party towards Social Democratic parties was to stab them in the back. You may be quite sure that if such a statement had been made by Dimitrov, Laski would have produced it."

On April 30 Pollitt published[26] the full B.B.C. monitored text of the Dimitrov speech pointing out that it nowhere contained the words or the concept of "stab in the back", and that Laski had not been the first to distort it.[27]

To Laski's question, why not disband the Communist Party and individually join the Labour Party, Pollitt replied that a Marxist party was essential, without it Communists as individuals could not make their full contribution to the thinking and activity of the Labour Party. Marxism provided the kind of knowledge which Laski himself had said[28] was needed—"Why we are socialists, and what we are going to do with our socialism". "Affiliation would bring Marxism into the Labour Party. There was no stab in the back policy, the Communist Party was fighting all tendencies to water down Labour's programme and would do all in its power to make nationalisation successful as the next stage on the road to socialism."

In May, Dimitrov asked Laski to publicly correct his mistake. Referring to the phrase "stab in the back", Dimitrov wrote: "It is very strange that you derive such a false conclusion; nowhere have I expressed this viewpoint in speeches or writing.... In the 1933 trial at Leipzig, with shackles on my hands, I defended to the best of my ability not only German Communists, but also the German Social Democratic Party, against the Hitlerites."[29] Laski remained silent.

In May, recorded support for affiliation included 7 national executives of trade unions, 11 Trades and Labour Councils, 85 local and 30 divisional Labour Parties.[30] The capitalist and official Labour publicity machines intensified their anti-affiliation campaign.

At the Conference Morrison, claiming to do so "much against my inclination", stated the Executive's case against affiliation.[31] The Labour Party believed in constitutional government, parliamentary democracy and civil liberty, the Communist Party did not. It was not only a party, it was also a conspiracy with open and secret members, orders from above, mysterious funds. It subordinated British interests to external ones, it organised espionage. If affiliated it would have access to secret documents. It supported Browden's desertion of socialism.

Affiliation was moved by the Engineers and seconded by the Fire Brigades. Debate was prevented by an immediate call for a vote. The vote was: For 448,000; against 2,678,000 Pollitt wrote[33] that opposition to affiliation was the counterpart to failure to face up to economic and political realities thus rendering the movement unprepared for the severe struggles ahead. This opposition had the support of the reactionary elements in Britain and the U.S.A. The defeat of affiliation was a blow at all who hoped to see the Labour Government carry through its full election programme.

Describing Morrison's attack as "unmeasured and filthy" Pollitt added that "the Morrison type always directed their full venom, not against capitalism, but against the Communists, whose policy was to strengthen the working class and its will to the conquest of power and Socialism."

The Labour Executive did not stop at rejecting affiliation. It put forward an amendment[34] to the Party's Constitution for the purpose of ruling out of order any future application by the Communist Party. Formally moved and put to the vote without debate, the amendment was carried by 2,413,000 votes to 667,000.

5. HOME POLICY.

Nationalisation[35]

In 1946 the Bank of England, coal, civil aviation, cable and wireless were nationalised; in 1947 electricity and inland transport; in 1948 gas. Steel, the one case where capitalist resistance was serious, not till 1951. Pollitt supported[36] these measures and made constructive proposals to remedy their weaknesses. He opposed the compensation as excessive in amount and as the burden of private profit borne by the industry or the taxpayer. The failure to provide government money for modernisation compelled the nationalised industries to load themselves with interest payments to capitalist financiers.

The nationalised industries were controlled by Boards without representatives of the public or the workers. The same Governor continued at the Bank of England, the Coal Board Chairman was an ex-coal owner. The Transport Commission had a civil servant as Chairman, three previous rail company directors, a Co-operator and an ex-Trade Union official. The Rail Executive were four railway officials, a retired General, an ex-Trade Union official. This "management by officials, headed by ex-Directors who are political enemies of Labour ensured a dominant capitalist outlook on all questions".[37]

The argument that ability counted and not politics, Pollitt described as "the social democratic failure to understand that the capitalist outlook is based on restriction of production, the socialist outlook on its expansion."[38] To Morrison's dictum that the Government should buy the best brains available, Pollitt said that success in nationalised industries depended not on buying capitalist brains but on drawing the workers into operational plans.[39]

Pollitt saw these differences turning on a fundamental question. Was post-war reconstruction to be a return to pre-war production directed by monopoly capital for its own profit? Or was production to be directed by the government to meet the people's needs? The former meant a new lease of life for capitalist imperialism; the latter a great democratic advance towards socialism.[40]

Pollitt drew up, in close consultation with leading miners, a plan for the nationalised coal mines.[41] To achieve the targets would need 100,000 more miners, better organisation, and a democratic administration combining national planning with consultation with the workers. Men would be attracted to mining only if wages and rations were increased, conditions improved, decent homes, training and a good medical service provided. Miners fully deserved such differential treatment. The best available machines and equipment needed for all mining processes should be bulk-produced in national engineering works no longer needed for war purposes. Coal production should be concentrated in the best pits. A special civil engineering force should be organised to open new pits or, where worth while, develop existing ones.

The Coal Board should have a majority of trade union leaders with the full confidence of the miners. Emergency Committees with power to carry through all measures necessary to prevent a coal crisis, should be formed of representatives of the Government, the miners, managers and deputies, with a leading miner as Chairman.

Production and Wages

Pollitt stressed that the purpose of production was not to pile up profits but to meet the people's needs. "Only increased production can ensure us from becoming a colony of U.S. big business."[42] To get more production the government must prove that workers would benefit from it. That meant action to raise wages, control prices, lessen taxes on necessities. Higher wages were essential, they had lagged far behind the cost of living, which had risen far more than shown by the official index. The government should not weaken the unions' power in collective bargaining, but it should set the example with its own workers, and intervene when employers refused increases. There should be a minimum base for all scales of wages, Trade Board rates should be raised, separate women's schedules should be replaced by the rate for the job.

Asked if this policy would mean inflation, Pollitt replied, "No, provided there is firm government control of prices." Nor need it increase prices provided profits were limited. "Low wages mean technical backwardness, high wages stimulate efficiency."

Planning

Pollitt envisaged[43] a Planning Commission of trade unionists, technical experts, civil servants and industrialists, with sub-commissions experienced in each industry. The plan would be subject to popular discussion and joint consultation. His central idea was that targets for each major industry, set for some years ahead, would cover production for home and export, modernisation, new industrial and social construction, in such quantity and quality as would raise the people's living standards and ensure Britain's place in world trade. These targets as a whole would be the basis for the provision of machines and buildings by the engineering and construction industries, for allocation of raw materials and controlled investment. Nationalised industries, including national war-time engineering factories, would be decisive in realising the plan; private industry would work within this framework, stimulated by government bulk orders. Prices and profits would be controlled. There were also proposals for distribution, agriculture, housing, taxation and foreign trade.

6. THE SQUATTERS.

In 1946 many homeless or intolerably overcrowded families moved in to occupy empty government-owned hostels or camps. When the movement spread to private property the Ministry of Health asked local authorities to cut off essential services and to secure the eviction of squatters.

On Sunday, September 8, some 400 homeless families occupied empty Kensington flats in Duchess of Bedford House, Melcombe Regis Court, Fountain Court and Abbey Lodge. This caused a national sensation. The London Committee of the Communist Party, which organised the action, pointed out that there were 250,000 homeless on the London County and Borough Council lists, while thousands of empty flats and houses were not requisitioned. Five Communist leaders were prosecuted for conspiracy—Ted Bramley, L.C.C., Westminster Councillors Joyce Allergant and Gabriel Carritt, Stepney Councillor Rosen, and Stan Henderson, a tenants' leader.

On September 12 a great crowd in Cranbourne Street, Leicester Square, heard Pollitt call for support for the squatters.[44] He pointed out that during the war the government, rightly, took over the needed buildings and land for a variety of war purposes. Churchill promised that with peace housing would be treated like a military operation, but that was not being done. Labour and material were found to fit out the Mall for the victory parade, and to house 40,000 Poles who ought to be back in their own country, but no extraordinary measures were taken to house our own homeless, except by the squatters. Instead of this being welcomed as showing fighting qualities against injustice, there was a press hue-and-cry against them and steps to evict them. To the press the workers were the salt of the earth when they suffered in silence, and "the mob" when they fought for their rights. It was the foreign policy and preparations for new wars that explained the snail's pace in de-requisitioning buildings. To the responsible Minister, Aneurin Bevan, Pollitt said, "If this action had taken place under a Tory Government, you would have used your power of invective against them, you would have called on the people to stand firm. Do not be stampeded now."

Pollitt proposed the withdrawal of proceedings against the squatters, no evictions, supply to them of light and heat; and that the government state the number of empty buildings suitable for temporary accommodation and what they proposed to do with them. On September 15, Pollitt stated that "the squatters had done much to speed up the housing programme". The Minister for Health had called on Councils to provide additional homes at the greatest possible speed: many responded by extended requisitioning. On the 17th, with a Court Order against them, the Kensington squatters marched out of the premises with band and banners.

The five Communists appeared at the Old Bailey before Mr Justice Sable on October 30. Ted Bramley defended himself, the others were defended by Sir Walter Monckton, K.C., who "out of sheer generosity left his lucrative civil practice to appear for the defence, conducted it with his usual conciliatory charm, and refused to accept a fee.[45] Bramley, explaining why the Communists had helped the squatters, gave details of how people were living. One family, a father, mother and five children aged 7 to 19 who went into Duchess of Bedford House, had come from one bedroom in which they all slept and one very small kitchen, both draughty and in bad repair. Prior to that they lived with a friend, 12 people in four rooms. The father was in the army from 1913 to 1945, was on the last boat out of France after Dunkirk, and in the invasion on D-Day. He knew of many similar cases. Building of new houses in London was appallingly slow, in one year the L.C.C. had built 382, six Borough Councils not a single one, while in the region, thousands of properties stood empty, and 29,610 licenses were issued for non-housing work.[46] The five were found Guilty and bound over for two years.

7. Year of Crisis.

In 1947 the cost of the foreign policy and the lack of planned economic reconstruction were reflected in a series of crises. Acute shortage of coal brought factory closures in January, intensified by a prolonged freeze until in February, $2^{1}/_{4}$ million workers were laid off. A mounting adverse balance of payments, premature exhaustion of the U.S. loan, largely due to a 40 per cent increase in U.S. prices, together with Marshall-imposed convertibility of the £, brought into sight the danger of the exhaustion of Britain's gold and dollar reserves. The Government refused to cut military and armaments expenditure but did cut social services and capital investment at home, lowered real wages and launched an export drive.

In January 1947 Pollitt prepared a memorandum[47] under the title "No Middle Way", reviewing the eighteen months of Labour Government. In addition to shortages and damage produced by the war, Britain had a specific problem. Pre-war, its exports paid for only half its imports, the remainder were in fact profit from investment abroad. These investments were lost during the war. This, together with U.S. penetration and colonial liberation, meant that to maintain the economy now needed an immense increase in exports. But production was held back by obsolete plant, lack of planning and manpower shortage. Solution of this problem required an all-round break with the imperialist past. The Labour Government was not making this break. It sought agreement with the vested interests, a "middle way" between capitalism and socialism. This meant transforming the election programme of reforms into a programme for reorganising capitalism at the workers' expense and resulted in nationalisation with huge compensation and no democratic control, continuation of imperialist foreign policy and alignment in a junior position with the U.S. "Events have proved there is no middle way. There is only one way of advance for the people—the Socialist way."

With no middle way there were only two possibilities. One was to reorganise the government, change its policy, go forward to a great economic reorganisation, co-operate with the Soviet Union, the new democracies and the colonial peoples. The other was to surrender to the monopolies at home, sink to dependence on American imperialism, become a vulnerable advanced base for war against European democracy.[48]

As discontent in the movement rose, some government changes were made, but only to strengthen the right wing. Pollitt wrote[49] that class-conscious workers tested in strikes and lock-outs were never promoted, the decisive government jobs went to inexperienced university newcomers with no practice in the daily struggle. "What do Messrs. Mayhew, Wilson and Gaitskell know of the struggle against capitalism?" The Easter trade union conferences and the majority of resolutions at the Labour Party Conference 1947 were critical of government policy. Pollitt called[50] for unity of all opposed to the present composition and policy of the Government so that the Labour Conference could give a lead "to transform the situation and rally the country". But the opportunity was lost, the left "capitulated from the start, failed to make any effective challenge" and right-wing domination continued.

8. LOOKING AHEAD.

In August 1947 Pollitt, in a pamphlet entitled *Looking Ahead*, made a new appraisal[51] of the relation of political forces. In the common effort of those standing for socialism, national liberation and democracy, lay the future of the common people against whom monopoly capital sought to align all reactionary forces. But "it is not a question of opposing one world against another, or one nation against another", such reactionary aims had to be defeated. "It is a question of inspiring confidence in the strength of mankind's progressive forces" so that the peoples in countries pursuing reactionary policies could call a halt to them and insist on governments promoting world co-operation. American imperialism "had taken the place of Hitler Germany, with different methods but the same aim—world domination". The Potsdam agreement had been violated to make Germany safe for big business. Marshall Aid was only for governments subservient to U.S. policy. British imperialism was junior partner to the U.S. in an "alliance" which opened her economy and markets to U.S. competition and made her a fixed aircraft carrier and front-line base for war against the U.S.S.R. The immediate hope of great power co-operation for peaceful democratic world advance had faded.

Britain had a crisis of under-production, no economic plan, modernisation lagging behind, private industry profiting from shortages. The Labour Government's economic policy was not solving the crisis but was endangering the enacted reforms and those promised. The Government argued that as we were not a totalitarian state, economic development could only proceed with the acceptance of both sides in industry. "But we ask, since when has the capitalist side accepted the aims the people voted for in 1945? Since when is it more interested in national recovery than in profit? Limiting its policy to what secures the voluntary co-operation of big business means that the government cannot do anything seen by the capitalists as a threat to their wealth and power." The talk about democracy was a cover for undemocratic capitalist methods. "The question is not whether labour should be directed: it is whether the capitalists should be directed to work within a national plan."

Pollitt, speaking "not as an outside critic but as a representative of the Communist Party which was working harder than any other to see that Labour's election programme is achieved", then re-stated the Party's constructive proposals emphasising the necessity for "a new kind of Government whose members have faith in their own movement and land, who are Socialists in theory and practice."

9. A LETTER TO THE PRIME MINISTER.

On August 28, Pollitt gave to the Prime Minister, Clement Attlee, the Communist Party's view of the crisis and the policy to solve it.[52] The salient points of the letter were:

"In two years you have carried important measures of nationalisation and reform, but stultified them by continuing a traditional Tory foreign policy which has made us dependent on a ruthless and aggressive

American imperialism. You have failed to put through any serious reconstruction at home, accepted the indefensible conditions of the American loan which have crippled British recovery, and turned down an agreement on Soviet trade which could have provided a large proportion of our essential imports.

"A position has been reached when the alternatives have to be faced. They are: a cut in the armed forces or an ever extending cut in the people's living standards; a basic change in foreign policy, or degradation of Britain to a colony of U.S. imperialism."

The Communist proposals: (1) Reduce the armed forces by half a million; bring home all troops from the East; (2) Negotiate new trade agreements with the U.S.S.R. and the new democracies; call a conference to utilise Empire resources for mutual benefit of the peoples and withstand the menace of U.S. imperialism; (3) A national economic plan and means to carry it out; (4) Emergency measures now to ensure a record harvest next year; (5) Tax capital, strict control of prices and profits, reduce workers' income tax.

"These measures require the removal of Ministers responsible for the present position, and their replacement by trusted representatives of the Labour movement who will carry through this policy.

"Future relations with America must be on the basis of no conditions and no attempt to dictate what policy or allies Britain must be associated with."

10. For a Left Labour Government.

"Britain faces a crisis. You have heard the Prime Minister put the Government's view. You have heard Churchill for the Tory Party. Now come and hear Pollitt give the Communist answer." This appeal was made in 200,000 leaflets, hundreds of loud-speaker announcements, and 10,000 stickybacks by the London Communist Party during the week when the T.U.C. was meeting.

Sunday, September 7 1947 was warm and fine; the crowds enjoyed the sunshine in Hyde Park, the hecklers were busy at Speakers' Corner. At 2.30 p.m. a large van with huge loudspeakers facing in four directions took up position on the grass West of Speakers' Corner. Soon the strollers were replaced by a purposeful gathering. 50,000 workers had come in answer to the Communist appeal. On the stroke of 3 p.m., Ted Bramley, London Secretary of the Party, announced Pollitt, who plunged straight into his speech.[53]

Serious and silent they listened for over an hour to his explanation of the crisis, and the Communist proposals for its solution. It was the analysis made in *Looking Ahead* expressed in popular terms. The crisis had taken the people by surprise, there was neither an adequate conception of what was at stake nor a conviction of urgency on a basic change of policy. "That is the result of Social Democracy, which disarms the working class at moments of greatest difficulty". The Government proposals were entirely inadequate. There was no middle way between imperialism and socialism. To solve the crisis required a double fight, first against our own capitalist class and its supporters in the Labour Government; second against the aggressive aims of American imperialism. "Why do the F.B.I. say that the appointment of Cripps as economic chief is on the right lines? If it was me that had the job, the F.B.I. would not be pleased, but paralysed." Instead of compromising with the employers, the Government should organise the nation's resources as was done after Dunkirk, and he recalled Attlee's statement on May 22, 1940 that complete government control was necessary "not over some person or some particular class, but over all persons—rich or poor, employers or workers—and over all property". He then explained the Communist proposals, stressing the need for mass pressure to reorganise the government. At the T.U.C. the left fought every inch of the way for a new policy: it did not win the majority, but it was a significant minority. "When workers fight for a policy there is always hope." But the Government speakers and the General Council advanced no working-class policy; giving them blank cheques would not produce the goods. "The Southport T.U.C. will give great encouragement to the capitalists."

In December Pollitt made a further re-appraisal of Communist policy, including the following:[54]

The Labour Government was now an active partner in the imperialist camp, carrying through a capitalist solution of the crisis. This required a change in Communist policy.

The Party correctly had exposed the reactionary nature of the Truman doctrine and the Marshall Plan, but it had been slow to recognise that U.S. imperialism had become the central driving force of world reaction. It had been correct to support the Labour Government for fulfilment of the election programme while opposing reactionary policies, but we were late in appreciating the full scale of the drift to the right and that the government had become an instrument of imperialism. It was correct to lead the fight for increased production, but we were slow to bring out that without a basic change in policy, no production effort could solve the crisis. The exposure of the disorganising role of social democracy, which at every decisive moment throws its weight on the side of the capitalists, was insufficient. The main danger now was to under-estimate the workers' readiness to fight for their demands.

The main tasks now were: to fully develop the struggle in defence of living standards and for peace; to help unite all the left forces in the movement, with the perspective of a new Labour Government based on the left and progressive forces in the Labour movement.

Pollitt explained that a Left Labour Government meant one whose policy served the interests of the working class and the broad mass of the people, not the rich. Its members would be Labour, Socialist and Communist men and women with proved capacity in working-class struggle and loyalty to socialist principles. Such a government could only arise from far reaching changes in the movement, not from any re-shuffle of existing leaders.

The basic change necessary was that the mass of organised workers should refuse to accept class-collaboration leadership and should go into action for their demands, with their trade unions playing a vital part. Alongside economic issues it was essential to preserve peace and defend democratic rights. For the mass struggle to reach its full height there must be working-class unity. "The united front of the left wing and the Communist Party is the only way in the long run to defeat the right wing and its policies."

Alongside leadership in the struggle for immediate demands there was needed the exposure of right-wing theory and practice. The similarity of Tory and right-wing Labour policies resulted from the fact that the right wing rejected socialism and protected capitalism, the result being to strengthen monopoly capitalism, not to reach socialism. There could be no fundamental advance by the workers while social democracy dominated the movement.

Particular issues had to be linked with general policy. The aim of united action was to win immediate practical gains and to secure a national policy to advance the workers' interests. The Labour workers, Councillors and M.Ps. who regarded loyalty to Labour as meaning loyalty to right-wing leaders, were not solid reactionaries. There was differentiation among them and mass struggle would sharpen it. M.Ps. who fought for a class policy should be supported; those who retreated should be criticised. Workers in struggle should pressurise M.Ps., trade unions should fight at selection conferences for candidates pledged to a working-class policy.

Communist Party activity was essential to realise these changes; it had to combine leadership in day-to-day struggle with basic Marxist explanation of the way forward to socialism. The Party had to overcome serious weaknesses—to end the illusion that grew after 1945 that the working class could advance without determined struggle against capitalism and the right-wing leaders; to end the sectarian outlook which held back united action; to overcome the outlook that economic issues were things in themselves, and to link them more closely with government policy. To lead workers in action the Party had to be firmly based in the factories, the winning of trade union positions was no substitute for basic Party leadership and organisation. To advance to political leadership of the working class the Party must win a decisive increase in local government and Parliamentary representation.

CHAPTER 23

THE LABOUR GOVERNMENT—1948–1951

*1. Anti communist offensive. 2. The 'Amethyst' affair. 3. Health,
4. Three happy occasions. 5. General election, 1950.
6. New—and old—Europe. 7. Tory victory.*

1. ANTI-COMMUNIST OFFENSIVE.

During 1948–50 the Labour leaders conducted a mounting anti-Communist campaign, alleging that the Soviet Union was a police state and that the C.P.G.B. was out to sabotage economic recovery and to disrupt the Labour movement. There were Ministerial speeches, Labour Party circulars, T.U.C. pamphlets, penalisation of Communists in the civil service, a virulent press campaign, expulsion of John Platts Mills,[1] a left-wing Labour M.P. in short, all the devices of a modern witch-hunt. Pollitt, in rebutting the allegations, showed that their purpose was to weaken the growing resistance to lower wages and longer hours.

The T.U.C. General Council announced, without evidence, that the Communists were out to wreck the recovery effort of Britain and of other countries who accepted the Marshall Plan.[2] Pollitt branded this as a lie, the Communist Party put forward an economic policy and a national plan for recovery, peace and higher standards of life. The Marshall Plan was not for Britain's recovery, but for American domination; the rearmament that went with it was not for defence, but for war on the Soviet Union. He listed facts to show Marshall in operation—dollar-financed revival of German and Japanese industry in competition with Britain; cuts in steel supplies to Britain; U.S. demands for cuts in British housing and social services funds; British production targets, capital projects using "aid", financial and trade policy all subject to U.S. control. According to a British Government document mid-1948 production was 20 per cent up on pre-war, while working-class standards were lower. "The workers' reward is increasing poverty, the shadow of war and a new offensive on their living standards".[3]

The General Council asserted that the Communist Party "never regarded the trade union movement as a means of organising workers for either the protection of those workers or to improve their standard of living."[4] Pollitt remarked that the General Council "had no criticism for Tory or Catholic activities in the unions, but reserved their spleen for the Communists." He then re-stated the Communist Party's stand for 100 per cent trade unionism: every worker a trade union member, strong factory and shop steward organisation, trades councils as local unifying centres; one union for each industry by amalgamation and federation; trade union affiliation to the World Federation; periodic democratic elections for all positions; Branch meetings to be made more attractive; vigilance against usurpation of powers by E.Cs.; the General Council to be nominated and voted for by the rank and file through the unions, thus ending intrigues to get leaders on without consultation with the members; repudiation of the wage freeze, demands for appropriate increases in each industry especially for the lower paid, the women, and the unskilled, equal pay for equal work; the unions to use their influence for peace, recognise that rearmament brings lower living standards, reject the idea that war scares are not bad if they bring contracts for munitions.

"It is not the Communists who are disrupting the trade union movement. It is the right-wing leaders who resort to anti-democratic methods to seek positions and authority in order to use them on behalf of capitalism, not on behalf of the interests of the movement."[5]

Communists on Trial in the U.S.A.

The U.S. Government charged twelve Communist leaders with "membership of an organisation that advocates overthrow of the government by force and violence"[6] The General Secretary of the Communist Party of the U.S.A., Eugene Dennis, made the main speech for the defence; the Court prevented him from delivering several sections of it. Pollitt, in a preface to the full text[7] described it as "magnificent and courageous". It showed the trial to be a pretext for outlawing the Communist Party, the indictment did not contain one specific charge or one scrap of evidence that the accused advocated or committed any act of violence. Calling for solidarity, Pollitt wrote, "Remember, men can be gaoled, but not ideas. You cannot lock up Marxism-Leninism."

The trial began in March 1949 and ended in October; the prisoners were found guilty, a verdict which Pollitt said was "a challenge to freedom of speech throughout the world". The defence lawyers were sentenced for contempt of Court—"in reality", wrote Pollitt, "for protesting at the judge's refusal to allow the defendants to state their case in full."[8]

In Australia

That October, the General Secretary of the Communist Party of Australia, L. L. Sharkey, was gaoled for three years. Pollitt in a protest to the High Commissioner said that Sharkey's crime was not the seditious words for which he was charged, it was his consistent fight against the Government's policy of dragging Australia in the wake of the American warmongers and his resistance to all attacks on living standards. "The trial and sentence aim to intimidate all who oppose the Government policies."[9]

A Libel Case in France

As the anti-Communist campaign mounted, certain French newspapers printed sensational matter from a book by one Jean Valtin, published in the U.S.A. in 1941 with a French edition in 1948. The International Communist movement and the Communist Party of France were portrayed with highly coloured detail as paid agents of the Soviet political police. Pollitt was described as a Comintern agent who had stayed at the home of Réné Cance, a leading Communist in Le Havre, at the same time as a Russian General Gussev. The French C.P. took legal action for libel. Pollitt was asked whether he would give evidence and agreed. He had seen the 1941 edition of the book. In a Statutory Declaration to be deposited in the French Court he declared that he had never been in Le Havre, never had any acquaintance with M. Cance, never stayed at his home and never met a General Gussev. There were significant differences between the American and English editions of Valtin's book. A chapter on England comprising 18 pages in the American edition was cut to six pages in the English, every reference to English Communists still living including Pollitt and Gallacher, was also omitted. Pollitt had been legally advised that some of the expurgated references were defamatory and had watched the English press with the intention of suing those responsible had these references been repeated. To his knowledge no English paper had dared to reproduce them.[10]

Prior to the trial, the French Communist daily published data including photographic copies of official Gestapo documents showing that Valtin's real name was Krebs, that in a Hamburg prison in 1937 he signed a declaration of willingness to work for the Gestapo, and had given information leading to the arrest of anti-fascist seamen.[11]

The case came up in a Le Havre court on June 7, 1948. Pollitt was present but was not called because the defence did not appear. The case was adjourned *sine die*. The non-appearance of the defence was in French procedure regarded as admission of inability to rebut the prosecution's case.[12]

2. The 'Amethyst' affair.

In April 1949 the Chinese People's Liberation Army, in the offensive destined to drive Chiang Kai-shek from the mainland, approached the mighty River Yangtse. It planned to cross at Chinkiang, some 60 miles from Nanking and 100 miles from Shanghai. No reply to its ultimatum having been received, the P.L.A. early in the morning of April 20 began shelling Kuomintang troops on the north bank and on islands in the river. Kuomintang war vessels returned the fire.

During this firing British warships appeared, were hit by shells and fired back at the P.L.A. *Amethyst* ran aground, she had 19 killed, 27 wounded; *Consort* 10 killed and 4 wounded; *London* 13 killed, 15 wounded; *Black Swan* 7 wounded. *Consort* had approached from Nanking, the others from Shanghai. The Kuomintang Government in February had informed the British that it could not guarantee the safety of their ships. It was notified of these movements, the P.L.A. was not, though the British Embassy had no difficulty in contacting them after the incident.

The official reason for sending *Amethyst* up the river was to relieve *Consort* stationed at Nanking. *The Times* wrote on April 27: "Why *Consort* could not have been revictualled by air remains a mystery," and "valuable lives have been lost without any apparent useful purpose". Attlee in the House on April 26, admitting that the time and place of the intended crossing by the P.L.A. were known, showed no awareness of the blunder—or worse—of sending British ships to the crossing place on the very morning the ultimatum expired. With typical imperialist arrogance he claimed that "*Amethyst* was on her lawful occasions".

The capitalist press made full use of the opportunity to turn grief and anger at the loss of British lives against the Communists and away from those responsible for sending the ships into danger.

It so happened that Pollitt was due to speak in Devon that weekend, at Dartmouth, seat of the Royal Naval Training College on Friday, April 22, next day at Dartington and on the 24th at Plymouth. Some Tory dailies took the unusual course of publicising these meetings, adding that sailors from Dartmouth and Plymouth were among those killed, and that the father of one of them would be at the Dartmouth meeting. It was clear that trouble was being fomented and that Pollitt was being put in the position of being accused of provocation if he kept his engagements or political cowardice if he cancelled. Without hesitation he decided to fulfil them, and without hesitation Peter Kerrigan decided to go with him.

After tea at the home of the Dartmouth Communist secretary, a woman with a young child, they found some 250 people at the meeting place.[13] On one side was the platform, against a wall; on the other the river Dart. Pollitt began with an expression of grief for the needless loss of life that had occurred and for twenty minutes held attention by his exposition of the Chinese revolution. Then, at a signal, the crowd began moving in on the platform. A man called out, "Let me have the mike". Pollitt refused. Several voices shouted, "Let him have it, it is Mr. Akhurst." Knowing this was the bereaved father, Pollitt said, "Certainly, when I've finished my speech and answered questions." He then answered questions which came from all sides, the hostile ringleader repeatedly urging that the speaker be thrown into the Dart. The crowd were now close around the microphone; one shouted, referring to Kerrigan, "There's his Russian bodyguard".

From his height of 6 feet plus, in a voice that momentarily awed the crowd, Kerrigan answered, "I'm Scottish". The crowd surged round the platform. One man kicked Pollitt at the bottom of the spine. Kerrigan jumped on him, both went down in a tangle. Pollitt received another kick—a police inspector warned the man responsible. To one more question, "What would you do if you were in *Amethyst*" Pollitt replied, "What I'm sure the boys are doing, asking the same question as many of you—what was *Amethyst* doing there?[14] and wondering who is responsible for causing needless loss of British and Chinese lives."

The crowd rushed the platform. Pollitt and Kerrigan were forced along the pavement, things looked very ugly. Then Mr. Akhurst called on the crowd to sing "God Save the King", and this was done. Some thought it was to celebrate Pollitt and Kerrigan being down and out. Others thought they had taken refuge in the police station and went to besiege it. They had in fact reached the local C.P. secretary's house, from which the police kept the re-gathering crowd at a distance. At midnight the police informed them that another crowd was camping at the Ferry Station to prevent them leaving in the early morning. Eventually a car took them to Totnes whence they walked to Dartington, arriving at 5 a.m.

The capitalist press sensationalised the evening's events with a reckless disregard for facts. Later Pollitt answered some of the inventions.

Press: Pollitt sought refuge in the police station,
Pollitt: I was never in the Dartmouth Police Station.
Press: Pollitt escaped by the back door of the house.
Pollitt: There is no back way out of the house.
Press: Pollitt was handed a piece of rope by Mr. Akhurst and invited to emulate Judas.
Pollitt: I did not see any rope. Mr. Akhurst was perfectly courteous to me. Later it was said that the rope and invitation were sent by registered post. If so, it has not yet arrived.

The Dartington meeting was in the village hall at 7 p.m. Earlier in the day, Pollitt was told by police that car-loads of people were coming from Dartmouth to break up the meeting and that the Chief Constable of Devon advised cancelling it. Pollitt declined. Over 300 people packed the hall, larger numbers were outside. The meeting was carried through. Pollitt spoke for fifty minutes and then replied to questions. A car provided by a local comrade was parked some yards away from the hall, to preserve its tyres. A hostile crowd lined up all the way to the car, shouting abuse; eggs were thrown and "an exquisitely dressed female with a look of hatred on her very hard and very county face" spat on Pollitt. They got away in the car, and arrived in Plymouth for a long night's sleep.

Plymouth centre had been blitzed, only a bit of the Market and the Corn Exchange, where the meeting was to be held, were left. A long queue was waiting, headed by sailors in uniform. When the doors opened, they surged in to occupy the front rows. Some naval officers were in civilian clothes. Admission cost 6d. Every seat was soon filled. A police officer remarked, "You're no businessman, Mr. Pollitt, you could have charged 5s. and filled it." When the doors were closed the crowd outside began shouting.

The Chairman, an ex-Navy man well respected in the town, introduced Pollitt, who spoke for fifteen minutes before heckling began. A crash was heard downstairs, a door had been broken down and more people crowded in till the police closed the entrance. The sailors, urged on by the same ringleader as at Dartmouth, moved their chairs closer to the platform. One shouted, "What about *Amethyst?* You daren't answer that!" Pollitt replied, "Certainly, if you give me silence to answer a serious question." They gave him two minutes, then not liking the answer, began shouting again. It was getting impossible to continue, but in a momentary silence, he got in "I thank those who came to listen. I wish those who came to interrupt would try it in East London or Glasgow. You may take it out of me, but you can never take China again. I declare the meeting closed."

A brick came through a window, pandemonium broke out. Metal chairs were flying, the sailors attacked the platform, fighting broke out in the hall. The platform party surrounded Pollitt and got him into a side room. The stewards got the worst of the battle till the police cleared the hall. It was now surrounded by people throwing stones and shouting "We want Harry", with lurid details of what they would do to him. When the pubs closed the crowd grew bigger than ever. A new attempt was made to force the doors. There were police casualties from bricks and stones. The scene reminded Pollitt of December 18, 1901, when Lloyd George, opposing the Boer War, made a getaway from a misguided and angry crowd.

The siege went on until about 11 p.m. when the police found another way out of the hall. During the war a special exit had been made in case anyone was trapped in the cellars. Reached through the boiler room, it led to a back entrance into the Market, where a car was waiting. It took them to the police station, where a C.I.D. officer remarked, "You know, Mr. Pollitt, we've not had a night like this since we had to protect Mosley from your fellows." It was one of those rare occasions when Pollitt had no reply. Six arrests had been made. Pollitt requested that no charges be made, "they are not the real organisers of the hostile demonstration." They caught the night train to London, and next morning were back at the Party Office.

The damage to the hall cost £23 8s 7d. This was paid by the local branch of the C.P. Their appeal raised £72 19s 7d., including £30 from the Party Centre. After paying all the costs the Branch returned £15 to Pollitt, and sent £15 to the *Daily Worker*. A local paper[15] had reported that Pollitt had been struck by a metal chair, and that the red flag had been torn off the platform. A responsible Communist who was present, Dave Goodman, wrote: "This was pure fantasy. Pollitt was not touched or struck by a chair; there was no red flag to tear off ... reporters have since agreed that they reported a yellow cloth covering the speaker's table, but a sub-editor changed it to a red flag." The ringleader of the disturbances was recognised by a local comrade as a Tory Party agent. At a big Tory rally in Plymouth on April 23, one Tory M.P. used language calculated to incite disorder, and a Tory prospective candidate was reported as saying of the Dartmouth crowd, "I applaud the action."[16] Among letters published in a local paper one read "If any more Reds appear in Dartmouth, I hope the worthy citizens will supply themselves with well-knotted rope ends to flog them through the town and into the river."[17]

A few days later Pollitt got a tremendous reception at the London May Day Rally, the crowd greeting him with "For He's a Jolly Good Fellow" and *The Internationale*.

The kicks in the spine resulted in months of discomfort and pain. Pollitt was in hospital being treated for a displaced disc when on November 16 the *Amethyst* crew marched through London to be banqueted at the Guildhall. At 10.30 p.m. the night nurse gave Pollitt a telegram. Despatched from Waterloo Station it read: "My feet may march today but my heart will not be there. Best wishes for a speedy recovery and return to the fight. A lonely member of the *Amethyst* crew."[18]

There was at the time considerable concern that Pollitt had been allowed to carry through these engagements made months before. Kerrigan himself later wrote: "It was lunacy for us to allow Harry to face this ordeal in such an atmosphere of hysteria whipped up by the press, and of all places in the very heartland of the British Navy. We were very self-critical and, if we had not been, we would have been reminded by comments from some of our brother Parties. During it all and afterwards, Harry always kept his sense of humour."

A sequel occurred at the 1965 Congress of the Communist Party when one of the delegates, an active Party member, acknowledged that he had been one of the sailors who broke up Pollitt's Plymouth meeting, "but had since seen the light."

3. HEALTH.

During 1947 and 1948 Pollitt suffered pain from an injury to the left knee sustained in an accident in Glasgow. Kicks in the spine during the Devon meetings aggravated the trouble. In summer 1949 he went to a Czech spa at Lazni Jescovik.

"I rise at 6.30 a.m. My masseur encases me in a very cold bath, my head covered by an ice-cold cap, peeps out of the top. It is almost like a coffin. I gather this is to make escape impossible. Smiling and wishing me 'an agreeable bath' my masseur leaves me feeling like Scott in the Antarctic. In 15 minutes he returns, presses Button B, the coffin lid is taken off, I lie down dripping wet and am covered with a linen sheet, expecting pennies to be put on my eyes, and mourners to pass solemnly by. But no, heavy blankets cover me, and with wishes for 'an agreeable sleep' the masseur leaves me for 30 minutes. Unwrapped, I feel I want to hop, skip and jump over mountains and do all they do in the Russian Ballet. Then, in dressing gown and feeling like Baron Rothschild, I repair to the dining room and despatch two eggs, bread, butter and jam.

"At 10.30 the masseur again wishing me 'an agreeable massage' gives me the works—rolls, punches, kneads and slaps. Then he leads me firmly to the shower, begins ice cold and works up to something like an Iceland boiling geyser, wishing me 'an agreeable shower'. Then I am dried, dress and have a smoke. At 11.30 the vapour bath for bronchitis, the lovely Czech lady assistant says, what I assume is to wish me 'an agreeable inhalation'. Then lunch. I eat all placed before me, and sleep for an hour.

"Then the foot bath, two of us, side by side with feet in a tub. Murmuring 'an agreeable footbath' my masseur touches knobs, and my feet and ankles are barraged alternately with ice cold and very hot water. I love it. When we are released I feel wonderful. Treatment ends for the day; tea is at 4 p.m., dinner at 7, bed at 9.30. The procedure is repeated each day, but on alternate days the first ice-cold bath is with radio-active water.

"The treatment is to tone up the heart, blood and muscles—and the spa is also dry. I have not felt so well in body and mind for years. The spa originated 100 years ago when a farmer observed that tired or injured animals made for the mountain streams and pools, stood in the water and emerged lively as crickets. Thinking the water had curative qualities, he experimented on his family, with amazing results. I forgot to tell you that I asked for a short hair cut, the barber shaved my head! Now I look as wonderful as I feel and in the bath they don't know which end is which."

This short treatment, however beneficial to general health, could hardly be expected to cure the knee and spine condition. Pain returned in the autumn, a prolapsed disc was diagnosed. The doctors rejected an operation. For five weeks Pollitt lay flat on his back and was then "fitted with a corset to strengthen the spine".

Then came the 1950 General Election campaign. He knew he ought not to have undertaken it, but "political circumstances left no alternative". The exertion undid the good results of the treatment, pain in knee and thigh became acute, he had to continue the corset. So in April he went to a Soviet clinic where he was immediately "put on a strict diet. Twelve professors examined me and found that for a man of advancing years my condition was sound, but there was trouble with blood pressure and heart. They would get the spine right without an operation, and I could do without the corset." Treatment included physio-therapy, massage, mustard, mud and hydro-sulphide baths, much walking, diet and no alcohol. "Shades of Mahon and Cripps! I wot of things vegetarian they never knew—carrots, cabbages, radishes, beetroots, prunes, and then all over again. Never again will I, a boilermaker who likes his pint, his dram, his fish and chips, laugh at vegetarians—not me. The results speak for themselves. The disc is back in place, the sciatic nerve practically healed and free from pain. The corset is now in the Revolutionary Museum. Some rheumatic trouble in the left thigh, they say, will be cured before they let me go. They add that my health is not my private concern. I have not tasted alcoholic liquor for five weeks. I feel fine and dandy, not an ounce of superfluous flesh."[19]

4. THREE HAPPY OCCASIONS.

In September 1949 Pollitt completed his twentieth year as General Secretary of the Communist Party, and in November 1950, reached the age of sixty. In July 1951 the thirtieth anniversary of the *Labour Monthly* was celebrated.

On September 11 1949 the St. Pancras Town Hall was full. After J. R. Campbell and Bob Stewart had outlined the twenty years, Pollitt made one of his most effective speeches.[20] Perfectly poised to the occasion, it established an identity of thought and feeling between speaker and audience. It revived memories of childhood experiences of poverty and injustice, recalled great events in working-class history. It sparkled with humour and throbbed with passion. Accepting the appreciation of his personal contribution, he transformed it into confidence in the working class and in the Communist Party. He honoured the fighters of the past, strengthened determination to sustain the struggle, and pointed the way to the socialist future.

He began, "I have received the greatest help from my comrades, in particular Tom Mann, Tom Bell, Albert Inkpin, Bob Stewart, J. R. Campbell, William Gallacher, and above all my comrade and side-kicker—could two men be more temperamentally unlike, proving the unity of theory and practice—R. Palme Dutt. I hasten to add, myself providing the theory and Raji the practice".

"It is great to be able to take it on the chin; to be able to laugh against yourself, above all, to have a persistent belief in the Revolution that nothing on earth can destroy . . . How often did Cripps say to me 'Is it still the next five years, Harry?', or Maxton 'Is it still round the corner?' My reply was always 'the next five years will see great changes and it is still round the corner'. How can you go on if you don't believe this? The revolution has been round the corner for me ever since I saw my sister Winnie die through poverty; since my mother held my head under a shawl taking me to work with her in the mill; since my days at the Socialist Sunday School in Openshaw."

After reiterating his declaration of faith in the working class, he concluded "They will transform Britain into the finest Socialist country in the world; end poverty, unemployment, class inequalities and war for ever. The Britain they govern will give complete independence to all the colonial countries, help our freed colonial brothers and sisters to transform their countries achieve socialist industrialisation and collective agriculture."

"This is the 'gleam' which the pioneers of our Labour Movement tirelessly followed, which inspired them to go to the street corners and market places to speak to a mere handful, gave them eloquence and burning fire to talk to their mates in workshops and homes. This is the certainty which enabled them to endure crushing poverty and victimisation, made persecution easier to bear, steeled them to break down barrier after barrier and build up working class education and power."

"It may seem all a dream today when the toiling millions are driven to make war for profit, territory and raw materials for their imperialist masters. But tomorrow will come; this dream will be translated into a living reality, and Britain become a green and pleasant land for its people to live in."

The celebration of his 60th birthday was on November 26. The drab Lime Grove Baths hall was transformed into a blaze of colour by flags, banners and streamers. In spite of a thick November fog every seat was taken, people stood at the back, in the aisles and round the platform. When Pollitt entered, with Marjorie, Brian and Jean, familiar as he was with ovations, the warmth of the prolonged welcome visibly affected him. Claude Berridge, militant leader of the London engineers and chairman of the London Committee of the Party, thanked him "for speeches which are a constant source of political education and inspiration, for invaluable guidance on London problems, for time and thought given to help hundreds of comrades overcome their difficulties".

Then for thirty minutes a stream of comrades mounted the platform with birthday gifts. The first was an overcoat from the London Committee. The Secretary, John Mahon, said, "We hope that in the bitterest weather it will keep you as warm as the feeling in our hearts for you." One Branch brought standard roses for his front garden, another a cheque to cover the cost of binding his files of periodicals, the representative of NAFTA 15 a cheque for £195 for shares in the *Daily Worker*. The Communist lawyers gave a silver plated teaset; the Communist bakers a giant cake inscribed in colour. Soon Pollitt was almost hidden from view by the growing pile of gifts: there were books, a coffee table, cases, travelling rugs, lamps, pens, shirts, smokes, bottles, boxes and more books.

When the Chairman asked for money for Pollitt Scholarships at Party Schools, £165 was handed in.

Pollitt began his speech of thanks by saluting the Russian socialist revolution—"that gigantic, mighty, incredible event". He ended, "We are on the winning side. What we stand for will transform these islands, banish for ever the cares and anxiety of poverty and unemployment, build up the glorious socialist society of happiness for the people which has inspired all that is best in the Labour movement."[21]

Congratulations came from 35 Communist and Workers Parties from multi-million parties in the Soviet Union and Peoples' China, from small parties such as Northern Ireland, Iceland and Cuba. Many went much further than formal official recognition of his sixty years. The Argentine Party spoke of his "embodiment of the British working peoples' struggle against the imperialist policy of the ruling class"; Austria recalled his fight "to prevent British imperialist intervention against the young Soviet Union"; Canada said the consistency of his efforts had "won a permanent place of honour in the hearts of class conscious workers all over the world"; Ceylon spoke of "a firm friend and a wise guide"; Cyprus of his "outstanding example to Communist and freedom fighters the world over"; Denmark of his record being "a strong and living testament of working class internationalism," Germany, "in 1914 imperialism plunged mankind into catastrophe, you raised the banner of internationalism;" Greece "thanks for all you have done and continue to do against imperialist intervention in our country"; Iceland thanks "for deep and never failing sympathy in our struggle;" Norway, "one of our closest friends who has made an important personal contribution to our work;" Pakistan of his "inspiring personality, revolutionary eloquence and patent love for the Indian people"; Spain, "unswerving defender of the cause of the Spanish people"[22]

Rajani Palme Dutt

During the celebration of the thirtieth anniversary of the founding of the *Labour Monthly,* Pollitt expressed his appreciation of Rajani Palme Dutt in more political terms than his earlier reference to his "comrade and side-kicker" and to their being "temperamentally unlike". This they certainly were.

Pollitt was short, stocky, affable, of working class origin and upbringing, leaving school at 13, a skilled workman, a master of the spoken word. Dutt was tall, long limbed, serious, of middle class background, winning scholastic distinction at Oxford, intellectual, author, editor, a master of the written word. Each possessed exceptional intellect and lucidity of expression. They were alike in their devotion to the working class, the Socialist Revolution and Marxism-Leninism, and in their determination to develop the Communist Party as the Marxist-Leninist party essential for the achievement of socialism in Britain.

This identity of purpose matured during the preparation of the Report of the 1922 Party Commission, and in the following years they continued to exchange ideas on major problems, greatly helped by Dutt's talented wife, Salme, who had long experience in the Bolshevik Party.

As early as 1923 they formed the opinion that the key leaders inherited by the Communist Party of Great Britain were not able to transform the party into an effective leadership of working class struggle, but Dutt's proposal that Politt should become the General Secretary was rejected by the E.C.C.I. The issue arose again with the 1928 challenge by Dutt and Pollitt to the E.C. majority, and in 1929, after discussion throughout the Party, Pollitt was elected as General Secretary.

A major political difference arose between Dutt and Pollitt in September 1939 when Dutt queried the correctness of Pollitt's analysis of the war. When the October E.C. changed the Party's position and put Dutt in charge of the Party Centre, relations between them were somewhat strained but not broken. Their full co-operation was resumed when Pollitt returned to the post of General Secretary.

In July 1951, Pollitt wrote[23] that "the contents of the *Labour Monthly* under the brilliant editorship of R. P. D. had won world wide fame and respect . . . had removed the reproach that the British Labour movement had never contributed anything fundamental to the thought of Marxism-Leninism" and advised those desirous of understanding the events of 1920–1950 that by going through the volumes of the *Labour Monthly* they would gain a real political education." The Notes of the Month, were eagerly awaited by agitators and propagandists in the Communist Party and far beyond its ranks because of "their penetrating analysis, merciless exposure of false arguments and policies, devastating denunciation of all that is harmful to the cause of Labour and their passionate defence of the present and future interests of the working people at home and abroad." The writer of the Notes, R. Palme Dutt, Pollitt described as "one who hates the rich and loves the poor, one who despises the nauseating pretensions of those who uphold capitalism, and places his services at the cause of those who suffer and die because of the accursed capitalist system. One who has the most profound sense of both real patriotism and proletarian internationalism," and specified "the treatment of every question of the struggle of the colonial peoples for their independence" as having gained respect in every colonial country.

5. GENERAL ELECTION, 1950.

In December 1948 Pollitt proposed that the Communist campaign for a socialist policy and a Left Labour Government should include contesting in 100 parliamentary constituencies. The 1949 municipal elections showed Tory gains from Labour and a fall in the Communist vote. Pollitt wrote[24] that the government policy had led to many Labour workers not voting and a swing back to the Tories by the less politically advanced among those who voted Labour in 1945. Dissatisfaction with the government was not yet expressed in votes for a left policy, and the Communists were not seen as an alternative. The future depended not on the choice between a Tory or a right-wing Labour Government, but "on the development of a fighting movement to defend the working class from capitalist attack and advance to a new government with a genuine working class policy, and including Communists."[25]

When the election date was announced, Pollitt in an article offered to a capitalist paper[26] presented Communist policy as the only alternative to the almost identical position of the Tory, Labour and Liberal Parties. The issue was not whether the Tory or Labour leaders would fight harder against Communism, it was whether Britain should move towards prosperity, happiness and lasting peace, or towards a great trade depression and an American organised war on the Soviet Union. West German and Japanese competition menaced British exports. The Tory-Labour-Liberal policy to maintain full employment was "to export more at competitive prices", meaning cuts in real wages and social services, thus reducing purchasing power at home and hastening the slump. The three major parties all approved the U.S. decision to make the H-Bomb, American occupation of Britain, and control of her policy, and the oppression of the colonial people and the war in Malaya. "Once the Tories tried to monopolise Patriotism, National Independence and the Union Jack: today, terrified by the advance of Communism, they eagerly sell British interests and national independence to the Wall Street millionaires." The article concluded by summarising Communist policy. It was not published.

With 100 Communists nominated, the B.B.C. grudgingly allocated $8^{1}/_{2}$ minutes on 15 February at 6.15 p.m., a time when many workers could not listen, a week before the poll. Much thought and more advice preceded the thirty-eighth, and final, draft of Pollitt's speech.[27] His main points were as follows:

If the Tories could abolish poverty and unemployment, why did they not do so when in power? Labour boasts of its policy of fair shares for all, but after five years of Labour Government the rich are richer and the workers' share of the wealth they produce is smaller. Sir Stafford Cripps admits that profits today are larger than ever.

Communist policy to avoid a slump, unemployment and war included: higher wages, benefits and pensions; lower prices, profits and military expenditure; freeing British trade from American restrictions; extended social services, particularly house building; extended nationalisation with workers' representation in control and limited compensation; Britain to leave the Atlantic war pact, ban nuclear bombs, and work for a permanent Five Power Peace Pact.

He rejected the idea that the Soviet Union menaced Britain. "They lost 7 million dead in the last war. It is not they who want war, it is the panic-stricken American millionaires." The U.S. Secretary for Defence committed suicide when he thought a fire alarm signalled a Russian invasion. He was said to have been insane, but the Americans and our Tory, Liberal and Labour leaders carry on his insane policy. The

Chairman of the U.S. War Appropriations Commission said that the U.S. should equip the soldiers of other nations to go "into the holocaust so that we don't have to send our boys".

Pollitt again contested in Rhondda East, and in the campaign "gave no sign of the pain he was suffering or the discomfort of the corset he had to wear" (Annie Powell). His election address again combined local and national issues.

Among the letters he received was one from the distinguished scientist, Professor J. D. Bernal, who wrote: "The candidates of no other party have raised, as you have, the real issues of the election—the need to stop the criminal drift to war and the madness of the hydrogen bomb. As a scientist I welcome your reference to the use of research in combating silicosis. At present, expenditure on health research is only one-fiftieth of the £86 million spent on war research. We could easily afford to spend ten times as much on health and make an enormous difference in the fight against all other diseases like tuberculosis, cancer and rheumatism." Arthur Horner wrote "To send you good wishes for success is unnecessary. You know that everybody in your constituency knows what I desire as the outcome of this election."[28]

The election stalwarts rallied once more, the meetings, though not so numerous, were solid in support. Pollitt noted changes—hundreds of miners families had left the valleys and "the women are now thinking for themselves, no longer waiting for their husbands to decide". But the mood was very different from 1945. Heads nodded when he said that nationalisation had not brought what the miners hoped; indeed their reward for record output was dismissals, closures and wage freeze. More nods when he proposed that miners be put on the Boards, that compensation and highly salaried officials be cut. But they were thinking of the threat of a Tory majority—a spectre given embodiment by the appearance of a Tory candidate in the Rhondda—and not of a new and leftward Labour advance.

The result was: Labour 26,645; Communist 4,463; Conservative 2,634; Welsh Nationalist 1,357. The defeat for Pollitt was part of a national setback: Gallacher and Piratin lost their seats as did the expelled Labour Independents.

The Communist election effort was the most wide-spread yet. 6 million election addresses were circulated; 97,000 copies of the programme, and 270,000 of an Election Special were sold. 5,381 meetings were held. The result was: Labour 315; Tory 297; Liberal 10; Communist 0; others 2.

Pollitt summarised this as a substantial Tory advance and the new Attlee Government as a thinly veiled coalition. Elimination of Communist and militant Labour M.Ps. meant a reactionary Parliament. "The main body of workers voted Labour to defeat the Tory offensive, but failed to understand that they were handing over their representation to those who were at one with Tory policy." But the record size of the Labour vote expressed determination not to return to the old days. The low Communist vote showed that the Party, not firmly rooted in the factories, was unable to counter the intense anti-Communist propaganda, and had under-estimated the need for deeper explanation of its attack on the right wing. The workers felt better off under Labour and feared a Tory return. In face of this fear the Communists were unable to counter the cry "Don't split the vote". But there was no future for the Communist Party in retreat from the electoral field, it was necessary to explain why it should be voted for, and by linking work on economic issues with the fight on policy, to develop industrial support into electoral support.

Pollitt emphasised that "the profound feeling of the people for peace forced the Tory and Labour leaders to break their conspiracy of silence on foreign policy. This feeling must be transformed into action against the war plans of British and U.S. imperialism."[29] Following the election he was foremost in the struggles against the imperialist wars in Malaya[30] and Korea.

Korea

On June 26, 1950, four days after a visit from a U.S. State Department representative, South Korean troops entered Northern territory at three points. The U.N. Security Council, without the Soviet Union's agreement, but with British acquiescence on hearsay evidence, declared North Korea the aggressor without hearing its case. The U.S. at once attacked the North with heavy bombing of towns, including the capital, Pyong-Yang. The Labour Government sent planes, ships and troops to take part in the war under U.S. command.[31]

Pollitt said: The U.S. imperialists have gone from preparation for war to direct acts of aggression—the most horrible, barbarous and inhuman manslaughter in Korea, where every fiendish and murderous device of modern war is being used in a war of conquest to restore landlordism and instal American control and a fascist dictatorship. It is preparation for further aggressive acts against China and gravely increases the danger of world war.[32]

Negotiate for peace

On the eve of the 1951 election, Pollitt defined the supreme question: "War or Peace? All other issues depend on the answer."[33] War was not inevitable, immediate negotiation on disputed questions would prevent the trend to war getting too strong to be stopped.

The talk about Russia threatening to attack, Pollitt described as "the Big Lie of today". It was the only Western argument for huge armaments, repeated by Tory and Labour leaders because both were committed to U.S. war plans. Reliance on armaments to preserve peace played into the hands of those who wanted war, put Britain under U.S. control, endangered her economic stability and imposed hardship on her people. There was no factual basis for thinking that Russia wanted war. The U.S. Ambassador in Moscow reported[34] no signs of war, Soviet army units were at peacetime strength, no extraordinary movements of troops or supplies, no restriction of civilian consumption of critical materials, no shifts of labour to war industry. *The Wall Street Journal*[35] wrote, "Grim warnings from the Pentagon are largely propaganda. They want Congress to appropriate the full 61 billion dollars they are asking for the current year. Actually military advisers and diplomats have no evidence of new Russian moves." The U.S. Economic Commission for Europe stated that the numbers per thousand of population on defence work were: Britain 82, U.S.A. 74, Soviet Union 49.[36] At a press conference[37] Truman said that the U.S. now relied on force rather than diplomacy in dealing with Russia. Asked did he mean force after the other fellow had used force first, Truman replied, "I did not say that".

Pollitt then listed the Soviet Union's proposals. On *atomic bombs*—prohibition of manufacture, destruction of all stocks; *other armaments*—reduce by a third; *Korea*—a cease fire on the 38th parallel to be a starting point for agreement; *People's China*—to be in the U.N; *Germany*—no rearmament in East or West, an all-German Assembly democratically elected, a German Peace Treaty, withdrawal of all foreign troops. On all these, the Soviet Union wanted to negotiate, the refusal came from the West. Yet the West claimed that the purpose of the armaments on which it had spent £4,700 million was to enable it to "negotiate from strength". Then why not begin to negotiate now?

Negotiations could lead to a Five Power Peace Pact, the free flow of trade, full employment based on the people's needs not on war preparations. Money freed from armaments could be used for great advances in housing, health and education and development of backward countries.

During the 1951 election, 67,000 copies of this pamphlet were sold.

6. New—and old—Europe.

Between 1946 and 1951 Pollitt attended meetings of eight European Communist Parties. The 1945 intervention of British Labour leaders to break Socialist-Communist unity revived the split in the working class in the direct interest of imperialism and reaction. In several countries the immediate post-war governments included Communists, and enacted some measures of democratisation and nationalisation. In 1947–48 the Marshall Plan stimulated a general reactionary offensive. Where it was accepted, Communist Ministers were dismissed, progressive measures halted, American control introduced, the economy subordinated to monopoly capitalist profit and militarisation. Where it was rejected, the reaction was deprived of power, democratisation speeded up, the economy planned to supply the people's needs, the advance to socialism begun.[38]

Sweden—May 1946:

Pollitt was in Stockholm for the XIII Congress of the C.P. of Sweden. Shops bulged with all varieties of goods, but prices had risen more than wages. The working class, just over half the population, had a majority in the two Chambers. There was a Social Democratic Government, but reactionaries held the key state positions. The Congress met in the Concert Hall on the main square. For such an occasion, the custom was to fly the flags of the nations on standards around the square. The C.P. wanted to include the tricolour of the Spanish Republic, the city authorities refused. The C.P. said they would leave the standard bare, and tell the people why. The authorities changed their minds—the flag was flown.

The Congress proposed the broadening of the Social Democratic programme to make possible an alliance with the middle class, achieve work for all, better living conditions and wider democratisation. This would break the power of monopoly capital and open the way to a peaceful transition to socialism.[39]

Spain—March 1947

To a leadership meeting of the C.P. of Spain, "so young in age, so mature in experience", Pollitt pledged continuation of C.P.G.B. support to the Republican cause. Illegally organised, the C.P. of Spain worked for the unity of all democratic forces to end the fascist dictatorship and allow the people to decide through free elections what regime they wanted.[40]

Italy—January 1948

Togliatti reported to the Milan Congress of the C.P. of Italy. Marshall Aid had brought two million unemployed, rising prices, new attacks on living standards, dismissal of the Communist Ministers, efforts to split the trade unions and break the Socialist-Communist alliance. The U.S. menaced Italian independence and peace. The C.P.I. worked for economic progress, national independence and a wide democratic movement. "British and U.S. pressmen who expected an adventurist policy were disappointed." At the Breda engineering works, 6,000 of the 16,000 workers were in the C.P. Ten thousand stood in the pouring rain to hear Pollitt and other visitors' speeches. When the workers in the large boiler shop heard from Pollitt that he was a boilermaker "their enthusiasm knew no bounds."[41]

France—1947–48

At the 1947 Congress of the C.P. of France, Pollitt found the main issue to be "the dangerous slide to the right of French policy". Reaction had gathered around De Gaulle, workers' living standards were attacked, democratic rights were being limited, "a course very different from that hoped for by the martyrs of the Resistance". Communist Ministers were dismissed, the Socialist leaders refused unity, their so-called "humanist socialism" in fact aided reaction. The Congress emphasised that the unity of all democratic and republican forces and Socialist-Communist co-operation was the only way to restore democratic government.[42]

In Paris on Bastille Day 1948, Pollitt at a great Communist meeting recalled Goebell's boast that the Nazis would erase 1789 from history, "but Hitler and Goebells have been defeated, 1789 is still commemorated." The British ruling class was traditionally hostile to revolution and democracy in France: Ernest Jones, the Chartist, had said that the poor and oppressed in England and the robbed and ruined in France "appertain to one country, one past, one present and one future."[43] Solidarity of the two peoples was needed to resist the Marshall Plan the governments had accepted.

Finland—August 1948

The C.P. had been legal since 1945, after 26 years underground. It worked through the Democratic League, third largest Parliamentary party. The Social Democrats were anti-Communist and refused a People's Front, the general election had returned a reactionary government which wanted Finland to be a police state and in the Western war bloc. The C.P. regarded the Mutual Aid Pact with the U.S.S.R. as the mainstay of Finnish independence. The Party's main weakness was in the battle of ideas. "Masses of workers know nothing of Marxism-Leninism except what the class enemy says about it."[44]

Czechoslovakia—1946 and 1949

At the 1946 Congress of the C.P., Pollitt saw the outlines of a new kind of Republic. Banks, mines, insurance, 85 per cent of engineering, 20 per cent of food processing were nationalised. Millions of acres of land were distributed to the peasants, German and collaborator property confiscated. The workers were directly represented throughout public administration and nationalised concerns. The government was based on a national front of democratic organisations. A provisional national Assembly was preparing a general election. The Congress planned to complete this national democratic revolution by economic and political reconstruction.

Pollitt spoke at a meeting of C.P. members in Prague; it filled the Town Hall Square and the streets around it. At Kladno he visited a steelworks where, of 6,000 workers, 4,000 were C.P. members. Under the Nazis the supervisory staff numbered 300; workers' control managed with eight. At the Benes mine he found, carefully tended with flowers, a monument to the miners killed by the Nazis. The miners now got violet ray treatment after their pit-head bath. "If our miners saw the treatment rooms, they would not know whether they were at the pit or in dreamland." At Brno, Pollitt was presented with a hunting rifle "the last word in craftsmanship". Back at Croydon, soldiers called it a marvellous job, but the Customs were adamant, in the absence of the necessary papers the rifle was detained.[45]

At the 1949 Congress Pollitt heard the account of the political crisis of February 1948. The right-wing parties wanted to accept Marshall Aid, halt nationalisation and agrarian reform, and avoid adoption of a new Constitution. On the 20th they withdrew their twelve Ministers from the government and with the support of British, French and U.S. reaction and reformist leaders, urged President Benes to form a government excluding the Communists. The Social Democrats decided their Ministers should not resign; the C.P. called on the President to accept the right-wing resignations and form a new government. On the 22nd 8,000 delegates from factory councils at a Congress, convened by the General Council of Trade Unions called for further reforms, an end to right-wing plots and a one-hour stoppage of work. On the 23rd, one million workers stopped work and elected Councils of Action. On the 25th the President formed a new government with 12 Communists, 4 Social Democrats, 2 National (Benes) Socialists, 2 People's Party, 1 Slovak Democrat, 1 Slovak Freedom Party and 2 non-party Ministers, with Gottwald, Communist, as Prime Minister.

The Congress endorsed Zapototsky's summing up of the 1945 and 1948 events as breaking the power of the capitalists and exposing their pseudo-democratic helpers. "This political victory transformed millions of working people into really free and equal citizens. It now confronts us with the main task—to crown political success with economic success."[46]

East Germany—July 1950

In July 1950 Pollitt was at the 3rd Congress of the Socialist Unity Party of Germany, formed at Easter 1946 by the fusion of the Communist and Social Democratic Parties in the Soviet occupied zone. The Socialist Unity Party's aim was to establish an anti-fascist parliamentary republic with a live and efficient democracy, and to destroy militarism and imperialism. By September 1947 the reaction had been deprived of economic and political power by the confiscation of the properties of war criminals and active Nazis and of the junkers' land. The division of land among small peasants and the nationalisation of large enterprises provided the basis for a democratic transformation of economic life. The III Congress met when the Soviet Union had handed over the administration of the zone to the newly-formed German Democratic Republic, the first German Workers' State.

There were fraternal delegates from 25 countries, and the Congress showed its "unfeigned joy" that the long isolation due to fascism and war from the international Communist movement was over. Many delegations from factories brought presents indicative of their production achievements. The Free German Youth delegation was 1,000 strong, in blue shirts and blouses, with band and banners, singing, clapping, then chanting "Peace and Friendship". Delegates from the newly constructed giant steel mill at Brandenburg brought a sample ingot of their first steel. Another delegation was from the People's Police, "a splendid body of young men and women, who look after the interests of the people". 1,500 Young Pioneers, each carrying a bunch of flowers, "filled the hall with beauty, colour and young life, expressing what I am sure life is going to be like for the whole people."

The veteran Wilhelm Pieck gave the report of the Executive; Otto Grotewohl spoke on peace and a democratic Germany; Walter Ulbricht on economic prospects. Pollitt commented that the Congress had opened a new perspective which would lead to a higher standard of life than the German people had ever known under capitalism.[47]

Hungary—February 1951

Pollitt was at the 2nd Congress of the Hungarian Working People's Party, established in 1948 by the fusion of the Communist and Social Democratic Parties. The political report was made by Mathias Rakosi, who spent 16 years in a prison cell in fascist Hungary. Pollitt had led a great campaign for his release, and Rakosi thanked him for it. Production in socialised industry was 35 per cent higher in 1950 than in 1949. Hundreds of new factories were being built and socialist methods of work being adopted. The key problem was agriculture. The large estates had been given to the peasants but primitive methods held back production. State and cooperative farming was just beginning. The platform and the floor were at one in their deep concern for peace. The country had suffered terribly during the war, every family had losses, everywhere the Germans had destroyed factories, bridges, buildings, forests. The idea that strengthening the country meant deterring the aggressor was widespread. At a machine station, the tractors bore the slogan "We Defend Peace—Forward to Socialism". A Congress delegate said, "Every ton of steel we produce is a blow at the aggressor."[48]

South Africa—A Non-event

In September, 1950, the *Cape Times* announced that Mr. Harry Pollitt was returning home on the *Caernarvon Castle* after a visit to Natal. This gave the South African authorities a shock, and they got cracking to find out what was on. It turned out that the report referred to a businessman who had lived in South Africa since 1913, and had been on holiday.[49]

7. Tory victory, 1951.

In October 1951 the Communist Party contested only ten constituencies. The B.B.C. refused time, the speech Pollitt would have made was printed,[50] however. And its theme was that a Tory majority would be a disaster, and that while the Communists put forward an alternative policy, the Labour leaders did not.

Tory policy would attack the workers in the interests of big business. They wanted to put back the clock in Eastern Europe, to restore freedom to landlords, capitalists and fascists. That could not be done without war. Churchill wanted closer relations with U.S.A. That meant more American domination, troops and air bases here. Another Tory leader wanted to halve food subsidies, that meant lower real wages and pensions.

The first necessity was peace through negotiation. The strongest evidence that the Russians had no aggressive aims was the fact that they had not attacked. They had repeatedly declared willingness to negotiate on arms reductions, banning the bomb and a Five Power Peace Pact. Britain should refuse cannon fodder for a U.S. war, send home the U.S. troops, stop the arms drive, and use the money saved to meet the people's needs.

The Communists exposed the wage-freeze swindle and led the fight against it. A real peace policy would release resources to solve the housing problem. Nationalisation should be extended, compensation cut, workers and technicians put in control.

A group of Communist M.Ps. would guarantee a determined battle for peace, the people's needs and socialist principles.

Idris Cox took Pollitt's place as Communist candidate for Rhondda East. In a supporting speech, Pollitt dealt with the view that to vote Communist would be disloyal to Labour. "This argument had to be met by Labour pioneers, such as Tom Mann, Keir Hardie and Ben Tillett. Had workers been loyal to Liberal-Labourism there would have been no independent working-class representation in Parliament and no strong trade unions for the unskilled . . . Today needs a similar fight against those trying to turn the Labour movement into an instrument of capitalism, and against the penetration of capitalist ideas into the working class, which the right wing seeks to achieve . . . To fight this, to vote Communist, to express the demand for a socialist policy, is not betrayal but real loyalty to working-class principles."[51]

The election gave the Tories 321 seats, Labour 295, though Labour had 13,952,105 votes to 13,718,069 for the Tories. The Liberals were down to

6, and apart from 3 Welsh Nationalists, there were no others.

Pollitt commented that the right-wing leaders had thrown away victory, a nation-wide united front would have defeated the Tories. "The organised workers and their families remained loyal to Labour believing they were safeguarding world peace. They instinctively feared Churchill as a war-monger. There was mass election activity by shop stewards, anti-Tory Committees in the factories and trade union branches. Local Labour Parties welcomed Communist help. The result of the Communist campaign was to win votes for Labour; in our constituencies we never broke through the fear of letting the Tory in."

"The new Tory Government represents big capitalists, financiers, aristocrats and militarists. Of 16 Cabinet Ministers, 7 went to Eton, 2 to Harrow, 1 to Winchester; there are 6 Lords and 9 Company Directors. Of the government as a whole, the first 66 appointed include 22 from Eton, 6 from Harrow, 6 from Winchester; 43 went to Oxford or Cambridge; 18 are peers."

The Labour Opposition was already showing defeatist tendencies. "The right-wing leaders cannot lead a fight, for on basic issues their policy is similar to that of the Tories."

The main task of the Communist Party was to help forward the fight of the Labour rank and file for a fundamental change of policy and to do more to explain what socialism would mean, and the need for a Marxist Party; the supreme duty was to prevent war.[52]

CHAPTER 24

THE BRITISH ROAD TO SOCIALISM

*1. Preparations and purpose.   2. Essence of the programme.
3. Response.   4. In place of Empire.   5. Democracy.*

1. PREPARATIONS AND PURPOSE.

Pollitt was the moving spirit in the preparation of the programme of the Communist Party, *The British Road to Socialism*, which first appeared in 1951. To appreciate the development of Communist thinking expressed in this programme it will be useful to recall previous efforts.

Four years discussion, with British Communists taking an active part, preceded the 1929 publication of the programme of the Communist International. It dealt on the world plane with the development of capitalism, its general crisis and the advance of revolution. In 1935 the Communist Party of Great Britain published its own programme, "For Soviet Britain". It analysed class relations in Britain, set out measures to realise socialism after the overthrow of capitalism by the workers, and envisaged the replacement of parliament and the state machine by democratically elected Councils of Workers' Delegates. This reflected the experience of Soviet Russia, the only socialist state then in existence.

Events overtook this programme, and a new draft was prepared reflecting changes in outlook due to experiences in the anti-fascist struggle. More closely related to British conditions, including the character of the labour movement, it set out measures to curb the monopolies and extend democracy. It spoke of the possibility of a working-class government based on a parliamentary majority. To overcome violent capitalist resistance to its democratic and socialist measures, this government would have to appeal directly to the working people, and organise their armed struggle. From then on a new Socialist State would develop on the basis of the mass organisations of the people, in whose hands real power would be. This draft was printed for the Party Congress called in 1939 but postponed owing to the war.[1]

In public discussion in 1945–47, Pollitt raised the question of how Britain would move from capitalism to socialism. He recalled that Marx and Engels had never laid down a blueprint for the transition, nor had the Communist Party claimed the Russian Revolution of November 1917 as a model for others. Then the Soviets had no choice other than to fight or be exterminated; armed intervention by the imperialists compelled them to use dictatorial methods. But in 1947 the world advance of democratic liberation and socialist forces made possible the "transition to socialism by paths other than that of 1917."[2] In some countries a peaceful transition was possible.

As to when socialism would become the issue in Britain, Pollitt said: "When the majority of the British people democratically decide that the time has come to replace capitalism by a socialist order."[3]

To the question whether, with the capitalist state in existence, the transition could come without civil war, Pollitt gave a qualified reply. The British state was certainly dominated by reactionary forces, but "to the degree that the united power of the Labour and progressive forces secures a parliamentary majority and a new type of government, changes can be made in the state and democracy extended."[4] These changes would include not only meeting the economic demands of the workers, but developing democratic control in industry, and democratising local government, the armed forces, the police and the state machine. New personnel from the Labour movement would be brought into controlling positions from which those who opposed the people's interests would be excluded.[5]

Pollitt distinguished clearly between the Communist concept of the possibility of peaceful transition, including the necessity to inhibit or defeat anti-democratic violence, and the reformist concept of inevitable gradual movement towards socialism without upheavals and struggles. "Marxists realise that the capitalist class resists every forward step made by the working class, and that only by struggle can victory be won."[6] "The advance to higher forms of democracy, to the full participation of the people in the administration of things, depends upon the organised power of the people making itself felt."[7]

On the question whether the capitalist class would accept the democratic verdict of the people, or organise violence against those who wished to transform society peacefully from capitalism to socialism, Pollitt made two points: first, that experience showed no ruling class allows power to slip from its influence without furious and prolonged resistance. Second, that the outcome would be decided by the unity and strength of the working class and democratic movements. "The fundamental issue remains the issue of power, the fundamental and only method ceaseless united struggle against capitalism."[8]

The ideas of democratic advance and peaceful transition were further enriched and clarified by the experiences of 1945–51, particularly the contrast between the consolidation of capitalism by the Labour Government in Britain and the advance to socialism by the popular democracies in Eastern Europe.

At a meeting of the C.P.G.B. Executive in July 1950, Pollitt proposed the drafting of a programme based on and applicable to British conditions and institutions, to "link our fight for immediate demands with a clear perspective for the future".[9] In January 1951 he presented such a draft entitled *The British Road to Socialism*. He described it as a long-term programme of how to get real power for the people and to solve once and for all their existing problems, thus distinguishing it from an immediate programme confined to issues arising in a current situation and also from a general election programme of demands for the coming parliament to carry through.

The draft outlined a perspective of decisive change giving power to the people and opening the road to socialism, an alternative to the continuation of capitalism and the problems it imposed. It showed the falsity of the argument that the Communists wanted to destroy democracy and parliament and to set up a totalitarian dictatorship. It proposed constructive measures by which an alliance of the workers and all progressives could guarantee jobs, wages, peace, extended democracy and a stronger, independent Britain.

When the Executive had adopted the text, Pollitt sent an explanatory letter[10] to the Communist Party members to assist in discussion and study of the programme, which answered four fundamental questions—"How can lasting peace be assured?", "How can Britain's independence be restored?", "What is the perspective for relations between Britain and the peoples of the present Empire after they have achieved independence?", "By what road can the British people advance to Socialism?"

The programme was published[11] in pamphlet form. In a Foreword Pollitt said its message was that "the people of Britain can look forward to a better future only if they take their country into their own hands. . . . It is a call to the whole Labour movement to struggle for the immediate interests of the working people and to safeguard their future interests in a Socialist Britain."

2. ESSENCE OF THE PROGRAMME.

In a number of public meetings Pollitt outlined the main ideas of each section of the programme.[12]

The Introduction contrasts the decline of Britain as a capitalist power with the advance of the countries where the workers rule. The Labour Government frustrated the people's hopes of 1945 by seeking to strengthen capitalism at the expense of the British and colonial workers and by subordination to American big business. "We attack, expose and reject the policy of the right-wing Labour leaders."

Peace: For a considerable period the decisive issue will be the struggle for peace. A third world war would bring catastrophe. We combat the idea that war is inevitable, our policy is based on the possibility of the peaceful co-existence of capitalism and socialism. We refute the charge that communism is to be imposed by aggression and conquest. Social transformation can come only through internal change in each country in accord with its conditions. The prosperity of the British people and their advance to socialism are bound up with the struggle of all peoples for peace and national independence. We put forward a British foreign policy to guarantee lasting peace. If the people are to advance, the Tories and their allies in the Labour movement, the right-wing leaders, must be fought and defeated.

National Independence: In practice, British political, economic and military policy is under American control. Communist policy is for Britain to be free, strong and independent, not subservient to any foreign power. It advocates national independence for all peoples of the British Empire, and that all British forces and administrations abroad be withdrawn and sovereignty handed over to governments freely elected by the people. On such a basis mutually beneficient relations would be possible between the British and the liberated peoples.

People's Democracy—Britain's Path to Socialism: Britain will reach socialism by her own road. The Communist Party does not aim to abolish parliament and set up soviets. The people can change parliament into a democratic instrument of the will of the majority. A people's government, based on a truly representative parliament, supported by a united working class and a popular alliance of all democratic forces, would be able to effect socialist nationalisation of the monopolies, develop a planned economy and by democratic reforms break the capitalist political domination. The people and their government would act decisively against any capitalist attempt to use force to maintain their privileges.

Socialist Nationalisation: In contrast to the capitalist nationalisation by the Labour Government, socialist nationalisation would remove the burden of rent, interest and private profit from industry, establish democratic administration at every level, and organise a nationally planned economy and a vast increase in production.

Social Services: This section indicates the main principles which would guide a People's Government in relation to housing, social insurance, health, education and the special needs of women and young people.

The Communist Party and the Way Forward: The way forward is through the united action of the working people for all their interests. The strengthening of the Communist Party, based on Marxism, is indispensable to the achievement of the programme.

Pollitt summarised[13] the programme as meaning that a great extension of the democratic rights and power of the people was essential to the building of socialism in Britain. To make possible the planned production needed to solve social and economic problems, there must be socialist nationalisation of the banks, the factories and the land. This would end the economic domination of the capitalist class. Parliament and the state machine, instead of being dominated by the propertied interests, would be in the hands of the people and serve their interests. This would end the political domination of the capitalist class. Freedom and independence of the colonial peoples from British imperialist exploitation, and of Britain from subservience to American domination, were both essential. Britain, thus changed from a capitalist democracy into a people's democracy, would be free to advance to socialism.

3. RESPONSE.

The programme received some publicity on the B.B.C. and in the national press. Four capitalist dailies gave it leading articles; the *Daily Herald* gave it eleven lines, the Labour weeklies no mention. Sales of the pamphlet in six weeks reached 150,000.

Thousands of Labour workers bought it, many took supplies and sold them. A frequent comment was, "this should be *our* policy." At discussions between Communist and Labour workers it emerged that what alienated many from the Communists was the idea that they wanted "violent revolution". There were objections to the proposal that the millionaire press be taken over by democratic organisations, it was feared that this would mean suppression of opinion. Questions frequently put included, "What guarantee is there that if a People's Government came to power it would carry out the programme?", "If we did not like what the Government did, would we be able to change it?", "If we break with America politically, could we still trade with her, and if not, could we do without that trade?", "Why do you oppose calling up reserves in Britain and not oppose Russian workers serving in their armed forces?"

At the many meetings where Pollitt explained the programme, he noted "close attention, you could have heard a pin drop". He described the response of the Communist Party members as "enthusiastic, they feel they have a powerful new weapon in their hands. After a discussion in a factory branch, one said 'Harry, this is our *What Is To Be Done*'." But he also had to record that many members seriously underestimated the significance of the programme, and had to warn against the tendency to focus discussion on particular formulations and thus "loose sight of the perspective of a fundamental solution of the people's problems".[14]

The programme attracted wide attention in the international Communist movement. Published in full in the international journal, and in the press of the C.P.S.U. and of the Polish, Hungarian, Czech and other parties, it aroused considerable controversy. At the 1951 Congress of the Hungarian Party Pollitt noted, "Fraternal delegates from 25 countries asked me about the programme. At a meeting at the Party School, I got 113 questions on it; at a meeting of Budapest Party functionaries, John Mahon got 151 questions."[15]

In his political reports to C.P.G.B. Congresses in 1952, 1954 and 1956, Pollitt included a re-statement of the key ideas in the programme and their significance in the current struggle, thus continually reminding the Party of its perspective for the realisation of socialism.

In 1956 Pollitt noted, "The C.P.G.B. was the first party outside the socialist countries to base a programme on the possibility of peaceful transition to socialism. It helped other parties, including those in Scandinavia and in the Dominions."[16]

In May 1956 Pollitt proposed further theoretical work. "There is a gap in our work. We have an immediate programme and a long-term programme: we have not seriously tackled the relation between the two." In connection with the People's Government, he asked for closer study of the class structure and relation of political forces; the relations between the working class and the professional and middle sections; and "the great political developments" and the extension of democracy necessary for the advance to a People's Government. On the policy of a Socialist Britain, he proposed a re-examination of the concept of the "fraternal alliance" with former colonial peoples in the light of the disintegration of the colonial system; of the supplies, resources and foreign trade needs of socialist industry; of party political life and relations in a Socialist Britain.[17]

4. IN PLACE OF EMPIRE.

To show Pollitt's concept of future relations between Socialist Britain and the liberated peoples of the one time British Empire, we give here an extract, somewhat abbreviated, of his speech at a Conference in 1954.[18]

"For scores of years the writers, poets and statesmen of imperialism have tried to deceive the people by talk of the glories of Empire, of the blessings it brings to all its peoples, of the Christian civilising mission of the imperialists. But they cannot hide the fact that the Empire is based on dreadful deeds and ghastly crimes. Its basis is the vilest barbarities committed against innocent peoples. It relies on brute force because it can never command the willing assent of those it oppresses. It violates every principle of Christianity and every humane, moral instict of mankind.

"We look forward to a future as different as day is from night. We see the mills of Lancashire turning out, not uniforms for British lads to fight and die in far off lands, but the fabrics needed by the freed colonial peoples. We see the great engineering factories of Britain ceasing to produce guns, tanks and planes for the slaughter of the colonial peoples, but sending locomotives, machine tools, electrical generators and motor vehicles to them. We envisage the ships of Britain's merchant navy, not loaded with troops, shells and poisonous chemicals, but carrying our goods to other countries and bringing theirs to us. Instead of piling up sterling balances out of the sweat and blood of Malayan plantation workers or African miners and small farmers, we see trade on the basis of equal exchange, and giving every assistance in our power to help the formerly backward countries to take their place amongst the foremost nations of the world."

Pollitt then replied to the argument that the crimes of British imperialism mean that the liberated colonial peoples will want no association with Britain.

"We fight not only for solidarity to destroy imperialism: we fight for it so that we can together build up the new classless society of socialism. Without such solidarity in helping to build the new society there can be serious setbacks.

"We must never forget that the class enemy when it has lost power does everything possible to regain it. That is why we have to stand, fight, and work together to win freedom and retain it."

"The association we have in mind is one that would at last enable decent British working people to visit India, or Malaya, or Kenya without a sense of the deepest shame. It would enable all to walk their lands in dignity and peace. It would begin to wipe out the memory of a shameful past and establish relations of brotherhood and comradeship in the great task of conquering nature and raising the social, economic and cultural standards of mankind."

5. Democracy.

Pollitt's approach to problems of freedom, liberty and democracy was based on the reality of the class struggle.

"I am a democrat, but not of the Whig tradition where the father's income came from Consols and the son owned the right to draw tribute from half the world and wanted freedom to go on doing it. These democrats played their part in the struggle against feudal privilege. But the period of Gladstonian democracy in Britain was based on the exploitation of the workers. Our democracy belongs to something more permanent in the life of our people—its essential element is that of struggle for the bettering of conditions. Remembering the cruel hours worked by our parents and the self-denial and courage shown by them that we might be clothed and fed, we realise that such improvements as we have seen are due in large measure to exercising our democratic right to organise, and if needs be, fight, in our trade unions."

Of the rights of free speech, organisation, to strike and to vote, the first targets of fascism, he wrote, "The essential guarantee of their existence is a strong and democratic trade union movement." Where these rights were abandoned by those who ought to have defended them, progressive and cultural forces were smashed down, barbarism advanced.[19]

He rejected as a distortion of Marxism the view that under capitalism the form of government was immaterial. The working class had made too many sacrifices for democratic rights to see them taken away. The very existence of trade unions represented victories won at great cost, the first act of fascism in power is to destroy workers' organisations. "The defence of democracy even though it rests on the basis of capitalist economy is one of the most important issues facing the people today."

"The British machinery of government offers any amount of opportunity for the very rich to put their will across as the will of the people, but it also gives the common people opportunities to protect their interests. In the struggle between fascism and democracy we cannot be neutral, we cannot pretend we have nothing to lose."[20]

For Pollitt the defence of democracy against fascism and authoritarian rule "did not mean the abandonment of the class struggle, but freedom to carry it forward" to a real people's democracy—complete democracy—where "the people will be able to rule themselves by rules they have agreed to abide by, and will be judged by those whom they have decided shall judge them". "From the rule of the working class among themselves in the factories, will arise the future ruling class of the country and with it will be allied all who believe in freedom and democracy. There will be no place for those who like many of our rulers today use demagogic phrases to maintain their own vast privileges against the workers and the middle class."[21]

That is why "Liberty is always the watchword of those who strive to prevent the march of the workers towards a new Socialist state of society, those who try to foment war against the one nation where the workers have conquered power. It is now the watchword of American Imperialism in its efforts to secure that world domination that we prevented Hitler obtaining."

"To the right-wing Labour leaders, democracy meant the system that kept workers under and capitalists on top. A democracy where workers had no say in running industry, only capitalists had managerial rights, and where workers were allowed to vote after their minds had been twisted or put to sleep by the B.B.C." When workers did think for themselves, as in France or Italy, then the electoral rules were changed. "The right wing charged the Communist Party with totalitarianism to cover their own hostility to any democracy that upsets capitalist control, and their denial of democratic rights in their own organisations. Anyone with Communist views is excluded from the Labour Party."[22]

In a discussion on "liberty" Pollitt exposed some of the shortcomings of capitalist democracy. A list of "liberties I would curtail" began with "the liberty to live by the exploitation of another man's labour". Others included the liberty "to conduct fascist or anti-semitic propaganda—to issue bonus shares to escape income tax—to reconstruct a battleship for royal tours and to extend Buckingham Palace while materials and labour to build workers' houses are urgently needed—to form breakaway unions to satisfy personal animosities—the liberty of the B.B.C. to deny to the Communist Party the right to state its views while giving other parties that right."

To the accusation that the Communist Party was opposed to liberty, Pollitt replied by quoting from the Party's rules—"Work to preserve, develop and utilise to the fullest extent the democratic rights of public speech, press, assembly, organisation, representation in parliament, local government and other public bodies in order to advance the best interests of the people and secure a government truly representative of the majority of the nation."[23]

Pollitt pointed to the class interest in the Tory and Liberal concept of liberty—what they wanted was "the liberty of capital to crush labour", they "made a fetish of the word while shamelessly exploiting the working class". "What liberties did they give to the millions in their colonies until the national liberation movements compelled concessions?" "Those loudest in protestations of being defenders of liberty when their class interests are not at stake, are the first to restrict it when they are—emergency powers and arrests in the general strike, repressive regulations in war."[24]

To the question—Why are Communists democrats? he replied, "Communist theory is based on the belief that the majority of the people should rule their own destinies."[25]

"Winning the battle of democracy means putting an end to the power of wealth over the lives and minds of the people."[26]

CHAPTER 25

TORY GOVERNMENT—1951-1955

*1. After the Tory victory. 2. For peace: against the war in Malaya.
3. For peace: against German re-armament and the nuclear bomb.
4. William Gee. 5. Trade union unity. 6. Book reviews.
7. General election, 1955. 8. A memorial to Marx.*

1. AFTER THE TORY VICTORY.

Faced with the grim prospect of five years of Tory Government, Pollitt called for active resistance, political and industrial, to Tory policy with the dual objective of immediate defence of peace and living standards and the perspective of forcing a general election to return a Labour Government with a socialist policy.[1] The right-wing Labour leaders' outlook was reflected in a *Daily Herald* cartoon of Attlee and Morrison turning gleefully away while Churchill and Eden took the "hot seat" in Parliament. It fell to the Communist Party to stimulate united action against Tory policies and to extend socialist consciousness in the labour movement. The only way to break the vicious circle of collaboration was for the labour movement, through its constituted authorities, to define a socialist policy, campaign for it and ensure that its M.Ps. and Ministers were willing and able, with mass support, to carry it into legislation and government. Pollitt was in no doubt about the magnitude of the task. "We face problems which require all our energy, determination and Marxist understanding to overcome."[2]

For the next five years, apart from enforced rests due to illness, Pollitt once more plunged into leadership of nation-wide political campaigns. The main aims were defence of world peace against the U.S.-British war drive; defeat of all attacks on wages, living standards and democratic rights; national independence for the colonial peoples; ending British subservience to U.S. imperialism; building working class unity and popularising socialism.

2. FOR PEACE: AGAINST THE WAR IN MALAYA.

In January 1952 Pollitt exposed the imperialist motives for the war begun by the Labour Government and intensified by the Tories against the Malayan struggle for national independence.[3]

In 1942 when the British abandoned Malaya to the Japanese, the *Daily*

Express wrote (15-1-42) of "the great tragedy ... we could have had a native defence force, but a pack of whisky swilling planters and military birds of passage forgot this side of the population. They handed it over to the Japanese together with the radio station and the stores." In contrast, the Malayan freedom fighters harrassed and fought the Japanese right up to the liberation of the peninsula in August 1945, a month before the British troops returned. Malayan fighters were decorated by Lord Louis Mountbatten and cheered in the Mall during the Victory Parade.

During the war they were promised self-government, a promise renewed by the Labour Government after the war. In response the Malayan People's Anti-Japanese Army laid down its arms, but the Labour Government began to restore colonial exploitation and repression. From 1945 to 1948 the Malayan people strove by peaceful means for their independence. When they rejected a constitution which denied them self-government, British military forces went into action against them, and a new Resistance began. In three years British forces totalled, by Churchill's admission, 102,000 men against a population less than that of Greater London. This showed the falsity of the British Government's claim to be conducting "a police action against a handful of bandits".

Pollitt listed the methods used in what was in fact a full-scale war. "Lincolns, Spitfires and Tempests in unremitting air offensive." "Napalm and flame throwers burn huts and villages, kill helpless old women and innocent children. The people are pursued by Alsatian wolf-hounds and head-hunting Dyaks. Armed planters shoot down rubber workers who organise for higher wages, In imitation of the Nazis, entire villages are razed to the ground. Half a million peasants are in concentration camps."

All this was done in the interests of the British rubber and tin capitalists, who secured enormous profits, and of the British Exchequer which benefited from the dollars gained by sales to the U.S.A.

3. For Peace: against German re-armament and the nuclear bomb.

While Pollitt continued to closely follow industrial events, his main effort was to further the popular campaign for peace. International in scope and intensified by the U.S. explosion of a hydrogen bomb and the resultant agonised deaths of innocent Japanese fishermen from radio-active fall-out, in 1954 there arose what Pollitt described as the "most profound, spontaneous and all-embracing upsurge of world public opinion ever witnessed"[4] against the nuclear horror. The French imperialists in Indo-China, after suffering reverses, found their main army trapped at Dien Bien Phu in 1954 and being hammered to pieces by the Viet Minh. The Americans were ready to intervene with atomic weapons against the liberation forces. Public opinion in Britain and France prevented these two governments agreeing to such U.S. action. Subsequent conferences at Geneva, with the entry of the Chinese People's Republic into the world discussions, resulted in a cease-fire in Korea and an armistice and treaty of independence in Indo-China, to the disgruntlement of the U.S.A. Pollitt was able to write of "great victories for the forces of peace",[5] though grave dangers still remained.

Foremost among these was the Anglo-American determination to re-arm Germany, nominally to share in "European defence", actually to provide an anti-Soviet army for the North Atlantic Treaty Alliance. In an attempt to soften public objection to a German army officered by Nazis, a so-called "European Defence Community" with an alleged international control, was thought up, but was defeated by French public opinion. The British-American imperialists then fell back on the proposal for a re-armed German Federal Republic within N.A.T.O., at the same time doing their best to conceal from their peoples the significance of the Soviet proposal of a European Collective Treaty guaranteeing all European countries against aggression and ending the division into two blocs.[6]

Early in 1954 trade union and co-operative conferences in Britain voted heavily against German re-armament. For the Tories to carry through their policy, Labour support was vital. Attlee, Morrison and Gaitskell went into action in a big way to get it, taking disciplinary measures against six Labour M.Ps. who were recalcitrant. The platform carried the day at the T.U.C. and Labour Party Conferences, though by small majorities. The British Peace Committee called for a mass Lobby of Parliament on January 25 1955.

Throughout 1954 Pollitt in speeches and articles had made clear what was at stake and in late autumn[7] he and John Gollan spoke to a nation-wide series of meetings arranged to give all members of the Communist Party the opportunity to fully equip themselves with the facts, and plunge into winning support for the Lobby.

For a trade union branch, the arguments of Labour leaders, of course, carried more weight than the Tories, and Pollitt answered them point by point.[8]

Pollitt: Two world wars had been started by the German militarists acting on behalf of the expansionist aims of the great German trusts, said Pollitt. Now these same trusts were to have put into their hands the power to start a third, this time a hydrogen-bomb war.
The right-wing: The Potsdam Declaration ensured that West Germany was ready to reconstruct life on a democratic and peaceful basis.
Pollitt: In West Germany the trusts and cartels have been fully restored; the Government and State Departments are full of Nazis, the Generals who will command the army are Hitler's Generals.
The right wing: The new West German Army will help N.A.T.O. in the defence of Europe.
Pollitt: If any defence of Europe is necessary it is absurd for only six states

to take it on. It is a matter for all Europe and that is what the Soviet Union has proposed.

The right-wing listed a number of countries as Soviet "territorial gains".

Pollitt: Estonia, Latvia and Lithuania had Soviets in 1917; later they were overthrown by German troops. In 1939 they were taken back by the Soviets in anticipation of German attack. "Half of Poland" was inhabited by Ukrainians, conquered by the Poles; Churchill approved its return to the U.S.S.R. in 1939. "Part of Finland" and "half of East Prussia" were taken in 1945 with full agreement by the West, as security measures for the U.S.S.R.

The right-wing spoke of massive rearmament and Soviet forces of $4^{1}/_{4}$ million in the Eastern Zone.

Pollitt: U.S. Joint Chiefs of Staffs in a press statement on February 20, 1953, put the Soviet forces at $2^{1}/_{2}$ million.

To the argument that as West Germany was now competing with Britain in the world market, her re-armament would hinder her export capacity and so benefit Britain, Pollitt said[9] "This is like saying that an escaped convict is trying to break into my house, so if I give him some dynamite that will stop him using his jemmy." History shows that capitalist states have always used armed force to back up their economic policy. When Hitler built up his army, German competition in world markets did not diminish, but increased. "It is the West German and British capitalists, the strongest supporters of German re-armament, who are the worst enemies of their own working people as far as wages and living conditions. That is why there is no separation between the fight for wages and the fight for peace."

The Lobby was the largest at the House of Commons on a foreign policy issue since the anti-fascist actions of 1937–39,[10] but with official Labour support the Tories went on with German re-armament.

4. WILLIAM GEE.

"By his death, one of the few remaining links with the pioneers of the labour movement has been broken." So said Pollitt at the funeral in May 1954 of his old friend and mentor, Bill Gee.

Born in Northampton in 1869 he worked as a newspaper boy, and later in a boot factory. Interest in the Bradlaugh case led him to politics and socialism. Aged 19, entirely self-educated, reading all he could of Marx, he joined the S.D.F. and was listed as lecturer and speaker. He was S.D.F. organiser for Scotland in 1900, E.C. member of the S.D.F. in 1907, and contested Ashton-under-Lyne in January 1910, polling 413 votes. He went with S.D.F. into B.S.P.[11]

"He was by universal recognition the outstanding street corner and market place exponent of Marxism in Britain" T. A. Jackson wrote "We of the old brigade all regarded him as Socialist Propagandist No. 1 of the British Isles, and admired him for his unflinching refusal to compromise." Recalling that once he succeeded in dividing a market place audience 50-50 with Gee, Jackson said, "I boast of this because no propagandist in England or Scotland ever did better in competition with Bill."[12] Another leading Marxist, Bill Joss, was "brought to socialism" by hearing Gee in Glasgow during the South African war of 1899–1901.[13]

Pollitt's first contact with Gee, then known as the "Socialist Dreadnought", was in 1908 when he spoke for the Openshaw Socialist Society. "Bill Gee was my idol; my secret hope was to become as good a speaker as he." Others at the Socialist Hall shared this appreciation. Ella wrote that Gee "could hold any audience: he made people laugh while he made his point, using phrases that stuck in the mind." Forty years later Albert Adshead remembered Bill's "lucid exposition of Marxist economics, he made it easy for me to grasp the theory of value."[14] Pollitt recognised Gee's personal kindness to him—"he advised me on reading, explained passages in Marx that I did not understand and took great interest in my political development."[15] He also noted shortcomings—Bill's "brutal frankness, unconcealed likes and dislikes".[16] "He was not easy to get on with, his temper had many rough edges. But his qualities as revolutionary socialist propagandist more than outshone his defects."

In 1911 Gee was lecturing in Coventry Market Square to audiences of 500 to 1,000. The course was on Marxist theory beginning on a Sunday night with "What is the Class Struggle?" and ending on Friday with "Why Socialism Must Come". Beginning at 7 p.m., "Gee, a great orator, held hundreds spellbound—not a murmur. Afterwards discussions went on till midnight." "The Salvation Army was called out to try to drown Gee. The crowd ran them off the Square. Police intervention also failed. Later they politely asked us to clear off by 10 p.m." The week's collections, mainly in coppers, totalled £44.[17]

Gee lectured on Marxist economics and on Marxist philosophy. The lecture titles in an economics course at West Ham, were: "Socialism and General Science", "Marxian Theory of Value", "Exchange of Commodities", "Circulation of Commodities", "Relative and Equivalent Forms of Value", "Production of Surplus Value, Absolute and Relative".[18] On Marxist Philosophy we have no headings, but the assurance that "every phase will be expounded."[19]

In his prime he was "tall, well built, with a bluff manner"[20] in later years "somewhat corpulent"[21] (Ben Ainley 14-5-49). An undated photograph[22] taken at Rossendale shows a well-developed head, the cerebrum capacious, the hair thinning, forehead broad and high, aquiline nose, firm chin and trimmed moustache, an expression of strength and resolution, shoulders sturdy, a chest broad.

Gee depended for his living on a share of the collections and the hospitality of the organisation who booked him. He advertised in the socialist journals for engagements. In 1917 he described himself as "W. Gee—Still the Red Revolutionist".[23]

In 1920 he was a member of both the British Socialist Party and of the Socialist Labour Party. He signed the manifesto of those in the S.L.P. who helped found the Communist Party, of which he became a member and on whose behalf he spoke.[24] But he opposed the united front and affiliation policies, and probably found Party discipline irksome. In 1923 he was expelled for supporting an organisation working against the C.P.[25]

These political differences did not prevent Pollitt from "remaining a good friend, helping him materially and finding time to go and see him when he went North".[26] In November 1924 Pollitt issued an appeal—"William Gee, 35 years a propagandist for Socialism—now illness threatens to deprive him of the physical capacity to carry on." Other signatories were George Lansbury, M.P., R. Hon. F. O. Roberts, M.P., Tom Kennedy, M.P., Jack Jones, M.P., Wm. Gallacher, Ben Tillett, Tom Mann, A. A. Purcell, and the Rev. R. W. Cummings.[27]

In December 1941 in Aberdeen, Pollitt was "really shocked" at the conditions in which Gee was living. "He is in a little back room in a dilapidated slum tenement, no fire, no coal, only an evil-smelling little oil lamp ... I know well the many shortcomings of this old stalwart, but he carried the Socialist banner at every street corner when the message was not so easy to popularise as now."[28]

This new appeal was sent to some fifty people of all shades of socialist thought, who were familiar with Gee's activities in his prime. The £73 6s. which came in was used to ease his immediate difficulties and gave him a weekly payment during the following year.[29] Pollitt's original intention to get accommodation for Gee in Northampton proved impractical—all his old friends had died or left the town, and it was crowded with evacuees.

From 1946 the appeal became an annual event and continued up to and including 1950.[30] Substantially the same list of about 65 names was used. Right-wing trade union officials and M.Ps., left wingers who had broken with the Communists, some themselves retired, continued along with Communists to respond with donations and appreciative letters.

For most of this period a leading Labour personality in Aberdeen, Duncan Fraser, Provost in 1947, kept in touch with Gee and, by agreement, saw that the funds Pollitt sent were correctly used. Gee would breakfast with him every Monday and usually showed him Pollitt's letters "with a degree of pride".[31] Gee struck up a pen friendship with Brian Pollitt, referring to him as "my dear little friend" and expressing pleasure that "in spite of parental dictatorship, he keeps his end up", adding, "I expect most of his faults are inherited."[32]

Gee began to show signs of failing health; in 1951 he was "in dire straits" and had to be taken to an infirmary. A few months later he began to lose control of his faculties. He died in May 1954.[33]

Pollitt concluded his oration, "When our Socialist cause shall have triumphed in Britain, as it will, it will be your pioneering work that helped to make it possible."

5. Trade union unity.

In autumn 1954 dissatisfaction with the policy of the leaders of the T.&G.W.U., including their expulsion of militants, resulted in some 10,000 dockers mainly in Hull, also in Liverpool, Birkenhead and Manchester leaving that union and joining the National Amalgamated Stevedores and Dockers, referred to as the "blue union" from the colour of its membership card. The N.A.S.D. had previously some 6,000 members, mainly in London, where it was represented on the Port negotiating machinery. In March 1955 the Merseyside Dock Labour Board withheld registration from men who had joined the N.A.S.D., and provoked a united struggle. In May 1955, the N.A.S.D. asked for representation on the negotiating machinery in the northern ports. The T.&G.W.U. refused, since to agree would have meant acquiescing in the N.A.S.D. organising its discontented members. The N.A.S.D. then called all its members out on strike. 16,000 responded and asked T.&G.W.U. dockers not to cross their picket line. About 4,000 T.&G.W.U. men, mainly in London, responded. The T.&G.W.U. leaders called on their 60,000 members to remain at work. A difference developed in the N.A.S.D., the London members, though out solid, did not agree with the strike. A personality clash in the leadership also took place. After six weeks the N.A.S.D. called off the strike without having gained its point.[34]

Pollitt repudiated the allegation that the Communists supported the breakaway from the T.&G.W.U., as a "slander and a lie". Such action could only lead to civil war between two unions to the benefit of the employers. Certainly the wrong policy of the T.&G.W.U. leaders was responsible, but the members could bring about changes in union policy and leadership. "It is a profound mistake to believe that Mr. Deakin is the T.&G.W.U. He is not. The union is much bigger and better than he ever was or will be." The way forward was not by inter-union strife, but by "unity in action by both unions to improve wages and conditions."[35]

Problems raised by the dock strike were discussed by Pollitt in an article and at a public meeting. He was critical of the T.&G.W.U. leaders and suggested a T.U.C. enquiry into the working of that union in the docks. This provoked a reply by the T.&G.W.U.'s new General Secretary, Tiffin.[36]

At the public meeting Pollit began by briefly referring to the lessening of international tension. And drew a moral. "If the working class has the power to change the policy of governments, it has the power to change the policy and leadership of its trade unions." Some workers still felt that less armaments meant less work, but "a working class that looks to war as a means to provide work does not know its own strength and has given way to political defeatism".

He explained the view of the Communist Party that the recent strike was misconceived, also making clear that no Communist Party member had passed the picket line, and that the N.A.S.D. was not a 1923 breakaway but had existed since 1872. Unity in action of all port workers, and both unions, for a common programme to improve wages and conditions was the "absolute prerequisite" to closer trade union unity, and a stronger docks' branch of the Communist Party would help to achieve it. Tiffin, made some acid comments[37] on this speech of Pollitt's, but was silent on the idea of joint union action.

In this period several strikes revealed the dangers of inter-union conflict or lack of solidarity, particularly the railway strike of the A.S.L.E.F. men when the N.U.R. remained at work, goods traffic was moved by road and mails by troops. From these experiences, Pollitt in a widely circulated article[38] argued that "the need of the hour is not more inter-union rivalry, but closer union unity than ever before."

Sections of this article were of more than current interest. There should be uncompromising rejection of any attempts to limit the right to strike. Workers took strike action only when they had a strong sense of grievance and felt that to strike was their only resource. Background causes were resentment at longer hours and increased exploitation at the same time that huge profits and dividends were flaunted, and often the protracted delays in considering their demands. Unofficial strikes usually followed a sudden attack by employers or failure by union leaders to act. The existing divisions and competition between unions and the occasional talk of breakaways were no service to the working class. Experience proved there was no short cut to developing more militant forms of trade unionism. The rank and file had the power, if they were prepared to use it at the workplace and in the union branches, committees and conferences, to make the needed changes.

To stimulate united action his proposals included: a national united trade union campaign for higher wages, shorter hours and 100 per cent trade unionism; every workplace to have its shop stewards committee; a sustained drive for amalgamation of unions with closely related trade interests and for better attended meetings; opposition to limitation of the right to strike, to poaching or breakaways; heal the division between the two trade union internationals.

6. BOOK REVIEWS.

Reviewing books of social and political interest, particularly political biographies, was one of the ways Pollitt expressed his interest in these subjects. The following four summaries are selected from the seven reviews he wrote during 1953-55.

Not Like This, by Jane Walsh, was "written in simple style, creating an atmosphere of cruel poverty, brutal realism, the capacity of working people to sacrifice, and their kindliness to one another. You feel the damp of the houses, understand what it is like 'never to feel full', the resentment at having to wear cast-off clothing, and at what it meant to be on the dole, or to make the extra sacrifices demanded by illness in the family." It brought back his own memories of Lancashire. A weakness was that the personal sufferings of the author had not yet evoked a desire to fight back in a collective way, or to question the cause of the sufferings, the social system. Nevertheless, if widely read it would stimulate resolution to unite in action against poverty, unemployment and war.[39]

John Gollan's *The British Political System* was "a brilliant and thorough exposure of the British State" with a particularly fine chapter on Parliament. It showed the truth of Marx's remark "the state is the executive committee of the capitalist class". Gollan listed the directors of twenty-eight powerful trusts occupying leading posts in the state machine; showed the Monarchy as a stronghold of the Tory Party; how the Tories had a permanent majority in the House of Lords whose "main role is obstruction of the House of Commons when Tory Governments are not in office." Gollan concluded that "The central issue of politics is political power. For almost a century it has been firmly in capitalist hands. Now capitalism's possession of political power is threatened by the democratic advance of the common people." Pollitt commented that British political institutions had been given their present form by the capitalists in order to preserve capitalism's political power; and that the Communists wanted to transform Parliament from a body dominated by defenders of capitalism into a democratic instrument of the will of the majority of the people.[40]

Tempestuous Journey: Lloyd George, His Life and Times by Frank Owen was described by Pollitt as "one of the most brilliant biographies", and he had learned more from it than from any other dealing with Tory, Liberal or Labour leaders. It covered the period from 1890 to 1945, one of the most fateful in British history, and with its wealth of documentation was indispensable to the student of that time. Pollitt commented on some aspects of Lloyd George's activities—"the struggles for a new kind of budget, against the Tory die-hards and big landlords; the steps towards National Insurance." "The conflicts between Lloyd George and Churchill over armed intervention against Soviet Russia in which Lloyd George comes out with cleaner hands than Churchill." "The indefatigable way in which Lloyd George produced an immediate solution of some crisis, or looked ahead in a manner not done today by Tory or Labour leaders". "His reactions to the war in Abyssinia and in Spain; his terrific underestimation of Hitler, his critical attitude after Munich to the whole government policy until June 1941."

Pollitt summed up Lloyd George. "He may have been a demagogue, but he had a turn for a blistering phrase, a popular analogy, an effective simile that those who today pretend to form public opinion might well envy." "Despite his protestations of love for the working man, he was at rock bottom the champion of monopoly capitalism, a very clever and brilliant leader. He may not have liked reading documents or sitting on committees but he knew what the documents should contain and what the committees should discuss." "Lenin in his great work *Left Wing Communism* quoted from Lloyd George, and declared "the reader will see that Mr. George is not only a very clever man but that he has also learned a great deal from the Marxists. We, too, have something to learn from Lloyd George."[41]

Referring to the impression of ceaseless intrigue, of personal fights for careers and power and of corruption conveyed by the book, Pollitt wrote: "If only the people had known this during the 1914–1918 war, the ghastly, needless sacrifice of tens of thousands at Passchendaele and the Dardanelles, the real situation, the conflicts between generals, there would not have been another war in 1939, for they would have taken the affairs of the country into their own hands."[42]

In October 1955, the first complete, unabridged edition of *The Ragged Trousered Philanthropists*[43] was welcomed by Pollitt who had read every edition of this famous novel of working class life, and "always felt that all that Robert Tressell wrote had not been published." Pollitt refers to Tressell's "picture of the terrible poverty and suffering of the workers through low wages, short time and unemployment; how they suspected each other of trying to get well-in with the charge-hand and the boss; of the bosses' greed and corruption; of the stinking hypocrisy of the ladies and gentlemen of the town trying to salve their consciences by dealing out tickets for soup kitchens and giving away old clothes." The socialist spokesman in the book "despised the crawlers, hated the rich bible-punchers who preached religion on Sunday and every minute of the working week exploited their workers, tricked them out of wages they were entitled to, extolled the virtues of Jesus Christ at the same time robbing the dead with their jerry-built coffins; and blaming workers for spending money on strong drink when they had not enough to buy bread." Tressell's hero was a craftsman, and Pollitt noted that craftsmen have always been in the vanguard for social advance. "The fact that they are skilled at their work, makes them more anxious to see a society where the full fruits of their craftsmanship are reflected in the life of the working people."[44]

7. GENERAL ELECTION 1955.

The peace movement and the economic struggles showed the growth of opposition to the Tory Government, but it chose its own moment for the general election in May 1955. Pollitt cut short a visit to People's China to speak in all the seventeen constituencies contested by the Communist Party. Salient points from these speeches follow:[45]

May 8. For G. J. Jones in Hornsey: In Moscow, British businessmen were given details of orders amounting to £400 million in three years that Russia wanted to place in Britain. But as the Tories take their orders from the U.S.A., licences were refused or delayed.

May 9. For Frank Foster in Hayes: Eden and the right-wing Labour leaders by re-arming West Germany violated the Anglo-Soviet Treaty, the U.S.S.R. had no course but to annul it.

May 10. For Bert Pearce in Birmingham, Perry Barr: The £15¾ million spent on the latest aircraft carrier could have paid for 388 primary schools each with 300 children. The £13 million spent on the base in Cyprus could have paid for 120 secondary schools each with 500 pupils.

May 11. For John Peck in Nottingham North: There are 34 U.S. air bases with 50,000 troops in Britain. *U.S. News and World Report* wrote in 1948—"U.S. bombers based on Britain could sweep all Europe up to the Ural mountains."

May 12. For Joe Bent in Southwark: Lavish pensions for retired Admirals, Generals and Air Marshals contrast to miserable sums for old people who can no longer work and have to eke out an existence that brings shame on the nation.

May 13. For Tom Rowlandson in Wigan: Loyalty is a fine thing, but loyalty to leaders who have abandoned socialism is disloyalty to the working class and to your wives and families.

May 15. For Peter Kerrigan in Gorbals and Finlay Hart in Springburn: Five or ten hydrogen bombs could destroy Britain. We should seize with both hands the Soviet proposal to stop all H. Bomb tests as a prelude to completely outlawing all nuclear weapons.

May 16. For Dave Bowman in Dundee West: In Malaya, terror bombing, starvation of villages, imported head-hunters, 650,000 in concentration camps, but the British imperialists cannot subdue the people. Yet Attlee says that imperialism is a thing of the past.

May 17. For A. Henderson in Dunbarton East: In the Youth Movement, Tory cuts in grants have brought a shortage of funds, facilities and leaders and a drastic decline in clubs and groups. For a fraction of the vast sums spent on arms there could be a great expansion of Youth facilities.

May 18. For Howard Hill in Sheffield, Brightside: The Tories threaten new anti-trade union legislation. No worker comes out on strike unless the sense of grievance is so strong that they feel no other course is open to them.

May 19. For Jock Nicolson in St. Pancras North: Strikes in mining and on the railways take place because their controllers have the mentality of generals, former coalowners and rail directors.

May 19. For Solly Kaye in Stepney: Successful planning of Britain's resources demands extension of nationalisation to engineering, shipbuilding, building materials, chemicals, banks and insurance, and the land of the big landowners.

May 20. For John Betteridge and A. Morris in Hackney Central and Stoke Newington-and-Hackney-North: The cost-of-living has gone up because both Labour and Tory Governments put profits before wages, allow combines to raise prices without limit and do nothing to clean up price rings or the huge rake-offs by middlemen.

Sun. May 22. For Annie Powell in Rhondda East: After 1945 there would never again have been a Tory Government in Britain had the Labour Government carried out the will of the people instead of trying to run the capitalist system better than the Tories could do.

May 23 & 24: For W. Lauchlan, at ten meetings in West Fife: Any objective comparison of our Party with other parties will prove that we alone have a policy in the interests of every working man and woman, young person, old age pensioner, a policy that will free Britain from American domination and put Britain in its rightful place as a great democratic and peace-loving power. We have thrown down the gauntlet to the Tories and to the right-wing Labour leaders whose electoral campaign is a disgrace.

The Labour vote fell by 1½ million, and the Tories were returned with an increased majority. Analysing this result[46] Pollitt pointed out that in 1945 Labour's parliamentary majority of 180 arose from the marked difference between Labour and Tory policy. In 1955 Labour and Tory showed no major difference and a Tory majority of 67 resulted. The Labour leadership failed to arouse the workers because they had the same policy as the Tories. The whole experience since the war showed that to make a serious fight against the Tories required the end of this bi-partisanship. Only in this way could the "Labour Movement, which fought for so long to establish its independence from Liberalism, now assert its independence from the even more disastrous tutelage of Toryism".

Pollitt then went on to the heart of the problem. The Labour Movement "can never establish its independence from the parties of the employing class unless its call to the working people is based on a class and socialist policy". At the root of the electoral loyalty of the millions who consistently voted Labour, was a class and socialist outlook. To maintain and extend this loyalty a class and socialist policy was essential. "The struggle for such a policy is the key to Labour's future." This struggle could only be successful if carried on in association with the Communist Party which, because it is based on Marxism, can distinguish the class issue in events and rouse the workers to support a policy simultaneously serving their immediate interests and advancing the struggle for socialism. The more this was done, the greater the support for the Left against the Right in the

Labour Party. "All bans on members of the Labour and Communist Parties need to be removed ... because they stand in the way of developing a more united and militant Labour Party." The Labour Left could itself set an example of unity based on a common programme and discipline. On occasions they appeared in public divided on fundamental issues, sometimes loyalty to personal careers was put before loyalty to socialist principles. Sometimes they avoided the battle expected by their followers. On German re-armament, and on the nuclear bomb, "if the left had stuck to their guns and carried the issue to the rank and file and to the affiliated organisations, they would have won a victory throughout the Labour movement and made certain of an election victory."

The growing political awakening manifested in trade union conferences and in trade union voting at Labour Party conferences could be a source of great strength to the Labour left in the fight against the right. Mass movement of struggle against Tory policies could end all the apathy resulting from bipartisanship, and lead to unity in thought and action against the employing class and the Tory Government.

8. A MEMORIAL TO MARX.

Karl Marx died on March 14, 1883. At the graveside in Highgate Cemetery a handful of friends heard his lifelong comrade Frederick Engels declare, "Marx was before all a revolutionary. . . . His name and his work will endure through the ages." The grave became a place of pilgrimage for socialists and communists from all over the world. Each year on March 14 representatives of socialist and working-class organisations laid flowers and heard a memorial speech. In the twenties and thirties workers with their banners marched from a nearby station to the cemetery.

There was often talk of a suitable memorial, but there were difficulties. Objection from Marx's senior heir, whose consent was legally necessary, held up any progress.[47] To accommodate a memorial and permit it to be approached meant moving the grave, for it was completely surrounded by others, and some yards from a narrow path. Thought turned to other forms of commemoration, and in 1933 a delegate conference and a public meeting decided to establish the Marx Memorial Library and Workers School.[48] Pollitt gave this proposal his full support, spoke at the meeting and was elected to the Committee. The Library was opened in October 1935.

It was 1950 before permission was gained to move the grave and to erect a monument. A nearby site, more spacious and suitable for a gathering, was conceded by the cemetery authorities. A Committee[49] of the Library invited designs, to be "of simplicity and sobriety, and international in appeal". The inscribed stone[50] from the original site was to be incorporated, and the ashes of Marx's brilliant daughter, Eleanor, were to be laid in the new grave.

From various designs submitted, that of Lawrence Bradshaw emerged. To resolve differences as to its merits, a meeting of artists, sculptors and architects was held, with Pollitt in the chair.[51] Bradshaw wrote. "Marx's head, hair and beard were to be in granite, his face in bronze. My original scheme for the plinth was a stone spiral, symbolic of the movement of progress brought about by the rule of the working class—upwards towards communism, the classless society. It was to be made of green Cumberland slate, with an earthy look about it."[52]

A lively discussion went on for two hours. Some approved what they felt would be "a concentrated and moving monument"; others thought it "erred on the side of over-boldness for the mood to be struck within a cemetery". Bradshaw recollected, "Barbara Niven supported my project; she told me that my attitude to opposition was so aggressive that it would be better for me to let her speak, which I did. Harry's opinion was that my drawing of Marx was the best he had seen, but that the proposed plinth would not be acceptable to the cemetery authorities who wanted the memorial to be inconspicuous." The outcome was general approval for the design of the bust, but the plinth to be rectangular. Later "Harry saw my sketch, and left it to me to work it out as I wished. The completed model went before the Committee who did not interfere with the design and encouraged me to do it the way I felt it should be done."[53] The final version was the head and shoulders of Marx in bronze, the base in grey stone. The inscriptions were "Workers of the World, Unite" and "Philosophers have hitherto interpreted the world differently, the task however is to change it."

On March 14, 1956 the unveiling was witnessed by some 250 people, including the Soviet Ambassador, other Socialist diplomats, two of Marx's great-grandsons, Frederick and Robert Longuet, the Memorial Committee, and many delegates from working-class organisations. Andrew Rothstein, Arthur Horner, Professor Bernal and Harry Pollitt spoke, flowers were laid.[54]

In his speech Pollitt said: "Marx's work endures not only in printed books but in the minds and hearts of hundreds of millions of working people all over the world. Others before him had dreamt of a new society in which all would co-operate for the common good. But to Marx the new society was more than a dream; it was a practical aim to be realised through the actions of men and women.... Today one-third of the human race, led by parties based on the principles and philosophy of Karl Marx, has won victory over capitalism and is marching steadily on to socialism and communism." [55]

CHAPTER 26

VISIT TO INDIA

1. Send off.   2. On board the 'Batory'.   3. India.   4. Congress of the Indian Communist Party.   5. Return.

1. SEND OFF.

On 21st November 1953 some 300 students, workers and professional people, mostly Indians, Pakistanis and Singhalese; also Iraqis, Egyptians, Syrians, Malayans, South Africans, Kenyans, Guianese and British, gave Pollitt a lively send off to his visit to India[1] as fraternal delegate from the Communist Party of Great Britain to the Third Congress of the Communist Party of India. Ben Bradley of Meerut fame was Chairman, R. Palme Dutt the principal speaker.

The enthusiasm for the C.P.I. was shown in the acclamation for a warm fraternal message and in the rapid collection (though all had paid for admission) of £157. 12s. 6d.for the Congress Fund. There was a message and a present for Pollitt on his 63rd birthday.

2. ON THE 'BATORY'.

Eighteen days on the Polish motor ship *Batory*[2] gave Pollitt the opportunity to rest in preparation for the strenuous programme inevitable in India. On a dismal November afternoon they left Southampton, the weather continued wet, cloudy and windy till they reached Egypt.

At Gibraltar scores of small boats appeared, displaying wares for sale. "Some passengers amused themselves making ridiculous bids without the intention of buying anything. I was told they were bum boats. I hope I will be pardoned if I say there were more bums on the ship than in the boats."

They passed Malta ablaze with light in the evening and in the early afternoon next day arrived at Port Said for an eleven hour stay. More small boats, "Looking at what they did not sell, one wonders how they live." From here a trip to Cairo was arranged, but Pollitt was refused permission to land, and two plain clothes men made certain that he did not. In the Red Sea the awnings went up, the crew appeared in white, sunbathing became a serious matter. Asked by a lady if he would mind rubbing her shoulders with a cooling oil, Pollitt at once obliged, but was somewhat annoyed when a request to do the same for her beautiful legs was made to a handsome young fellow who had come along.

Pollitt's name in the passenger list aroused varied feelings. Two deputations of Indians, of whom many were on board, thanked him for his work for colonial liberation. He was pleased when an Indian lady said she was proud to meet him, but not so pleased when another one, having asked him to tell her all about communism, had only one question: "Mr. Pollitt, how can you square your principles with travelling first class and not third?" An American lady was seen reading *The Rosenberg Letters*, her husband had heard Pollitt speak in London, they were two of the first victims of the McCarthy anti-communist campaign.

At his table he was the only Britisher not wearing formal dinner dress, and looks were exchanged as much as to say "He's letting the flag down, but what can you expect?" One lady's comment was "What is Mr. Pollitt going to India for? Isn't there enough trouble in the world without him starting more?" To those who asked him directly why he was going, he replied "To try and strengthen the bonds of peace and friendship between the British and Indian peoples, and make some contribution to help wipe out memories of Britain's shameful role in India in the past."

His pleasure in the company of children and readiness to do baby-minding were soon appreciated. One little lad, having been allowed to use his typewriter, said that as his dad had three typewriters, he would ask him to send one to Pollitt. At this, the lad's mother said, "Mr. Pollitt, my husband will laugh his head off, he is a police inspector." Another mother asked him, rather sternly he thought, "Are you Mr. Pollitt the Communist?" He pleaded guilty, adding "I hope you don't think I've been contaminating your baby." Next morning she said "I had to laugh at your remark last night. My sister is in your Party in England, and my brother in the Communist Party in India."

There was a daily round of entertainments and James Mason in "The Long Memory" reminded him of his own recitations of the Lancashire poets at Sunday School gatherings, and he found to his satisfaction that he could recall, after more than fifty years, the words of "The Owd Pedlar", "Bowkers Yard", and "The Drunkard". But he failed on "An Ode to the Sun" of which he could manage only the line "Come on, owd lad, we're reet glad to see thee". At Port Said a local magician came aboard, asked a passenger to step forward, and then put his hand into the man's waistcoat and produced six chickens. Pollitt commented, to himself, "If we could do that with new members for the Communist Party, what problems would be solved." One night during dinner the voice of Paul Robeson came over the tannoy system, conversation died down. When someone started to talk, the lady who had questioned Pollitt's intentions in India, got quite angry, and said "Please be quiet, Paul Robeson is the greatest singer in the world." Another night at a fancy dress dance a lady "just a teeny weeny bit tiddly" who had never before spoken to him said "Harry, I like you." He explained that he was an old married man with two grown up children.

She exclaimed "What does that matter between friends?" It was another of the rare occasions when he was at a loss for a reply.

The other British passengers were mainly "Old India Hands" and lamented the passing of Empire, "they don't knuckle under as they used to do." But the new age was also represented. A young engineer going to do maintenance work in India appeared every evening in shirt sleeves and open neck and did not care what anybody thought about it, a party of Dundee workers were going out for specialist work in the Calcutta jute mills, a Lancashire father looked after his eight children "All steps and stairs, without batting an eyelid and proud as a peacock."

Pollitt struck up a congenial friendship with the famous Indian animal trainer, Damoo Dhotre, returning to India after 16 years absence, to buy six tigers at 2,500 dollars each. Pollitt having been a circus fan from his early years, there was plenty to talk about—Chapman's circus with Wallace, the man-eating lion from Darkest Africa, which featured at the Gorton Wakes every first week in September, then Lord John Sanger, Chipperfield, Bertram Mills and Tom Arnold. He remembered Dhotre and his animals at the Blackpool Tower in 1914, but it was a sad memory for the trainer who recollected, "Because of the war I received instructions that all my wild animals and dangerous snakes had to be killed. It broke my heart to see the animals I loved so well being shot." Dhotre explained that he believed in training animals by love and affection, at night when all was quiet he sang and talked to them. In and out of cages for 38 years, if he had a mishap it was his own fault and not that of the animals. He said, "The golden rule for the trainer is, always remember that a wild animal is never, never tamed, it is only trained. Forget this and you may not get another chance."

Pollitt thoroughly enjoyed the trip, the time passed too quickly. Towards the end more and more people came up to speak to him, the word had got round that he was not a bad sort of fellow, made jokes, and never minded looking after babies. The last day before Bombay one of the ship's officers and the two youngest members of the crew, a girl and a boy, came to tell him how glad the crew were that he was on their ship, and presented him with a card signed by all members of the crew and a handsome volume of photographs. "Some of the happiest days of my life were spent on board the *Batory*", he wrote later.

3. INDIA

Bombay

After a night wakeful from excitement at what was to come, Pollitt was on deck at dawn on December 12 as they approached Bombay.[3] The sun rose from behind the hills to starboard, on the port side the city with its hills and buildings became clearer every moment. At 7 a.m. the ship was

Harry's father, Samuel Pollitt, and his mother, Mary Louisa at the age of 65.

At the Church of England School in Market Street, Droylsden: Harry Pollitt is the third boy from the left in the back row.

3. An early photograph of Harry's sister Ella—and one taken many years later.

4. Harry Pollitt in 1917, aged 27.

5. An early portrait of Mary Louisa Charlesworth, Harry Pollitt's mother.

Harry and Marjorie Pollitt
on honeymoon in 1926.

Marjorie Pollitt.

8. Benson's Mill in Accringto[n]

9. The Socialist Hall in East Manchester, built in 1905. A board over the door (shown inset) proclaims it the headquarters of the East Manchester Lads' Club.

10. A presentation among Gorton Tank boilermakers in 1930. Left to right, front row: Jack Dent, Harry Harrison, Jack Allan, Thomas Kaye (under-foreman, Boiler Shop), William Unsworth (marker off chargehand, Boiler Shop), Jack Allan's father, James Knowles, Walter Wilkinson, Frank (family name not traced), Harry Greenwood (secretary of 'Manchester No. 3 Boilermakers' Club'); second row: Jack Cork, Jack Unsworth, and—ninth along the row—Arnold Kidd (a founder member of the committee which built the Socialist Hall).

11. Harry Pollitt at the Trades Union Congress at Scarborough in 1925.

12. A typical portrait of the 'thirties.

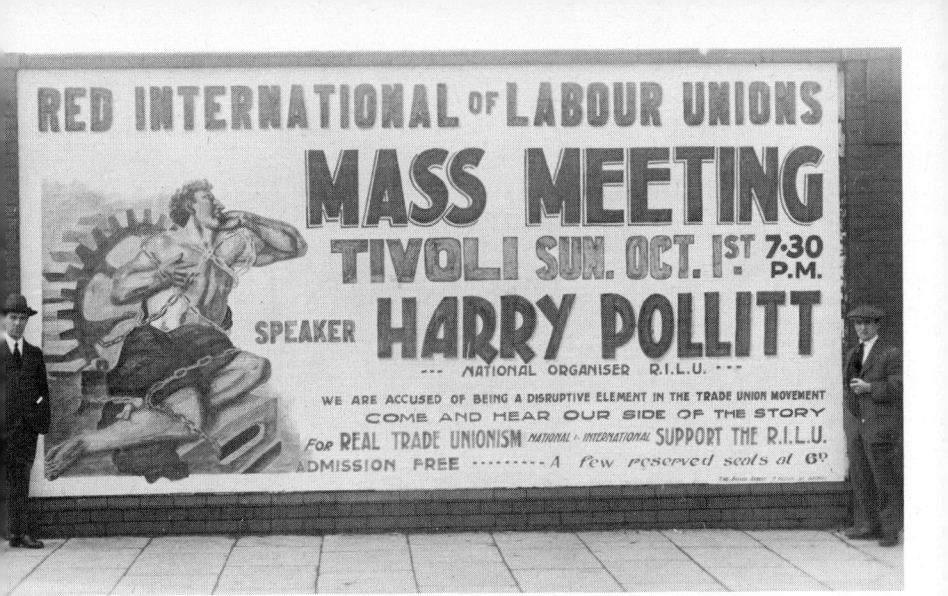

Harry Pollitt, left, standing beside the gigantic Red Trade Union poster in Paxton Street, Barrow-in-Furness in 1922.

Harry Pollitt (second from left) leading the procession past Charing Cross to a mass meeting of unemployed in Trafalgar Square on March 4, 1934.

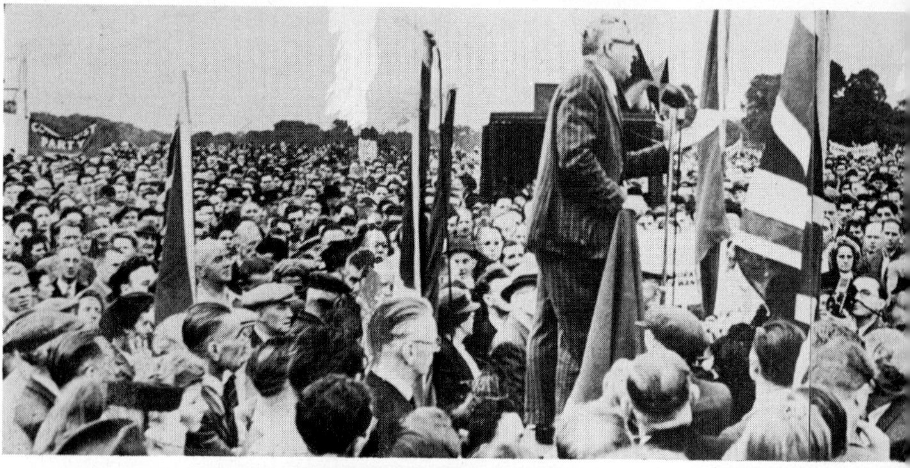
PARTY

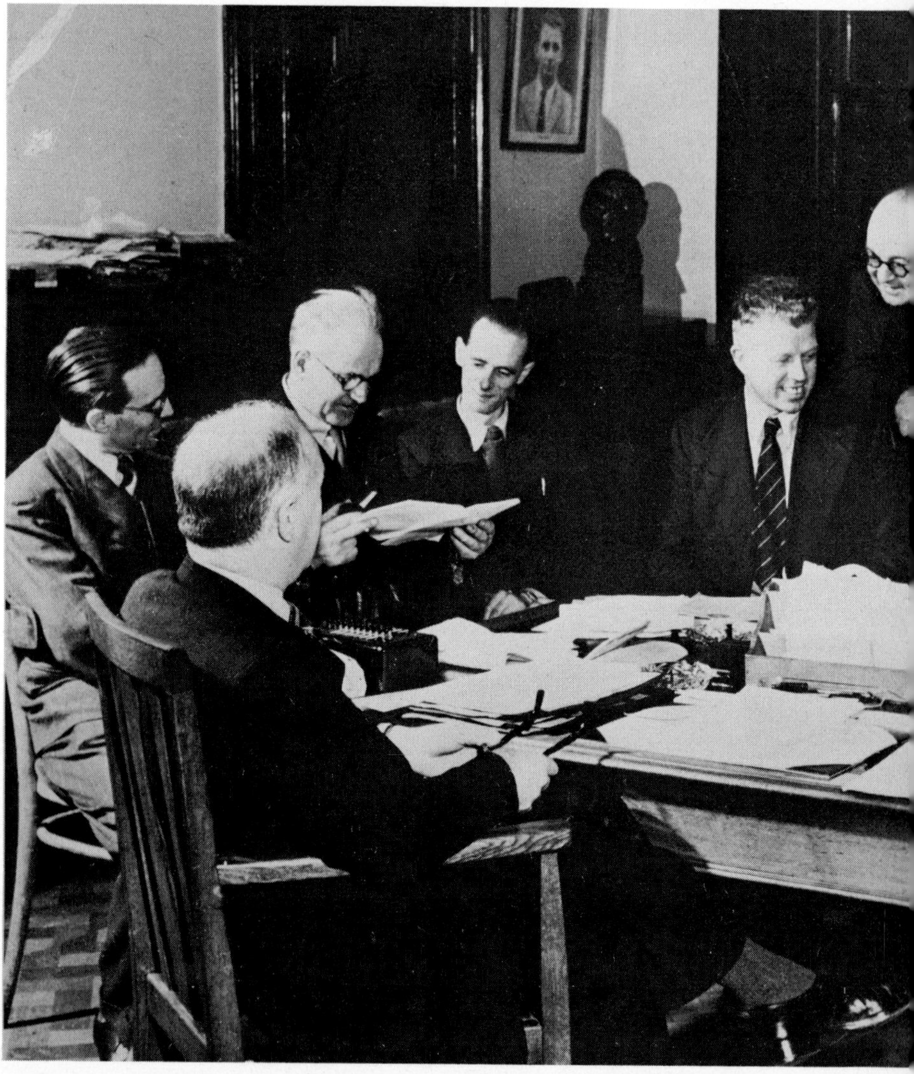

15. Harry Pollitt addressing a rally in Hyde Park on Sunday, September 7, 1947.

16. A meeting of the Political Bureau of the Communist Party of Great Britain. Harry Pollitt in the chair, and (left to right) J. R. Campbell, William Gallacher, John Gollan, Peter Kerrigan, Bill Rust, R. Palme Dutt, Ted Bramley and Emile Burns. The portraits on the wall are of Lenin and the writer Ralph Fox, who was killed in Spain.

17. Seeing Tom Mann off to Canada on April 17, 1936. In the front row, left to right: Nat Watkins, Harry Pollitt, Tom Mann, Mrs Elsie Mann and Wal Hannington.

Two photographs of Harry Pollitt with the British Battalion in Spain, on the Ebro Front.

19. A rally in support of Greek Democracy, in Upper St Martin's Lane.

20. Harry Pollitt (centre) with Ted Hill and others at a Boilermakers' Society presentation in 1956.

1. In China in 1955—a photograph is being taken.

2. Ella Pollitt (front) with Marjorie behind (left), during a visit to a Soviet school.

23. A celebration in Battersea of Harry's sixtieth birthday in 1950. Behind him (left) are his wife Marjorie and his children Jean and Brian.

24. Addressing a meeting in Melbourne, New South Wales, Australia.

5. At the Lirico Theatre, Milan, during the Italian Communist Party's Congress on January 7, 1948. Left to right: Palmiro Togliatti, Harry Pollitt, Maurice Thorez.

6. Listening while a disabled pensioner puts his case.

27. The Soviet ship 'Harry Pollitt' in London docks, not far from the scene of the 'Jolly George' incident.

moored, at 9 a.m. disembarkation began. Hundreds of workers appeared on the quay and repeated shouts of "Welcome Harry Pollitt" brought a look of disapproval to the faces of the "old Indian hands". Going through the customs all the luggage porters came to shake his hand, immediately outside he was greeted by leaders of the Indian Communist Party, in the streets he got a tremendous ovation. He walked through ranks of enthusiastic workers, banners and Red Flags, was garlanded every few steps arriving at the waiting car literally weighed down with flowers. His first words to the press were given wide publicity: "I hope my visit will strengthen the bonds of friendship between the people of India and the people of Britain."

The pattern of the next few days was to be repeated many times during his stay in India,—a welcome by huge crowds and by representatives of organisations, visits to sites and buildings recalling significant events in India's history, talks with Communist, trade union and civic personalities, and speeches to great meetings, with the added satisfaction of finding his speeches reported at considerable length in papers of various political shades.

There was much to see in Bombay. The heat was great and it was a relief to be provided with a cotton jacket and trousers. Sipping lime juice at a café table on the Malabar Hill, there was a splendid view of the bay, the marine drive and the surrounding sea. Bombay had for centuries been the principal seaport on the western coast of India. The first Europeans to come were the Portuguese, and in 1661 the city went to Charles II as part of the dowry of his Portuguese bride. When the Suez Canal was opened, Bombay became the main British entry to India. The city was splendidly sited on the seaward spit of an island, the docks on its eastern side in a wide estuary, the west and south looked out on the Arabian Sea.

The British established extensive cotton mills and later the main base of the Royal Indian Navy. In 1928 the cotton workers, 100,000 strong came out on strike for six months, and established a revolutionary trade union which became a leading force in the growth of militant trade unionism throughout the Indian industrial centres. In February 1946, Indian naval ratings mutinied, set up a strike committee, seized the ships and the shore establishments, hoisted the flags of the national independence movement and marched through the streets of the city amid the delirious enthusiasm of the people. It was notice to quit for the British Raj.

Among the places visited by Pollitt were the nearby seaside resort of Juhu, St. Xavier's College, and the house where Ben Bradley, defendant at the Meerut Conspiracy Trial, had lived. Juhu had golden sands and a beautiful bay. It had become known all over India when in 1924 Gandhi recuperated there after an acute attack of appendicitis in prison. Pollitt saw performing monkeys, mongooses and numerous snake charmers. A group of young workers from Bombay were sunbathing and singing; one of them, who had been at the docks the day before, recognised him and, telling him that they belonged to the Young Workers League, asked him to meet the others. After shaking hands, they sang for him.

At St. Xavier's College he had to share the limelight with some wrestlers, one giant having challenged all and sundry, and defeated them one by one. There was then a prolonged interval before another opponent came forward. When he did, there was a failure to agree about "rewards", the match was off, and the angry crowd stormed the stage and set it on fire. This College recalled to Pollitt the memory of an old friend, Shapurji Saklatvala, the first Indian to become a member of the British House of Commons, and the first Communist M.P. to be returned by an English constituency. Saklatvala was born in Bombay, educated at St. Xavier's, studied law, and was called to the Bar in London in 1905. He became a convinced supporter of the Russian Socialist Revolution and a foundation member of the Communist Party of Great Britain. Pollitt described him as of "amazing vitality, unrivalled abilities as an orator and exponent of the revolutionary principles of the Communist International".[4] In Battersea North, which he represented first as a Labour man and later as a Communist, he was known in every working-class street as "Sak"; he placed his legal ability and untiring energy at the disposal of anyone in trouble, and his frequent meetings were crowded with men, women and even children, who absorbed his simple but eloquent explanations of the class struggle.[5] He made the cause of Indian national freedom known all over Britain, and received a tremendous reception when he visited India in 1927.

It was the conditions in the working-class areas which made the deepest impression upon Pollitt. "The appalling poverty and dreadful housing conditions surpassed anything I had ever seen, even in the West Indies. What a commentary on the greed and rapacity of the British Imperialists that after the millions of pounds they have extorted from the workers these conditions still exist". And every night thousands who had not even one of these miserable shelters, slept in the streets. "It will be a long time before I forget what I saw", he wrote; and long after he had returned to Britain, he would wake with a start during the night, the recollections of Indian poverty returning in his dreams.[6]

Ben Bradley was repeatedly asked after. "His name is a legend here, scores of comrades have mentioned him." Pollitt had been foremost in Britain in popularising the idea of sending organisers to help the Indian trade unions, and throughout the four years of the Meerut conspiracy trial he never ceased to champion the cause of the 31 prisoners, including Bradley.

Pollitt received plenty of evidence of the determination of the Indian workers to struggle for trade union demands, national freedom and socialism.

He visited the publishing headquarters of the Communist Party of India, and found that the Party workers who lived there, very frugally, with their families, were turning out a daily newspaper and a stream of pamphlets, leaflets and books, work of a high standard, though they had no linotypes or modern equipment. He also saw the offices of the Bombay Committee of the C.P.I. and of the cotton workers trade union, which had so appreciated Ben Bradley's work that he, an Englishman, had been elected to responsible positions.

Pollitt's first meeting in India was on a Sunday evening, December 13, warm as an English August, the streets full of colour from the beautiful saris of the women, the variety of costumes and headgear, the white clothes of the men. It was held on the Kamgar Maidan, a vast open space, thousands squatting on the green and thousands more standing as far as the eye could see. Ajoy Ghosh, the general secretary of the C.P.I., took the chair. There were some fifty garlands from every section of the working-class movement. It was dark by the time the garlanding was finished and Pollitt was called upon to speak. "There were just two lights on the platform, it was a strange experience to speak to a great audience that you could not see, who enthusiastically applauded as the main points of my speech were translated."

Next night the public meeting was in a hall seating 1,500 and crammed to the doors with the speeches relayed to hundreds outside. Pollitt was asked to "please make a long speech," it was a special audience and all understood English. "You could have heard a pin drop throughout the proceedings. The intense attention inspired me to put into my speech everything I knew after my long experience of public speaking. I spoke for 1³/₄ hours, when I finished no one stirred. The chairman declared the meeting at an end. Still no one stirred, only cries of 'Please speak a little longer'." But he was exhausted after speaking so long in such heat. Then the *Internationale* was sung in Hindhi, but still the audience would not go. Pollitt, emulating Tom Mann, called for "Three cheers for a lasting peace, and loud enough to be heard in Washington". They were so given, and the meeting ended.

The ample press reports of both speeches stressed his remarks about the increasing U.S. domination of British policy, his support of the opposition to the U.S. arms bases in Pakistan, and his pride in the defeat of the U.S. in Korea. They headlined also his remark that "if the United Kingdom, India, the U.S.S.R. and China stand together for peace, there will be no third world war". He repulsed an attempt to present him as bringing "instructions" to the Communist Party of India, by the remark that "The C.P. of India is perfectly capable of taking care of itself".

Delhi—Amritsar—Jullundur—Agra

Four crowded days and nights followed, journeys by air and car, Delhi Old and New, Amritsar, Jullundur, Agra.

Delhi, imperial centre in the Saracen and Moghul times, and later capital of British India. Old Delhi with its fabulous palaces, mosques, domes and minarets, New Delhi with the British built Residences of the Viceroy and high officials, the Parliament House and the Secretariat.

The airport tarmac was invaded by welcomers, in addition to garlands there were numerous bouquets, white and gold marigolds being much in evidence. After a brief drive round the city, Pollitt was given a seat in the Distinguished Strangers Gallery in the Parliament House and listened to a debate. British procedure was somewhat in evidence; M.Ps coming out to the lobbies to meet people who had asked for them looked "as if the cares of the world rested on their shoulders alone". He was introduced to one of the Communist M.Ps, Sadhan Gupta, who had just unexpectedly won a by-election in Calcutta. His blindness did not prevent him giving a lifetime of service to the working people.

In the evening at a meeting of Communist Party members Pollitt spoke on the situation in Britain, Gupta spoke on the recent by-election. Pollitt wrote, "His English was perfect, and what a lovely voice he has. When he finished, the comrades cried 'Give us a song" and he did, then he led the singing of the *Internationale*'.

Later that night he was shown a newspaper report stating that the Ceylon authorities had banned his entry and circulated 10,000 copies of his photograph, so that the police could recognise him. They had taken seriously his remark at Southampton that he would "enter Ceylon by emulating the biblical gentleman who parted the seas and walked through them".

Next day at Amritsar the airport welcome included peasants who had come twenty miles or more, the local Communist M.P., representatives of organisations, and the author Mulk Raj Anand, on holiday in his native town. After the garlanding, Pollitt's first thought was to visit the Garden commemorating the massacre of 1919. He marched there at the head of a huge procession with red flags, laid a wreath on the simple white stone monument on its raised platform and stood for two minutes in silence which "was what I thought all that is best among the British people would expect me to do".

In 1919 the site of the present Gardens was a waste space, called the Jalianwala Bagh.[7] About the size of Trafalgar Square, it was surrounded by eight-foot high walls, behind which were houses. It was entered only through a narrow lane. The Government of India at that time had taken repressive action against popular discontent in the Punjab. On April 10 the Amritsar district magistrate siezed two popular local leaders and held them incommunicado. Crowds marched on the European quarters to demand their release. Police barred the way and fired, some demonstrators were killed. Back in the city there was violence and arson, five Europeans were killed. Then all public meetings were banned. On April 13, the Hindu New Year's Day, a crowd variously estimated at six to ten thousand gathered in the Jalianwala Bagh. The news reached the British Commanding officer, General Dyer.

Without any further enquiry, Dyer decided that this was defiance of his ban. Taking with him fifty riflemen and some machine guns he set off to the Bagh. According to his own statement to the Commission of Enquiry which sat later, he deliberately made up his mind to take such action as would "strike terror into the whole of the Punjab".

The narrowness of the entrance lane prevented him from using his machine guns, so he deployed his riflemen, and "without a word of warning opened fire at about ten yards range from the dense crowd". "For ten consecutive minutes he kept up a merciless fusilade on the seething mass of humanity caught like rats in a trap, vainly rushing for exit or lying flat on the ground to escape from the rain of bullets which he personally directed to the points where the crowd was thickest". Having fired 1,650 rounds and almost exhausted his ammunition, he marched away. He had—according to later official figures—killed 379 people and wounded 1,200. Dead and wounded alike were left on the ground, he did not consider it his "job"—his own word—to do anything about them.

Two days later Dyer proclaimed martial law, and promulgated an order that all Indians passing a lane in the city where a missionary had been assaulted during the disturbances, must crawl on all fours. All over the Punjab were arrests of national leaders, and "promiscuous floggings and whippings".

For his infamous action General Dyer was never even reprimanded, let alone punished. The Lieutenant Governor of the Punjab, Sir Michael O'Dwyer, gave his official approval. The Parliament and the authorities in London condoned. Of this massacre, Nehru later wrote "I realised ... how brutal and immoral imperialism was and how it had eaten into the souls of the British upper classes".

From the Gardens, Pollitt was taken to the Golden Temple, a sacred shrine of the Sikhs, where he was shown the treasure of gold and jewels kept in the innermost recesses, and presented with a scarf and two religious symbols. After lunch at Khuba College, the Principal took him round and he met many of the 1,600 students and one of the most well known veterans of the Indian struggle, Buba Sohan Singh, 83 years of age and bent almost double from the privations of 35 years in prisons and numerous hunger strikes. Pollitt wrote, "As I looked at him I thought how little we in Britain know of sacrifice for the Cause." Passing through parts of the city which looked as though they had been heavily bombed, he was told it was the result of communal riots following the partition of 1947. Amritsar being only 16 miles from the India-Pakistan border the flow of refugees both ways had been accompanied by heavy losses of life and property.

It was a cold night but many thousands came to the open-air demonstration, squatting on the ground, tall handsome bearded men in multi-coloured turbans, women in brightly coloured dresses. There were songs, recitations, a play about the struggle against the landlords and money lenders. Pollitt received a framed Address of Welcome, and the highest honour the Punjab can give a guest, a Sword of Honour. After the meeting, a fifty mile drive to Jullundur, where the Party headquarters for the Punjab are situated.

Next morning a discussion with some 200 of the leading comrades of the province, visits to the offices of the Party and of the Party paper, and many pressing invitations to visit Kashmir, which had to be regretfully declined. Then back to Delhi airport, to drive in a jeep 125 miles to Agra, and arrive covered in dust at ten minutes to midnight.

"A dream of my boyhood about to be realised. Through the outer portals, and there in the light of an almost full moon—the Taj Mahal. I have not the command of language to describe the scene. I can only say that it took my breath away to gaze at its extraordinary loveliness". The guides explained its history. Built by command of the Emperor Shah Jehan as a memorial to his beloved wife who died in 1629, twenty-two thousand men worked on it for 18 years. "I suppose we shall never know its cost in blood and lives, but there it is, a striking commentary on the craftsmanship of those times, and even more on the appalling conditions in the villages where the people lived."

Having seen the Taj in the moonlight, they decided they must see it again next morning in the sunlight. Outside their hotel a man was playing on pipes and a great cobra was swaying in response to the music. "Again the marvellous sight of the Taj, this time glorious in the sun rays pouring on to the white marble and dazzling our eyes, but we agreed it was loveliest in the light of the moon."

After a rather hasty walk through the great fort of Agra, within whose walls stand the palace and audience hall of Shah Jehan, they mounted the jeep again for the return to Delhi. The driver, a Sikh comrade who fought with the British army in Italy during the Second World War, had been chosen to take part in the victory parade in London, but when his political opinions became known he was not invited.

The daylight journey revealed the terrible poverty in the villages through which they passed. "Never did I think such poverty existed. You read statistics and words and try to imagine what it is like, but you have to see this awful soulsearing poverty of the people and the houses they live in, to understand what the reality means. It drove me into an uncanny depression, I tried to think what I would do if my people had to endure such conditions. The bitterness of thought, the hatred of the rich landowners and money lenders was profound. The scene in village after village was only relieved by the colourful dresses of the women who seemed in this manner to challenge the whole of their ghastly and squalid surroundings. We passed caravans drawn by bullocks and camels. We saw hundreds of monkeys and parrots, and a field where hundreds of vultures were gathered, they seemed to be saying 'We'll get you yet for tolerating such conditions'."

Some ten miles from Delhi they saw the Kutab Minar, a graceful tower of magnificent workmanship, erected early in the thirteenth century, standing 238 feet high. It tapers gracefully from a base diameter of 47 feet, to 9 feet at the summit. Inside is a winding staircase, but remembering the Monument in London, Pollitt decided not to make the climb.

The evening mass rally in Delhi was held in front of the Great Mosque, one of the largest in India, another reminder of Shah Jehan. No light but that of the full moon, and again thousands squatting on the ground and beyond them thousands more standing.

Before leaving Delhi Pollitt was invited by Nehru to his home, where they had a friendly talk. The press gave considerable space to Pollitt's speeches at Delhi and Amritsar emphasising his support for India's peace policy and quoting under "Sayings of the week" his remark that "It is better to have five years of negotiations between five powers for peace rather than one day of atomic war".

Calcutta

For sheer size the welcomes in Calcutta were the greatest of the tour. The airport was a seething mass of working people, the garlands uncountable. "I could not see an inch before me, I was a mass of flowers from head to foot." After fifteen minutes drive the road was blocked by another crowd, refugees from East Pakistan, their poverty unmistakeable, they brought their flowers, many women and little children offered a single blossom. Pollitt was moved to tears.

It was Sunday December 20 and at 4 p.m. the greatest demonstration the Communist Party ever had in Calcutta gathered on the Maidan, estimated next day by the press at 150,000 to 200,000, larger than that for the Prime Minister the previous Sunday. Mounting a raised platform for the people to see him, Pollitt could not see where the audience ended. He spoke for an hour, then a translation was made, the *Internationale* was sung and three cheers given for peace. "Then the problem was to get to the car. I had seen Randolph Turpin defeat Sugar Ray Robinson, I had seen a wrestling match in Bombay, and I got back to my hotel feeling as if I had taken a principal part in both contests."

Next day a speech to the Provincial Conference of the Communist Party, then a visit to the Party offices, bookshop and press, where everything was hand set, including the daily newspaper. Flowers again, this time including one called "night of fragrance" like a small lotus with an enchanting perfume.

"The afternoon was dreadful. I visited the dock, ship-repair, jute and engineering areas. I saw the so-called hostels where Indian seamen live while waiting for a ship. Never have I seen anything like it. The worst slum in Britain is a paradise compared with it. The most depraved human being in Britain would not keep a dog under such conditions as Calcutta workers have to live. After seeing the seamen's hostels, I went through the working class streets but I could not bear to go into any more 'houses', what I saw from the outside was enough. Human beings with hearts that can beat and minds that can think were never meant to live in such conditions. There is blood and infamy on every penny of the profits the shipping companies and the jute millionaires have extorted from the Indian workers. There are rich West Ends and poor East Ends in every capitalist city, but surely to whatever Gods there may be, there cannot be any greater contrast between the two than here in Calcutta.

"Then 'back to the other Calcutta'—the neon lights, the great palaces, the posh hotels, the boulevards, the lovely parks and lakes, the monuments to such creatures as Lord Canning, the arch-robber Clive and Queen Victoria. A late meal in a hotel patronised by British, all in evening dress, still making their ill-gotten gains out of the exploitation of the Indian people. One thing I wish I could do to them, not murder or violence, just make them eat and sleep in the conditions of the working people who live in the other Calcutta."

"At 4 a.m. next morning, on the way to the airport, how many thousands stretched out sleeping in the streets? It is pitiful, and large rats move about among them. I suppose I should have begun to get used to it, but I can't, it shocks me."

Hyderabad

The air journey from Calcutta to Hyderabad included a wait at Nagpur where two Englishmen of Noel Coward's "Mad Dog" type were talking loudly. Said one, "Have you read Pollitt's speeches? Why the devil did they let the fellow in, what's he up to?" As the plane descended at Hyderabad a mass of people with red and blue flags could be seen. The two "Mad dogs" exchanged glances as much as to say "My God, he must be with us."

The State Government lodged Pollitt in its Guest House, situated in beautiful ornamental grounds, once the Residence of the British Minister. Again smothered in flowers he rode there in a car preceded by a motor-cycle with two lads and a red and a blue flag, and followed by bicycles and buses with the rest of the welcomers.

On the way to the hall for the public meeting, he saw small factories and workshops, surburban villas of the rich and the houses of workers and peasants. There were women pulling lawnmowers in posh gardens, working in rice fields, breaking stones for road repairs, carrying heavy burdens in the streets, coming out of factories, and in all cases their saris were of beautiful and varied colours. "The contrast between rich and poor is as deep in Hyderabad as elsewhere in India, but this mass of colour helps to soften the squalor and poverty."

Pollitt's speech at the evening meeting got great publicity in the press which reported the presence of numerous leading personalities of the town. A youngster of eighteen presented a garland amid great applause. He had been sentenced to death during the Telegana disturbances, then reprieved and put on parole. When Pollitt's speech ended, the people would not go away, he had to leave by a back exit.

Next morning he was received in the offices of the Democratic Front, founded in 1951 when the Communist Party was illegal, and consisting of trade unions, democratic and socialist political parties and independent groups. In the general election of 1951–2 it won a quarter of the seats in the State parliament and seven in the central parliament. Its M.P.s were present in the building, formerly the headquarters of the Nizam's Commander-in-Chief, when Pollitt spoke on the position in Britain and answered many questions.

During a session of the State Parliament, Pollitt was ushered into the Distinguished Strangers Gallery, and then invited to the room of the Chief Minister who gave him a cordial welcome.

Under the Nizam's rule Hyderabad had experienced some of the worst forms of feudal exploitation and repression to be found in all India and in consequence great struggles of the peasants had taken place. As a result the State prisons held 150 comrades, 85 of them in the town prison. Pollitt received permission to enter—and leave—this prison, and to see fifteen of them in groups of five. They were peasants or students, in their twenties or thirties. Of this experience he wrote later: "When the last five were brought in and we had shaken hands, there was a long silence. Then one, still under the death sentence, exclaimed 'You are an old man, I always thought you were a young man'. I laughed, but was it a compliment or a back hander? Another comrade struck me by his thoughtful manner, he was serving twenty years, I asked him whether he was married and had children. A tear came into his eye as he replied 'No, but my mother visits me once a month and I am proud to say that she has collected more signatures for a peace petition than anyone else in Hyderabad'. Under such circumstances, what could you say or do? I am not ashamed to say I did it. Time was up, the comrades went back, I hope the happier for my visit. All of them asked me to thank D. N. Pritt Q.C. for what he did to save some of them from the hangman's noose. I came out resolved to work harder than ever for their release."

The last evening in Hyderabad was devoted to speaking to a meeting of the members of the Communist Party.

Madras—Madurai

The temperature was 85 degrees in the shade when Pollitt alighted at

Madras airport, across the building ran a huge banner "Welcome to Harry Pollitt". This time the flowers were mainly pink roses, there were showers of petals and many children handed him a single flower, an orange or a lime. There was no time to see the city, the first settlement of the British in India, for at 8.20 p.m. on Christmas Eve the train left for Madurai where the Congress was to be held. It moved out punctually, the station crowded with working people giving a send off to the Congress delegates and the leaders of the C.P.I.

A red flag firmly secured to his carriage window signalled his whereabouts to the hundreds waiting on the platform at a station about an hour's run from Madras. There were garlands, speeches, autograph signing. This happened at twelve stations where they stopped, at one they reached at 4 a.m. thousands had been waiting all night.

At 7.20 a.m. on Christmas morning the train pulled in at Madurai. The station, the great square outside it and the nearby streets were jammed with 20,000 people. A Guard of Honour was ready for inspection, a platform had been erected and by it stood a great elephant bearing two red flags emblazoned with hammer and sickle. Unusually, it was raining, and Pollitt was accused of bringing Manchester weather with him.

He found Madurai a fairly large city, with many famous old temples, a huge textile plant, an important railway centre. It was a stronghold of the Communist Party. The heat was greater, the people darker of skin and more scantily clothed. Magnificent buildings housed the bank and the textile firms, many people were crowded in festering hovels. "What craftsmanship and labour went into the great temple and the king's palace, while hundreds have nowhere to lay their heads! I find it impossible to rhapsodise about Art when before me is a long queue of half-starved men, women and children, waiting to be handed a bowl of soup. I cannot work up feelings of awe when I look up at the huge sacred tank and all around are little children with hunger swollen bellies and beggars hideous with 'religious' white paint smeared over their faces. No wonder the people have such splendid traditions of struggle. No wonder the Red Flag flies over one working class area I visited and none dare to pull it down.

"Back in my room I read a newspaper report of a speech by the Chief Minister of Madras. He deplored 'petty thieving' and impressed upon the people their duty 'to respect their conscience'. After all the robbery by the British imperialists and now by Indian princes, capitalists and landlords, that advice is a piece of infernal impudence".

4. Congress of the Communist Party.

The Congress met at a time when it was especially important to define the Party's political line because in a general election the Indian National Congress had for the first time failed to receive its then customary overwhelming majority vote.

The Congress met in a theatre in a working-class area, opening at 11.30 a.m. December 27. Passing between lines of applauding workers, the delegates found a Guard of Honour drawn up outside the hall. At the entrance, Dr. Muzuffar Ahmed, a founder member, hoisted the red flag to the top of a standard, while a flock of doves were released. Ahmed was one of the four accused in the first "Communist Conspiracy" trial at Cawnpore in 1924, and later at Meerut was sentenced to transportation for life. Inside, the platform background was a huge red flag emblazoned in silver with the hammer and sickle. As soon as the Presidium was elected, its members, the Party leaders and the fraternal delegates led the whole Congress in solemn procession to file past a memorial column to those Communist Party members who had been done to death in the struggle. The first resolution passed was in honour of the fallen and of those in prison.

Thirty-five fraternal parties were represented. Pollitt was among those who spoke on the first day, and received an ovation. After referring to the thirty years of co-operation between the Indian and British Communist Parties and paying tribute to India's efforts for world peace, he pointed to the increasingly aggressive actions of American and British imperialism. In 1947 the upsurge of the Indian people had compelled British imperialism to abandon direct rule and to compromise with the Congress in an effort to maintain the maximum hold possible and to avert a popular revolution. But they still had a strong grip on India's resources and drew from her a large tribute. A new menace had also arisen. American imperialism had outstripped Britain in the Indian market and was seeking to draw India into an economic and financial stranglehold.

The illusions of 1947, that liberation from imperialism had been won and the road opened to solve India's problems, had been outlived. Growing hardship among workers and peasants, crisis in agriculture, abandonment of the nationalisation programme, admission of foreign monopolies to the economy, corruption in business and congress circles had given rise to mass unrest, reflected in the heavy fall in Congress votes.

The six million votes cast for the Communist Party of India and its allies showed that the Indian people were searching for a new path. Only the programme of the C.P.I. and its allies set out that path. The road lay through struggle for leadership of the working class and the people, strengthening and unifying the C.P.I., building a mass united trade union movement of the working class, developing the peasant struggle against the landlords, an alliance of the working class and peasantry, and a united democratic front of all sections for national independence, peace and the solution of economic problems.

He concluded with a comprehensive review of the struggle in Britain.[8]

The same day Pollitt, at an interview with the press, who were not admitted to the Congress, again rebutted the idea that he had come to give instructions. "The Communist Party of India", he said, "by its long devotion to the cause of the Indian workers by hand and by brain, has proved itself completely capable of looking after its own affairs."

Pollitt attended every session of the eight-day Congress, two going on till midnight and one till 5 a.m. In the main debates he noted the seaching and critical mood among the delegates, with several hundred amendments to each of the principal documents.[9]

The Congress made clear its perspectives for the establishment of State governments of democratic unity, through majorities in the legislatures and the development of the mass movements of the people, and its belief that such governments could be secured within the existing constitution, provided that the united front of the workers, peasants and all democratic forces was achieved. In general the resolutions got fair press publicity, but one paper wrote of the "intention to use the parliamentary facade to conceal preparations for armed rebellion" and that the purpose of the united front was "to deceive the allies of the party."[10]

Invited to address the Congress prior to its close, Pollitt began by saying he had never seen a Congress where the mass of the workers showed such interest in the proceedings. The Congress had taken resolute steps to eliminate weaknesses in the party, and the political resolution gave the lead on how to fight to improve the working and living conditions of the workers and peasants, to strengthen the struggle for national independence and world peace, to strengthen India's economic basis and enhance her role in the world. On these issues allies had to be won, the united front built, the C.P.I. made stronger and with a firm base in the factories and villages. The main danger was the menace of a third world war, the issue not whether the main enemy of India was British or American imperialism, but how the C.P.I. was to mobilise the people to ensure that India's vast influence was used for peace against the U.K.-U.S.A. war bloc.

The day before the final session of Congress there was a great march through the town. Madurai was transformed; the people had responded to the call of the local C.P., houses, shops, rickshaws, stalls, windows, buildings and streets were red with bunting. In brilliant sunshine thousands of men, women and children lined up for the march, an ocean of red flags moved in the breeze. People had come from a hundred miles around, hundreds of bullock carts brought peasant families, special trains were packed, thousands more came on foot.

Waiting for the march to begin, Pollitt noticed that one of the many temples was decked with red flags, and that some of the officials were carrying them. He asked, "Are you Communists?" The reply was "No, but the working people here don't get sufficient wages, many are unemployed. We sympathise with the Communist Party because it fights for the poor."

The procession moved off headed by the elephant with its red flags, its keeper on its back, proud and dignified, monarch of all he surveyed. Through streets lined with watchers, it took three hours to reach the meeting place and an hour to pass the platform. "It was estimated that some 250,000 people were at the rally. Men in whites, women and children in their best saris, with flowers in their hair. I have never seen anything like it in any part of the world. From the platform on all sides stretched a vast sea of humanity."

Pollitt had the honour of being the first of the four speakers. "How I wished I could speak in the Tamil language to this overwhelming crowd who demonstrated their love, affection and trust for and in the Communist Party of India, and what it means to them."

The local press noted two of his points: "It was not part of the creed of Communism to advocate violence. The real advocates of violence were the British, French and American imperialists who were putting it into practice in Malaya, Africa, British Guiana, Korea and Indochina." And "The people of Pakistan should learn from the experiences of Britain and France and tell the Americans before it was too late that under no circumstances would they allow foreign troops or air bases on their soil."[11]

Next day Congress ended and Pollitt returned by train to Madras, and was seen off by Ghosh and Dange by plane to Bombay. He had travelled 2,000 miles in India by air, car and train, and had spoken to over half a million people. In all the heat—it was 91° in the shade in Bombay—he had to wear the metal corset necessitated by his spine condition. The mosquitos had not helped. "I have been bitten by every mosquito in India, and by fraternal delegations of these pests organised from other countries." He was glad to take it easy and get some early nights. There were interviews and personal talks, but the only formal occasion was a reception where many prominent personalities thanked him for his speeches about peace and the danger from the U.S.-Pakistan pact.

A telegram from the Communist Party of Australia asked him to go that way home and call on them, but it was too late; he was booked on the *Strathmore* via Suez leaving next day.

The very last evening saw the sole victory over prohibition. Comrade Sanyal, who had looked after him throughout the tour, "came rushing into my room, the light of triumph in his eye. 'Harry, I've got you a drink at last, and no regulations broken' and he produced a bottle of Halls Wine. It tasted like nectar to me, despite its having been made in Bow, where I once worked in Fowler's boilershop, holding my nostrils when crossing Stinkpot bridge to get there."

In a final interview with the newspaper *New Age* he expressed some of the thoughts arising from his experiences. "My dominant impression is that of the appalling conditions of so many Indian workers and peasants. I have never in my life seen such a contrast between the conditions of rich and poor. It has brought home to me the vast debt the people of Britain have yet to pay to the working people of India for the shameful robbery and exploitation by British Imperialism for nearly 200 years. I have seen amazing demonstrations of the love and trust of the Indian workers and peasants for the Communist Party of India, arising from the devoted services it has given and will continue to give to them. I realise the gigantic tasks the C.P.I. has to solve, but of its ultimate success there can be no doubt.

"I wish the democratic, progressive and peace-loving people of India every success in their activities to improve the material, educational and cultural level of India's toiling millions. I hope my visit has strengthened the bonds of peace and friendship between the British and Indian peoples and that I have convinced those who listened to me that there is another Britain than that of the Clives, Hastings, Dyers and Churchills."

5. Return.

He would not agree to any mass send-off, but the press was there in force and the faithful comrade Sanyal was with him until visitors had to leave the ship, which moved out at 3 p.m. on January 7 1954. The home journey was pleasant despite some untoward events. Two stowaways were found; one of the crew jumped overboard in the Red Sea and could not be saved; and there was a death and burial at sea. A lady at his table gave him a meaning look as she remarked that there appeared to be a Jonah on board. Pollitt landed at Tilbury on January 24 1954 to be welcomed by Marjorie, Jean, Brian, and a group of friends.

Of his stay in India he said he had been received everywhere with respect and affection. "Nothing has been too much for the comrades to do for my comfort. I appreciate it more than words can convey and look upon it as a tribute to the British Communist Party."

The visit had been a great success. Harry had received the greatest popular welcome ever accorded to an Englishman in India.

The experience had a very deep effect upon him. A few months later at the Conference of Communist and Workers' Parties in the sphere of British Imperialism, he said: "You know I recently paid a visit to India. As long as I live, as long as I have breath in my body, I never want to see again the things I saw in that great country. They are seared like red hot irons on the tablets of my memory. I felt dishonoured and ashamed, and bereft of the power of expression. I thought of what I would feel and do if my wife and son and daughter had to live as I saw other mothers and children doing. I think of what the peoples of Korea went through, and the terrible plight of the peoples of Malaya and Kenya at the present time.

"I also rejoice that the lesson of our time is that there is nothing in the world that can now stop the onward march of the British people and their allies in the countries oppressed directly and indirectly by British Imperialism from reaching their goal.

"In comradeship, love and affection we greet them all."[12]

CHAPTER 27

CYPRUS—1954

*1. Storm over Cyprus. 2. A long day. 3. The old and the new.
4. 8th Congress of A.K.E.L. 5. Tired but happy. 6. Pendant.*

1. STORM OVER CYPRUS

In March 1954 Pollitt went to Cyprus for the Congress of the Progressive Party of the Working People, generally known as A.K.E.L., the initials of its Greek name. Cyprus had one similarity with India, the dominating factor in public life was the popular determination to achieve independence. The British took Cyprus over from the Turks in 1878, annexed it in 1914, and had ruled it as a Crown Colony since 1925. Makarios, Archbishop of Cyprus, later to become world famous for his successful defiance of the British, and as the first President of the Republic of Cyprus, was emerging as the popular leader. A.K.E.L., a legal party formed in 1941 as successor to the Communist Party of Cyprus, illegalised after 1931, had become the recognised political representative of the workers and peasants. In the May 1953 municipal elections it had 46 per cent of the votes cast, gained the majority in Limassol, Famagusta and Larnaca, and in alliance with other progressives gained Paphos and Kyrenia.[1]

A.K.E.L.'s relations with the Communist Party of Great Britain in the common anti-imperialist struggle were all the closer because of the Cypriot communities in Britain. The British rulers had never been able to provide work in Cyprus for all who needed it. Considerable emigration took place, much of it to Britain, cohesive Cypriot communities arose in London, Manchester, Glasgow and other cities. Most Cypriots in Britain intended to return to their beloved island, and retained their connections with it. Many had been members of A.K.E.L., continued to support it, and in London sustained their Greek language paper *Vema* (Truth). They found that of the British political parties, only the Communists consistently opposed imperialism. Many of them joined the Communist Party of Great Britain, which had cordial relations with A.K.E.L.

Pollitt had for many years personally assisted the Cypriot struggle by his political initiatives, speeches and writings. In 1928 he published[2] an exposure of conditions in Cyprus: mass unemployment with neither relief nor public works; no legal maximum working day; 12 to 14 hours daily worked in the mines and elsewhere; no legal minimum wage; no workmen's compensation except for fatal accidents in mines where the employer might have to pay up to £100 in final settlement. The government had dissolved workers' organisations; there was a strict police surveillance, Communists and sympathisers were not allowed to work in the mines.

In 1931 Pollitt called for "Hands Off Cyprus" and solidarity action. The Governor had dictatorially enforced a Bill rejected by the Legislative Council, military police fired on a peaceful demonstration of protest. This led to a widespread upheaval in which the Governor's House was burned. Though no-one on the government side was killed or even wounded, British troops and police killed ten people, ten were deported for life, and over 2,000 imprisoned.[3]

Early in 1946 Pollitt received details of the arrest of trade union leaders in Cyprus, followed by heavy sentences. Subsequently, on March 5, a Labour M.P., Mr. Leslie Solley, raised the matter in the House. He quoted from the documents on which the prosecution was based and from the Court proceedings. The President of the Court asked, "Is Marxist theory a crime?" The Solicitor General replied "According to Cyprus law, yes". The President: "Is possession of Marxist books a crime?" The Solicitor General; "Yes". Solley commented, "It is fantastic that when Labour rules at Westminster, socialism is a crime according to the law of Cyprus."[4]

2. A LONG DAY

March 2 was a long day for Pollitt. The B.E.A. Viscount left London two hours late. Lake Geneva sparkled in the sun, the Alps were snow clad, Rome under heavy rain, the lights of Athens passed, and a midnight arrival at Nicosia. Outside the airport a great crowd shouted "Welcome to Harry Pollitt"; there were handshakes and pats on the back from all sides. Greeted by the A.K.E.L. General Secretary, Ezekias Papaioannou, and the Mayors of Limassol and Larnaca, he was loaded with bouquets and carried shoulder-high to the waiting car, soon filled with violets, carnations, daffodils, marigolds and irises. At the A.K.E.L. headquarters, more people, more flowers, more greetings. Replying, Pollitt said he hoped his visit would strengthen the bonds of friendship between the working peoples of Cyprus and Britain.[5]

Papaioannou and Pollitt were old friends, the former had lived for some years in London, was well-known in the trade unions as a Cypriot spokesman, and had served on the London Committee of the C.P.G.B. At a hotel they talked over the problems facing the coming Congress, and Papaioannou outlined the position of Cyprus.

The population was of mixed nationalities, 77 per cent Greek, 18 per cent Turkish, 5 per cent Armenian, Maronites, British and others. The Greeks were Orthodox Christians, the Turks Mohammedans. Villages tended to be either Greek or Turk, in all towns there were Turkish quarters. Not only the dominant British imperialists were interested in

Cyprus; so were the Americans, N.A.T.O., and the governments of Greece and Turkey. With the Turkish coast 40 miles north, Syria 60 miles east, Egypt 280 miles south, the Greek islands 300 miles west, Cyprus was a desirable base for those interested in the oil, strategy and politics of the Arab lands, the Dardanelles, the Suez Canal, the route to India and the Persian Gulf. Great areas of the Mediterranean, North Africa, Asia Minor, even the Black Sea were within reach of aircraft or missiles based on Cyprus.

From earliest recorded history the Greeks populated Cyprus, but the Pharoahs, Assyrian and Persian kings, Roman and Byzantine Emperors had at various times seized and lost it. Then came Saracens, Anglo-Normans, Lusigans, Venetians and Turks, all seeking wealth from conquest, war and trade. Always the peasants in the fields, the fisherman on the coast, the craftsmen and labourers in the cities carried on their backs the soldiers, merchants, nobles and kings. The people remained tenaciously Greek, the Orthodox Church a political and religious factor in the survival of their Greek spirit. Only after the Turkish conquest of the sixteenth century did a settled Turkish population appear.

The ancient Greeks had it that Aphrodite chose the coast of Paphos to emerge from the sea. If so, she chose well. Later came a less amiable visitor, none other than St. Paul. But it was St. Barnabas who did most for the island. The discovery of his remains, with a copy in his own hand of the Gospel of St. Matthew, resulted in the Byzantine Emperor confirming the autonomy of the Church of Cyprus, and granting to the Archbishop rights hitherto reserved to the Emperor himself, including wearing a cape of imperial purple and signing his name in red ink. The later Turkish conquerors were evidently impressed, they respected the autonomy of the Church and acknowledged the Archbishop as the official representative of the Greek Cypriots.

3. THE OLD AND THE NEW

Pollitt took the opportunity to see the island and the people, old and new side by side. A walk through the Cyprus Museum in Nicosia was a journey in time from the tools of the iron and bronze ages, to the ceramics and sculpture of the Greco-Roman era. Many exhibits had come to light by archeological excavation, others by chance discovery, or by earthquake. A link with Britain was a bronze statue, the head so life-like it appeared to speak, arms and hands adding a persuasive gesture—that of the Roman Emperor Septimus Severus, who died at York in A.D. 211.

On the Venetian walls of Nicosia a monument marked the spot where in 1571 a Turkish soldier first planted the banner of the Crescent. The cathedral of St. Sophia was converted by the Turks into a mosque, two high minarets took the place of the Gothic spires. Pollitt took off his shoes to cross the mat-covered floor of the pillared hall. From the minarets came a voice calling the faithful to prayer—but it was relayed by loud-speakers, no-one any longer climbed the hundreds of steps to the top.

Then a glimpse of the new. Pollitt inspected the Medical Clinic built by the trade unions to serve the workers. With doctors and surgeons, wards and dispensary, it sought to make up for the failure of the British rulers to provide a public health service. Then on to the modern printing plant and editorial offices where the A.K.E.L. daily newspaper, *Neos Democratis*, was produced.

Nicosia is well situated for travel all over the island by car. Pollitt went first to Kyrenia on the northern coast. From the summit of the pass 1,250 feet above sea level the penetrating light and the vapour-free air revealed the coast stretching east and west, mile after mile of white and gold beaches. On one side the blue green of the sea—on the other the green and grey of forested mountains, overhead the cloudless Mediterranean blue. In the far distance the snow-capped peaks of Asia Minor. Immediately below, Kyrenia seemed to float in its own sea of trees and flowers, a cluster of fishing boats in the old harbour, dominated by the walls and towers of the crusaders' castle. As the car descended, the enormous walls of the fortress on Mt. Hilarion came into view on the left, the graceful arches of the half-ruined Abbey of Bellapais on the right. In the modern outskirts of Kyrenia, Pollitt commented, "You have to hand it to the English with money to spend; they know the best places to live in" as he saw the number of lovely houses in magnificent surroundings occupied by well-to-do English.

The next ride was south to Famagusta, through agricultural land protected by mountains from northern winds and partially irrigated. At the village of Vateli, and again in Lysi, Kondea and Kalopsida, peasants with their wives, children and old people, were waiting with a smiling welcome and gifts. Pollitt wrote: "I made a brief speech of thanks. As I looked at bodies, wracked with hard work, and took the hands, hard as wrought iron, of men and women, I thought—'these are the real people'." In contrast was Dekhelia, one of the British military bases. For the single men, well-built brick barracks; for families two story houses; for the officers still better houses. For the Service Corps and the Ordnance, huge stores and workshops. For the Command, great headquarters, canteens, clubs, recreation. Money poured out like water for British military requirements, no concern for Cypriot housing or farming.

In Famagusta, a speech in the street being illegal, Pollitt spoke inside the packed headquarters of A.K.E.L. and waved from the balcony to a cheering crowd. Sightseeing was brief, along the 50 feet high Venetian built walls of the old town, the carved lion of St. Mark still looking down into the harbour which received the fleeing remnants of the Crusaders after the fall of Acre. At the Othello Tower, Pollitt asked if it was true that Desdemona was murdered there. An expert assured him that she was, though in which room was not known, and in impeccable English criticised

Shakespeare for having appropriated the story from an Italian writer. The Famagusta Council had an A.K.E.L. Mayor, who took Pollitt to see some of their achievements—new flats for workers, a home for the aged, a sports stadium, and almost ready for opening, a People's Seaside Centre, with sandy beach and every facility for sea and sun, bathing, refreshment and entertainment.

The return to Nicosia was via Larnaca, a quiet town with many gardens, palm lined beaches and the ancient Monastery of Stavrovouni, founded by the mother of Constantine, the Emperor who made Christianity the state religion of the eastern Roman empire. Again an A.K.E.L. Mayor received Pollitt at the municipal centre and explained ambitious plans for street improvements, housing, sanitation and a public library.

Next day at Lefkonico, east of the capital, Pollitt chatted with many peasants and spoke to a crowded meeting in the A.K.E.L. hall. He was surprised that among the welcome handshakes was one from a police sergeant who had a reserved seat—not that he supported A.K.E.L., but because the British authorities insisted that a police representative be present at every public meeting. Later Pollitt went with the crowd to the bridge across the little river to lay flowers in honour of three comrades killed when police fired on a demonstration in 1945.

Salamis, on the coast north of Famagusta, told a different story. Said to have been founded by a Greek hero of the Trojan war, it was for centuries a city state and commercial centre. Twice sacked and burned, it was finally reduced to ruins by an earthquake and a tidal wave. Pollitt saw a gleam of white columns and huge stone blocks in the now submerged harbour. The ruins of the Roman period included a great forum, baths, villas, a theatre seating thousands, and a 35 mile long aqueduct, evidences of the luxury of the wealthy, but giving no clue to the lives of the slaves who did the work.

4. 8TH CONGRESS OF A.K.E.L.

The Congress opened in the Loucoadi Cinema in Nicosia at 7 p.m. on March 5. Under the blue and white flag of Greece and the red flag of the international working class, the upstanding delegates sang the battle hymn of A.K.E.L. and honoured those who had given their lives in the struggle. Of the many messages of greeting, the most prolonged applause was for those from comrades held in concentration camps. A delegation from villages all over Cyprus, in their national costumes, saluted the Congress and brought gifts for Pollitt, flowers and fruit, an inscribed banner, a primitive plough known 2,000 years ago and still used in some localities today.

The keynote was struck by Papaioannou, when in reply to the British complaint of Cypriot unwillingness to undertake joint responsibilities with them, he said: "We are ready, now, to assume full responsibility for a Cyprus free of all imperialist influence and control." That A.K.E.L. stood for the unity of the Cypriot liberation struggle was shown by the adoption of a programme expressing the interests of all sections of the working people and of the island community, Greek and Turk, as a whole.

The British colonial secretary had boasted that he would never allow the creation of a communist state within the British empire. In his fraternal speech Pollitt commented: "He does not know what he is talking about. No power on earth can crush the fight for the national independence of all oppressed peoples; that is the lesson of Korea, Malaya and Kenya." Pledging continued solidarity from the British movement, Pollitt recalled that before the Second World War the Cypriot workers and peasants toiled from sunrise to sunset. Now they had substantial improvements in living-standards and democratic rights, thanks to their militant solidarity and to the leadership of A.K.E.L. Referring to the growing danger from imperialist plans to militarise the island, and to the interpretation of self-determination as meaning immediate union with Greece, Pollitt said: "Your fight for national independence is made more difficult by the existence today in Greece of a government that serves the interests, not of the Greek people, but of its foreign masters." This warning was fully justified by later events. Among his impressions Pollitt noted the youthful character of the Congress, its political unity, determination to increase A.K.E.L.'s membership, and to champion the cause of the workers and peasants.

5. Tired, but happy.

After the Congress Pollitt went to Paphos in the south west. The day was a religious festival and a general holiday; the ride was through lovely valleys, over mountains, and for many miles along the coast. The crops were already a foot high, the fruit trees in bloom, everywhere the villagers were out enjoying the holiday. "But behind the beauty is tragedy. We pass through mining villages: some years ago the miners lost a four months' strike, now no trade union is allowed by the American company. Any miner trying to form one is victimised. In another foreign-owned mine, eight hours underground is the rule, men are compelled to work overtime and Sundays without extra pay. Approaching Paphos we pass through villages looking as though they had been bombed, they were devastated by last year's earthquake, it is pitiful to see them." Paphos, a town of 17,000 people, centre of a rich area growing grapes, currants, sultanas, figs, almonds and bananas, had suffered heavily from the earthquake, thousands were living in army huts. Pollitt was taken sight-seeing: to the catacombs, 3,000 B.C; the column to which St. Paul was tied to receive 39 whip lashes for his preaching; the castle where the Turks incarcerated prisoners, a dreadful place; the Tombs of the Kings, dug deep through solid rock in 2,500 B.C. In the largest tomb he saw where the Kings and Queens were laid, where their slaves had to die when their owners passed away. There was a public meeting that evening, the British military authorities issued an order that no soldier attend, "but I was glad to note that quite a few of the lads were present and I hope they enjoyed the evening as much as I did".

From Paphos to Limassol, where the Mayor, an old friend, Comrade Partasides, showed off the marble Town Hall with great pride, then took Pollitt to see the trade union offices, medical clinic and dispensary, and introduced him to the Councillors. At a great public meeting the reception moved Pollitt to tears. "I am greeted by lovely children with doves and flowers, delegates from women's organisations who hand me exquisite needlework, and by workers and peasants with more gifts. All the prominent citizens are present. I can only hope my speech made them feel that all their trouble and kindness was worthwhile. I used no notes, spoke straight from the heart, if you know what I mean. Arrived back at Nicosia, very tired but very happy."

In four days, apart from the Congress, he had spoken in 25 towns and villages and met people, Greek and Turk, from all sections.

6. PENDANT

In October 1955 after the appointment of Field Marshal Sir John Harding as Governor of Cyprus, Pollitt wrote[6] "Those who describe this appointment as 'an act of war' are quite right. Harding has stated his absolute determination to restore law and order and compared the situation in Cyprus with that in Malaya and Kenya. The British imperialists intend to transform Cyprus into a military base ... since 1878 their contribution to development of the island has been practically nil, but the moment it became clear that the Egyptian people were no longer prepared to tolerate British occupation, millions of British money has been poured into Cyprus to construct aerodromes, military camps and headquarters, submarine bases."

In December, Harding ordered the banning of A.K.E.L.—which had denounced terrorism and called for united open mass struggle—and the arrest of its leaders. Pollitt called for mass protest in Britain against "this most desperate and shameful step".

In 1956 the British exiled Makarios. In 1959 he returned in triumph, in 1960 he became President of the Republic of Cyprus.

CHAPTER 28

THE C.P.S.U. 20th CONGRESS

1. Previous C.P.S.U. Congresses.   2. The death of Stalin.   3. The 20th Congress.   4. For a balanced view on the Soviet Union.

1. Previous C.P.S.U. congresses.

Pollitt was steadfast in the view that the success of socialism in the Soviet Union and that country's consequent role as a leading world power were vital to the future of the working class everywhere. He followed with close attention developments of Soviet policy and the proceedings of C.P.S.U. Congresses. He was present at the 15th and 16th Congresses, which recorded decisive advances in socialist construction and collective agriculture, and the political defeat of opponents of the general line.[1] He was not at the next two, but spoke in October 1952 at the 19th Congress, the first to be held after the war and the last during Stalin's life.

The 19th Congress was held in the Great Hall of the Kremlin. Pollitt recalled that the 3rd Congress of the Communist International had met in this hall, and noted that the removal of the ornate decoration, then so prominent, had revealed a new dignity and beauty in the lines of its structure. In the galaxy of Communist leaders present from 44 countries all over the world, were such famous veterans of the Communist International as Stalin and Molotov from the U.S.S.R., Liu Shao-chi from China, Gottwald from Czechoslovakia, Rakosi from Hungary, Pieck from Germany, Thorez from France, Pasionaria from Spain, Pollitt from Britain.

The discussions on the political report, the Five-Year Plan and the new Party Rules, were summed up by Pollitt as "a landmark in triumphant Soviet progress, decisions which would change the face of the Soviet Union, usher in a new era of Communist construction, a turning point in history".[2]

When all other business had been dealt with, Stalin spoke. He was brief, his speech was directed to the delegates from fraternal parties and concluded:

"Formerly the bourgeoisie championed bourgeois democratic freedoms and in doing so created for itself popularity among the people. Now, gone is the 'freedom of the individual', the rights of the individual now are recognised only in the case of those who have capital, while all other citizens are regarded as human raw material fit only for exploitation. The principle of equality of people and nations has been trampled underfoot;

it has been replaced by the principle of full rights for the exploiting minority and no rights for the exploited majority of citizens. The banner of bourgeois democratic freedoms has been thrown overboard. You, representatives of the Communist and democratic parties, will have to pick up this banner and carry it forward if you wish to rally around yourselves the majority of the people. There is no one else to pick it up.

"Formerly the bourgeoisie was considered the head of the nation, it championed the rights and independence of the nation. Now, the bourgeoisie sells the rights and independence of the nation for dollars. The banner of national independence and national sovereignty has been thrown overboard. You, representatives of the Communist and democratic parties will have to pick up this banner and carry it forward if you wish to be patriots of your country, if you wish to become the leading force of the nation. There is no one else to pick it up.

"That is how matters stand at present."[3]

In reporting this speech,[4] Pollitt said, "Every sentence and thought was not merely perfectly phrased, but was delivered with a tremendous confidence that made everyone present feel stronger and happier because it betokened such a profound sense of international solidarity, and how all Communist Parties the world over helped each other. When Comrade Stalin ended with the slogan 'Long Live Peace Between the Nations of the World!' 'Down with the Warmongers!' there was a spontaneous outburst of cheering that moved everybody who took part in it. There can be no doubt that Stalin evokes something in every Communist that makes you feel as if you could move mountains and no finer theme could have been chosen for this closing stage of the 19th Congress."

2. The death of Stalin.

Joseph Stalin, Chairman of the Council of Ministers of the Soviet Union and Secretary of the Central Committee of the C.P.S.U., died on March 5, 1953 at 9.50 p.m. Moscow time, after a severe illness. He was aged 73 years and 4 months. Pollitt and Peter Kerrigan took turns in the Guard of Honour in the House of Trade Unions, where one and a half million people passed before the bier. The funeral was on March 8 in the Red Square.[5]

At a memorial meeting in London Pollitt, in an account of Stalin's life and achievements[6], included some brief quotations which he felt were particularly appropriate to the occasion.[7]

1904: "For the victory of the proletariat the uniting of all workers *without distinction of nationality* is necessary."

1905: "What is scientific socialism *without the working-class movement?* A compass, which if left unused will only grow rusty and then will have to be thrown overboard. What is the working class movement without scientific socialism? A ship without a compass, which will reach the other shore in any case, but would reach it much sooner and with less danger if it had a compass. Combine the two and you will get a splendid vessel which will speed straight towards the other shore and reach its haven unharmed."

1935: "Millions of working people, workers and peasants, labour, live and struggle. Who can doubt that . . . these people accumulate vast practical experience? . . . Hence we leaders of the Party and the Government must not only teach the workers, but also learn from them."

1935: "The indisputable successes of socialism on the construction front . . . demonstrated that the proletariat *can* successfully govern the country *without* the bourgeoisie and *against* the bourgeoisie; it *can* successfully direct the whole of the national economy *without* the bourgeoisie and *against* the bourgeoisie; it *can* successfully build socialism in spite of capitalist encirclement."

1941, July 3: "History shows that there are no invincible armies and never have been." The fascist armies "can be smashed as were the armies of Napoleon and Wilhelm."

1945, at the Victory Celebration: "I propose a toast for simple, ordinary, modest people, those who kept our great State machine going in all branches of science, national economy and military affairs. There are very many of them, tens of millions of people. They are modest people. Nobody writes anything about them. They have no titles and few of them hold ranks. But they are people who support us as the base supports the summit. I drink to the health of these people—our respected comrades."

1951, in an interview with Emil Ludwig, a German writer: "Marxism in no way denies the role played by outstanding personalities or the fact that man makes history . . . But men do not make history according to some fantastic ideas that come into their heads ready made. Each new generation finds itself in the presence of determined conditions which existed when this generation was born. And the 'great men' are only great in so far as they know accurately these conditions and how to modify them."

3. THE 20TH CONGRESS.

After Stalin's death Malenkov became Prime Minister. In June, Beria, the Security Chief, was arrested; in September Khrushchev became First Secretary of the C.P.S.U. Early in 1954 a Commission of Investigation headed by Pospelov enquired into security activities under Stalin. Following its discoveries of many injustices and abuses, numbers wrongfully convicted were released and rehabilitated. In February 1955 Bulganin became Prime Minister. These events heightened world interest in the 20th Congress in February 1956.

Pollitt attended all the open sessions, but not the closed session. The two major reports were by Khrushchev on the political situation, and by

Bulganin on the Sixth Five-Year Plan. On the Moscow radio, Pollitt answered questions on his impressions.[8] He noted that the tremendous confidence in the future was based on the past achievements including full employment, no slumps, and a stable cost of living. Khrushchev had most convincingly shown the Soviet desire for peace and the possibility of peaceful co-existence; war was no longer inevitable if the peoples used their power to prevent it. He welcomed the forthcoming visit of Khrushchev and Bulganin to Britain as a strengthening of peaceful relations and trade.

Pollitt's report to the C.P.G.B. members[9] focused on the constructive policies decided by the Congress—the concepts of peaceful co-existence, "war is not inevitable"; the possibility of new forms of transition to socialism, in some countries peaceful transition; the greatest plan ever known for continued advance by the Soviet people in the economic, political and cultural spheres; the "resolute sweeping aside of everything outmoded and hindering advance".

It was now an indisputable fact, which capitalism had been powerless to prevent, that socialism had emerged from within the bounds of one country and become a world system. Two opposite world economic systems, the capitalist and the socialist, developing according to different laws and in opposite directions, the sphere of capitalist exploitation contracting and socialism's position expanding—what new tremendous strength the world Labour movement could draw from this. After outlining the significance of the Five Year Plan, he quoted Khrushchev; "No one can intimidate us or compel us to renounce the defence of peace, democracy and socialism. We march forward on the path charted by Lenin. Hundreds of millions of men and women inspired by the ideas of a just social system, of democracy and socialism, are rallying around us and our friends. Under the banner of Marxism-Leninism the Communist Party of the Soviet Union will lead the Soviet people to the triumph of Communism." These were the things on which attention should be concentrated; they were "the background on which the cult of the individual should be considered".

At this stage Pollitt was aware only of the references to "the cult" in Khrushchev's political report. None of the foreign delegates had been invited to the closed session[10] at which what was known as Khrushchev's "secret speech" was made, nor had they been informed of what transpired there.

In March the capitalist press began printing sensational reports of "revelations of the crimes of Stalin". Most Communists gave little or no credence to these reports, for the capitalist press had continually lied and slandered the Soviets ever since they won power in 1917. But during March information from Moscow made clear that Stalin had made serious theoretical and political errors and that under his direction the Party Rules and Soviet law had been continually violated.

4. For a balanced view on the Soviet Union.

In articles and speeches[11] Pollitt consistently, and without any attempt to minimise or excuse, recognised that the exposure of Stalin's mistakes and his responsibility for abuses, had come as an unexpected shock to the whole C.P.G.B. and to other Communist Parties. He strove "for a balanced view, for an understanding of what has happened, for the defeat of the attempts by the enemies of socialism to take advantage of the situation."

The depth of the shock and concern arose from the esteem in which Stalin was held for his fight for the socialist industrialisation of the Soviet Union and the collectivisation of its agriculture, for the carrying through of the first two Five-Year Plans in a way which laid the basis of victory over fascism. It was during these difficult years of intense strain that Stalin began the denial of collective leadership which hardened into a system of personal power. This, accompanied by his theory of the intensification of the class struggle after the workers' victory over capitalists and landlords in a socialist country, led "to major mistakes".

With the system of personal power and the accompanying "cult of the individual", Stalin "placed himself above the Party, the Government and the people". He did not call full, regular meetings of the Central Committee; there were only meetings of groups of members working in separate departments. The Party Rules were violated, the Party's role belittled, the "cult" led to the stultification of intellectual life and the absence of independent thought and creative work.

The theory of the intensification of the class struggle was put forward in a one-sided way by Stalin. It is true that where the people win political power the old ruling class fights back harder than ever and that world reaction tries to destroy the new power. The other side is that the building of socialism brings new opportunities to win allies, within the country and internationally. Stalin's one-sided view led him to a false outlook of dependence on the security forces, instead of on the people. Hence in his last twenty years, the security forces operated above the Party and the Government, and abused their power. "We are all deeply shocked to learn that many who were represented as traitors to the people's cause were victims of deliberately organised violations of justice, and were in fact devoted Communists."

Other mistakes of Stalin having serious consequences were in agricultural policy, the failure to heed timely warnings of Hitler's attack in 1941, the failure to settle differences with Yugoslavia by fraternal discussion in 1948. On the latter issue the C.P.G.B. was misled by evidence later stated to be fabricated, "We now withdraw our attacks on Tito and Yugoslavia."

The shock of the disclosures was emotional as well as political, and the wound went deep. Pollitt recorded as a political weakness the fact that at every meeting to hear a report on the 20th Congress he had felt that "the principal aims of this historic Congress have not been listened to, understood, or their significance for the working people of the world realised", because attention focused on the past role of Stalin. "To get a balanced view was not easy, but it was necessary, for we are above all a fighting Party aiming at ending Tory rule and helping the British people advance along the road to socialism."

Enemies of Communism claimed that the disclosures meant that all they had said about the Soviet Union was true and all the Communists had said was false. But, said Pollitt, the facts showed that the Soviet Union had established the socialist system and proved it superior to the capitalist system, and that "whatever the weaknesses and mistakes, the basic Marxist principles have been proved correct and confirmed again and again. In condemning errors and abuses we must never forget that they occurred within the framework of socialist advance".

To such questions as "How could it happen?", "What were other Party leaders doing?", Pollitt replied that only the Soviet comrades could give a full answer, but he drew attention to the circumstances in which the historic task, against almost unbelievable odds, of building socialism had been undertaken by the Soviet Communists. "They came under the bitter fire of the whole of world capitalism, and the former ruling classes of their own country. Threats, blackmail, economic boycott, continuous plots, war itself—nothing was too grim or ruthless for world reaction. The Soviet people, Government and Party had to steel themselves to beat back these ferocious attacks, and a degree of bitterness and ruthlessness, not their choice but imposed by world reaction, became necessary, for without it the revolution could not have survived." Then came the rise of fascism, Hitler's aggression in Spain, a dress rehearsal for the Second World War, till it looked in 1939 as though Hitler would stride roughshod over the whole world. "This does not excuse what Stalin's mistakes resulted in, because Lenin faced similar problems but always preserved Party democratic practices and collective leadership. But it helps to explain how it could have happened."

"Stalin's prestige in the eyes of the people was such that any fight against his wrong methods would have divided the nation, such a division at critical moments could have proved fatal. It may be judged that other Soviet leaders regarded it as their duty to preserve Party unity and rally the people behind the Party's correct general line to defeat fascism and so lay the basis for the positive development opened by the 20th Congress."

While dealing with the Stalin issue, Pollitt also indicated that the C.P.G.B. could gain from the discussion generated by the 20th Congress, and could strengthen itself, particularly in the field of theory. In its concern with immediate problems the Party was apt to deal insufficiently with underlying questions of principle. Much had yet to be done in applying Marxism to British problems, he suggested more study of the democratic and labour movements, more thought on the transition from the present political situation to one where a People's Government could be elected.

At the C.P.G.B. Congress in April 1956, Pollitt, in addition to his political report, gave in private session a report on the 20th Congress. After searching questions, it was unanimously accepted.

CHAPTER 29

PARTY CHAIRMAN

1. *The 24th Congress of the C.P.G.B.*   2. *People's China.*   3. *Hungary, 1956.*   4. *C.P.G.B. Special Congress, 1957.*   5. *Old friends.*   6. *Health, 1953–1958.*   7. *Vision of the future.*   8. *A talk with Ho Chi Min.*

1. THE 24TH CONGRESS OF THE C.P.G.B.

At the C.P.G.B. 24th National Congress in March 1956 Pollitt's political report, in addition to the presentation of policy, dealt more searchingly than ever before with the unsolved problem of the small size of the Party.

The Party's undoubted influence resulted mainly from the activity of a comparative few able to influence the decisions of shop stewards committees and trade unions, rather than from public activity conducted by the Party itself. The small number of members was usually regarded as inevitable and led to activity being restricted to what could be done through other organisations, instead of popularising the idea of a mass political party seeking to lead the working class to socialism.

"This vicious circle", said Pollitt, "can only be broken by a great increase in our work in the factories." The Tories did not fear opposition limited to Parliament, they did fear mass movement of the working class. That knowledge should inspire Communists to bring about a great change of outlook in the factories, where the daily clash of ideas takes place, and where the workers feel their power and can organise it. The factories are at the heart of the immediate struggles, and also of the advance to socialism. Communists should give leadership on the daily issues and also open up thoughts in the workers' minds about what socialism is and how to achieve it. The more the Party grows in the factories the greater possibilities of increasing electoral support. Millions will not regard the Party as a political force unless it expresses its policy in the local Councils and in Parliament.[1]

The National Congress normally imposed a strain upon the General Secretary; this time it was intensified by the issues arising from the 20th Congress of the C.P.S.U. Pollitt was far too human a person to regard the Stalin disclosures with personal detachment, they were as painful for him as for thousands of other responsible Communists, and he was fully aware that they were giving rise to new and complex problems for the Party.

Immediately following the Congress, he showed visible signs of physical exhaustion. On April 25 he experienced a loss of ability to read following a haemorrhage behind the eyes. The medical advice was imperative—immediate rest. So, being in his 66th year, he felt it in the best interests of the Party to tender his resignation from the post of General Secretary, but once his health was restored he would gladly fulfil any responsibilities entrusted to him by the Executive Committee.

The Executive reluctantly agreed to accept the resignation[2] and recorded deepest appreciation and warm thanks for his outstanding leadership. It sent best wishes for his speedy recovery and asked him to continue to play a major role in the leadership of the Party as its Chairman, a member of the Political Committee, and one of its principal public spokesmen. The comrade elected as the new General Secretary was John Gollan.

In the middle of May, Pollitt embarked on the "Batory" once more, for a complete rest. He returned much better, and on June 25 wrote that his "sight was improved, but not fully restored". Not until July 21 could he say he was "able to read for the first time since April 25". In mid-August he was back at work in the Party Centre, and cracked "the obituaries were a bit exaggerated".

From the health angle the principal gain for Pollitt was the relief from the daily pressure on so many matters to which the General Secretary was inevitably exposed. He still had a regular schedule—the Political Committee every Thursday morning, the Chairmanship of the Executive Committee meeting—a two-day affair every second month.

The repercussions of the 20th Congress continued, rising to a crisis following the events in Hungary in October 1956. During this period the major responsiblity for policy was, of course, that of the new general secretary, John Gollan; but Pollitt continued to be one of the collective leadership and a popular spokesman of the Party.

2. PEOPLE'S CHINA.

In September 1956 Pollitt with William Gallacher and George Caborn respresented the C.P.G.B. at the 8th Congress of the C.P. of China, the first Congress since the liberation. It represented 10,700,000 members organised in half-a-million branches. At the foundation congress in 1921 twelve delegates had represented 57 members. Pollitt was among the delegates from 56 fraternal parties welcomed by Mao Tse-tung and Liu Shao-chi with the toast of "International Communist Friendship".

Three major reports dealt with the political situation and the Party's tasks, the proposed new consitution, and the Second Five Year Plan.

In his extensive report back from China Pollitt said that the political keynote was struck by Liu Shao-chi when he said "The establishment of the People's Republic of China signifies the virtual completion of the bourgeois democratic revolution and the beginning of the transition from capitalism to socialism." "This transition would be carried through by hundreds of millions of liberated and organised working people, bringing about, step by step, socialist industrialisation and the socialist transformation of agriculture, handicrafts and commerce, and would take a long time." The political life of the state, said Liu, was based on the fact that "the People's Republic has lifted several hundred million people, hitherto insulted and injured, suffering from cold and hunger, from the position of slaves to that of masters." For the first time in China's long history, the State guaranteed the life and liberty of worker and peasant, honoured their labour, gave women equal status with men. In international affairs it was made clear that China "desires peace and to be allowed to make her full contribution to help make it permanent;" that she stood with the socialist countries and the anti-imperialist movements of Asia, Africa and Latin-America; that the aims of U.S. imperialism are "under the pretext of fighting Communism, to suppress its own people and to interfere in and control the vast areas between the socialist countries and the U.S."

In his fraternal speech Pollitt congratulated the Chinese Communists on "epoch making achievements which have transformed the lives of hundreds of millions of people in China and have contributed to a new world situation." The liberation, the establishment of a government representative of the people, and China's advance on the road to Socialism he described as "one of the greatest events of all times".

This occasion was Pollitt's second visit to China, the first was in 1955 when his tour, recorded in detail in a diary, was cut short by the British general election. His third visit in 1959 on the occasion of the celebration of the tenth anniversary of the liberation enabled him to record great changes. Of the new industrial areas of Shanghai he wrote "a forest of new construction extended as far as the eye could see, thousands of workers were erecting factories, flats, shops, everything needed for communal life based on socialist industry." A new machine building factory at Peng Pu was turning out rolling machines, paper making machines, coke making and foundry equipment. The shipyard had been mechanised. Formerly limited to 50 ton coastal vessels, it was now building river craft of 2,000 and 5,000 tons, ocean going vessels of 8,000 tons, two large train ferries, and even submarines. The record was a 5,000 ton ship built in 5 months and 5 days. Pollitt enjoyed his tea on a newly completed 1,200 ton ship going up the Yangtze for far away Chung-king.

He noted too that the Shanghai plan involved reducing the city population to 3 million by dispersing the other 3 million to productive activities in the surrounding provinces. The new People's Commune at Ma Chiao comprised 10,650 households, 48,500 persons, and grew wheat, rice, rape, cotton, vegetables and dairy produce on its 4,886 hectares. It had workshops, small factories, pumping stations, agricultural equipment, but only six tractors. It provided 326 communal dining rooms, 251 nurseries, 44 kindergartens and 109 schools, junior, primary and middle.

Its seven Health Centres had 70 doctors. It had its own broadcasting and telephone service, library, film and cultural units. Its formation in 1958 was the outcome of five years' experience in co-operative farming. The quantity and quality of production, and the living standards, were rising. Production was organised in 31 brigades, in 7 management areas with a total of 275 production teams. Each peasant received income in cash and kind, according to the work he contributed. The Commune, the Chinese comrades said, was proving superior to previous forms of co-operative farming.

3. Hungary, 1956.

The 1956 events in Hungary may be seen in three phases: after the 20th Congress of the C.P.S.U. prolonged discussion and division in Party and Government; from October 23 to November 3 an outburst of popular discontent and a steady growth of counter-revolutionary activities; then the emergence of counter-revolution into the open and its defeat by the new Kadar government in Hungary with the aid of Soviet troops. Throughout these events Pollitt continued to work for full and frank discussion from which the C.P.G.B. could form a balanced view and emerge politically and ideologically stronger.[3]

He contrasted the developments in Hungary with those in Poland. In both countries discussions following the 20th Congress of the C.P.S.U. had revealed mistakes and abuses, both faced economic difficulties, both experienced a popular upsurge for democratisation. In Poland, following a strike and clashes at Poznan, the Party was united, recognised the legitimacy of the people's complaints, made drastic changes in policy and leadership to put things right and kept in close touch with the workers.

But in Hungary the Party was rent by a struggle between the Rakosi and Nagy groups. When Nagy was for the first time Prime Minister, he went too far in lossening controls and made promises he could not fulfil. This intensified the internal struggle. Rakosi resumed leadership, but after the 20th Congress it became clear he could not face up to what was necessary. His removal in July led to an increasing division in the Party's leading circles, during which no effective fight was made against wrong theories which began to spread among the intellectuals or against the propaganda of hostile elements who exploited genuine grievances for their own ends.

On October 23 a popular demonstration in Budapest took place; some of the demands were to remedy genuine grievances, others were of an anti-Soviet and anti-Jewish character. Simultaneously armed groups seized the radio station, the airport, newspaper and Party offices; in the north-west armed men seized Gyor, set up a "Liberation Centre" and opened the frontier with Austria to admit emigré and reactionary forces. London newspapers[4] wrote of "a revolt plotted for a year", "hundreds of insurgents armed with machine guns, pistols and grenades", "counter-revolution in Hungary".

From the first news of October 23, Pollitt recognised an "extremely serious situation, a temporary setback to our cause". Three facts had to be recognised—the desire of the people to condemn and put an end to official abuses of socialist legality and to extend democracy; that the Party was disorganised and taken by surprise; that well organised and armed counter-revolution had seized its opportunity.

American imperialism, through organisations set up under the 1949 Intelligence Agency Act and the 1951 Mutual Security Act, had spent hundreds of millions of dollars on propaganda, military training of emigrés and refugees, subversion and sabotage against the socialist countries, with aims clearly stated in responsible capitalist newspapers. The *Sunday Times*[5] described military training for "specialised" duties; the *Manchester Guardian*[6] reported political training "of the new élite that will take over the People's Democracies upon their 'liberation' ". The *New York Times*[7] quoted General Lucius Clay: "The way to bring peace is to produce revolutions in the countries behind the Iron Curtain." From West Germany, Radio "Free Europe", staffed by emigrés under U.S. control, continuously broadcast incitement to subversion and sabotage; pro-fascist and extreme ring-wing para-military formations of emigrés were held ready for action. October was chosen because the reaction felt that it had gained enough ground to take advantage of popular discontent, hoped also for revolt in Poland, and calculated that the differences between Britain and France and the Soviet Union over the Suez Canal would deepen.

After October 23 the Nagy Government moved rapidly from an equivocal position, through one concession after another to the reaction, to open association with counter-revolution. Armed bands fortified their position in the heart of Budapest, Nagy made no effort to mobilise the workers, called in the Soviet troops, then asked them to withdraw, while the reaction inflamed nationalist feeling. He allowed the public emergence of anti-socialist, anti-Soviet and pro-fascist organisations, brought more right-wingers into his government, and proposed that Hungary withdraw from the Warsaw Pact. On November 1st four Communist Ministers left Nagy and formed a new, revolutionary government.

On November 3, with the Soviet troops gone, the counter-revolution threw off its mask. Mindzenty, Cardinal, Prince Primate, recognised leader of reaction, broadcast a political appeal for the end of socialist and popular power, the restoration of capitalism and landlordism, and Western intervention. All over the country extremist gangs began a white terror against communists and trade unionists. A fascist group seized the office of the Foreign Ministry.

On November 4, Kadar, Prime Minister of the Revolutionary Workers and Peasants Government, announced its programme for the defence and further advance of socialism, called the organised workers into action and asked the Soviet troops for aid against the counter-revolution. With tranquillity restored, the Kadar Government put an end to the abuses, extended democracy, and resumed the advance to socialism.

Throughout these events Pollitt did all he could to promote well-informed discussion. In the chair at the C.P.G.B. Executive meetings, including an enlarged session attended by seventy leading comrades, he facilitated the expression of all viewpoints. The capitalist press and radio spoke of a fight for freedom by Hungarian patriots, sought to spread dissension within the C.P., and to rouse public prejudice against it.

At public meetings some of the most frequent questions Pollitt dealt with included:

Q: Why were Soviet troops in Hungary at all?
H.P: From 1945 to 1955, by agreement with the Western Powers until the Potsdam Agreement was broken by the formation of N.A.T.O. and Western German re-armament. From then on under the Warsaw Pact, the mutual security measure of the socialist countries in reply to N.A.T.O.
Q: Why don't the Russians leave Hungary to settle its own affairs?
H.P: For the Soviet troops to leave at this time would mean abandoning the Hungarian workers and peasants to the armed Hungarian reaction acting with political and military support from Western imperialism. Experience in Greece has shown the result of such a combination—a fascist dictatorship and a militarised regime. The Soviet intervention has not only saved Hungary from fascism, but has also saved Europe from the menace of a new base for aggressive fascism and imperialism being set up in its very heart.

4. C.P.G.B. Special Congress, 1957.

These events in Hungary intensified controversy arising from the Stalin disclosures, the Party lost 7,000 members, a fifth of its total.[8] Most members wanted self-critical examination of how the violations of socialist legality had come about and to ensure the prevention of their recurrence, but some, in their desire to defend the socialist achievements of the Soviet Union, were unwilling to admit the seriousness of the abuses; others saw the abuses as the main issue and thought them inherent in the Soviet system. It was alleged that C.P.G.B. leaders had known of the violations and had concealed them. Proposals were made for basic changes in the Party's attitude of support for the socialist countries, in its programme and to abandon its Marxist principle of organisation, democratic centralism. A Special Congress in April 1957 had before it documents on policy, programme and inner-Party democracy which, prepared after Party-wide discussion, gave full scope for controversy.

The Political Report was made by John Gollan and, for the first time since 1925, Pollitt was Congress Chairman. To steer 500 delegates through four days intense discussion is always an exacting task, needing a strong sense of fair play, a combination of tact, firmness and a thorough knowledge of procedure. On this occasion the tense political atmosphere made the Chairman's task even more onerous than usual, and the capitalist press were there in force to make the most of any division.

In the outcome, much of the discontent was expressed in emotional terms. One delegate, a shop steward, wanted "a different front bench" and a "British party with a British policy"; another, a well-known professor, asked with vehemence, "Is it not the truth that the leadership knew what was going on and kept quiet?" When a political case was made for a Minority Report on party democracy, it got 23 votes, with 472 for the Majority Report, with 15 abstentions. An appeal against expulsion was rejected by 486 votes to 31, with 11 abstentions.[9]

As chairman, Pollitt's task was to ensure the correct conduct of the debate, and this he did scrupulously. On several occasions tempers rose: he was always calm. One delegate recollected, "He called delegates by name to come and make their point. When an E.C. member ignored the red light, Pollitt said 'Please stop, you have exceeded your time'. In a heated discussion, one speaker was insulted by a delegate on the floor. Harry intervened with 'Such things should not be said'. There was never any challenge to his ruling, everyone acknowledged his authority and fairness."[10]

5. Old Friends

Alice Jones

One of Pollitt's valued possessions was a reproduction of a Walter Crane cartoon, a print from a wood block in reddish brown ink. It had belonged to Alice Jones, who got it at a rally of the Social Democratic Federation at which Walter Crane was present and autographed the copy for her, in addition to the printed signature. She later gave it to her daughter, Alice Loveman, and her husband, and when they suggested Harry for whom she had great affection might like to have it, she readily agreed. Harry was delighted to receive it, had it framed in oak, and hung on his office wall. The design showed a winged female figure, "Freedom", pointing through an archway to a pleasant prospect of countryside with river and hill illuminated by the rays of a rising sun, inscribed "Co-operative Commonwealth". Before her stands a worker, child on shoulder and wife by his side gazing through the archway. A pendant ribbon on the left is inscribed "Socialism—The World for the Workers and the Fullness Thereof".

Alice Jones,[11] born in Deptford on January 1, 1876, went to work at the age of 12; at 19 she joined the Social Democratic Federation, sold *Justice* and *Merrie England,* worked with H. M. Hyndman and Harry Quelch, once sat on the platform with Karl Marx's daughter Eleanor. At 23 she met

Tom Mann at a London meeting where he spoke in support of the Chicago martyrs. She joined the Labour Choir formed by Elsie Mann. In 1912 she was in the British Socialist Party. She supported the Russian socialist revolution from the start, was active in the "Hands Off Russia" campaign, formed a local Communist League which merged with the Communist Party on its foundation in 1920. In the General Strike of 1926 she was a delegate to the Lewisham Council of Action. In the years of mass unemployment she defended the interests of the unemployed on several Labour Exchange Committees, also organising a meal for unemployed who took part in the First of May marches to Hyde Park. Associated with the First of May Committee since before the 1914 war, she later was responsible for arrangements for caring for children while the demonstration was in progress, providing a maypole, games, entertainment and refreshment. In 1936 she was arrested while helping to block the road to a fascist march in South-east London. At 75 she lost the use of her right hand due to a shock at the death of her youngest son. She at once set about learning to write with her left, entered an essay competition run by the London Communist Party and won honourable mention with her essay on Dimitrov. She had married at 19 Jimmy Jones, a socialist printing worker at the Twentieth Century Press at Clerkenwell Green, where *Justice* and later Lenin's *Iskra* were printed, in the building now named Marx House. They had two boys and four girls, a happy family, all associated with her political ideas; four of them joined the Communist Party.

Pollitt knew her well and admired her spirit, energy, directness and organising ability. He would always seek her out for a handshake on May Day, and sent a warm letter of congratulation on her 80th birthday. Alice Jones outlived Pollitt, and died on October 20, 1965, aged 89 years 10 months.

Wilhelm Pieck

Wilhelm Pieck, President of the German Democratic Republic, veteran of the Communist International, celebrated his eightieth birthday on January 3 1956, and personally invited Pollitt to attend. The evening of the 2nd saw a great torchlight march past of the youth of Berlin, the President standing for several hours to take their salute. At 7 a.m. on the morning of the 3rd., delegations from organisations all over the Republic and from twenty other countries began to stream through the Presidential House to give greetings and receive a smile, a handshake and a few words. Among them Pollitt met many old friends, Voroshilov and Stassova from the Soviet Union, Pasionaria from Spain, Kuusinen from Finland, Chu Teh from China, Koplenig from Austria and Marcel Cachin from France. The reception continued all day till at 6 p.m., a celebration meeting began in the National Opera House, Pollitt on the Presidium. The highlight was Cachin's speech; "this frail veteran of 86 years of age brought the entire audience to its feet as he described the recent electoral advance of the Communist Party of France—the best birthday present Wilhelm Pieck could have."[12]

6. HEALTH, 1953–1958.

In November 1953 came a deterioration in Pollitt's health; he had to wear the corset all through his Indian tour, "the hardest time of my life—heat, mosquitos, mouth ulcers, nearly killed with work, and the rubbing of the corset skinning my tummy."[13] In July 1954 he was again in a Soviet clinic, and again a rigorous diet and curative exercises produced in two weeks "a change almost beyond recognition; blood pressure down to normal, no bags under the eyes, no need for sleeping tablets or concoctions to rub into neck or spine. The corset taken away. I sleep on a wooden plank bed, have gone from 40 cigarettes a day to 8; don't see and don't want strong drink. I do all the doctors order, never was there a more disciplined patient—perhaps because there's nothing else to do."[14]

After nine weeks he was home again, but while he realised the causes for the improvement in his condition, he did not change his habits. "You can't teach an old dog new tricks", he said,[15] and went on doing three men's work. From then on it was a repetition of overwork, return of pain and high blood pressure, treatment with good results gradually wearing off. In May 1956, complete exhaustion and a haemorrhage behind the eyes led to temporary loss of vision. In April 1957 his spine was "as bad as ever."[16] Another spell in a Soviet clinic was not so successful, pneumonia developed. On return to London he was again in hospital, and in August was "reconciled to the fact that they can no nothing for my left leg; will have to grin and bear it". For some months he did ease up, and did no speaking until he delivered the Marx Memorial Lecture in 1958. He got a great reception, but the next morning sustained a minor stroke. He was taken at once to hospital. He made a rapid recovery but had to regularly take a drug to reduce blood pressure. A side effect was to cause mental depression.[17]

7. VISION OF THE FUTURE.

In January 1959 Pollitt attended the 21st Congress of the C.P.S.U., called to discuss one major question—the Soviet long-term plans for future economic and social development, presented by Khrushchev in a six-hour report. Unprecedented increases in production, living standards and cultural advance, to be achieved not by longer or more intense labour, but by applying science and technology, meant, Khrushchev declared, that the Soviet Union would outstrip the capitalist countries both in total production and in production per head of the population. Pollitt noted Mikoyan's remark that the report's title suggested a dry, economic subject, but "it sounded like a magnificent symphony of Communist construction," and Kuusinen's that "the plans were multi-stage political rockets that will with great precision put our country into the Communist orbit."[18]

In reporting on this Congress Pollitt expressed his confidence that the quantitative increases planned meant the beginning of qualitative advance from socialism to communism. The application of science to production, while increasing productivity, demanded new skills of hand and of brain. Higher standards of education and personal creative initiative were essential. The elimination of differences between manual and mental labour was beginning. The application of scientific research, machines and electrification in agriculture, the modernisation of farm and village life would assure the nation of adequate food supplies and begin the elimination of differences between town and countryside.

A sign of the continuous advance of Soviet democracy was the active interest of the people in the pre-congress discussions: 70 million took part; 7 million spoke in meetings; 670,000 made proposals; press and radio received 650,000 letters. In the state and municipal departments, alongside the officials. voluntary organisations and workers' delegates were undertaking increasing responsibilities in administration and control.

The Communist construction going forward in the Soviet Union would Khrushchev had emphasised further advance the world influence it had gained by being the first to blaze the trail to socialism and becoming one of the most powerful countries in the world. Fulfilment of the plans would, in Khrushchev's words, "raise the Soviet Union to such heights that nobody will have any doubts left of the great advantages possessed by communism over moribund capitalism".

The magnificent perspectives opening out for the Soviet people enhanced the significance of Khrushchev's concluding call, "Long Live World Peace" and of the Congress declaration that "a real possibility of excluding world war from the life of society will take shape, even while capitalism still exists in some parts of the world. This will be socialism's inestimable contribution to man's history, the realisation of mankind's most cherished hope and aspiration."

Recalling that H. G. Wells had once described Lenin as "the dreamer in the Kremlin", Pollitt added, "Now Lenin's dreams are coming true."[19]

8. A TALK WITH HO CHI MIN.

In October 1959, during a visit to China, Pollitt had a talk with Ho Chi Min.[20] They were old friends, having first met at the Third Congress of the Communist International.

Ho described the situation in the Democratic Republic of Vietnam as "steadily improving". The land reform was being carried through, 20 per cent of the peasants were in co-operatives, many more in Mutual Aid Societies. There was enough food and no need to import rice. The remaining difficulties were being overcome with help from the Soviet Union and other socialist countries. But in the South things were very bad, there was a reign of terror, production was low, the peasants were with the Communists on the land question, peasants and bourgeoisie were dissatisfied with the U.S. intervention. The general tasks of the Communist Party were to build up the economy in the North, to work for re-unification, and the honouring of the Geneva agreements, and to oppose the U.S. dominated South-East Asia Treaty Organisation.

In Laos things were critical. U.S. intervention sought to break up the agreement between Pathet Lao, the peoples front, and the Royal Government, and to make Laos a military base for a general offensive in Indo-China. Pathet Lao had great influence, it fought for the Geneva Agreements, against U.S. penetration, and wanted friendly relations with the Royal Government. Vietnam had not sent arms to Laos.

There was need for international observers, journalists and peace supporters, to report objectively in Vietnam and Laos.

CHAPTER 30

AUSTRALASIA—1960

*1. The invitation. 2. New Zealand. 3. New South Wales.
4. Queensland. 5. Victoria. 6. Sydney. 7. Last voyage.
8. Last Tributes.*

1. THE INVITATION.

In March 1960 Pollitt accepted an invitation from the Communist Party of Australia to tour that country. The dates also enabled him to attend the Conference of the Communist Party of New Zealand.

The evening of April 8 saw a small gathering of his family, including Ella, who had come from Stockport, and close friends, to wish him good travelling and success. There was plenty of laughter and jokes, but also an unspoken apprehension. When Ella sang at his request the songs she had sung so often when they were young, tears came to his eyes and hers. Everyone present knew that his decision to go was an act of international solidarity, that he had put aside considerations of his own health and wellbeing, and that he would give all he had to inspire every meeting, every gathering and every individual he met with understanding, determination and confidence in the victory of socialism and the communist cause.[1]

He had long wanted to see Australia, in whose working people he saw a new force of great importance to the international labour movement. He desired to make his contribution to deepen solidarity between the two parties.

His flight to New Zealand was interrupted by a stop at Sydney on April 11, and he was warmly greeted by a group of comrades headed by L. L. Sharkey and Dick Dixon, General Secretary and President of the Communist Party of Australia.[2] They recalled earlier meetings and talked about arrangements for his tour. Interviewed by *Tribune*, the C.P.A. paper, Pollitt said his visit "was the fulfilment of a life's desire and he hoped to learn a great deal". Asked about Britain, he said that the public were "greatly interested in the approaching Summit talks and the Soviet Union's disarmament proposals". After a night's sleep the flight continued to Auckland.

2. NEW ZEALAND.[3]

Arriving in Auckland on the 12th., Pollitt found that the other fraternal delegates to the Communist Party Conference were Chen Yu from

People's China and L. Aarons from Australia. An Australian delegate was usual, but it was the first time that Britain or People's China had been represented. A delegate from the German Democratic Republic had been refused a visa.

The Conference opened on the 14th, the 42 delegates including 4 women. Pollitt and the other fraternal delegates were received with enthusiasm and elected to the Presidium. Unauthorised transmitting devices were discovered and removed on the first and also on the second days. In his speech, Pollitt dealt with the problems facing capitalism in Britain, and described the Prime Minister, Harold MacMillan, as a "capable, centre-of-the-road politician" who advocated that Tory policy should follow a middle way between two extremes, socialism and reactionary capitalism, both unacceptable to the British people. But under his policy the rate of exploitation of the workers was higher than ever, most married women now went to work, and the basic industries on which Britain's prosperity had been built—coal, shipbuilding and textiles—were in permanent crisis. MacMillan recognised "a wind of change", but it was more like a tornado. On the main issue before the delegates, their attitude to the New Zealand Labour Party, he would only remind them that it would be a great mistake to regard it as "one homogeneous reactionary mass" or to fail to find means of working together with the rank and file.

A public meeting at the Town Hall followed. It was full in spite of pouring rain. "It was like a Lancashire audience; I had the honours of the longest time, and got to work in the old style. Everyone was delighted." And he got a standing ovation.

The Party Executive gave a dinner for the fraternal delegates at the Grand Hotel. The manager, being amiable, brought round a large box of cigars. The word went round that Harry liked a good cigar, so even the non-smokers took a couple, and he was stocked up for a week.[4]

His public meetings in the South Island were at Dunedin—where the local paper described him as "a 5'5" dynamo"—Port Chalmers, Christchurch and Greymouth. At all of them, and in smaller gatherings, he met many he had known in Britain, particularly Scots, engineers and miners. "I've lost count of how many". He was impressed by the distances, Auckland to Dunedin nearly 1,000 miles, and by the absence of the traditional slum housing and industrial dereliction familiar in Britain. Then back to North Island for meetings in Wellington and nearby Lower Hutt. He was billed to speak at Porirua, but the hall booking was cancelled by the authorities on the grounds that a political meeting could not be allowed on the 25th, Anzac Day.[5]

Before leaving Auckland on the 28th for the 1,100 mile flight to Sydney, he went to see Mrs. McLaurin, whose son Geoff, a volunteer in the International Brigade, had been killed in action in Madrid in December 1936. He took her a bunch of flowers.

He was pleased with his tour, "record attendances and a good press gave the Party a lift".[6] The New Zealand comrades responded to his "eloquence and the political content of what he said. He never dressed-up or watered-down his opinions to suit his audience. He aroused great respect and liking."[7]

3. NEW SOUTH WALES.

On the 28th he was back in Sydney to an enthusiastic welcome at the airport, the crowd included leaders of the Communist Party of Australia and of several trade unions;[8] an interview with the press and TV was on two channels that night. The C.P.A. had arranged a car for him and a comrade to drive and see to his needs. This comrade, H. T. Johnson, known as Johnno, was a "wharfie", the Australian term for docker, released from the job by union request. The choice proved a happy one; Johnno had the human warmth that Pollitt liked, they got on famously.

The C.P.A. had booked hotel rooms, but Pollitt preferred the informality of a private house, so after a couple of days they were fixed up at the home of a Central Committee member, Jack Hughes. The family were away, they had the house to themselves. Johnno got the breakfast; other meals they took out. Each evening Pollitt wrote his notes of the day's events. He did not watch TV, but listened to the news on the radio, particularly B.B.C. overseas at 11 p.m. His favourite spot for a chat and a drink was at the trade union club where he met workers of all trades. On the Friday evening he was a Guest of Honour, along with Soviet trade union delegates at the traditional May Day Festival Ball.

That year, May 1st fell on a Sunday, and Pollitt was the principal guest speaker at the traditional meeting on the Domain, an open ground in Sydney's largest park. He declined to go to the meeting by car, saying that he always "marched with the Party on May Day and would do so now." So he was placed along with Lance Sharkey and J. B. Miles at the head of the Communist contingent, enjoyed the reception he got from the bystanders, waved back, joined in the singing, and generally had a good time. At the Domain a huge crowd was waiting.

Awaiting his turn to speak, Pollitt's mind went back to the first trade unionists who trod this Domain[9]. It was September 4, 1834. A column of heavily shackled men escorted by armed soldiers were marching to the George Street barracks. They had disembarked from the convict ship, *Surrey*, its cells so crowded that no man could lie down full length during the 111 days' journey. Among them were five farm labourers from the village of Tolpuddle, sentenced to transportation for seven years. Their offence? Administering an oath to men joining a trade union. The evidence? Supplied by informers sent by the local magistrates in collusion with the Home Secretary. The circumstances? Their employers after promising to raise their wage of 9s. a week to the County level of 10s., cut it first to 8s., and then to 7s.

From the Sydney barracks they were dispersed to work for farmers whose power over them was despotic. One, James Loveless, was sent to Strathallan, 300 miles south-west of Sydney. He had to walk. The two Standsfields, Thomas the father and John the son, were sent north to Backwater in the Hunter valley; later the father was sent to Williams River. James Brine went to Glendon, also in the Hunter Valley. These three were later held without charge in Newcastle gaol. The fifth man, James Hammett, was "sold for £1 like a slave", and had to walk 400 miles to his master. The sixth Man of Dorset, George Loveless, had been shipped to Tasmania.

But their fellow trade unionists at home had not forgotten them. Agitation for their release went on without pause, petition after petition, demonstration after demonstration. M.Ps. repeatedly raised their case. On March 14 1836 a more enlightened Home Secretary secured them a full pardon.

Two sentences in the relevant correspondence sound a modern note: "The leaders of the Orange Lodges, the Duke of Cumberland and the Duke of Gordon are far more guilty than the labourers, but the law does not reach them, I fear", and "The Duke of Cumberland and Lord Wynford have been doing the same thing only with much more cunning."

Pollitt began his first speech in Australia with a characteristic sentence—"Today all over the world millions have marched to demonstrate their faith in the working class, their desire for a lasting peace, their re-dedication to the struggle under the glorious Red Flag for the abolition for all time of poverty, unemployment and war."

Newcastle

After the speech, Johnno drove a hundred miles north to Newcastle, a centre of steel and coal, the second industrial city of New South Wales, where May Day was traditionally celebrated on the first Monday in May. A colourful procession marched for three miles to the Sports Ground, where there were refreshments, games and athletics. The day wound up by a concert and cabaret show with 400 guests.[10]

Pollitt was one of the thousand marchers who with many trade union banners, forty floats and two bands, were watched by 10,000 people lining the route. It was hot and tiring, but Pollitt refused the offer of a lift, saying he would "march as long as my legs will carry me". The workers on the march liked his spirit, summed up by Johnno as "the gutsiest Pommy I ever met".

It was the largest May Day procession for ten years and the Boilermakers got the award for the largest contingent. Twenty ships' crews were represented among the seamen, who won the award for the best display, with many posters and more than twenty national flags. There were several aspirants, each with appropriate costume and attendants, for the honour of being the May Queen. The crown went to the Water Board employees' candidate. The tactful judges gave two political awards—to the Labour Party for their float; to the Communist Party for their display.

Having enjoyed the day, they returned to Sydney for a few days' relaxation, Pollitt spending time in the homes of several comrades and talking to others at the trade union club or on the beaches.

Wollongong

On the Friday they drove south to another industrial town, Wollongong, also on the coast, J. B. Miles, a member of the Central Committee of the C.P.A. going with them. There was a dinner at the Workers' Club, attendance of 100 had to be limited to invitation so there were many disappointments. It was a representative gathering: the majority of the coalmines on the coast had someone there, and Pollitt found many he had known in Britain.

The evening meeting filled the Town Hall, the biggest hall in the city. In the chair was Steve Quinn, the State organiser of the Boilermakers, who commented: "Harry gave of his very best, his speech, his fantastic memory and his delivery kept the vast audience completely attentive." At that time Britain was one of the seven countries making up the European Free Trade Association as distinct from the six in the European Economic Community. Pollitt began his explanation of this question by remarking, "You have heard the saying that people are at sixes and sevens. Well, that is just what is happening in Europe today."

Next day was devoted to an outing, a dozen carloads of comrades, and a grand picnic on the beach at Kiama, to the south of Wollongong. Then three more days sightseeing and visiting in and around Sydney, with L. L. Sharkey, Jim Healey and others often coming on car trips to scenic spots.

Northern New South Wales

On the 11th, with Joe Bailes and Johnno, Pollitt set off on the 600 mile car journey to Brisbane, going first to Newcastle, where miners, boilermakers and others packed the Wintergarden Theatre to hear him. After calling on Arthur Horner's daughter Joan and her family at their home in Weston, they turned inland and took the New England Highway for 150 miles to Tamworth, where they drove round a sheep station. Another 60 miles brought them to Armidale with its colleges and university. Turning toward the coast, they crossed the New England mountain range "4,500 feet high . . . and very cold" to Bellingen. After giving a short talk at a social gathering organised by the local C.P.A. branch Pollitt expressed a wish to see a dairy factory, and this was arranged for the next morning. The night was spent in a hotel.

After the dairy factory and farm, another 150 miles, this time on the Pacific Highway, brought them to Ballina, a lovely seaside spot, where they dined in a motel and had an early night.

Of this journey Joe Bailes wrote: "Harry loved the miles and miles of sandy beaches, the surf, the bright sunshine, the beauty of the kiddies playing almost naked, the sun-tanned men and women, carefree and happy. When we stopped for a rest, he would be quite wrapped up in what he saw, the blue hills or the golden beaches, and would talk about what socialism would do for the people."

4. QUEENSLAND.

Next morning the 14th, they entered Queensland at Coolangatta, met by the State Secretary of the C.P.A., Ted Bacon, and lunching at a beer garden overlooking a surf beach before completing the remaining 60 miles to Brisbane. There it was hot and sunny, and the comrades had arranged an evening gathering to welcome Pollitt at the Waterside Workers Hall, where he spoke for 40 minutes. "It was a most enthusiastic and lovely night."[11] Among the 300 present was a British migrant, Joyce Slater, who had joined the C.P.G.B. in 1936 in Birmingham after hearing Pollitt call for aid to Republican Spain. She introduced her 16-year old son, Victor, a regular subscriber to the *Daily Worker*. Inspired by Harry's conviction of the coming world-wide triumph of socialism, the Slaters decided on the spot to organise a house meeting for him in their locality, on the west side of Brisbane.

On the 15th, another 70 miles took Pollitt and Johnno to Nambour, the northernmost point of the tour. They went over a comrade's farm in the surrounding country where sugar cane, banana and pineapple were growing. Then inland to Glasshouse Mountain and Crohamhurst Observatory, a centre for the recording of meteorological data. The director, Lennox Walker, and his wife, made Pollitt very welcome, explained the system of daily international contact with other observatories set up by his predecessor, Inigo Jones, who devoted his life to weather forecasting. He also painted in oils, and Pollitt was shown the views of the plateau on which the Observatory stood, painted on the slab walls of the original wooden house.

The next four days were occupied with political functions interspersed by the personal chats, "sometimes visiting old comrades at the back of beyond" which he delighted in. At the Brisbane Trades Hall, the Secretary of the Queensland Trades and Labour Council had arranged a gathering for him to meet leading personalities from the trade unions and the Labour Party. He was the guest of the Miners Federation at Ipswich, some

40 miles from Brisbane, where he spoke to a social gathering, and again found people he had known in Britain. He attended a session of the Queensland State Committee of the C.P.A., and highly approved their decision to re-issue the Party's Queensland paper, commenting "without a regular newspaper you fight with one hand tied behind your back".

The farewell gathering was on the 19th at the house of Alex MacDonald; a hundred people came, and he was presented with a record of "Reedy River". Next day he left by air for Melbourne.

In Queensland Pollitt remarked on the vast stretches of land without buildings. "You travel hour after hour and never see a house." He was also intrigued by the old style Queensland houses, built high off the ground to allow a current of air underneath. The new houses of the affluent were in conventional style with air conditioning.

On this journey Johnno commented, "Harry was a tiger for Party work. It was not that the Party worked him too hard, it was impossible to restrain him. He wanted more meetings. 'I want to talk to people; that's what I came for', he said. I gained the impression that he felt he had not much time left and wanted to put all he had into every minute."

5. Victoria

After the hot sunshine of Brisbane, he found Melbourne "like Manchester, cold and raining". But there was nothing cold about his welcome at the airport or at the evening social in his honour. There was also a press conference. "The boys tried it on and found I wasn't born yesterday." He stayed with Ted Hill, a namesake but no relation of his old friend in England. Provided with a car and a driver, he wrote to Marjorie, "They look after me like a long-lost brother; its very nice to be made such a fuss of."

The highlights of his fifteen days activity in Victoria were a great meeting in the Melbourne Town Hall and a reception at the Trades Hall. He was twice on the TV, first for "a Robin Day type of interview, but he'll get as good as he gives", second for a "Meet the Press" feature.

Melbourne Town Hall claimed to possess the largest organ in the world, but its fame in the international labour movement was due to its association with Tom Mann. On his 80th birthday on April 15, 1936, it flew the Red Flag in tribute to his great work for trade unionism and socialism during his seven years in Australasia. Four years as organiser for the Victoria Labour Party, Tom Mann was also founder and secretary of the Socialist Party of Victoria. Later he was famous all over Australia for his part in the great miners' strike at Broken Hill. In 1908 he wrote in the Melbourne Labour paper, "We avowed ourselves straight out international revolutionary socialists", and Pollitt's great meeting carried on this tradition.

May 24 saw the Town Hall crowded. Pollitt had come at a moment of political tension. On the eve of summit talks an American spy plane had been sent over Soviet territory, where it was promptly forced down. The Soviet demand for an apology and a guarantee of no more such flights was refused by the U.S. President. Pollitt charged the U.S. with wrecking the Summit talks and showed the spy plane flight as part of the American strategy of aggression. He recalled that when Khrushchev and Bulganin came to Britain in a new Soviet cruiser, a British intelligence agent had got himself killed trying to examine it from underneath; the British Prime Minister apologised for the action. Said Pollitt, "What was good enough for the British should be good enough for the Americans." He went on to deal with socialism, saying, "I know of no country with such a glorious future as Australia once the working class has power in its hands . . . We are winning, whatever the capitalist class does, it cannot stop the onward march of humanity." He sat down to an ovation. The resolution called on the Federal Parliament to dissociate Australia from U.S. aggressive policy. The collection was announced as £A 984, and a man in the audience at once made it up to £A 1,000.

Other meetings included a lunch with the staff of the C.P.A's paper *The Guardian*, where Pollitt outlined the story of the restarting of the *Daily Worker* after the wartime banning and bombing, and a miners' meeting followed by a Social—"They were all Scots"—at Monthaggi, 70 miles along the coast.

But though the enthusiastic audiences saw no sign of it, a shadow was falling. He had spells of giddiness, then a haemorrhage behind the eyes, "my glasses are almost useless". He was examined by Dr. Egal White, a Party member, who insisted that he cut down his activities. He reluctantly agreed to cancel meetings at Adelaide and Perth, but refused to cut short his Melbourne fixtures and expressed determination "to do my last few meetings in Sydney, whatever anyone says."[12]

The next Melbourne highlight was a reception at the Trades Hall given by six metal, building and maritime trade unions.

A victory atmosphere pervaded this event. The port employers and the Industrial Court had tried to impose compulsory Sunday labour by suspending dockers who refused to obey orders to do this work and fining the union £500 for supporting them. Two nation-wide stoppages induced the government to think again; a tripartite conference declared Sunday work to be voluntary—a win for militant solidarity.

Prior to his TV session on May 29, Pollitt wrote "there is a lot of interest; I hope to keep my end up". In the course of his remarks he referred to the Communist Party as "an integral part of the Labour movement". This brought from a Federal Labour leader, Mr. Calwell, the assertions that there was an "unbridgeable gulf" between Labour and Communism, and that "Communist ideology is that of world domination".[13] An immediate rebuttal by Pollitt and Hill was not published. An election was in the offing, the Liberals were charging Labour with Communist associations.

Dr. Egal White had understood that Pollitt would not appear at this TV session, and was surprised and alarmed when he did so. He hastened to warn Pollitt that he was "working up for another stroke and would be unlikely to make such a good recovery as he had done earlier". Once more Pollitt agreed to rest, and two days later spoke to 400 seamen, writing to Marjorie, "The doctor would have a fit if he knew". After this, he did relax for two whole days, enjoying the beauties of the coast, Geelong and the surf beaches with a final Social farewell on June 1. On the 3rd he flew back to Sydney.

6. SYDNEY.

At Sydney airport, Johnno was waiting to take him to the C.P.A's permanent political school in a large house on the bank of the Georges River near Minto. He spoke to the students in session, spent time with them informally, then returned to the Hughes house. He went to a meeting of the C.P.A.'s Sydney Committee, and to a cadres' gathering. It was clear he was not well, but he refused the proposal of the C.P.A. leaders that he drop everything, rest for a week, and fly home. He had decided to go by sea, "the four week journey would be an excellent rest, and he would arrive home ready for Party work". He would speak at the Trades Hall on the 8th and cancel other engagements. Three days later, driving round Sydney, his vision became blurred. At the eye hospital the doctors wanted to keep him in, but he refused. He admitted not taking the blood-pressure tablets prescribed for him in England.[14]

On the morning of the Trades Hall meeting he said to Johnno, "Drive me around, anywhere, don't talk, I just want to think." Johnno drove to Newcastle and back. Pollitt, absorbed in thought, made none of his usual comments on the scenery. Back in Sydney in time for the meeting, he was once more his usual jovial self.[15]

It was the last advertised meeting, a crowded hall, Dick Dixon in the chair, Lance Sharkey among those on the platform. There was an ovation for Pollitt when he was introduced, a second when he concluded his speech, a third when the C.P.A. State Chairman, Alf Watt, presented him with a banner of greetings from the C.P.A. to the C.P.G.B. Pollitt spoke "for an hour and a half without notes". His speech punctuated with repeated applause reached its climax with an appeal to non-members to join the C.P.A. "so that in your day and generation the reins of power will be in the hands of the working class. Communists dedicate their lives to the cause of the world's working people. The capitalist interests hate and slander the Communist Party because they are frightened of what we have done and what we can do. The aim of Communism is to bring beauty, colour and dignity into the lives of the people; men and women like you have done marvels in the Soviet Union and People's China. When power is in their hands, the people of Britain and Australia will compete on which will most speedily transform their island into one on which the sun of joy will never set."

He spoke once more at a mass meeting of dockers, then went on to their Federation Office, where he met their officials and those of other unions. The Treasurer, Stan Moran, wrote: "He entertained us with reminiscences of Lenin, Tom Mann, Ben Tillett, Willie Gallacher, and others."

His steamship ticket sent from London now arrived, and departure was fixed for June 20. There were some quiet days of sight-seeing, a 250 mile trip to Canberra, the federal capital, another to the Blue Mountains, many friendly talks, and then the final round of farewells, including an evening at the home of Jim Healey, where many leading trade unionists were present, and one arranged by the Central Committee of the C.P.A. at the home of Bert Chandler.

There was a special meeting of the C.P.A. Political Bureau to hear his impressions and observations. He spoke from notes and undertook to write an article based on his report. He stressed the positive results of his tour, the big public meetings, TV and radio sessions, press interviews, talks with trade union leaders, and so on. He drew attention to the many British migrants who attended his meetings and the possibilities of Party work in this field. He spoke of the derisive and contemptuous way the word "politician" was used by Party members and workers and warned that Communists were "also politicians and could become parliamentarians." He also stressed the significance of work among young people.

Of the tour as a whole Lance Sharkey said it "rendered a high service to the cause of the working class. Everywhere audiences responded to your eloquence in international goodwill, peaceful relations and advance to socialism. Australians will long remember the visit of Harry Pollitt." Dick Dixon wrote: "He became widely known and very popular; the mass media were compelled to recognise him. He acquitted himself impressively in radio and TV interviews, and received extensive press publicity. The tour, successful in every sense, helped to strengthen the bonds between the Communist Parties of Australia and Britain."

All through the tour he wrote frequently to his family. Of his letters Marjorie said, "they breathed happiness and fulfilment in a good job well done, with full recognition for it and good comradeship, a fitting climax to his life's work." His last letter to Jean included a characteristic sentence, "Thank goodness I have paid my way here and in New Zealand, and that's a load off my mind."[16]

In his farewell message to the C.P.A. Pollitt said, "I am sure my visit has been a success and will have done much to draw our Parties and peoples closer together" and expressed his "warm thanks to the General Secretary, President and all comrades of the Communist Party of Australia for the kindness and hospitality I have received during my stay."

7. Last voyage.

On June 20 Pollitt boarded the P. and O. liner *Orion*.[17] The C.P.A., thoughtful to the last, had arranged for Johnno to travel with him to Freemantle, the last Australian port of call on the long journey to England. Many passengers, hearing he was on board, came to speak to him. He was invited one evening to dine at the captain's table, the crew got permission to send representatives to have a talk with him. A cable from Marjorie told him that Brian at Cambridge had gained first class honours in the Economics Tripos Part I. He was so pleased he at once went to the ship's shop and bought for Brian the best available electric shaver. During the stop at Melbourne, C.P.A. comrades, including Dr. Egal White, came aboard. When Pollitt recalled with some disapproval that in a Soviet clinic he had had "the leech treatment", Dr. White said, "Harry, that treatment helped keep you alive the past four years, it thins the blood."

Late in the afternoon of June 24, *Orion* arrived at Port Adelaide and representatives of the C.P.A's State Committee came on board to greet Harry.

The active members of the C.P.A. in South Australia included an engineering worker, Joc Goss, a migrant from London where his sterling qualities had gained him respect and influence in the Communist Party and in the engineering union. He has described[18] the eagerness with which Pollitt's visit was awaited. "I followed with intense interest the reports of his great meetings in Sydney and Melbourne. Pictures of Harry in his characteristic stance revived memories of speeches greeted with thunderous applause in crowded halls that stirred me when a lad of twenty-one and greatly influenced my future life. When I was told that Hindmarsh Town Hall had been booked for him, it was difficult for me, even at 50 years of age, to contain my tremendous excitement. I cannot recall any event I looked forward to with greater anticipation. Harry Pollitt was going to speak in Adelaide!"

The enforced cancellation caused great disappointment, but it was recognised as essential, though it was not known how serious his illness was. The State Committee had arranged a small informal gathering of leading comrades with whom Pollitt could chat if he felt like it: he accepted the invitation. Let Joe Goss continue:

"The great day arrived. We foregathered at the home of a lovable, modest and respected comrade, Dr. David Caust and his wife Tess. A huge fire burned in the grate, the atmosphere was warm and cosy. Harry was due any moment, he and Johnno were coming in a taxi. It pulled up outside, there were voices. The door opened. Harry and Johnno stepped into the room. Harry looked round and extended his hand. When it became my turn to grasp it, he looked at me. 'Well, if it isn't Joe Goss!'

"There were introductions all round. Alan and Jean Finger, Elliott Johnston, Ralph Maddern, Eddie Robertson, Jim Moss and of course,

David and Tess Caust. Harry came over, asked me what I was doing, and we sat down by the fire. After my brief story, he answered my string of questions about comrades in London, members of the A.E.U., and others with whom I grew up in the youth movement.

"Our talk was brought to an end by the announcement that dinner was served. We all took our seats. After a nice meal, with jokes, questions and anecdotes across the table, Harry was asked if he would like to say a few words. He rose to make the last speech he would ever make. 'My compliments to the cook' he said, 'it was a delightful meal. I have enjoyed this visit to your country and have met some wonderful people, people who will soon be among the new rulers of Australia. The world of capitalism is coming to an end, the world of socialism is at hand, the dreams of those who fought throughout the ages for progress and human brotherhood will begin to become reality.'

"He recounted some of his early experiences, and some of the mistakes made by that devoted group of Communists in Britain in its early years. He expressed in a very matter of fact way forebodings about his own future. 'My eyes are not what they should be. I can't read the papers, and feel very cut off. I have a lot of experience and I think I know myself. This gives me the feeling that my sight will not improve.'

"Harry expressed gratitude to the Australian comrades for their warm hospitality, and to Johnno who had looked after him and attended to his needs. He was very glad to have seen Ralph Maddern and Joe Goss again. He concluded with a characteristic peroration that reminded me of the countless times I had heard him round off a speech in a way that brought his audiences to their feet. 'This is a vast and rich land of sunshine and limitless resources. When the people take it into their hands they will transform it into a veritable paradise.'

"After he sat down there was casual conversation with Harry as the centre. Then Alan Finger proposed that Harry should get back early for a good night's rest. He called on us to show our appreciation in the usual way: we certainly did. Both Dr. Finger and Dr. Caust wanted Harry not to return to the ship but to go into hospital, but he declined; he wanted to get back to England and home. He thanked us once more. Took his leave with handshakes all round, and was driven by Alan and Jean Finger back to the ship."

What were his thoughts in the quiet of his cabin that night? Whose birthday was June 25? Here's to him, and all the good comrades in many lands! Australia had meant a great effort, but it had all been worth while. Tom Mann would have approved. His heart, one may imagine, warmed with recollections of the greetings, the handshakes, the sunshine, the blue hills, the happiness of the bathers on surf beaches, the crowded meetings, the close attention to his speeches, the applause.

What a long way he had come: what great changes the workers had wrought in the world since those far off days when, going to the mill on a winter morning, his mother covered his head with her shawl against the driving rain. As real as the events of the day rose his memory of his first visit to Soviet Russia, he felt again the firmness of Lenin's handgrip, the intensity of purpose in the young Socialist Republic. He had followed every step of its progress, the years of effort, the agony of war, the tears of victory. Now no force in the world could stop its onward march; triumphant socialism was opening the way not only to the stars but to a new life of brotherhood and peace on earth.

Next morning, the 25th at 8 a.m., *Orion* left Port Adelaide. On Sunday, the 26th seated in a deck chair after breakfast, while *Orion* was steaming through the Great Australian Bight, he suffered a stroke and was taken to the ship's hospital. About 2 a.m. next morning, without recovering consciousness, Harry Pollitt died from cerebral thrombosis.

8. LAST TRIBUTES

In Australia and New Zealand the sense of shock felt by thousands at the unexpected death of a deeply loved friend was expressed in obituary messages from trade union and Communist leaders and workers[19], and in the observance of two minutes' silence at seamen's and other meetings. In Auckland a memorial meeting included the tape of his Congress speech, music and the showing of coloured slides. The last of these showed him waving farewell from the doorway of the plane on which he left Auckland. As it came on the screen all present rose and sang *The Internationale*.

In Britain, the *Daily Worker* printed numerous messages. Arrangements were immediately made for the body to be flown to London.

In London on July 9, workers began to assemble at a traditional spot near Golders Green station for the march to the Crematorium. Black streamers hung from the red flags and the banners of organisations. Representatives of fraternal parties[20] and of national executives were at the head. When the motor cortege arrived, all were silent, tears gathered in the eyes of men and women who had faced unmoved police batons, prison, bombs and battle. The cortege slowed to marching pace, the 7,000-strong procession followed, silent all the way to the crematorium. There the coffin, wrapped in the banner of the Communist Party was borne into the Chapel by some of those closest to him[21]. The organist played "How Beautiful They are" from Rutland Boughton's "The Immortal Hour". The last farewells were spoken by John Gollan, Willie Gallacher, Sir Richard Coppock, Daniel McGarvey, Roger Garaudy for the French Communist Party, and P. N. Pospelov for the Communist Party of the Soviet Union. The voice of Paul Robeson moved all hearts as he sang "England Arise" and then Harry's favourite song, "Joe Hill". The speeches[22] and the singing were relayed to the thousands unable to enter the Chapel. As the coffin disappeared from view the strains of "The Internationale" sounded, first softly then rising to a note of exultation to express the determination of all present to continue the struggle for the aims to which Harry had devoted his life.

A few extracts[23] from the numerous tributes to Pollitt may give an idea of the sentiments expressed.

A Catholic neighbour: Never was a man more worthy of the love and esteem in which he was held by so many. Somehow birthdays without a card from Uncle Harry, and our ritual visit on Christmas Day will never seem quite the same again.

Reginald Bridgeman: I am one of the millions who owe much of my own thoughts to Harry because his summary of a problem or an emergency made clear how it was to be understood and dealt with.

The Executive of the South Wales N.U.M: The miners loved Harry Pollitt and they will never forget his courage and fighting spirit.

The Workers Circle Division 9: We have always taken pride in the fight he conducted on behalf of the oppressed, among whom the Jews were counted.

The Central Committee, C.P.S.U: The Soviet people will ever preserve the happiest memories of Comrade Pollitt as a true and great friend of our country, a tireless fighter for strengthening friendship between Britain and Soviet peoples.

The Communist Party of Austria: He was a model of internationalism, which plays so great a part in the British working-class movement.

Wallace Johnson: He helped me to find my way in this country and in my appeal to the Privy Council against a conviction for sedition in the Gold Coast in 1936. He has laboured hard, may his soul rest in peace.

Ted Hill, General Secretary, Boilermakers Society: He never sought fame or fortune; instead he carried on the fight for socialism, irrespective of the consequences. He died as he lived, fighting for the cause he so dearly loved.

London No. 11 Branch Boilermakers Society: He could have attained the highest of places in the trade union movement or in commerce, but he had dedicated himself to alleviate the workers' lot, and he was known and respected the world over for it.

Prisoners of Franco: Through walls and bars comes sad news of the death of Harry Pollitt. We make heartfelt homage to this cherished Communist fighter, the loyal friend of the Spanish political prisoners.

The Labour Research Department: He understood the value of research; in his hands facts became dynamite.

D. N. Pritt, K.C: I try not to think of Harry's death, but rather of his life with its splendid examples of courage and vision, which gave such great help to so many, including myself.

Among the memorial meetings, that at Manchester Free Trade Hall on July 16 was outstanding. Leading Lancashire personalities were present from the Boilermakers, Electricians, Engineers, Foundry Workers and Railwaymen, and from the Labour and Communist Parties. Associated with the meeting were the Mayor of Barrow, Alderman Miller, a former Lord Mayor of Manchester, Alderman Tom Regan, and a former Labour M.P. for Gorton, Will Oldfield. Among the speakers were Sam Wild, one time Commander of the British Battalion in Spain.

In January 1962, a sculpture of the head of Harry Pollitt, the work of Lawrence Bradshaw, cast in bronze, was unveiled at the Head Office of the C.P.G.B. Marjorie, Jean and Brian were among those present. The sculptor sought to portray the ceaseless and passionate mental effort characteristic of Pollitt. This departure from the usual reproduction of a photographic likeness of the head aroused controversy as well as appreciation.

July 1970 saw a commemoration of the tenth anniversary of his death by the deposition of the ashes behind an inscribed plaque in the Wall of Memory at Golders Green, alongside similar records of George Allison, Tom Mann and William Rust. A meeting in the hall was addressed by John Gollan and by Fred Bateman of the Boilermakers Executive. In the audience were Marjorie Pollitt, Brian Pollitt and Harry's sister Ella. Prior to this ceremony an article[24] by Betty Reid, who worked closely with Pollitt for twenty years, recalled "his great warmth and affection for ordinary people, whose lives he understood, with whose aspirations he sympathised and for whom he never lost that respect which is the antidote to cynicism and despair".

The same year saw a sepia and brown Soviet postage stamp bearing the head of Harry Pollitt with a symbolic representation of the *Jolly George* incident of 1920.

In 1971 came a most moving Soviet tribute, the naming of a 13,500 ton motor freighter *Harry Pollitt*, built at Warnemunde in the German Democratic Republic, highly automated, engines of 9,500 h.p. from eight cylinders, speed 17 knots. Facilities for the crew of 46 included a swimming pool. On her first voyage, to Cuba on July 30, she called at London's Royal Albert Dock, a stone's throw from where the *Jolly George* was struck. John Gollan presented her captain with a replica of the bronze head of Pollitt by Lawrence Bradshaw. Veterans of the C.P.G.B. and others welcoming the ship were greeted by the Soviet Ambassador, Mikhail Smirnovsky. A sister ship was named *William Z. Foster* in tribute to the American Communist leader, who was a great friend of Harry Pollitt.

CHAPTER 31

HARRY POLLITT
A Retrospect

*1. A man of integrity and compassion.   2. A trade unionist.
3. A socialist and communist.*

1. A MAN OF INTEGRITY AND COMPASSION.

A warm and attractive personality, political acumen, a natural bent for leadership, care for others, superabundant energy and an unfailing sense of humour were Pollitt's main characteristics.

Stocky, sturdy, shoulders square, back straight, chest and arms developed by his use of the plater's hammer, he possessed a strong physique, and complete self-control. Normally his appearance was cheerful, friendly and modest; under stress it expressed determination, sometimes grimly.

Lawrence Bradshaw, who studied scores of photographs when sculpting his memorial bust and had seen him in action during twenty-five years, wrote: "The face was Anglo-Saxon, square and strong, the forehead broad, the foreskull large in volume. The eyes exceptionally alive, conveyed a strong challenge. The thick, black eyebrows, resembling George Robey's were not used for comic effect as Robey's were, but helped to fix attention when he spoke. These eyebrows and the whole physical quality of the face expressed above all vitality, also humour, shrewdness and resilience. The mouth was warm and human. There was strong resistance to anger, he did not lose his temper even in the fiercest discussion. In later years the face lost certain inequalities indicating internal strain and was quite balanced. The personality became very powerful, more than life size, the expression on guard but always warm and human. There was no mask, no trick smile, no trace of hypocrisy. Face, head and neck were those of a fighter, but balanced and tolerant.[1]

By temperament he was equable, buoyant, extrovert and courageous. In physical danger he did not flinch; if his work made a risk necessary, he took it. His political and moral courage stood up to all tests. He could get on speaking terms with all types of people. He enjoyed life to the full, got the utmost out of it and put his utmost into it. The blackest situation did not depress him but redoubled his fighting spirit. He liked a joke, had an inexhaustible supply of funny stories. He liked social gatherings, and often led the singing of popular songs. His sister recalled "socials, flat as flat, when Harry appeared they lifted as though a spark had kindled a fire".[2] He never lost his youthful liking for the circus, music hall and variety. Jig-saw puzzles stimulated him; he first assembled the edge pieces, then heaps according to colour, and he "got more ideas out of doing them than anything else".[3] His health, aided by a strong digestion and the habit of physical activity, was good, apart from occasional bronchitis and exhaustion due to overwork. He took a nightly steaming hot-water bath, and in later years Turkish baths. He made no pose of perfection, cheerfully admitting smoking too many cigarettes, enjoying a good cigar and sometimes drinking more than was good for him.[4] After a motor accident in 1947 a deterioration in health set in, aggravated by kicks received in Devon in 1949.

His intellect was perceptive, quick to assess the factors of a situation and the essence of a problem. Detail was mastered, his mind was uncluttered. His analysis led to a synthesis, to positive action. Rapid and sure in his own judgment, he could be impatient with doubters. Sometimes, though rarely, he regretted a too quick decision, but did not like re-opening a question. His mental work was thorough, facts had to be well established, reasoning comprehensible, and conclusions clear. He had an exceptional flair in political matters based on sound working-class instinct, a vast store of knowledge and continuous study. His rare errors of judgment, seen in hindsight, sprang from overestimation of positive factors.

He had an inborn sense of the value of individuals, recognised their good qualities and that each could make a contribution to the great cause, but did not always allow for the fact that his appreciation might not be shared by others.

All his life he was a voracious reader, particularly of political histories and the memoirs and biographies of political leaders[5]. Marx and Lenin he studied closely, keeping his own notes of references and quotations. But he also read westerns and crime stories, for, as he said to another student of serious works, "If you don't sometimes read such, the mind gets moribund".[6] His exceptional memory, enhanced by systematic note-making and copying, enabled him to recall whole paragraphs of special interest. "I close my eyes and can see the print", he said.[7]

His work was planned, tasks set out for each day and week, people drawn in to help, progress noted. Without such a collective method he could never have done the amount he did. In financial matters he was meticulous; a personal phone call made from the office, he paid for; when he made a financial appeal, as for Bill Gee, every donation was receipted and an account sent to each donor.

In the words of a Birmingham comrade, "Harry had a tremendous big heart which carried a great love for the whole of working mankind."[8] Suffering or oppression, of an individual or a people, aroused his indignant protest and desire to help. This response was part of his make-up, from boyhood when he collected "Saturday pennies" for a family with two sons stricken with tuberculosis, to maturity when memories of poverty seen in India made him "wake in the night unable to forget the hunger-emaciated bodies sleeping in the streets".[9] Along with sympathy for the victim went antipathy for the aggressor, whether a capitalist waxing rich on war profits, or an imperialist general ordering fire on unarmed crowds in the colonies. That the evil was far away or the crime committed on people of a different colour did not deter him; he spoke with the same passion for the class-war prisoner in the U.S.A. as in Britain, against exploitation in South Africa as in South Wales.

His hatred of fascism was a burning fire. He saw it as the organised attempt of the exploiting class to "return to the dark ages", "to eradicate the instincts of pity and tenderness".[10] For him the future of democracy and socialism depended on the political and military defeat of fascism. He well knew the cost of victory. He continually spoke of the endurance and heroism of "some lad home from convoy work; some airman forced down in the sea, his raft drifting for days before rescue"; of "the risk entailed, the menace to health of the women in the powder-filling factories"; "the nightly death toll of our bomber pilots"; "the agony, sorrow and travail of this people's war". He did all he could to secure the Second Front against Hitler, as he had done to strengthen the International Brigade against Franco.

Consideration for others ran through his daily life. A meeting with him in charge finished sharp on time—"the workers like their drink", he said. After a meal in a comrade's house he always washed up, a habit not appreciated by every husband. A comrade in hospital would be sure of a visit if Harry was within reach. Informed of a comrade's funeral, he attended if he could. Old friends, colleagues, all on the staff at the Party Centre each year received a birthday card from him. If going away, he arranged for the cards to be posted in good time. He marked the fiftieth or sixtieth birthdays of active colleagues by a letter appreciating their record.

He never lost the rare quality of compassion. Seeing a comrade at her desk in the Party Centre, and knowing her mother to be in hospital and not expected to live, he said, "The work will be here when your mother has gone. Go and sit with her." A shop steward convenor with an exceptional record had a serious illness. Efforts to get him a holiday in a socialist country fell through. "Harry came with a car and took him and his wife to Hastings where he had fixed them up for a month."[11] After the war in Spain he personally checked that incapacitated members of the British Battalion and dependants of those killed were not in want. In the Second World War he wrote personally once a quarter, typing the letters himself at home, to all Party comrades in the fighting zones. During the bombing of London, if returning home after a meeting they passed rescue work, or if bombs fell near his house, he went to lend a hand. Among questioners at one of his Marx lectures was an old comrade who had lost the ability of intelligible expression, his efforts were painful to hear. Pollitt referred to him by name, said he would repeat the question for all to hear, himself formulated it, and answered. On May Day Harry was always early at the starting point of the march. One "old timer" after another came up to him to be greeted by name and a handshake and have a brief chat.[12] Perhaps only those who, old after long service in the cause, feel passed by and forgotten, can fully understand what that handshake meant.

For Pollitt the most effective way to influence people was the spoken word. He described himself in *Who's Who* as "propagandist". In 1941 he wrote:[13] "In these times propaganda is not only meant to inform and explain, but also to arouse and inflame, to show what fascism means in all its appalling brutality, in such a way that those who listen not only believe, but want to go out and do something about it." At doing just that Pollitt was supremely capable. His apparently effortless ability to command the concentrated attention of an audience resulted from prolonged preparation, knowledge in depth of his subject, and palpable sincerity.

He never shouted or strained. His voice was clear and carried far, a gesture was rare, emphatic when it came. He used simple English words, his phrases conveyed an image at once recognisable. He did not talk down to his audience, parade his erudition, or use political shorthand; wit and humour sprinkled in the speech drove home a point or gave the audience a momentary relaxation from concentration.

He would speak to any serious audience but was happiest in a meeting of workers, his own class, with whom he completely identified himself. They wanted enlightenment on their problems, encouragement for their efforts and informed confidence in the justice of the cause: all this Pollitt gave them in full measure. Rejecting demagogy, he appealed to reason. But reason convinced does not yet mean action, for that, the heart too has to be won. Pollitt knew how to win workers' hearts.

In the spirit of Tom Mann, Pollitt carried on the tradition of popular oratory, expressing the people's feelings and the aspirations they found difficult to put into words. He added something new, pointing the way to working-class power and socialism by presenting Marxist-Leninist ideas in everyday language. He began with familiar facts, then showed their significance in terms of class relations. The listeners realised that their hardships and frustrations were the lot of millions, they identified themselves with their class in the struggle he so vividly described; they understood that their future was bound up with the world-wide movement to end all exploitation. A political development took place in their minds, they saw more clearly what had to be done.

In an age when pelf and place are in ample supply for political deserters from the working class, and the Labour movement is so frequently used as a ladder to climb into Establishment status, Pollitt's loyalty to his class and to communism stands out for all to see.

From the early twenties onward, his qualities and popularity would have ensured his rapid advance to high position in the Labour movement, had he chosen to conform to the prevailing opportunism. He refused to do that; others might find specious arguments to cover the surrender of working-class principle, not he. For him, the gleam of the socialist future was not a mere phrase in a peroration, he devoted his life to working for its realisation.

Turning down in 1923 an offer from Bevin of a well paid job[14] provided he would "toe the line in your official duties" Pollitt replied, "Nothing doing, I am very happy in my work for the revolutionary movement and the Communist Party." Commenting on his refusal of a safe Labour seat, his sister Ella wrote: "He was a man of integrity and had a real feeling that what the Communist Party stood for was the only hope for the workers. He never forgot his own class, never sought the company of those outside it, he believed that if you were really fighting on behalf of the workers, such people did not welcome you socially."[15]

His political integrity sprang from his personal integrity; in his mind feeling, thinking and action were a unified sequence. Poverty and injustice had to be fought, not merely resented and deplored. It was this inner-unity that impelled Trevor Evans to write, "Almost as obvious as his Lancashire warmth was his tremendous atmosphere of sincerity. One felt in Harry Pollitt's presence that here was a man whose private world was enviable in its strength and consistency."[16]

2. A TRADE UNIONIST.

Pollitt liked to talk to trade unionists who consulted him and if he gave advice it was down to earth. He advised an apprentice just initiated into the Boilermakers Society, "Learn the trade properly, become a good craftsman and earn the respect of your fellow workers."[17] A hospital worker was anxious to make her points clearly in her union branch but nervous of standing up to speak. "Well then," he said, "stand up now and tell me about it."[18] To a Communist who had to deal with officials who had left the Communist Party he said, "Its better to speak even if you call each other names, than not to speak at all."[19] His advice was often but not always followed. In 1948, after Shinwell was dismissed from the Ministry of Mines, the chairman of the Coal Board talked with Pollitt who advised him, "Resign, with every other member who does not believe in nationalisation and let the industry be run by those who do".[20]

Not only rank and file members recognised Pollitt's exceptional understanding of union affairs. Abe Moffatt, for over thirty years a militant leader of the Scottish miners, wrote: "Many trade union leaders welcomed and appreciated assistance from Harry Pollitt. He never tired in writing speeches and drawing up resolutions, this assistance did not only apply to Communists. One need only read the presidential speech of Will Lawther at the 1947 Annual Conference of the Miners to see the hand and guidance of Pollitt. That was before Lawther was knighted, after which his speeches were in complete contradiction to that of 1947. Pollitt wrote more pamphlets and made more speeches than any other person on trade union unity, higher wages, better conditions and the change to Socialism. No one impressed more strongly on Communists the need to be active members of their union, to attend regularly their union branch meetings and to work alongside their fellow trade unionists, including Labour Party members".[21]

Pollitt saw trade unionism as the developing force of the organised workers, embodying their past experience, expressing their present needs, nurturing their aspirations for the future.

The major elements in his thinking on trade unionism may be summarised in four concepts:[22] that the unions are basically the workers' organisations to defend their interests and to pursue the class struggle; that the development of their full potential strength is held back by the right-wing leaders' acceptance of capitalism and rejection of a fight against it; that the union membership in the factories and the union branches has the power to end right-wing domination; that the Communist Party has an indispensable contribution to make to the further development of trade unionism.

Class struggle

The unions' origins went back to the early decades of the industrial revolution. Their strength was rooted in the collective of the workers, in their ability to combine and if necessary to withdraw their labour. The employers had the aid of parliament and the state forces. The organised workers became the major force in winning shorter hours, better standards of life, legality, freedom of speech, the right to vote, and on two occasions preventing wars.[23] They formed their own parliamentary party and raised it to the strength necessary to form a Labour Government. They also sustained many defeats, betrayals and retreats, but these were transient, the struggle for a better life was always resumed. Another gain of far-reaching consequence was the definite if slow growth of unity and class-consciousness. But none of the gains was secure, the capitalist class was always ready to seize an opportunity to regain lost ground.

Under the pressure of events the unions began to move from a craft or sectional basis towards organisation by industry. In the political arena they defended their democratic rights and strove to influence legislation and government policy. Some unions in addition to wage demands began to demand such measures as workers' control in industry, nationalisation, and state direction of the economy.

As we have seen above[24], Pollitt was in the forefront of trade union activities to improve wages and hours. But he also asked: Are these conflicts to go on for ever, do we not owe it to our children to change society so that exploitation of man by man would be ended? Then there would be no poverty, unemployment or war, the workers would be secure, enjoying the full fruits of their labours, and for that purpose, he argued again and again, socialism was necessary.

Pollitt was forthright in declaring that the circumstances of their struggle imposed on the trade unions a duality of aim. To raise the standard of living they had to organise the workers in all grades and all industries, and to promote their united action. But because capitalism in crisis is bound to continually attack the workers, it was also necessary to move towards a strategy which would first challenge and then end monopoly capitalist domination of industry and the state.[25]

Pollitt realised that while some unions were moving towards such aims, their full adoption by the trade union movement would need great advances in policy, organisation and leadership. A socialist outlook and a consistent militant policy would have to replace the prevalent reformism. Industrial and class unity were needed in place of sectionalism. A Labour Government was vital but it had to have an over-all majority and be backed by a mass militant movement in the country. Its policy must "not be that of guardians of capital, but that of fighters for the cause of Labour".[26] These advances would not be made easily or rapidly; in addition to propaganda they would need "many years of steady organised activity" in the trade unions.[27] Pollitt expressed his conviction that the advances would be made, within the unions, by the membership.

Events would widen the trade unionist outlook. Parallel to the growth of monopoly capital and its transnational organisation of production, the trade unions would grow in numbers and cohesion. Technological changes would bring closer together skilled and unskilled, manual and white collar workers, and would facilitate the extension of trade unionism to administrative, professional and even managerial fields.

In contrast to the crisis-free growth of the economy and the standard of living in the socialist countries would be the repeated crises of capitalism and its attempts to solve them at the workers' expense.

Class collaboration

The essence of class-collaboration as practised by the right-wing leaders of the trade unions and the Labour Party was to reject the class struggle against capitalism. They limited their demands to what the capitalists could concede while maintaining their legal right and political power to exploit the workers. This policy diverted the unions from the class struggle and sowed dissension in their ranks.[28]

Pollitt did not mince words in criticising the advocates of this policy, but he raised the controversy above personalities and argued for the interests of the movement as a whole. The trend to collaborate had deep roots in the movement. For decades the craft unions had combined tenacious defence of the economic interests of their own members with political subordination to the Liberal Party and acquiescence in imperialist exploitation of the colonial peoples. In the 1914-18 war the right-wing leaders entered Lloyd George's government and surrendered the right to strike. In 1924 Ramsay MacDonald proved that a Labour Government could carry on Tory policy, and to impose this pattern on the Labour Party he secured the total exclusion of Communists from its organisations. His allies were the right-wing trade union leaders who in 1926 betrayed the general strike and later, fearing further class confrontations, abandoned the right to strike against capitalist rationalisation. Pollitt wrote: "While the workers sacrificed to build up their trade unions . . . the dominant class with their skill in governing succeeded in utilising these organisations for the purpose of defending their own class interests".[29] MacDonald's rejection of the class struggle "also meant the abandonment of socialism as the objective of the movement"; and "to abandon the socialist aim is the road to destruction of the Labour movement".[30]

Union Membership

Whatever the collaborating leaders might decide, Pollitt emphasised that the union members in the factories and branches had the last word. The shop stewards movement in the first world war, the unofficial strikers and rank and file movements in the early thirties had breached the collaboration agreements. Pollitt laid great stress on workshop organisation and industrial unionism because he saw the factory as the front line of trade unionism.

On the job every worker, irrespective of grade, sex, age, nationality, religion or political views, was exploited for capitalist profit, therefore every worker should be a trade unionist. On the job a national agreement was not enough, it could not cover the frequent changes in techniques or in management policy. Workshop organisation was necessary to secure unity of purpose among the workers and to elect shop stewards who would form an all-factory leadership. The stewards were able to negotiate with the management from a position of strength because the workers could decide, if they felt it necessary, to withdraw their labour. Wages and conditions were primary, but no issue arising within the factory or from without was too small or too great to be discussed if the workers felt that it affected them. The workshop organisation, Pollitt said, was an example of democracy in action. The workers discussed the issue and voted on a viewpoint and also on what action should be taken. It was for them to decide whether or not they should withdraw their labour, and to accept or reject terms for resumption of work.

Pollitt wanted the democratic practices of informed discussion, decision by majority vote and solidarity in action applied throughout the unions, from workshop floor to national conference, and executive. All union positions should be filled by periodic democratic elections. To him "democracy was the lifeblood of trade unionism" and he wanted the removal of any and all restrictions upon it, because "trade union democracy hastens the victory of the working class".[31] This applied particularly to the removal of the bans on the right of the members to vote for Communists and militants if they so wished, for all union positions, including those of delegates to and candidates of the Labour Party.

Leadership was an essential factor at all levels of the union. Pollitt saw no need for antagonism between leaders and members if consultation was adequate, democratic procedures observed, and candidates for election were allowed to declare their policies. But if the leadership became bureaucratic, failed to inform and consult the members, or to heed their decisions, then antagonism was bound to develop.

Pollitt held the view that the unions should move toward a position where the General Council of the Trades Union Congress, acting in accordance with Congress decisions, became a general staff for the trade union movement as a whole. He thought that the T.U.C. should elect to the General Council "the most tried, trusted and experienced leaders, who know what the class struggle is and are convinced socialists with a working-class outlook".[32] Such results could only be attained if the election of delegates to the T.U.C. itself and the Congress election procedure were both democratised.[33]

Pollitt saw the struggle for full democracy through the trade union movement as "the fight for the very future of trade unionism".[34]

The Communist Party

Pollitt argued that the activity of a mass political party based on the scientific socialism of Marx and Lenin was indispensable for the future of the trade unions.

The spontaneity sufficient for trade union action in earlier times was no longer enough when capitalism was in crisis and decay, and the struggle between workers and their employers had merged with the complexities of world politics. Trade unionists could not afford to leave their future to be decided by a handful of leaders, or to uncritically accept sophisticated phrases intended to deceive them. They needed a realist analysis of class interests, they needed facts to combat the misinformation put out by the capitalist media, they needed socialist ideas in order to make their own decisions on what policy served their interests.

All this could only be got from a party which had a scientific understanding of the contradictions in capitalist development and of the perspective to working-class power and socialism.

3. A SOCIALIST AND COMMUNIST.

In his youth socialist ideas took deep root in Pollitt's mind, he never forgot Snowden's phrase, "Poverty, unemployment and war can be abolished only when the means of production, distribution and exchange are publicly owned and controlled".[35] Robert Blatchford argued the case for this public ownership with an unequalled thoroughness, felicity of popular expression and warmth of human sympathy. But on the crucial question, how to attain socialism, Blatchford had frankly admitted being negative. To the establishment of a socialist state he had "given least attention", he thought that "socialism will grow up naturally out of our surroundings . . . come by paths unseen by me and develop in ways I do not dream of".[36] In his mind, as in those of other socialist propagandists of that time—William Morris being an exception—the concept of organised working-class power as pre-requisite for socialism was either absent or misconceived as a reformist parliamentary Labour majority. This weakness led Pollitt to comment that Blatchford's works gave "an elementary understanding of socialism but did not steel one to do battle with the capitalist system"[37], and that in general "the early theories of socialism did not give political consciousness and understanding because socialism was, so to speak, placed on a pedestal, removed from current class struggles and unrelated to them".[38]

It was when Pollitt read Marx and Engels on the class struggle and the nature of the State that the way to socialism became clear. Earlier socialists "dreamed of the future abolition of the ills and sufferings of mankind but Marx showed how capitalism would be overthrown and socialism established and that only the working class could lead the struggle against the bitter resistance of the capitalist class . . . He gave the working class confidence in its own strength, theory to guide its struggles, a deep sense of international solidarity . . . With Marx socialism made a leap forward, it became a science."[39]

"For those fighting in the depths of difficulty and depression, in slums or sickness, unemployed or under-nourished, amid victimisation, abuse, oppression, illegality; for the pioneers of the Labour movement of all countries, Marx lit up the skies of the future with the gleam of socialism. That gleam preserved them from despair, taught them how to suffer defeat yet return to the battle, impelled them on to forge that future at whatever cost to themselves."[40]

Marx and Lenin opened for Pollitt the grand perspective of working-class advance to political power, socialist construction and the classless society. Asked "Why are you a Communist?" Pollitt replied, "Because I want a society where there is no exploitation of man by man, where all forms of imperialism are abolished and war is outlawed." Social ownership of the means of production would make possible a planned economy with no unemployment and no crises. Women would be emancipated. The freedom of colonial peoples and the end of state rivalries would secure world peace. The State would give priority to the care of youth and the relief of the aged from anxiety. New techniques and nuclear energy would lighten toil and increase leisure. Art, science and culture would offer limitless pleasure and enlightenment to all working people. From socialism, humanity would "advance to the classless society of communism where nature would be at man's service, culture blossom as hitherto unknown, abundance reign, the watch-word be 'from each according to his ability, to each according to his need' ". He added : "I have been a Communist since I was sixteen, now I am sixty-six. Every experience in my lifetime has strengthened my faith and confidence in communism."[41]

Marx's view of international working-class solidarity was expressed throughout Pollitt's political activity. Such solidarity was neither an act of charity nor a luxury; it was a political necessity because the contest between labour and capital was world-wide and would be decided by world forces. His unflinching support for the Soviet Union was based on facts. There the means of production, distribution and exchange were wholly in the hands of the people and the economy planned in their interests, so there was neither class nor racial antagonism. The exploitation of man by man had been abolished. The Soviet Government was a really socialist government, its interests were economic prosperity and lasting peace for its peoples and for the world. "Any other aim would be alien to the conception of socialism for which the Soviet people have been working, fighting and dying since they conquered power." These facts gave rise to deadly hatred in the minds of the capitalist class and their social-democratic allies. They conducted the anti-Soviet slander campaign to split the international labour movement and strengthen their own hold on the working class. "You cannot be a real socialist and an enemy of reaction and at the same time assist a struggle against the Soviet Union, however much you pretend to protest only against the tactics of certain Soviet leaders. The attitude to the Soviet Union and its people is the real test of devotion to socialism on the part of all who call themselves socialists."[42]

To realise Marx's perspective the working class required its own political party completely independent of capitalist influence and capable of leading it to the conquest of political power. Reading Lenin, Pollitt learnt that the Bolsheviks, organisers of the victory of November 1917 in Russia, had a different kind of party from the socialist parties in Britain and had built it by resolutely waging the class struggle. Comparing the Bolshevik victory with the fact that in Britain capitalism still ruled after more than a century of working-class struggle, Pollitt concluded that British Labour would only attain its objective when "the active socialists in its ranks were organised and disciplined as the Bolsheviks were, and like them armed with a consistent working-class theory enabling them to judge events in relation to the fight for socialism."[43] He welcomed the formation of the C.P.G.B. as a declaration of intent to transform the founding organisations into such a new type of party.

In 1922 he helped to formulate proposals[44] as to how this could be done and some progress was made, but not till he became general secretary in 1929 was there a sustained effort by the collective leadership to complete the transformation. The thirties were a decade of class struggles. The workers faced intensified attacks on their standards and saw with alarm the advance of fascism, actively aided by the "National" Government. Their rising desire for united resistance was frustrated by the official Labour policy of collaboration enforced by disciplinary measures and bans on Communists. The Communist Party stood for united action but it was small in numbers and largely isolated. It was also hampered by wrong tendencies—a misconception of unity, resulting from the belief that Labour organisations could never be drawn into action without official sanction; lack of confidence that Labour organisations could themselves break through collaboration; retreat from trade union activity when class collaboration became official policy. To meet the challenge, Pollitt and the collective around him made changes in policy and methods of leadership so as to impel the Party into activity among the workers in industrial disputes, unemployed marches, rank and file movements, nation-wide joint campaigns for unity and mass anti-fascist actions.

From each Party Congress there now emerged a general line of policy expressing the immediate and long-term interests of the working people. To popularise this policy and develop action for it gave common purpose to the Party members whatever their ability or field of work. Enthusiasm greeted the publication of the long-talked-of *Daily Worker*, and supporters rallied to defeat the wholesalers' boycott by themselves selling it. Morale rose as the Party felt itself acting as a single political force, able to reach far beyond its own ranks through its daily paper.

A new emphasis was placed on organisation. After the collectively worked out policy, Pollitt insisted that "every possible measure be taken to convince our members that it is correct, so that they are able to fight for it".[45] He set the example in his own speeches and writings, and initiated occasional "political letters" to promote discussion in the branches. Leading comrades under his direct guidance were responsible for helping branches get into personal touch with factory workers, discuss their problems and assist them. When selecting a comrade to do a job, he took into account qualities and temperament, as well as experience. He explained what was wanted in political terms, then encouraged them to get on with it, with the admonition: "Do what you think best and be ready to take the consequences." When he criticised it was to clarify and not to reproach. He got good results from committee work by ensuring adequate preparation, ventilation of viewpoints, definition of differences, and clear decisions. His organisational leadership proved effective in drawing a high proportion of members into activity, helping comrades to develop their abilities, and bringing forward new cadres and leaders.

When publicly explaining[46] what was meant by "the party of a new type", he drew on British working-class history. The first struggles were not for revolutionary power but for trade union rights—the shorter working day—the franchise—democratic demands: but they helped advanced workers to realise that a final solution of such problems required "a revolutionary policy leading to emancipation from capitalism". In the permanent organisations which came later, two trends were in conflict. One proposed to "redress social grievances without danger to capital or profit", and to do so through class collaboration. It gave rise to parties of the old type, disapproving of class struggle, seeing parliament as the medium for piecemeal reforms and confining political action to elections. The other trend "proclaimed the necessity of a total social change", meaning the abolition of capitalism and its replacement by socialism. It sought to do so through class struggle and therefore required a party of a new type, "a conscious political instrument developed by the working class to fight for its immediate interests and also for the conquest of power and the building of socialism". The old type of party saw each struggle for an immediate demand as a thing in itself. But Marx wrote that "the Communists in the movement of the present also represent and take care of the future of that movement",[47] which Pollitt read as meaning "support for immediate struggles not only to secure practical gains for the workers but to deepen their class consciousness, extend their unity, and build their revolutionary party".[48]

Pollitt began his secretaryship with a party of 3,000 in disarray. Ten years later it was a united political force with influence in factories and trade unions and 16,000 members whose energy and devotion were recognised by its opponents. It had by experience and determination found ways to give public leadership in the great anti-fascist upsurge. It retained its cohesion during the exceptional difficulties of the first two years of the Second World War and after the summer of 1941 reached record heights[49] of public work, factory organisation and a membership of 50,000.

The actions of the majority Labour Government of 1945–50 revealed the depth of the right-wing commitment to imperialism and the strength of its grip on the Labour movement. In setting the aim of achieving a new Labour Government with a left policy, Pollitt defined the essential task of the Communist Party as "to advance to the position of leading the working class, especially in mass action in defence of its conditions, and ending the domination of the workers movement by Social Democracy . . . a task we have not yet approached within measurable distance of fulfilling".[50]

In the following years he repeatedly stressed the need for a much larger Communist Party. "When we convince factory workers to come into our party in whole groups; when we build a thousand factory branches equal to our present best, then we lay the decisive basis for winning the struggle for socialism."[51] "Unless and until the Communist Party embraces in its ranks hundreds of thousands of members so that its influence and leadership extends to the majority of the working class, Socialism will not come on the order of the day as a practical possibility for Britain".[52] "At the heart of every problem we face is the size, activity and influence of the

Communist Party... Our capacity to give the leadership the movement needs is limited by our present size... The need for the Communist Party is not yet widely understood."[53]

He explained why the party must be based on the factories. In contrast to the Labour Party's concentration on an electoral machine divorced from the factories and the daily struggle against capitalism, the Communist Party "gives priority to political and organisational work in the factory because the class struggle begins at the point of production. There the worker is continuously exploited... the factory is the real centre of political thought and discussion." It was a hangover from social democracy that "many of our members do not understand that the factories are all-important".[54]

"We are still at the stage where comrades individually give leadership in the factories... while we may make progress on immediate issues through our present methods, we shall never by this means alone win the majority of workers to accept our basic political ideas. For that there must be large-scale activity by the Communist Party branches in a public and organised manner."[55]

The growth of the Communist Party and the development of political class consciousness would not come automatically. "The fight for immediate demands is seen as a thing in itself and not as a means of developing the political consciousness of the workers and drawing them into the Party to fight for the interests of the *whole class* and not merely one section."[56]

"As long as workers see only immediate struggles or sectional interests, they may see the need for individual Communists but not see the need for the Communist Party... the working class does not spontaneously develop a political, socialist consciousness out of separate, or even a series of separate struggles."[57]

"The factories are the heart not only of the immediate struggles but of the advance to socialism. To help the movement take the path of *The British Road to Socialism* depends on changing the outlook of the key sections of the factory workers. Therefore our work should be to give leadership in the daily struggles and open up thoughts in the workers' minds about socialism and how we can achieve it."[58]

Pollitt stressed the significance and complexity of the task of building a mass Communist Party when he said: "The problems facing revolutionary workers in Britain in essence can be reduced to the single one: how to agitate, educate and organise the workers to build up their revolutionary proletarian party which can lead them forward to the conquest of power and the establishment of socialism."[59]

He did not live to see this aim realised, but he proved in fact that the principles of modern Communism expressed in British terms are not only acceptable to workers, professional people and youth, but enable them to develop political activity, loyalty to socialism and zeal in its cause which are an indispensable source of strength to the labour movement.

What were the political results of Pollitt's activities? What influence did he have on the working class and on the course of events? A full answer will not be possible, at least in the view of the present writer, until socialism is a fact in Britain, but a preliminary estimate may be offered.

To use his own words, Pollitt's appeal was to "serious-minded workers". His name attracted audiences to fill the largest halls in Britain. He gave them an education in politics, a popular presentation of basic Marxism, and a reasoned case on current issues which he always related to the objective of socialism. He roused and sustained the will to direct action, that first step on the road to working-class power. Drawing on the heritage of the past, recalling the deeds of the Tolpuddle Martyrs, the Chartists, the socialist pioneers, he helped the workers to strive for the future, the abolition of capitalism and its replacement by socialism. Internationalist to the core, he was English in his absolute refusal to acquiesce in defeat, his persistence in sustaining the struggle in most adverse circumstances, his unshakeable confidence in the final victory. By imbuing thousands of "serious minded" workers with this class-conscious outlook and socialist purpose, Pollitt and his associates initiated mass movements which decisively influenced the course of events on three historic issues.

The first was in 1920 when the "Hands Off Russia" movement compelled the government to abandon its plan for war on Soviet Russia. The second was in the early thirties when thousands of workers by independent strike action broke through the right-wing leaders' attempt to reduce the Labour movement to an auxiliary to big business and the state. The third was in the late thirties when the anti-fascist working class, by direct action against the will of the official Labour leaders, defeated blackshirt fascism in Britain, manned the British Battalion to fight for Republican Spain, and ended official Labour support for "non-intervention". This mass feeling later helped to compel Chamberlain's resignation and to prevent pro-Hitler elements in the ruling class from retaining control of policy. These three achievements expressed in varying degrees the power of united working-class action so consistently advocated by Pollitt.

Throughout the struggles on immediate issues Pollitt sustained his contribution to the future socialist development of the Labour movement—his leadership of the Communist Party, his ceaseless activities for united action, his initiation of the programme for socialism in Britain.

He applied Marxism-Leninism to British conditions and problems, to him the Communist Party was an integral part of the labour movement, a creation of the working class. The independent activity of the Communist Party was essential to enable Labour to end its subordination to policies designed to perpetuate capitalism and imperialism. These policies were imposed by the right-wing leaders whose domination was buttressed by undemocratic bans on trade unions, Communists and Lefts, and by an unspoken ban on scientific socialist education, Marxism. Right-wing domination could only be broken from within, by the advance of the Left to a majority in the affiliated organisations and the Conference. The political work of the Communist Party, particularly in the factories and the trade unions and in the field of ideas, was indispensable to such a Left advance, for which the driving force must come from mass struggle against capitalist policies and authoritarianism, and from the wide extension of socialist consciousness. Pollitt directed the work of the Communist Party to defeat Liberal and Tory influence over the movement, to end sectionalism, to strengthen democracy, to win the majority for socialist policies.

The programme *The British Road to Socialism* showed how the working class, the majority of the nation, together with all democratic forces, could conquer political power and use it to construct socialism, by methods of democratic mass action and electoral victories in accord with British traditions.

"Socialism", said Pollitt, "will become the issue in Britain when the majority of the British people democratically decide that the time has come to replace capitalism by a socialist order."[60] The conditions for realising socialism he defined as "a people ready to fight for it, a capitalism that cannot go on in the old way and a working-class leadership that can really organise and lead"[61] He saw the socialist programme as "a call above all to the whole Labour Movement to recall its glorious traditions of struggle for the immediate interests of the working people and to safeguard their future interests in a Socialist Britain".[62]

NOTES ON CHAPTERS

Abbreviations used in the Notes and in the Appendices are listed below p. 539.

NOTES ON CHAPTER 1.

1. Tom Mann *'From Single Tax to Syndicalism,'* 1913.
2. *Reynolds News*, 4-5-90 and 11-5-90; *Star* 5-5-90. This demonstration was seen by Frederick Engels: he wrote that "The grandchildren of the old Chartists are entering the line of battle." Marx's daughter Eleanor was the moving spirit of the Eight Hours League. At its foundation in 1889 the second International Association of Working Men called for demonstrations on May Day in all countries to demand the legal eight hour day.
3. John Burns *The Liverpool Congress 1890.*
4. Tom Mann and Ben Tillett *The New Trade Unionism* 1890.
5. Data on Droylsden from Speke and Whitty *History of Droylsden;* on No. 14 from Ella, Miss W.J. Brown and *SMT.*
6. Sylvia Pankhurst *The Suffragette Movement* p. 129.
7. Marriage Certificate.
8. In a letter dated 26-3-70 James Jarvie graphically describes the relation of smith and striker:

    "The striker stands at the opposite side of the anvil to the smith. He uses long shafted hammers grasped in both hands, the weights vary according to the strength of the blow required: one about 3½ lbs. weight, a 'plying' hammer for light work; a second about 7 lbs. a 'fore' hammer; a third of 14 lbs. for heavy blows, known as a 'Monday' hammer as its use produces the depressive feeling experienced on a Monday morning when contemplating the thought of a week's work ahead.

    "The smith and the striker both render blows upon the hot iron or a tool shaping the iron, the skill is in synchronising each blow so as to avoid the hammers clashing. The smith uses a much lighter hammer wielded with one hand, the other hand grasps the tongs in which the iron or steel is held. Heavy jobs which cannot be done at an anvil are forged on a power hammer or press. These can render a blow of say 3 cwts. up to a goliath of some tons. We also have power presses of 5,000 tons' pressure. The method of work then varies as between smith and striker. The smith (or forger) will handle the hot metal, either by tongs or a 'porter bar'. The job will usually be held up by a crane sling, and the smith will move the job under the hammer while the blows are being struck. Such forging usually requires large tools to shape the job. The striker holds these tools under the hammer by means of a long handle, while the smith inserts the hot iron or steel into the tool. The hammer renders the blow and the metal is shaped.

"The above description illustrates that the 'striker' is not just a 'mate' who fetches and carries tools for the craftsman. Smith and striker are a team whose integrated efforts are necessary to produce a job. For this reason smith and striker, unlike many other crafts, divided the wages by a recognised proportion. Of each 20s. earned, 12s. went to the smith and 8s. to the striker."

9. Details on Samuel and Mary Louisa from Ella and *SMT*.
10. School details from Miss W.J. Brown, Mrs. Kennerley, Ella and *SMT*.
11. Lancashire dialect poets Benjamin Brierley and Samuel Laycock were Harry's favourites. On his 1953 Journey to India he was able to recite "The Owd Pedlar", "Bawton's Yard" and "The Drunkard", but his memory failed on Laycock's "Ode to the Sun". The full text will be found in *Collected Writings of Samuel Laycock*, W.E. Clegg, London, 1900. The first stanza runs. . . .

> Hail, owd friend! Aw'm fain to see thi:
> Wheer hast t'been so many days?
> Lots of times aw've looked up for thi
> Wishin aw could see thi face.
> The little childer reawnd abeaut here,
> Say they wonder wheer tha'rt gone;
> An they wanten me to ax thee
> T'show thisel' as oft as t'can.

12. Miss Jessie Rathbone—*R*.
13. *S.M.T.*
14. *Letters to Bill No.3.*
15. The cutlooker—Woven material coming off the loom was called a "cut", the looker examined it for faults.
16. This Branch is recorded in the I.L.P. directory as represented at the Annual Conferences of 1899, 1901, 1902, and as Openshaw and Gorton in 1903. Membership fluctuated around 100.
17. Mr. James Acton—*R*. The building was demolished in 1971 to make way for a Social Service centre.
18. This may have been in 1901 when Noel records speaking in Manchester and Dukinfield. *An Autobiography*, Conrad Noel.
19. *Gorton Reporter*, 21-7-1906, 4-8-1906, 11-8-1906.
20. Dr. Pankhurst and his wife Emmeline were public figures in Manchester. In 1883 he contested a Manchester by-election as an

Independent polling 6216 to the Tory 18,188; in 1895 he stood as I.L.P. Socialist for Gorton. Polling 4,261 to the Tory 5,865 in 1894 she topped the poll in Openshaw for the Board of Guardians. In 1903 she launched the Women's Social and Political Union which later began its public campaign by organised interruption of Winston Churchill at a Liberal meeting. The three daughters, Adela, Christine and Sylvia were all active suffragettes, Sylvia was also a Socialist. See *The Suffragette Movement*, Sylvia Pankhurst, 1931.
21. In the *D.W.* 20-12-1952 H.P. gives the date 1906, in several speeches he says "at 16". The date 1909 in *S.M.T.* may be a printer's error, at that time H.P. was fully involved in the Openshaw Socialist Society.
22. *Clarion* first mentioned the O.S.S. in 19-10-1906. See Appendix No. 1.

NOTES ON CHAPTER 2.

1. Data on Gorton Tank from *S.M.T.*, R. Allcroft—*R.*, Vic Summers—*R*, *Magazines* of LNER, Dec. 1927, GWR 1914, GCR 1905-6, and George Dow *The Great Central III*.
2. H. Fleet—*R.*
3. Writing in *G.C.R. Journal* 1905-6, Nos. 3, 5, 6, 7.
4. Ted Hill verbally to J.M., 14-8-1969.
5. R. Allcroft—*R.*
6. At that time evening classes were held in a building dating from 1858, known successively as the Mechanics Institute, the Droylesden Institute and the Educational Institute. Later used as Council offices. It was demolished in 1970.
7. The Manchester School of Technology in 1918 was renamed the Municipal College of Technology, functioning as a Faculty of the University of Manchester. In its Jubilee Year, 1952, it published an illustrated account of its origins and growth from which this data is taken. Later it became the Institute of Science and Technology of the University.
8, 9. M.S.T. *Calendar* 1910-11 and Records.
10. Verbatim Report in *Industrial Syndicalist*, January 1911. H.P. bought this paper regularly.
11. *S.M.T.*
12, 13. Vic Summers—*R.*
14. Data on movement from *Gorton Reporter*, *Manchester Guardian* Jul.-Sep. 1911.
15. R. Coppock to J.M. verbally.
16. *Gorton Reporter*, 12-8-1911.
17. *Gorton Reporter*, 14-10-1911.
18. Gorton Branch Proposition and Minute Books.
19. *S.M.T.* 31.
20. *S.M.T.* 32.
21,22,23 *S.M.T.* 58-61.

NOTES ON CHAPTER 3.

1. It may have been the end of 1906.
2. *Labour Leader* 20-1-1905.
3. *Gorton Reporter* 9-12-1905.
4. *Gorton Reporter* 3-10-1908.
5. All four stones were later defaced.
6. If any leaflets were printed on this press, no copy has been found. An edition of Bonar Thompson's memoirs *An Agitator of the Underworld* (16pp. 2d.) was printed on it, probably in the early twenties.
7. *Clarion* 30-10-1908; 6-11-1908. Ella. The County Forum had previously met in this building. Later Labour College lectures were given there. It finally became a Kardoma cafe and was demolished in 1970.
8. Data from *SMT, Clarion,* Ella.
9. A packet printed on two sides read: "When you are reading your *Clarion, Justice* or *New Age*, 1d. weekly from all newsagents, smoke a 'Red Flag' Cigarette", and "Guaranteed hand-made from pure tobacco, no dust, fine aroma, a sweet and cool smoke, made by Socialists for Socialists, Lewis Lyons & Sons, 79, Cephas Street, London."
10. *S.M.T.* 43.
11. *S.M.T.* 43.
12. *S.M.T.* 45.
13. Vic Summers—R. D.N. Pritt, *Autobiography I*, Oldham lecture *Clarion* 17.11.11.
14. From *Forum Echoes*, an account mainly in rhymed verse by a constant attender, S. Pulman, published by Abel Heywood, Manchester 1910. Foundation date from a 1954 programme, copy in Manchester CRL. In 1970 the Forum was still extant, its Secretary was Mr. J. Skelton.
15. *S.M.T. Forum Echoes*.
16. Charles Marks to J.M.
17. *Solo Trumpet*, T.A. Jackson, pp.84-86.
18. *Plebs* 1921, July, December.
19. Charles Marks to J.M.
20. *S.M.T.*
21 Charles Marks, tape in possession of E. Frow.
22. *S.M.T.* 41.
23. The precise date is not known, H.P. probably took over after the death of Alf Gerring in August 1909. A memorial ceremony was held in the Hall in December 1911 for Gerring and for Fred Crossley who died in the preceding February. Gilbert Roberts spoke and following a Socialist Custom unveiled a wall plaque and two pictures. Mrs. E. Davies recalls that such pictures were chosen for beauty and were not in any way funereal. On this occasion the choice was "Cupid and Psyche" and "La Belle Dame Sans Merci."
24. *Clarion,* 25-8-1911.
25. D.N. Pritt *Autobiography I.* p.12.
26. H.P.P. and *S.M.T.*

27. Full text in H.P.P. One side in *SMT*. The whole leaflet is reproduced above.
28. V.I.Lenin, *Collected Works*, Vol. V, p. 353.
29. H.P.P.
30. *S.M.T.* 12-13.
31. *Clarion*, 4-8-1911.
32. *Manchester Guardian*, 2-10-1911.
33. *S.M.T.* p.45.

NOTES ON CHAPTER 4.

1. R. Allcroft—*R*.
2. *Gorton Reporter*, 5-10-1912.
3. *S.M.T.* 53.
4. Advertised in *Justice* and *Clarion*.
5. Ella—*R*.
6. Quotes from *Justice* weekly reports.
7. Wm. Gallacher, *MSS*.
8. *Syndicalist*, July 1912.
9. *Justice*, 16-11-1912.
10. *Justice* 12-10-1912; *Gorton Reporter* 12-10-1912.
11. *Gorton Reporter* 14-9-1912, R. Allcroft—*R*.
12. *S.M.T.* 54.
13. *Justice* 18-5-1912, 8-6-1912.
14. *Justice* 13-7-1912.
15. H.P. in LM. Jan. 1951.
16. R. Allcroft—*R*. H. Fleet—*R*.
17. *The Syndicalist*, Jan. 1912.
18. *Manchester Guardian* 10-5-1912; *Weekly Citizen* 11-5-1912; Dona Torr *Tom Mann*, p.43.
19. Dick Coppock—*R*.
20. H.P. records in *S.M.T.* that he first took the Chair when "about seventeen" for Miss Boltansky lecturing on Eugenics, though Jack Unsworth says in a letter that it was for a speaker from Stockport named Bashden "in January". *Clarion* mentions Miss B. lecturing on "Eugenics and Socialism" on 5-2-1911 and, without mentioning the subject, on 21-10-1911. *Justice* reports her as Mrs. McKellen on "Education & Heredity" on 23 and 30-11-1912 and 7-12-1912, and *Clarion* on "The Biological Aspect of the Woman Question" on 16-11-1913. Her husband, Thomas Moult (McKellen) wrote to H.P. on 29-8-1949 recalling their meeting at Margaret Street when "you were introduced by me to Jack London's *Iron Heel*, and took his hero, Ernest Everhard, into your heart, dedicating your own life to the same great cause—and how earnestly, devotedly and nobly you have kept your vow is plain when you have completed 20 years as Secretary to the Communist Party". He adds that his wife has been doing educational work in Mexico for ten years.
21. Quotes from HP's review of *The Iron Heel* in *Challenge* 19-11-55.
22. *Clarion* 26-5-1911.
23. *S.M.T.* 49.

24. In August 1970 Mr. Lawson, owner of a Handforth cycle repair shop to which *Clarion* cyclists brought their machines, directed the present writer to the site of the Clubhouse, now replaced by a modern house. The Handforth Clubhouse should not be confused with nearby Handforth Hall, nor with Valley Ford Clubhouse some miles away, both still extant.
25. *Clarion*, 26-5-1911.
26. *Clarion* 26-5-1911.
27. *Clarion* 26-5-1911.
28. *Clarion* 28-3-1913.
29. *S.M.T.* 50 (but the date is in error).
30. *T.U.C. Report* 1915, pp.112-121.
31. *Clarion* 17-10-1913.
32. *Collected Works XIX*-332.
33. *T.U.C. Report* 1915.
34. *Clarion* 3-10-1913.
35. *Clarion* 14-11-1913.
36. *Clarion* 21-11-1913.
37. The Liverpool meeting was on 1-12-1913, organised jointly by socialists and trade unionists. The programme—a copy is in possession of E. and R. Frow—quotes Larkin's speech on 22-11-1913—"While this accursed wages system lasts, let us see to it that we get the highest wages we can force from the employers, that we compel them to recognise the best possible conditions. Let us forget that we are sectionalised, forget class lines of demarcation, forget the sex-distinction in the workshop and live according to the truest spirit within us."
38. *S.M.T.* 48.
39. *S.M.T.* 51-52.
40. It was spoken of by J. Grierson, Openshaw delegate to the Communist Unity Convention.
41. *Justice* 16-4-1914.
42. Conference *Report.*
43. *Justice* 30-4-1914.
44. H.M. Hyndman *Further Reminiscences*, 1912. pp.247 & 459.
45. H.P. to Frank Jackson 15-5-1953.
46. Political data from B.S.P. Conference Reports and *The Call.* Personal data from Roberts' daughter Muriel. At the Annual B.S.P. Conferences he was delegate from Openshaw in 1913, 1914, 1918, 1919, from Paisley in 1916 and 1917. There was no national conference in 1915. In 1912 and 1920 he was not a delegate. At the Communist Unity Convention in 1920 he represented Stalybridge B.S.P.
47. After 1920 Pollitt appears to have lost touch with Roberts, whose health deteriorated through a long spell of unemployment. In 1924, sponsored by the N.U.W.M. and endorsed by the Gorton Trades Council, he was elected for the Kirkmanshulme Ward to the Board of Guardians, serving till 1927. After great difficulties he got work cleaning trams at Hyde Row Depot. He died on 28-9-1933 leaving a widow, three daughters and one son.

NOTES ON CHAPTER 5.

1. *S.M.T.* 64.
2. *S.M.T.* 67.
3. Mrs. Davies—*R.*
4. Minute Book.
5. Minute Book: Text of appeal in *Justice* 28-1-1915. It argues that Britain was forced to go to war by the German attack on Belgium; she fought to defend small nations, and that peace is not desirable or even arguable till Belgium and France are free of invaders and Germany forced to pay compensation. Thirty signatories included Belfort Bax, Ralph Hartley, H.M. Hyndman, Dan Irving, Jack Jones, Bert Killip, John Stokes, Will Thorne and Ben Tillett. There is no record of any draft reply by Pollitt.
6. R. Allcroft—*R.*
7. *Engineering Heritage Vol. I.* Whitworth Exhibition 1966.
8. W. Hannington, *Industrial History in Wartime*, p.35.
9. E. Tomkinson—*R.* (Frow memo.)
10. Letter in H.P.P. from F. Perreman, Southampton I.L.P.
11. Sir George Askwith, *Industrial Problems and Disputes.*
12. *SMT* 70. In his 1954 review of Owen's biography of Lloyd George Pollitt recalled that Macnamara brought him "a blistering message from Lloyd George about my patriotic duty, and he got one back about his."
13. *S.M.T.* 73.
14. *Southampton Times*, 2-10-1915.
15. *S.M.T.* 75.
16. *Southampton Times* 9-10-1915.
17. *S.M.T.* 76, and H.P. in *Workers Dreadnought* 24-4-1920.
18. *Monthly Report*, Oct. 1915.
19. Sir George Askwith *Industrial Problems and Disputes.*
20. Up to July 1916 there were 1,006 convictions for strike activities and 10,645 for breaches of working conditions. W. Hannington, *Industrial History in Wartime*, p.63.
21. *The Worker* 22-1-1916.
22. Alderman Tom Regan, then a delegate, was definite in this recollection that in 1917 Pollitt, too, was a delegate to the Trades and Labour Council. The Minute Book of the Gorton Boilermakers shows they were not affiliated that year, so Pollitt could only have represented the local B.S.P. The B.S.P. Minute Book for 1917 is silent on the matter; that of 1918 records a branch decision on 4-1-18 to discuss affiliation at the next meeting; but in that year Pollitt was in London.
23. *S.M.T.* p.85.
24. *Gorton Reporter*, 19-5-1917.
25. D. Lloyd George, *War Memoirs.* IV-1491 (1933 edition) II-1150 (1938 ed).
26. *Gorton Reporter*, 26-5-1917.
27. J.B. Jeffreys *The Engineers.*
28. *Daily News*, 4-6-1917.

29. Leeds Convention *Official Report.*
30. *The Call.* 12-7-1917.
31. *The Call.* 9.8.1917 and 13-9-1917.

NOTES ON CHAPTER 6.

1. *Looking Ahead*, 41.
2. Proclamation of the Soviet Congress, Lenin's reports and speeches in Lenin *Collected Works*, XXVI—239-265.
3. *Looking Ahead*, 41-42.
4. Engels, *Conditions of the Working Class in England in 1844.*
5. Frances Trollope, *Michael Armstrong.*
6. *The Times* 10-8-1819.
7. Data on Peterloo and quotes from Donald Reed *Peterloo*, and C.P.G.B. *Peterloo.*
8. John Sanders, *Manchester.*
9. Engels as above; Marx *Capital I*, particularly Chs. X and XV. Pollitt would also have got information from such 1d pamphlets as C.A. Glyde *Liberal and Tory Hypocrisy.*
10. Engels, p.191.
11. The following data are from Marx's full account in *Capital I*. The factory Acts 1833 to 1853 set maximum daily working hours for Children (in 1833 aged 9 to 13, later 8 to 13) young persons (13 to 18), women (over 18):

Act	Children	Young Persons	Women	Normal Working Day incl. 1½ hours meals
1833	8	12	–	5.30 a.m. to 8.30 p.m.
1844	8	No change	12	
1847	No change	10 (as from 1-5-1848)	10	60 hour week
1850	No change	10½ (uniform hours, relays banned)	10½	6 a.m. to 6 p.m. Sats. 6 a.m. to 2 p.m.
1853	8 (within same hours as young persons)	No change		

Night work outside normal working day was forbidden in 1833 for all under 18, and in 1844 for women. Hours of adult males, or for motive power, were not regulated. In 1878 factory labour was forbidden for children under 10, in 1918 for under 14.

12. Cecil Driver in *Tory Radical, the Life of Richard Oastler*, gives a full account of Ten Hours agitation and of the anti-Poor Law struggle.
13. Ferrand, a Tory M.P. in the House 27-4-1863 quoted in *Capital I*, p.263, Marx.
14. *Gorton Reporter* 22-2-1908.
15. *Clarion* 30-5-1913.
16. Margaret Blunden, *The Countess of Warwick.*

17. Hewlett Johnson, *Searching for Light.*
18. CPGB *Our History* No. 31.
19. Sir Richard Coppock described to the author how a group including Harry Pollitt and himself went knocking on the doors selling the 1d edition. "We had a large supply on a van, money was put into bags, no change was given."
20. Hewlett Johnson, as above.
21. Data and quotes from Randolph S. Churchill. *Lord Derby, King of Lancashire.*
22. *DW* 18-4-1959.
23. Data from Morton and Tate, *The British Labour Movement*, T.L. Humberstone, *Battle of Trafalgar Square,* and E.P. Thompson, *William Morris.*
24. Data from J.J. Terrett, *Asquith and the Featherstone Massacre.*
25. R. Page Arnot, *The Miners,* p.240.
26. Phillip S. Bagnell, *The Railwaymen;* "Llanelly firing", *Reynolds News,* 20-8-1911.
27. Data from Ian Hambling, *Short History of the Liverpool Trades Council;* W.H. Lee, *The Great Strike Movement of 1911; Clarion* 28-8-1911; *Manchester Guardian* 14-8-1911.
28. Data from G. Dangerfield, *The Strange Death of Liberal England.*
29. Quotes from Lord Roberts 12-2-1914 in the Lords; Bonar Law in the Commons 23-3-1914; *The Morning Post* 26-3-1914 quoted by Dr. R. Dunstan, Barrister-at-Law in *Communist Review* Dec. 1925.
30. Emmet Larkin, *James Larkin,* p.212.
31. The fourteen were Patrick Pearse, Thomas J. Clarke, Thomas MacDonagh, Joseph Plunkett, Michael O'Hanrahan, Willie Pearse, Major John MacBride, Eamonn Ceant, Con Gilbert, Michael Mallin, J.J. Heaston, Thomas Kent, James Connolly, Sean MacDearmada—see Brian O'Neil, *Easter Week,* Lawrence & Wishart, 1936.
32. *S.M.T.* 69.
33. John Terraine, *Western Front.*
34. Randolph S. Churchill, *Lord Derby.*
35. *Looking Ahead,* p.42.

NOTES ON CHAPTER 7.

1. At 239, East India Dock Road, under Whiffens, the photographer, opposite Cotton Street near Blackwall Tunnel. J. O'Donaghue—*R. H.P. Letters.* In 1919 he lodged with Mrs. Griffiths, Plaistow. Percy Glading—*R.* and from 1920 till 1925, at 85, Central Park Road, East Ham.
2. Openshaw B.S.P. *Minute Book.*
3. *S.M.T.* 282.
4. Frank Jackson—*R.*
5. David Mitchell *The Fighting Pankhursts* p.83.
6. *S.M.T.* 109-110.
7. *Workers Dreadnought.*
8. *Daily Sketch,* 2-5-1919.

9. *S.M.T.* 93.
10. H.P.P.
11. This Council, an offshoot of the Plebs League and the London Labour College, later became a delegate body of trade unions and other workers' organisations and was renamed London Council for Independent Working Class Education, a term considered more self-explanatory than the word "Marxist". *Plebs*, July 1920 announced its formation with J. Burns as Hon. Secretary, R. Holder as organiser. Later John Mahon was Hon. Secretary.
12. The lecture headings were: Introduction—From Mark to Manor and Feudalism; Fall of Feudalism and Rise of Mercantile Era; Early Manufacturing Period; Modern Capitalism; What of the Future? The recommended books were: Ashley's *Economic Organisation of England*; Gibbins' *Industrial History of England*; Craik's *Outline of the Modern Working Class Movement*; Starr's *A Worker Looks at History*, and Cole's *World of Labour*. H.P.P. Circular, syllabus.
13. Percy Glading—*R.* and 50th birthday letter from H.P.
14. Harry Brown—*R.* Pollitt recommended reading *Six Centuries of Work and Wages* by James E. Rogers, from 1884 to 1912—it had 11 editions. Robert Bailey, a contemporary student in Hornsey described this book as "an economic, social and political survey from the 13th to the 18th century, based on factual records of prices, food, wages and rents. It deals with attempts to regulate wages by legislation, successfully resisted by the people in the 14th and 15th centuries, but resulting in the 16th to 18th centuries in their great impoverishment. The author criticises accepted historians for their 'fables and guesses' and adds 'Had there been any inclination to search into the doings of the mass of our forefathers instead of skimming the froth of foreign policy, wars, royal marriages and the personal character of the puppets strutting the stage of public life, I might have dispensed with this marshalling of facts and figures.'"
15. H.P. to J.T. 26-1-1945.
16. *S.M.T.* 109.
17. H.P. in *Prison Notebook*, somewhat abbreviated.
18. *S.M.T.* quotes an article from this paper. Ted Hill, Harry Brown and T. Crawford all remember buying it, but no copies have come to light.
19. *S.M.T.* 93.
20. Frank Jackson—*R.*
21. H.P.P. Leaflet.
22. *S.M.T.* 98.
23. *S.M.T.* 92.
24. *Workers Dreadnought* 1-2-1919. *The Times* 27-1-1919.
25. *The Times* 29-1-1919.
26. *S.M.T.* 97.
27. *S.M.T.* 97.
28. H.P.P. original of letter.
29. Boilermakers *Monthly Report* Dec. 1922.
30. Ted Williams—*R.*
31. *Monthly Report* 1919-20.

32. *Workers Dreadnought* 27-3-1920.
33. *The Masses* No.1. Feb. 1919.
34. Frank Jackson—*R.*
35. *The Call*, 28-11-18.
36. *Workers Dreadnought* 23-8-19, 4-10-19, 17-1-20.
37. *Solidarity*, Dec. 1918.
38. H.P.P. leaflets.
39. Frank Jackson—*R.*
40. *Justice* 1-1-1914.
41. *S.M.T.* 107. T.A. Critchley *History of the Police.* Sir Nevil Macready, *Memoirs II* 403. A leaflet issued by the N.U.P.P.O. (copy in Birmingham C.R.L.) claims that in an interview with Lloyd George on 31-8-1917 the union E.C. was promised a wage increase, the ending of victimisation, and that while the union could not be recognised during the war, non-recognition was temporary. On 12-9-1918 the Home Secretary agreed that the men could join the union and that as a wartime measure a representative Board, independent of the union be set up. The union was asked to assist in working out details with Macready. London members of the union E.C. were elected to this Board. The leaflet then claims that Macready broke the agreement and the constitution of this Board by refusing to allow further elections on an all-in basis and set up another Board elected on the basis of three different ranks. Most of the men refused to have anything to do with this new Board. Spackman was dismissed for opposing this violation of the agreement. The Government's Police Bill then legalised the Macready Representative Board and compelled its acceptance as a Police Federation, thus illegalising the union.
42. *N.U.P.P.O. Magazine* Aug. 1919.
43. Sir Nevil Macready, *Memoirs II.* 403.

NOTES ON CHAPTER 8.

1. *Lessons of the Revolution* by N. Lenin. 52pp. Petrograd. Jan. 1918. *Secret Diplomatic Documents and Treaties.* 48pp. Petrograd Jan. 1918. *To the Toiling Masses,* 4pp. Lenin, Chicherin, Trotsky. No imprint.
2. *The Call,* 18-10-1918.
3. *S.M.T.* 112.
4. *Are You a Trade Unionist?* Lenin, Chicherin. 8pp. 1d. People's Russian Information Bureau, London.
5. Industrial Workers of the World, mainly based in U.S.A. but with a few Branches in Britain.
6. Conference *Official Report. S.M.T.*
7. T.U.C. *Report* 1919. Labour Party Conference *Report* 1919.
8. *Workers' Dreadnought* 10-5-1919. Front page article by H.P. headed "Dockers Beware".
9. No comprehensive record of his activities appears to be available. *S.M.T.* mentions efforts to interrupt Lord Cecil at Birmingham Town Hall; an unsuccessful counter-meeting to Lloyd George at Sheffield; H.P. deputising for Col. Malone at Edinburgh, his first meeting in

Scotland "Not so red as I expected". *Call* reports H.P. speaking at the Free Trade Hall on 2-11-1919. In an obituary speech on Walter Grainger, a boilermaker, H.P. mentions his help in forming a Hands Off Russia Committee in Newcastle-upon-Tyne in Sept. 1919.
10. Letter in H.P.P.
11. *S.M.T.* 109.
12. *S.M.T.* 112.
13. Joe Leigh—*R.*
14. Letter in H.P.P.
15. *S.M.T.* 114.
16. *S.M.T.* 115.
17. H.P. *A War Was Stopped.* Also *SMT.*
18. Fred Thompson *D.W.* 23-4-51.
19. Full text of Hands Off Russia Appeal "To the Organised Workers of Great Britain" in *Call,* 20-5-1920.
20. Hands Off Russia *Circular* 21-7-1920. Copy in H.P.P.
21. Labour Party Conference *Report* 1921.
22. *The World Crisis: Aftermath.* p.269.
23. Labour Party Conference *Report,* 1921.
24. *A War Was Stopped,* p.3.

NOTES ON CHAPTER 9.

1. The founding organisations were: B.S.P.; Communist Unity Group, a section of the Socialist Labour Party; South Wales Communist Council, and a number of local Socialist Societies and Communist groups. The Workers Socialist Federation did not attend. See the Convention *Official Report* and James Klugmann *History of the C.P.G.B.* Vol. I.
2. *S.M.T.* 123-4. Lenin in *Left Wing Communism* Collected Works.
3. *The Times* 21-2-1921 reported H.P. at Kentish Town saying that the only way to fight unemployment was "to get hold of the property the capitalists now possessed."
4. *S.M.T.* 125.
5. *S.M.T.* 119.
6. Report of IV Congress.
7. *S.M.T.* 150.
8. *S.M.T.* 156.
9. *Report of the Party Commission,* C.P.G.B. 1922. Issued to members.
10. *S.M.T.* 155-6.
11. At that time the Central Committee elected a Political Bureau and an Organising Bureau. Details in Klugmann I.
12. *S.M.T.* 165.
13. R.P. Dutt in *Times Literary Supplement.* 5-5-1966.
14. *Workers Weekly* 23-5-1924. 30-5-1924.
15. For details of this and subsequent Labour Conference discussions on Communist Affiliation, see the *Reports* of 1922, 1923, 1924, 1925, 1926 Conferences. A brief summary of all decisions appears in the 1926 *Report* Appendix vii. Text of Pollitt's 1922 speech in SAS, I.

16. *Inprecorr* 16-10-1924.
17. *Workers Weekly* 17-10-1924.
18. *Workers Weekly* 2-11-1923.
19. VII Congress *Report*, p.157.
20. 1923 General Election; Unionist 11,025, Ferguson, local Labour Independent 10,021, Liberal 4,662.
    1924 May by-election: Unionist 15,488, Ferguson, Labour, endorsed by National E.C. but not supported "owing to developments during the contest", 11,167; Liberal 1,372 (L.P. Conference Report, 1924).
21. *Communist* 25-11-1922.
22. *The Worker*, 1-12-1923.
23. Fred Douglas—*R*.
24. *Workers Weekly* 17-10-1924.
25. *The Miner* 25-10-1924 and *Workers Weekly* 31-10-1924.
26. Tom Mann *Russia in 1921* RILU British Bureau.
27. Mrs Davies—*R*.
28. Tom Regan—*R*.
29. Leaflet HPP.
30. *SMT* 142. Price informed JM that the essence of the conversation would be found in his book, *My Three Revolutions*.
31. *The Worker*, 5-8-1922.
32. *S.M.T.* 66. *Workers Weekly* 2-6-1923.
33. *L.M.* Aug. 1923.
34. *Inprecorr* 7-6-1923.
35. *The Worker* 13-12-1924.
36. *Workers Weekly* 31-3-1923.
37. Letter in H.P.P. There does not appear to by any record of action taken.
38. *S.M.T.* 191.
39. *S.M.T.* 192.
40. *Workers Weekly* 22-2-1924.
41. *Manchester Guardian* 28-1-1924.
42. *S.M.T.* 193.
43. Mick Jenkins, *R.*—Unpublished script.
44. *S.M.T.* 195.
45. See Chapter 10.
46. *S.M.T.* 196. Full text in *Workers Weekly* 25-7-1924.
47. *S.M.T.* 197.
48. Chairman's Address to VII Congress C.P.G.B.
49. *S.M.T.* 198.
50. *LRD Monthly Circular*.
51. Eva Reckett—*R*.
52. *Workers Weekly* (6-6-1924) printed a photograph of Rose Cohen and her report of a visit to Faustova, a village 60 versts from Moscow. Some years later her husband and she were arrested. This was a great sorrow to Harry, who did not believe her guilty and made every effort to get her case reviewed, without result.
53. Eva Reckitt—*R*.

NOTES ON CHAPTER 10.

1. *S.M.T.* 127. H.P. *Brief History of the Minority Movement.* Full account in Losovsky *The International Council of Trade and Industrial Unions.* The Provisional Committee used this title. In Britain it was *Red Trade Union International.* The first World Congress decided on *Red International of Labour Unions.*
2. Leaflet dated 3-11-1920.
3. *SMT* 127.
4. Full account of Black Friday in Klugmann II.
5. *Brief History of the Minority Movement.*
6. *Solidarity,* 18-2-1921.
7. *Solidarity* 1-4-1921.
8. *SMT* 129.
9. Original in H.P.P.
10. At this Conference the present writer for the first time heard Pollitt.
11. On 8-6-21 at the House of Commons a debate took place between H.M. Hyndman and the Duke of Northumberland, on "The Cause of Industrial Unrest". In his reply the Duke referred to the London Committee of the R.I.L.U. adding "There are nine of them. Then we come to a very interesting gentleman, Harry Pollitt. He deserves special notice". The above quote is from a verbatim report which was published by the S.D.F.
12. MacManus, *Chairman's Report,* Nov. 1921.
13. *Western Evening Herald,* Plymouth 1-6-1921. *Daily Herald* 2-6-21.
14. *S.M.T.* 131.
15. *S.M.T.* 134-139.
16. Following the precedent of the First International.
17. *S.M.T.* 141.
18. Losovsky, *Report of First Congress RILA.*
19. *S.M.T.* 141.
20. *Constitution of the R.I.L.U. and of the British Bureau.*
21. Losovsky, as above.
22. *T.U.C. Report* 1921. S.M.T. 142.
23. Letter in H.P.P. and S.M.T. 157.
24. These activities are partly reported in *All Power* and in *The Worker.*
25. Photo in *All Power.* Nov. 1922. See also illustration section below.
26. *Brief History.*
27. *All Power,* Jan. 1922. From then till July 1924 there were 31 issues.
28. Text in *All Power* Sept. 1922. Note in *Communist* 9-9-22.
29. *Brief History.*
30. *Solidarity,* 4-3-1921.
31. Alec Squair—R.
32. H.P.P.
33. Wal Hannington *The Insurgents in London.*
34. In March or April 1922.
35. *Communist,* 30-9-22.
36. *All Power,* Nov. 1922.
37. J.D. Lawrence and Ness Edwards in *LM* Apl. and Aug. 1923.

38. *Strike Bulletin, The Docker* No.1. July 10; No.2. July 15.
39. Data from *The Docker, Workers Weekly*, HPP, *S.M.T.* 164.
40. No copies appear to be available.
41. These *Open Letters* were duplicated. 4-8-1923 and 11-8-1923, *The Times* 8-8-1923 gives text of first.
42. CPGB circular letter 19-2-24 signed by HP.
43. *Daily Herald*, 23-2-1924.
44. Data from *Daily Herald* 22-3-1924, 1-4-1924, 2-4-1924, *Workers Weekly* 28-3-1924, *The Worker* 3-5-1924.
45. *The Worker.* 9-8-24.
46. *Workers Weekly* 15-8-1924.
47. H.P. unpublished article in H.P.P.
48. How the national conference arose may be seen in *Minutes and Annual Reports* 1922 and 1923 of the Birmingham Trades and Labour Council and in the Birmingham *Town Crier.* 30-6-22 14-7-22, 20-10-22.
49. *Daily Herald* 16-10-1922, *All Power* Nov. 1922. H.P. in *L.M.* Nov. 1923. L.R.D. *Monthly Circular* Nov. 1922.
50. H.P. in *L.M.* Nov. 1923.
51. *S.M.T.* 169 and printed folder.
52. *Daily Herald* 19-11-1923, Birmingham *Town Crier.* 23-11-23 H.P. unpublished article in H.P.P.
53. *L.M.* Sept. 1922.
54. TUC *Report, SAS*, I.
55. *All Power* Aug. 1922.
56. *L.M.* Sept. 1924.
57. *Workers Weekly* 21-9-1923 and *Communist Review* Oct. 1923.
58. N.M.M. Manifesto, full text in First Conference Report.
59. N.M.M. First Conference Report.

NOTES ON CHAPTER 11.

1. Losovsky, *British and Russian Workers.*
2. Reported in *The Worker* 31-1-25.
3, 4, 5. H.P. at VII Congress C.P.G.B., pp.7, 66, 69.
6. *Workers Pictorial News*, Apr. 1925 printed a photo of Pollitt showing the uncollected rail ticket to his workmates.
7. *SMT*—200 *The Times* 3-4-25.
8. *Workers Weekly* 27-3-25.
9. Original in HPP.
10. During the 1927 libel action against Pollitt, see Chapter 12-3 a prosecution witness was involved in a brawl and subsequently died from a fractured skull. Pollitt received the following letter: "My dear Pollitt, I have read with interest the enclosed, and would advise you that after careful consideration this has been placed to your credit and will be settled—when the time is ripe—in a befitting manner. Yours faithfully, J. Rowlandson". SMT 202, original in HPP. (inclosed was a press cutting reporting the death—JM).
11. *The Times* 3-4-25 reported the police court proceedings and 24-4-25 the Assizes.

12. *S.M.T.* 202.
13. Copy in H.P.P.
14. Conference *Report* p.299.
15. Chairman's Address VII Congress C.P.G.B.
16. A full account is in R. Page Arnot's *The Miners: Years of Struggle.*
17. *S.M.T.* 204.
18. *The Times* 3-8-25.
19. *Hansard* 6-8-25.
20. *Workers Weekly* 7-8-25.
21. *S.M.T.* 204. *W.N.* 2-8-58.
22, 23. TUC *Report.*
24. *S.M.T.* 205-6-7.
25. *L.M.* Oct. 1925.
26. Published in April 1924, ratified by the Labour Government in August. A product of the Allied Commission on Reparations, it provided for Allied control of German credit, customs and excise, and railways, and for taxes and interest charges to raise £125 mn. annually. Pollitt wrote that "by reducing Germany to a slave colony it means a wholesale offensive on the wages and conditions of the whole working class."
27. Data and quotes from *L.P.C. Report.* Also see H.P. in *Inprecorr* 15-10-25 and Pollitt's speech in *SAS* Vol. I.
28. *SMT* 210.
29. M.P. to J.M.
30. M.P. in *D.W.* 25-3-57.
31. M.P. to J.M.
32. *S.M.T.,* 208.
33. H.P. to W.D. Buxton 14-10-25. Letter in HPP; it was seized by police in their raid on N.M.M. office, and later returned.
34. HPP.
35. *Weekly Despatch* 11-10-25.
36. The twelve were: Eight members of the Political Bureau—Tom Bell, J.R. Campbell, William Gallacher, Albert Inkpin, Arthur MacManus, J.T. Murphy, Harry Pollitt, William Rust, and four others—R. Page Arnot, E.W. Cant, Wal Hannington and Tom Wintringham. The *Daily Mirror* 16-10-25 stated that the Cabinet had considered approximately 40 names.
37. *S.M.T.* 208.
38. Gallacher *MSS.*
39. *Workers Weekly* 6-11-25.
40. *Workers Weekly* 20-11-25.
41. *Workers Weekly* 27-11-25.
42. *Workers Weekly* 20-11-25. *The Times* 17-11-25.
43. E.S. Fay *Life of Mr. Justice Swift* 176. *The Times* 19-11-25.
44. Three CPGB pamphlets *The Communist Party on Trial*—speeches of *Harry Pollitt, Wm. Gallacher, J.R. Campbell.*
45. *Pollitt's Defence,* also in *SMT* 211.
46. *The Times* 25-11-25.
47. Quotes in this paragraph from E.S. Fay as above 178-9.

48. 1926 *Cmd* 2682.
49. Prison incidents are from *SMT* 248-252 and also Gallacher *MSS*.
50. *Workers Weekly* 12-3-26.
51. Quotes in letter from John Hill to H.P. 31-8-26. HPP.
52. *S.M.T.* 13.
53. Data and quotations in this section are from H.P.'s *Prison Notebook*, HPD.
54. L.M. Oct. 1926.
55. The Council's chairman, E. Friend, J.P., presided, Wal Hannington spoke, Tom Mann replied. The songs were *The Internationale, Red Army March* and *The Red Flag*. The Programme, copy in HPP, included a tabloid history of the L.T.C. compiled by Frank Smith.
56. A Programme, autographed "Albert, Wally, Winnie, Harry, Marjorie and Julia, in commemoration of Wandsworth November 1925—September 1926" is in *HPP*.
57. Sources Conference *Report*, H.P. pamphlet *What Margate Means*, also as an article in *Communist Review* and *SAS* I.
58. *S.M.T.* 254 and *The Worker* 29-10-26.
59. *The Worker* 7-11-26.
60. *Workers Weekly* 12-11-26.
61. A full account of Spencer affair in R. Page Arnot as above.
62. *SMT* 254 *Workers Weekly* 26-11-26.
63. C.P.G.B. *Notts. United* 1937.
64. *S.M.T.* 255.

NOTES ON CHAPTER 12.

1. NMM view in Open Letter to delegates in *The Crisis of Trade Unionism*. See also HP in *LM* Feb. 1927.
2. H.P. in *The Worker* 21-1-27.
3. *Trade Union Leadership*.
4. *Is Trade Unionism Played Out?*
5. Andrew Conley, 1926 TUC *Report*: see also *The Worker* 10-9-26.
6. These anti-democratic measures ranged from prohibiting branches from associating with the MM in any way whatever—even reading correspondence—to disbandment of branches and expulsion of members. Unions involved included: Ban on correspondence—N.U.R., T. & G.W.U., R.C.A., Shop Assistants. Ban on standing for official positions—R.C.A., Shop Assistants, N.U.G.M.W., N.A.T.S.O.P.A., Boilermakers. Quashing of elections of M.M. members in spite of majority ballot—E.T.U., Scottish Miners, N.U.G.M.W. Disciplinary action against members criticising official policy in M.M. press—Boot & Shoe, Bakers. Expulsion of M.M. members—S.A.U., N.U.G.M.W., Garment Workers, ASW. In the A.E.U. attempts by E.C. to penalise and restrict members rights were more than once quashed by the Final Appeal Court.
7. Declaration of the Minority, *The Worker* 16-9-27.
8. So-called because the employers' representatives were led by Sir Alfred Mond and those of the T.U.C. by Ben Turner.

9. *LM* Feb. 1928.
10. *L.M.* Aug. 1928.
11. N.M.M. *Pollitt's Reply to Citrine.*
12. Full details in *Barriers of the Bureaucrats, Fife Breaks Through* David Proudfoot and J. McArthur, Miners M.M. 1929. The wrecking of the Scottish Miners Union by the defeated right wing officials led to the formation of the United Mineworkers of Scotland. In 1936 after a change of leadership in the M.F.G.B. unity was restored in Scotland, militants were elected and took positions in Fife.
13. Adopted by II World Congress, pamphlet CPGB.
14. See Chapter 14-7.
15. Other members—Earl Browder, USA Trade Union Educational League and Jacques Duclos, France, MP and metalworker.
16. *The Worker* 15-7-27.
17. Tom Mann *What I saw in China* NMM.
18. *The Worker* 18-2-27.
19. Emil Burns in *LM* Sept. 1929.
20. N.M.M. *British Imperialism.*
21. Quoted in *S.M.T.* 188. Originals in HPP.
22. *S.M.T.* 257.
23. "Havelock Wilson . . . entered into mutual arrangements with the shipowners . . . no seaman could get a job without a union ticket . . . there was deep suspicion that in return for this monopoly Wilson had entered into a pact not to demand higher wages and better conditions." (Trevor Evans, *Bevin,* p.142.) Also HP at 1927 TUC. "Contrary to Law" *The Times* 12-5-26
24. Havelock Wilson *My Stormy Voyage Through Life.* 206.
25. Two pamphlets were published in several languages, *The Struggle of the British Seamen* by George Hardy, and *Havelock Wilson Exposed* by G. Atchkanov. The English editions were published by the Seamen's Minority Movement.
26. N.U.S. *The Real Truth About the Soviet Government;* also in *The Seaman,* 26-2-27.
27. *S.M.T.* 257.
28 to 39. Quoted from transcript of shorthand notes of trial. Copy in HPP.   28 from Day 2, p.16.   29 from Day 4, p.91.   30 from Day 2.   31 from Day 4, p.36.   32 from Day 7   33 from Day 9,. p.44.   34 from Day 7, p.31.   35 from Day 9, p.47.   36 from Day 4   37 from Day 11, p.26.   38 from Day 9, p.66.   39 from Day 11, p.63.
40. *S.M.T.* 262.
41. *The Times* 21 and 25.2.28.
42. The following are mainly recollections of J.M. who from 1925 worked in the M.M. Headquarters.
43. A file of this paper from Mar. 1928 to June 1929 is in HPP, but lacks Sept. and Oct. 1928.
44. *Evening Standard* 19-7-28.
45. Frank Wild—*R.*
46. *The Worker* 15-4-27. See Appendix No. 10.

47. Sources: Mrs Kathleen Eves, his eldest daughter; NMM publications; Scott trial transcript; TRS letters to JM; JM—R.
48. In *The Boilermaker* July 1928 H.P. wrote that at a boilermakers meeting in Coventry a member of the Labour E.C. said that they had told the Boilermakers E.C. that they "ought to be ashamed to allow a man like Pollitt to represent them", and they had promised to see what could be done.
49. *Daily Telegraph* 25-3-27.
50. *Monthly Report* Nov. 1927.
51. Pollitt to Hill 23-12-27.
52. Circular Letter 3-1-28 in *S.M.T.* 181.
53. *Monthly Report* Mar. 1928.
54. *Monthly Report* Apr. May. 1928
55. *Letter* 11-5-28—copy in HPP.
56. Pollitt to Hill 24-6-28.
57. Hill to Pollitt 10-7-28.
58. H.P. in *The Boilermaker* July 1928.
59. *The Worker* 19-10-28.
60. *S.M.T.* 277.
61. *Communist* 9-9-22.
62. Pollitt to Cook 25-10-28, copy in HPP. Cook wrote in *Sunday Worker* 21.10.28 "all faults in trade union structure, methods, voting etc. are the fault of the members".
63. Cook to Pollitt, original in HPP.
64. Compare Cook in his pamphlets *Is It Peace?*, *Mond Moonshine*, *Mond's Manacles*, with Cook in *Forward* 9-3-29 and *L.M.* June 1929.
65. Speech at Dawdon 2-5-29 verbatim in *HPP*.
66. See *LM* June 1929.
67. *SMT* 277 Account of Cook's death aged only 46 in Arnot's *The Miners* III P540.
68. Byron, *Poetical Works*, Epigrams, Oxford U.P.
69. *The Worker* 22-3-29.
70. *Leaflet* in HPP.
71. *The Worker* 3-5-29.
72. *Leaflet* in HPP.
73. H.P. in *L.M.* May 1929.
74. Jim Ancrum in *L.M.* Sept. 1929.
75. *Workers Life* 12-7-29, 26-7-29, 16-8-29.
76. *L.M.* May 1929.
77. H.P. in *R.I.L.U. Magazine*, Aug. 1929.
78. *L.M.* May 1929.
79. *S.M.T.* 267-269.
80. *S.M.T.* 269.
81. *SMT* 267.
82. Quoted by Francis Williams *A Pattern of Rulers* p.64.
83. Francis Williams, as above, 68, 82, 97.
84. *S.M.T.* original in HPP.
85. *S.M.T.* 278-9.
86. *What Margate Means*, The reference to "middle class liberals" is

primarily to Ramsay MacDonald and his close associates. Light on MacDonald's relations with the Liberals was thrown in 1958 by the publication of details of a secret electoral deal in 1903 between R. MacDonald, then secretary of the Labour Representation Committee and Jesse Herbert on behalf of Herbert Gladstone, the Liberal Chief Whip. The agreement covered some 35 constituencies in which the Liberals agreed not to oppose Labour candidates. It bore fruit in 1906 when Labour won 29 seats, in 24 of which Liberals did not contest. Details, taken from unpublished Gladstone papers in the British Museum, are given by Phillip P. Poirier in *The Advent of the Labour Party*, 1958. (Allen and UNwin). See also RPD, '*Notes of the Month*', LM, Oct. 1958.

87. Summarised from the documents in C.P.G.B. *Communist Policy in Great Britain*, a full report of IX Plenum British Commission.
88. P. Braun *At the Parting of the Ways*.
89. *Workers Life*, 16-3-28 and 6-4-28.
90. In a 6000 word report based on IV RILU Congress documents, he was not present. Copy in HPP.
91. Report of VI Congress in *Inprecorr*
92. *Workers Life* 11-1-29.
93. *Workers Life* 23-1-29, *Inprecorr* 1929-96, X Congress documents in CPGB *The New Line*.
94. Dated 27-2-29, copy in HPP.
95. *C.R.* Oct. 1929.
96. *Inprecorr* 1929-885.
97. *Workers' Life* 26-7-29 and 16-8-29.
98. Report X Plenum in *CR* 1929.
99. Tapsell in *Inprecorr* 1929-1363.
100. *SMT* 284.

NOTES ON CHAPTER 13.

1. Preparatory discussion in WL. Aug. 16, 23, 30; LM. Aug., C.C. Resolution CR. Sept. H.P. on X Plenum E.C.C.I. in CR. Oct.
2. CPGB *Resolutions of XI Congress* includes ECCI letter. HP's report in WL, 6-12-29. His reference to atmosphere in speech on *Twenty Years As General Secretary*.
3. HP in *The Road to Victory*.
4. Reports of ECCI XI and XII Plenums in pamphlet form, that of RILU Central Council in *RILU Magazine*, 1-2-32, the same issue discusses the XII Plenum economic resolution. HP's speech at XI Plenum in *CR*. Jun. 1931, at XII Plenum in *CI*, 1932, Nos. 17/18. See also reference to XII Plenum in *The Road to Victory*.
5. *The Road to Victory*.
6. Text in *CR*. Feb. 1932, and as pamphlet. See also HP in *Party Organiser*, Mar. 1932, and HP's summary in *The Road to Victory*.
7. HP in *CI* 1-1-33, and *The Road to Victory*.
8. Joe Leigh—*R*.
9. H.P. in *L.M.* Jan. 1931.
10. *The Worker* 28-11-30.

11. *The Worker* 5-12-30.
12. Joe Leigh—*R*.
13. H.P. in *L.M.* Jan. 1931.
14. *Address* and *Special* in HPP.
15. *Recollections* in this and following paragraphs are those of Joe Leigh.
16. Summarised from C.C. *Resolution*, Dec. 1931.
17. H.P. reply to discussion at XII C.P.G.B. Congress.
18. Data from HP in *D.W.* Jul. 16, 28, 24, 30, Aug. 12, Sept. 8, 21, 24; *The Worker* Aug. 1, 15; Lock-Out edition of *The Boilermaker*, 24-7-31, 14-8-31.
19. Data from Leaflets and Bulletins of the Cotton MM and Solidarity Movement; HP in *CR* Jun 1932; *Inprecorr* 1932, p.839; *СПХ*-616. HP notes of visit to Burnley in Feb. 1932 in HPP and *Cotton Workers Leader* Nos. 8 and 9 1933.
20. Joe Leigh—*R*.
21. HP at XIII Plenum.
22. *The Busman's Punch*.
23. HP in *RILU Magazine* 1-2-33; in same issue a full account by George Renshaw *The London Busmens Strike*, also reprinted as pamphlet.
24. N.M.M. *The Workers Charter*. See also series of six *Charter pamphlets*.
25. N.M.M. E.C. Resolution Dec. 1930 HPP.
26. H.P. in *The Worker*, 11-4-31.
27. H.P. in *The Worker*, 14-2-31.
28. HP in *Road to Victory*, 1931 with resolutions of the Convention.
29. *R.I.L.U. Magazine*, 1-2-32.
30. Data in Trevor Evans' *Bevin*, pp.142-3; Fred Thompson in *The Worker* 12-7-29, 26-7-29, 9-8-29; *Labour Research*, Aug. 1929.
31. *R.I.L.U. Magazine* 1-2-32.
32. Abe Moffatt—*R*.
33. J.M.—*R*.
34. Unpublished notes. HPP.
35. Report and reply in *The Road to Victory* 1932.

NOTES ON CHAPTER 14.

1. *I Accuse Baldwin*.
2. Fred Douglas—*R*.
3. Idris Cox—*R*.
4. N.M.M. *Why Mardy Was Expelled*.
5. Data on the campaign from *D.W.* 7-3-33 to 29-3-33.
6. Data from *D.W.* 26-8-33, 28-8-33, 30-8-33, 31-8-33, 1-9-33, and *SMT* 282.
7. HP in *The Communist Party and the Labour Party* 1935.
8. Brockway's remark in *The Coming Revolution*, his presidential address.
9. A full report of this debate in C.P.G.B. *Which Way for the Workers?*
10. *R.P.C. Bulletin*, Aug. 1932.
11. *DW* 30.7.32. A CP "appeal to militant delegates" said: whether the break with the Labour Party was fundamental would be shown in action; the *New Leader* had done "nothing to help" in industrial

disputes; "there is no genuine middle way between reformism and communism".
12. *L.M.* Aug. 1932.
13. At XII Plenum E.C.C.I. Sept. 1933.
14. *The Road to Victory.* CPGB.
15. Order in HPP, Tom Mann in *DW* 17-10-32 and 19-10-32.
16. *Irish Daily Telegraph* 16-10-33.
17. *Manchester Guardian* 16-10-33.
18. Report in *The Way Forward.* H.P. speech in full in *Into Action.*
19. Mass street battles with police in Sheffield and elsewhere compelled the government to suspend this part of the Act.
20. *Western Mail* 24-2-34.
21. Idris Cox—*R.*
22. D.N. Pritt *From Right to Left.*
23. *DW* 6-7-34.
24. *DW* 3-7-34.
25. Data on Assizes from DN Pritt as above pp. 145-8.
26. Data on Meerut in Clemens Dutt *The Meerut Trial,* Ben Bradley *Trade Unionism in India,* also *The Prisoners Reply, Meerut Conspiracy Case,* all published by the Meerut Prisoners Defence Committee, London, secretary Percy Glading. Statement by Lester Hutchinson in *Meerut Trial,* Manchester Meerut Defence Committee. For list of prisoners names see Appendix No. 9.
27. Quoted by Brecher in *Nehru: A Political Biography.*
28. National Archives of India, quoted by Brecher, p. 152.
29. Abbreviated from text in HPP.
30. H.P. to Ted Hill 13-6-34 in HPP.
31. *D.W.* 14-6-34.
32. *DW* 9-7-34, 13-7-34.
33. See below, pp. 416-7.
34. A facsimile of these Rules was reproduced by the Society in 1934.
35. *D.W.* 18-8-34.
36. Data on the celebration from *Centenary Souvenir* and R. Allcroft—*R.*
37. *DW* 20-8-34.

NOTES ON CHAPTER 15.

German Elections Parties	No. of M.Ps. Nov. 1932.	Mar. 1933.
Nazis	196	288
Nationalists	51	52
	247	340
Social Democrats	121	120
Communists	100	81
	221	201
Others (mainly right and Centre)	116	106
Total number of M.Ps.	584	647 After Communists outlawed – 566
Needed for majority	293	324 " " – 284

In November 1932 the Nazi vote was 11.7 mn. a drop of 700,000 compared with the previous election. The Communist vote was 6 mn., an increase of 700,000. In Berlin the three leading parties were Communist 860,000; Nazi 719,000; Social Democrat 646,000.

2. A full account in *The Burning of the Reichstag*, Official Findings of the Legal Commission of Enquiry; Chairman D.N. Pritt, K.C., London, Sept. 1933.
3. CPGB letter to L.P. headed, "Joint Action in Britain", enclosing copy of CI appeal March 8 in DW and reprinted as folder March 1933.
4. *Daily Telegraph*, 10-9-34.
5, 6. J.M.—R.
7. CPGB *September 9th*.
8. C.P.G.B. *A Hell of a Business*, Memorandum. *Dynamite in the Dock*, Pollitt's evidence.
9. *L.M.* Oct. & Nov. 1935.
10. *Outline History of the Communist International*, 364. The ban imposed in 1933 had been lifted "having lost justification", see letter Adler to Cachin 16-11-34.
11. *LM* Oct 1935.
12. HP's speech at CI VII Congress in *Inprecorr* 1935-1403, also *Unity against the National Government*.
13. H.P. to Rhondda miners 15-9-35, HPP.
14. *Inprecorr*, 1935-1328.
15. *D.W.* 4-10-35.
16. The five parties were British, Czech, Danish, Dutch and Swedish (Braunthal, *History of the International* II 482.
17. *C.R.* Dec. 1934.
18. XIII C.P.G.B. Congress.
19. H.P. *Election Special*.
20. HPP.
21. *Porth Gazette* 9-11-35.
22. At C.C. meeting Jan. 1936.
23. H.P. to Middleton, 25-11-35.
24. CP pamphlet *Forward*.
25. Middleton to H.P. 27-1-36.
26. Summarised from *Unity, Peace and Security*.
27. *Le Populaire* 21-11-35.
28. *Aeroplane* 4-3-36.
29. *I Accuse Baldwin*.
30. *L.M.* May 1936.
31. *The Path to Peace*.
32. *L.M.* May 1936 and *The Path to Peace*.
33. From Conference *Reports*.

34. The National Administrative Council, equivalent to an Executive Committee.
35. The C.I. Constitution provided for affiliation and representation of parties which though not yet Communist were in sympathy with C.I. aims.
36, 37. Notes in HPP.
38. The March 1934 joint meeting agreed to co-operate on eleven issues: fascism, war and unemployment; National Hunger March and Congress; May Day; Anti-fascist and anti-war activities in factories; the Sedition Bill; Release of Meerut prisoners; T.U.C. Resolutions; Mining and Textile issues; the European Anti-fascist Conference; the Labour Camps; communication on grievances or published criticisms.
39. HP at ILP Conference 1935.
40. *New Leader* Jun 1933.
41. *Controversy* first issue Nov. 1933.
42. Of the RPC leaders who joined the CP, Eric Whalley was killed in action in Spain 1937; Jack Gaster, and CK Cullen held leading posts for many years, the former a member of the London District Committee and elected in 1946 with Ted Bramley to represent Stepney on the LCC; Hilda Vernon active locally and later secretary of the British Vietnam Committee.
43. Sources:1 *Young Socialist* Aug 1936, Dec 1940; MP to JM; Mrs Ivy Tribe—*R*; Stanley Harrison *Alex Gossip* p.63. There were ten precepts—Be friendly to your school fellows remembering that they will be your fellow workers in life; Love learning which is the food of the mind; Make every day worth while by good and useful deeds and kindly actions; Honour the good, be courteous to all, bow down to none; Do not hate or speak evil of anyone; Do not be revengeful, but stand up for your rights and resist oppression; Do not be cowardly; Be a friend to the weak and love justice, the wealth of the world is produced by labour and should be shared, each according to his needs; Observe and think in order to discover the truth; Do not believe what is contrary to reason and never deceive yourself or others; Do not think that because we love our own country we should hate other nations or wish for war; Work for the day when all men and women will be free citizens of the world and live in peace.

NOTES ON CHAPTER 16.

1. *Left Review*, Dec. 1936.
2. *Inprecorr*, 1936-931.
3. *Spain and the T.U.C.* H.P. quoted evidence of German and Italian ships in Lisbon unloading munitions for Franco, and Viscount Churchill's report of identification in Spain of German bombs and planes.
4. *Save Spain from Fascism.* After taking Badajos, Franco slaughtered Government supporters en masse. *The Times* 17-8-36, wrote of "1,200 shot in cold blood"; the *Manchester Guardian* 17-8-36, "2,000 executed by the rebels." From Lisbon, *Reuter* 18-8-36 "Executions continue."

5. Isabel Brown—*R.* also article *Thirtieth Anniversary CPGB*. Data on Linaria from *Shields Gazette* 27-4-37, and Alex Robson—*R.* on London engineers, *LR.* Mar. 1939.
6. See HP *Save Spain from Fascism, Arms for Spain, Spain and T.U.C*, also *Inprecorr* 1936-930, 959, 1001, 1254, 1272.
7. *D.W.* 31-8-36.
8. R. Bishop *Inprecorr* 1936-1273.
9. Summarised from *Spain and T.U.C.*
10. *Inprecorr* 1936-1254, 1272.
11. Quoted in *Arms for Spain.*
12. Hans Kahle *WNV* 1942-438.
13. HP at XIV CPGB, Congress May 1937.
14. Data from *Book of XV Brigade*; Kerrigan *The CP and the Spanish War.*
15. Report of Fifth visit—HPP.
16. Jim Ruskin—*R.*
17. Frank Ayres—*R.*
18. Sam Wild—*R.*
19. Letters and data in HPP.
20. Don Brown—*R.*
21. *In Memory of Ralph Fox*, *CI* XIV-869; speech at London CP Congress June 1938.
22. Following data and quotations, unless acknowledged otherwise, are from the full text of Pollitt's reports in HPP, published in part in *DW* on his return, in *Pollitt Visits Spain*, in *WNV* 1958 Aug. 23, Sep. 13 and 20. *Inprecorr* Aug. 1936 to Feb. 1939 contains a wealth of political and factual material on the fascist war in Spain.
23. Account based on *Book of the XV Brigade*, Letters from Peter Kerrigan in HPP, W. Rust *Britons in Spain*, and Sam Wild—*R.*
24. Frank Ryan, *Book of the XV Brigade.*
25. D. F. Springhall quoted in *In Memory of Wilf Jobling.*
26. *Daily Mail* 31-3-37.
27. *C.I.* 1937—869.
28. Luis Prestes was General Secretary, CP of Brazil.
29. HP wrote "Arthur", *Book of XV Brigade*, gives "Robert".
30. At Annemasse, France in June 1937, LSI and CI delegates agreed to demand the restoration to the Spanish Republic of her international rights. Later the LSI and the National Council of Labour withdrew support from "non-intervention".
31. Frank Ayres—*R.*
32. Frank Ayres—*R.* Nan Green—*R.*
33. Data on Albacete, JM.—*R.*
34. Copy in HPP.
35. Quoted in Rust, *Britons in Spain*, 164.
36. *Inprecorr*, 1938-487.
37, 38. *Inprecorr*, 1938-591.
39. XV Congress CPGB. Sept. 1938.
40. HP in *W. N.* 1942-178.
41. *Volunteer for Liberty*, 5-9-38. Sam Wild—*R.*
42. *Defence of the People.*

43. *Spain, What Next?* Also in *SAS* II.

NOTES ON CHAPTER 17.

1. H.P. in *W.N.* 1958-503 and HPP.
2. Full text in *The Unity Campaign.*
3. H.P. in *W.N.*
4. Report in *The Unity Campaign.*
5, 6 HPP.
7. The Workers Party of Marxist Unification (POUM) issued a weekly bulletin titled *The Spanish Revolution*, in English. In HPP is a copy of Vol. I, No. 1, dated Barcelona 21-10-36, which includes the following: "The struggle in Spain is not between democracy and fascism, but a phase of the world wide battle between fascism and socialism. Nothing less than a proletarian revolution is being carried out in our country today." Referring to the government of Catalonia, "it is necessary to form a government of a working class character, with representatives of left petty bourgeois parties. From committees of workers, peasants and soldiers for which we are pressing, will spring the direct representation of the new proletarian power." "The POUM, FAI and CNT are the only strictly socialist revolutionary organisations. All other parties are in the war but not in the revolution." "The rearguard is the revolution and the vanguard is the war. A workers government or council in Madrid would give the antifascist struggle an impulse which would bring incalculable advantages."
8. *D.W.* 4-11-37.
9. Unless otherwise acknowledged data are from MSS in HPP, apparently a fuller version of the article in *World News.* 1958-462.
10. Full text (D) in HPP.
11. Typed draft in HPP.
12. The speakers were Norman Angell, the Dean of Canterbury, Sir Stafford Cripps, Lloyd George, Victor Gollancz, Harry Pollitt and John Strachey. Paul Robeson sang. Lloyd George's speech in *The Times* 25-4-1939.
13. *Inprecorr* 1936-312.
14. *DW* 11-6-37.
15. *DW* 24-9-37.
16. Copy in *HPP.*
17. Data from *United We Stand.*
18. CP Manifesto in *DW* 15-1-38; HP's speech *DW* 22-1.38.
19. Summary based on CP statement *The Peoples Front* 21-5-38.
20. Speech on 11-6-38 at London CP Congress, in *LM* July 1938, and pamphlet *Unity and the People's Front,* London C.P.
21. Data from HP *Austria.*
22. Data and quotes from HP's pamphlets *Czechoslovakia and Britain,* May 1938; *Czechoslovakia* Sept.; *Czechoslovakia Betrayed,* Oct.
23. *Repudiate Munich* 30-9-38 copy in HPP.
24. *DW* 26-10-38.
25. HPP.

26. Marjorie Pollitt—*R*.

Notes on Chapter 18.

1. Notes in HPP.
2. The following quotes and summary are from H.P's pamphlet *Can Conscription Save Peace?*
3, 4. *Picture Post* 5-8-39.
5. The pageant for which all work was voluntary was organised by the Arts Committee of the London District C.P., staged by Andre Van Gyseghem, scenario by Montagu Slater, musical director Alan Bush.
6. Text in HPP and in *DW* 28-8-39.
7. H.P.P.
8. C.P.G.B. *How to Win the War*, 32 pp., includes full text of Manifesto of 2-9-39.
9. *News Chronicle* 16-9-39.
10. The following summary is compiled from notes in HPP.
11. For a full exposition of the C.I. view see the ECCI Manifesto of 6-11-39 and G. Dimitrov *Communism and the War*.
12. CC. Manifesto *D.W.* 7-10-39. *The Times* 12-10-39.
13. *D.W.* 13-10-39.
14. Telegram from, and H.P. letter dated 12-10-39 to *News Chronicle* in HPP.
15. H.P. to Joan Thompson.
16. *Western Mail* 16-10-39.
17. Those mentioned are in HPP. That from Mary Louisa is dated 11-10-39.
18. Letter dated 18-11-39 in *D.W.*
19. Text of Stalin in *Soviet Weekly* 14-2-46. Salient paragraphs, abbreviated, are: "The principal fascist states, Germany, Japan, Italy, before attacking the allied countries, destroyed the last remnants of bourgeois-democratic liberties at home ... trampled underfoot the principle of sovereignty and free development of small countries ... declared for all to hear that their aim was world domination and the extension of the fascist regime to the whole world; while by the seizure of Czechoslovakia and the central provinces of China the Axis states demonstrated that they were ready to carry out their threat concerning the enslavement of all freedom loving nations. In view of this, as distinct from the first world war, the second world war from the very outset assumed the nature of an anti-fascist war, a war of liberation, one of the tasks of which was to re-establish democratic liberties. The entry of the Soviet Union into the war against the Axis states could only strengthen—and did actually strengthen—the anti-fascist and liberating character of the second world war".
20. On Commercial TV 30-4-56 interview with Frank Owen in 'Seconds out' 10.25pm.
21. Summary based on Pollitt *How to Win the War* and notes of speeches in

HPP; the CI view from the Manifesto of 6-11-39 and G. Dimitrov *Communism and the War.*
22. Letters in HPP.
23. Julius Jacobs—*R*. Gladys and Sid Easton recollect having seen the urn with the inscription; when the present writer visited the grave in 1970 it had disappeared.

Notes on Chapter 19.

1. *Forward* 11-11-39.
2. Abe Moffatt—*R*.
3. David Ainley—*R*.
4. HPP *Manchester Guardian* 2-12-39.
5. Data on meetings from advertisements and reports in *D.W.* and notes in HPP.
6. HP in letter to E. Frow.
7. *Election Address.*
8. On 19-3-40 Chamberlain stated in the House that in addition to sending huge supplies to Mannerheim, Britain had ready a force of 100,000 men "heavily armed and equipped" to fight Russia. The Soviet breach of the Mannerheim Line and the peace of March 12 frustrated Chamberlain's plan.
9. Lawrence Bradshaw—*R*.
10. J.M.—*R*.
11. *D.W.* 28-3-40.
12. *L.M.* May 1940.
13. Letters in HPP.
14. Postgate to H.P. 26-3-40 and 1-4-40 in HPP.
15. J.M.—*R*.
16. Full text in HPP.
17. *The War and the Labour Movement* 12-6-1940; *Wages Policy* 24-12-40; and *Letters to Bill* No. 1. *The War and the Workshops* 17-6-40, No. 2 *What Is Russia Going to Do?* 17-7-40. No. 3 was written but apparently not published.
18. Draft in HPP.
19. Text in *L.M.* Nov. 1940.
20. The *Official Report* of the Convention includes Chairman's Address by Harry Adams; speeches by D.N. Pritt, K.C. M.P., and W.J.R. Squance moving resolutions on Policy and on Campaign, points from speeches in discussion, text of resolutions, messages of support, and analysis of credentials. Nehru's daughter, Indira, was among the visitors. A series of pamphlets subsequently explained the Convention's programme.
21. *L.M.* Feb. 1941.
22. *War Cabinet papers 1941-45,* quoted in *Morning Star* 1-1-72.
23. *Manchester Guardian* 10-2-41.
24. *WNV* 1941-202.
25. Quotes from *Tom Mann—A Tribute,* pamphlet by HP.
26. Ted Hill—*R*.
27. H.P. in *China Diary* 1955, unpub.

28. *LM* June 1941.
29. H.P. Broadcast 28-6-45.
30. Official documents in HPP show that the application was referred to the District Shipyard Controller, an official of the Ministry of Labour and National Service, who rejected it on July 15. On July 25, Pollitt appeared before the Poplar Local Appeal Board. They recommended release, which was granted on Aug. 8.
31. Ted Hill—*R*.
32. *The Times* 19-2-42.
33. Text in HPP *MG* 27-6-41.
34. *Political letter* 8-7-41.
35. *Britain's Chance.*
36. *A Call for Arms.*
37. *W.N.V.* 1941-514.
38. *Smash Hitler.*

Notes on Chapter 20

1. Full presentation in HP speech at Stoll Theatre 28-12-41.
2. *Smash Hitler.*
3. *Britain's Chance.*
4. At C.C. meeting, 1-8-41.
5. *Call for Arms.*
6. H.P. in *Manchester Guardian*, 22-8-41.
7. *W.N.V.*, 1941-597.
8. H.P. in *Manchester Guardian*, 22-8-41.
9. *W.N.V.*, 1941-597.
10. *L.M.*, Oct. 1941.
11. *Daily Herald*, 8-8-41.
12. *W.N.V.*, 1941-513.
13. *WNV* 1941-514.
14. *DW* 22-11-54.
15. *HPP.*
16. See TUC *Report* 1941 and RPD in *LM* Oct 1941.
17. *W.N.V.* 1941-597. *L.M.* Oct. 1941.
18. *Daily Mail*, 8-9-41.
19. *L.M.* Oct. 1941.
20. Data and quote from *New Builders Leader*, Oct. 1941.
21. Full text (D) issued by C.P.G.B. 28-12-41.
22. *W.N.V.* 1942-2.
23. *Smash Hitler.*
24. *L.M.*, Oct. 1941.
25. HP at Stoll, 28-12-41.
26. *Smash Hitler.*
27. Stoll, 28-12-41.
28. *L.M.*, Oct. 1941.
29. Data in *L.M.*, Nov. 1941.
30. *W.N.V.*, 1942-81.

31. *W.N.V.*, 1942-113.
32. *W.N.V.*, 1942-129.
33. *W.N.V.*, 1942-227.
34. *The Way to Win.*
35. *W.N.V.*, 1942-293.
36, 37. *Speed the Second Front.*
38. A.P. quoted in *W.N.V.*, 1942-309.
39, 40. *W.N.V.*, 1942-323.
41, 42. *W.N.V.*, 1942-333, 303.
43. *W.N.V.*, 1942-344.
44. *W.N.V.*, 1942-345.
45. *W.N.V.*, 1942-353.
46. *W.N.V.*, 1942-366.
47. *Pravda* on Sept. 1 quoted in *W.N.V*, 1942-369.
48. HP in *LM* Oct. 1942 and pamphlet *Deeds Not Words.*
49. *W.N.V.*, 1942-417, 419.
50. *The Times*, 22-5-42.
51, 52. *Deeds Not Words.*
53. In serial form in *Sunday Express.* (3-2-46, 10-3-46, 24-3-46).
54. Quoted in CPGB *The Communists Were Right*, May. 1946.
55. *Deeds Not Words.*
56. In speech to Moscow Soviet reported in *WNV* 1942-444.
57. *Political Letter*, 13-11-42.
58. *W.N.V.*, 1943-249.
59. Full text in *Where Does Britain Stand?* on which the following summary is based.
60. *W.N.V.*, 1943-337.
61. Evidence at the *Nuremburg Trial, The Times*, 28-11-45.
62. Robert Bailey—*R.*
63. Conference *Report.*
64. To his brother Robert.
65. Data from Robert Bailey.
66. *W.N.V.*, 1944-193.
67. Full text in *Documents* XVII CPGB.
68. H.P. to Joan Thompson, 14-7-44.
69. *D-Day.*
70. Stoll, 28-12-41.
71. Kingsway Hall, 24-1-42.
72. *W.N.V.*, 1942-187, 193.
73. Nehru in cable dated 13-4-42 to India League, text in *W.N.V.* 1942-231.
74. At CPGB National Conference, May 1942: report in *The Way to Win.*
75. *W.N.V.*, 1942-326.
76. HP in Preface to *The Indian Communist Party* by P.C. Joshi.
77. Dated 27-7-42. The text signed by Pollitt is in HPP: it is not clear whether the letter was sent or whether it was overtaken by events.
78. Text in *W.N.V.* 1942-349.
79. *W.N.V.*, 1942-339.
80. *W.N.V.*, 1942-357.

81. Report in *W.N.V.*, 1942-364.
82. Full text of letter in *Documents XVII CPGB*.
83. These notes are extracts from some of H.P.'s letters to Joan Thompson, who in June 1944 was in hospital with arthritis when the building was hit by a flying bomb. She had to be dug out of the ruins and was the only patient in her ward to survive. Her legs and ankles were irreparably injured. There are gaps in the sequence of the available letters, in HPP.
84. The first consumers co-operative in Britain was founded in this Lancashire town in 1844.
85. *W.N.V.* 1945-7 gives the total as 104; at 90 of these the results were 834 new members for the C.P., literature sales £289, collections £3,737.

Notes on Chapter 21.

1. *How to Win the Peace.* The chapter headings were: 1. We are the Future; 2. Unity and Victory; 3. Post-War Years; 4. "Last Time and Now"; 5. The Advance to Socialism; 6. The Problem of Production; 7. Who are the People? 8. Britain for the People; 9. Peace and World Security; 10. India and the Colonial Countries; 11. The General Election; 12. The Unity of the Labour Movement; 13. Conclusion.
2. The quotes are from *How to Win the Peace,* mainly pp.86, 91 and 92. Subsequent events showed that in *How to Win the Peace* and in his view of the Crimea Conference, Pollitt tended to under-estimate the danger that capitalist reaction in co-operation with official Labour would "rupture the war time alliance." In December 1947 he referred to "lateness in appreciating the full scale of the drift to the right."
3. In *W.N.V.* 1944-305, and HPP. Official German sources sought to blame Allied bombing for the deaths of Thaelmann and Breitscheid. *The Times* 19-9-44 exposed contradictions in Nazi statements, one dated the alleged bombing of Buchenwald as Aug. 28; another as Aug. 24.
4. The poem, without author's name, is in HPP. An account of Ernst Thaelmann's life in Anna Seghers *Ernst Thaelmann* 1932, a full and documented account by Walter Wimmer in *BZG* 2/1972 German Democratic Republic. These confirm Pollitt's summary, with some minor corrections in dates.
5. Speaking at Ipswich on 5-12-44, reported in *W.N.V.* 1944-394.
6. *W.N.V.* 1944-393.
7. In *Life* 12-5-47 Churchill wrote about the order he sent at 2 a.m. on 6-12-44 to General Scobie that he "should no longer consider himself neutral between the Greek parties, but on the contrary support the Premier Papandreou and shoot at the Communists without any hesitation." He went on "for forty days we waged a stubborn struggle for the life and soul of Athens ... two or three British divisions gradually entered the city. We liberated house after house from the Communists, hurling them back with heavy losses." Quoted by Dr. Bilbo at Political Committee of U.N.A. and by H.P. in 1948.

8. *The Times* (6-12-44) wrote that E.A.M. is "composed of the Communist Party, the Socialist Party, the Union of Popular Democrats, the Agrarian Party, the Socialist Workers' Party, the Greek Socialist Union, the Party of Social Democracy, the Workers and Peasants Party, the Left-wing Liberals, and many other organisations and individuals." For description of right-wing activities see *The Times* 7-12-44 and 9-12-44.
9. For data and documentation see *Churchill's New Order in Greece*, Hermes Press, London 1945. *Report on Greece* by Gerald Barry, Editor, *News Chronicle*, Feb. 1945.
10, 11. Tony Ambatielos—*R.*
12. The demonstration was called by the League for Democracy in Greece. Other speakers included Dr. Haden Guest, H.N. Brailsford, Sir Compton Mackenzie, Lord Strabolgi.
13. W.N.V. 1944-413.
14. Conference *Report.*
15. *Pollitt Answers Foot.*
16. H.P. in *Weekly Letter* (D), 4-5-45.
17. *Report* XVII C.P.G.B. Congress.
18. *The Times,* 2-12-44.
19. *W.N.V.,* 1944-394.
20. *Manchester Guardian,* 23-11-44.
21. *W.N.V.,* 1944-413.
22. *Crimea Conference.*
23. *Answers to Questions*: The eight questions were—1. What do you consider the basic changes in the world situation? 2. Will not the causes of war remain as long as capitalism remains? 3. Is it possible to carry out economic co-operation, or must it break down through interimperialism rivalry? 4. Can we reconcile the Crimea perspective with our understanding of the basic contradictions within capitalism? 5. Is planned capitalism possible and under what conditions? 6. What changes are taking place in the State that facilitate democratic advance? 7. Is a peaceful transition to socialism possible? 8. What common interest in the post-war period will make national unity possible?
24. *W.N.V.,* 1945-89.
25. Conference *Report*
26. *W.N.V.,* 1946-261. HP wrote of "Russia's 15 m casualties." *Soviet News* 9-5-72 quoted Marshall Grechko in *Pravda* stating "20 m dead".
27. Speech in *L.M.,* July 1945.
28. Full text in leaflet and *DW* 29-6-45.
29. Silicosis, petrification of the lungs by silica dust in anthracite, was scheduled as an industrial disease in 1935. Before then no compensation was paid. Pneumoconiosis, petrification due to coal dust was not scheduled till 1943. These diseases were commonly called "miners' anthrax". There were instances of men, even brothers, working side by side, of whom some would contract the disease; others would not.
30. Data on Rhondda from E.D. Lewis, *The Rhondda Valleys* and the Borough of Rhondda *Official Guide.*

31. In 1946 the Regional Survey claimed that Rhondda coal reserves were 1,071 tons. The National Coal Board in 1949 planned two projects. One to employ 2,800 men at Maerdy to produce 1 mn. tons annually from the 120 mn. tons estimated to be there; the other to employ 2,500 men to produce 1.2 mn. tons at Fernhill from the 80 mn. tons there. (E.D. Lewis, p.271).
32. During the 1910 strike, 600 police under orders of the Chief Constable of Glamorgan, were reinforced by 500 Metropolitan police and also troops. At Tonypandy on 8-11-10, at Aberaman on 13-11-10 and again at Tonypandy on 21-11-10 there was a combination of brutal batoning by police and "gentle persuasion" with the bayonet. See R. Page Arnot, *The Miners*. A photo of Fusiliers and Huzzars at Pontypridd on 9-11-10 was reproduced in the *Daily Worker* on 18-2-50. During the national railway strike of 1912 troops at Llanelly fired on miners and railwaymen.
33. Full text of Lenin's letter in *British Labour and British Imperialism* p. 271 L & W, London.
34. At the end of 1972 only three collieries were working—Maerdy in Rhondda Fach; Fernhill in Rhondda Fawr; and Lewis in Merthyr. (Official Guide).
35. The following recollections were given verbally to JM in 1973 by Annie Powell, unless otherwise acknowledged, and by Mrs. Roberts, Ebby Thomas and George Baker.
36. Ebby Thomas—*R*.
37, 38. Mrs. Roberts—*R*.
39, 40. HP to Joan Thompson.
41. George Baker—*R*.
42. Data on campaign from report of Idris Cox, the organiser, in HPP.
43. *Leader and Gazette* 14-7-45.
44. Data on speeches from notes in HPP.
45. *Leader and Gazette* 14-7-45.
46. Idris Cox—*R*.

Notes on Chapter 22.

1. *Political Letter*, 1-8-45.
2. XVIII C.P.G.B. Congress.
3. *Professional Workers* and XVIII C.P.G.B. Congress.
4. C.P.G.B. XVIII Congress.
5. Report to EC CP 13-12-47 in *WNV* 1947-577.
6. in 1945 *Looking Ahead* p. 33.
7. This summary is based on HP's notes and report (D) dated 6-9-45 in HPP.
8. The British Stock Exchange *Year Book 1944* gave data showing the interlocking of British financial interests with the Dutch oil kings.
9. *Why You Should be a Communist*.
10. Byrnes quoted by D.N. Pritt, *The Labour Government*.
11, 12. Notes in HPP and in *W.N.* 1958-491.
13. *Labour's Foreign Policy*. At the XVIII CPGB Congress W. Rust said

Bevin was "No. 1. for removal" from the Government. Pollitt said this was not the Party's policy, which was that "changes in government policy should be brought about by pressure from the whole Labour movement." *D.H.* 27-11-45.
14. In *Daily Herald*, 5-2-46.
15. *The Times*, 6-3-46 wrote: "Mr. Churchill also said that UNO must immediately begin to be equipped with an international armed force . . . Since the end of the war a shadow had fallen on the scene; nobody knew what Russia and its Communist international organisation intended to do in the immediate future . . . An iron curtain has descended across the continent."
Also *DW* 9-3-46.
16. Quote by D.N. Pritt, *The Labour Government*.
17. On 10-3-46, reported in *W.N.V.* 1946-81.
18. *LM* July 1946.
19. On 22-1-48 in a review of foreign policy.
20. C.P.G.B. XX Congress.
21. *LM* Jan. 1947.
22. *Double Diploma*, pp.xii and 179, Hutchinson, London, 1968.
23. Speech at Memorial Hall, 10-4-46. HPP.
24. In his pamphlet *The Secret Battalion: An Examination of the Communist Attitude to the Labour Party*. and in *Daily Herald* 9-4-46.
25. Laski fails to give any source for this alleged instruction by Lenin. Close students of Lenin, have no knowledge of it.
26. *Laski's Mistake.*
27. HP refers to an article by Alistair Forbes in the *Sunday Dispatch*. (This commentator quoted four words from Dimitrov, gave them a context from his own imagination, and ascribed the result to Dimitrov.)
28. In a speech to the Kilmarnock Fabian Society reported in the *Kilmarnock Standard*, 12-1-46.
29. Earl Browder, General Secretary of the C.P. U.S.A. in 1944, had assumed a basic change in the character of imperialism, and a consequent long term perspective of class peace after the war. On this analysis the C.P. U.S.A. dissolved itself as a political party. At the XVIII CPGB Congress in 1945. Pollitt said in his political report that the Executive of the CPGB "resisted definite attempts to import Browder's basic ideas into our Party." (*Congress Report,* p. 7).
30. *D.W.* 11-5-46.
31. CPGB. *Affiliation Bulletin*, 13-5-46.
32. Conference *Report.*
33. *L.M.* July 1946.
34. Conference *Report.*
35. D.N. Pritt in *The Labour Government* gives a detailed and documented account of both the home and foreign policy.
36. 37 XIX, C.P.G.B. Congress.
38. In a Memorandum to C.P. of Sweden, in HPP.
39. *Britain Will Make It.*
40. XIX, C.P.G.B. Congress.
41. *Plan for Coal* and *Report* to XIX C.P.G.B. Congress.

42. *Britain Will Make It.*
43. XIX C.P.G.B. Congress. *Report.*
44. *The Squatters.*
45. D.N. Pritt in *L.M.*, Sept. 1969.
46. C.P.G.B. *Bramley's speech.*
47. In HPP dated 30-1-47 in answer to a request from the C.P. Sweden.
48. XIX, C.P.G.B. Congress.
49. *L.M.* Apr. 1947.
50. *C.R.* May 1947.
51. *Looking Ahead* from which the quotes in this section are taken. Over 40,000 copies were sold at 2s. then a considerable price.
52. Full text *W.N.V.* 1947, p. 397; proposals in *The Times* 1-9-47.
53. Text in HPP.
54. Report to Executive Committee CPGB on 13-12-47. Full text in W.N.V. 1947-577.

Notes on Chapter 23.

1. In April Platts Mills, M.P. for Finsbury, sent a telegram signed by 21 Labour M.Ps. wishing success to the Italian Socialist Party who were contesting in a General Election in agreement with the Communist Party.
2. In pamphlet *Defend Democracy,* Nov. 1948.
3. *Trade Unionists—What Next?*
4,5. In *Tactics of Disruption,* Mar. 1949, to which Pollitt replied in *W.N.V.* 2-4-49 in an article with the same heading.
6, 7. CPGB *American Communists on Trial.*
8, 9. *W.N.V.* 1949-506.
10. Data from materials in HPP. The book was titled *Out of the Night;* English edition by Heinemann London 1941.
11. *L'Humanite,* 14, 15 & 16 May 1948.
12. *L'Humanite,* 6, 7 & 8 June 1948.
13. Data on the incidents in Devon from the extensive notes in HPP except where otherwise stated.
14. *The Times* 25-4-49.
15, 16. *Western Morning News,* 25-4-49.
17. *Dartmouth Chronicle,* 29-4-49.
18. Original in HPP. D.N. Pritt in his Memoirs refers to his readiness to defend before a court-martial a sailor in HMS *London* who gave notice that he would refuse to obey any order to fire on the Chinese Communists.
19. Quotations from *letters* by H.P. to Margot Heinemann, in HPP.
20. Printed as a folder, *Twenty Years as General Secretary.*
21. *D.W.* 27-11-50 and J.M's recollections.
22. CPGB *World Greetings to Harry Pollitt.*
23. The following quotes are from H.P. in *L.M.* July 1951.

24. *Political Letter*, 20-5-49.
25. XXI C.P.G.B. Congress.
26. Sent on 9-2-50 to Mr. Frank Owen, Editor of the *Daily Mail.* Copy in HPP.
27. Text in *The Listener* 23-2-50 and *DW* 16-2-50.
28. Letters in HPP, Bernal 17-2-50, Horner 18-2-50.
29. *Political Letter*, 13-3-50.
30. Malaya is dealt with below in Chapter 25-2.
31. D.N. Pritt, *The Labour Government*; also in *Light on Korea.*
32. *Peace Depends on the People.*
33. *Negotiate Now.*
34. *U.S. News and World Report*, Dec. 1950.
35. *Wall Street Journal*, 3-8-51.
36. Gaitskell on 25-9-51 quoted the first two figures, but omitted the third, *Negotiate Now*, p. 12.
37. After Ottawa, 20-9-51.
38. There were Communist Ministers in the immediate post-war governments of Austria, Belgium, Denmark, Finland, France, Greece, Iceland, Italy, Norway and San Marino. Following Marshall Aid these Ministers were dismissed or resigned in refusal to acquiesce in anti-popular measures. *The Times* 12-12-72 quoted Mitterand: "Communists have governed in ten Western European countries. Apart from Greece they left power normally".
39. Report of visit (D) in HPP, also *W.N.V.* 1946-188.
40. *W.N.V* 1947-148.
41. H.P. in *W.N.V.* 1948-36.
42. Notes in HPP. *WNV* 1947-301.
43. *People's Paper*, 17-2-1848.
44. *W.N.V.* 1948-408.
45. Data and quotes from *Impressions of Czechoslovakia. W.N.V.* 1946-171 gave the results of the May elections: 114 Communist M.Ps., 55 Benes Socialists, 47 People's Party, Catholics, 36 Social Democrats. The votes in the Czech lands were: Communists 2,205,658; Benes Siociasts 1,298,917; People's Party 1,126,777; Social Democrats 862,494—and in Slovakia: Democrats 988,275; Communists 490,257, Freedom 67,575, Labour 49,983.
46. H.P's report of the 1949 Congress did not appear in *WNV* presumably because on pp. 281 and 295 that journal published lengthy summaries of Gottwald and Zapototsky. See also Klugmann in *W.N.V.* 1948-107.
47. *W.N.V.* 1950-377.
48. J.M. in *W.N.V.* 1951-124.
49. HP's *Weekly Letter* (D) 22-9-50.
50. *Undelivered Broadcast* Oct. 1951.
51. Notes in HPP.
52. Folder *After the Election* Nov. 1951.

NOTES ON CHAPTER 24.

1. *Draft Programme*, 1939.
2. *Looking Ahead*, 88-91.
3. *Answers to Questions*, 39.
4. *Answers to Questions*, 33.
5. *Looking Ahead*, 86-87.
6. *Looking Ahead*, 93.
7. *Answers to Questions*, 33.
8. *Looking Ahead*, 90, 92.
9. *C.R.*, Feb. 1951.
10. *Political Letter*, 30-1-51.
11. *The British Road to Socialism*, first published as a 22 page pamphlet, price 3d. in January 1951, three times reprinted. In April 1952 the XXII Congress adopted a revised version, published as a 4d. pamphlet. In 1957 the XXV Congress remitted a new text to the Executive which adopted it in January 1958. Published as a 6d. pamphlet it was reprinted in March and May. After Pollitt's death there were further editions.
12. Speech in HPP.
13. Notes in HPP.
14, 15. *D.W.* 9-3-51. HP's *Report* on II HWPP.
16, 17. *W.N.V.* 1956-281.
18. *Allies For Freedom.* Report of the II Conference of Communist and Workers Parties within the sphere of British Imperialism. London, April 1954.
19. From HP's article in a symposium *Why I am a Democrat*, 1939. edited by Sir Richard Acland, M.P.
20. From Notes for a Debate on Liberty, in HPP.
21. *Why I am a Democrat*, as above.
22, 23. Notes as above.
24. From HP's *Marx Memorial Lecture* 14-3-1958.
25. Notes as above.
26. Lecture as above.

NOTES ON CHAPTER 25.

1, 2. *Political Letter* 10-11-51.
3. Data and quotes from *Stop the War in Malaya*. Also see HP in *WNV* 1950-390 and 1951-307 on the Labour Governments "wholesale destruction of villages, shifting populations into concentration camps, marshalling workers on estates and mines into guarded compounds ... one vast forced labour camp, being drained of its rubber and tin under the gun muzzles to serve the US war machine."
4, 5. *W.N.V.* 1955-1.
6. *In Defence of Peace.* See also *The Nazis Shall Not Pass.*
7. Text in HPP. The twenty meetings were attended by 7,948 active members, DW 28-1-55.
8. *In Defence of Peace.*
9. At Birmingham, 11-1-55.
10. Entry to the House was stopped at 7 p.m., mounted police forced away

the crowd; some 10,000 marched to Montague Place where several thousand were waiting to hear Pollitt. Police estimated that in total 17,000 took part. (D.W. 26, 27-1-55).
11. *Reformers Year Book* SDF Reports.
12. TAJ to HP. 15-12-41.
13. Joss to HP, 1941.
14. Adshead to HP, 20-12-47.
15. Obituary speech by HP.
16. *S.M.T.* 43.
17. Frank Jackson, a member of the SDP Branch who organised the meeting and was present, Marx Library *Bulletin*, July 1973.
18. *New World*, Apr. 1913.
19. *Clarion*, 2-2-13.
20. *Leaven of Life*, 14.
21. Ben Ainley—*R*.
22. In HPP.
23. *Call*, 26-7-17.
24. *Communist*, 28-10-20.
25. *Workers Weekly*, 18-11-23.
26. Ella—*R*.
27. *Workers Weekly* 13-11-24.
28. In HP's appeal dated 13-12-41.
29. Letters, receipt stubs and balance sheet in HPP.
30. Amounts totalled 1941 £73.6s. 1946 to 1950 £28.10s. £63 £55.3s. £77.11s. £58.8s.
31. Fraser to HP.
32. Gee to HP.
33. Letters and data in HPP.
34. *DW.* 17-5-55 to 5-7-55.
35. In an interview in connection with the breakaway of Hull dockers from the T&GWU, autumn 1954. Text in HPP.
36. *DW* 15-7-55 *What Next in the Docks?* reprinted as leaflet, copy in HPP, advertising meeting at Canning Town Public Hall 10-8-55. On 29-7-55 *DW* printed comment by Tiffin and rejoinder by HP.
37. Tiffin's comment circulated in full by P.A., part in *Daily Telegraph* 11-8-55 with report of meeting. Report also in DW 11-8-55. Notes of Pollitt's speech in HPP.
38. *DW* 17-6-55, *The Lessons of the Strikes*; twice reprinted as a folder.
39. *D.W.* 26-2-53.
40. *D.W.* 15-4-54.
41. Reference by Lenin in *Collected Works* XXXI-82.
42. *D.W.* 22-11-54.
43. An abridged version of *The Ragged Trousered Philanthropists* by Robert Tressell was published in 1914 and in 1916. The original full text was first published by Lawrence & Wishart in 1955, and was reviewed by Harry Pollitt. F.C. Ball in *Tressell of Mugsborough* gives data to support his view that the author's real name was Robert Noonan. See also excerpt from a further book by Ball, *More Light on Tressell*, in *MTD*. 1967, p. 177.

44. W.N. 1955-767.
45. Items from notes in HPP.
46. *Marxist Quarterly* July 1965.
47. At this time Marx's grandson, Jean Longuet, was the senior heir; he was a socialist, but antipathetic to Marx. When he died, his younger brother was favourable to the memorial project.
48. *Manchester Guardian* 13-3-33.
49. The Committee consisted of Andrew Rothstein, R. Palme Dutt, Peter Kerrigan and John Morgan. Later Harry Pollitt was added, and Arthur Horner became treasurer of the fund. The public appeal raised the £12,500 cost. Some Minutes, etc. are in possession of Andrew Rothstein.
50. This stone names Jenny von Westphalen, Marx's wife; Karl Marx; Harry Longuet (grandson), and Helene Delmuth. The ashes of Eleanor Marx were for many years in the safekeeping of the Social Democratic Federation; then the British Socialist Party, and finally of the Communist Party.
51. On 14 October 1954.
52, 53. Lawrence Bradshaw—*R*.
54. Reports of the ceremony are in *D.W.* and *Manchester Guardian* 15-3-56, *Highgate Express* 16-3-56, *WN* 1956-186.
55. *W.N.* 1956-186 and H.P's speech (D).

NOTES ON CHAPTER 26.

1. Calendar of dates: 1953, Nov. 24 Southampton; Dec. 12-15 Bombay; 16-19 Delhi, Amritsar, Jullandur, Taj Mahal; 20-21 Calcutta; 22-23 Hyderabad; 24 Madras; 25-Jan. 4 1954 Madurai; 1954 Jan. 5-7 Bombay; 24 Tilbury.
2. Incidents on the *Batory* from *H.P.'s Diary*.
3. Unless otherwise stated, data on the tour are from HP's *Indian Diary* and his scrapbook of cuttings and photographs from the Indian press. HPP.
4. *Inprecorr* 1936-174.
5. J.M.—*R*.
6. *H.P.* to J.M.
7. Data and quotes on Amritsar massacre from Sir Valentine Chirol's article in *The Times*, 17-5-21, including quotes from Dyer's evidence to the Commission of Enquiry. Comment by Nehru quoted by Brecher in *Nehru, A Political Biography*.
8, 9. In addition to the published *Indian Diary* there are detailed notes of the CPI Congress proceedings, including his own and some other speeches, in HPP.
10. *Hindustani Times* 23-1-54.
11. *Free Press Journal* 5-1-54.
12. Conference *Report*, p. 135.

NOTES ON CHAPTER 27.

1. Papaioannou in *Allies for Freedom*.
2. *The Worker*. 21-9-28.
3. E. Joannides *The Case for Cyprus* 1937.
4. *W.N.V.* 1946-87.
5. Data on HP's activities in Cyprus and quotations, unless otherwise stated are from HP's Cyprus Diary, partly published *DW* March 1954 plus some historical and descriptive material gained by J.M. in a visit to Cyprus in 1966. Data on British rule in Cyprus in E. Joannides *The Case for Cyprus* 1937.
6. *D.W.* 1-10-55.

NOTES ON CHAPTER 28.

1. XV Congress was in Dec. 1927, XVI Congress in Apr. 1929. There is no record of HP being at XVII in Jan. 1934 or XVIII in May 1939.
2. *W.N.V.* 1952-517.
3. Somewhat abbreviated; full text in *W.N.V.* 1952-505.
4. *WNV* 1952-517.
5. *DW* 9-3-53.
6, 7. HP's speech at a London memorial meeting on 25-3-53, *In Memory of Joseph Stalin and Klement Gottwald* from which the following quotes are taken.
8. Full text in HPP.
9. In London, 12-3-56, text in HPP.
10. On 25-2-56. In June 1956 *The Manchester Guardian* published what purported to be a full text of *Khrushchev's* speech to the closed session. The text was supplied by the U.S. Information Service.
11. *D.W.* 24-3-56; *W.N.* 1956-246 *W.N.* 1956-278, on which the following summary is based.

NOTES ON CHAPTER 29.

1. Political Report to XXIV Congress C.P.G.B.
2. Meeting on 12-5-56 report in *W.N.* 1956-324.
3. The following summary is based on HP's notes for reports to two meetings.
4. e.g. *Daily Mail*, 25-10-56.
5. *Sunday Times*, 25-6-50.
6. *Manchester Guardian*, 1-12-51.
7. *New York Times*, 29-6-52. Quotes 4 to 7, and many others from British and US papers in *Hungary: Background Notes* (D) CPGB 8-11-56.
8, 9. Congress *Report*, reports in *The Times* 20, 22, 23-4-57.
10. John Ashton, a delegate,—R.
11. Data on Alice Jones from her papers seen by J.M. and from her daughter Alice Loveman.
12. HP in *W.N.* 1956-32.
13. HP to Joan Thompson.
14. HP to George Matthews.
15. To JM.

16. HP to Joan Thompson.
17. MP—*R*.
18, 19 *W.N.* 1959-121 and HPP.
20. Notes in HPP.

NOTES ON CHAPTER 30.

1. Gladys Easton—*R*.
2. This general account of HP's tour of Australia has been compiled from letters, the press, and personal recollections, as follows: Letters: HP to Marjorie, Jean, and John Gollan; to Marjorie from R. Dixon, Ralph Maddern, W. McDougall, Stan Moran, Joyce Slater. CPA papers: Sydney *Tribune*; Melbourne *Guardian*. Capitalist papers: Melbourne *Herald*; Newcastle *Morning Herald*. Recollections written to JM by: Marjorie Pollitt, and by J.W. Bevan, Joe Bailes, R. Dickson, R. Gibson, Joe Goss, H.T. Johnson (Johnno), Steve Quinn, Alf Watt. Of the weekly summary of HP's notes of each day's events, mentioned by Johnno, there is no trace among his effects.
3. The N.Z. account has been compiled from letters of HP to Marjorie, Jean and John Gollan; tape recording of HP's speech to Conference; recollections of G.E. Jackson, *Wellington Evening Post*, 16 & 17-4-60 and Dunedin *Evening Star* 20-4-60.
4. G.E. Jackson—*R*.
5. *Evening Post*, 17-4-60.
6. At the time of Pollitt's visit ideological differences had not developed into the subsequent breach with the C.P. of China. After the latter had put forward in 1966 their alternative "General Line for the International Communist Movement", the Communist Party of New Zealand split. The dominant leadership followed Mao Tse-tung, those loyal to Marxism-Leninism formed the Socialist Unity Party of New Zealand. G.E. Jackson, previously Chairman of the C.P.N.Z. became National Secretary of the S.U.P., which was later joined by many who left the C.P.N.Z., including members of its National Committee.
7. G.E. Jackson—*R*.
8. Alf Buckley, General Secretary of the Boilermakers Society of Australia, advised of Pollitt's visit by Ted Hill, then General Secretary of the British Boilermakers, brought the matter before his Federal Executive, who agreed to "extend suitable hospitality to Bro. Pollitt," and to notify the Branches so that they could also contact him. (Ex. Circular 7/60). During his stay Pollitt met the Federal Executive, and wrote to Marjorie that he "found the Boilermakers in Australia very active, everywhere to the fore in the Labour Movement." In 1969 when Marjorie arrived to settle in Australia, the Boilermakers helped her.

Other national officials who assisted in Pollitt's tour included Jim Healey, Gen. Sec. of the Waterside Workers, and Laurie Carmichael, Vice Pres. of the Amalgamated Metal Workers.

9. Data from T.U.C. *The Martyres of Tolpuddle* 1934.
10. *Morning Herald* 3-5-60.
11. Joe Bailes—*R.*
12. HP to MP.
13. *Herald* 30-5-60.
14, 15. Johnno.
16. 16-6-60.
17. Built at Barrow in 1935, *Orion* was 23,371 tons gross, a twin-screw vessel with Parsons single reduction geared turbines. She "provided a complete break with the traditional, had one funnel and one mast." Her interior design was another innovation, "from lamp-shades to lay-out of public rooms, all was placed in the hands of one man." Orient Line *Little History.*
18. Joe Goss—*R.*
19. In the CPA papers and letters to MP.
20. These were Australia, Belgium, Bulgaria, China, Cyprus, Czechoslovakia, Denmark, Finland, France, Holland, Hungary, Iceland, Northern Ireland, Norway, Poland, Romania, Sweden, USSR.
21. The bearers were J.R. Campbell, R.P. Dutt, Peter Kerrigan, John Mahon, George Matthews and Brian Pollitt.
22. Text of the speeches in CPGB, *Harry Pollitt, A Tribute.*
23. Most of these letters and others in *Harry Pollitt,* as above. LRD obituary in *Labour Research* Aug 1960.
24. *Comment,* 1970-405.

NOTES ON CHAPTER 31.

1. Lawrence Bradshaw—*R.*
2. Ella—*R.*
3. HP to Joan Thompson 6-11-40.
4. Ella—*R.*
5. HP in *DW* 22-11-54.
6. John Wood—*R.*
7. J.M.—*R.*
8. W. Brain—*R.*
9. Marjorie Pollitt—*R.*
10. HPP Speech in honour of Thaelmann Oct 1944.
11. Charlie Wellard—*R.*
12. J.M.—*R.*
13. *LM*—Oct 1941.
14. HPP and *SMT.*
15. Ella—*R.*
16. *Daily Express* 28-6-60.
17. Ray Offley—*R.*
18. Louise Ross—*R.*
19. Sid Easton—*R.*
20. Margot Heinemann—*R.*
21. Abe Moffat—*R.*

22. From his articles in LM 1922 on to his last writings in *MTD* Aug. 1958 and his synopsis in 1959 for a book on trade unionism, Pollitt consistently put forward these concepts. Synopsis in Appendix 7.
23. During the American civil war there were great demonstrations against intervention on the side of the slave owners. In 1920 war on Soviet Russia was prevented, see Chapter 8.
24. Particularly Chapters 7, 9, 11, 15.
25. *MTD* Aug. 1958.
26. *Workers' Weekly* 17-10-24.
27. *The Meaning of Margate*. In this pamphlet Pollitt makes a full analysis of the results of the 1926 Labour Party Conference.
28. Synopsis *Reply to Citrine*.
29. *Workers Weekly* 15-8-24.
30. *The Meaning of Margate* and *Reply to Citrine*.
31. Synopsis.
32, 33. *MTD Aug. 1958* and *Synopsis*.
34. Synopsis.
35. *S.M.T.*
36. *Merrie England* pp. 104-6.
37. 661 *Clarion* readers answered the question "Who was Britain's greatest benefactor?" The top ten were—Darwin 136, Caxton 103, Cromwell 52, Shakespeare 35, Robert Owen 27, Charles Dickens 22, Geo. Stephenson 14, Lord Shaftesbury 12, Prof. James Simpson 12, James Watt 11, and next Simon de Montfort 10. Of Socialists chosen, Robert Owen 27, Karl Marx 6, Keir Hardie 4, Bernard Shaw 4, William Morris 3, Victor Grayson 1, Ernest Jones 1. (*Clarion* 4-1-07) Blatchford's own choice was Guy Fawkes.
38. Lecture 14-3-39.
39, 40. Lecture 14-3-52.
41. Speech 12-12-56 HPP.
42. *Looking Ahead* pp. 41 to 43.
43. *Why You Should be a Communist.*
44. *Report* of the Party Commission.
45. Report to XII Congress CPGB.
46. Lecture 10-2-37 HPP.
47. *Communist Manifesto.*
48. Lecture 10-2-37.
49. On March 31 1944 members registered, excluding those serving in the Forces, totalled 47,513; details in Report of E.C. to 17th Congress.
50. Report XXI Congress CPGB.
51. Report XXII Congress.
52. Report XXIII Congress.
53. Report XXIV Congress.
54. Report XXII Congress.
55. Report XXIV Congress.
56. Report XXI Congress.
57. Report XXIII Congress.
58. Report XXIV Congress.
59. *SMT* 14.

60. *Answers to Questions p. 39.*
61. *Political Letter 1-8-45.*
62. Foreword to the first edition of the *British Road to Socialism.*

APPENDIX 1

HARRY POLLITT'S EARLY READING

"All his life he loved books" as Ella said and the roots of his enduring and developing ideas of the Socialist revolution sprang from his early reading of progressive and socialist periodicals, penny pamphlets and the writings of Robert Blatchford, William Morris and Karl Marx.

In December 1891, Samuel Pollitt was in Manchester carrying his baby son in his arms when he first heard the call "Buy the *Clarion*, Blatchford's paper." Said Samuel to Mary Louisa, "Here, hold our Harry while I buy this paper", and he went on buying it till 1914. He also read the *Freethinker*, and in Openshaw, when they were delivered to the house on Fridays, Harry "rushed for them both". Blatchford was no Marxist, but the *Clarion* gave Harry what it gave to thousands—a fearless exposure of the social injustices and economic oppression by capitalism, and a popular, closely reasoned case for the social ownership and control of production. Of this flair for simple explanation of capitalism, Mary Louisa commented, "I saw the light of day, all was made plain and simple." Life was to prove, alas, that it was by no means so simple. H. M. Hyndman's *Justice*, though founded earlier, in 1884, never attained the wide appeal of the *Clarion*, but it helped Harry to grasp basic Marxist economics. In the *Freethinker*, the National Secular Society's journal, first published in 1881, Harry read reasoned criticism of superstition and official hypocrisy in society, and a concern for recognising social facts.

In 1910–11, reading Tom Mann's *Industrial Syndicalist*, he found a series of expository articles by Tom and his circle of militants, on the problems of industrial mass action as a means of approach to socialism, often sharply defining the reality of the class struggle.

Harry broke with both Blatchford and Hyndman when in 1914 they supported the imperialist war. From 1916 *The Call* championed socialist internationalism and later the Bolshevik Revolution. When in London in 1918, Pollitt also read and wrote for Sylvia Pankhurst's *Workers Dreadnought*.

For the decades around the turn of the century, the penny pamphlet was a major means of political education for workers. The national organisations of socialists, radicals and progressives published them in a steady stream, many were also printed by local presses, particularly in Lancashire and Yorkshire. Pollitt read all he could lay hands upon, many he preserved, re-read and quoted. "I have said many 'Long Lives' in my time, but I will never get tired of saying 'Long Live the Penny Pamphlet!'"

Among those he re-read many times was *Liberal and Tory Hypocrisy* by C. A. Glyde of Bradford, a city councillor and guardian. Its 32 pages of small print are an arsenal of facts on the exploitation, oppression and deception of workers by both ruling-class parties. It makes a case for an "independent socialist and trade unionist party, the only hope of the workers." It gives the Manchester speech of Ernest Jones, after his release from prison, nearly two years in solitary confinement. Pollitt's interest in the great Chartist was stimulated by this account, and in later years he read all he could about him. This pamphlet ran to fourteen editions. Glyde wrote three others—*Britain's Disgrace—A Plea for Old Age Pensions*; *The Misfortune of Being a Working Man*; *A Peep Behind the Scenes at a Board of Guardians*. The sales totalled 260,000 copies.

Other early pamphlets quoted or preserved by Pollitt included:

John Burns *Speech from the Dock*. 1886, XX Century Press, London.
Victor Grayson, MP *Appeal for Socialism*. Peoples Press, Stockport. *Destiny of the Mob*, Workers Press, Huddersfield.
Daniel De Leon *What Means This Strike?* 1898, USA. *Reform or Revolution*. 1896
George Loveless *Victims of Whiggery*, Central Dorset Labourers Committee. 1837
James Nathan *Was Jesus Christ a Socialist?*
John Lincoln Mahon *A Plea for Socialism*. 1856. 1d
William Morris *Monopoly—How Labour is Robbed*. 1891, Socialist League. *Chants for Socialists*. 1892. *Useful Work Versus Useless Toil*, Freedom Library
William Morris *Why I Am a Communist*. 1894, Liberty Press. Written at the request of James Tochatti after Morris had broken with the Anarchists, Tochatti owned the Liberty Press
John Ruskin *Unto This Last, Sesame and Lillies*, Collins Penny Library.
James Tochatti *Social Conditions and Character*. 1896, Lberty Press
Mary Marcy *Shop Talks on Economics*. 10c. USA. 1911

Publications of Charles H. Kerr, Ltd, the socialist publishers of Chicago, were prominent on the literature stall at Margaret Street ("We clubbed together to buy everything they got out"—*SMT* 56). Pamphlets preserved by Pollitt in a bound volume included six from the "Pocket Library of Socialism" issued monthly at 5 cents: No 10 C. H. Kerr *Morals and Socialism* and E. Belfort Bax *The Odd Trick*; No 22 R. La Monte *Science and Socialism*; No 27 Rev W. T. Brown *The Relation of Religion to Social Ethics*; No 35 A. M. Simons *The Philosophy of Socialism*; No 44 Jack London *The Scab*; No 56 Paul Lafargue *Economic Evolution*; also Rev C. H. Vail *The Mission of the Working Class* 2c; Eugene Debs *You Railroad Men*; Paul Lafargue *The Right to be Lazy* 10c; W. Liebknecht *No Compromise, No Political Trading*.

Socialist books recollected by Pollitt include:

Robert Blatchford *Merrie England, Britain for the British, Not Guilty*: "I knew them off by heart" (*SMT* 34)
Karl Marx *The Communist Manifesto, Theory of Value, Value, Price and Profit, Wage Labour and Capital, On the Erfurt Programme, Capital, Vol. I*
Frederick Engels *Conditions of the Working Class in England in 1844. Socialism, Utopian and Scientific*
Louis Baudoin *Theoretical System of Karl Marx*
Paul Lafargue *Social and Philosophical Studies*
Prince Kropotkin *Fields, Factories and Workshops. The State*
William Morris *News from Nowhere*
Jack London *The Iron Heel* (and "all I could get")

It would be ridiculous to think that Pollitt was only interested in political reading. Whether he read his father's copy of *Decline and Fall of the Roman*

Empire we don't know, but he did use the *Chambers Dictionary*, and Ella remembered him earlier entranced in *Butterfly* and *Comic Cuts* and in numbers of the penny series, *Books for the Bairns* and *Lewis' Readings*. For horrors there was the *Police Gazette*, which specialised in murders, often illustrated.

Later came science, history, poetry and general literature, got mainly from the Public Libraries: Haekel *The Riddle of the Universe*, unspecified volumes from the Social Science Library USA, Gibbins' *Industrial History of England*, Green's *History of England*, "publications of the Rationalist Press". Poetry included Burns, Morris, Rossetti, Shelley and Yeats. Favourites were Fitzgerald *Omar Khayam* and Oscar Wilde *Ballad of Reading Gaol*, and the ballads of the Lancashire poets recited at Sunday Schools and remembered all through his life. He particularly favoured Samuel Laycock's *Warblin's Fro' an awd Songster*, but we do not know if he included the "Droylsden Bard," James Burgess. Then Arnold Bennett, George Meredith, Robert Service, Samuel Smiles' *Self Help*, Thackeray and H. G. Wells ("my last tanner on *Kipps*").

The reading listed above is limited to works mentioned by Pollitt mainly up to 1914. During the war he mentioned Norman Angell *The Great Illusion*, *War, What For?* (author unknown), and J. T. W. Newbold *How Europe Armed for War*.

Pollitt first read Lenin in 1919: in the summer, the *Appeal to the Toiling Masses*; in October, *The State and Revolution*.

Harry Pollitt liked, as did other socialist speakers of his young days, to quote at an appropriate moment in a speech, a passage from a writer or a verse from a poem, to emphasise a point, stress an appeal, or uplift the spirit of his hearers. His notes included a large number of such extracts, of which the following is a brief selection. We begin with Ernest Jones, the great Chartist, one of whose poems was first brought to Pollitt's notice in Glyde's pamphlet *Liberal and Tory Hypocrisy*:

From Ernest Jones

>Men counted him a dreamer? Dreams
>Are but the light of clearer skies—
>Too dazzling for our naked eyes.
>And when we catch their flashing beams
>We turn aside and call them dreams.
>Oh, trust me, every thought that yet
>In greatness rose and sorrow set
>That Time to ripening glory nurst
>Was called an "idle dream" at first.

>* * *

>We're low—we're low—we're very, very low,
>As low as low can be;
>The rich are high—for we make them so—
>And a miserable lot are we.

We plough and sow—we're so very very low
That we delve in the dirty clay,
Till we bless the plain with the golden grain
And the vale with the fragrant hay.
Our place we know—we're so very low.
T'is down at the landlord's feet:
We're not too low the bread to grow,
But too low the bread to eat.

We're low, we're low—we're very very low,
Yet from our fingers glide
The silken flow and the robes that glow
Round the limbs of the sons of pride.
And what we get and what we give
We know—and we know our share.
We're not too low the cloth to weave
But too low the cloth to wear.

"The Song of the Low"

* * * *

The land it is the landlord's,
   The trader's is the sea,
The ore the usurer's coffer fills,
   But what remains for me?

The engine whirls for master's craft
   The steel shines to defend,
With labour's arms, what labour raised
   For labour's foe to spend.

The camp, the pulpit and the law
   For rich men's sons are free;
Theirs, theirs is learning, art and arms,
   But what remains for me?

The coming hope, the future day
   When wrong to right shall bow.
And but a little courage, man
   To make that future—NOW!

"Song of the Future"

* * *

They think us dull, they think us dead.
   But we shall rise again.
A trumpet through the land shall ring.
   A heaving through the mass
A trampling through their palaces
   Until they break like glass.

"Peace and Plenty"

* * *

"Men of Manchester—From 18,000 pulpits 18,000 parsons are this day preaching the gospel of the rich. I stand here to preach the gospel of the poor. Surrounded by the temples of Mammon, I stand here to preach the democracy of Christ—for Christ was the first Chartist, and democracy is the gospel carried into practice. . . . Within our towns lie 2,500 millions of wealth—they belong to a few hundred money lords. Within our factories, machine power equal to 800 million hands belongs to a few thousand manufacturers. Around you lie 77 million acres of land; they belong to 30,000 landlords. The land and the wealth on its surface has been created by God and the working man. By whom is it enjoyed? By the devil and the rich idler."

(Speech on release from prison, 1850)

From Louis Aragon

Two extracts from the French Communist poet—the first a verse from the poem "The Poet to His Party".

> My Party's given me back my memory and my sight
> I had forgotten things that even children know—
> How red my blood was and how French my heart.
> My Party's given me back my memory and my sight.

The second from the poem in honour of Gabriel Peri, French Communist leader shot by a Nazi German firing squad in 1941. Aragon explains that he wrote the poem in illegality to mark the second anniversary of the murder, and that the details were not based on fact—Peri was buried at Suresnes not at Ivry—but on a popular legend which had reached him "as in the time of the troubadours, from mouth to mouth, across a France devastated and in the grip of mercenaries."

> And at the graveyard of Ivry
> In vain they lock the gates each night.
> Somebody comes with flowers bright
> To lay before Gabriel Peri.
>
> A gleam of sky where all is still,
> The sun is good when it shines through,
> The rain and memory's eyes are blue
> For him that violence did kill.
>
> Do you remember, you who fired,
> The way he sang that morning chill?
> Why, you've not put the fire out, still
> Its flaming though it seems expired.
>
> Yes, in the graveyard at Ivry
> He's singing still, he's singing still.
> There will be other dawns, there will
> Be others like Gabriel Peri.

From William Morris

      What is this, this sound a rumour?
      What is this that all men hear,
    Like the wind in hollow valleys
        When the storm is drawing near;
    Like the rolling on of ocean
        In the eventide of fear?
        Tis the people marching on.

    Hark, the rolling of the thunder
    Lo, the sun! and lo, thereunder
    Riseth wrath and hope and wonder
      And the host comes marching on.

                "The March of the Workers"

           *   *   *

Come join the only battle wherein no man can fail,
  Where whoso fadeth and dieth yet his deed shall still prevail,
  Ah come, cast off all fooling for this at least we know,
    That the dawn and the day is coming
    And forth the banners go.

From Byron

    Now half-dissolving to a liberal thaw
      But hardening back when 'ere the morning's raw;
    With no objection to true liberty,
      Except that it would make the Nations free.

    But these are deeds which should not pass away
      And names that must not wither

    Yet freedom yet thy banner torn but flying
      Streams like the thunder storm against the wind;
    The trumpet voice though broken now and dying
      The loudest still of tempests leaves behind;
    Thy tree hath lost its blossoms, and the rind
      Chopped by the axe looks rough and little worth,
    But the sap lasts, and still the seed we find
      Sown deep even in the bosom of the North:
    So shall a better spring less bitter fruit bring forth.

                "Childe Harold"

From Edward Carpenter

> England Arise! The long, long night is over,
> Faint in the East behold the dawn appear.
> Out of your evil dream of toil and sorrow,
> Arise, O England for the day is here;
> From your fields and hills
> Hark the answer swells—
> Arise, O England, for the day is here!
>
> "England Arise"

From James Connolly

"We are out for Ireland for the Irish. But who are the Irish? Not the rack-renting, slum renting, slum owner landlord, the profit grinding capitalist, not the sleek and oily lawyer, not the prostituted pressmen, the hired liars of the enemy. Not those are the Irish upon whom the future depends, but the Irish working class, the only secure foundation upon which a free nation can be reared...."

* * *

"The stronger I am in my affection for national tradition, literature, language and sympathy, the more firmly rooted am I in opposition to that capitalist class which in its soulless lust for power and gold would bray the nations as in a mortar."

(in "Forward" 22.8.14)

From John Mitchell, Irish rebel, 1848

"If any man talks to you of religious sects when the matter in hand relates to civil and political rights, to administration of government or distribution of property, depend upon it, though he wear a coronet, he means to cheat you."

From Ella Wheeler Wilcox

> Who is a Socialist? It is the man
> Who strives to formulate or aid a plan
> To better earth's conditions. It is he
> Who having ears to hear and eyes to see
> Is neither deaf nor blind when might roughshod
> Treads down the privileges and rights which God
> Means for all men; the privilege to toil,
> To breathe pure air, to till the fertile soil—
> The right to live, to love, to woo, to wed,
> And earn for hungry mouths their meed of bread.

From Wordsworth

> Milton! Thou shouldst be living at this hour:
> England hath need of thee
> She is a fen of stagnant waters.

He would quote from a source we have not traced:

> Men of England, ye are slaves,
> Though ye rule the roaring waves,
> Though ye shout from sea to sea
> 'Britons everywhere are free'.

And to conclude with a smile, from *Hilaire Belloc*

> Lord Finchley tried to mend the electric light
> Himself. It struck him dead; and serve him right!
> It is the business of the wealthy man
> To give employment to the artisan.

Harry Pollitt was fully aware of the importance attached by relatives and friends to the funeral ceremony and when, as he often was, he was invited to speak on such an occasion, he would not hesitate to alter other engagements to meet the request. From his early association with the National Secular Society, he retained a copy of two funeral orations from which for some years he often quoted. The first extract is from one by Austin Holyoake, the second by Annie Besant. (The extracts are abbreviated.)

"He leaves to his sorrowing relatives and friends a legacy in the remembrance of his virtues, his services, his honour and truth. . . . He worked out for himself the problem of life and no man was the keeper of his conscience. His religion was of this world—the service of humanity his highest aspiration. . . . There is not a flower that scents the mountain or the plain, not a rosebud that opens to the morning sun, but ere evening comes may perish. Man springs up like a tree: at first the tender plant, he puts forth buds of promise, then blossoms for a time and gradually decays and passes away. His hopes may wither and be blown about by the adverse winds of fate; but his efforts, springing from the fruitful soil of wise endeavour, will fructify the earth, from which will arise a blooming harvest of happy results to mankind. . . ."

"Sad is death at all times. It were heartless to deny the sadness and the gloom cast by death, and the tears that drop into the open grave sully no courage nor have to mankind ought of shame. Since Death must come to all to whom life has come, while it were cruelty not to sorrow, it were cowardice to break into despairing repining. While we give tears to the dead, let us from the grave turn back to life which still has its duties, if for a while it has lost its glory and its joy. The message from this open grave is one of love and work. Of love that binds us be gentle to the living that we need to drop no tears of remorse over the dead. Of work, that life is uncertain and brief, that all we can do to help and improve our generation must be done now, while this priceless treasure of life is ours . . ."

In later years he often concluded a funeral oration with the following words, from a Soviet writer.

> "Man's dearest possession is life, and since it is given to him to live but once, he must so live as not to be seared with the shame of a cowardly and trivial past; so live as to have no torturing regrets for years without purpose; so live that, dying, he can say 'All my life and all my strength were given to the finest cause in the world, the liberation of mankind'."

Where music was possible he often suggested the Russian Revolutionaries' Funeral March, though the words were not usually sung.

> Our banners are lowered, they droop on the street,
>   And the pulse of our sorrow is marked by our feet.
> We bring to a rest that their life never knew
>   Our comrades who fought and died to free the many from the few.
>
> Yet we will not mourn them as lost to the fight,
>   Nor death shall defeat them whom none can defeat.
> Our dead shall live on in the fight we maintain
>   Their impulse still drives us, their tradition still sustain.

(English Text by Randall Swingler)

APPENDIX 2

OPENSHAW SOCIALIST SOCIETY 1906–1911

It is regrettable that little evidence of the activities of the OSS is extant. All that is in print seems to be irregular reports in "The Movement" pages of the *Clarion*, a few references in the *Gorton Reporter*, a copy of the November 1911 election leaflet preserved by Harry Pollitt, and his recollections in *SMT*. The present writer was given additional information as recollected by early members of the OSS, mainly by Mrs. Elizabeth Davies and Harry Pollitt's sister Ella; also by Sir Richard Coppock and Vic Summers. No copy of Rules, Aims, Constitution, Membership Card or Minute Book seems to have survived.

The earliest socialist organisation in Openshaw appears to have been the ILP. Its Gorton Branch was represented at the Annual Conference from 1894 onwards; its Openshaw Branch from 1889. It was the Openshaw ILP that Harry's Aunt Emily and Mary Louisa joined about 1902. Harry joined the ILP Socialist Sunday School. A leaflet shows that he acted the part of Mr. Merryman in an operetta, *Lazyland*, about that time. In 1906 he himself joined the Openshaw ILP. The Gorton Trades and Labour Council—Openshaw was part of the Gorton Parliamentary constituency—acted as the co-ordinating body for all sections of the movement on both industrial and political matters, including elections, city council affairs and industrial disputes. The ILP was affiliated, so was the Gorton Branch of the Boilermakers of which Harry was a member. The Openshaw Socialist Society was formed on the initiative of the ILP: what is not clear is the political motivation for the decision to give it a name of its own.

Early in 1905, the Openshaw ILP announced (*Labour Leader*, 20.1.05) plans and fund raising to "build a new clubhouse, a palatial edifice." Nearly a year later, the site having been secured, John Hodge, the adopted Labour candidate for Gorton, opened a grand bazaar to raise money to build this clubhouse in Margaret Street (*Gorton Reporter*, 9.12.05).

The first public mention of the OSS was the announcement that in October 1906 it would hold a series of public lectures at the ILP Hall in Old Lane, with the intention "to win Openshaw for Socialism". It continued to work from that address until its own hall in Margaret Street, begun in March 1907, was open for activity in Sept. 1908. Throughout this period, John Hodge, Labour MP since December 1906, continued to be associated with it, and his agent was at an OSS public meeting at Whitworth Hall. All this suggests, not an intention to split, but rather to broaden the socialist organisation in Openshaw by providing premises larger and more attractive than those at Old Lane.

But a split was not long in coming. The return in 1906 of 29 Labour MPs organisationally independent of the Liberals, stimulated division on what they should say and do. Many thought they were far too moderate, the extent of the discontent was shown by the return in a Colne Valley by-election in 1908 of Victor Grayson, a militant, in opposition to the wishes of the official Labour leadership, a victory received with enthusiasm by the OSS. How the split developed is described by Pollitt (briefly in *SMT*; in more detail in notes in mss.). After a period of growing dissatisfaction with official Labour policy, the OSS on 10 June 1909 voted by 107 to 100 for secession from the ILP; on Sept. 2nd for secession from the Trades Council; on Oct. 10 the following year, prior to the municipal elections, the OSS refused permission for the Labour candidate to address its members. In August 1911, it seceded from the Board of Guardians Committee and began practical preparations to put up its own candidate as a "Revolutionary Socialist". It did so in November, the ILP then called for the formation of a new ILP Branch in Openshaw.

Of the Committee of the OSS, Alfred Gerring was the first secretary, given much help by Jim Crossley. After Gerring died in August 1909, Harry Pollitt became secretary. The date of his election is not known. Mrs. Davies does "not remember anyone being secretary between Alf Gerring and Pollitt" (HPP). The leading political personalities were undoubtedly Gilbert Roberts, Jim Crossley, Albert Adshead, Jack Grierson, Jack Munro, Jack Unsworth and Harry Pollitt, probably they made up the Committee. There was no permanent Chairman. Charlie Openshaw was the Literature Secretary, Ted Somerset, the Treasurer, Jack Unsworth the Propaganda Secretary.

The OSS was associated with the Manchester Socialist Representation Committee, which signed the convening notice for the Unity Conference to launch the British Socialist Party. The notice read, in part: "The basis of agreement must be the socialisation of the instruments of production, distribution and exchange." (*Clarion*, 18.8.1911). OSS delegates to the Unity Conference were Jim Crossley and Jack Munro. Their report was endorsed by the OSS, including agreement reached by the conference on the aims of "Socialisation of the means of production and distribution; transformation of capitalism into collective or communist society; not a reformist but a revolutionary party, fighting the class war through to a finish." (*Clarion*, 6.10.1911).

This formulation probably met the OSS view that the new Party should not be just a fusion of other socialist groups with the SDF, but should have a revolutionary edge against reformism.

No Register of Members is known to have survived, but in 1970 Mrs. Elizabeth Davies, *née* Holt, who joined the OSS in its early days and continued membership all through the BSP and the CPGB, compiled a list from her notes and recollections for inclusion in this volume. Together with some additional data from Harry Pollitt's *Serving My Time*, Ella's letters, Richard Allcroft, Sir Richard Coppock and Vic Summers, the list gives at least a partial picture of the kind of people who made up the OSS.

Those known to have continued into the BSP are marked with an asterisk; those into the CP with a second asterisk. The list is grouped as follows: first, those known to have made up the active core, political or social; second, those who made a frequent if not continuous contribution; third, those of whom only the name is known. The first group were mainly skilled workers, trade unionists, with a few "white collar" professionals and some small shopkeepers. At that time it was not unusual for some workers to seek relief from the factory grind and discipline in running a backstreet shop or an insurance round. In this group a high proportion of husbands and wives were both members, as were their sons and daughters. The homes of socialist families were often open to one another and the movement, particularly after the *Clarion* organisations developed, carried on an active and varied social and cultural life. The names total some 116. At peak the membership was about 300. We may assume that Mrs. Davies would remember the most active and frequent attenders. The high proportion of metal workers may be noticed.

ALBERT ADSHEAD** was an insurance agent; his wife DORA** a teacher of blind children. She was a daugher of another socialist stalwart, TOM HALPIN** who kept a drapers shop.

The CROSSLEY family, father, mother, five sons—Alf, Jim**, Percy**, his wife, Stanley, Fred, and a daughter Nellie** were devoted, opening their home to speakers or others who needed shelter. Jim became "a kind of elder brother" to Harry Pollitt, and a leading member of the CP. Fred died aged 21.

There were three FLEMINGS, Will*, Maggie*, and their son, Dick.

ALF GERRING, boilermaker at the Tank and the first Secretary of the OSS, married Harry Pollitt's Aunt Emily**. Their daughter Amy* married another member, CHARLIE COLLINS*, and lived next door to the Pollitts in Melba Street.

RALPH HARTLEY* a speaker and occasionally Chairman.

DICK HOLLINS* and his two sons FRED* and HAROLD* were all engineers.

EDMOND HOLT** was a founder of the Rubber Workers Union and a foundation member of the ILP. His father was a founder of the Spinners Union. His daughters Alice** and Elizabeth** were also members. Alice had married JACK CALDER** a furnishing trade worker; Elizabeth's husband was ERNEST DAVIES*, engineer.

MR.** and MRS.** JOLLY.

JACK MUNRO*, a sheet-metal worker was, along with Jim Crossley, an OSS delegate to the Conference which founded the BSP. Later he was from 1936 to 1944 Secretary of the Manchester and Salford Trades Council.

The four OPENSHAW brothers—Charlie**, Frank*, Willie* and Walter* were all engineers. Charlie was the Literature Secretary, and a cycling pal of Harry's.

As well as Harry Pollitt**, Mary Louisa** and Ella** were also active, as was

Ella's husband, STANLEY SWIFT**, a printer till he was incapacitated by illness. ANGUS POLLITT, no relation to Harry, was secretary of the Vocal Union.

Of GILBERT ROBERTS** we have written at length; his wife was also a member and two of his daughters were interested. Later, one married DAVID AINLEY who became President of the London Co-operative Society.

JOE ROYAL*, Conductor of Choir.

ERNEST TOMKINSON** was an insurance agent; his wife MARY ELLEN** kept a small shop.

JIM* and JACK UNSWORTH** were both platers, one in the Engineers Union, the other in the Boilermakers. Jack's second wife was HILDA GREGORY** whose father** and mother** were members.

Mr. WARBURTON* for a period Treasurer and his wife*.

ARTHUR WHITTAKER* a joiner, his wife* and their son Fred** and his wife Edith*.

The second grouping were also mainly skilled men, trade unionists, with a sprinkling of "white collar" workers and small shopkeepers.

Building workers were Mr. BOWCOCK, whose wife also belonged, and TOM PICKERING*, GEORGE HIBBERT* and TOM SMITH*, the first two voluntarily laid and polished the dancing floor of the Socialist Hall. DICK COPPOCK*, a bricklayer, later a trade union official, and his wife STELLA.

The metal workers included: BOB DAVIES; JIM FELLOWS, Chairman of Works Committee at Astbury's Carriage & Wagon Works, and his wife*; HARRY FISHER* on the Committee of the Land & Building Society; JACK GRIERSON** a foreman at Armstrong-Whitworths; GEORGE PEET**, later a leader of the National Shop Stewards Movement, arrested under DORA in 1917; TED SOMERSET* a foundry worker, his nephew TOM SLACK, electrician; VIC SUMMERS** who came from Sheffield in 1910, Mr. STADEN and his wife, a midwife; TOM STENNET*.

The small shopkeepers included TED MORT* and his wife*, grocers; Mr. & Mrs. WINKLE, greengrocers; Mrs. BROWN*, a fish-and-chip shop.

Mr.* and Mrs. SMART* with a family of three girls and one boy RALPH* who was killed in the 1914–18 war.

CHARLIE BLUNT* caretaker.

ANNIE LEE* later first Labour woman on Manchester City Council and first woman Alderman.

Mr.* and Mrs.* WILD.

Office workers were WILL CARTER and his wife MABEL, and TOM MOSS*. CISSIE HIGNETT was a teacher. BILL DAVIES* a chemist, Mr. DAVY a solicitor, SARAH GREENHALGH an artist, WALTER MOSS an actor, DICK GREENWOOD a manager, SAM RAINES* a warehouseman.

The third grouping:

 CLAUDE ABLE* ASE
 JENNY ARMSTRONG*
 BOB BALDWIN
 Mr. & Mrs. CHARLTON*

WILL CRANE, ASE
HARRY GILBERT*
NELLIE GODDARD*
J. GRAINGER
WILL GREENHALGH*
BOB MACLEAN* ASE
Mr.* and Mrs.* PENNEY
RALPH ROWBOTTOM*
TOM SMITH* ASE
ALBERT STARKEY*
RAY* and AMY* WILLS
BEN WOOD* ASE (went to Australia)
TED WOOD, in Dramatic Society

APPENDIX 3

CONGRESSES OF CPGB WITH DATA ON HARRY POLLITT

1st	1920 Jul	London	Present as visitor, not delegate
2nd	1921 Jan	Leeds	Not recorded present
3rd	1921 Apr	Manchester	Not recorded present
4th	1922 Mar	London	Report on United Front; elected to Party Commission
5th	1922 Oct	Battersea	Elected to Executive Committee (re-elected at all subsequent Congresses up to and including 26th)
6th	1924 May	Manchester	Moved resolution on National Minority Movement
7th	1925 May	Glasgow	Member of Presidium; Opening speech; Report on International Trade Union Unity (Congress Report)
8th	1926 Oct	Battersea	Report on Labour Party Conference
9th	1927 Oct	Salford	Report on Labour Party Conference (*WL* 14.10.27)
10th	1929 Jan	Bermondsey	Moved resolution on political levy
11th	1929 Nov	Leeds	As general Secretary, moved Political Resolution (*WL* 6.12.29)

From the 12th to 24th Congress Pollitt presented the Political Report and replied to the discussion, except as stated below. The title of the printed report is given

12th	1932 Nov	Battersea	*The Road to Victory*
13th	1935 Feb	Manchester	*A Call to All Workers*
14th	1937 May	Battersea	*It Can Be Done*
15th	1938 Sep	Birmingham	*For Peace and Plenty*

Originally prepared for Autumn 1939, the 16th Congress was postponed due to the outbreak of war. In 1942, May, a National Conference was held. Pollitt's Report was entitled *The Way to Win*

16th	1943 Jul	London	*Unity and Victory*
17th	1944 Oct	Shoreditch	*Victory, Peace, Security*
18th	1945 Nov	London	*Communist Policy for Britain*
19th	1947 Feb	London	*Britain's Problems Can Be Solved*
20th	1948 Feb	London	*For Britain Free and Independent*
21st	1949 Dec	Liverpool	*Communisty Policy to Meet the Crisis*

Pollitt absent due to illness: his report was read by W. Gallacher, MP, and J. R. Campbell replied to the discussion

22nd	1952 Apr	London	*Britain Arise*
23rd	1954 Apr	London	*The Challenge to Labour.* John Gollan replied
24th	1956 Apr	London	*The People Will Decide.* John Gollan replied. In the private session HP reported on the CPSU 20th Congress

After the 24th Congress Pollitt resigned as General Secretary and was elected Chairman

25th	1957 Apr	Hammersmith	HP in the Chair
26th	1959 Mar	London	HP in the Chair

APPENDIX 4

CONGRESSES OF THE COMMUNIST INTERNATIONAL AND
PLENUMS OF THE EXECUTIVE COMMITTEE (ECCI)

An asterisk indicates HP present

Communist International

1st	Congress	1919 Mar	
2nd	Congress	1920 Jul	
3rd	*Congress	1921 Jun	HP visitor for last few days, *SMT*
1st	*Plenum ECCI	1922 Feb	HP Trade Union question
2nd	Plenum	1922 Jun	
4th	Congress	1922 Nov	
3rd	*Plenum British Commission	1923 Jun	HP left before Commission concluded
4th	Plenum	1924 Jan	
5th	Congress Org Bureau	1924 Jun 1924 Nov	HP not present but elected to ECCI *Inpre* 1925—136
5th	*Plenum	1925 Mar	

6th	Plenum	1926 Feb	Resolution on Britain CPGB *Orders from Moscow?*
7th	Plenum	1926 Nov	
8th	Plenum	1927 May	
9th	Plenum	1928 Feb	Dutt–Pollitt alternative thesis at British Commission, but HP not present
6th	Congress	1928 Jul	HP elected to ECCI, *Inpre* 1547
10th	*Plenum	1929 Jul	HP speech, *Inpre* 885, article in *CR* Oct
	*Enlarged Presidium	1930 Feb	HP report. Resolution on CPGB, *Inpre* 411
11th	*Plenum	1931 Mar	HP speech on Youth, *Imprecor* 669, report *CR* Jun, MB
12th	*Plenum	1932 Aug	HP speech in *CI IX*—612 and pamphlet *Next Steps in Britain*, MB
13th	*Plenum	1933 Nov	HP speech in *Imprecor XIV*—129, *CI XI*—69 and pamphlet *Soviet Power*
	*Presidium	1934 Oct	HP speech on Britain, *CI XI*—911
	*Presidium	1935 Mar	HP speech on United Front, *Outline History* 364
7th	*Congress	1935 Jul	HP on Presidium. Speech in *Labour Monthly* Oct and Nov, *Imprecor* 1403, *CI XII* 789, 897 and pamphlet
	*Secretariat	1936 Sep	HP in debate on Spain, *Outline History* 416
	1943 CI dissolved		

CONGRESS AND SESSIONS OF THE RED INTERNATIONAL OF LABOUR UNIONS

An asterisk indicates HP present

1920 Jul	After two preliminary meetings of trade union leaders from several countries, convened by the All-Russian TUC, a provisional International Council of Revolutionary Trade and Industrial Unions was formed	
*1921 Jul	First World Congress of the Red International of Labour Unions, HP among British delegates	
1922 Nov	2nd World Congress	
1924 Jul	3rd World Congress	
*1924 Nov		HP in RILU delegation to 6th Soviet TUC
1928	4th World Congress	HP in absence, elected to Central Council
*1929 Jun	Executive Bureau	HP reports on NMM (*RILU Magazine*, I—313)
1930 Aug	5th World Congress	
1930 Dec	6th Session Central Council	
*1931 Nov	8th Session Central Council	HP speech in *RILU Magazine*, 1932 Feb
*1935 Aug	Executive Bureau	HP co-operated with Abe Moffatt
1936	RILU Unity Commission	HP a member
1937	RILU apparatus dissolved	

APPENDIX 5

ARTICLES, BOOKS AND PAMPHLETS BY HARRY POLLITT

Articles are listed by year and month. After one mention of full title of periodical, initials are used with Roman numerals for bound volumes. Title of article is followed by page number or month.

HP's articles in *The Worker, Workers' Weekly, Workers' Life* and *Daily Worker* would make too long a list. Apart from comment on current events, their political essence was usually expressed in a weekly or monthly periodical.

Publications are by the CPGB unless otherwise stated, when BB is by the British Bureau of the RILU; DAC the Dependents Aid Committee for the British Battalion of the International Brigade; LW Lawrence and Wishart, London; MB Modern Books, London; NCMC National Congress and March Council; NFTC National Federation of Trades Councils (prior to that sponsored by TUC); NMM National Minority Movement; NUCC National Unity Campaign Committee.

Other abbreviations used:

Bklt = booklet. BR = Book review. D = duplicated. EA = election address. F = folder. L = leaflet signed by HP. np = not priced. NS = new series of volumes. Pref. = Preface or foreword only by HP. SAS-I or -II = the item or part is reprinted in *Selected Articles & Speeches*. SMT = item reprinted in *Serving My Time*. FLP = *For Lasting Peace* (journal of the Cominform).

1911

L Municipal election leaflet *Socialism or Social Reform* drafted for Openshaw Socialist Society (SMT)

1915

L Appeal of Boilermakers Strike Committee, Southampton (SMT)

1919

Boilermakers Monthly Report (*Official journal* Boilermakers Society): London District Committee Report—Feb Apr Jun Aug Sep, Amalgamation—Jun, Hands Off Russia—Jul, Trade Unions and Politics—Sep Oct, Acceptance for nomination as Parliamentary Candidate—Apr

Workers Dreadnought (Weekly, Sylvia Pankhurst) Dockers Beware—May 10 (also SAS-I), Shipbuilding and Increased Output—Sep 13

Masses (monthly, W. F. Watson) My message—Feb

The Consolidator (River Thames Shop Stewards Movement) Open letter to the Minister of Labour—Feb 14 (SMT)

1920

Boilermakers MR: Time for Action—Feb, Workers, Own the Machine!—Apr, May, Wanted a National Conference—Sep, Boilermakers and the National Labour Movement—Nov

WD Autocracy of the Boilermakers—Mar 27, Southampton Boilermakers 1915 Strike—Apr 24, Supplement

Boilermakers MR Buy the *Daily Herald*—Feb, Moscow or Amsterdam—Mar, A Cry from Russia, Famine!—Sep, Wage Reductions and Higher Profits—Nov, Thanks for TUC Votes—Jun

1921

Solidarity Vol. V: Red or Yellow International—Feb 18, Labour Conference on Unemployment—Feb 23, Ship Joiners Strike—Apr 1, To Hell With This Enquiry (Shipyard and Engineering Wages)—Apr 15, Report at Barrow—Apr 15, London Conference—May 13

Trades Union Congress Annual Report: Speeches, Disarmament 298, Russian Famine 350, Forty-four hour week 392

Labour Monthly (a magazine of International Labour) I: None

Communist Review (monthly) I:—None

International Press Correspondence English Edition I: Oct—Dec None

1922

Boilermakers MR: Strikes—Sep, Election Address for EC—Apr, Thanks for TUC votes—Jun, Election Address for London District Delegate—Nov,

TUC Speeches: US coal strike 326, Duties of General Council 404, Forty-four hour week 431 (also SAS-I)

Labour Party Annual Conference: Speeches in Report Russian Social Revolutionary Prisoners 194, Communist Party Affiliation 196 (SAS-I) 199

LM II: Jan–Aug, Oct–Dec none, Future of the TUC General Council—Sep

All Power (Monthly, British Bureau RILU) I: Open Letter to Frank Hodges—Aug

Inpre II: Engineers' Lock-out 275, Situation in England 447, Miners Conference at Blackpool 461, Labour Movement in England 469

The Communist (Wkly): Aug 26 To all Railway Workers; Sep 23 Why Sydney Webb Smiled; Sep 30 A Challenge (Shipyard Wages); Nov 25 Report on Scottish *Daily Communist*

Pamphlets etc

F   RILU London Committee, Organisation and Policy (SMT) np.

Report on Party Organisation by R. P. Dutt, H. Inkpin and H. Pollitt np

1923

Boilermakers MR: Is Trade Unionism Played Out?—May. The Growing War Danger—Nov. Thanks for Votes for London Delegate—May

TUC speeches: General Council 298 Italy and Greece 313

LPAC Speeches: New Socialist International 183, French Occupation of the Ruhr 184, Opponents 185, CP Affiliation 188

LM IV: None

LM V: Issues before TUC—Sep Trades Council Conference—Nov

CR IV: Lessons of Plymouth TUC—Oct

Inpre III: Undelivered speech to Hamburg Conference of 2nd and $2\frac{1}{2}$ Internationals 398

Pamphlets etc
F   Second Annual Conference of Trades Councils, Chairman's Address   np 8pp.   NFTC   (SMT)

1924

Boilermakers MR: Unemployment, Russia and Ourselves—Jul
TUC speeches: Labour Government 287, International Trade Union Unity 311, 314, 356, 367, Industrial Workers Charter 356, Compulsory Arbitration 488
LPAC Speech: Communist Party 127
LM IV: Trades Union Congress Sep
CR IV: The Party Conference Feb
Inpre IV: British TUC—Sep, Labour Party Conference—Oct

Pamphlets etc
Article in Unity Symposium, NMM 2d. 40pp

1925

Boilermakers MR: The Furness Withy Patriots—May
TUC Speeches: Premises and Research 364, Unemployment 397, Trade Union Aims 437, Dawes Report 55, Imperialism 554
LPAC Speeches: The Communist Party 182, Labour Party and the Nation 223, Debate on Pollitt Kidnapping 299
LM VII: Scarborough TUC—Oct, SAS-I
Mineworker (Fortnightly, Mineworkers Minority Movement): Article Sep 19
CR V: None
Inpre V: Role of Soviet Trade Unions 181, Scarborough TUC, Liverpool Labour Party Conference 1099

Pamphlets
Pref. Report of 2nd Conference NMM   NMM 2d. 32 pp.; Communist Party on Trial, Pollitt's Speech for the Defence   (SMT)   2d. 32 pp

1926

Boilermakers MR: Thanks for Solidarity While in Prison—Sep
LPAC Speeches: Chairman's Attack on Miners 172, Communist Party 185, 186, The Labour and Socialist International 191, Mining Crisis 194, By-elections 249
LM VIII: A Message—Oct
CR VII: Labour Party Conference—Nov

Pamphlet
What Margate Means, 1d. 14 pp.   Also SAS-I

1927

TUC Speeches: Non-political Trades Unionism 271, Future Policy 307, Minority Movement 324, Relations with Russia 371, Seamen's Union 456
LM IX: Conference of Executives—Feb, Trade Unions Bill—Jun, Paris Congress IFTU—Sep, Edinburgh TUC—Oct

CR: As from Feb 1927 name changed to *The Communist*
The Communist II: Problems before Edinburgh TUC—Sep
Inpre VII: None
Book, *RILU and Tenth Anniversary of Russian Revolution*: Article by HP, British Labour and the Russian Revolution, NMM 1/6 134 pp

Pamphlets etc
Pref. What's Wrong in the Engineering Industry? NMM 2d
Pref. What's Wrong in the Textile Industry? NMM 2d
In SAS-I: *A Brief History of the Minority Movement* reprinted from *The Worker*, Aug 12, 19, 26

1928

Boilermakers: In a circular letter 3.1.28, full text in SMT, HP replied to the attack on him in the *MR* Nov 1927
LM X: Industrial Peace—Feb, Minority Movement Congress—Aug
The Communist III: Ourselves and the Labour Party—Mar, Swansea TUC—Sep, Should We Pay the Political Levy?—Dec
Inpre VIII: None
RILU Magazine I: None

Pamphlet
Pollitt's Reply to Citrine, 1d. 20 pp, SAS-I

1929

LM XI: General Election and Class struggle—May, Future of Revolutionary Trades Unionism—Aug
Communist Review NS I.: Lessons of Tenth Plenum ECCI—Oct
Inpre IX: War Provocation on Chinese Eastern Railway 725, Hands Off the Soviet Union, speech at ECCI 10th Plenum 885, Minority Movement 6th Annual Conference 997, Belfast TUC 1128, CPGB and 12th Anniversary Russian Revolution 1296
RILU Magazine I: Towards NMM Conference—Aug, The 6th NMM Conference—Oct

Pamphlets
The War Danger, speech in Report of 6th Annual Conference NMM 2d. 40 pp
Pref. On Strike: A Word to Workers in Dispute, NMM ½d
Pref. British Imperialism NMM 2d. 48 pp
EA Seaham Harbour (SMT)

1930

LM XII: The Struggle Ahead—Apr, Nottingham TUC—Oct
CR II: CP and Mining Crisis—May, CP and Workers Charter Campaign—Nov
Inpre X: Nottingham TUC 954, Conference of United Mineworkers of Scotland 1005
RILU Magazine: None

Pamphlet The Workers Charter, NMM ½d. 16 pp
(In *SAS-I Three Years of Mondism* reprinted from *The Worker* May 23 Jun 6 Jun 13)
EA: Whitechapel and St. Georges

1931
LM XIII: The Communist Party and the Whitechapel By-Election—Jan, The Eve of Charter Convention—Apr, Anti-war day—Aug, The Charter Fight against all Cuts—Oct
CR III: Towards the National Charter Convention—Mar, Report on Eleventh Plenum ECCI—Jun
Inpre XI: Speech at XI Plenum ECCI—669, The War Danger, Aug 1—729
RILU I NS: The Charter Convention—Jul 1, The Bristol TUC—Sep 15

Pamphlets
Struggle or Starve, XI Plenum ECCI—YCI Report, HP on youth   MB 2d   NMM 1d 16 pp
Pref.   The Road to Victory, Charter Convention   NMM 1d 16 pp
Pref.   Free Soviet Labour and Forced Capitalist Labour   MB 2d 46 pp
EA: Whitechapel and St. Georges

1932
LM XIV: Trade Unions and the Fight—Mar, The Bradford ILP Conference and After—Aug
CR IV: Building the Bolshevik Party in Britain—Mar, The Cotton Fight Today—Jun, The War and the Tasks of the CPGB—Jul, Newcastle TUC—Sep, Work of the Communists in South Africa in the Trade Unions—Dec
Party Organiser I: How Party Work can be Improved—Mar, Know What Goes on in the Factory—Dec, 12th Congress Decisions on the Railways—Dec
Inpre XII: International Solidarity Against War and Intervention 433, Lancashire Textile Strike 839
Communist International IX: Speech at Twelfth Plenum ECCI 612
RILU II NS: Speech at Eighth Central Council *RILU* 68

Pamphlets
Which Way for the Workers? Debate with Fenner Brockway   2d 32 pp
Next Steps in Britain, Speech to XII Plenum ECCI, MB 2d 88 pp
Bklt: The Road to Victory, Report to XII Congress CPGB   SAS-I   6d 94 pp

1933
LM XV: Manoeuvres of the TUC—Jan, BR Memories of Lenin—Apr, The New Attacks and the Need for Unity—Nov
CR V: Party Congress and Railwaymen's Fight—Jan, Communists and ILP—Feb, United Front in Britain—Apr, Coming Battles and United Front—Jun
Inpre XIII: Tasks of YCL of Great Britain 584
CI X: Twelfth Congress CPGB A New Turn—Jan, Anti-Soviet Policy of

British Imperialism and the Protest Movement—Jul 15, Struggle of the CPGB Since XII Plenum—Nov 1
RILU III NS: Left Manoeuvres of Trade Union Leaders—Feb 1

Pamphlets
Towards Soviet Power, Thirteenth Plenum ECCI 3d 38 pp
EA: Clay Cross
Pref. The Condition of the Working Class in Britain by Allen Hutt L & W

1934

LM XVI: None
CR VI: The Labour Party's Peace Policy—Aug, United Front Next Steps—Dec
Inpre XIV: Report to 13th Plenum ECCI on United Front in Britain 129, Lessons of Sep 9 1259 (also SAS-I), United Front for Spanish Workers 1584 Thirteenth Congress CPGB 1673, Rescue our Comrade Rakosi 1748 SAS-I
CI XI: Speech at 13th Plenum ECCI 69, Labour Party, ILP and CPGB 377, The CPGB since the 6th World Congress CI 733, United Front in Britain, Speech to Presidium ECCI 911

Pamphlets
The Way Forward—Speech to United Front Congress NCMC 1d 16 pp
Into Action—CP Proposals for United Front Congress SAS-I 1d 16 pp
Labour and War 1d 24 pp

1935

LM XVII: Seventh Congress CI—Oct Nov
Inpre XV: International Solidarity Day 587, The Arms Commission 588, The War Danger in Abyssinia and the British Working Class 1224 (SAS-I), Fight for Unity in Face of War 1319, Speech at 7th Congress CI 1403
CI XII: United Front—What Next? 12, Reply to discussion at 13th Congress CPGB 196I, LP Derby Conference 441, Fiftieth Anniversary *Jolly George* 509, Influence of Soviet Construction on Workers in Capitalist Countries 635, Speech at 7th Congress CI—Parts 1 & 2 789, 897
Bk *We did not Fight*, Symposium Cobden Sanderson London. Article by HP *The Dockers Said "No"* (later reprinted as pamphlet *A War Was Stopped*)

Pamphlets
We Can Stop War (part in SAS-I) 1d 16 pp
A Call to All Workers, Report to 13th Congress CPGB 3d 80 pp
A Hell of a Business Memorandum to Arms Commission 1d 16 pp
Dynamite in the Dock Evidence before Arms Commission (SAS-I) 1d 30 pp
Unity Against National Government Speech at 7th Congress CI (SAS-I) 1d 32 pp
Labour Party and Communist Party
EA Rhondda East

1936

LM XVIII: The Communist Party and Unity—Feb, A Working Class Peace Policy—May, The Antikainen Trial—Sep
Discussion I: Forward from Edinburgh and Sheffield—Nov
Left Review II: Building the People's Front 797
The Eye (House journal L & W): No 5   BR   The Founding of the First International
Tom Mann's 80th Birthday Souvenir   Greetings from HP   6d
Trade Union Information (NMM) II: For a United Labour Movement—May
Inpre XVI: CPGB Central Committee meetings 41 (SAS-I), 110, 749, Obituary for Saklatvala 174, CP Affiliation to LP 215, Thaelmann Must be Freed 312, Against the Baldwin Government War Policy 487, The Movement to Overthrow the National Government 670, Situation in Palestine 780, Abandonment of Sanctions (SAS-II) 789, Defend the Spanish Republic 930, To the Aid of the Spanish People 959 (SAS-II), Truth Behind the "Red" Atrocities 1001, Labour Party Conference and Embargo on Arms for Spain 1254, The Fate of the Working Class is in Our Hands (Sheffield Conference CPGB) (SAS-II) 1272, United National Front in India 1342, October Revolution Lessons for British Workers 1344, Fight Against German Fascism and its Agents 1358
CI XIII: Tribute to Saklatvala—126, Against Instigators and Abettors of War—215, People's Front in Britain—455

Pamphlets
   Forward, Report to CC CPGB   1d 16 pp
   I Accuse Baldwin   1d 16 pp
   The Path to Peace   2d 32 pp
   Unity, Peace, Security—Reply to Morrison   1d 16 pp
   Save Spain from Fascism   1d 16 pp
   Arms for Spain   1d 30 pp
   Spain and the TUC   1d 16p
   A War Was Stopped   1d 14 pp
Pref.   Coffin Ships by Ted Hill   1d 12 pp
L   Communist Affiliation, Correspondence LP & CP   np 4 pp

1937

Boilermakers MR: Appeal Against Disqualification for TUC—Apr
LM XIX   BR: Forward from Liberalism—Mar, Next Stage in the Fight for Unity—Jul, What Next in Britain?—Oct, Twentieth Anniversary Russian Revolution—Nov
Discussion II: What is the Position?—Oct
Inpre XVII: 51st Birthday Ernst Thaelmann 405, International Spain Week 509, International Unity Can Bring Peace to Spain and Europe 594, Spain is the World at the Crossroads 668, Japanese Murder of Women and Children 933, Twentieth Anniversary Lessons for British Workers 1144, Twentieth Anniversary and Great Britain 1253, Passionaria, Leader of the Spanish Proletariat 1291
CI XIV: In Memory of Britons Fallen in Spain 869, Land of Socialism and Capitalist Britain 1242

Pamphlets
The Unity Campaign, Cripps, Pollitt (SAS-II) & Maxton   NUCC 2d 34 pp
Truth About Trotskyism (jointly with R. P. Dutt)   2d 36 pp
It Can Be Done, Report & Reply 14th Congress CPGB   6d
Salute to the Soviet Union (SAS-II)   2d 32 pp
Labour's Way Forward   1d 16 pp
Save Peace Aid Spain   1d 16 pp
Pref. This Is Our City (Manchester) M. Jenkins   1d 16 pp

1938

LM XX: Eve of Indian National Congress (with R. P. Dutt and Ben Bradley)—Mar, Unity and People's Front—Jul, The People's Movement—Oct
Discussion III: Significance of Teruel—Feb
Party Organiser I   NS: Eliminating Weaknesses in Branch Life—Aug
Inpre XVIII   Renamed *World News & Views* as from No. 33—Jul 2 1938: French CP Ninth Congress 17, Speech to All-Party Conference on Spain 22, If we Fail Spain Who Will Help Us? 24, The Coming General Election 53, Save Spain Save World Peace 150, Crushing the Traitors 309, Dimitrov, United Front and Popular Front 455, A Stroke of Genius 684
WNV: Czechoslovakia and Britain 822, CPGB and Present Situation 1038, Plot Against Czechoslovakia 1097, Anti-fascist Unity Grows in Britain 1302
CI XVI: British People and Czechoslovakia No 7

Pamphlets
Pollitt Visits Spain, Dec 1937   DAC   2d 32 pp
Austria (SAS-II)   1d 16 pp
Czechoslovakia and Britain   1d 16 pp
For Unity in London, Speech at London CP Congress   3d 34 pp
Czechoslovakia   1d 16 pp
Czechoslovakia Betrayed (SAS-II)   1d 16 pp
Peace and Plenty, Report to CPGB 15th Congress   SAS-II   6d 192 pp
Pref. Books & Pamphlets, How to Sell Them
L   People's Front, Reply to LP—May   np 2 pp
L   Popular Front, Letter to Labour Party affiliates—Jun   np 2 pp
Pref. Jack Coward   *Back from the Dead*   1d 32 pp

1939

LM XXI: The Communist Crusade—Feb, Karl Marx 56th Anniversary—Apr, After Southport—Jul
WNV XIX: In Honour of the British Battalion 32, Speech at Left Book Club Rally 488, Statement 1028, Declaration 1118
CI XVII: None
Bk   *Why I Am a Democrat*   Symposium L & W, London   Article by HP

Pamphlets
Defence of the People (SAS-II)   1d 16 pp
Spain: What Next? (SAS-II)   1d 16 pp
Can Conscription Save Peace?   1d 16 pp
Will It Be War? (SAS-II)   1d 32 pp
How to Win the War   1d 32 pp

1940

LM XXII: After Six Months, What Now?—Apr, BR Where Mr. Gollancz Has Gone—Jun, The People's Parliament—Dec

WNV XX: Communist Party and Labour Party 419, Hour of decision 538, Call for the People's Convention 559, New Stage in our Struggle 725

Book: Serving My Time: An Autobiography L & W (Several reprints)

Pamphlets
  The War and the Labour Movement   1d 12 pp
  The War and the Workshop: Letters to Bill No 1   1d 16 pp
  What is Russia Going to Do? Letters to Bill No 2   1d 16 pp
  Wages—A Policy   2d 24 pp
EA. Silvertown

1941

LM XXIII: People's Convention, What Next?—Feb, India, A Call to the British People—Jan, The Way to Victory, Second Front—Oct

WNV XXI: New Hope, New Unity, New Power 24, The Dull Thud 71, Situation in the Labour Party 113, Tom Mann, a Tribute 177, Gollancz's Uneasy Men 188, Tom Mann's Funeral 202, James Connolly, Irish leader 238, Daily Worker and the War 255, Preface to *Lenin on Britain* 383, The Future Depends on You 465, Do It Now 513, "Smash Hitler" Fund 525, 568 582 600, The Most Urgent Need 545, Bring Labour's Battalions Into the Fight 561, Strengthen the Government 597, Tanks for Joe 625, Britain's Part 734, Working Class Unity for Victory 774

Pamphlets
  Smash Hitler Now   1d 16 pp
  Tom Mann, a Tribute   1d 8 pp
  A Call for Arms   1d 16 pp
  Britain's Chance Has Come   1d 16 pp
PL For the Defeat of Fascism   np 2 pp
  Report of the Peoples Convention—speech HP   3d

1942

LM XXXIV: Communist Party and the Fight for Victory—Jan, We Hold the Key to Victory—May, BR Britain in the World Front—Jul, Deeds Not Words—Oct

WNV XXII: We Rely on You 24, Never Forgive or Forget 33, A Year of Ban on the *Daily Worker* 51, Great Changes Must and Will be Made 81, Churchill Must Act 113, New Government Must Have a New Policy 129, Labour Party Conference 175, Jose Diaz Obituary 178, On With the Campaign 197, Make Victory Certain 204, Unity for Victory in 1942 225, Communist Party and Mr. Morrison 236, Unity for Victory in 1942 225, The Youth of Britain 237, Report to CPGB National Congress 250, Lift the Ban Without Delay 257, The Danger to Britain 265, Anglo-Soviet Alliance 273, Letter to Secretary for War 283, The Government Must Act 321, Greetings to India 326, George Measures Obituary 334, India 339, A Price Will Be Paid 353, India, A Letter to Churchill 357, Labour Leaders Attack

Unity 372, Tom Bell's Sixtieth Birthday 392, Labour Must Act 417, Russian Revolution 25th Anniversary 433, BR Soviet Documents of Nazi Atrocities 458, W. Gallacher, MP 492

Pamphlets
  The World in Arms   2d 16 pp
  Into Battle: The Call of May Day   2d 18 pp
  The Way to Win, Report to CPBG Conference   6d 64 pp
  Speed the Second Front   2d 16 pp
  Deeds Not Words   2d 16 pp
Pref. Indian Communist Party   6d 34 pp

1943

LM XXV: CP Affiliation to LP—Feb, Final Word on Unity—Jun
WNV XXII: On Guard 9, What the British People Think of the Red Army 51, May Day 137, Policy of the CPGB 174, Coal 203, Burn Hitler out of Existence 249, Our Treasury of Literature 272, Building the Communist Party 317, Industrial Unrest and its Causes 321, Labour's Responsibility 337, Three Power Conference 353, 393

Pamphlets
  Miners' Target   2d 16 pp
  Workers of Britain Unite!   2d 20 pp
  Coal (Speech to Sixteenth Congress CPGB)   1d 8 pp
  Italy—Now Smash On!   1d 8 pp
  Unity and Victory, Report & Reply 16th Congress CPGB   9d 64 pp
  Where Does Britain Stand?   3d 22 pp
L   Revolution in Shipbuilding (reprint from *Unity* CP Ireland)
Pref.   CP and Labour Party: Correspondence and Statement   2d 16 pp
L   Affiliation, Letter to LP—Mar   np 2 pp
F   Affiliation Bulletin, Article by HP on "What Is At Stake?"—Apr 20   np 4 pp
F   Affiliation Bulletin, Article HP Letter to LP May 6   np 4 pp
PL   Our Victory and Unity Campaign—Aug 18   np 4 pp

1944

LM XXVI: Teheran in Deeds—Aug
WNV XXIV: Roll Call 22, Letter on Election Truce 31, May Day 137, Tom Bell Obituary 162, Youth and the Labour Movement 177, Speed Victory 193, Letter to LP on General Election 275, Letter to Marcel Cachin 305, A Reply to Morrison 393

Pamphlets
  Pollitt Answers on Communist Policy   2d 16 pp
  Take Over the Mines   3d 24 pp
  D Day   1d 8 pp
Bklt   How to Win the Peace   2/- 96 pp

Victory, Peace, Security Report Reply Seventeenth Congress CPGB   1/-
64 pp
Pref.   The CP of France   6d 32 pp
Pref.   When the Fire Burns Red poems by V E Crosland   6d 16 pp
Pref.   Tom Mann by Dona Torr (L & W)   1/6 48 pp
Pref.   British Soldier in India, Clive Branson's Letters L & W   2/6 120 pp
L.   End Jew-baiting, reprint from DW   2 sides

1945

LM XXVII: Lessons of the Labour Conference—Jan, Communist Party and the Election—Jul
WNV XXV: National Unity 89, Into Battle with Confidence 161, Potsdam Conference 241, Eighteenth Congress Discussion 337, Message to CPSU (B) 349, Winning the Peace, Reply at Eighteenth Congress 393

Pamphlets
    Crimea Conference Safeguard of Future   3d 16 pp
    Pollitt Answers Foot (Coal)   2d 16 pp
    Answers to Questions   1/- 48 pp
    Why You Should Be a Communist   4d 32 pp
    Communist Policy for Britain: Report & Reply to 18th Congress CPGB   1/-
80 pp
F   Wages   2d 4 pp
PL   Now We Face the Future   np 4 pp
Pref.   Prefabrication and the Shipyard Trades   3d 16 pp
Pref.   Liberate Spain by Passionaria   3d 12 pp
Pref.   Italy's New Path   3d 26 pp
PL   A Personal Letter to Every Communist Mineworker   np 4 pp
EA   Rhondda East

1946

LM XXVIII: CPGB Congress—Jan, Outlook After Bournemouth—Jul, After the Brighton TUC—Dec
CR 1946: The Communist Party and the Nation—Mar
WNV XXVI: Long Live the *Daily Worker* 9, Letter to LP 25, Churchill's Fulton Speech—Sabotage 81, The "Imperceptible Revolution" 177, CP of Sweden 13th Congress 188, A New Situation 305, Our Fund 329, 387, 411, Empire Communist Conference 369

Pamphlets
    Professional Workers   3d 32 pp
    Laski's Mistake   2d 16 pp
    CP Czechoslovakia 8th Congress   1/- 48 pp
    Britain Will Make It   6d 32 pp
F   Professional Workers
F   Labour's Foreign Policy   1d 4 pp
F   *Daily Herald* Poison Pens   1d 4 pp
F   The Squatters   1d 4 pp
Pref.   Steel   3d 14 pp

514

PL Affiliation Campaign—Jan 3 np 2 pp
Affiliation Bulletin article by HP, Labour Needs the Communists, May np 4 pp

1947

LM XXIX: BR "Bevin" by Trevor Evans—Jan, How to Reorganise the Government—Apr
CR: Prospects for 1947—Jan, The Immediate Political Struggle—May
WNV XXVII: CP Fighting Fund 10, 23, 35, 71, 119, 156, 180, 215, 239, 287, 335, 372, 442, 503. Free the Indian Communist Leaders 40, R. Stewart 70th Birthday 77, CPGB 19th Congress Reply to Discussion 87, Making Austria Democratic 135, Democratic Spain is Rising 148, Jack Owen 60th Birthday 176, CP France 11th Congress 301, Message to CP USA 308, Independence 311, Britain and Marshall Policy 315, Letter to the Prime Minister (on crisis) 397, Russian Revolution 30th Anniversary, Letter to Stalin 508, Report to EC on Crisis 577
Booklet Looking Ahead 2/- 128 pp

Pamphlets
Britain's Problems Can Be Solved, Report to 19th Congress CPGB 6d 32 pp
Plan for Coal 3d 16 pp
Pref. We Speak for Freedom, Report of First Conference of Empire Communist Parties 2/6 92 pp

1948

LM XXX: The Margate Conference—Oct
CR: Yugoslavia—Aug, USSR and its Communist Party—Nov
WNV XXVIII: CP Fund 11, 25, 76, 183, Morrison and Marshall 33, CP Italy 6th Congress 36, Ben Bradley 50th Birthday 44, The Price of Bevin 45, Wigan By-Election 75, Centenary of the *Communist Manifesto* 145, Scarborough Labour Party Conference 217, CP and the Catholics 249, Situation in Yugoslavia CP 295, Trade Unions and Nationalisation 357, CP Finland 8th Congress 408, Smash the Attack on Living Standards 413, Trial for the Twelve US Communists 461

Pamphlets etc
Britain Free and Independent, Report and Reply CPGB 20th Congress 9d 52 pp
The Miners Next Step 3d 16 pp
Trade Unionists, What Next? 3d 16 pp
F Save Britain from War, Speech to YCL Congress 1d 4 pp
F Where is Labour Going? 1d 4 pp
Pref. *The English Revolution* by A. L. Morton 3d
PL Party Initiative and the Mass Movement 1d 4 pp
L Trade Unions and Communism np 2 sides

1949

LM XXXI: None
CR: The Trade That Britain Needs—Sep
WNV XXIX: The Communist Party 109, CP Fund 227, 230, 368, 419,

592, Attitude of British Workers to War on USSR 133, Tactics of Disruption 161, BR New China, New World 244, Death of Georgi Dimitrov 325, CP and the Slump, Reply to Cripps and Foot 326, Idris Cox 50th Birthday 346, T. A. Jackson 70th Birthday 398, EC Letter to HP on 20 Years as General Secretary CPGB 429, International Tributes to HP on 20 Years as General Secretary 435, Greetings to Marcel Cachin 454, Result of US Communist Trial 505, Protest Against Sentence on L. L. Sharkey CP Australia 505

Pamphlets
 Communism and Labour Report to EC CPGB 1/- 48 pp
 Those Russians 2d 16 pp
 Communist Policy to Meet the Crisis, Report to 20th Congress CPGB 1/- 64 pp
F Twenty Years Fight for Socialism np 4 pp
F The tactics of Disruption 1d 4 pp
PL After the Elections 1d 4 pp
Pref. Speech of Eugene Dennis in Trial of US Communists 6d 32 pp

1950

LM XXXII: BR Crisis of British Empire—Feb, Brighton TUC—Oct
WNV XXX: Message to CP West Germany 13, Doris Allison 50th Birthday 35, CP and General Election 38, Death of Mrs. Stewart 133, In Memory of Dimitrov 304, Socialist Unity Party of Germany 3rd Congress 377, On Bandits and Terrorists 390, New Stage in Fight for Peace 493, EC letter to Pollitt on 60th birthday 558, Extracts from HP speeches 559, Sinews of Peace 566, R. Page Arnot 60th Birthday 603, For Peace and British Independence 605
CR: The Fight for a Working Class Policy—Apr, Our Tasks (Political Letter, May)—Sep. Also P. Kerrigan on Pollitt's 60th birthday—Dec
Booklet Thirtieth Anniversary CPGB Article by HP
FLP: The General Election Feb 10, After the General Election Apr 7, May Day April 28, Korea Jul 21, For Peace and Working Class Unity Aug 18, Brighton TUC Sep 29, Margate LPC Oct 20, New Stage in Fight for Peace Nov 3

Pamphlets
 Welfare State or Warfare State? DW 3d 16 pp
 Fight for Peace and Working Class Unity 3d 24 pp
 Peace Depends on the People (Report to EC) 6d 38 pp
 World Greetings to Harry Pollitt on his 60th Birthday 6d
PL Forward With Confidence np 4 pp
L For Peace: Appeal to Members of the Labour Party np 2 side
EA Rhondda East

1951

LM XXXIII: BR Old Friends to Keep by T. A. Jackson—Jan, Thirty Years of the Labour Monthly—Jul
 CR: A New Perspective—The British Road to Socialism—Feb, Five Power Pact—May, New Mood in the Labour Movement—Sep

WNV XXXI: New Year Message 1, Alan Bush 50th Birthday 11, CP Fund 23, 90, 169, 318, 515, Theodore Rothstein 80th Birthday 138, Warmongers Say: Watch Out for Peace 141, Message to 7th Congress CP Italy 142, Finlay Hart 50th Birthday 146, BR *Coal and the Miners* by George Allison 146, BR *Rise Like Lions*, WG 168, Unite Now to Defeat Tories, Report to EC 177, Five Power Pact 249, CGT Giles 60th Birthday 277, Scotland's Fine Example 275, CP Malaya 20th Anniversary 307, Claude Berridge 50th Birthday 350, Message to 16th Congress CP Australia 370, John Mahon 50th Birthday 530, William Gallacher 70th Birthday 549

Pamphlets etc
   Open Letter to a Trade Unionist   3d 16 pp
   Negotiate Now   1d 16 pp
PL   British Road to Socialism   1d 4 pp
F   Appeal to Members of LP   1d 4 pp
F   Unite Now to Defeat the Tories   1d 4 pp
F   The Broadcast I Would Have Delivered   np 4 pp
F   After the Election: A Fighting Policy for Labour   1d 8 pp
F   Why Britain Needs the CP   1d 4 pp
Pref.   *Frederick Engels in Manchester*, M. Jenkins   6d
Pref.   *The British Road to Socialism*   3d
Pref.   Georgi Dimitrov—Selected Articles and Speeches   L & W   12/6
Reprint of Art in *LM 30th Anniversary*   21s   1952
LM XXXIV: Year of Decision—Jan, A Policy for Labour—Sep
CR: None
WNV XXXII: Issues before 22nd Congress CPGB 41, The Fight for Unity 73, R. Stewart 75th Birthday 92, Greetings to Rakosi 60th Birthday 122, Reply to Discussion at 22nd Congress 169, CP Fund 227, CP Denmark 17th Congress 270, Hymie Lee 50th Birthday 309, E. Taylor 60th Birthday 383, Rumania's Eight Years 389, Ernest Brown 60th Birthday 458, Beattie Marks 50th Birthday 479, Olive Arnot 60th Birthday 495, Report of 19th Congress CPSU 517, CP and the Labour Movement 529, Study the Success of our Scottish Comrades 555

Pamphlets etc
   Stop the War in Malaya   3d 12 pp
   Britain Arise: Report to 22nd Congress CPGB   1/- 52 pp
   The Nazis Shall Not Pass   3d 12 pp
PL   Issues Before the 22nd Congress CPGB   1d 4 pp
F   Open Letter to Students   2d 4 pp

1953

LM XXXV: None
CR: Marxism in the British Labour Movement—Apr
WNV XXXIII: Why the Czech Trial? 5, Build the CP, Strengthen the *Daily Worker* 87, Palmiro Togliatti 60th Birthday 152, Clemens Dutt 60th birthday 174, What US Domination Means to Britain 195, Dona Torr 70th Birthday 202, Nikes Zacharides 50th Birthday 211, Hymie Fagan 50th Birthday 254, International Trade Union Unity 301, 315, CP Ceylon 10th

Anniversary 310, Speak Out for Britain 325, Preliminary Agenda for Margate LPC 351, James Gardiner 60th Birthday 371, Youth After Bucharest 389, Minnie Bowles 50th Birthday 444, A Shameful Outrage in British Guiana 482, Walter Ulbrecht 60th Birthday 509, A Beacon to All Who Want Peace 531

Pamphlets
   A Policy for Labour   3d 12 pp
   In Memory of Stalin and Gottwald   6d 16 pp
   What Do Miners Need?   3d 12 pp
   Labour, What Next?   3d 12 pp

1954

LM XXXVI: A Common Policy for Labour—Jan. Also reviews of HP's *Selected Articles and Speeches* Vol I by R. Stewart—Feb, Vol II by Peter Kerrigan—Aug
   CR replaced by *Marxist Quarterly*
   WNV changed to *World News I*: Britain's Shameful Heritage 115, Journey to India 173, 192, Role of the CP 181, Socialist Unity Party, Germany 4th Congress 313, British Road to Socialism, Chart of the Future 483, CP Czechoslovakia 10th Congress 519, National Independence for the Colonies 543, German Rearmament, Victory in the Balance 741, World News and You 783

Books
   Selected Articles and Speeches by Harry Pollitt   Vol I 6/- 180 pp. Vol II 5/- 142 pp

Pamphlets
   The People on the March   3d 16 pp
   Indian Diary   1/- 32 pp
   Challenge to Labour: Report to 23rd Congress CPGB   1/- 55 pp
Bklt   Allies for Freedom: Second Empire Conference
      of Communist Parties   6/- 148 pp: Speeches incl. HP
   In Defence of Peace   4d 16 pp

1955

LM XXXVII: How Labour Can Win—A Policy—Jan
   WN II: Prospects for Labour 1, Working Class Unity is Greater than the H-Bomb 219, Working Class Unity Can Defeat the Tories 462, Socialism or Mugsborough 767, Thirty-eight Years 850, The Opportunities of our Time 946, 1956 Will Be a Year of Action 961
   MQ II: Tory Victory and Labour's Future—Jul

Pamphlet
   The Communist Party and the Labour Party   3d 12 pp
F   Lessons of the Strikes, reprinted from DW   np 4 pp

1956

LM XXXVIII: Tom Mann Centenary—Apr
WN III: W. Pieck 80th Birthday Celebrations 32, CPSU 20th Congress Speech by HP 136, CPGB 24th National Congress, part of HP's Political Report 210, CPSU 20th Congress and the Role of Stalin 246, 278

Pamphlets
   The People will Decide—Report to CPGB 24th Congress   1/- 56 pp
L   Labour Must End the Bans   np 2 pp
D   Report on VIII Congress CP of China   np 20 pp f'scap

1957

LM XXXIX: None
WN IV: Dockers Beware 696
MQ replaced by *Marxism Today* (monthly) I: October Revolution and British Labour—Oct

1958

LM XL: None
WNV V: Four Points 33, Our Would-be Conquerors 132, BR Correspondence of the Grand Alliance 169, Dutchmen on Britain 389, Wanted, Trade Union Summit Talks 412, Memoirs: Left Book Club Period 462, Ernest Bevin 491, Cripps, Pollitt, Maxton Unity Campaign 503, Struggle of the Spanish People, Dress Rehearsal for World War 526, With the International Brigade 563, 574, Literature, a Political Weapon 724, British Road to Socialism, Remedy for Frustration 1555
MTD II: Whither Trade Unionism?—Aug
World Marxist Review (monthly, journal of the International Communist Movement) I: Creative Factor in World History No 3

Pamphlets
   None

1959

LM XLI: None
WN VI: Illusion and Reality, Labour Policy 33, How To Spike the Tories' Guns 57, CPSU 21st Congress 106, 121, What Lenin Taught Us 223, Message to Iraqi Communists 231, China Revisited 578
MTD III: None
WMR II: Problems of War, Peace and the Socialist International No 6

1960

LM XLII: No articles. A memorial tribute 8 pp plus two letters written by HP to the Boilermakers MR in 1920, included in August number, also reprinted as a folder
WN VII: Eden Bit Off More than he Could Chew 139, Literature in Scotland 153, Story of the *Jolly George* 221
MTD IV: Tribute to HP by R. Stewart—Aug
WMR III: Memorial Tribute—Aug
WMR III: Memorial Tribute—Aug

Pamphlet
   Harry Pollitt—A Tribute   1/- 32 pp

APPENDIX 6

DIARY OF MAIN EVENTS

1890	Nov 22	Born at 14, Wharf Street, Droylsden
1894		Entered at King Street Infants School
1895		Entered Junior School
1897		Transferred to British School Market Street
1898		Saw Chapmans Circus at Gorton Wakes
1900		First job, spare time in rag store Wharf Street. Moravian and other Sunday Schools
1902		Walked to Ashton for examination for half-timers. First job half time at Bensons Mill
1903		At Openshaw ILP Sunday School hears first Socialist lectures—Philip Snowden, Conrad Noel. First seaside holiday at Lytham
	Nov 22	Finished school, whole time at Bensons
1904		Evening School at Droylsden
1905	Oct 2	Started at Gorton Tank
1906		Made member of Openshaw ILP
	Dec	Put up window bill for John Hodge. Moved to 4, Melba Street, Higher Openshaw
1907		Began as apprentice plater. Evening courses at Whitworth Hall
1908		First public speaking
1909		Took Metal Plate course at Manchester School of Technology
1910		Gained City and Guild Ordinary Certificate in Metal Plate
	Nov	Heard Tom Mann debate with Frank Rose. Helped campaign to organise labourers. Attended Manchester County Forum
1911	Sep	Classes in Structural Iron & Steel and Mathematics
	Jul	Helped in labourers' strikes
	Nov	Drafted election leaflet for Openshaw Socialist Society. Given Marx's *Capital I* as 21st birthday present
1912		Secretary Openshaw BSP. Speaker in Lancashire and Yorkshire; Clarion Cyclist; reads Jack London's "Iron Heel". Made member first class Boilermakers Society Gorton Branch; works in various Lancashire boiler shops.
1913		Delegate to BSP Annual Conference; Spoke at York Annual Meet of Clarion Cycling Club; deputised for Jim Larkin at Grimsby
1914		Worked at Beyer Peacock's, Gorton, and left rather than pay for spoilt work; in Aug. spoke against the war; meetings broken up
1915		Resigned Secretaryship of Openshaw BSP. Shop Steward at Armstrong Whitworth; fights dilution

	June	Started at Thorneycrofts, Southampton
	Sep	On Strike Committee, fined for breach of Munitions Act
1916	Feb	Started at Nicolson's, Northam
	Nov	Back to Manchester boiler shops
1917	May	Active in engineering strike
	Jul	Spoke in Stephenson Sq. for peace
	Nov	At once supported Bolshevik Revolution
1918		Started in London ship-repair; transferred to London No. 11 Boilermakers; joined and spoke for Workers Socialist Federation; distributed Lenin's "Appeal to the Toiling Masses" and "Are You a Trade Unionist?"
	Oct	Helped found River Thames Shop Stewards Movement
	Dec	On Boilermakers London District Committee. Spoke for Arthur Henderson in coupon election
1919	Jan	Took classes on Industrial History and Economics; Elected Secretary of Boilermakers District Committee, organiser for RTSSM and leader of strike; Wrote for Boilermakers *Monthly Record*
		Moved action resolution at national conference for "Hands Off Russia"; elected to committee to carry out resolution
	Feb 16	Spoke for Carpenters' amalgamation
1919	May	Appealed to port workers not to handle munitions for use against Soviet Russia. Art in *W.D.* Dockers Beware
	June	Helped form enlarged National Committee for Hands Off Russia
	Sep	Becomes its National Organiser, and travelled all over country for Hands off Russia Committee
	Oct	Read Lenin's *State and Revolution*
	Dec	Returned to shipyard—"can do more for Russia in the docks"
1920		Series of meetings and leaflets in docks to stop munitions; HP sacked for refusing to work on barges for war material
	May 1	Spoke for London May Day Committee in Hyde Park and Albert Hall
	May 10	Dockers, with union backing, struck the '*Jolly George*'
	Jun–Aug	'Hands Off Russia' activities culminated in official Labour call for Councils of Action; government yielded and dropped intervention
	Aug	Present as visitor at founding conference CPGB
	Dec	Began work for British Bureau Red International of Labour Unions
1921	Jan	Secretary London Committee RTUI Lodges at 18 Central Park Rd E6
	Feb 18	Spoke at Poplar Town Hall "to form Branch of CPGB"
	Feb 23	Boilermakers delegate to Labour Conference on Unemployment
	May 7	Spoke at London Conference for delegate to First World Congress RILU
	May 20	Arrested for speeches at Plymouth, fined £10

	Jul	At III Congress CI and I Congress RILU handshake with Lenin; first meeting with Losovsky and others
	Sep	Boilermakers delegate at TUC Cardiff champions policy of RILU
	Oct	Reported on RILU and Russian Famine to London Conference
	Dec	Boilermakers delegate to LP–TUC Conference on Unemployment
1922	Jan	Edited and published first issue of *All Power*
	Feb	CPGB delegate to ECCI 1st Plenum
	Mar	Opened discussion on United Front at 4th Congress CPGB; elected to Party Commission
	Jun	Boilermakers delegate to 22nd NLP Conference in Edinburgh; speaks for Communist affiliation
	Jul	In Germany speaking for CP Germany
	Sep	Delegate to 54th Southport TUC. Moved resolution on 44 hour week
	Oct	Signed report of Party Commission to 5th Congress CPGB; elected to EC, on Organisation Bureau in charge of industrial work
	Nov	Spoke with John Hodge at Gorton, explains why not standing in General Election. Editor Scottish edition *Daily Communist*. Represented EC at Conference to establish London District CPGB
1923	Feb	Assisted R. Palme Dutt in editing *Workers Weekly*
	Mar	Spoke in West Ham against deportation of Irish
	May	Attends 3rd Plenum ECCI
		Spoke for CP Germany
	Jun	On delegation to fusion conference of Second and Two-and-a-Half Internationals from International Committee Against Occupation of the Ruhr. At ECCI 3rd Plenum, but left before British Commission. Full-time member of Political Bureau CPGB. Delegate to 23rd NLP Conference; spoke for Communist affiliation
	Jul	Spoke for and edited bulletin for unofficial strike in London Docks; opposes break-away union
	Aug	Gave up Secretaryship of RILU British Bureau
	Sep	In charge of CPGB campaigning and organisation. Delegate to 55th Plymouth TUC. Urged united action.
	Oct	Proposed as Labour candidate for Paisley; not adopted. Relieved of duties as National Organiser CPGB
	Nov	Presided at Second Annual National Conference of Trades Councils
1924	Jan	At Lenin's funeral and Guard of Honour and banner-bearer for CI
	Feb	Spoke for unofficial shipyard strikers at Southampton; elected to EC Labour Research Department
	May	At 6th Congress CPGB moved resolution on Minority Movement, and spoke to Women's Conference

	June		Elected to ECCI at 5th Congress
	Jul		Drafted Appeal to Forces for *Workers Weekly*
	Aug		Elected Hon. General Secretary of National Minority Movement by inaugural conference
	Sep		Delegate to 56th TUC at Hull; spoke for militant policy
	Oct		Delegate to 24th NLPC, opposed anti-Communist measures. In general election helped Bob Stewart, Communist Candidate in Dundee
	Nov		At 6th Conference Soviet Trade Unions at ECCI
	Dec		Spoke for CPG in election campaign
1925	Jan		Reported on International Trade Union Unity at NMM National Unity Conference
	Mar		Kidnapped by fascists at Liverpool
	May		Delivered Chairman's address and reports on international trade union unity at 7th Congress CPGB
	Aug		Disqualified as candidate for Boilermakers E.C. Spoke on Aims and Objects of NMM at 2nd Annual Conference
	Sep		Delegate to 57th Scarborough TUC, spoke on resolution on Imperialism
	Oct		Delegate to 25th Liverpool NLPC. Challenged Macdonald's policy; spoke against ban on Communists as trade union delegates. 10th, married to Marjorie Brewer. Home at 63, Dresden Rd N9. 14th, arrested with 11 other Communist leaders
	Nov		Tried at Old Bailey, sentenced to 12 months in second division, sent to Wandsworth Prison
1926	Apr		Issued with Prison Notebook
	Sep	10	Released from Wandsworth
		12	Welcomed by mass rally in Hyde Park
	Oct		Delegate to 26th Margate NLPC, Opposed re-affirmation of Liverpool anti-Communist decisions. Spoke to locked-out miners in Leicester, Notts. and Derby
	Oct	16	At 8th Congress CPGB reported on LP policy
	Nov	7	Spoke at Albert Hall on Anniversary
		21	Banned from speaking at Derby
1927	Feb		Spoke at founding conference of League Against Imperialism in Brussels. Moved to 78, Tollington Park N4
	Mar		Spoke at funeral of Arthur MacManus
	Apr		Challenged Bromley on slander of MM. Bromley silent
	May		Spoke for May Day Committee in Hyde Park and Albert Hall
	Aug		Spoke at 4th Annual Conference NMM on International trade Union Unity
	Sep		Delegate for last time at 59th TUC. Signed statement for the Minority
	Oct		Delegate to 27th NLPC for last time. At IX Congress CPGB. Tried for criminal libel of Scott, a seaman backed by Havelock Wilson. Ordered to pay £100 costs. HP's reply to attack in Boilermakers *Monthly Report* refused publication.

	Nov		On rank and file delegation to Soviet Tenth Anniversary; taken ill on tour with appendicitis.
	Dec		Ended work in shipyard till 1941
1928	Jan	3	Circularised Boilermakers with reply to EC attack; with R. P. Dutt signed thesis for 9th Plenum ECCI
	Feb		Appealed against conviction on Scott; lost
	Mar		Prohibited by Boilermakers EC from standing for election to TUC or NLPC
	May		Spoke in Hyde Park
	June		Wrote NMM pamphlet *Reply to Citrine*
	Jul		Signed invitation to establish British Section League Against Imperialism. Published exposure of irregularities in Boilermakers' ballot
	Sep		Spoke at demonstration outside 60th Swansea TUC
	Oct		Appealed personally to A. J. Cook to stand firm as militant
	Dec		At 8th Soviet TUC
1929	Jan		Representative of ECCI at 6th National Convention CP USA. At 10th Congress CPGB. Moved resolution for payment of Political Levy
	Mar		Helped Dawdon miners against wage cuts
	May		In General Election was Communist candidate at Seaham Harbour against Ramsay MacDonald
	Jun		At 12th Congress CP Germany
	Jul		Spoke at 10th Plenum ECCI and at 2nd Congress of League Against Imperialism. Helped form Meerut Defence Committee in London
	Aug		At 4th Conference NMM. Spoke on war danger; resigns honorary Secretaryship, is elected Vice-President. Elected General Secretary CPGB. Began preparations to issue *Daily Worker*
	Nov		At 11th Congress CPGB gave Political Report
1930	Jan		Refused government permission to attend Meerut Trial as witness for defence
	Feb		Reported to ECCI
	May		Wrote *Three Years of Mondism*
	Aug		Launched campaign for a Workers' Charter
	Oct		At 2nd Annual Conference UMS. Spoke in Trafalgar Square for Charter Campaign
	Dec		In Whitechapel by-election as Communist candidate
1931	Feb		At 7th Annual Conference NUWM
	Mar		At 11th Plenum ECCI
	Apr		Opened discussion at Charter Convention
	May		On May 1st Spoke in Hyde Park. At Congress CP of Belgium
	Jul		Assisted London Boilermakers strike
	Aug		Spoke at National Conference of Charter women
	Oct		In General Election Communist candidate for Whitechapel

	Nov		Spoke at RILU 8th Central Council, clashes with Losovsky
1932	Jan		Described Japanese attack on Manchuria as "commencement of a new world war"
	May		Debated with Fenner Brockway at Memorial Hall
	Jul		Spoke outside ILP Conference at Bradford
	Sep		Reported at 12th Plenum ECCI. Helped in Lancashire cotton workers strike
	Nov		Gave political report at 12th Congress CPGB
	Dec		Assisted in London Lightermen's strike
1933	Jan		In by-election in Rhondda East assisted Arthur Horner, the Communist candidate
	Feb		Spoke at Shoreditch to welcome Tom Mann on release from prison
	Mar		Circulated CI manifesto for united front against fascism and made unity proposals to LP, ILP, TUC and Co-operative Party. Speaks at Conference to found Marx Memorial Library and Workers School
	May		At first joint meeting CP–ILP for united front
	Jul	30	Spoke in Hyde Park for Anti-war Movement
	Aug		In by-election at Clay Cross was Communist candidate against Arthur Henderson
	Oct		Deported from Belfast
	Nov		At 13th Plenum ECCI
	Dec		Signed appeal for National Hunger March and United Front Congress
1934	Feb		Arrested with Tom Mann after speeches in Glamorgan, and charged with Sedition. At National United Front Congress, HP's speech read by William Gallacher
	June		Made proposals to help London Boilermakers on strike
	Jul		With Tom Mann on trial at Swansea; case dismissed
	Aug		On March and at dinner at Centenary of Boilermakers Society
	Sep	9	Spoke in Hyde Park at huge demonstration to "drown Mosley in a sea of working class activity"
	Nov		Proposed Communist support for Labour candidates willing to support immediate demands. During the year, date not known, speaks for CP of Ireland at Rathmines Town Hall, Dublin
1935	Jan		Spoke at Shoreditch on 5th Anniversary of *Daily Worker*
	Feb		Reports at 13th Congress CPGB
	Mar		Spoke at ECCI on United Front
	Apr		Spoke as CP representative at ILP Annual Conference
	May		Presented evidence and spoke at Arms Commission
	Aug		Spoke at 7th Congress Communist International
	Sep		Spoke in Rhondda against war on Abyssinia. Along with Czech and French Communist leaders appointed by CI to discuss joint action for peace with Labour and Socialist International
	Oct		Appealed to Labour Party Conference for common action

	Nov		In General Election was Communist candidate in Rhondda East. Applied to LP for Communist affiliation
1936	Mar		Appealed for Ernst Thaelmann
	Apr		Spoke at dinner for Tom Mann on 80th Birthday
	May	1	Spoke in Hyde Park and at Shoreditch
	June		Refused visa for South Africa
	June	4	Debate with Tory MP at Oxford Union
	Jul		Called for aid to Republican Spain
	Aug		Condemned "non-intervention" as "treason to democracy and peace"
	Sep		At ECCI spoke for aid to Spain, including International Brigade
	Oct		Reported at National Conference CPGB, "The fate of the working class is in our hands"
1937	Jan		With Stafford Cripps and James Maxton launched CP–ILP–SL Unity Campaign at Manchester
	Feb		Spoke for Left Book Club at Albert Hall. First visit to British Battalion in Spain
	May		Reported at 14th Congress CPGB
	Jul		Second visit to British Battalion in Spain
	Sep		In Paris with CP France. Protested at Japanese bombing of Chinese cities.
	Dec		Third visit to British Battalion in Spain. At 11th Congress CP of France
1938	Jan		At Aberdeen launched Communist crusade for unity
	Feb		Spoke for Left Book Club at Albert Hall
	Mar		Wrote pamphlet on Hitler annexation of Austria—sale 100,000 copies
	Apr		Fourth visit to British Battalion in Spain
	May		Argued with Labour Party to support People's Front
	Sep		Reported to 15th Congress CPGB. Fifth visit to British Battalion in Spain. Issued 1,000,000 leaflets for repudiation of Munich Agreement
	Oct		Wrote pamphlet on Czechoslovakia—sale 130,000 copies. Ordered by doctors three months rest
	Nov	6	Spoke at 21st Anniversary Rally Empress Stadium. Cruise for health in Caribbean
	Dec	30	Returned to London
1939	Jan	8	Spoke at Empress Hall Rally on return of British Battalion
	Mar		Spoke at Lambeth on "Spain, What Next?"
		14	Delivered Marx Memorial Lecture at St. Pancras
	Apr		Spoke for Left Book Club with Lloyd George at Empress Hall
	Jul		Spoke at Pageant of Chartism at Empress Hall
	Aug		Spoke at London Rally on German-Soviet pact and coming war
	Sep		Wrote pamphlet on the measures necessary to secure the victory of democracy over fascism

	Oct	Maintained his view of the war, was removed from post of General Secretary when EC changed its line and declared the war to be imperialist. Later Pollitt accepted the majority decision and explained it at public meetings
	Nov	At funeral of his mother
	Dec	Helped Eric Gower, Communist candidate in Stretford by-election
1940	Jan	At by-election in Southwark spoke for Labour Anti-war candidate
	Feb	At by-election in Silvertown was Communist candidate
	Mar	Published autobiographical book, *Serving My Time*
	Jun 23	After Dunkirk spoke at huge London rally, "France has fallen, the people must act—arm the workers"
	Aug	Spoke at celebrations for 20th Anniversary CPGB including presentations to foundation members
	Oct	Signed appeal for People's Convention. Campaign in Fife
	Dec	Spoke at London Rally for People's Convention
1941	Jan	Delegate to the People's Convention
	Mar	At Dunbarton by-election spoke for Malcolm McEwen, Communist candidate. At funeral of Tom Mann
	Apr 21	Started work in London ship repair
	Jun	At EC declared support for People's War following Hitler attack on SU and Churchill's pledge of aid; restored to position of General Secretary
	Jun 26	Spoke at big meeting in Central London
	Aug 9	Released from ship-repair by Ministry of National Service. Visited Lloyd George
	Dec 7	Visited Bill Gee in Aberdeen, shocked at his condition
	22	Issued appeal for Bill Gee
	28	Spoke at Stoll Theatre, London on "Programme for Victory" relayed to 10 other meetings
1942	Jan 24	Spoke for Indian Independence
	28	Welcomed Government changes, but "only a beginning"
	May 3	Spoke to 20,000 in London, "Into Battle"
	23	Spoke for "Win the war programme" at CPGB National Conference in London. Regretted Cripps' declaration that "nothing more can be done on India"
	24	Spoke to 50,000 in Trafalgar Square for Second Front
	Jul 26	Spoke for Second Front to 60,000 in Trafalgar Square
	Aug	Welcomed legalislation CP India; urged Churchill to reopen negotiations with Indian leaders. Criticised Churchill for delaying the Second Front
1943	Jul	Reported at 16th Congress CPGB
	Oct	Warned against re-emergence of "die-hard Tories thinking only of their class interests" after the Nazi defeat at Stalingrad
1944	Jan 9	Spoke to 2,000 in Hackney, "London part of the battle-field"
	Feb	Wrote pamphlet *Take Over the Mines*

	Feb 13	Spoke at Coliseum on Anniversary of Jarama
	Jul	Wrote letter to all Communists in the Forces
	Sep	Spoke at Coventry to launch fund for Tom Mann Memorial Hall
	Oct	Spoke in memory of Ernst Thaelmann. Reported at 17th Congress CPGB
	Dec 9	Spoke in protest on Churchill attack on Greece. Published policy for democratic advance in *How to Win the Peace* and raised question of how Britain would move from capitalism to socialism
1945	Feb	Welcomed decisions of Crimea meeting
	Apr	Spoke for CP France in Paris
	May	Welcomed Labour decision to end coalition, and urged anti-Tory unity
	Jun	Broadcast speech for General Election; is Communist candidate in Rhondda East
	Aug	Declared Communists will "help the Government to carry out Labour's declared policy". Delegate to Congress of CP of Norway
	16	Spoke at Stoll Theatre for 25th Anniversary CPGB
	Sep	Pointed out that Bevin's foreign policy did not correspond with Labour's programme
	Nov 14	Talked with Ernest Bevin at Foreign Office. Reported at 18th Congress CPGB. Replied to coalowners by advocating nationalisation
1946	Jan 6	Spoke at Albert Hall for *Daily Worker*
	,, 20	Spoke to Communist professional workers
	Feb	Called for change in the foreign policy
	Mar	Condemned Churchill's Fulton speech
	Apr	At 8th Congress CP Czechoslovakia
		Spoke at Memorial Hall exposing Morrison intrigue against Communist affiliation; exposes Laski's falsification of Dimitrov
	May	At 13th Congress of CP Sweden
	Sep 12	Spoke for London Squatters
1947	Jan	Reviewed eighteen months of Labour Government to show "there is no middle way"
	Feb	Reported to 19th Congress CPGB
	Mar	At Empire Conference of Communist Parties
	Jul	In car accident in Glasgow; knee injured
	Aug	Made new political appraisal in *Looking Ahead*
	Sep	Spoke in Hyde Park on necessity for a new, left Labour Government
	Dec	Developed new perspective in Communist policy following from estimate of Labour Government as "an active partner in the imperialist camp, carrying through a capitalist solution of the crisis"
1948	Jan	At 6th Congress CP Italy
	Feb	Reported to 20th Congress CPGB

	Mar	Spoke at Albert Hall for Centenary of Communist Manifesto
	Apr	In Paris on Valtin case
	May 1	Spoke in London at "banned" May Day march
	June	In Le Havre on Valtin case
	Jul	Fitted with special boot for leg injury
	14	Spoke in Paris for CP France
	17	On deputation to Alex Gossip for 85th Birthday
	Aug	At Congress CP Finland
		Proposed aim at for 100 Communist candidates at next General Election
	Dec 16	At Congress Polish Workers Party
	20	At Congress CP Bulgaria
1949	Apr	HP physically assaulted at meetings in Devon coinciding with the Amethyst affair
	May	Great reception for HP at London May Day rally. At 11th Congress CP Czechoslovakia
	Jul	In Sofia for funeral of Dimitrov
	Aug	In clinic in Czechoslovakia for treatment
	Sep	At celebration of twenty years as General Secretary CPGB
	Oct	Defended the arrested Communist leaders in USA
	Nov	In hospital for prolapsed disc
	Dec	Report to XXI Congress CPGB read by W. Gallacher, MP
1950	Jan 9	Resumed work after hospital
	Feb	In General Election given $8\frac{1}{2}$ mins. on BBC as Communist spokesman; Communist candidate for Rhondda East
	Mar	Called for "profound feeling of people for peace to be transformed into action against the war plans of British and US imperialism"
	Apr	In clinic in Soviet Union
	June	Spoke for CP France in Paris
	Jul	At EC of CPGB called for preparation of new Party Programme. At 3rd Congress Socialist Unity Party of Germany
	Sep	Spoke at Empress Hall for 30th Anniversary CPGB
	Nov 22	Received world wide congratulations on 60th birthday
	26	Spoke at London celebration for 60th birthday
1951	Jan 2	Spoke at Berlin celebration of W. Pieck's 75th birthday. At CPGB EC presented draft of *The British Road to Socialism*
	Feb	At 2nd Congress Hungarian Working People's Party
	Mar	Visit to Czechoslovakia with John Gollan
	22	Issued appeal for seven arrested dockers
	Jul	Wrote on 30 Years of the *Labour Monthly*
	Sep	Holiday in Romania
	Oct	Defined "war or peace" as the supreme issue of the general election; speaks in Rhondda East for Communist candidate Idris Cox. Broadcast refused by BBC published as leaflet

	Nov	Called for resistance to Tory policy
	Dec 25	At Wm. Gallacher's 75th Birthday celebration
1952	Jan	Exposed the imperialist motives of the British war on the Malayan people
	Apr	Reported to 22nd Congress CPGB
	May	At 17th Congress CP Denmark
	June	At Marjorie Pollitt's 50th birthday
	Jul	Headed Communist march through East London and spoke at Stratford
	Oct	At 19th Congress CPSU
1953	Mar	At funeral of Stalin; and spoke at Memorial meeting in London
	Nov	In hospital for treatment of back
	24	Boarded *Batory* for Bombay
	Dec 12	Bombay, 16–18 Delhi, Amritsar, Jullundur
	19	Aggra, Taj Mahal; 20–21 Calcutta; 22–23 Hyderabad 24 Madras; 25 Madura
	28	3rd Congress Communist Party of India
1954	Jan 7	Sailed from Bombay for home
	24	Arrived Tilbury
	Feb 2	Interviewed by British Columbia TV
	Mar 3–7	At 8th Congress Working People's Party of Cyprus (AKEL) and tour of island
	30	At 4th Congress Socialist Unity Party of Germany
	Apr	Reported to 23rd Congress CPGB
	May	At funeral of Bill Gee in Aberdeen
	Jun 11	At 10th Congress CP Czechoslovakia
	24	In clinic in USSR
	Aug 1	At opening of Agricultural Exhibition in Moscow
	30	Returned to London
	Dec	Again speaking at meetings
1955	Feb	Spoke in Albert Hall for 25th Anniversary *Daily Worker*
	Apr 12–25	Tour of China; Peking, Nanking, Shanghai, Hangchow, Canton, Wuhan
	May	General Election, spoke for Communist candidates. Spoke for trade union unity in strikes and against breakaways
1956	Jan 2	In Berlin for 80th Birthday W. Pieck
	Feb 20	At 20th Congress CPSU. Not at closed session
	Mar 12	Reported to London Communists on 20th Congress CPSU, argued for a balanced view on the Soviet Union
	14	Spoke at Marx's grave and unveiled monument
	30	Reported at 24th Congress CPGB
	Apr 16	At Poplar Civic Theatre on Tom Mann
	30	Spoke on Commercial TV
	May 12	Elected CPGB Chairman on retiring from General Secretaryship. Doctors ordered complete rest; leaves for cruise on *Batory*
	June 25	Returned from cruise, but sight not fully restored
	Jul	On CP delegation to CPSU

	Aug		"Back at desk—obituaries a bit exaggerated"
	Sep		At 8th Congress CP China
	Oct		Analysed events in Hungary and defends the Kadar Government
1957	Feb	16	At celebration 80th birthday Bob Stewart
		17	At 21st Birthday Party for Brian Pollitt
	Mar		Meeting with Polish Workers Party
	Apr		In the chair at 25th Congress CPGB. Again in hospital with back trouble
	Aug		Again at desk
	Oct	20	"First speech for many months" at Abe Moffat's birthday
	Nov		At Moscow celebrations of Anniversary
		19	In Czechoslovakia for funeral of Pres. Zapototski
	Dec		Returned to London after treatment at Sochi
1958	Mar	14	Delivered Marx Memorial Lecture, later suffered a "minor stroke"
	Nov	9	Spoke at London meeting for Anniversary
	Dec	18	Granted superannuation benefit by Boilermakers
1959	Feb		At 21st Congress CPSU
	Mar		In chair at 26th Congress CPGB
	Sep		In Peking for 10th anniversary celebrations; talked with Ho Chi-minh
	Oct		In Sochi for treatment
	Nov	7	In Moscow for Anniversary
1960	Apr	9	Left London for Australia and New Zealand
		11	Stopped at Sydney, greeted by Australian CP leaders
		13–27	In New Zealand, at Congress CP New Zealand and spoke in Auckland, Dunedin, Greymouth, Christchurch, Wellington, Lower Hutt, Porirua
		28	Great welcome at Sydney Airport
		29	Guest of Honour at Sydney May Day Ball
	May	1	On Sydney May Day march and speaker at rally on Domain
		2	On Newcastle May Day march
	Jun	19	Public and trade union meetings, social events, personal talks, TV and radio sessions, press interviews, sightseeing in New South Wales (Sydney, Wollongong, Newcastle, Tamworth, Armidale, the New England Range, the Blue Mountains and the coast), Queensland (Brisbane, Nambour, Crohamhurst), Victoria (Melbourne, Monthaggi, Geelong) and Canberra.
	Jun	20	Left Sydney for home on *Orion*
		24	A dinner at Adelaide
		26	A stroke while *Orion* in the Bight
		27	Died in the ship's hospital

APPENDIX 7

POLLITT'S LAST WRITINGS ON TRADE UNIONISM

In 1958 Pollitt re-raised basic questions in an article entitled "Whither Trade Unionism?" (*Marxism Today*, Aug 1958). He spoke of "chaos and confusion in policy", of the General Council's "sectionalism and repudiation of class solidarity" during the recent London busmen's strike. His proposals did not make the hoped for impact; they "were met by a conspiracy of silence among those interested in suppressing constructive ideas coming from the Communist Party". As Tory plans for wage restraint, unemployment and legal action against the unions developed without effective counter-measures by the TUC, he began work on a book on trade union problems. Only the synopsis, of which a summary follows, was completed.

1. *At the Crossroads*

The opening theme is the present power of the trade unions and "their enormous potential strength". Fearing this power, the employing class through numerous agencies makes continuous efforts to determine the course to be taken by the unions. The attitude of the union leaders is mainly defensive; that of the big employers is aggressive. Impelled by intensified competition, technological revolution, and the advance of socialism, they intensify the exploitation of labour, seek to shackle the democratic movement of which the unions are a decisive part and threaten union gains and rights. Room for sectional settlements narrows, the class and political role of the unions becomes decisive.

2. *Class Collaboration or Class Struggle*

Next, the two main trends revealed in recent conflicts are analysed—class collaboration practised by the right-wing leaders and the line of struggle called for by increasing numbers of union members. The right-wing policy of seeking only temporary gains for sections of workers inevitably brings acceptance of sectionalism and rejection of a class approach, acceptance of capitalism and rejection of a fight against it. The left, with the Communists as their most consistent spokesmen, seek to advance at the expense of the employing class both the immediate and the long term interests of union members. This means a continuous struggle for working class unity and against capitalism. In organisation the right favours bureaucracy and attacks existing levels of democracy. The Communists are for maximum democracy to bring the mass of the union members into discussion and action, and for maximum unity to bring the greatest strength to bear. The right, while itself giving political support to reformism, argues either "no politics in the unions" or "don't use industrial strength for political ends." The Communists are for political struggle against capitalism because the final solution of trade union problems requires socialism.

3. *Wages and Hours, the Crucial Question*

The unions should fight unitedly for higher wages and shorter hours for all, including women, youth, unskilled and low paid workers. Wage increases now, not in the distant future, would benefit all British people, except the monopolists who want to solve the crisis at the expense of the workers.

To secure united action, the unions have to reject arguments used by the employers and repeated by the right-wing. They claim that higher wages are against the national interest because by raising export prices they lose orders and cause unemployment. The reply is that low wages never solved the export problem, and the biggest menace to jobs is failure to raise the people's purchasing power. If the unions agree that higher wages can only come out of higher productivity, they accept as permanent the existing division of the national income as between wages and profits. That means accepting capitalism as permanent. Nor is there any guarantee, apart from union action, that increased productivity will lead to higher wages and shorter hours. It usually leads first to redundancy, then to more production from fewer workers under greater pressure and with a smaller total wage bill. Wage restraint under a Labour Government does not "give Labour a chance": it gives monopoly capitalism a chance. The right-wing seeks to avoid a clash with monopoly, and this leads to loss of working class support and the return of a new Tory Government.

4. *Shop Stewards and Factory Struggle*

Chapter IV is devoted to organisation on the job, where agreements become meaningful and the interests of workers and employers inevitably clash. To negotiate with the management the workers elect shop stewards whose strength lies in their representative character. They speak and act as the workers collectively decide, report to the workers the results of negotiations, and take such further action as the workers decide. This is workshop democracy in action, its power depends on the workers' unity, class outlook and readiness to withdraw their labour if need be. As the shop stewards are the biggest obstacle to the class collaboration policy, they become the main target of attack by the employing class.

The strength of the shop stewards compelled their recognition in most unions as part of the official machinery. The right-wing price for this recognition is to impose artificial divisions, limited activity, and separation from politics.

Workshop organisation is in no sense an alternative to the trade union; on the contrary it can make a major contribution to ensuring that the union fully serves the workers' interests and that members make full use of their democratic rights. Since "factory self-sufficiency holds no prospect of solving the workers' problems", shop stewards will also be involved in social and political as well as economic questions.

5. *One Union for each Industry*

The employers in each major industry are organised as a single body and act as such. They have other advantages; a powerful press, their Tory Party, and state support. There is no comparable organisation of the workers, the sectionalism of the unions plays into the employers' hands. The General Council, itself reflecting and acquiescing in this sectionalism, does not seriously campaign for amalgamations. Some industrial federations of unions have national negotiating machinery which is a step towards a common front against the employers, but their policy is often a compromise between conflicting unions. These federations tend to be substitutes for amalgamation rather than an impetus to it. Pressure for amalgamations now can make substantial advances towards one union for each industry, with provisions in it for the needs of sections with special problems.

6. *Democracy is Strength*

Democracy is described as "the very lifeblood of trade unionism". Any weakening of democracy "weakens the unity and leadership of the struggle, impairs the fighting strength, opens the way to employers and Tory attacks, develops frustration and cynicism among the members." The struggle for full democracy "is the fight for the very future of trade unionism."

Essentials of trade union democracy in the fields of policy, elections and organisation are: All members to have the right to formulate policy; the democratically elected annual or biennial conference to decide policy binding throughout the union. Executive and District decisions to be made known, members to have the right of appeal. All members to have the right to elect and be elected; Executive, District and Branch Committees, and all officials to be periodically elected. A majority of delegations to TUC, Labour Party and other such conferences to be lay members. Shop Stewards to be officially recognised and protected, and to have the right to District meetings. The Branch structure to be based on the place of work wherever possible.

Anti-democratic measures such as bans on Communists to be abolished. Pollitt declared "The Communists stand for trade union democracy because they stand for the class struggle, for the victory of the working class over the exploiting class, because they understand that trade union democracy hastens the day of that victory."

7. *A True General Staff for Labour*

In conditions of today organised solidarity is vital in every important struggle; the unions have to confront the big employers with their united strength. This requires a different conception of leadership from the class collaboration hitherto dominant in the General Council majority, whose policy has in fact been in opposition to the wishes of the union membership and has been carried through by conference manoeuvres, "statesmanlike" speeches to hold the unions back from struggle, and dubious methods of election of the General Council.

Elsewhere, Pollitt says more precisely what he has in mind. "We will stick to our early conception of a General Council of the TUC, as the class leadership of the movement as a whole. . . . It should consist of the most tried, trusted and experienced leaders, those who know what the class struggle is, are convinced socialists, with a working class outlook that nothing can corrupt. . . .

It should act as a Cabinet of the trade union movement, leading it in accordance with the decisions of the TUC. . . . Such a General Council would have many obstacles to overcome. It would have to abolish sectional prejudices and examine every issue from the standpoint of class and not craft. But such obstacles are in the main self-imposed and could be overcome".

The election practices the end of which he demanded, included—bargaining for seats, absence of competitive elections in some groups, mis-use of the bloc vote—"you vote for our man and we'll vote for yours"—failure to consult the union membership and to allow them to vote before nominating candidates for the General Council.

The synopsis continues—instead of advocating capitalist ideas in politics and economics, the General Council should conduct widespread education and propaganda exposing the falsity of these ideas. It should promote industrial unionism and bring into the unions the millions still unorganised. It should work for united action and a single Trade Union International. Instead of witch-hunting against militants and Communists, it should promote full democratic practices throughout the movement.

8. *A World-wide Struggle*

Trade unionists of all countries could cope better with world problems if a single united Trade Union International replaced the present World Federation of Trade Unions and International Confederation of Free Trade Unions. The WFTU stands for world trade union unity, the ICFTU, formed by the US and British trade union leaders as a breakaway from the World Federation, supports NATO and is anti-Soviet and anti-Communist. Yet within it are national trade union centres with millions of members who do not support cold war policies.

A single International could make a great contribution to ensure that workers of one country do not compete with those of another, that help is given to organise trade unions in colonial countries, that bans on east-west trade are lifted, the gigantic waste on arms production ended, and above all that the road to a third world war is barred. Much could be gained by the unions of socialist and capitalist countries sharing experiences and knowledge.

The perspective should be democratic pressure for as much unity of action as possible now on common problems, and a conscious progress towards amalgamation and one trade union International.

9. *Trade Unionism and Socialism*

The final chapter recalls that years ago many trade unions realised that it was the capitalist system which prevented the workers obtaining all they desired from life—work, leisure, high living standards, knowledge, enjoyment. These unions saw the need for a government of their own to end the exploitation of man by man. "That is why Socialism is inscribed on our banner."

Those who do very well out of capitalism—employers, bankers, landlords—go to any lengths to prevent the movement making progress in its socialist aim. "The right-wing leaders succumb to this pressure, they either abandon the socialist aim or so distort it as to in effect abandon it"—for example, replacing socialist nationalisation by state shareholding in big capitalist firms. "The abandonment of the socialist aim is the road to destruction of the Labour movement."

The alternative is to carry forward the tradition of those pioneers of the trade union movement who, while defending every immediate interest of the workers, never failed to see the socialist goal. That alternative is outlined in the Communist Party's programme, *The British Road To Socialism*.

The synopsis makes clear that the purpose and spirit of the book as a whole would have been that of the conclusion of the article already mentioned. "It needs to be remembered that the capitalists always seek to solve their problems at the expense of the working class and are only successful in doing so because of the existing reactionary leadership and out of date and divided trade unions. . . . There can never be any let-up in the struggles of the working class. Capitalism in decay is bound to attack the workers more and more. It will more and more continue to divide and rule. We have it in our power to prevent this if we will. . . . No sectional interest, no personal position or craft outlook ought to be allowed to stand in the way of the full unity and power of the workers being used. The tremendous changes in the structure of capitalism, its strategy and tactics, its more blatant use of the state machine and the reactionary Labour leaders, demands a tremendous change in the situation, strategy and tactics and leadership of the whole trade union movement."

APPENDIX 8

TWO FABRICATIONS

1947

In the House of Commons on December 10, 1947, John McGovern, MP said that on one occasion Pollitt amazed Maxton and himself by saying, in reference to J. B. Figgins and Joe McMillan, "I have instructed both to deny that they are members of the Communist Party, although they were secret members." (Hansard, 10-12-47, quoted in *Railway Review*, 19-12-47).

Pollitt wrote to the Speaker: "I wish to categorically deny having made any such statements to Mr. McGovern . . . never on any occasion did I have conversation in the company solely of Mr. McGovern and the late James Maxton." To Figgins he wrote: "There is not a word of truth in the assertion of Mr. McGovern either in relation to yourself or the late Mr. Joe McMillan."

Figgins published the correspondence (*Railway Review*, 19-12-47).

1974

On 18 November 1973, Mr. D. Harding, the industrial correspondent of the *Sunday Telegraph*, wrote that in 1926 Harry Pollitt had said, "Do you think we care a damn about the interests of the miners? What we are interested in is the road to revolution."

The allegation was repeated in a letter to the *Daily Telegraph* and in an article in *The Spectator* by Mr. Edward Pearce, a Labour candidate. Mr.

Harding, challenged by Reuben Falber, the assistant secretary of the Communist Party, to name his authority, after some delay stated that the statement had been made in a conversation in the Lobby of the House of Commons with the correspondent of the *Morning Post*, Mr. Peaker, "six weeks after the general strike of May 1926". Mr. Peaker had written the words down "within minutes of leaving Mr. Pollitt in the presence of Mr. John Baker White, who was willing to speak of the meeting should Mr. Falber's pursuit of the truth take him that far" (Harding in *Morning Star*, 1-3-74).

The fabricators of Mr. Harding's phantasy had forgotten that six weeks after the general strike, Harry Pollitt was in Wandsworth Prison. He was not released until 26 September, 1926.

APPENDIX 9

THE MEERUT PRISONERS

Sentenced to Transportation:
For Life:
Muzaffar Ahmed, TUC Vice-President, Secretary WPP Bengal. Foundation member CPI. In 1924 sentenced to four years prison*
For 12 years:
S. A. Dange, TUC Assistant Secretary, Bombay Textile Union General Secretary, WPP EC member. In 1924, four years.*
S. V. Ghate, Bombay Municipal Workers Vice-President*
K. N. Joglekar, Railworkers Union Organiser, WPP EC member
R. S. Nimbkar, Bombay Textile Union Vice-President, WPP General Secretary
Phillip Spratt, TUC EC member
For 10 years:
Ben F. Bradley, Bombay Textile Union EC member, WPP EC member, Bombay Textile Strike Committee treasurer. Member of British AEU.
S. S. Mirajkar, British India SN Co Staff Union Secretary, WPP Bombay secretary*
Shaukat Usmani, WPP Bombay paper editor. In 1924 four years. In 1929 Communist Candidate in Spen Valley
For 7 years:
D. Goswani, Calcutta Juteworkers Union organiser
P. C. Joshi, WPP Secretary United Provinces, Editor*
Abdul Majid, militant
For 5 years:
G. M. Adjikari, WPP writer and journalist*
M. G. Desai, WPP journalist, editor Bombay Spark*
S. S. Josh, WPP President*
A. Prasad, militant in Bombay

Sentenced to rigorous imprisonment

For 4 years:
  Gopal Basak, Bengal Textile Union official
  G. Chakravarty, East India Railway Union official
  Lester Hutchinson, Bombay Textile Union Vice-President, WPP paper editor
  S. H. Jhabwalla, Railway Union official
  R. P. Mitra, Bengal Jute Workers Union General Secretary
  K. N. Sehgal, Congress Committee Punjab, previously sentenced to three years for sedition.

For 3 years:
  A. A. Alwe, Bombay Textile operative
  S. Huda, Bengal Transport Workers secretary
  R. Kasle, Bombay Textile Union official
  L. R. Khadam, militant
  Goura Shakner, WPP official

Died in prison:
  D. R. Thengi, TUC EC member, Arsenal Workers Union president

Acquitted:
  S. N. Bannerjee, WPP; K. Ghosh, Bengal Union official; V. N. Mukhargi, WPP; D. Singh, WPP

The 1924 sentences were at a trial in Cawnpore of founding members of the CPI.

* = present at CPI Third Congress

(Source: *Meerut Trial, the Facts*, by C. P. Dutt, Meerut Defence Committee, London.)

ABBREVIATIONS
used in the Notes and Appendices

ORGANISATIONS AND INSTITUTIONS

AEU	Amalgamated Engineering Union
ASW	Amalgamated Society of Woodworkers
BB	British Bureau (of the Red International of Labour Unions)
BSP	British Socialist Party
CC	Central Committee
CI	Communist International (Third International, or Comintern)
CNT	Confederacion National de Trabajo—Spanish National Confederation of Labour
CPA	Communist Party of Austria
CPGB	Communist Party of Great Britain
CPI	Communist Party of India
CPSU	Communist Party of the Soviet Union
CRL	Central Reference Library
DAC	Dependents' Aid Committee
EAM	Ethniko Apeleutherotiko Metopo—National Liberation Front, the political wing of ELAS, the anti-fascist resistance army in Greece
EC	Executive Committee
ECCI	Executive Committee of the Communist International
ETU	Electrical Trades Union
FAI	Anarchist Federation of Iberia
ILP	Independent Labour Party
LCC	London County Council
LP	Labour Party
LPC	Labour Party Annual Conference
LRD	Labour Research Department
LTC	London Trades Council
MB	Modern Books (publishers)
MFGB	Miners' Federation of Great Britain
MM	Minority Movement (also NMM)
MST	Manchester School of Technology
NATSOPA	National Association of Operative Printers and Assistants
NFTC	National Association of Trades Councils
NUGMW	National Union of General and Municipal Workers
NUPPO	National Union of Police and Prison Officers
NUR	National Union of Railwaymen
NUS	National Union of Seamen
NUWM	National Unemployed Workers' Movement
OSS	Openshaw Socialist Society
PA	The Press Association
RCA	Railway Clerks' Association

RILU	Red International of Labour Unions (Profintern)
RTSSM	River Thames Shop Stewards' Movement
SAU	Shop Assistants' Union
SDF	Social Democratic Federation
SDP	Social Democratic Party
SL	Socialist League
SLP	Socialist Labour Party
SU	Soviet Union (USSR, Union of Soviet Socialist Republics)
T & GWU	Transport and General Workers' Union
UMS	United Mineworkers of Scotland

JOURNALS, PUBLICATIONS

BZG	Berliner Zeitung
Cmd	Command paper
CR	Communist Review
DH	Daily Herald
DW	Daily Worker
Inprecorr	International Press Correspondence
LM	Labour Monthly
MR	Monthly Review
MTD	Marxism Today
RPC Bulletin	Revolutionary Policy Committee (ILP) Bulletin
SAS	Harry Pollitt: *Selected Articles and Speeches*, Lawrence & Wishart, London, 2 vols, 1954
SMT	Harry Pollitt: *Serving My Time*, Lawrence & Wishart, London, 1940
WL	Weekly Letter
WN	World News (formerly World News and Views)
WNV	World News and Views (later World News)

PERSONS

AP	Annie Powell
JM	John Mahon
JT	Joan Thompson
MP	Marjorie Pollitt
RPD	Rajani Palme Dutt
TAJ	Thomas (Tommy) A. Jackson
TRS	Thomas Robert Strudwick

SPECIAL INFORMATION SOURCES

HPP	Harry Pollitt's papers. These include papers preserved by him, mainly notes or texts of his speeches, drafts of articles, diaries, notebooks

and correspondence. But they are by no means complete enough to be called an Archive. To them have been added additional papers, mainly correspondence, press cuttings, election addresses, given to the author during the writing of this book.

R   Personal recollections, written or given verbally to the author.

INDEXES

GENERAL INDEX

Affiliation (to Labour Party), 42–4, 87, 132, 137, 199, 316–18, 263
aggression, 201, 209, 210, 239, 247, (indirect) 249, 289, 298, 347, 351, 421
agriculture, 180, 306, 320, 392, 396, 400, 405, 412; socialist a., 396, 400, 405, 412
"Amethyst", H.M.S., 327, 330–2
Anglo-American bloc (Special Relationship), 313, 315
Anglo-German Naval Treaty, 200, 244
Anglo-Soviet Treaties, 269, 270, 273, 277, 314, 318
anti-Semitism, 356, 406
armed forces (*see* Organisations Index: armies; *and below*, soldiers, etc.)
armaments (*see also* disarmament), 102, 181, 192, 194, 262, 322, 364, 335
Armstrong Whitworth (*see* Names Index; firms)
Arms Export Ban, 194–5
"Aurora", battleship, 54
Austin Motors (*see* Names Index: firms)
Atlantic Charter, 287
Atlantic Pact, 339

banks, -ers, 155, 165, 180, 262, 352, 535–6
"Batory", s.s., 372, 374, 404
Black Friday, 99, 101, 106, 117
bloc vote (in trade unions), 133, 535
Bloody Sunday, 61
Bolshevism, ists (*see also* Organisations Index: Communist Parties), iii, 54, 121, 128, 145
British Battalion (Spain), 210–31
British-Franco-Soviet Pact, 247–8
building industry, workers (*see* industries & trades)
busmen (*see* industries & trades)

Campbell Case, the, 95
capitalist press, 142, 145, 150, 193, 194, 216, 260, 353, 159, 408 (*see also* Publications Index)
capitalists, -ism (*see* classes)
capitalist encirclement, 398

Chartism, -ists, -ter, 6, 126, 163–4, 173
child labour, 9, 130
Christianity, 21, 268, 354, 367, 390–1
civil disobedience (non-co-operation), 288–90
civil liberties, 53, 317 (*see also*) freedoms)
classes, 14, 22–8, 49, 110, 155, 189, 283–7, 291, 295, 326, 336, 349–50, 354, 364, 367, 442
 capitalists, -ism (bourgeois, employers, owners, shareholders), 2, 7, 9, 11, 17, 32, 38, 40, 54–7, 61–7, 71–7, 83, 98, 91, 94–5, 101–9, 111–19, 123–8, 130–7, 142, 154–9, 162–9, 171–4, 180–4, 190–8, 201, 204, 206, 251, 258–9, 260, 262–5, 267–8, 283, 289, 294–6, 300, 301, 308, 309, 311–9, 320–5, 332, 335, 350–7, 361, 365, 366–9, 371, 382, 384, 386, 398–9, 401, 404, 407–8, 411–15, 416, 422, 431, 334, 436–7, 439, 441, 443
 "big business", 83, 125, 282, 300, 319, 323, 366
 feudalism, 355
 landowners, -lords, 55, 63, 165, 180, 185, 341, 345, 369, 354–5, 400, 407, 535
 "middle class", middlemen, small traders, 130, 132, 140, 156, 235, 354, 356
 monopolies, -ists, 155, 164, 275, 282, 296, 315, 322–6, 342–3, 349, 352, 367, 385, 436, 533
 peasants, 182, 383, 285, 294, 297, 400, 405, 408, 413
 serfs & slaves, 87, 119
 workers (working class, labour, proletariat) *see also* industries & trades; and Organisation Index: trade unions), 2, 17, 38, 53, 56, 58, 86, 89, 91–6, 125–6, 129, 131–2, 136–9, 140, 165, 167, 175, 179, 181–4, 191–9, 201–9, 244–8, 251–8, 260–6, 271, 275, 283–4, 295–6, 305, 311–19, 322, 326, 335–9, 342–3, 347, 349, 350–7, 364–8, 370–1, 376–7, 384–5, 387, 393–7, 400–7, 417, 422, 427, 432–9, 440–4, 533

class collaboration, 101, 119, 130, 173, 202–3, 326, 436, 441
class struggle (conflict, war), 45, 62, 95, 101, 103, 115, 120, 125, 132, 140, 154–7, 160, 199, 356, 362, 374, 400, 434–42, 534, 536
classless society, 371, 438–9
clothing workers (*see* industries & trades)
coal (*see* industries & trades, miners)
Coal Commission, 66
collective bargaining, 305, 319
colonies, 83, 125–6, 131, 138–9, 140, 145, 165, 181, 202, 232, 247, 250, 265–6, 287, 294–5, 315, 322, 338–9, 351, 353, 335–9, 436, 438, 535
Combination Acts (*see* Laws)
Communism, -ists (*see also* Organisations Index: Communist Party), 55, 77, 84, 88, 91, 94, 99, 107, 112, 114, 120–6, 132, 139, 144–8, 152, 157–9, 160–7, 170, 175–7, 180–5, 192, 196–9, 200, 203, 207, 210, 228, 235, 241–2, 247, 256–61, 269, 270, 275, 294, 298, 308, 314, 316, 323–6, 340–8, 366, 371, 373, 390, 394, 397–9, 400–3, 411, 436, 439, 440–6, 536
concentration camps (*see* imprisonment)
Conservatives (*see* Tories)
Corn Laws (*see* laws)
cotton workers (India), 377
Councils of Action, 82
counter-revolution, 67, 192, 250, 254, 406–8
Crimea Conference, 303
crises (of capitalism), 162, 294–5, 321–5, 329, 349, 385, 436–7
"cult of the individual", 390, 399, 400–1

Dawes Plan, 120
democracies, new, people's, 318, 322, 350, 356, 405–7
democracy, 55, 147, 155, 207–8, 211, 225, 234, 239, 241–9, 250, 254, 264–5, 303, 317, 319, 322–8, 342–6, 349, 350–8, 360, 366, 385–6, 394–7, 401–8, 431, 436–7, 440, 444, 532, 534
democratic centralism, 408
dictatorship, 199, 313, 351; fascist, 244, 408; proletarian (*see* working class power)
disarmament, 101–2, 342, 414 (*see also* rearmament)
dividends (interest), 105, 352, 364

Easter Rising 1916, 62
education, 125, 151, 197, 258, 295, 342, 352, 368 (*see also* schools)
Education Acts (*see* laws)
Eight-hour Day (*see* hours)
elections: *1907–11*, 31–2; *London*, 61; *1922–4*, 88–90; *1929*, 152–6; *Whitechapel*, *1930–1*, 164–6; *Rhondda, Clay Cross*; 179–81; *1935*, 197–8; *Stratford, Silvertown, 1939–40*, 257–9; *1945*, 304–10; *1950*, 338–40; *1951*, 347–8; *1955*, 367–70, 442; *Cyprus, municipal, 1953*, 359
Emergency Powers Act (*see* laws)
Emergency Regulations, 99, 113, 357
employment (full), 301, 303, 308, 339 342–3, 350, 535
engineers (*see* industries & trades)
"equal pay for equal work", 328
European Defence Community, 328
European Collective Treaty, 360

factories, 2, 3, 18, 37, 56, 59, 86, 159, 173, 176, 185, 207, 266, 296, 326, 348, 352, 403, 431, 434, 440–2, 533
Factory Acts (*see* laws)
factory committees, 119
factory inspectors, 58
fascists, -sm (*see also* nazis, -ism), 91, 112, 115–17, 120, 166, 175, 179, 192–8, 200–9, 210–8, 220, 225–9, 132–9, 240–9, 250, 255, 259, 260–2, 226, 269, 271, 274–5, 278, 280, 282, 286, 289, 294, 297–9, 301–4, 309, 312–14, 341, 346–9, 356, 361, 398, 401, 407–8, 440
Finish-Soviet conflict, 259
Five Power Peace Pact, 339, 342, 347
Five Year Plans (Soviet), 175, 396, 399, 404
food, 3, 4, 5, 6, 8, 59, 181, 265, 271, 301
forced labour, 140
foreign policy, 313–16, 321, 324, 341, 352
freedom fighters (*see* Resistance)
freedoms—individual, press, speech, thought, 192, 265, 296, 255–7, 290, 434
"Foster, William Z." s.s., 2, 428
French (*see* nationalities, nations)

General Strike 1926, 128, 131, 137, 141, 147, 156, 163, 357, 436
general strikes, 44, 59, 77–8, 83, 90, 104, 111, 172

543

Geneva Agreements (Vietnam), 413
Germans (*see* nationalities, nations)
German Peace Treaty, 342
German-Polish Non-Aggression Pact, 247—8, 250–4
German-Soviet Non-Aggression Pact, 247–8, 250–1, 254
Governments (Cabinets, States):
 British: 30–2, 82, 111, 117–18, 125–6, 142, 184, 208, 210, 230, 241, 249, 279, 314, 324, 338, 344, 350, 356; Labour, 89, 94–5, 108, 113, 133, 139, 152, 155–8, 160–7, 171–2, 180, 190, 197–9, 200, 232, 303, 311, 315, 318–19, 322–5, 350–2, 358–9, 369, 436, 441, 533; Left Labour (project), 239, 241, 311, 325, 338; Labour Progressive (project), 295; Liberal, 62, 306; National, 125, 128, 181, 192, 196, 202, 232, 239, 240; Tory (Conservative), 132–3, 157, 187–8; Chamberlain, 209, 238, 250–8; Churchill, 262, 265, 269, 271, 280–3, 303–6, 321, 348, 367–9, 533; People's Front (project), 239, 254, 262–3, 352–4, 402; Revolutionary Workers' (project), 58, 88, 154–8, 160–4, 198; Working Class (project), 340
 Catalan (Spain), 234
 China, Kuomintang, 330; People's, 342
 Cyprus, Legislative Council, 350
 Czechoslovakia, 344–5
 Finland, 344
 France, 82, 208; Blum, 209, 230, 241, 344, 360
 Germany, 191, 360, 408; Nazi, 191
 German Democratic Republic, 345–6
 Greek, Royal, 298; National 299
 Hungary, 344; Kadar, 406, 408; Nagy, 407
 India, 271; National Govt., 288, 290, 307; Provisional Nat. Govt., 288–9; Hyderabad Govt., 382; State Govts., 386
 Ireland, 62; Free State, 92; Provisional Repub., 62
 Laos, Royal Govt., 413
 Malaya, 358–9
 Poland, 83
 Spanish Republic, 206, 208, 210; Negrin, 216, 228, 230, 343
 Sweden (S.D. Govt.), 343
 USA, 328, 359, 413, 421
 USSR (Council of Ministers), 74, 82, 257, 260–3, 342, 361, 397–9, 413, 439
 Vietnam Democratic Republic, 412

"Hands off Cyprus", 390
"Hands off Russia", 65, 68, 72–83, 204, 410, 447
"Harry Pollitt", s.s., 428
Health, hospitals, safety, 59, 185, 295, 308–9, 340, 342, 352, 393
High Commissioner (Australia), 328
Hitlerism (*see* nazism)
Home Rule (Ireland), 62
hours of work, 1, 5, 12, 58, 72, 102, 110–13, 117, 137–8, 155, 172, 197, 264, 266, 295, 327, 439, 365, 367, 389, 394, 434, 533
housing, 43, 59, 110, 164, 172, 180–1, 185, 239, 258, 307–8, 320–1, 327, 342, 347, 352, 356
Hunger Marchers (Means Test), 183–4, 203 (*see under* Organisations: NUWM)

imperialism, -sts (*see also* war, imperialist), 44, 46, 63, 94, 119–20, 125, 138–9, 140, 154–6, 165, 178, 192, 196, 201–2, 232, 244, 249, 250–1, 254, 262, 272–3, 280–9, 294, 297, 311, 313, 319, 322–5, 330, 337, 341–5, 349, 353–5, 358, 376, 379, 384–8, 393–5, 408, 436, 438, 441, 443
imprisonment (*incl.* concentration camps), 49, 172, 187, 190, 192, 220, 233, 237, 270, 296, 301, 329, 359, 390
Indian Naval Mutiny, 375
Independence Movement (National Liberation), 131, 138, 182, 196–7, 202, 250, 254–5, 287–9, 290, 294, 298–9, 322, 323, 343, 350–9 360, 389, 396
industries & trades (*see also under* trade unions):
 agriculture, 295, 305
 banking, 295, 369
 building, 110, 113, 133, 369
 busmen (*see* transport trade unions)
 clothing, 167, 181
 dockers, 1, 15, 16, 99, 107–8, 113, 118, 147, 164, 178, 264, 297, 318, 364, 415, 421–3
 electricity, 1, 295, 302, 318

industries & trades—*contd.*
  engineers, 1, 103, 106, 114, 117, 179, 181, 275, 302, 318, 336, 369
  gas, 1, 295, 318
  iron & steel, 150, 275, 305, 317, 417
  lightermen, 170, 178, 249
  match girls, 1
  miners, 37, 44, 56, 61, 88, 98–9, 101–7, 113, 115, 118, 125, 132–3, 141, 151–5, 162, 164, 167, 172, 179, 180–5, 232, 262, 292, 295, 300–8, 318–19, 321, 324, 339–40, 369, 389–90, 394, 415–18, 420–1
  seamen, 128, 299, 354, 382, 418
  shiprepair, 168–9, 181, 188
  shipyards, 106, 109, 155, 181, 188, 268, 369, 415
  textile, 154, 164, 167, 169, 181, 415
  transport, 98–9, 113, 117–18, 154, 262, 275, 295, 297, 305, 318; buses, 167, 173; railways, 1, 4, 14, 20, 27, 302, 369
infantile mortality, 364
interest (*see* dividends)
internationalism, 42, 44, 47, 101–2, 263, 266–7, 329, 337, 397, 404, 477, 443
international trade union unity, 112–15 (*see also* Organisation Index, trade unions, international)
intervention: Russia, 79, 366; Spain, 207, 209, 210, 443; Hungary, 407; Vietnam, 413

"Jolly George" s.s., 81–2, 81–5, 178, 246, 259, 428
juries, 117, 125
jute workers (India), 187

Labour Movement (*see also* Organisation Index: Labour Party), iii, 15, 31, 44, 62–3, 67, 74, 67, 82–3, 88, 95, 101, 104, 121, 125, 131, 134, 152–6, 161 166, 176, 192–5, 202–3, 212, 225, 232,–6, 244, 249, 251, 258–9, 260–2, 265, 280–3, 295; German, 297, 302–9, 322–7, 340–1, 347–9, 350–2, 358, 362, 366, 369, 370, 399, 421, 432, 438, 441, 443, 536
  leadership: official, right-wing, 75, 85, 154, 162, 180, 192–6, 231, 248, 259, 272, 304, 308–9, 314–15, 322, 326–7, 342, 348, 351–2, 356, 358, 360–1, 336, 368–9, 434, 440–3, 536; left, militant, 133, 235, 239, 311, 316, 326, 328, 340, 370

land, 155, 352, 369
laws:
  Civil Authorities (Special Powers) Act, 183
  Combination Acts, 50, 58
  Education Acts, 6
  Eight-hour Act, 152
  Emergency Powers Act, 134, 191, 265
  Factory Acts, 18, 48, 263
  Intelligence Agency Act (USA), 407
  Mines Act, 18
  Munitions of War Act, 49–51
  Mutual Security Act (USA), 407
  Reform Act, first, 58
  Sedition Acts, 181, 203
  Trade-Union Act, 316
  Unemployment Act, 185, 188, 203, 212
League of Nations, 210
lease-lend, 313
Leninism (*see* Marxism)
Liberals, -ism, 25, 36–7, 61–2, 89, 94, 131–2, 155–6, 164–6, 180, 192, 207, 218, 225, 235, 237, 240, 259, 298, 311, 348, 357, 421; National Liberals, 89
living standards, 324–9, 344–7, 358, 361, 369, 405, 434, 436, 535
lock-outs, 40, 61, 73, 80, 95, 104–9, 111, 113, 115, 322

Marshall Plan (Aid), 315, 321–7, 342–5
Marxism, -ists (-Leninism), 31–3, 44–5, 67, 94, 127, 183, 202, 235, 239, 250, 284, 291, 306, 315, 317, 337–8, 344, 348, 350–8, 361–2, 367–9, 370–1, 390, 399, 400–1, 408, 432, 443–4
Marx Memorial Lecture 1953, 411
Means Test (*see* Hunger Marchers)
Meerut Trial, 337–8, 375–6, 385, 537–8
miners, mines (*see* industries & trades)
Mines Act (*see* laws)
Monarchy (*see* Royalty)
Mondism, 137, 151, 154, 171, 184, 189, 282
monopolies, -ists (*see* classes)
Munich Agreement, 242
Munitions of War Act (*see* laws)
Mutual Aid Pact (USSR-Finland), 344
Mutual Assistance Pacts, 201

nations, -alities (*see also* Governments): Abyssinia, 263; America, 207, 217, 222–3, 271, 280, 281, 286, 345, 351–2, 358, 373, 377, 387, 391, 405;

nations, -alities—*contd.*
   Arab, 165, 222, 277 (*see also* Moors); Armenia, 390; Australia, 416–25; Belgium, 207, 214–15, 261; Britain, *passim*, 54, 207, 253, 372, 390; Bulgaria, 80; Burma, 288; Canada, 217, 222–3; Ceylon (Singhalese), 372; China, 136, 182, 415; Cyprus, 368, 389–95; Czech, 242; Denmark, 81; Egypt, 372, 395; Gold Coast, 427; Finland, 257; France, 54, 91, 112, 126, 130, 207, 214, 222, 233–4, 258, 261, 263, 247, 345; Germany, 54, 73, 90–2, 112, 131, 213, 229, 233, 241–58, 261–3, 276–7, 285–6, 308; German Democratic Republic, 345–6; Greek, 247, 313, 390–1, 394; Hungarian, 406–8; Indian, 165, 182, 187–8, 227, 263, 287, 373–5, 386; Irak, 372; Ireland, 60, 92, 150, 155, 182, 217, 262; Italy, 230–3, 246, 263, 343; Japan, 287, 303, 305; Jews, 164–5, 246, 427; Kenya, 372; Malasia, 372; Meronite, 390; Moor, 207, 213–17 (*see also* Arab); Norway, 107; Pakistan, 372; Poland, 82–3, 233, 247, 250–1, 320; Portugal, 375; Romania, 247; Russia, 64–6, 90, 121, 130–1, 142, 149, 221, 235, 241–79, 303–8, 353; Scotland, 331; Slavs, 207; South Africa, 372; Spain, 207, 231 *et seq.*, 419; Sudeten German, 242; Syria, 372; Wales, 219

national independence (*see* independence movement)
National Insurance, 366
nationalisation, 72, 132, 152, 155, 194, 232, 262, 295, 300–8, 317–18, 322–3, 339–47, 352, 369–70, 433–4, 536
Naval Pact, Anglo-German (*see* A.-G. Naval Treaty)
nazism, hitlerism, -ites, 196, 249, 260, 276, 279, 291, 294, 296, 303, 345, 359
Nazi M.P.s, 191–2
Non-intervention (*see* intervention)
North Atlantic Treaty Organisation, NATO, 360
nuclear weapons, 339–42, 359–60, 368

opportunism (*see* reformism)

parties (*see* Organisations Index)
peace, 6, 53, 55, 165, 183, 201–2, 208, 211, 225, 235, 238–9, 241–8, 251, 261, 263, 230, 232, 236, 294–5, 298, 302–5, 308, 320, 325–8, 339, 341–8, 350–2, 355, 358–9, 360–1, 367, 373, 386, 397, 399, 412, 438
"Peace & Plenty", 239
peaceful coexistence, 351, 339
peaceful transition to socialism, 343, 350–1, 399
pensions, 5, 180, 232, 304, 339, 347, 368
Peoples Communes (China), 405
Peterloo, 28, 55, 57, 60
planning, 283, 291, 301, 305, 319–27, 343, 352, 369, 438
police (CID, Scotland Yard, Special Branch), 41, 44, 61, 75, 99, 104, 117, 123–8, 134, 142–4, 150, 174, 182–7, 193–4, 242, 274, 306–7, 331–2, 343, 349, 373, 390, 393
police strike, 74
Poor Law (*see* laws)
Popular Front, 234, 240
Potsdam Agreement/Declaration, 315, 360
prices, 51, 130, 168, 181, 264–5, 295, 300, 303, 309, 320, 343
"production, distribution & exchange", 438–9
production, 71, 203, 265, 275–6, 280, 291, 300, 318–19, 323, 325, 352, 411–12, 438, 442, 535
profits, 22, 32, 38–9, 57, 63, 105, 117, 130, 136, 149, 178, 194–5, 258, 262, 275, 282–3, 295, 300–1, 306–9, 318–19, 320–4, 336, 339, 342, 352, 359, 364, 431, 436, 441, 533
Progressive Alliance, 303–4
Public Assistance (Relief), 169

Radicals, 27
railwaymen (*see also* Organisations Index: trade unions), 56, 61, 98–9, 106–7, 111–18, 173, 180
rationalisation, 138, 154, 162, 184 (*see also* production)
rearmament, 44, 200, 328, 347, 360–1, 370, 408
reduction of armed forces, 123, 127 (*see also:* Arms Export Ban, disarmament)
religion, 25–6, 307, 327 (*see also* Christianity
Reform, 57

Reform Act, first (*see* laws)
reformism (opportunism), 31, 43–4, 55, 101, 130, 157–8, 163, 173, 176, 182, 188, 196, 202–3, 345–6, 350, 438, 441, 532
Rego (*see* Names Index: firms)
"Release the Twelve", 127
rent, 105, 110, 130, 303
reparations, 120
Republicanism, Spanish, 207, *et seq.*
Resistance, the, 244, 298, 301–2, 309, 314, 337, 344, 359
Royalty, 57, 123, 125, 141, 180, 187, 229, 298, 366; Indian, 383–4; Cyprus, 391
Revolution, -aries (red), 20, 32, 36, 44, 52, 63–6, 73, 80, 88, 91, 102–3, 108, 112, 117, 120, 126, 130, 137, 145–6, 157, 172, 175, 182, 188, 199, 204, 237, 363, 370, 385–6, 407, 433, 441–2
Russians (*see* Governments, nationalities)

sailors, 197–9, 201
sanctions, 197–9, 201
schools (*see also* education), 6, 7, 9, 10, 185
Second Front, 271–9, 280–3, 288, 311
self-determination (*see also* Independence Movement), 58, 359
ship-building, -repair (*see* industries & trades)
shop stewards, 44, 49, 51, 171, 189, 262–3, 365, 436, 533–4
Social Democracy, -ats, 31, 55, 92, 157, 173, 175, 191, 246–7, 317–18, 325–6, 345, 439, 441
Social Security (benefits, relief, services), 181–4, 295, 302–8, 322–7, 334, 352
Socialists, -sm, -movement, iii, iv, 6, 14–19, 25, 28, 33, 36–9, 43–4, 47, 53–5, 60, 62, 74, 78, 80, 86, 91, 103, 114, 122–4, 137, 140, 147, 165, 181–2, 192–7, 204–7, 240–1, 247, 255, 259, 267, 269, 287, 289, 294–8, 301–3, 317–19, 322, 325–6, 335, 337, 343, 347, 349, 350–8, 362–3, 369, 370–1, 376, 390, 396, 399, 403–7, 412, 414, 420, 423, 427, 431–9, 441–4, 532–6; international, 439; Left, 363–9; Right, 364; Scientific, 397–8, 444; (*see also* Organisations Index)
Socialist Republic (State) (USSR), 55, 294, 336–7, 426, 439

Socialist Revolution, 376, 410
Socialist construction, 438
Socialist legality, 408
soldiers, armed forces, troops, 28, 50, 53, 61–6, 81, 90–8, 119, 123, 125, 128, 130, 138–9, 187, 306, 324, 350, 353, 340, 408
Soviets (power, democracy), 82, 196, 352, 412 (*see also* USSR)
"Special Relationship" (Britain-USA) (*see* An.-Am. bloc)
standards of life (*see* living standards)
State of Emergency, 98
State Power, 63, 113 (*see also* working-class power)
strikes (*see also* General strike, police strike), 2, 15, 20, 28, 31, 36–7, 43, 48–9, 52, 61, 73–5, 95, 99, 104–5, 108, 111, 113, 115, 120, 128, 132, 146, 152, 158, 163, 167–9, 170–1, 178, 181, 189, 190, 299, 322, 355, 364–5, 369, 375, 420, 436, 552
suffrage, 11, 56–7, 355
suffragettes, 47
Summit Talks, 414
Syndicalists, 43

taxes, 130, 185, 265, 320, 324, 357
ten-hour day (*see* hours)
textile workers (*see* industries & trades)
tithes, 130
Tories (Conservatives), 11, 15, 27, 32, 44, 54, 90, 94–5, 99, 124, 126, 131, 134, 155, 159, 163, 165, 168, 181, 240, 254, 259, 282, 295, 303–9, 323–7, 333, 338, 340–1, 347–8, 352, 357–8, 360–1, 366–8, 415, 426
totalitarianism, 356 (*see also* Dictatorship)
trade, international agreements, 320, 324, 399
trade unions, -ism, -ists, movement, 2, 7, 21–2, 47–4, 49, 51–4, 57, 65, 70–88, 98–109, 113, 117–18, 129, 136–8, 147, 159, 160, 163, 167, 169, 171, 173, 176, 179, 232, 238, 241, 262–7, 284, 296, 300, 310–19, 320, 322, 367–8, 355–6, 360, 368, 370–1, 376, 390–5, 416–18, 420–3, 434, 436, 440–4, 533–5; leaders, 48, 62, 109, 115, 118, 132, 134, 156, 158, 163, 167, 173, 185, 187, 195–9, 203–5, 228, 316, 326–8, 363–5, 436, 447, 532; left, militant, revolutionary, 72–5, 103, 109, 112, 119, 129, 146, 154, 169–73, 179, 187–90, 242, 261,

547

trade unions, -ism, -ists, movement
—*contd.*
276, 363–5, 375, 421, 433, 436, 440, 444, 532; Soviet t.u.s., 416; unity, international, 111–12, 151, 171, 196–7, 365, 436, 459, 535 (*see also* united action, un. working class, unity)
transport (*see* industries & trades)
Treasury Agreement 1915, 72
trials, 30–1, 123–7, 141–3, 184, 187, 235, 328–9, 390
Triple Alliance, 118
Trotskyism, 234
Truman Doctrine, 315, 325
Tsarism, 52–4, 125

unemployed, -ment, 25, 57, 68, 71, 85–9, 101–8, 110–13, 120, 123, 138, 147, 155, 160, 163, 167, 172, 174, 179, 180, 184, 190, 218, 232, 239, 258, 266, 285–7, 336, 369, 343, 367, 386, 389, 417, 436–7, 440, 533 (*see also* Organisations Index: NUWM)
united action, 91–2, 101, 125–6, 195, 358
United Front, 86, 158, 182, 193–8, 366, 363, 386
UK-USA bloc, 386
United Nations, 283
united working class, 110, 201, 231–2, 312, 352–8
unity, 85, 116, 246, 259, 267, 283, 296–7, 303–8, 350, 364–5, 370, 434, 436, 440–3, 533–5
unity campaign, 234
Unity Convention, 84
unity, Socialist-Communist, 199, 294, 312

Versailles Treaty, 192, 200
victimisation, 16, 52, 176, 336

volunteers (Spain), 209 *et seq.*
voting (*see* bloc vote, suffrage)

wages, 4, 9, 10–19, 22, 45, 51, 56, 67, 72, 98, 102–18, 120, 130, 137, 146, 152–5, 163, 167–9, 172, 179, 184, 188–9, 202–5, 258, 295–6, 301–5, 319, 322, 327, 340–7, 350, 361, 364–7, 389, 394, 434, 533
war, 46–7, 112–13, 121, 126, 154, 163, 175–9, 185, 192, 195, 201–2, 212, 234, 242–58, 262, 271, 277, 282–7, 290, 294, 297, 306, 319, 320, 327, 336–9, 340–1, 360, 366, 399, 412, 417, 431, 436–9; anti-fascist, people's 206 *et seq.*, 254, 269, 271 *et seq.*, 286, 471; First World War, 46–53, 436; imperialist, 44–9, 51, 62–3, 83, 91–5, 102–3, 126, 250–1, 341, 346, 358–9; Second World War, 178, 394, 401, 431, 441; South African (Boer) War, 352, 362
War criminals, 345
Warsaw Pact, 407–8
women, 319, 328, 352, 395, 405, 415, 438 (*see also* suffragettes)
workers' control, 55, 113, 129, 155, 295, 345, 434
working-class power, "proletarian dictatorship", 55, 63–4, 77, 88, 101, 110–15, 165, 181, 183, 189, 232–4, 255, 260
world market, 125, 361
world trade union unity (*see above*, trade unions, international unity)

Young Community League, YCL, 284
Young Pioneers (GDR), 346
youth, 264, 284, 352, 368, 422, 438

Zinoviev letter, 75

NAMES INDEX

Aarons, L., 415
Acabel, P., 213
Acton, J., v
Adams, H. P., 129
Adamson, Rt. Hon. W., M.P., 89
Adler, V., 197
Adshead, A., 362

Ahmed, Dr. M., 385
Ainley, B., v, 362
Ainley, D., v, 257
Akhurst, Mr., 330–1
Alexander, W. (Bill), 222
Allaun, F., M.P., 255
Allan, W., v.

Allen, W. G., v
Allcroft, R., v, 14, 190
Allergant, J., 320
Allison, G., 138, 172, 428
Ambatielos, B. & A. (Tony), v, 299
Amery, Rt. Hon. L. C., M.P., 280
Anand, Mulk Raj, 378
Anders, Gen., 314
Anderson, Rt. Hon. Sir J., 264
Angus, J., v
Archbishop of Cyprus (*see* Makarios)
Armstrong Whitworth (*see* firms)
Arnot, R. P., iv, 96, 158
Ash, E., iv
Askwith, Sir G., 49
Astor, Lady N., 278
Attlee, Rt. Hon. Major C., M.P., 222, 270, 311–16, 323, 325, 330, 340, 358, 360
Austin Motors (*see* firms)
Ayres, F., v, 222
Azana, Pres. M., 230

Bacon, T., 419
Bailes, J., v, 418–19
Bailey, H. H., 284–6
Bailey, R., iv, 284
Baker, Rt. Hon. P. Noel, M.P., 222
Baldwin, Rt. Hon. S., M.P., 158, 175, 181, 202
Ball, John, 94
Barber, H., 229
Barbusse, Henri, 237
Bateman, F., 428
Bates, R., 216
Baxter, S., 183
Beall, Mrs. F. M. M., v
Beauchamp, K., iv
Beauchamp, V., 72, 112
Beaulieu, P. L., 129
Beaverbrook, Lord, 309
Beech, R., 141, 143
Bell, J. A., v
Bell, T., 84, 127, 159, 335
Bell, Mr. (lecturer), 129
Benes, President, 345
Benn, Col. W., M.P., 126
Bennett, Sir H. C., 117
Bensons (*see* firms)
Bent, J., 368
Beria, L., 359
Beritz, M., 27–8
Bernal, J. D., Prof., 340, 371

Berridge, C., 369
Betteridge, J., 369
Bevan, Rt. Hon. A., M.P., 233, 280, 299, 321
Bevan, J. W., v
Bevin, Rt. Hon. E., M.P., 50, 81, 102, 105–8, 119, 174, 208–9, 239, 262–5, 277, 299, 311–16, 433
Beyer Peacock (*see* firms)
Birkenhead, Lord, 124
Biron, Sir C., 123
Bismarck, 297
Blackwell, T., 72
Blake, William, 56
Blatchford, Robert, 4, 24–5, 38, 235, 338
Bloom, J., iv
Blum, Leon, 209, 262
Boltansky, Miss, 24, 35, 38
Booth, Charles, 20
Boughton, Rutland, 426
Bower, F., 260
Bowles, M., v
Bowman, D., 368
Boyle, D., 217
Bracken, Rt. Hon. B., M.P., 273
Bradlaugh, Charles, 361
Bradley, B., 138, 188, 372–7
Bradley, S., 69
Bradshaw, A., 35
Bradshaw, L., v, 259, 371, 428–9
Bradsworth, Dr., 224
Brailsford, H. N., 218
Bramley, F., 40
Bramley, T., 193, 280, 320–4
Breitscheid (Germ. SD), 296–7
Brent, J., 217
Brewer, Marjorie (Mrs. Pollitt), 121
Bridgeman, R., v, 427
Bright, F., 255
Brine, J., 417
Brockway, F. (Lord), 181–2, 202–3, 218, 239
Bromley, J., M.P., 79, 145–6
Browder, E., 317
Brown, D., v
Brown, E. & I., v, 167, 207
Brown, G., 216
Brown, H., 67
Brown, Mrs. L., v
Brown, Mrs. W. J., v
Browne, F., 210
Brownlee, J. T., 50
Bulganin, Premier, N., 388–9, 421
Burns, E., iv, 9, 171
Burns, J., 61

Butcher, Capt. H. C., 279
Byron, Robert (Lord), 152

Caborn, G., 414
Cachin, M., 197, 410
Calder, Mrs., v
Calwell, M., 420
Campbell, D., v
Campbell, J., 292-3
Campbell, J. R., 95, 124, 145, 187, 252, 335
Cance, R., 329
Canning, Lord, 382
Cant, E., 108
Carritt, G., 320
Carson, Lord, 124
Casato, Col., 230-1
Casement, Sir R., 141
Cassell, Prof. G., 120
Castlereagh, Viscount, 152
Caust, Dr. D. & Mrs. E., 424-5
Chamberlain, Rt. Hon. Sir N., M.P., 207-9, 225-6, 230-9, 240-62, 443
Chandler, B., 423
Chaplin, S., 196
Charles II, 375
Charlesworth, E. (Aunt Emily), 4
Charlesworth, Granny, 4, 5
Charlesworth, M. L. (Pollitt, mother), 3
Charlesworth, W., 3
Chen Yu, 415
Chiang Kai-Shek, 329
Chicherin, G. V., 476-7
Churchill, Rt. Hon. Sir W., M.P., 61, 82, 89, 145, 155, 200-5, 263-9, 270-9, 280, 281, 288, 298-9, 302-9, 311-15, 320, 324, 347-8, 350, 359, 361, 368, 398
Chu Teh, 410
Citrine, Sir W., 126, 137, 208-9, 218, 239, 282, 312
Clark, Gen., 279
Claus, R., 237
Clay, Gen. L., 407
Clive, Robert, 382-8
Clynes, Rt. Hon. J. R., M.P., 112
Coates, W. P., 79
Cockran, N., v
Cohen, N., 216
Cohen, R., 96
Cole, G. D. H. & M., 96
Collins, M., 92
Connolly, J., 40, 62
Cooney, R. (Bob), 229
Copper, Rt. Hon. Duff, M.P., 251

Copeman, F., 222
Copic, Lt. Col., 222; (Cdr.), 227
Cornforth, M., iv
Coppock, Sir R. (Dick), v, 11, 18-19, 25-6, 37, 426
Cox, I., v, 179, 307-9, 397
Crane, Walter, 25, 429
Cramp, C. T., 78
Crawford, T., v
Cripps, Rt. Hon. Sir S., M.P., 232-5, 253, 256, 312, 325, 334, 339
Crome, Dr. L., 221
Crossleys (see firms)
Crossley, J. & P., 26-7, 33, 39, 46-7, 52, 138, 256
Cullen (ILP), 204
Cumberland, Duke of, 417
Cummings, R. W., 363
Cummings, Lt., 229
Cunningham, J., 214-15

Daladier, Premier E., 231, 242, 254, 259
Dalton, Rt. Hon. H., M.P., 218
Daly, P., 219
Dange, S. A., 387
Davies, Mrs. B., 5
Davies, S. O., M.P., 103, 150, 290
Day, F., iv
Day, W., 69
Deakin, A., 361
Dean of Canterbury, Manchester (see Johnson, Hewlitt)
de Gaulle, Pres. C., 344
del Vayo, A., 227
Derby, Earl & Lady, 60
Despard, Mrs., 132, 155
Devine, P., 179
Dhotre, D., 374
Diaz, J., 128
Dickens, Charles, 123
Digges, A., v
Dimitrov, G., 197, 199, 201, 235-7, 316-17, 410
Dixon, Sir P., 315-16
Dixon, R. (Dick), v, 414, 422-3
Docherty, M., v
Dollfuss, Chancellor E., 240
Douglas, F., v, 89
Dunbar, M., 216-17, 221
Dunbar-Nasmith, Sir M., 267
Dutt, R. P., iv, v, 85-7, 96, 157-8, 161-2, 251, 255, 260, 335-8, 372
Dutt, S., 225, 337
Dyer, Gen., 379, 388

Easton, G. & S., v
Eaves, K., v
Eden, Rt. Hon. Sir A., M.P., 251, 315–16, 358, 368
Edward VII, 141
Edwards, T., 229
Egelnick, M., iv
Elliott, J. B., iv
Engels, F., iii, 27–8, 34, 57, 199, 216, 349, 370, 438
Ercoli (*see* Togliatti, P.)
Evans, H., 224
Evans, T., 315, 433

Falber, R., 537
Ferguson, A., v, 88, 48–9
Fimmen, E., 424–5
Finger, A. & J., 424–5
firms:
    Armstrong Whitworth, 20, 47–8, 51–2
    Benson's Mill, 2, 5, 13
    Beyer Peacock, 20, 22
    Charles Kerr (Chicago), 34
    Clothiers, 167
    Crossleys, 20
    Frasers, 68
    ICI, 193–4
    Nicholsons, 51
    Rego, 167
    Thomas Acton, II
    Thorneycrofts, 49, 51
    Vickers, 193–4
Figgins, J. B., 536
Fisher, H., 39
Fleet, H., v, 13–14
Fleming, M., 47
Fletcher, Lt. G., 221, 229
Flint, H., 190
Foot, Rt. Hon. M., M.P., 314
Foot, R., 300–1
Foster, F., 366
Fowkes, E. H., iv
Fox, Ralph, 212
Fox, Councillor, T., 19
Franco, Gen. F., 206–9, 213, 218, 224–5, 230, 243
Fraser, D., 363
Fraser, Mr. Justice, 117
Frasers (*see* firms)
French, S., iv
Frow, E. & R., iv
Fry, Lt. A. J., 214
Fry, H., 220

Gaitskell, Rt. Hon. H., M.P., 322, 340
Gallacher, W., M.P., 52, 84–9, 169, 123–8, 145, 161–2, 182, 184, 198, 200, 266, 270, 293, 305, 329, 335, 344, 363, 404, 423, 426
Galligaris, G., 221
Gandhi, Mahatma, 284, 294, 375
Garaudy, R., 426
Garibaldi, 36
Gaster, J., iv, 182, 204
Gates, J., 227
Gee, W. (Bill), 25–6, 35–6, 43, 361–3, 430
George V., 101
George, Rt. Hon. D. Lloyd, M.P., 235, 272–3, 332, 366, 436
Gering, E. J. & M., 10, 14, 23, 26
Ghosh, A., 377, 387
Gibbon, E., 4
Gibbons, J., 224
Gibson, R., v
Gilchrist, J., 69
Glading, P., v, 121–2, 138, 291
Glading, R., iv
Godfrey, J., 260
Goebbels, P., 344
Goering, H., 279
Gollaglee, C., iv
Gollan, J., iv, 360, 366, 404, 408, 426, 429
Gollancz, V., 234–6, 256
Gooch, G. P., 129
Goode, Principal W. T., 79
Goodman, D., 332
Gordon, Duke of, 417
Gosling, H., M.P., 107, 164
Goss, J., v, 424–5
Gossip, A., 110, 204–5, 256
Gottwald, K., 345, 396
Gough, S., 79
Gramsci, A., 237
Gray, Mr. (debater), 27
Grayson, V., 24, 31–3
Greaves, W. McG., 27
Green, N., v
Greenwood, Rt. Hon. A., M.P., 249
Gregory, Lt. W., 229
Grenfell, Cdr., 79
Grigg, Rt. Hon. Sir J., M.P., 280
Grotewohl, O., 346
Guest, Dr. H., M.P., 280
Gupta, S. (Indian M.P.), 378
Gusev, Gen., 329

Hague, Councillor S., 18, 19, 36
Haldane, J. B. S., 221, 257
Halifax, Lord, Rt. Hon., 280

Halkett, G., 229
Halpin, T., 24
Hamilton, Duke of, 268–9
Hammond, J. L. & B., 129
Hanlon (Jun.), 229
Hannington, W., 99, 103–4, 127, 131, 144, 309
Hardie, Keir, M.P., 347
Harding, D., 534, 537
Hardy, G., 144, 293
Hardy, Fd. Marshal Sir J., 395
Harris, Air Marshal, 278
Hart, F., iv, 368
Hart, Dr. T., 222
Hart, Capt. L., 274
Hastings, Sir P., K.C., 95
Hastings, Warren, 388
Hawkins, A. H., 132
Hayes, J., 74, 79
Healey, J., 418, 423
Heinemann, M., v
Henderson, A., 368
Henderson, Rt. Hon. A., M.P., 51, 65, 157, 180–1
Henderson, S., 320
Hess, R., 268–9
Hewlett, W., 100, 306
Hicken, H., 150
Hicks, G., 108, 115, 123, 202
Higginson, Coun. T., 18–19
Hill, H., 368
Hill, T. (Australia), 421
Hill, Ted (Lord), v, 140, 148, 267, 268, 420, 427
Hitler, A., 181, 191–8, 200–8, 218, 225–8, 237, 240–9, 252–8, 262–9, 272–7, 281–7, 291, 298–9, 315, 366, 400–1, 431, 443
Hoare, Rt. Hon. Sir S., M.P., 262, 280
Ho Chi Minh, 412
Hodge, J., 15, 23–4, 88
Hodge, P., 89–90
Hodges, F., 87, 116
Hogg, Sir D., 123–4
Hollins, D., 26
Holmes, W., 291
Hopkins, H., 282
Horner, A., 171, 179, 180, 198, 251, 266, 306–9, 340, 376, 418
Horrabin, F., 232–3
Hughes, J., 416
Humphreys, Sir T., 123, 141
Hunt, "Orator", 57
Hurd, R., 217
Hutchings, S. C., v

Hutchinson, W. H., II
Hyndman, H. M., 25, 42–4, 409

Ibarruri, D. (Passionaria), 209, 396, 410
Inkpin, H., 84, 85, 126–7, 161, 256, 260, 335
Inkpin, A., 85
Ironside, Gen., 67, 262
Irving, D., 43

Jacobs, J., v
Jackson, F., iv, 65, 77, 163
Jackson, T. A. (Tommy), 25, 37, 361–2
Jagger, J., M.P., 112
Jarvie, J., iv
Jenkins, M., v
Jodl, Gen., 283
Johnson, Very Rev. H., 11, 59, 60, 291
Johnson, H. T. (Jonno), 416–19, 420–5
Johnson, W., 427
Johnston, E., 424
Jones, A., v, 409
Jones, E., 344
Jones, F. G., 21, 35–6
Jones, G., 419
Jones, G. J., 368
Jones, Jack, M.P., iii, 367
Jones, Jim, 410
Joss, W. (Bill), 362
Joynson Hicks, Rt. Hon. Sir W., M.P. (Lord Brentwood), 124

Kadar, Premier J., 406–8
Kapp, Gen., 90
Kaye, S., v, 369
Keiley, P. H., 22
Keats, J., 291
Kennedy, T., M.P., 43, 363
Kennerley, Mrs. J., v
Kenton, L. & L., 222
Kerensky, A., 54
Kerr, C. (see above, firms)
Kerrigan, P., iv, v, 213, 215, 229, 330–3, 368, 357
Khruschchev, N., 398–9, 411–12, 421
Kidd, A., G. & W., 4, 10, 14, 21, 26
King of Italy, 291
King & Queen, England, 229
Kirkwood, D., M.P., 132
Kleper, Gen., 212
Klugman, J., iv
Knight, Mrs., 257
Knight, T., 73, 99
Koplenig (Austrian C'st), 410

552

Krebs (see Valtin, J.)
Kuusinen, O., 410, 412

Lafargue, P., 28
Laithwaite, W. H., iv
Lambert, L. B., 69
Lansbury, G., M.P., 74, 127, 132, 141, 251, 363
Lansbury, N., 256
Larkin, J., 37, 40–1
Laski, H., 233–4, 252, 312–17
Lauchlan, W., 369
Laval, P., 261
Lawrie, H. H., 15, 18–19, 31, 252
Lawther, Sir W., 112, 433
Leaper, Sir W., 227
Learmouth, Pte, 217
Legge, H., 18, 19
Leigh, B. & J., v
Lenin, V. I., iii, 31, 40, 47, 54–5, 76–7, 80, 84, 92–4, 100, 157, 260, 297, 306, 316–17, 367, 399, 401, 410–12, 423, 426, 430, 437, 439
Letsky, B. M., v
Lewis, B., v
Lin Shao Chi, 396, 405–6
Lismer, T., 72, 256
Lissagaray, iii
Lloyd George, Rt. Hon. D., M.P., 49, 51, 82–3, 251, 272, 316–17, 372
Loban, J., 229
London, Jack, 38, 103
Londonderry, Lord, 152, 154
Longuet, F. & R , 371
Losovsky, A , 101–1, 126, 158, 173
Loveless, J. & G., 417
Loveman, A. & J., v, 409
Low, David, 145
Ludwig, Emil, 348
Lumley (local CP), 153
Luxembourg, Rosa, 47, 147
Mabon, F., v
Mabon, J., 221, 334, 336, 353
McArthur, J., v
MacBride, M. G., 92
McCarthy, 373
MacCrue, E., v
MacDonald, A., 420
MacDonald, Rt. Hon. J. R., M.P., iii, 11, 35, 87–8, 95, 120–1, 126, 151–8, 161, 163, 175, 187–8, 199, 436
McDougall, Ian, iv
McDougall, W., v
McGahey, M., iv
MacGarvey, D., iv, 421

McGhee, W., 205
MacGovern, J., M.P., 536
McGuire, W., 205
McIntyre, H., v
McIlroy, P., 217
McKellan, Mrs., 38
MacLaine, W., 103
McLaurin, Mrs., 415
McLaurin, G., 415–16
MacLean, J., 79
McLean, W., iv
McLerie (of Glasgow, in Spain), 218
MacManus, A., 89
MacMillan, J., 536
MacMillan, Rt. Hon. H., M.P., 415
Macnamara, Dr., 49
McNeil, Rt. Hon. H., M.P., 314
Macready, Gen. Sir N., 75
Maddern, R., v, 421, 425
Mainwaring, H. H., 179–80
Makarios, Archbishop, 389, 395
Malenkov, G. M., 398
Malone, Col., M.P., 79
Mann, Mrs. E., 292, 410
Mann, Tom, 1, 17, 18, 23, 37, 38, 43, 73, 78–9, 90, 95, 99, 100–3, 108, 113, 121, 138–9, 172, 179, 183–9, 200, 238, 256, 260, 266–7, 313, 335, 347, 363, 377, 410, 420–8, 432
Mannerheim, Marshal, 258
Mao Tse-Tung, 404
Marklew, E., 35, 41
Marks, B., v
Marks, C., v, 27, 28
Marmontel, S. F., 16
Marshall (see General Index: Marshall Plan)
Martin, Dr., 3
Marx, Eleanor, 371
Marx, Karl, iii, 22, 27–8, 32–6, 57–9, 199, 216, 235, 344, 366, 370–1, 430–9, 441
Masters, S., 210
Matthews, G., v
Mayhew, Rt. Hon. C., M.P., 322
Maxton, J., M.P., 88, 134, 140, 185, 202, 204, 212–14, 335, 536
Mehring, F., 47
Mellor, W., 22–4
Menon, K., 227, 256, 266, 290
Meredith, George, 36
Meynell, Francis, 85
Miaja, Gen., 222, 230–1
Middleton, J. S., 218
Mikoyan, A., 44

Miles, J. B., 416, 418
Miller, Ald., 428
Miller, W. (Bill), v
Mindzenty, Cardinal, 407
Modesto, Col., Gen., 225–6, 229
Moffat. A., v, 477
Molotov, V., 247, 251, 313, 396
Mond, Sir A. (Lord Meltchett), 137
Moody (of MM), 145
Moore-Brabazon, Rt. Hon. Lt. Col. J. R., M.P. (Lord), 273–9
Moncton, Rt. Hon. Sir W., K.C., M.P., 320
Moran, S., v, 423
Morel, E. D., M.P., 89
Morgan, L. H., 28
Morley, J., 25
Morris, A., 319
Morris, William, iii, 25, 39, 60, 65, 94, 438
Morrison, Rt. Hon. H., M.P., 117, 200, 208, 262–6, 274, 302, 317–18, 358, 360
Morton, "Old Man", 15
Mosley, Sir O., 186, 193–6, 200, 203, 246, 302, 332
Moss, J., 424
Mountbatten, Lord L., 290, 359
Munroe, J., 33
Murphy, J. T., 98, 103, 159
Murray, J., 183–4
Murray, Coun. T. and A., 229
Musgrove, J., 33
Mussolini, B., 181, 207–8, 218, 221, 225, 237, 242, 244, 281

Nagy, Premier, 406–7
Negrin, Premier, 216, 229–31
Nehru, Pandit J., 187, 227, 287–8, 379, 381
Newbold, W., 89, 103
Nicholson, J., 368
Nicholsons (*see* firms)
Niven, B., 371
Nizam of Hyderabad, 383
Northern Ireland, Duke of, 99
Nutt, M. & I., iv

O'Casey, Sean, 260
O'Daire, P., 216, 229
O'Dyer, Sir M., 379
Offley, R., v
Oldfield, V., M.P., 428

Oliver, K. C., 141–2
Openshaw, C., 26, 31
Owen, F., 316
Owen, Robert, 94

Pankhurst, A. (Emmeline), 11
Pankhurst, E., 11
Pankhurst. S., 66, 76
Papandreou, G., 298–9
Pappaionnou, E., iv, 30, 33
Papworth, A. F., v, 171
Parker, Inspector, 260
Parsons, H., 283
Parsons, O., v, 96
Partassides, Mayor (Limassol), 395
Passionaria (*see* Ibarruri, D.)
Patterson, Pte., 217
Paul, E. & C., 66
Paul, W., 35
Paynter, W., v
Pearce, Bert, 368
Pearce, E., 530
Pearse (Irish rebel), 62
Peaker (*Morning Post* correspondent) 537
Peck, J., 368
Peet, G., 52, 79
Pertini (It. Soc.), 237
Petain, Marshal H. P., 261, 301
Phillips, Morgan, 312–16
Pieck, W., 201, 346, 391, 410–11
Piratin, P., M.P., 255, 340
Platts-Mills, J., M.P., 327
Pollitt family:
　Brian, son, 204–5, 291–2, 336, 363, 358, 424, 428
　Ella, sister, iv, 3, 4, 7, 10, 34, 38, 291, 362, 414, 428, 433
　Emily, aunt (married Gerring), 10, 14, 25–6
　Harry, *passim*.
　Jean, daughter, v, 181, 204–5, 226, 290–1, 336, 388, 420, 422–4, 428
　John, grandfather, 3, 4
　Marjorie, wife (*née* Brewer), iv, 121–2, 132, 155–6, 204, 290–2, 336, 388, 420, 422–4, 428
　Mary Louise (mother, *née* Charlesworth), 3, 4, 5, 6, 8, 10, 23, 25–6, 32, 129, 204, 253–7, 335, 426
　Samuel, father, 3, 4, 5, 6, 7, 23
　Stanley, brother, 3
　Winnie, sister, 3, 5, 8, 335
Pollitt, H. loco. engineer, 4

Pollitt, H. student, 4
Pollitt, J. B., boilermaker, 4, 190
Pospelov, P. N., 398, 426
Postgate, R., 85, 132, 260–1
Pountney, E., 285
Powell, A. & T., v, 306, 340, 388
Prince Regent, 57
Prince of Wales, 123
Pritt, D. N., K.C., M.P., v, 186, 233, 254, 383, 427
Pugh, A., 120
Purcell, A. A., 78, 98, 112, 115, 363
Putterel, Rev. J., v, 259

Quelch, H., 25, 43, 409
Quelch, T., 73, 103, 110
Quinn, S. V., 418
Quinton, H., iv

Rakosi, M., 346, 396, 406
Ramsay, Capt. A. H. M., M.P., 72, 154
Ratcliffe, H., 49, 190
Rathbone, Miss J., 9
Raven, A., 217
Ravera, C., 237
Reading, Lord (Viceroy of India), 187
Reckitt, E., v, 96, 256
"Red Dean" (see Johnson, Very Rev. H.)
Regan, Alderman T., v, 90, 428
Reid, B., iv, 428
Renshaw, W., iv
Ricard, E., 189
Roberto (It. Lib. Repub.), 237
Roberts, Fd. Marshal Lord, 62
Roberts, F. O., M.P., 363
Roberts, G., 26, 34, 44
Roberts, J., 49
Roberts, M., v
Roberts, Mrs., v
Robertson, E., 42
Robeson, Paul, 373, 426
Robson, A., v
Robson, R. W., iv, v, 210
Roosevelt, Press. F. D., 282, 303–4
Rose, F., 17
Rosen, Cllor., 320
Rosen, R., v
Rosmer (Fr. t.u.s.), 98
Ross, W. & L., v
Rothstein, A., iv, 371
Rowlandson, D. H., 116–17
Rowntree, B. S., 20
Runciman, Lord, 241
Ruskin, J., v

Rust, W. (Bill), 127–8, 159–60, 220, 224, 478
Ryan, Capt. F., 214–17

Sable, Mr. Justice, 320
Saklatvala, S., M.P., 132, 376
San Carolo, Mrs., 35–6
Sanyal (Ind. CP), 387–8
Savage (MM), 145
Scheer, J., 237
Scott, D., 140–3, 147
Sedley, W., v
Selkirk, R., v
Sell, H., 74
Senior, J., iv
Sexton (TUC), 112
Shah Jehan, Emperor, 380–1
Shakespeare, William, 128
Sharkey, L. L., 328, 414, 416, 418, 422–3
Shaw (Int. Textiles), 116
Shaw, G. B., 140, 260
Shinwell, E. (Lord), 112, 433
Simon, Rt. Hon. Sir J., M.P., 210, 262, 280
Singh, B. S., 379
Skelton, J., v
Slater, H., 221
Slater, J., v, 419
Sleigh, B., 25
Smirnovsky, M., 423
Smith, F., 103
Smith, H., 133
Snowden, Rt. Hon. P., M.P., iii, 11, 57, 163, 199, 437
Stamp, Sir J., 120
Solley, L., M.P., 390
Somerset, T., 26
Sorgue, Mme., 35
Spackman, Bro., 79
Speedley, J., v
Spencer, G. A., M.P., 134, 141, 145, 199
Spencer, W., v
Sprague, K., v
Springhall, D., 215, 251
Squair, A., 99, 100
Stalin, J. V., 253, 269, 274, 276, 280, 303, 396–403, 408
Stansfield, T. & J., 417
Stassova, E., 410
Stevenson, Miss (Ll. George's Sec.), 273
Stewart, R. (Bob), 88–9, 335
Stitt, K., 259
Strachey, Rt. Hon. J., M.P., 32, 234
Strauss, G., M.P., 233

555

Strudwick T. (Tommy), v, 141, 143, 146–7
Strudwick R., 147
Strurrock, W. (Bill), 108
Sullivan, S., K.C., 141
Summers, V., v
Sverma (Int. del.), 197
Swales, A. B., 119
Swift, Mr. Justice, 123, 124
Sylvester, Mr. (Ll. George's sec.), 273

Talbot, Mr. Justice, 186
Tanner, J., 69, 72, 79, 99
Tapsell, W., 222, 224
Taylor, Dr., 211
Taylor, J., 7
Taylor, T., v
Tazzaman (Williamson), 223
Terracini (It. C'st), 237
Thaelmann, E., 189, 229, 237, 296–8
Thiel, T., 74
Thomas, E., v
Thomas, Rt. Hon. J. H., M.P., 101–2, 119–20, 123, 140, 199
Thompson, B., 81, 99, 107
Thorez, M., 197, 201, 297, 301, 396
Thorneycrofts (*see* firms)
Thurtle, E., M.P., 273
Tiffin (T & GWU), 365
Tito, J., 400
Titt, Councl. F., 11, 20; Alderman, 190
Tillet, B., 102, 112, 266, 347, 363, 423
Tochatti, J., 65, 69
Togliatti, P. (Ercoli), 201, 343
Tomkinson, E., 48
Tomsky, M., 98
Tranmael (Norw. SD leader), 313
Tressell, R., 367
Trevelvan, Rt. Hon. Sir C., M.P., 233
Tribe, I., v
Trollope, F., 56
Trotsky, L., 76, 89, 203
Truman, Press. H., 304, 314, 325, 342 (*see also* General Index: T. Doctrine)
Turner, (Sir) Ben, 137
Turnhill, G., 212

Ulbricht, W., 346
Unsworth, W. (Bill), 14
Unsworth, J., 14, 20, 26

Valtin, J. (Krebs), 329

Varley, F. B., M.P., 134
Vaughan, J., 132
Vernon, H., 204
Viceroy of India (*see* Lord Reading)
Victoria, Queen, 382
von Hindenburg, Fd. Marshal, 191
von Papen, F., 175
von Paulus, Gen. F., 382
von Schushnigg, Chenc. K., 240
Voroshilov, K., 410

Walker, Mrs., 75, 80
Walker, H., 224, 229
Walker, L., 419
Walker, M., 66, 108
Walsh, J., 366
Warner, Sylvia Townsend, 206, 207
Ware, H., 11
Warwick, Lady, 59
Watkins, G., 223
Watkins, N., 103, 133, 144, 256
Watt, A., v, 10, 422
Watson, W., 217
Watson, W. F., 73
Webb, W. (Bill), 73
Weir, G. & S., 67
Wellard, C., v
Wellington, Duke of, 57
Wells, H. G., 104, 412
West, J., 129
Whalley, E., 220
Wheatley, Rt. Hon. J., M.P., 88
White, J. B., 537
White, Dr. E., 421–4
Whitehead, W. (Bob), 27
Whitney, A., 48, 65, 190
Whittle, Mrs, 27
Whitworth, Sir J., 16, 48
Wild, (MM) 145
Wild, S., v, 211–12, 114, 428
Wild, Sir E., 143
Wilkinson, E., M.P., 90, 103
Williams, F., 155
Williams, R., 79, 98–9, 134
Williams, T., iv
Wilson, A., v
Wilson, Mrs. D., v
Wilson, Rt. Hon. H., M.P., 322
Wilson, H., 140–1, 147, 174
Wintringham, T., 122; (Cap.), 214
Wood, J., v
Wood, Rt. Hon. Sir Kingsley, M.P., 262
Wooley (MM), 145
Worrall, T., 190

Wynford, Lord, 417

Yeats, W. B., 291
Young, Cdr. E., 233
Young (MM), 145

Zak, W., v
Zangwill, I., 79
Zapototsky, 345
Zetkin, C., 47
Zinoviev, G., 90

ORGANISATIONS INDEX

Admiralty (*see also* Navy), 49, 62, 113–14, 267, 333
"All-in" International (*see under* Internationals)
Amalgamated Engineering Union (*see* Trade Unions, Engineers)
Amalgamated Society of Boilermakers (*see* Trade Unions, Boilermakers)
Anglo-Russian Trade Union (Unity) Committee, 115–16
Armies, Belgian, 261; British (including various branches and RAF), 57, 60–1, 75, 81, 98, 212, 273, 279, 280, 285, 291, 319; Chinese, Red, Peoples' A., 235, 329; Kuomintang A., 330; German, 76, 201–9, 273, 275, 279, 280, 283, 285–6; Russian, Red, Soviet, 55, 80–2, 251, 259, 275–6, 278, 280, 283, 251, 253, 259, 309, 392; White, 76
Arms Enquiry (USA), 195
ASLEF (Locomotivemen) (*see* Trade Unions)

Bank of England, 200, 305, 318
Benson (*see* Name Index, firms)
Blackshirts (Brit. fascists), 116–17, 186, 192–3, 198
Boards of nationalised industries, 313, 340
Boilermakers' Union (*see* Trade Unions, Boilermakers)
Bolshevik Party (*see* Communist Parties, Soviet Union)
British Battalion (*see* Spain)
British Broadcasting Corporation (BBC), 193, 271, 273, 298, 317, 339, 347, 251, 257, 416
British Embassy (China), 330
British Joint Labour Aid Committee, 90
British Medical Association, BMA, 184
British Military Mission to Baltic, 79
British Occupied Zone (Germany), 314
British Peace Committee, 366

British Raj (India), 375
British Socialist Party, BSP, iv, 27, 33–7, 41–53, 65, 74, 77, 84–5, 161, 361, 363, 410
British Transport, v

Cabinets (*see* General Index: Governments)
Central Election Committee (Rhondda), 179
Chartists, Charter, 59, 74, 171, 245, 344, 443; Convention, 246
Churches, 6–7, 130, 194; Cyprus, 391
Clarion organisations, 24–5, 33–4, 36, 38–9, 40, 74, 76
Coal Board, 300, 318–19, 433
Coal Commission, 120, 129
Committee of Enquiry (Amritsar), 379
Committee of Action 1930, 108
Communist International, 44, 56, 73, 78, 84, 90–4; *3rd Cong.*, 100, 108, 125; *6th Cong.*, 156–8, 160–2, 169, 175, 182, 192, 195; *7th Cong.*, 195–204, 210–11, 234, 250–5, 297, 314, 338, 410, 412
Communist League, 410
Communist Parties, iv, 5, 45, 94, 108
Belgian, 174
Australian, 328, 414–24
Austrian, 427
British (CPGB), 80, 84; *4th Cong.*, 85; *5th Cong.*, 86; *6th Cong.*, 86, 94, 118, 121–2; *7th Cong.*, 123–5, 132, 136–7, 144, 150–3; *8th Cong.*, 156; *9th Cong.*, 157–8; *10th Cong.*, 159–60; *11th Cong.*, 161–3, 166, 171; *12th Cong.*, 175, 178, 182, 183–4, 192, 199, 202–4; *1926 Cong.*, 209–10, 232, 239, 242, 246, 249, 252, 256, 260, 266, 268–9, 272, 277, 279, 280–7; *Cong. 1941*, 302, 306, 311–17, 336–8, 341, 343, 349, 350, 354, 358, 363, 365, 369, 370, 385, 389, 402–8, 410, 419, 422, 425, 427–8,

Communist Parties—*contd.*
433, 435, 422, 426, 536; London Dist., 144, 215, 320, 390; Candidates, 36, 39, 122, 156, 160–6, 179–80, 197–8, 258–9, 304–10, 338–44, 367–70; M.P.s, 132, 157, 197, 340, 376; Women's Committees, Dept., Conf., 87; Young Communist League, 124, 144, 160, 215, 584
Chinese, 194
Cyprus (AKEL), 339, 390, 395
Czechoslovakian, 344–5, 353
French, 209, 262, 329, 344, 411
German, 90–2, 237, 296–7, 317
GDR (Socialist Unity P.), 345
Greek, 299
Hungarian (Working Peoples' P.), 346, 353, 406
Indian, 372–7, 380–8
Italian, 221, 237, 343
New Zealand, 414
Poland, 353
Russian (*see* Soviet)
Soviet (Bolsheviks, CPSU), 47, 54, 66, 78–9, 81, 93–4, 100, 354, 396–402, 406, 411, 426–7
Spanish, 215, 217, 223, 228, 230–1, 343
Swedish, 343
USA, 250, 317
Conferences of Communist & Workers' Parties, 337, 388
Conference of Foreign Ministers, 313
Conservatives (*see* Gen. Index: Tories)
Convention, Leeds (*see* "Hands off Russia")
Co-operatives, 1, 9, 10, 43, 98, 153, 255, 283, 292, 318, 360, 409
Co-operative Party, 112
Council of Action, 246, 259; Czechoslovakia, 345, 410
Council of Ministers (USSR) (*see* General Index: Governments)
Councils of Workers' Delegates, 349
Councils of Workers & Soldiers, 53, 78
Courts of Enquiry, Mines, 118; wool, 167

Defence Committee (Wales), 186
Dependants' Aid Committee (*see* Spain)
Democratic Front (Hyderabad), 383

Eight Hour Day Committee, 1
European Economic Community (EEC), 418

European Free Trade Association (EFTA), 418
Exchequer (British), 359

Fabian Research Dept., 95
Fabian Society, 42
Fascists, British (*see* Blackshirts); German (*see* National Socialists)
Federation of British Industries, FBI, 111, 178
First of May Committee, 258, 410
Foreign Office (and Minister), 75, 192; Soviet, 76
Free German Youth (GDR), 346

German Social Democrats (*see* Social Democrats)
Gestapo, 329
Gorton Trades & Labour Council (*see* Trades Councils)
Guardians, 108, (Yorks), 134
Greek Communists (*see* Communist Parties); liberation, EAM, EDES, 298–300; Royalists, EDES, 248–9, 298

"Hands off Russia" campaign, 78–9, 80–3
High Court, 58, 141
House of Commons (*see* Parliament)
House of Lords, 366
Hunger Marchers (*see also* NUWM), 142, 156, 184–5

ICI (*see* Names Index: firms)
Independent Labour Party, ILP, 6, 10–11, 19, 23–4, 31–3, 42–5, 65, 77, 121, 139, 181; *1932 Cong.*, 182; *Rev. Pol. Ctee.*, 182–4, 192, 234, 238; *1935 Cong.*, 204, 232; *Nat. Admin. Council*, 202–3
India League, 266, 290
Indian National Congress, 287, 289, 384
Indian Union, 288
International Brigades (*see* Spain)
International Ctee. of Action v. French Occupation of Ruhr, 91
International, "All-in", 203–4
International, First, 216
International, Second, Amsterdam, Labour & Socialist, 31, 45, 47, 91, 182, 197, 199, 201–4, 217–18
International, Third (*see* Communist International)

International, Two-and-a-half, 91, 182
International Labour Defence, 155
International Relief, 90
International Socialist Bureau, 42
International Workers of the World, IWW, 77
Irish Nationalists, 62–3
Irish Republican Army, IRA, 214–16
Ironworkers' Union (*see* Trade Unions)
Italian Socialist Party, 47

Labour Council, Salford, 189
Labour Educational Council, London, 87
Labour Exchange, 68
Labour Independent candidate, 340
Labour, National Council of, 98, 208–9
Labour Party, Australia, 418, 427, 434–7
Labour Party, Britain, iii, 15, 24, 36, 42–3, 47, 65, 78, 82, 104, 106, 116, 120–1, 131–2, 141, 153, 156, 180, 182, 184, 192, 199, 202, 205, 215, 218, 232–3, 238, 240, 252, 277, 283, 302–5, 313–17, 327, 339, 350, 352, 356, 360, 370; Candidates, 3, 32, 42, 72, 88, 165–6, 178, 180, 340, 347, 536; Conferences *1916*, 43; *1917*, 78; *1922*, 87, 112; *1923*, 86–7; *1924*, 87; *1925*, 117, 120; *1926*, 132, 147; *1927*, 148; *Brighton*, 197; *1936*, 208, 299; *1944* 303; *1945*, 313; *1947*, 322; *1965*, 333, 444, 459; Executive, 82, 87–8, 120, 149, 157, 199, 202–3, 232, 239, 308, 318; M.P.s, 19, 24, 31, 33, 58–9, 79, 109, 129, 164, 280, 314–15, 326–7, 339–40, 358, 360, 363, 428; Parliamentary Labour Party, 82
Labour Research Dept., 95–6, 140, 427
League Against Imperialism, 139, 216
League of Nations, 194, 197, 201, 209, 238, 241
Legislative Council (Cyprus), 390
Left Book Club, 234, 236, 255
Left Socialist Revolutionaries (Russia), 54
Liberal Party, 302, 339, 436
Liberation Centre (Hungary), 406
Lister Brigade (*see* Spain)
Lock-out committees, 164
London County Council, LCC, 321
London Trades Council (*see* Trades Councils)

Malaysian People's Army, 350
Manchester County Forum, v, 27–8

Manchester School of Technology, 4
Marx Memorial Library, 370
Medical Aid Committee (*see* Spain)
Meerut Defence Committee, 187
Merseyside Dock Labour Board, 364
Metropolitan Radical Federation, 60
Mining Association, 300
Ministers of the Crown, 194; Aircraft Production, 279; Health, 320; Information, 273; Labour, 265, 268; Lord Chancellor, 62; Munitions, 49–50, 52
Minority Movement, v, 87, 103–4, 111–14, 119, 122–4, 126, 131, 136–8, 140–59, 167–9, 170–6, 284–5
Mond-Turner Conferences, 137

National Police & Prison Officers Union (*see* Trade Unions: NPPOU)
National Shop Stewards & Workers Movement, 73, 276
NUR (*see* Trade Unions, Railwaymen)
NUBTO (*see* Trade Unions, Builders)
National Minority Movement (*see* Minority Movement)
National Unemployed Workers' (Committee) Movement (*see* Unemployed)
National Socialists, Nazis, 191–2, 200, 240; Sudeten, 241, 248, 254, 260–1, 344
Navy, Royal, 209 (*see also* Admiralty)
Navy, Royal Indian, 375
Non-Intervention Committee (*see* Spain)
North Atlantic Treaty organisation, NATO, 360, 391, 408, 535

Old Bailey, 321
Openshaw Socialist Society, OSS, iv, 11, 14, 24–8, (candidate 1910) 31–3, 42, Appendix
Organisation for Maintenance of Supplies, 120

Pan-Pacific TUC, 138
Parliament, House of Commons, 1, 16, 18–19, 33, 42, 44, 54–8, 72, 81, 95, 99, 104, 118, 126, 131, 142–5, 154, 188, 199–200, 249, 273, 278–9, 287, 313, 340, 344, 347, 349, 352–7, 360, 366, 369, 376, 379, 403, 434, 441, 536–7; Indian 383
Pathet Lao, 413
Peace Front, 238, 241
People's Army (*see* Spain)

Peoples Convention, 265
Peoples' Food Committees (India), 290
Peoples Front, 207, 212, 231-9, 344
Peoples Militia (*see* Spain)
Peoples Vigilance Committee (London), 264
Planning Commission, 320
Police (*see* General Index)
Port Conciliation Committee, 267
Port of London Authority, 67
Political Prisoners Committee, 92
Pollitt Scholarship, 336
POUM (*see* Spain)
Prisoners of Franco, 427
Production Committees, 275-6, 301

Radio Free Europe, 407
Rail Executive, 318
Red Army (*see* Armies)
Reform Union, 89-90
Register of Shipping, 142
Relief Fund for Russian Famine, Russian Famine Relief, 90, 102
Republican Congress Party (Ireland) 216
Republic, Spanish (*see* Spain)
Reserves, currency, 321
Rhondda local authorities 174
RILU (*see* Trade Unions)
River Thames Shop Stewards, (*see* Shop Stewards)
Royal Commission on Private Arms Manufacture, 194
Royal Naval Training College, 330
Royalty, 67, 158, 194, 298, 375

Scotland Yard (*see* police)
SEATO, 413
Security Council (*see* United Nations)
Shop Stewards Committees, Movement: national, River Thames, 69, 70-9; Manchester, 72; Woolwich Arsenal, 33, 72; Coal, Transport, 142
Social Democratic Federation (Britain), 33, 37
Social Democratic Parties: Australia, Victoria, Labour Party, 420; Australia, Victoria, Socialist Party, 420; Czechoslovakia, Social Democrats, 345; Denmark, Socialist Party, 312; Finland, Social Democrats, Socialists, 344; France, Socialist Party, 312; Germany, Social Democrats, 34-5, 317, Indep. SDs, 90;
Italy, Socialist Party, 343; Norway, Labour Party, 312-13; Spain (*see* Spain); Sweden, Social Democrats, 343
Socialist League, 65, 232, 238
Socialist organisations, 33; parties, 192, 195
Socialist Sunday Schools, 10-11, 14, 25-6, 34-5, 122, 158, 204, 255-6, 335
Solidarity movement (with Lancs cotton w.), 169-70
Soviets, Cong. of, 54
Soviet Information Bureau, 100
Soviet TUC (*see* Trade Unions)
Spain, 206-34
  British Battalion, International Brigade, 207, 210-13, 216, 219, 223-9, 234, 245, 428, 443; XV Brigade, 210, 219, 221, 227-8
  Friends of Spanish Republic (South Africa), 212
  International Brigade (*see also above*, British Battalion), 210-14, 220-1, 231, 245-6, 416, 431; Garibaldi Battalion, 238; Lister Brigade, 214
  Medical Aid, 207, 222
  Non-Intervention, 208, 227
  Peoples Army, 220
  Peoples Militia, 210
  Police, 206
  POUM, 234
  Republic, 211, 216, 223-7, 230-1, 343
  Socialist Party, 208, 217
  Wounded & Dependants' Aid Fund, Brit. Aid Ctee, 212, 246
Squatters, 320-1
State Dept. (USA), 315
Steel Smelters' Union (*see* Trade Unions)
Stock Exchange, 232
Strike committees, 19, 20, 50-1, 61, 107-9, 113-14

Tolpuddle Martyrs, 443
Tom Mann Memorial Hall, 292
Tories, Conservatives, 271, 283, 299, 302, 314, 333, 339, 368, 371
Trade Boards, 319
Trades (& Labour) Councils, 103-4, 109, 110-13, 120, 131-2, 137, 262, 317, 328; Birmingham, 110; Gorton, 10, 30, 52, 90; London, 131; Manchester & Salford, 20; Queensland, 414; West Ham, 92
Trades Union Congress, TUC, 1, 40-2,

Trades Union Congress (TUC)—*contd.*
  78–9, 82, 91; *1921*, 101–8; *1868*,
  110; *1922*, 111–12; *1923–4*, 112–18;
  1925, 119–21, 128, 134; *1926*, 137;
  1928, 138, 144, 147, 148, 151, 171,
  174, 192, 194, 203, 229, 238, 274,
  282–3, 312; *1947*, 324–7, 360, 364,
  431, 534–5
 All-India TUC, 187
 General Council 101–2, 106, 110–11,
  118, 126, 136–8, 147–9, 171, 208,
  325, 327, 437, 534–5
 Executives' Conferences, 118, 136
 General Federation Conference, 12
 Militant League, 176
 Revolutionary T.U. Opposition, 173
 Special T.U. Conference (London), 42
Trade Unions:
 AEU, ASE, Engineers, 11, 17, 52, 79,
  106, 118–19, 145, 266, 276, 302, 309,
  317, 424–7
 Amalgamated Soc. of River & Water-
  side Workers, 108
 ASLEF (Locomen), 79, 302, 365
 Blacksmiths, 71
 Builders, NFBTO, 11
 Boilermakers, iv, 4, 14, 20–2, 49, 51,
  70, 79, 87, 101, 105, 112, 128, 144–9,
  168, 188–90; Australia, 417–18,
  427–8, 433; Disputes Committee,
  189; Branches: *No. 2*, 149; *No. 11*,
  70, 72, 149–50, 190, 427; *Dundee*,
  89; London Dist., 70, 168, 190,
  267–8; Paisley, 88; Woolston No. 1,
  190
 Carpenters, 74
 Distributive Trades, 304
 Electricians, ETU, 75, 302, 304, 427
 Firemen, 302, 317
 Foundrymen, 427
 Furnishing Trades, NAFTA, 98, 110,
  204; *London No. 13*, 256; *No. 5*, 336
 General & Municipal, NUGMW, 137
 Ironworkers, 71
 Miners, MFGB, NUM, 10, 103, 117–
  18, 134, 179, 302–9, 427; Australia,
  414; Durham 153; Fife 89; Mans-
  field, 133–4; Mardy, 179; Notts,
  134, 138, 159; Scotland, 137, 174;
  S. Wales, 437
 Painters, 72, 302
 Police, 74
 Railway Clerks Association, 42
 Railwaymen, NUR, 78, 101, 304, 365,
  427

 Seamen, National Union of, 140–1,
  174
 Ship Construction, 71
 Shipwrights, 71
 Shop Assistants, 284–5
 Smiths & Strikers' Union, 5
 Steel Smelters' Union, 15
 Stevedores & Lightermen, 107, 364–5
 Transport Workers, T & GWU, 98,
  107–8, 118, 134, 141, 170–1, 174,
  285, 369; Irish, 60, 79
 United Cloth Workers, 174
 Vehicle Builders, 302
 Workers' Union, 15, 18
Trade Unions, International
 Amsterdam International, ICFTU,
  IFTU, 98, 101–2, 112–16, 201, 535
 Red International, RILU, iii, 91,
  98, 100–10, 111–12, 138, 146–7, 158,
  162, 174–6, 256, 306; British
  Bureau, v, 91, 98, 100–2, 106, 109,
  111, 113, 126, 158; London Ctee.,
  102, 109; Unity Commission, 115
 WFTU, 328, 525
 United Trade Union International,
  120, 535
Trade Unions, foreign: Czech TUC,
  345; Norwegian TUC, 345; Soviet
  TUC, 115, 137; International of
  Seamen & Harbour workers, 147,
  174
Traffic Combine, 171
Transport Commission, 318
Transport House, 197, 240, 301
Triple Alliance, 95

Ulster Volunteers, 62
Unemployed: London Conference, 105;
 Nat. Unemployed Workers' (Com-
 mittee) Movement, NUWM, 104–5,
 120, 144, 184–5; Unemployed Com-
 mittees, 102–4, 113
United Nations, 282, 289,ʹ 290, 342;
 Security Council, 341
United Working Class Party (Spain), 217
Unity Conference (Norway), 312
USA: Chief of Staff, 361; Economic
 Commission for Europe, 342; State
 Dept., 339, 341; War Appropria-
 tions, 340

Vickers Ltd. (*see* Names Index, firms)
Viet Minh, 359

War Office, 81
Welsh Nationalists, 308, 340, 348
Womens Social & Political Union, 11
Worker-Peasant Party (India), 187
Workers' Charter, Six Points, Convention, 171–2
Workers' Circle Div. 9, 427
Workers' Committees, 70, 72, 77, 99, 103–4, 113, 144
Workers' Control Committees, 202
Workers' International Relief, 130, 133
Workers' Socialist Federation, 66, 76, 79, 80, 81
Workers' Suffrage Federation, 66
Workers' Travel Association, 2
Works Committee, 274

Young Communist League (*see* Communist Parties)
Young Workers League (India), 376

PLACES INDEX

Aberdeen, 238, 363
Abyssinia, 181, 196–8, 201, 231, 241, 266
Adowa, 147
Africa, 139–40, 182, 197, 230, 279, 283, 290, 354, 387, 403; Algeria, 280; Kenya, 119, 355, 388, 394–5; North A., 279, 280, 285; (Alamein, 280); South Africa, 126, 140, 212, 266, 354, 387, 431
Albania, 241
Albert Hall (*see* London)
Altrincham, 10, 48
America (*see* Central & South America, USA)
Amsterdam, 175
Archangel (*see* USSR)
Argentina (*see* Central & South America)
Ashton-under-Lyne, 2, 11, 23–7, 36–8, 46, 311
Asia Minor, 391
Australasia, 17, 414–26
Australia, v, 219, 226, 328–9, 387; Adelaide, 421, 424, 426; Brisbane, 418–19, 420; Broken Hill, 420; Melbourne, 420, 424; Newcastle, 417–18, 422; Perth, 421; Queensland, 419–20; Sydney, 414–16, 418, 420, 422, 424; New South Wales, 417–18; Victoria, 420
New Zealand, v, 147, 216, 414–16, 423, 426; Auckland, 414–15, 426; Christchurch, 415; North Island, 415; Wellington, 415
Austria, 91, 199–203, 231, 236, 239, 240–1, 245, 249, 357, 410, 427
Azores, 242

Baku (*see* USSR)
Balkans, 91, 245, 314
Baltic (*see* USSR)
Barbados (*see* Central & South America)
Barrow-in-Furness, 103, 428
Belfast, (*see* Ireland)
Belgium, 174–5, 199, 283, 302; Brussels, 174–5, 139
Birkenhead, 364
Birmingham, 42, 110, 220, 229, 258, 293, 368, 419
Blackpool, 292, 374
Black Sea (*see* USSR)
Bolton, 199
Bolivia (*see* Central & South America)
Bombay (*see* India)
Bradford, 182
Brazil (*see* Central & South America)
Brighton, 197
British Guiana (*see* Central & South America)
Brno (*see* Czechoslovakia)
Brussels (*see* Belgium)
Broken Hill (*see* Australia)
Budapest, 353, 406–7
Burmah, 287

Caerphilly (*see* Wales)
Cairo, 372
Calais (*see* France)
Calcutta (*see* India)
Cambridge, 348, 424
Canada, 219, 337; Quebec, 286
Canton (*see* China)
Cardiff (*see* Wales)

Central & South (Latin) America, 139, 194, 405; Argentina, 337; Barbados, 242; Bolivia, 194; Brazil, 216; British Guiana, 367; Caribbean, 242; Panama Canal, 242; Paraguay, 194; Venezuela, 242
Ceylon, 337, 378
Chenies St. (*see* London)
Cheshire, 39, 60
Chicago (*see* USA)
China, 138–9, 162, 172, 175, 182, 194, 197, 201, 235–9, 291, 294, 329, 333, 337, 341–2, 359, 368, 377, 396, 404–6; Canton, 138–9, 238, 266; Chinkiang, 329, 405; Hankow, 138–9; Hongkong, 176; Nanking, 238, 329–30; Shanghai, 238, 329–30, 405; Yangtse river, 329, 405
Clarion buildings (*see* Openshaw)
Clay Cross, 180
Clyde, River, 51, 79
Colne Valley, 24, 31
Constantinople, 66
Cornwall, 292
Coventry, 292, 362
Crewe, 42, 184
Crimea (*see* USSR)
Croydon, 345
Cuba, 331, 428
Cyprus, 219, 337, 389–95; Famagusta, 389, 392–3; Kyrenea, 389, 392; Larnica, 389–91; Limassol, 389–90, 395; Nicosia, 390–5
Czechoslovakia, 196, 200, 236, 240–9, 255, 333–4, 344–5, 396; Brno, 345; Kladno, 345; Prague, 345

Dardanelles, 63, 367, 391
Dawdon, 152–7
Derby, 42, 133–4,
Denmark, 337
Devonshire (including Dartington & Dartmouth), 150, 330–2, 430
Dien Ben Phu, 122
Dover, 293
Droylsden, 3–5, 10–16, 23, 255–6; Bensons Mill (see Names Index: firms); Co-operative Hall; 11; Moravian Church, Settlement, Square, 8, 10, 255; Mottram Old Hall, 8
Dublin (*see* Ireland)
Dumbarton, 368
Dumfries, 112
Dundee, 89, 215, 368

Durham, 152–3
Dutch East Indies, 207–8

Earby, 169
Eastham Locks, 41
Edinburgh, 178, 229, 258
Egypt, 139, 152, 181, 299
Empire, 262, 287, 351–4, 374, 399
Europe, 123, 131, 209, 249, 266, 271, 274, 277–8, 282, 303 (Victory) 304, 308, 305; Centrel, 241, 251; People's Democracies, 313, 322, 350, 361

Far East, 178, 238
Farne Island, 268
Featherstone, 61
Fife, 89, 137–8, 174, 198, 369
Finland, 243, 257–9, 278, 361, 364, 410
France, 50–1, 63, 101, 112, 192, 195, 199, 201, 204–9, 225, 228–9, 241–9, 251, 254, 259, 261–2, 283, 294; Annemasse, 217–18; Calais, 174–5, 201, 210; Dunkirk, 261, 321, 325; Maginot Line, 261; Paris, 215, 261, 272, 301, 364; Somme, 63; Vichy, 261, 301

Gallipoli, 51, 63
Geneva, 359
German Democratic Republic, 345–6 (*see also* Germany, Berlin)
Germany, 43, 66, 76, 90–1, 112, 131, 162, 173, 175, 181, 189, 191–9, 200–9, 225, 236, 240, 243–4, 249, 251, 254–5, 274, 278, 280–6, 290, 303–4, 323, 327, 337–9, 342, 345–6, 360–8, 370, 396; Berlin, 91–2, 96, 208, 237, 304, 410, 415, 428; East Prussia, 34; Halle, 92; Hamburg, 91, 144, 297, 329; Leipzig, 92, 235–7, 317, 301, Munich, 242–4, 277, 297, 301, 366; Potsdam, 323, 360; Reichstag, 35, 191, 237, 366; Rhineland, 200; Ruhr, 91, 112; Weimar Republic, 91
Gibraltar (*see* Spain)
Glasgow, 43, 81, 86, 103, 148, 204, 217–18, 238, 257, 352–3, 362, 368, 389; Gorbals, 368; Kelvingrove; 86; St. Andrews Hall, 257; Motherwell, 89, 217; Springburn, 368
Gorton, 15, 18, 20, 23, 31, 52, 80, 90, 190, 428; Tank (loco works), 4, 12–19, 22, 26

563

Greece, 298–9, 302–3, 309, 313–14, 337, 391, 408; Athens, 298–9, 300
Greenhithe, 82
Grimsby, 41–2

Hamburg (*see* Germany)
Hankow (*see* China)
Harwich, 175
Hastings, 431
Heysham, 183
Hucknall, 133
Huddersfield, 302
Hull, 107, 112, 364
Hungary, 66, 278, 346, 353, 396, 404, 406–7
Hyde, 22, 24; Socialist Church, 59

Iceland, 337
India, 119, 138, 140, 163, 172, 181–2, 187, 197, 236, 250, 255, 265, 272, 276–7, 287–90, 296, 303, 337, 355, 372–87, 391, 429; Amritsar, 377–9; Bombay, 187, 374–7, 387; Calcutta, 187, 374, 378, 381–2; Delhi, 377–8, 380–1; Jallundur, 377, 388; Madras, 384, 387; Meerut, 372–6, 385, 138, 187; Punjab, 378–90; Telegana, 383
Ireland, 41, 62, 72, 92, 149, 164, 181–3, 265; Dublin, 40–2, 62, 92, 183; Limerick, 149; N. Ireland, 152, 183, 337; Ulster, 62
Isle of Wight, 92
Italy, 91, 181, 196–9, 221, 225, 278, 302, 314, 343, 356; Rome, 281; Sicily, 285–6

Japan, 126, 139, 147, 162, 175–8, 181, 192, 194, 201, 238, 248, 282, 287–8, 301, 327, 339, 358–9
Kenya (*see* Africa)
Korea, 178, 341–2, 360, 377, 387–8, 394 •

Lanark, 137
Lancashire, 3, 4, 8, 14, 36, 54–7, 60, 169, 257–8, 354, 427
Lancaster, 258
Laos, 413
Latin America (*see* Central & South America)
Leeds, 17–18, 52, 78, 92, 266
Leith, 88, 126, 178
Levenshulme, 22

Liverpool, 1, 28, 36, 38, 41–2, 46, 61, 75, 86, 108, 116, 119, 212, 217, 258, 364
London, 1, 42, 60–2, 65, 74–5, 61, 81, 84, 88, 99, 102–7, 116–19, 122, 145, 149, 156, 158, 160–4, 170–1, 175, 178, 182–8, 193, 198, 207, 209, 215, 217, 223, 234, 256, 258, 266, 268, 272, 276, 278, 292–3, 297, 301, 308, 320–1, 324, 333, 336, 354, 364, 373, 376, 379, 380, 389, 416, 425–7; Albert Hall, 73, 79, 128, 235; Battersea, 376; Bermondsey, 172, 189; Blackwall Ship repair yard, 67, 70; Bow, 68, 80; Cable St., 170; Chenies St., 158, 261; Chiswick, 70, 258; Clerkenwell Green, 105, 410; Deptford, 409; Empress Hall (Stadium), 232, 236, 242, 245, 273; Fulham, 204, 256; Golders Green Cemetery, 420, 428; Gravesend, 81; Graving Dock, 68, 287; Hackney, 369; Hammersmith, 65–6, 278; Harrow, 345; Hayes, 367; Hendon, 258, 290, 292; Highgate Cemetery, 370; Hornsey, 284, 368; Hyde Park, 65–6, 81, 95, 100, 105, 127–8, 131, 184–5, 193, 258, 264, 324, 410; Kensington, 320–1; Kentish Town, 65; King George V Dock, 67; King Street (CP Centre), 84–6, 131, 150, 332, 386, 428, 431; Lambeth, 99, 230; Limehouse, 273; Mall, the, 320, 359; Marx House, 410; Marylebone, 121; Montague Place, 269; Northumberland Ave., 105; Old Bailey, 122–3; Oxford St., 193; Poplar, 65, 67–9, 80, 84, 267; Port of London, 59; Queens Hall, 193, 242; St. Katherines Dock, 67; Scotland Yard, 75 (*see also* General Index: police); Silvertown, 258–9; Southwark, 146, 368; Stepney, 160, 170, 258, 369; Stoke Newington, 369; Stratford, 67; Teddington Lock, 67; Tilbury, 67, 70, 108, 116, 144, 188; Trafalgar Square, 60–1, 73, 104–5, 127, 193, 277–8, 280, 299, 378; Vallance Rd., 165; Victoria Park, 65; Wandsworth (prison), 127–9, 537; Walworth, 146; Wembley, 119, 392; West Ham, 122, 189, 258, 362; Westminster, 320; Whitchapel, 164, 166, 222; Woolwich 67, 73, (Arsenal) 135

Lytham, 10

Maidstone, 92
Malaya, 140, 287–8, 339, 341, 354–9, 368, 387–8, 394–5
Manchester, 2, 3, 4, 9, 11, 16–17, 20–8, 33–8, 40–1, 51–9, 60, 78, 87, 93, 98, 166, 170, 189, 203, 216, 222, 232–3, 255–8, 278, 291–3, 364, 389, 427–8; Free Trade Hall, 93, 232, 427; St. Peters Fields (Peterloo), 57; Stevenson Square, 19, 53
Manchuria, 178, 235
Mansfield, 133
Margate, 132, 147
Mediterranean, 391
Meerut (*see* India)
Melbourne (*see* Australasia)
Memel, 244
Merseyside, 258, 364 (*see also* Liverpool)
Middlesbrough, 278
Midlands, 133–4
Moravian institutions (*see* Droylsden)
Morocco, 206
Moscow (*see* USSR)
Motherwell (*see* Glasgow)
Murmansk (*see* USSR)

Natal, 247
Near East, 298
Newcastle upon Tyne, 103, 258, 292
Newcastle (*see* Australasia)
New South Wales (*see* Australasia)
New York (*see* USA)
New Zealand (*see* Australasia)
North Africa (*see* Africa)
Northam, 51
Northampton, 118, 361, 363
North Wales (*see* Wales)
Norway, 312–3, 377; Oslo, 312
Nottingham, 133–4, 229, 258, 368

Old Bailey (*see* London)
Oldham, 27, 37–8
Openshaw, iii, 2–4, 18–19, 23, 26–9, 31, 38, 41–7, 51–2, 59, 65, 77, 84, 90, 335, 362; Clarion organisations, 25; Margaret Street (Socialist) Hall, 20–5, 34, 38–9, 47, 79, 362
Oslo (*see* Norway)
Oxford, 212, 293, 337, 348

Pakistan, 337, 377, 381, 387
Palestine, 139, 165

Panama Canal (*see* Central & South America)
Paraguay (*see* Central & South America)
Passchendaele, 367
Pearl Harbour, 287
Pendleton, 37
Persian Gulf, 391
Phillipines, 287
Plymouth, 99, 112–13, 330–2
Poland, 80–2, 85, 91–2, 196, 247–9, 251, 255, 314, 361, 406–7
Portland, 92
Port Said, 372
Portugal, 206, 209, 299
Pyong Yang, 341

Quebec (*see* Canada)

Rangoon, 288
Red Sea, 372
Rochdale, 292
Romania, 241, 247, 293
Rossendale, 372
Ruhr (*see* Germany)
Russia, Soviet (*see* USSR)
Russia, Tsarist, 91, 94, 101, 114, 131

St. Albans, 293
Salford, 37, 81, 185
Scandinavia, 354 (*see also* countries)
Scotland, 88, 292, 361 (*see also* town names)
Seaham Harbour, 152, 154, 161
Seraing, 171
Sheffield, 42, 258, 368
Shrewsbury, 116
Singapore, 276, 287–8
Skoda Arms Works, 241
South Africa (*see* Africa)
Southampton, 49–51, 62, 102, 109, 190, 238, 260, 378
South Wales (*see* Wales)
Soviets, Soviet Republic (*see* USSR)
Spain, Republic, v, 91–8, 192–9, 206–31, 240–8, 255–8, 299, 314, 337, 343, 361, 396, 401, 406, 408, 419, 427–8, 431, 443; Albacete, 210–13, 220–5, 232, 282; Aragon, 210, 219, 221; Asturias, 206; Badajos, 210; Barcelona, 206, 210, 225–30, 234; Balearic Isles, 227; Basque Country, 210; Catalonia, 213, 230, 234; Ebro, R., 219, 226–9, 230; Gibraltar, 208, 327; Guernica, 210; Jarama R., 213–16; Madrid, 206,

Spain, Republic—*contd.*
   210–19, 221–4, 230, 416; Pyrenees, 211, 213; Valencia, 313–15, 318, 224, 230
Stockholm, 343
Strangeways Prison, 37
Stretford, 257
Suez, 175, 391, 407
Sweden, 343
Switzerland, 199, 292
Sydney (*see* Australasia)
Syria, 391

Tangier, 208
Tolpuddle, 416
Totnes, 331
Trinidad, 242
Turkey, 247, 791
Tyneside, 160

USA (America), 131, 195, 195, 239, 249, 250, 254–5, 266, 273, 278, 280–3, 289, 294–5, 300, 312–15, 318, 321–9, 339–43, 347, 351–8, 360–9, 377, 385, 387, 394, 405, 413, 421, 431; Boston, 207; Chicago, 34; Fulton, 313–14; New York, 217, 299; Pentagon, 342

USSR (Russia), 52–4, 64–7, 70–9, 82–3, 91, 93, 100, 102, 115, 123, 126, 131, 137–8, 141–2, 148, 155, 178, 181, 188, 192, 195, 200–1, 208, 218–19, 226, 238–9, 241–9, 250–9, 260–5, 268–9, 270–8, 282–3, 289, 294–5, 303, 309, 312–15, 322–7, 334–9, 341–6, 360–1, 371, 376–7, 396, 402–8, 410–14, 421–8, 439, 443; Archangel, 61, 76; Baku, 76; Baltic, 76, 207, 257, 361; Black Sea, 76, 391; Crimea, 80, 303; Estonia, 361; Kiev, 81; Lativa, 92, 361; Leningrad (Petrograd), 52, 54, 67, 100, 257–8, 272; Winter Palace, 54; Lithuania, 92, 361; Minsk, 76; Moscow, 54, 87, 90, 92, 96, 100, 141, 149, 166, 181, 204, 228, 231, 250–1, 260, 270, 272, 275, 278, 342, 368; Hall of Columns, 92–4, 397, Kremlin, 93, 100, 396, Red Square, 93, 274, 397; Murmansk, 76; Narva, 100; Novorossik, 141, 143; Petrograd (*see* Leningrad); Reval, 100; Sebastopol, 277; Siberia, 101; Stalingrad, 277–8, 280, 283; Tula, 100; Ukraine, 192, 252, 366; Vladivostock, 76; Voronesh, 277; Yalta, 303

PUBLICATIONS INDEX

(See also Appendix I and V)

All Power, ed. H.P., 103, 106, 109
Appeal to the Toiling Masses, Lenin, 76, 80

British Electoral System, J. Gollan, 366
British Gazette, 270
British Road to Socialism, 349, 351, 442–4, 536
Busmen's Punch, 171

Call, 51, 85
Cape Times, 51, 85
Capital, K. Marx, iii, 32
Challenge, 265
Clarion, 4, 10, 24, 59
Communist, 86
Consolidator, 69

Daily Communist (Scot.), 88
Daily Express, 193, 358–9

Daily Herald, 67, 153, 194, 277, 316–17, 353, 358
Daily Telegraph, 238, 536
Daily Worker, 162–3, 170, 175, 178, 188, 197, 211, 229, 242, 257, 265, 270–1, 277–8, 305, 332, 336, 419, 421
Daily Worker (USA), 214
Decline and Fall of Roman Empire, E. Gibbon, 4
Don't Shoot, Tom Mann, 95
Dream of John Ball, William Morris, 14

Evening News, 253

For a Soviet Britain, 349
Frethinker, 4, 10
French Revolution, H. P. Adams, 129–30
Freheiten (Norway), 312

Guardian, 421

Hansard, 531
History of Our Times, G. P. Gooch, 129
History of the Chartist Movement, J. West, 129–30
How to win the Peace, H.P., 294
How to win the War, H.P., 249

International Press Correspondence, 91
Irish Worker, 37, 40
Iron Heel, Jack London, 38
Iskra, 410

Justice, 33–4, 46–7, 409–10

Labour Monthly, 131, 265, 335, 338
Labour Weekly, 132
Left News, 234
Left-wing Communism, Lenin, 367
Lessons of the Revolution, Lenin, 76
Letters to Bill, H.P., 263
Looking Ahead, H.P., 322–4

Manchester Guardian, 79, 193–4, 407
Marxism Today, 532
Merrie England, R. Blatchford, 59, 235, 409
Mineworker, 103
Monthly Report, (Boilermakers), 148
Moral Tales, Marmontel, 16
Morning Star, 57
Morning Post, 145, 537

Neos Democratis, 392
New Age, 387
New Propeller, 265
New York Times, 407
News Chronicle, 14, 277
News from Nowhere, W. Morris, iii, 39
Nine Elms Spark, 117
Not Like This, Jane Walsh, 366

Open Letter to the Fighting Forces, 5

Paris Commune, Lissargaray, iii
Poor Man's Guardian, 130
Pravda, 278
Prison Notebook (unpub.), H.P., 129

Ragged Trousered Philanthropists, R. Tressel, 367
Railway Review, 536
Reply to Citrine, H.P., 137
Reynolds News, 275
Richard Cobden, P. L. Beajulieu, 129
Rosenberg Letters, 373
Rote Fahne, 91

Seafarer, 141–2
Serving My Time, H.P., 259–61
Socialism Utopian and Scientific, F. Engels iii, 27
Solidarity, 64, 99, 103
Spectator, 536
Sunday Express, 280
Sunday Telegraph, 536
Sunday Times, 407
Sunday Worker, 132, 151
Syndicalist, 37

US News and World Report, 368

Vema, 389

Who's Who, 432
Wages, Price and Profit, K. Marx, 22
What is to be Done?, V. I. Lenin, 353
Wall Street Journal, 342
Women's Dreadnaught, 66, 80
Worker, 103, 152
Workers' Dreadnaught, 66, 69
Workers' Weekly, 86, 94, 108, 122–3
World News and Views, 265